MULTICULTURAL
LAW ENFORCEMENT

MULTICULTURAL LAW ENFORCEMENT

Strategies for Peacekeeping in a Diverse Society

SECOND EDITION

Robert M. Shusta
Deena R. Levine
Philip R. Harris
Herbert Z. Wong

Prentice
Hall

Upper Saddle River, New Jersey 07458

Library of Congress Cataloging-in-Publication Data

Multicultural law enforcement: strategies for peacekeeping in a diverse society / Robert
M. Shusta . . . [et al.].—2nd ed.
   p. cm.
  Includes bibliographical references and index.
  ISBN 0-13-033409-X
  1. Police-community relations—United States. 2. Discrimination in law
enforcement—United States. 3. Multiculturalism—United States. 4. Intercultural
communication—United States. I. Shusta, Robert M.

HV7936.P8 M85 2002
363.2'3—dc21   2001024941

Publisher: Jeff Johnston
Executive Editor: Kim Davies
Production Editor: Lori Dalberg, Carlisle Publishers Services
Production Liaison: Barbara Marttine Cappuccio
Director of Production & Manufacturing: Bruce Johnson
Managing Editor: Mary Carnis
Manufacturing Buyer: Cathleen Petersen
Design Director: Cheryl Asherman
Cover Design Coordinator: Miguel Ortiz
Cover Designer: Kevin Kall
Cover Photo: © Tracey L. Williams/Courtesy of Somerset County Police Academy, North Branch, NJ,
   Dr. Richard Celeste, Deputy Chief, Executive Director.
Marketing Manager: Ramona Sherman
Assistant Editor: Sarah Holle
Composition: Carlisle Communications, Ltd.
Printing and Binding: R. R. Donnelley & Sons

Pearson Education LTD.
Pearson Education Australia PTY, Limited
Pearson Education Singapore, Pte. Ltd.
Pearson Education North Asia Ltd.
Pearson Education Canada, Ltd.
Pearson Educacíon de Mexico, S.A. de C.V.
Pearson Education—Japan
Pearson Education Malaysia, Pte. Ltd.

10 9 8 7 6 5 4 3 2 1
ISBN 0-13-033409-X

To the many law enforcement professionals who have contributed to this book and, by their actions, have demonstrated the professionalism that is required in our multicultural society.

And to our families, especially the late Dr. Dorothy L. Harris, whose tolerance and support made it possible for us to reach our goal.

CONTENTS

FOREWORD   xiii

PREFACE   xv

ACKNOWLEDGMENTS   xvii

PART ONE   *Impact of Cultural Diversity on Law Enforcement*   1

1   MULTICULTURAL COMMUNITIES: Challenges for Law Enforcement   3
Overview   3
Commentary   3
Introduction   4
Diverse Society   8
Interplay between Police Incidents and Culture   17
Mini Case Studies: Culture and Crime   20
Police Knowledge of Cultural Groups   22
Prejudice in Law Enforcement   23
Racial Profiling   29
Community-Based Policing   33
Summary   35
Eight Tips for Improving Law Enforcement in Multicultural Communities   36
Discussion Questions and Issues   36
References   38

2   THE CHANGING LAW ENFORCEMENT AGENCY: A Microcosm of Society   40
Overview   40
Commentary   40
Introduction   41
Changing Workforce   42
Ethnic and Racial Issues within the Workforce   44

Women in Law Enforcement   51
Gays and Lesbians in Law Enforcement   58
The Chief Executive   67
Summary   71
Discussion Questions and Issues   71
References   72

3   **MULTICULTURAL REPRESENTATION IN LAW ENFORCEMENT: Recruitment, Retention, and Promotion   73**
Overview   73
Commentary   73
Introduction   74
Recruitment of a Diverse Workforce   74
Retention and Promotion of a Diverse Workforce   85
Summary   88
Discussion Questions and Issues   89
References   89

PART TWO   *Training in Cultural Understanding for Law Enforcement*   91

4   **PREPARATION AND IMPLEMENTATION OF CULTURAL AWARENESS TRAINING   92**
Overview   92
Commentary   92
Introduction   93
Cultural Awareness and Cultural Diversity Training   95
Design and Evaluation of Cultural Training   102
External Consultants and Trainers   106
Law Enforcement Agency Models for Cultural Training   108
Administrative Guidelines for Cultural Awareness Training   109
Summary   111
Discussion Questions and Issues   112
References   113

5   **CROSS-CULTURAL COMMUNICATION FOR LAW ENFORCEMENT   114**
Overview   114
Commentary   114
Cross-Cultural Communication in the Law Enforcement Context   115
Cross-Cultural Communication Attempts   116
Language Barriers and Law Enforcement   121
Attitudes toward Non- or Limited-English Speakers   123
Interviewing and Data-Gathering Skills   126

Nonverbal Communication   127
Male–Female Communication in Law Enforcement   131
Summary   133
Discussion Questions and Issues   134
References   136

PART THREE   Cultural Specifics for Law Enforcement   137

6   LAW ENFORCEMENT CONTACT WITH ASIAN/PACIFIC AMERICANS   138
Overview   138
Commentary   138
Introduction   139
Asian/Pacific American Defined   139
Typology of Asian/Pacific Americans   141
Historical Information   142
Demographics: Diversity among Asian/Pacific Americans   145
Asian/Pacific Americans' Key Motivating Perspectives   147
Labels and Terms   150
Myths and Stereotypes   151
The Asian/Pacific American Family   154
Cultural Influences on Communication: Verbal and Nonverbal Styles of
    Asian/Pacific Americans   157
Key Issues in Law Enforcement   159
Summary of Recommendations for Law Enforcement   162
Discussion Questions and Issues   163
References   164

7   LAW ENFORCEMENT CONTACT WITH AFRICAN AMERICANS   166
Overview   166
Commentary   166
African American Culture   167
Historical Information   167
Demographics: Diversity among African Americans   169
Issues of Identity   171
Group Identification Terms   172
Myths and Stereotypes   172
Cross-Racial Perceptions in Law Enforcement   174
The Black Family   174
Language and Communication   177
Key Issues in Law Enforcement   182
Summary of Recommendations for Law Enforcement   190
Discussion Questions and Issues   192
References   194

8 LAW ENFORCEMENT CONTACT WITH LATINO/HISPANIC AMERICANS 195

Overview 195
Commentary 195
Introduction 196
Latino/Hispanic Americans Defined 196
Historical Information 197
Demographics: Diversity among Latino/Hispanic Americans 199
Labels and Terms 201
Typology of Latino/Hispanic Americans 202
Myths and Stereotypes 202
The Latino/Hispanic American Family 206
The Role of the Man and the Woman in a Latino/Hispanic American Family 206
Cultural Influences on Communication: Verbal and Nonverbal Styles of
    Latino/Hispanic Americans 209
Key Issues in Law Enforcement 211
Summary of Recommendations for Law Enforcement 217
Discussion Questions and Issues 218
References 219

**9 LAW ENFORCEMENT CONTACT WITH ARAB AMERICANS AND OTHER
MIDDLE EASTERN GROUPS 221**

Overview 221
Commentary 221
Middle Easterners Defined 222
Historical Information 225
Demographics 226
Differences and Similarities 226
Stereotypes 228
Islamic Religion 231
Family Structure 233
Cultural Practices 235
Key Issues in Law Enforcement 240
Summary of Recommendations for Law Enforcement 245
Discussion Questions and Issues 247
References 248

10 LAW ENFORCEMENT CONTACT WITH AMERICAN INDIANS 249

Overview 249
Commentary 249
Historical Information and Background 250
The Question of American Indian Identity 252
Tribes, Reservations, and Mobility of Native Americans 253
Differences and Similarities among Native Americans 254
Language and Communication 257
Family-Related Issues 260

Key Issues in Law Enforcement   262
Summary of Recommendations for Law Enforcement   269
Discussion Questions and Issues   271
References   271

PART FOUR   *Response Strategies for Crimes Motivated by Hate/Bias*   273

11   HATE/BIAS CRIMES: Insights and Response Strategies   274

Overview   274
Commentary   275
Historical Perspectives   275
The Hate/Bias Crime Problem   277
Victims of Hate Crimes   287
Jews and Anti-Semitism   288
Gay and Lesbian Victimization   292
War-Related Hate Crimes   296
Law Enforcement Response Strategies   297
Summary   302
Discussion Questions and Issues   302
References   303

12   HATE/BIAS CRIMES: Reporting and Tracking   304

Overview   304
Commentary   304
Defining the Problem   305
Hate Crimes Data Collection   306
Monitoring Hate/Bias Crimes and Incidents   312
Hate Crimes Laws   313
Trend Monitoring in Multicultural Communities   316
Trends to Monitor: STEEP Typology   319
Summary   321
Discussion Questions and Issues   321
References   322

13   HATE/BIAS CRIMES: Investigations, Control, and Victimology   323

Overview   323
Commentary   323
Introduction   324
Hate/Bias Crime and Incident Investigations   324
Hate/Bias Crime Prosecution   329
Hate/Bias Crime and Incident Control   331
Hate/Bias Crime and Incident Victimology   348
Summary   350
Discussion Questions and Issues   351
References   352

PART FIVE Cultural Effectiveness for Peace Officers 355

14 PEACE OFFICER IMAGE AND CULTURAL SENSITIVITY 356

Overview 356
Commentary 356
Impact of Images on Human Behavior 357
Twenty-First-Century Peace Officer Images 366
Cosmopolitan Public Servants 368
Community-Based Approach to Policing 370
Culturally Sensitive Peacekeeping 372
Summary 382
Discussion Questions and Issues 383
References 384

15 POLICE OFFICER PROFESSIONALISM AND PEACEKEEPING STRATEGIES IN A DIVERSE SOCIETY 386

Overview 386
Commentary 386
Police Leadership in Professionalism and Synergy 387
Regional or Statewide Cooperation in Law Enforcement 390
Career Development and Professional Opportunities 397
Peacekeeping Strategies in Multicultural Societies 399
Organizational Trends in Law Enforcement 413
Summary 417
Discussion Questions and Issues 418
References 419

APPENDIX A   MULTICULTURAL COMMUNITY AND WORKFORCE: ATTITUDE ASSESSMENT SURVEY 423

APPENDIX B   CULTURAL DIVERSITY SURVEY: NEEDS ASSESSMENT 429

APPENDIX C   LISTING OF CONSULTANTS AND RESOURCES 435

APPENDIX D   SELF-ASSESSMENT OF COMMUNICATION SKILLS IN LAW ENFORCEMENT: COMMUNICATIONS INVENTORY 440

GLOSSARY   441

INDEX   445

FOREWORD

Communities and police agencies across America have struggled for many years with the issues of race, ethnicity, and gender. In the past 20 years, these struggles have been even more complex and challenging as larger numbers of non-English-speaking legal and illegal immigrants have come to America seeking economic, religious, or political freedoms. In addition to the obvious communication problems, law enforcement professionals frequently encounter cultural tensions between the new immigrants and both majority and minority Americans as neighborhoods begin to change.

There are those who would argue that little progress has been made in policing given the widespread racial disturbances in recent years and the continuing debate over "racial profiling" as reflected in the following news stories:

> Black men stopped by police while driving on highways around the Motor City are more likely than their white neighbors to be searched without their consent, a study by the Michigan State Police has found. (APB News.com July 21, 2000)

> The first comprehensive study of racial profiling by a major police department found that motorists in San Diego are more likely to be pulled over if they are black or Latino. (APB News.com October 2, 2000)

Clearly, the effective policing of multicultural communities remains an enormous challenge. However, there is good reason for optimism as police agencies become more diverse, enhance training, improve language skills, and seek to build strong partnerships with ethnic and racial communities. To be sure, police departments have changed but, like society as a whole and its important institutions, have failed to keep pace with the rapid changes in the diversity of our communities.

Multicultural Law Enforcement: Strategies for Peacekeeping in a Diverse Society is a chronicle of both the progress that has been made and the enormous challenges that face policing in America in the new millennium. In five major sections, the second edition of this book addresses all of the key multicultural issues facing the police today and well into the future. It looks at the makeup of the police organization itself, training, professionalism, and the unique aspects of a number of specific cultures. The text provides practical and useful guidance on how the police can more effectively work with these cultural groups inside their organizations as well as in the community. Each chapter in the section on specific cultures sets forth the historical context of police relationships and identifies the key issues that must be addressed. The first edition of the book was on the cutting edge of these issues for the police and the second is even more valuable as police have become more sensitive to the importance of effectively policing our multicultural communities.

Multicultural Law Enforcement serves as an excellent model of strength of diversity. The authors themselves represent a diverse team in terms of their culture, gender, and other backgrounds. In addition, they have enhanced their diversity by reaching out to a wide range of experts on the areas in which they write. They have produced a magnificent volume that will continue to be of tremendous value to the police, students, and the community as law enforcement wrestles with the enormous challenge of policing in a democratic society. It is also a natural and comfortable fit with the community problem-oriented policing philosophy that so many police agencies have adopted throughout America.

This philosophy depends on engaging the community in a strong partnership that focuses on the problems that create the environment for crime, violence, drug abuse, and disorder. To do so, the police must understand and work with our diverse communities. *Multicultural Law Enforcement* is an important tool to enable them to understand cultures in a way that will be invaluable to building these critical partnerships.

Darrel W. Stephens, Chief
CHARLOTTE-MECKLENBURG POLICE DEPARTMENT
CHARLOTTE, NORTH CAROLINA

Authors' Note:

Chief Darrel W. Stephens is an accomplished government executive with 32 years of experience in policing that began as a police officer in Kansas City, Missouri, in 1968. His distinguished career includes work as Assistant Chief of Police, Lawrence, Kansas; Chief of Police, Largo, Florida; Chief of Police, Newport News, Virginia; Executive Director, Police Executive Research Forum; and Police Chief and City Administrator, City of St. Petersburg, Florida. He has served as a consultant, writer, and speaker throughout the country, promoting progressive policing approaches throughout his career. He is currently Chief of Police of Charlotte-Mecklenburg, North Carolina, a department with 2,000 employees, serving a city and an unincorporated area of over 600,000 people.

The authors of *Multicultural Law Enforcement* are honored that Chief Stephens' words introduce our readership to the message of our textbook.

PREFACE

This second edition of *Multicultural Law Enforcement: Strategies for Peacekeeping in a Diverse Society* is a tribute to all our readers who enthusiastically received the original work. It is a textbook for police departments and academies, colleges, and universities. It is also designed to assist all levels of criminal justice representatives in understanding the pervasive influences of culture, race, and ethnicity in the workplace and in multicultural communities. The text again focuses on the cross-cultural contact that police officers and civilian employees have with citizens, victims, suspects, and coworkers from diverse backgrounds. This second edition also includes new or expanded material on the following: hate crimes; community-based policing; undocumented immigrants and immigrant women; urban dynamics; women, gays, and lesbians in law enforcement; and a substantial discussion of racial profiling. We include updated demographic data using the most current population estimates and projections available to date.

Throughout these pages, we stress the need for awareness, understanding of cultural differences, and respect toward those of different backgrounds. We encourage all representatives of law enforcement to examine preconceived notions they might hold of particular groups. We outline for police executives why they should build awareness and promote cultural understanding and tolerance within their agencies.

An increasing number of leaders in law enforcement agencies and their employees have accepted the premise that greater cross-cultural competency must be a key objective of all management and professional development. Demographic changes have had a tremendous impact not only on the types of crimes committed but also on the composition of the law enforcement workforce and the people with whom officers make contact. To be effective, police executives must understand the diversity in their workforces and in their changing communities. Professionalism today includes the need for greater consideration across cultures and improved communication with members of diverse groups.

In an era when news is processed and accessed immediately, the public is exposed almost daily to instances of cross-cultural and interracial contact between law enforcement agents and citizens. So, too, have community members become increasingly sophisticated and critical with regard to how members of diverse cultural and racial groups are treated by public servants. Employees of police departments and other agencies entrusted with law enforcement find that they are now serving communities that carefully observe them and hold them accountable for their actions.

This new edition has been updated and expanded to provide practical information and guidelines for law enforcement managers, supervisors, officers, and instructors. With cross-cultural knowledge, sensitivity, and tolerance, those who are charged with the responsibility of peacekeeping will improve their image while demonstrating greater professionalism, within the changing multicultural workforce and community.

Robert M. Shusta, M.P.A.
Deena R. Levine, M.A.
Philip R. Harris, Ph.D.
Herbert Z. Wong, Ph.D.

A supplementary *Instructor's Manual* is available for this text.

ACKNOWLEDGMENTS

This second edition has benefited from contributions by the following people and organizations:

Hillel B. Levine, Ph.D., Graphic Artist
Castro Valley, California

Darrel Stephens, Police Chief
Charlotte-Mecklensburg Police Department
Charlotte, North Carolina

Ondra Berry, Deputy Chief
Reno Police Department
Reno, Nevada

Mitchell Grobeson, Retired Sergeant
Los Angeles Police Department
Los Angeles, California

David Barlow, Ph.D., Associate Professor
University of Wisconsin
Madison, Wisconsin

Gary Weaver, Ph.D., Faculty Member
School of International Service
American University
Washington, D.C.

George Simons, Ph.D., President
Simons International
Santa Cruz, California

Kenneth L.Whitman, Chief
California Department of Justice
Sacramento, California

Bob Harrison, Chief
Vacaville Police Department
Vacaville, California

Brian Harris, Detective
Houston Police Department
Houston, Texas

Robert Lewis, Sergeant
San Diego Police Department
San Diego, California

Ilana Lipsett, Editorial Assistant
University of California, San Diego
San Diego, California

Margo Dunlap, Research Assistant
University of California, Berkeley
Berkeley, California

Donya Fernandez, Language Rights Attorney
Employment Law Center/Legal Aid Society
San Francisco, California

Drew Setter, Lobbyist
Native American Concerns Legal Organization
Legix Organization
Native American Indian Lobbyist Firm
Albuquerque, New Mexico

Susan Jones, Lieutenant
Concord Police Department
Concord, California

Gregory Jones, Personnel Director
City of Concord
Concord, California

We owe special thanks to the following individuals for their helpful insights:

Steven Wallace, Ph.D., California	Sari Karet, California
Ron Martinelli, Ph.D., California	Judge Lawrence Katz, California
Sergeant P. Andrash, British Columbia, Canada	Thomas Kochman, Ph.D., Illinois
Major David Barton, Missouri	Sergeant Mark Jabour, Michigan
John Levelle, California	Char Miller, Ph.D., Texas
Alixa Naff, Ph.D., Washington, D.C.	Officer Darryl McAllister, California
Professor Danilo Begonia, California	Susan Miyahira, Ph.D., California
Chung Chuong, California	Dinh Van Nguyen, California
Jonathan Levine, Ph.D., Michigan	Alicia Powers, California
Officer Mohamed Berro, Michigan	Oscar Ramirez, Ph.D., Texas
Officer James Caggero, California	Victoria Santos, California
Deputy Lori Brimmage, California	Audrey Shabbas, California
Joe Canton, Ph.D., California	George Thompson, New Mexico
Darrell Standing Elk, California	Reverend Onasai Veevau, California
Officer Steve Fajardo, California	Norita Jones Vlach, Ph.D., California
Inspector E. Grandia, British Columbia, Canada	James Zogby, Ph.D., Washington, D.C.
Chief Thomas Hall, Virginia	John Zogby, Ph.D., New York
Jim Kahue, Hawaii	Susan Miyahira, Ph.D., Hawaii

We are grateful to the following people for reviewing the manuscript for the first edition of *Multicultural Law Enforcement: Strategies for Peacekeeping in a Diverse Society:* Major Craig Masterson, New York State Police Academy; Wayne Madole, Ed.D., Broward Community College, Ft. Lauderdale, Florida, and T. F. Adams, Rancho Santiago College, Santa Ana, California.

We would also like to thank the following people for reviewing and critiquing the first edition and for providing suggestions for our second edition: Steve Christiansen, Green River Community College, Washington; Ellen Cohn, International University, Florida; James Albrecht, John Jay University, New York; and Alejandro del Carmen, University of Texas at Arlington, Texas.

MULTICULTURAL
LAW ENFORCEMENT

PART ONE

Impact of Cultural Diversity on Law Enforcement

1 MULTICULTURAL COMMUNITIES: CHALLENGES FOR LAW ENFORCEMENT
2 THE CHANGING LAW ENFORCEMENT AGENCY: A MICROCOSM OF SOCIETY
3 MULTICULTURAL REPRESENTATION IN LAW ENFORCEMENT: RECRUITMENT, RETENTION, AND PROMOTION

Part One of *Multicultural Law Enforcement* introduces readers to the implications of a multicultural society for law enforcement, both within and outside the police agency. The changing population law enforcement representatives encounter is described in Chapter 1, and differing views on diversity are discussed. Using three case studies, Chapter 1 exemplifies how the presence of different cultures can affect the very nature and perception of crime itself. The authors present the subject of prejudice and its effect on police work, providing specific examples of its consequences in law enforcement. Examples of racial profiling are given, along with an explanation of and suggestions for professional police stops. The authors also discuss community-based policing and provide examples of departments with and without community partnerships. The chapter ends with suggestions for improving law enforcement in multicultural communities.

Chapter 2 discusses demographic changes that are taking place within law enforcement agencies, as well as racism in the law enforcement workplace and responses to it. In addition to data on ethnic and racial groups, this chapter provides information on women and on gays and lesbians in law enforcement institutions across the country. The authors illustrate the realities of the new workforce and the corresponding need for flexibility in leadership styles.

Chapter 3 discusses challenges in recruitment, retention, and promotion of police personnel from various racial, ethnic, and cultural backgrounds. The authors present strategies for recruitment, emphasizing the commitment required by law enforcement chief executives and the need to look inward—that is, to assess the level of comfort and inclusion that all employees experience in a given agency. If the levels are not high, hiring, retention, and promotion will be difficult. Chapter 3 describes the pressing need facing all agencies to build a workforce of highly qualified individuals of diverse backgrounds and in which all people have equal access to the hiring, retention, and promotion processes.

Each chapter ends with discussion questions and a list of references. The following appendixes correspond to the chapter content in Part One.

Appendix A   Multicultural Community and Workforce: Attitude Assessment Survey
Appendix B   Cultural Diversity Survey: Needs Assessment

1

MULTICULTURAL COMMUNITIES:

Challenges for Law Enforcement

OVERVIEW

In this chapter we discuss challenges facing law enforcement related to the growing multicultural population in the United States. Chapter 1 begins with the need for an increased understanding of the diverse populations, both immigrant and U.S.-born ethnic communities, with which law enforcement officials interact. The discussion of our mosaic society incorporates a brief historical perspective on immigration. Three mini case studies illustrate the points of contact between a person's culture and a particular crime or offense. We present practical reasons why officers should have an understanding of the cultural backgrounds of the groups they commonly encounter. Next, we discuss the subject of prejudice, including racial profiling and the need for law enforcement professionalism. Community-based policing is discussed, along with its implications for positive relations and contact with diverse immigrant and ethnic communities. The chapter ends with tips for improving law enforcement in multicultural communities.

COMMENTARY

The 21st century will be the century in which we redefine ourselves as the first country in world history which is literally made up of every part of the world.

—Mr. Kenneth Prewitt, Director of the U.S. Census Bureau

A multicultural community is one made up of many different ethnic and racial groups. The word *multiculturalism* does not refer to a movement or political force, nor is it an anti-American term. Multiculturalism and diversity are at the very heart of America and describe accurately the demographics of our nation in the twenty-first century. Law enforcement officials—those whose professional ideal is to protect and serve people equally from all backgrounds—must face the challenges and complexities of a diverse society. Many police procedures and interactions with citizens can be complicated by diversity. A lack of knowledge of cultural differences can result in inadvertent violation of individuals' rights. Further, officers must ensure that their prejudices are in check and that no biased thought (common to all human beings) is acted on. The following quotes provide a national perspective on the mandate of law enforcement:

> *Initial Report of the United States of America to the United Nations Committee on the Elimination of Racial Discrimination*
>
> As a functioning, multi-racial [and multicultural] democracy, the United States seeks to enforce the established rights of individuals to protection against discrimination based upon race, color, national origin, religion, gender, age, disability status, and citizenship status in virtually every aspect of social and economic life. . . . The federal government has established a wide-ranging set of enforcement procedures to administer these laws, with the U.S. Department of Justice exercising a major coordination and leadership role on most critical enforcement issues. (September 2000)
>
> *Interview with Deputy Chief Ondra Berry, Reno, Nevada, Police Department*
>
> Law enforcement is under a powerful microscope in terms of how citizens are treated. Minority and ethnic communities have become increasingly competent in understanding the role of law enforcement, and expectations of law enforcement for professionalism have been elevated from previous years. In an age when information about what happens in a police department on the East Coast speeds across to the West Coast in seconds, law enforcement officials must be aware. They must be vigilant. They must do the right thing. (Berry, 2000)

INTRODUCTION

The United States, compared to virtually all other nations, has experienced unparalleled growth in its multicultural population. Reactions to these changes range from appreciation and even celebration of diversity to an absolute intolerance of differences. In its extreme form, intolerance resulting in crimes of hate is a major law enforcement and criminal justice concern. From this perspective alone, multiculturalism cannot be ignored. Yet beyond hate crimes, law enforcement is faced with other challenges related to diversity that require knowledge and skills to handle cultural barriers. As community-based policing has increasingly become the norm in the United States, police department management is viewing communities in partnership roles. In doing so, many are now acknowledging that understanding diversity can play a significant and positive role in the effectiveness of law enforcement in multicultural communities. Many officers now understand that their contact with citizens from certain backgrounds is tinged with negative historical "baggage." In addition, law enforcement professionals have had to face widely disparate views that minorities and nonminorities hold toward the criminal justice system. Finally, law enforcement as a profession has had to come to terms with police practices reflecting prejudice on the part of some officers.

> *Changing America: Crime and Criminal Justice,* by the Council of Economic Advisors for the President's Initiative on Race
>
> Besides perception of discrimination in the criminal justice system, lack of racial and ethnic diversity among those working in criminal justice may also undermine the perceived legitimacy of the system. . . . Differences in perceptions about the fairness of the police, the courts, prisons, and jails among racial and ethnic groups have been widely noted. National survey data indicate that blacks are more likely than whites to believe that the criminal justice system treats blacks more harshly, and some research based on particular groups or cities finds that both whites and members of minority groups believe that discrimination on the basis of race or ethnicity is a problem in the administration of the criminal justice system. (Council of Economic Advisors for the President's Initiative on Race, 1998)

Beyond perceptions and actual incidents of differential treatment, strategies to enforce the law with one's own cultural group may very well result in unsuspected difficulties with another group. The acts of approaching, communicating, questioning, assisting, and establishing trust with members of different groups require special knowledge and skills that have nothing to do with the fact that "the law is the law" and must be enforced equally. Acquiring knowledge and skills that lead to sensitivity does not imply preferential treatment of any one group; rather, it contributes to improved communication with members of all groups. The goals on a personal level in multicultural law enforcement should be to become more comfortable with groups and communities different from one's own and to treat people fairly and with respect. Twenty-first-century professionalism in the criminal justice system implies increased sophistication in responding to people of all backgrounds.

The Melting Pot Myth and the Mosaic

Multiculturalism (also referred to as *cultural pluralism*) violates what some consider to be the "American way of life." However, from the time our country was founded, we were never a homogeneous society. The indigenous peoples of America (the ancestors of the American Indians) were here long before Christopher Columbus "discovered" them. There is even strong evidence that the first Africans who set foot in this country came as free people, 200 years before the slave trade from Africa began (Rawlins, 1992). Furthermore, the majority of people in America can claim to be the children, grandchildren, or great-grandchildren of people who have migrated here. Americans did not originate from a common stock. Until fairly recently, America has been referred to as a *melting pot,* a term depicting an image of people coming together and forming a unified culture. One of the earliest usages of the term was in the early 1900s, when a famous American playwright, Israel Zangwill, referring to the mass migration from Europe, said,

> America is God's crucible, the great Melting-Pot where all the races of *Europe* are melting and re-forming. . . . Germans and Frenchmen, Irishmen and Englishmen, Jews and Russians—into the Crucible with you all! God is making the American! (Zangwill, 1908).

This first use of the term *melting pot* was not designed to incorporate anyone except Europeans. Did the melting pot ever exist, then, in the United States? No, it never did. Yet people still refer to the belief, which is not much more than a romantic myth about the "good old days." African Americans, brought forcibly to this country between 1619 and 1850, were never part of the early descriptions of the melting pot. Likewise, Native American peoples were not considered for the melting pot. It is not coincidental that these groups were nonwhite and were therefore not "meltable." Furthermore, throughout our past, great efforts have been made to *prevent* any additional diversity. Most notable in this regard was the Chinese Exclusion Act in 1882, which denied Chinese laborers the right to enter America. Early in the twentieth century organized labor formed the Japanese and Korean Exclusion League "to protest the influx of 'Coolie' labor and in fear of threat to the living standards of American workingmen" (Kennedy, 1986, p. 72). Immigration was discouraged or prevented if it did not add strength to what already existed as the European-descended majority of the population (Handlin, 1975).

Even at the peak of immigration (late 1800s), New York City exemplified how different immigrant groups stayed separate from each other, with little of the "blending" that people often imagine took place (Miller, 2000). Three-fourths of New York City's population consisted of first- or second-generation immigrants (including Europeans and Asians); 80 percent did not speak English, and there were 100 foreign-language newspapers in circulation. The new arrivals were not accepted by those who had already settled, and newcomers found comfort in an alien society by choosing to remain in ethnic enclaves with people who shared their culture and life experiences.

The first generation of every immigrant and refugee group seeing the United States as the land of hope and opportunity has always experienced obstacles in acculturation (i.e., integration) into the new society. In many cases, people resisted Americanization and kept to themselves. Italians, the Irish, eastern European Jews, the Portuguese, Germans, and virtually all other groups tended to remain apart when they first came. Most previously settled immigrants were distrustful and disdainful of each newcomer group. "Mainstreaming" began to occur only with children of immigrants (although some people within certain immigrant groups tried to assimilate quickly). For the most part, however, society did not permit a quick shedding of previous cultural identity. History has never supported the metaphor of the melting pot, especially with regard to the first and second generations of most groups of newcomers. Despite the reality of past multicultural disharmony and tension in the United States, however, the notion of the melting pot prevailed.

The terms *mosaic* and *tapestry* more accurately and idealistically portray a view of diversity in America. They describe a society in which all colors and backgrounds blend in harmony to form society as a whole, but one in which groups are not required to lose their characteristics in order to "melt" together. The idea of a mosaic portrays a society in which all races and ethnic groups are displayed in a form that is attractive because of the very elements of which it is made. Each group is seen as separate and distinct in contributing its own color, shape, and design to the whole, resulting in an *enriched* society.

Reactions to Diversity: Past and Present

Accepting diversity has always been a difficult proposition for most Americans (Miller, 2000). Typical criticisms of immigrants, now and historically, include "They hold on to their cultures," "They don't learn our language," "Their customs and behavior are strange," and "They form cliques." Many newcomers, in fact, have historically resisted Americanization, keeping to ethnic enclaves. They were not usually accepted by mainstream society.

Are the reactions to newcomers today so different from people's reactions to earlier waves of immigrants? Let's look at reactions to the Irish, who by the middle of the nineteenth century constituted the largest group of immigrants in the United States, making up almost 45 percent of the foreign-born population. Approximately 4.25 million people left Ireland, mainly because of the potato famine. Many of these immigrants had come from rural areas but ended up in cities on the East Coast. Most were illiterate; some spoke only Gaelic (Kennedy, 1986). Their reception in America was anything but welcoming, exemplified by the plethora of signs saying, "Jobs available, no Irish need apply," which could be seen frequently.

> The Irish . . . endure[d] the scorn and discrimination later to be inflicted, to some degree at least, on each successive wave of immigrants by already settled "Americans." In speech and in dress, they seemed foreign; they were poor and unskilled and they were arriving in overwhelming numbers. . . . The Irish found many doors closed to them, both socially and economically. When their earnings were not enough . . . their wives and daughters obtained employment as servants. (Kennedy, 1986, p. 18)

If this account were rewritten without specific references to time and cultural group, it would be reasonable to assume it describes contemporary reactions to newcomers. One could take this quotation and substitute *Jew, Italian,* or *Polish* at various points in history. Today, it could be used in reference to Cubans, Somalis, Afghans, Mexicans, Haitians, Serbs, or Ethiopians. If we compare immigration today with that during earlier periods in U.S. history, we find similarities as well as significant differences. In the past few decades, we have received people from cultures more dramatically different than those from western Europe. For example, many of our "new Americans" from parts of Asia or Africa bring values and languages not commonly associated with or related to mainstream American values and language. Middle Easterners bring customs unknown to many U.S.-born Americans. (For cultural specifics, refer to Chapters 6 through 10.) Many refugees bring scars of political persecution or war trauma, the nature of which the majority of Americans cannot even fathom. The relatively mild experiences of those who came as voluntary migrants do not compare with the tragedies of many of the more recent refugees. True, desperate economic conditions compelled many early European immigrants to leave their countries (and thus their leaving was not *entirely* voluntary). However, their experiences do not parallel, for example, war-torn eastern European refugees who came to the United States in the 1990s.

Disparaging comments were once made toward the very people whose descendants would, in later years, constitute much of mainstream America. Many fourth- and fifth-generation immigrants have forgotten their history (Miller, 2000) and are intolerant of the "foreign ways" of various groups. *Every* new group seems to be met with some suspicion and, in many cases, hostility. Adjustment to a new society is and has always been a long and painful process, and the first-generation immigrant group suffers, whether Irish, Jewish, Polish, Afghani, Laotian, Filipino, or Russian. It must also be remembered that many groups did not come to the United States of their own free will but rather were victims of a political or economic system that forced them to abruptly cut their roots and escape their homelands. Although grateful for their welcome to this country, such newcomers did not want to be uprooted. Many new Americans did not have any part in the creation of events that led to the flight from their countries.

DIVERSE SOCIETY

In *One America in the 21st Century: Forging a New Future,* data showed that although racially and ethnically diverse groups have made progress with respect to the indicators used to measure the quality of life, they still face barriers to full inclusion in American life. In the area of civil rights enforcement, the Advisory Board to the President's Initiative on Race (1998) made the following recommendations:

> Strengthen civil rights enforcement
> Improve data collection on racial and ethnic discrimination
> Strengthen laws and enforcement against hate crimes

A diverse society obviously makes any law enforcement officer or manager's job more difficult. Racial tensions, cultural background, and ethnicity are bound to complicate many police procedures and encounters with citizens. It would be naive to "preach" to law enforcement officers, agents, and managers about the value of diversity when day-to-day activities are complicated by diversity. But the longer it takes to understand the influences of culture and ethnicity on behavior, the longer every police procedure and encounter between the police and the multicultural public will remain complicated. At a minimum, there must be a basic acceptance of diversity on the part of all criminal justice representatives as a precursor to improving interpersonal relations and contact across cultural, ethnic, and racial lines.

The Overlap of Race, Culture, and Ethnicity

Before entering into a discussion of demographics of various minority and immigrant groups, we must mention how, in this twenty-first century, demographic estimates and projections are likely to fall short of counting the true mix of people in the United States. In Chapters 6 through 10 of this book (culture-specific chapters), we discuss characteristics and law enforcement–related issues of Asian or Pacific Americans, African Americans, Latino or Hispanic Americans, Arab Americans and other Middle Eastern groups, and American Indians. This categorization is merely for the sake of convenience; an individual may belong to two or more groups (as represented in the chapters). For example, a black Latino may identify himself or herself as both black and Latino. Race and ethnic background (e.g., in the case of a black Latino) are not necessarily mutually exclusive. *Hispanic* is considered an ethnicity, not a race. Therefore people of Latino descent can count themselves as part of any race. An individual who in the 1990 census counted himself or herself as black and now chooses both black and white is considered one person with two races in the 2000 census ("Multiracial Data in Census Adds Categories and Controversies," *San Francisco Chronicle,* December 10, 2000, p. A-14). Law enforcement officials need to be aware of the overlap between race and ethnicity and that many individuals consider themselves to be multiracial.

> Everyday, in every corner of America, we are redrawing the color lines and are redefining what race really means. It's not just a matter of black and white anymore; the nuances of brown and yellow and red mean more—and less than ever." ("Redefining Race in America," *Newsweek,* September 18, 2000, p. 38)

Americans come in many shades and mixtures today in our heterogeneous society, in which an amalgam of races, cultures, and ethnic groups is commonplace. The first photo in the mentioned *Newsweek* article shows a child whose ethnicity is Nigerian, Irish, African American, Native American, Russian Jewish, and Polish Jewish (from parents and grandparents). Her U.S. census category may be simply "other." When we interpret population statistics, we have to understand that the face of America is changing. In 1860 there were only three census categories: black, white, and quadroon (a person who has one black grandparent, or the child of a mulatto and a white). In 2000 there were 30 broad census categories, from Asian Indian to other Pacific Islander. According to the *Newsweek* article there were 11 subcategories under Hispanic ethnicity. When the 2000 census results are published, 63 racial combinations will be possible ("Multiracial Data in Census Adds Categories and Controversies," *San Francisco Chronicle,* December 10, 2000, p. A-14). The challenges to accurate counting of the population result because "the census has a very distinct purpose to collect broad data on (populations). It's not there for collecting people's identity" (Eric Rodriguez, director of the Economic Mobility Project of La Raza, quoted in *San Francisco Chronicle* article). A Princeton University study (also cited in the article) estimated that in early 2000, 16.5 million people (or 6 percent of the U.S. population of 275 million) are multiracial.

Changing Population

Changes in population characteristics between 1990 and 2000 reveal some trends (see Exhibit 1.1); Exhibit 1.2 presents graphically the relative sizes of various ethnic populations. According to population projections, by 2050, 75 percent of the U.S. population will be white (this includes individuals indicating white and Hispanic categories) compared to an estimate of 82 percent in 2000. The non-Hispanic white population will be the slowest-growing race group. In 2050, 15 percent of the population will be black; 9 percent Asian and Pacific Islander, and 1 percent American Indian, Eskimo, and Aleut. The Hispanic origin population will increase to 25 percent, and the non-Hispanic white population will decline to 53 percent (Exhibit 1.3). According to demographic predictions "minorities" will become the majority in the United States by 2010.* This demographic shift has already occurred in some large

---

*Demographic shifts call for corresponding changes in terminology associated with groups in the population. Wherever possible, we have attempted to replace the words *minority* and *minority groups* with different terms.

Exhibit 1.1 Population trends by race and Hispanic origin, in thousands.

	1990	2000	CHANGE	PERCENT CHANGE
White, not Hispanic	188,596	196,806	8,210	4%
Hispanic origin	22,571	32,640	10,069	45%
Black, not Hispanic	29,404	33,551	4,147	14%
Asian and Pacific Islander, not Hispanic	7,090	10,565	3,475	49%
American Indian, Eskimo, and Aleut, not Hispanic	1,804	2,055	251	14%
Total	247,661	273,562	25,901	10%

Source: U.S. Bureau of the Census. (2000, October). *Resident Population Estimates by Sex, Race, and Hispanic Origin: April 1, 1990, to July 1, 1999, with Short-Term Projections to September 1, 2000.* Washington, D.C.: U.S. Bureau of the Census.

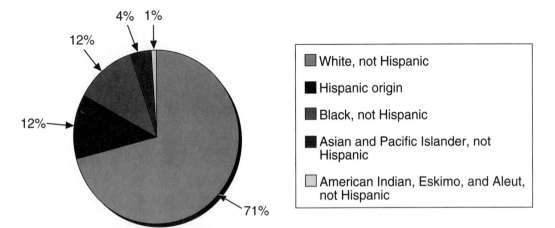

Exhibit 1.2 Population by race and Hispanic origin, 2000.

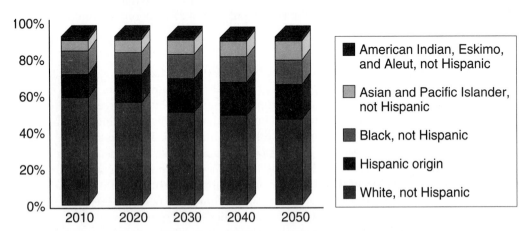

Exhibit 1.3 Population projections by race and Hispanic origin in stacked Percentages. *Source:* U.S. Bureau of the Census. (1996). *Population Projections of the U.S. by Age, Sex, Race, and Hispanic Origin 1995–2050. Current Population Reports.* Washington, D.C.: U.S. Bureau of the Census.

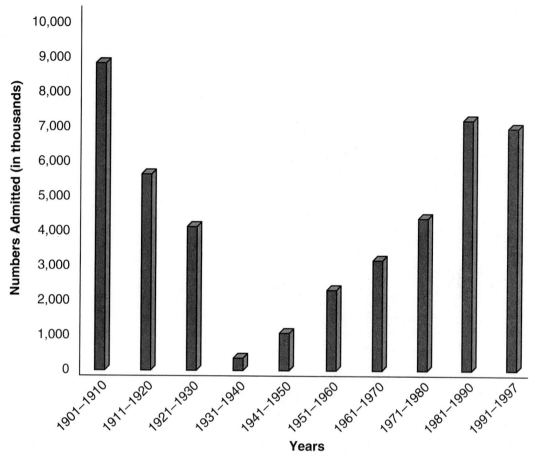

Exhibit 1.4   Immigration, 1901–1997. *Source:* U.S. Bureau of the Census. (1999). "FY 1996 U.S. Immigration and Naturalization Service, Statistical Yearbook, Annual and Releases," in *Statistical Abstract,* Washington, D.C.: U.S. Bureau of the Census.

cities across the country and in a number of areas in California, where the minority has become the majority. This change has had a huge impact on many institutions in society, not the least of which is law enforcement.

Immigrants

Immigration is not a new phenomenon in the United States. Virtually every citizen, except for indigenous peoples of America, can claim to be a descendent of someone who migrated (whether voluntarily or not) from another country. Immigration levels in 1990 reached their highest in 70 years when the number of immigrants surpassed 1.5 million (Exhibit 1.4). In addition, immigrants in the 1980s and 1990s came from many more parts of the world than those who arrived at the turn of the twentieth century (Exhibits 1.5 and 1.6). The U.S. Census Bureau reported in April 1998 that approximately 25.8 million U.S. residents (9.7 percent of the population)

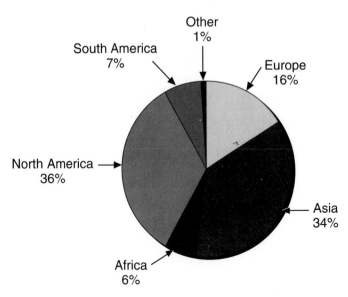

Exhibit 1.5 Immigrants admitted to the United States by region of birth, fiscal year 1996. *Source:* U.S. Bureau of the Census. (1999). "FY 1996 U.S. Immigration and Naturalization Service, Statistical Yearbook, Annual and Releases," in *Statistical Abstract.* Washington, D.C.: U.S. Bureau of the Census.

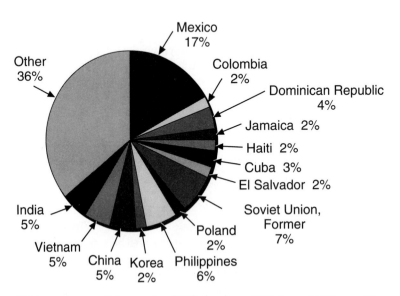

Exhibit 1.6 Immigrants by country of birth, fiscal year 1996. *Source:* U.S. Bureau of the Census.(1999). "FY 1996 U.S. Immigration and Naturalization Service, Statistical Yearbook, Annual and Releases," in *Statistical Abstract.* Washington, D.C.: U.S. Bureau of the Census.

had been born in other countries. This foreign-born population included 27 percent from Mexico, 4.4 percent from the Philippines, and 4.3 percent from China and Hong Kong. (These estimates were based on a March 1998 survey of legal and illegal immigrants and naturalized citizens.) In 1995 over half a million foreign-born persons came from each of the following countries: Canada, China, Cuba, the Dominican Republic, El Salvador, Jamaica, Korea, Germany, Great Britain, and Poland. California had the largest foreign-born population in 1995—over 7.7 million persons, or one-quarter of all California residents. New York ranked second in the number of foreign-born inhabitants, with 3 million. Other states with large numbers of foreign-born people include Texas (2.1 million), Florida (2 million), New Jersey (1.1 million), and Illinois (1 million) (U.S. Bureau of the Census, 1997). As of September 2000, nationals from the People's Republic of China submitted the highest number of asylum applications, followed by Colombians and Haitians (Immigration and Naturalization Service, 2000). (Immigrants who have obtained asylum are people who feared persecution in their own country and came to the United States seeking a safe haven, or a sanctuary in which they are safe from arrest. The basis of their persecution is usually political or religious.)

Even though most Americans (except indigenous peoples) have been immigrants at some time in their lineage, anti-immigrant sentiment is common. Especially in a time of recession, many people, including some police officers, perceive that immigrants are taking jobs away from "real Americans" (forgetting that legal immigrants are also "real" Americans). However, the issues surrounding immigration are not as clear-cut as they may at first appear. Despite the problems that are inevitably created when large groups of people have to be absorbed into a society, some immigrant groups stimulate the economy, revitalize neighborhoods, and eventually become fully participatory and loyal American citizens. Nevertheless, if an officer has an anti-immigrant bias, negative attitudes may surface when that officer interacts with immigrants, especially under stressful circumstances. When officers are under pressure, negative attitudes become apparent and their communication may become unprofessional. Indeed, some have claimed that officers with whom they have been in contact do not attempt to understand them or demonstrate little patience in communicating or finding a translator. (See Chapter 5 for a discussion of communication problems.)

In addition, officers must be aware of "racial flash points" that are created when immigrants move into economically depressed areas with large and diverse populations. Some people feel that immigrants' moving into certain urban areas displaces economically disadvantaged groups or deprives them of access to work. (It is beyond the scope of this chapter to discuss the validity, or lack thereof, of this sentiment.) Thus law enforcement representatives may see hostility between, for example, blacks and Korean or Arab immigrants in such cities as Los Angeles, New York, and Detroit. Although officers cannot be expected to solve these deep-seated problems, they may find themselves in situations in which they can serve as cultural mediators, helping each group to increase understanding and toleration of the other. For example, police can point out that a Korean grocer's not smiling and greeting a customer warmly is not necessarily a sign of hostility but rather a cultural trait. (The behavior may also be an expression of distrust, but that is not always the case.)

When a person complains that an Arab liquor store owner does not hire outside his or her community, officers can explain that it is usually because the business is a small, family-run operation in which employees are family members. Of course, not all problems are cultural, but with an understanding of immigrants' backgrounds, officers can help explain points of tension to members of other ethnic groups. The more direct contact officers have in ethnic and immigrant communities, the more knowledge they will gain about cultural differences that may have an impact on law enforcement.

Undocumented Immigrants

There are two major groups of undocumented immigrants: those who cross U.S. borders without having been "inspected" and those who enter the country with legal documents as temporary residents but have violated their legal admission status by extending their stay. Initially, Mexicans and other Latin Americans come to most people's minds when they hear the terms *illegal alien* and *undocumented worker.* Additionally, however, people from the Dominican Republic enter through Puerto Rico; since Puerto Ricans are U.S. citizens, they are considered legal. Therefore, officers may be in contact with "Puerto Ricans" who are actually from the Dominican Republic and have therefore come to the United States under an illegal pretext. People from other parts of the world may come to the United States on a tourist visa and then decide to remain permanently (e.g., Canadians).

Some undocumented "aliens" come to the United States hoping to remain legally by proving that they escaped their homeland because of political repression, claiming that if they were to return, they would face persecution or death (i.e., they are seeking asylum). People who are often deported as undocumented arrivals are those who come as "economic refugees" (i.e., their economic status in their home country may be desperate). Undocumented aliens generally have few occupational skills and are willing to take menial jobs that many American citizens will not accept. They fill economic gaps in various regions where low-wage labor is needed.

Outer appearances are not an accurate guide to who has legal status and who does not. Both illegal and legal immigrants may live in the same neighborhoods. Formerly illegal aliens can become legal through Immigration and Naturalization Reform Acts. For example, 300,000 illegal immigrants from Guatemala and El Salvador were legalized in May 1999, as were others from the countries of the former Soviet Union. Most of these illegal immigrants had escaped repressive regimes in the 1980s and 1990s.

Illegal immigrants lack documents that would enable them to obtain legal residence in the United States. The societal consequences are far-reaching. Law enforcement officials, politicians, and social service providers, among others, have had to deal with many concerns related to housing, education, safety, employment, spousal violence, and health care. The illegal segment of the immigrant population poses some difficult challenges for law enforcement officials. Trojanowicz and Bucqueroux (1990) state:

> [Illegal immigrants] pose a difficult challenge for police, because fear of deportation often makes them reluctant to report crimes committed against them—which also makes them easy prey. They can also fall victim to crimes related to their vulnerability—

scams including extortion, fees for phony documentation. . . . Because so many arrive with little or no money and have difficulty making a living, undocumented aliens often cluster in low-income, high-crime areas (p. 246).

The principal barrier to establishing trust with undocumented immigrants concerns their fears about being reported to the Immigration and Naturalization Service (INS). The argument supporting leaving illegal immigrants alone (unless they have committed a criminal act or are creating a disturbance) is based on the perspective that tracking down and deporting illegal workers is technically the job of the INS and not the police. Police department managements have to create policies related to turning in illegal immigrants to the INS. Sometimes the trust of the entire community (illegal and legal immigrants) is at stake. Donya Fernandez (2000), Language Rights Attorney in San Francisco, California, suggests that police departments make it known to immigrant communities when they have decided not to turn in illegal immigrants to the INS. When this is known, there may be less fear of the police when it comes to reporting crimes.

Undocumented Immigrants: Demographic Information. As of October 1996 an estimated 5 million undocumented immigrants were residing in the United States. California was the leading state of residence, with 40 percent of the undocumented population. The seven states with the largest estimated numbers of undocumented immigrants—California (2.0 million), Texas (700,000), New York (540,000), Florida (350,000), Illinois (290,000), New Jersey (135,000), and Arizona (115,000)—accounted for 83 percent of the total population of undocumented immigrants in October 1996 (U.S. Statistical Yearbook of the INS, 1996).

Mexico is the leading source country of undocumented immigration to the United States, and the undocumented population has grown at an average annual level of just over 150,000 since 1988, constituting about 54 percent of the total undocumented population (see Exhibit 1.7). The 15 countries with 50,000 or more undocumented immigrants in 1996 accounted for 82 percent of the total population. The large majority, over 80 percent, of all undocumented immigrants were from countries in the Western Hemisphere. About 2.1 million immigrants, or 41 percent of the total undocumented population in 1996, are nonimmigrant overstays. (They entered legally on a temporary basis and failed to depart.) The proportion of the undocumented population who are overstays varies considerably by country of origin (U.S. Statistical Yearbook of the INS, 1996).

Immigrant Women: Victims of Domestic Violence and Fear of Deportation

Batterers of immigrant women exert power and control to dominate and isolate their abused family members. . . . The Battered Immigrant Women's Protection Act of 1999 . . . will go far toward furthering the original purpose of the Violence Against Women Act's (VAWA's) immigration provisions—freeing battered immigrant women abused by citizen and lawful permanent resident spouses or parents to report the abuse to police, to seek help and to prosecute their abusers for the multiple crimes they commit against family members. . . . Helping battered immigrant women escape abuse and bring their abusers to justice will reduce domestic violence in our communities and will ensure that the citizen children of immigrant parents have the same opportunity to live lives free of domestic violence that VAWA sought to provide to all domestic violence victims. (Orloff, 2000)

Exhibit 1.7   Illegal immigrant populations (data for 1995–1996). *Source:* Department of Justice, U.S. Department of Justice Immigration and Naturalization Service. Washington, D.C.

COUNTRY OF ORIGIN AND ESTIMATED NUMBERS

All countries	5,000,000	Colombia	65,000
Mexico	2,700,000	Ecuador	55,000
El Salvador	335,000	Dominican Republic	50,000
Guatemala	165,000	Trinidad and Tobago	50,000
Canada	120,000	Jamaica	50,000
Haiti	105,000	Pakistan	41,000
Philippines	95,000	India	33,000
Honduras	90,000	Dominica	32,000
Poland	70,000	Peru	30,000
Nicaragua	70,000	Korea	30,000
Bahamas	70,000	Other	744,000

U.S. RESIDENCE AND ESTIMATED NUMBERS

All states	5,000,000	Colorado	45,000
California	2,000,000	Maryland	44,000
Texas	700,000	Michigan	37,000
New York	540,000	Pennsylvania	37,000
Florida	350,000	New Mexico	37,000
Illinois	290,000	Oregon	33,000
New Jersey	135,000	Georgia	32,000
Arizona	115,000	District of Columbia	30,000
Massachusetts	85,000	Connecticut	29,000
Virginia	55,000	Nevada	24,000
Washington	52,000	Other	330,000

Immigrants have been particularly vulnerable to domestic violence victimization. Research has found that 34 to 49.8 percent of immigrant women experience domestic violence over the course of their lifetimes (Rodriguez, 1995). Ironically, many of the women who have come to the United States to escape repression or poverty in their country of origin live with constant abuse in their new lives. Domestic violence is thought to be more prevalent among immigrant women than among U.S. citizens (Anderson, 1993).

Jang and colleagues (1995) offer the following explanations for the high rate of domestic violence experienced by immigrant women:

1. Immigrant women may suffer higher rates of battering than U.S. citizens because they come from cultures which accept domestic violence, or because they have less access to legal and social services than U.S. citizens. In addition, immigrant batterers and victims may believe that the penalties and protections of the U.S. legal system do not apply to them.

2. A battered woman who is not a legal resident, or whose immigration status depends on her partner, is isolated by cultural dynamics which may prevent her from leaving her husband or seeking assistance from the legal system. These factors contribute to the higher incidence of abuse among immigrant women.

3. Some obstacles faced by battered immigrant women include: a distrust of the legal system arising from their experiences with the system in their native countries; cultural and language barriers; and fear of deportation.

4. A battered immigrant woman may not understand that she can personally tell her story in court, or that a judge will believe her. Based on her experience in her native country, she may believe that only those who are wealthy or have ties to the government will prevail in court. Batterers often manipulate these beliefs by convincing the victim he will prevail in court because he is a male, a citizen or that he has more money (p. 313).

Domestic violence is a secret nobody wishes to discuss, and when a woman is an undocumented immigrant, she feels she has no protection. A 1991 survey conducted by the Coalition for Immigrant and Refugee Rights found that approximately one-third of Hispanic women suffered some form of domestic abuse—physical, emotional, or sexual. Many of the women in the study were employed, whereas their spouses were not, creating a volatile domestic situation. This change in family roles whereby the wife works, along with other factors, often creates desperate and violent home environments for immigrant women from around the world.

The phenomenon of new immigrants (whether women or men, legal or illegal) presents challenges to law enforcement officers working the streets. Immigrants must learn a great deal about U.S. laws, the law enforcement system in general, and the role of police officers. Many immigrants fear the police because in their native countries police engaged in arbitrary acts of brutality in support of repressive governments (e.g., in Central America). In other countries, citizens disrespect police because they are poorly educated, inefficient, and corrupt and have a very low occupational status (e.g., in Iran). The barriers immigrants bring to the relationship with police suggest that American officers have to double their efforts to communicate and to educate. A further challenge for law enforcement is that for the reasons mentioned, new immigrants often become victims of violent crimes. In part, the acculturation and success of immigrants in this society depend on how they are treated while they are still ignorant of the social norms and laws. Those who have contact with new Americans will need extraordinary patience at times. Adaptation to a new country can be a long and arduous process.

INTERPLAY BETWEEN POLICE INCIDENTS AND CULTURE

With community changes have come shifts in the concerns of law enforcement and criminal justice, as well as the nature of some crime and reactions to police tactics. Without knowledge of citizens' cultural and national backgrounds, law enforcement officers in today's society are likely to experience baffling incidents and to observe citizens' surprising reactions to police tactics:

The City of Spokane, Washington, paid a Gypsy family $1.43 million in 1997 to settle a civil rights suit over an illegal police search. The most controversial element of the case was the body search of the 13 family members, male and female, including a number of people who were not targets of the investigation. The family claimed that the unmarried girls who were searched were now considered defiled and unclean in the Gypsy culture. As a result, they could never marry another Gypsy. In fact, the entire household was considered contaminated, a family patriarch testified, and was soon after ostracized and unwelcome at weddings and funerals. (Alison Renteln, expert in cultural diversity and the law [University of Southern California political science professor], as reported in "Cultural Sensitivity on the Beat," *Los Angeles Times,* January 10, 2000, p. A12).

A Danish woman was jailed in 1997 for leaving her baby in a stroller outside a Manhattan restaurant—a case that focused international attention on New York City Police Tactics. . . . [T]he woman and the baby's father were charged with endangering a child and were jailed for two nights. The 14-month-old baby girl was placed in foster care for four days before she was returned to her mother. The incident precipitated a war of words between Danish newspapers and city administrators. Copenhagen columnists called New York police "Rambo cops." Pictures wired from Denmark showed numerous strollers [with babies] parked outside cafes in view of their parents. ("Cultural Sensitivity on the Beat," *Los Angeles Times,* January 10, 2000, p. A12).

An understanding of accepted social practices and cultural traditions in citizens' countries of origin can provide officers with the insight needed to understand and even predict some of the reactions and difficulties new immigrants will have in America. However, some customs are simply unacceptable in the United States, and arrests must be made in spite of the cultural background. Regardless of the circumstances, immigrant suspects need to be treated with respect; officers and all others in the criminal justice system must understand the innocent state of mind the citizen was in when committing the "crime." For example, female circumcision is illegal under all circumstances in the United States but is still practiced in certain African countries. The Hmong, mountain people of Southeast Asia (and particularly Laos), have a tradition considered to be an acceptable form of eloping. "Marriage by capture" translates into kidnap and rape in the United States. This Hmong tradition allows a male to capture and take away a female for marriage; even if she resists, he is allowed to take her to his home, and it is mandated that he consummate the union. Perpetrators of such crimes in the U.S. must be arrested.

In interviews with a deputy public defender and a deputy district attorney, a legal journal posed the following question: Should our legal system recognize a "cultural" defense when it comes to crimes? The deputy district attorney's response was, "No. You're treading on shaky ground when you decide something based on culture, because our society is made up of so many different cultures. It is very hard to draw the line somewhere, but [diverse cultural groups] are living in our country, and people have to abide by [one set of] laws or else you have anarchy." The deputy public defender's response to the question was: "Yes. I'm not asking that the [various cultural groups] be judged differently, just that their actions be understood according to their own history and culture" (Sherman, 1986, p. 33).

If law enforcement's function is to protect and serve citizens from *all* cultural backgrounds, it becomes vital to understand the cultural dimensions of crimes. Obviously, behaviors or actions that may be excused in another culture must not go unpunished if they are considered crimes in this country (e.g., spouse abuse). Nevertheless, there are circumstances in which law enforcement officials at all levels of the criminal justice system would benefit by understanding the cultural context in which a crime or other incident occurred. Law enforcement professionals must use standard operating procedures in response to specific situations, and the majority of these procedures cannot be altered for different groups based on ethnicity. In a multicultural society, however, an officer can modify the way he or she treats a suspect, witness, or victim given knowledge of what is considered "normal" in that person's culture. When officers suspect that an aspect of cultural background is a factor in a particular incident, they may earn the respect of—and therefore, cooperation from—ethnic communities if they are willing to evaluate their arrests in *lesser* crimes. (See the section "Police Knowledge of Cultural Groups" later in this chapter.)

Many officers say that their job is to uphold the law, but it is not up to them to make judgments. Yet discretion (to not take a citizen into custody) in *lesser* crimes may be appropriate. When officers understand the cultural context for a crime, the crime will and should be perceived somewhat differently. Consider the Sikh religion (a strict religious tradition followed by a minority of people from northern India), which requires that its followers wear a ceremonial dagger, a sacred symbol, at all times, even during sleep. Consider Pacific Islanders having barbecues in their garages, where they roast whole pigs. And consider a Vietnamese family who eats dog. When officers understand the cultural context within which a "crime" takes place, then it is much easier to understand a citizen's intent. Understanding the cultural dimensions of a crime may result, for example, in not taking a citizen into custody. At times (with lesser crimes), this may be the appropriate course of action and can result in the preservation of good police–community relations.

Before looking at specific case studies of incidents and crimes involving cultural components, we present the concept of culture and its tremendous impact on the individual. All people (except for very young children) carry cultural baggage, including, to varying degrees, members of culturally and racially diverse groups in a given society. (The degree is determined by their own conscious and unconscious identification with their group and their relative attachment to their cultural group's traditional values.) Being influenced by cultural baggage is a natural human phenomenon. Much of who we are is sanctioned and reinforced by the society in which we have been raised. According to some experts, culture has a far greater influence on people's behavior than any other variable (e.g., age, gender, race, and socioeconomic status) (Hall, 1959), and often this influence is unconscious. It is virtually impossible to lose one's culture completely when interacting in a new environment, yet change will inevitably take place.

The Definition of Culture

Although there are many facets of *culture,* the term is defined as beliefs, values, patterns of thinking, behavior, and everyday customs that have been passed on from generation to generation. Culture is learned (not inherited) and is manifested in largely unconscious and subtle behavior. With this definition in mind, consider that most children have acquired a general cultural orientation by the time they are five or six years old. For this reason, it is difficult to change behavior to accommodate a new culture. Many layers of cultural behavior and beliefs are subconscious. Additionally, many people assume that what they take for granted is taken for granted by all people ("all human beings are the same"), and they do not even recognize their own culturally influenced behavior. The anthropologist Edward T. Hall (1959) said, "Culture hides much more than it reveals and, strangely enough, what it hides, it hides most effectively from its own participants." In other words, people are blind to their own deeply embedded cultural behavior.

To further understand the hidden nature of culture, picture an iceberg (Ruhly, 1976). The only visible part of the iceberg is the tip, which typically constitutes only about 10 percent of the mass. Like most of culture's influences, the remainder of the iceberg is submerged beneath the surface. What this means for law enforcement is that there will be a natural tendency to interpret behavior, motivations, and criminal activity from the officer's cultural point of view. This tendency is due largely to an inability to understand behavior from alternative perspectives and because of the inclination toward *ethnocentrism* (i.e., an attitude of seeing and judging all other cultures from the perspective of one's own culture). In other words, an ethnocentric person would say that there is only one way of being "normal" and that is the way of his or her own culture. When it comes to law enforcement, there *is* only one set of laws to which all citizens must adhere, whether native-born or not. However, the following case studies will illustrate that culture does affect interpretations, meaning, and intention.

MINI CASE STUDIES: CULTURE AND CRIME*

The following mini case studies involve descriptions of crimes or offenses with a cultural component. If the crime is a murder or something similarly heinous, most people will not be particularly sympathetic, even with an understanding of the cultural factors involved. However, consider that understanding other cultural patterns gives one the ability to *see* and *react* in a different way. The ability to withhold judgment and to interpret a person's intention from a different cultural perspective is a skill that will ultimately enable a person to identify his or her own cultural blinders. Each case study describes an increasingly serious crime—from driving under the influence to child abuse to murder.

Mini Case Study 1: Driving under the Influence?

The following case, among others, was the subject of discussion in an officers' course in ethnic understanding in a San Francisco Bay Area police department ("Officers Being Trained in Ethnic Understanding," *San Jose Mercury News,* November 29, 2000, p. A3).

> A Tongan man living in [the Bay Area] was arrested on Highway 101 on the Peninsula in August 1999 for driving under the influence of *kava*, a relaxing elixir popular with Pacific Islanders. But a hung jury effectively acquitted [this man] in October. The jury determined, in part, that police didn't fully understand the effect and the importance of the drink. Tongans, Samoans, and Fijians say the kava ritual is an integral part of life, a way to share information and reinforce traditions. And they say it doesn't affect their ability to drive any more than soda pop.

---

*Discussion questions corresponding to each case study are found following the summary of this chapter.

Mini Case Study 2: A Tragic Case of Cross-Cultural Misinterpretation

In parts of Asia, there are medical practices unfamiliar to many law enforcement officials (as well as medical practitioners) in the West. A number of these practices result in marks on the skin that can easily be misinterpreted as abuse by people who have no knowledge of these culturally based medical treatments. The practices include rubbing the skin with a coin ("coining," "coin rubbing," or "wind rubbing"), pinching the skin, touching the skin with burning incense, or applying a heated cup to the skin ("cupping"). Each practice leaves highly visible marks, such as bruises and even burns. The following is an account of a serious misreading of some very common Southeast Asian methods of traditional folk healing on the part of U.S. school authorities and law enforcement officials.

A young Vietnamese boy had been absent from school for a few days with a serious respiratory infection. His father, believing that "coining" would help cure him, rubbed heated coins on specific sections of his back and neck. The boy's condition seemed to improve and he was able to return to school. Upon noticing heavy bruising on the boy's neck, the teacher immediately informed the school principal, who promptly reported the "abuse" to the police (who then notified Child Protective Services). When the police were notified, they went to the child's home to investigate. The father was very cooperative when questioned by the police and admitted, in broken English, that he had caused the bruising on his son's neck. The man was arrested and incarcerated. While the father was in jail, his son, who was under someone else's custody, apparently relapsed and died of his original illness. On hearing the news, the father committed suicide in his jail cell. Of course, it is not known whether the father would have committed suicide as a response to his son's death alone. The tragic misinterpretation on the part of the authorities involved, including the teacher, the principal, and the arresting police officers, provides an extreme case of what can happen when people attribute meaning from their own cultural perspective.

Cultural understanding would not have cured the young boy, but informed interaction with the father could have prevented the second tragedy. All of the authorities were interpreting what they saw with "cultural filters" based on their own belief systems. Ironically, the interpretation of the bruises (i.e., child abuse) was almost the opposite of the intended meaning of the act (i.e., healing). Even after some of the parties involved learned about this very common Southeast Asian practice, they still did not accept that it existed as an established practice and they could not fathom how others could believe that "coining" might actually cure illness. Their own conception of medical healing did not encompass what they perceived as such "primitive treatment."

Ethnocentrism is a barrier to accepting that there *is* another way, another belief, another communication style, another custom, or another value that can lead to culturally different behavior. Ethnocentrism often causes a person to assign a potentially incorrect meaning or attribute an incorrect motivation to a given act. Consider how the outcome could have differed if only one person in the chain of authorities had viewed the bruises as something other than abuse. The tragic outcome of serious cultural misunderstandins might have been averted.

Mini Case Study 3: Latino Values as a Factor in Sentencing*

In a court of law, a cultural explanation or rationalization (i.e., a cultural defense) rarely affects a guilty or not-guilty verdict. Nevertheless, culture may affect sentencing. Consider the following case, in which, according to Judge Lawrence Katz (2000), cultural considerations lessened the severity of the sentence.

A Mexican woman living in the United States became involved in an extramarital affair. Her husband became outraged when the wife bragged about her extramarital activities at a picnic at which many extended family members were present. At the same time, the wife also made comments about her husband's lack of ability to satisfy her and how, in comparison, her lover was far superior. On hearing his wife gloat about her affair, the husband left the picnic and drove five miles to purchase a gun. Two hours later, he shot and killed his wife. In a case such as this, the minimum charge required in California would be second-degree murder. However, because the jury took into consideration the cultural background of this couple, the husband received a mitigated sentence and was found guilty of manslaughter. It was argued that his wife's boasting about her lover and her explicit comments made specifically to emasculate him created a passion and emotion that completely undermined his *machismo,* masculine pride and honor. To understand the severity of her offense, the law enforcement officer and the prosecutor had to understand what it means to be humiliated in such a manner in front of one's family, in the context of Latino culture (Katz, 2000).

The purpose of these three mini case studies is not to discuss the "rightness" or "wrongness" of any group's values, customs, or beliefs but to illustrate that the point of contact between law enforcement and citizens' backgrounds must not be ignored. Officers must be encouraged to consider culture when investigating and presenting evidence regarding an alleged crime or incident involving people from diverse backgrounds. *This consideration does not mean that standard operating procedures should be changed, nor does it imply that heinous crimes such as murder or rape should be excused on cultural grounds.* However, as a matter of course, officers need to include culture as a variable in understanding, assessing, and reporting certain kinds of incidents and crimes.

POLICE KNOWLEDGE OF CULTURAL GROUPS

Law enforcement representatives have the ultimate authority to arrest or admonish someone suspected of a crime. According to Judge Katz (2000), "discretion based on cultural knowledge at the police level is much more significant than what happens at the next level in the criminal justice system (i.e., the courts)." Individual po-

---

*This mini case study involves homicide. In pointing out how the judges and jury were influenced, in part, by the defendants' cultural background (i.e., with regard to sentencing), the authors do not imply, in any way, that the crime was justifiable on cultural grounds. The purpose of this example is to illustrate, yet again, how culture plays a part in decision making at various levels in the criminal justice system.

lice officers have the possibility of creating positive public relations if they demonstrate cultural sensitivity and respect toward members of an ethnic community. Judge Katz cited the example of police contact with the San Francisco Bay Area Samoan community, in which barbecues and parties can include a fair amount of drinking, resulting in fights. In Judge Katz's opinion,

> The police, responding to neighbors' complaints, could come in with a show of force and the fighting would cool down quickly. However, word would spread that the police officers had no cultural understanding or respect for the people involved. This would widen the gap that already exists between police and many Pacific Islander and other Asian groups and would not be a way to foster trust in the Samoan community. Alternatively, the police could locate the leader, or the "chief," of this group and let that person deal with the problem in the way that he would have handled the conflict in Samoa. There is no question about the chief's ability to handle the problem. He has a prominent role to play and can serve as a bridge between the police and the community. The *matai* is also a resource; he is an elder who has earned the respect of the community.

The heads of Samoan communities are traditionally in full control of members' behavior, although this is changing somewhat in the United States. Furthermore, according to traditional Samoan values, if a family member assaults a member of another family, the head of the family is required to ensure punishment. (National Office of Samoan Affairs, 1984). Given the power entrusted to the chiefs, it is reasonable to encourage officers first to go through the community and elicit assistance in solving enforcement problems. This recommendation does not imply, in any way, that groups should be left to police themselves; instead, understanding and working with the leadership of a community represents a spirit of partnership.

The awareness of and sensitivity to such issues can have a significant impact on the criminal justice system, in which police have the power to either inflame or calm the people involved in a particular incident. According to Judge Katz (2000), "Many cases, especially those involving lesser offenses, can stay out of court." He asks, "Do you always need a show of force? Or can you counsel and admonish instead?" In certain types of situations, such as the one described earlier, officers can rethink traditional police methods in order to be as effective as possible. This involves knowledge of ethnic communities and a desire to establish a positive and trustworthy image in those communities.

PREJUDICE IN LAW ENFORCEMENT

The following questions were asked of police officers participating in a cultural diversity program:

> "Raise your hand if you are a racist." Not a single officer raised a hand.
> "Raise your hand if you think that prejudice and racism exist outside this agency." Most officers raised their hands.
> The instructor then asked with humor: "Then where were you recruited from?" (Berry, 2000)

When discussing the implications of multicultural diversity for police officers, it is not enough simply to present the need to understand cultural background. Whenever two groups are from entirely different ethnic or racial backgrounds, there is the possibility that prejudice exists (because of fear, lack of contact, ignorance, and stereotypes). To deny the existence of prejudice or racism in any given law enforcement agency would be to deny that it exists outside the agency.

What Is Prejudice?

Prejudice is a judgment or opinion formed before facts are known, usually involving negative or unfavorable thoughts about groups of people. Discrimination is action based on prejudiced thought. It is not possible to force people to abandon their own prejudices in the law enforcement workplace or when working in the community. Because prejudice is thought, it is private and does not violate any law. However, because it is private, a person may not be aware when his or her judgments and decisions are based on prejudice. In law enforcement, the expression of prejudice as bias discrimination and racism is illegal and can have tragic consequences. All police must consider the implications of prejudice in their day-to-day work as it relates to equal enforcement and professionalism.

It is not uncommon to hear in diversity or cross-cultural workshops for officers sentiments such as the following: "We've already had this training (i.e., on prejudice). Why do we need to go over it again and again?" As with other training areas in law enforcement, such as self-defense and tactics, the area of prejudice needs to be reviewed on a regular basis. One only has to read the headlines periodically to see that the problem of prejudice and racism in law enforcement is not yet solved. For example, in November 2000 the *New York Times* reported that racial profiling was routine in a large agency in the Eastern part of the U.S. (racial profiling is discussed later in this chapter). It is not our intention to single out any particular department but to state directly that prejudice has not yet disappeared from law enforcement. Although police chiefs cannot *mandate* that their officers banish prejudicial thoughts, this subject should be dealt with seriously. While some police officers say they have every right to believe what they want, the chiefs of all departments must be able to guarantee, with as much certainty as possible, that no officer will ever act on his or her prejudices. All officers must understand where the line is between prejudice and discrimination, whether in the law enforcement agency with coworkers or with citizens. It becomes eminently clear that prejudice in the law enforcement agency must be addressed before it turns into racism and discrimination. Indeed, an agency cannot be expected to treat its multicultural population fairly if people within the agency are likely to act on their prejudiced thoughts.

How Prejudice Influences People

Prejudice is encouraged by stereotyping, which is a shorthand way of thinking about people who are different. The stereotypes that form the basis of a person's prejudice can be so fixed that he or she easily justifies his or her racism, sexism, or other bias and even makes such claims as, "I'm not prejudiced, but let me tell you about those

___ I had to deal with today." Coffey et al. (1982) discuss the relationship between selective memory and prejudice:

> A prejudiced person will almost certainly claim to have sufficient cause for his or her views, telling of bitter experiences with refugees, Koreans, Catholics, Jews, Blacks, Mexicans and Puerto Ricans, or Indians. But in most cases, it is evident that these "facts" are both scanty and strained. Such a person typically resorts to a selective sorting of his or her own memories, mixes them up with hearsay, and then over-generalizes. No one can possibly know all refugees, Koreans, Catholics, and so on. (p. 8)

Indeed, individuals may be so convinced of the truths of their stereotypes that they claim to be experts on "those people." One of the most dangerous types of prejudice can be subconscious. Subconscious prejudice (sometimes referred to as character-conditioned prejudice) usually runs deep; the person with this character deficiency may hold hostile attitudes toward many ethnic groups (not just one or two). People who tend to mistreat or oppress others because of their prejudices often were mistreated themselves, and this experience can leave them extremely distrustful of all others. In addition, people who have strong prejudices can be insecure and frustrated because of their own failures. Consequently, they blame or scapegoat others. They have a great deal of stored-up anger that frequently began to build up in childhood because of dysfunctional relationships with their parents. Quite often, people in racial supremacist organizations fit the description of the *extremely* prejudiced person for whom mistrust and hate of all others is a way of life.

Another type of prejudice is acquired during "normal" socialization. This type of prejudice results when a person belongs to a group that holds negative views of other specific groups (e.g., southern whites and blacks, Arabs and Jews, Chinese and Japanese, Puerto Ricans and Mexicans). When there is a pattern of prejudice within a particular group, the "normal" person is the one who conforms to the prejudice. From childhood, parents pass on stereotypes of the out-group in the child's mind because of their "normal" prejudices. By adulthood, the person who has learned prejudice against a particular group can justify the prejudice with rationalizations (Coffey et al., 1982).

However, not everyone in a given group holds prejudices common among the rest of the members of the group. According to Coffey et al., some people are more susceptible than others to learned (or culture-conditioned) prejudice. Those more likely to be prejudiced include (1) older people, (2) less educated people, (3) farmers and unskilled or semiskilled workers, (4) residents of rural areas or small towns, (5) people uninterested in civic affairs, and (6) people of low socioeconomic status.

Police Prejudice

Deputy Chief Ondre Berry (of the Reno, Nevada, Police Department) conducts diversity training for law enforcement and repeatedly conveys this message to officers:

> If you are normal, you have cultural blind spots which will give you an unbalanced view of people who are different from you. Officers must look at themselves first before getting into situations in which they act upon their biases. (Berry, 2000)

Police prejudice received a great deal of attention in the latter half of the 1990s—so much so that it was addressed as a topic of concern in the President's Initiative on Race:

> Racial disparities and prejudices affect the way in which minorities are treated by the criminal system. Examples of this phenomenon can be found in the use of racial profiling in law enforcement and in the differences in the rates of arrest, conviction, and sentencing between whites and minorities and people of color. (Advisory Board to the President's Initiative on Race, 1998)

Law enforcement professionals have recognized, especially as they enter the twenty-first century, that prejudices unchecked and acted on can result in not only citizen humiliation, lawsuits, loss of jobs, and long-term damage to police–community relations but in personal tragedy as well. Sometimes, training can be successful in changing behavior and possibly attitudes. Consider the example of firing warning shots. Most officers have retrained themselves to refrain from this action because they have been mandated to do so. They have gone through a process of "unfreezing" normative behavior (i.e., what is customary) and have incorporated desired behavior. Thus explicit instruction and clear directives from the top can result in profound changes of police actions. The success of mandated change is supported by Fletcher Blanchard, a social psychologist at Smith College, who conducted and published research findings on fighting acts of bigotry (*New York Times,* September 16, 1991, pp. C-1 and C-8). His contention is that clear policies that *unequivocally* condemn racist acts or forms of speech will prevent most manifestations of prejudice. Asking a citizen, "What are you doing here?" just because he or she is of a different background than those of a particular neighborhood is not acceptable. Officers will listen to these specific and unambivalent directives coming from the top, even if their personal biases do not change. As Blanchard explains: "A few outspoken people (e.g., in an organization/agency) who are vigorously anti-racist can establish the kind of social climate that discourages racist acts. It may be difficult to rid an officer of his or her stereotypes, but not acting upon prejudices become[s] the mandate of the department."

Peer Relationships and Prejudice

Expressions of prejudice in police departments may go unchallenged because of the need to conform or to fit into the group. Police officers do not make themselves popular by questioning peers or challenging their attitudes. It takes a nonconformist to voice an objection or to avoid going along with group norms. Some studies have shown that peer behavior in groups reinforces acts of racial bias. For example, when someone in a group makes ethnic slurs, others in the group may begin to express the same hostile attitudes more freely. This behavior is particularly relevant in law enforcement agencies given the nature of the police subculture and the strong influence of peer pressure. Thus law enforcement leaders must not be ambiguous when directing their subordinates to control their expressions of prejudice, even among peers. Furthermore, according to some social scientists, the strong condemnation of any manifestations of prejudice can at times affect a person's feelings: Using pressure from authorities or peers to keep people who are prejudiced from acting on those biases can, in the long run, weaken the prejudice itself, especially if the prejudice is not virulent. People conform. Even if they are still prejudiced, they will be reticent to show it. National authorities have become much more vocal about dealing directly with racism and prejudice in law enforcement as an institution, especially in light of the quantity of allegations of racial profiling in police departments across the country.

A process of socialization takes place when change has been mandated by top management and a person is forced to adopt a new standard of behavior. When a mistake is made and the expression of prejudice occurs, a police department will pay the price (in adverse media attention, lawsuits, citizen complaints, human relations commissions involvement, or dismissal of the chief or other management). Government officials' public expressions are subject to a great deal of scrutiny. Berry-Wilkinson, a lawyer and expert on harassment issues, cited the case of a prosecutor who was publicly reprimanded for a hallway comment to another lawyer during a murder trial: "I don't believe either of those chili-eating bastards." The court stated: "Lawyers, especially . . . public officials, [must] avoid statements as well as deeds . . . indicating that their actions are motivated to any extent by racial prejudice" (*People v. Sharpe,* 789 p.2d 659 [1989], Colorado, in Berry-Wilkinson, 1993, p. 2d). Berry-Wilkinson's concluding statement following the reporting of this case reads: "What once may have been acceptable is now definitely not and may bring discipline and monetary sanctions. While public employees may be free to think whatever they like, they are not free to say whatever they think. A public employee's right to free speech is not absolute" (Berry-Wilkinson, 1993, p. 2d).

When officers in a police department are not in control of their prejudices (in either their speech or in their behavior) the negative publicity affects the reputation of all police officers (by reinforcing the popular stereotype that police are racists or bigots). Yet because of publicized instances of discrimination, officers become increasingly aware of correct and incorrect behavior toward ethnic minorities.

Beginning in 1990, a California police department was besieged by the press and outraged citizens for over two years because six police officers had exchanged racist messages on their patrol car computers, using the word *nigger* and making references to the Ku Klux Klan. The citizens of the town in which the incident took place ended up conducting an investigation of the department to assess the degree of racism in the institution. In their report, the committee members wrote that the disclosure of the racial slurs was "an embarrassment and a crushing blow" to the image and credibility of the city and police department. In addition, citizens demanded the chief's resignation. In a cultural diversity workshop (April 13, 1993) some of the officers said they believed that the entire incident was overblown and that there was no "victim." These officers failed to understand that the use of derogatory terms alone is offensive to citizens. Officers who do not grasp the seriousness of the matter may not realize that citizens feel unprotected knowing that those entrusted with their safety and protection are capable of using such hateful language. While the language is offensive, the problem is more with the attitudes it conveys. Such incidents are extremely costly from all points of view; it may take years for a department to recover from one incident connected to an officer's prejudice or racism.

Officers need to be aware that anything they say or do with citizens of different backgrounds that even *hints* at prejudice automatically creates the potential for an explosive reaction. Here the experience of the minority and the non-minority do not even begin to approach each other. An officer can make an unguarded casual remark and not realize it is offensive. For example, an officer can offend a group member by saying "You people" (accentuating a we-they division) or by implying that if a member of a minority group does not fit a stereotype, he or she is exceptional (e.g., "She's Hispanic, but she works hard" or "he's black, but very responsible").

Members of culturally diverse groups are up against the weight of history and tradition in law enforcement. Ethnic groups have not traditionally been represented in police work (especially in top management), nor have citizens of some ethnic groups had reasons to trust the police. The prejudice that might linger among officers must be battled constantly if they are to increase trust with ethnic communities. The perception of many ethnic group members is that police will treat them more roughly, question them unnecessarily, and arrest them more often than they arrest whites. Awareness of this perception is not enough, though. The next step is to try harder with ethnic groups to overcome these barriers. The African American psychiatrist Wendell Lipscomb (1993), who himself experienced biased treatment from officers in his younger years, advises officers to go out of their way to show extra respect to those citizens who least expect it. He suggests "disarming" the citizen who has traditionally been the object of police prejudice and who *expects* rude or uncivil behavior from the officer.

Beyond eliminating the prejudice manifested in speech, police management can teach officers how to reduce or eliminate acts of bias and discrimination. A large metropolitan police department hired several human relations consultants to help assess community–police problems. The chief insisted that they ride in a police car for four weekends so that they would "appreciate the problems of law officers working in the black ghetto." Every Friday through Sunday night, the consultants rode along with the highway patrol, a unit other officers designated as the "Gestapo police." When the month ended and the chief asked what the consultants had learned, they replied, "If we were black, we would hate the police." The chief, somewhat bewildered, asked why. "Because we have personally witnessed black citizens experiencing a series of unjust, unwarranted intimidations, searches, and series of harassments by unprofessional police." Fortunately, that chief, to his credit, accepted the feedback and introduced a successful course in human relations skills. After this training, the officers demonstrated greater professionalism in their interactions with members of the black community.

When it comes to expressions of prejudice, people are not powerless. No one has to accept sweeping stereotypes (e.g., "You can't trust an Indian," "All whites are racists," "Chinese are shifty," and so on). To eliminate manifestations of prejudice, people have to begin to interrupt biased and discriminatory behavior at all levels. Officers have to be willing to remind their peers that ethnic slurs and offensive language, as well as differential treatment of certain groups of people, is neither ethical nor professional. Officers need to change the aspect of police culture that discourages speaking out against acts or speech motivated by prejudice. An officer or civilian employee who does nothing in the presence of racist or other discriminatory behavior by his or her peers becomes a silent accomplice.

RACIAL PROFILING

Many police officers know not to act on the prejudices they hold. But the nature of prejudice is such that some people are (1) not aware of their prejudices or biases and (2) make inferences and take actions toward certain groups based on these biases. Today, most law enforcement agencies are dealing with the sensitive issue of "racial profiling," or "driving while black or brown" (DWB). Racial profiling, a practice in which police stop motorists on the basis of their race, has become a controversial issue nationwide. African Americans, Hispanics, and other racially diverse group members have known about racial profiling for years; near the end of the twentieth century the truth about the frequency of racial profiling became more widely known and shocked (mainly) nonminority Americans and awakened law enforcement as a profession. (Although it is not a new practice, the term itself began to be used increasingly in the latter half of the 1990s.) What is racial profiling?

> Racial profiling is the use of traffic offenses as an excuse—a pretext—to stop, question, and search . . . minority drivers in numbers far out of proportion to their presence on the road. Police use this practice because there are officers who believe that having black or brown skin is an indication of a greater risk of criminality, and they therefore view . . . minorities as potential criminals. Skin color becomes evidence: the upshot is that [many] African Americans and Hispanics become suspects every time they engage in the most common and prototypically American act: driving. Law enforcement officials try to explain profiling away as a rational response to crime, or as an efficient approach to policing. . . .[S]kin color is used as evidence against innocent people every day. (D. Harris, 2000, p. 1)

Citizen discontent and lawsuits against law enforcement often originate today as a result of *profiling suspects*. Various agencies, from U.S. Customs to traffic police, have used this method supposedly to prevent crime by stopping and examining persons deemed to be suspicious based on a profile of criminal types, especially with regard to carrying drugs illicitly. Law enforcement professionals need to be critical and introspective when analyzing this problem of racism and prejudice in the profession:

> How did racial profiles develop?
>
> Could the originator of the profiles indeed be racist or be one who is operating on misconceptions and stereotypes about people, usually a stereotypical generic version of blacks or Hispanic or Latino group members?
>
> Could distortions in the "eye of the beholder" cause innocent citizens to suffer this humiliation and possible arrest?

Law enforcement profiling affects blacks and Hispanics (as well as other minority groups) from every walk of life, every vocation, and every level of the socioeconomic ladder. There is a great deal of confusion as to why this happens. Officers can make stops for numerous reasons, some of which are somewhat minor (e.g., one of two taillights is out, a license plate light is out). Police must have reasonable suspicion or probable cause for stopping a vehicle. That certain group members are stopped disproportionately to their numbers and without regard to their background suggests that some untrained and biased officers are making inferences about violators of the law based on skin color. Consider the widespread allegations of racial profiling:

Tickets Tainted by Race (headline from the *Akron Beacon Journal* [Ohio], August 13, 2000)

Canton-area black residents were more than four times as likely as white residents to receive a traffic ticket from the Canton Police Department.

Race-Based Arrest Profiles Attacked: Skin Color Increasingly a Factor in Highway Drug Searches (headline from the *Detroit News,* June 3, 1999)

A new report calls racial profiling in traffic stops a serious problem nationwide, while a local police chief wants departments to keep track of motorists' race when they issues tickets.

San Diego Police Found to Stop Black and Latino Drivers Most (headline from the *New York Times,* October 1, 2000)

While blacks are 8 percent of the driving age population in San Diego, they accounted for 12 percent of the traffic stops and 20 percent of those searched. Hispanics, who are 20 percent of the driving age population, made up 29 percent of the stops and 50 percent of the searches.

Racial Profiling Routine, New Jersey Finds (headline from the *New York Times,* November 28, 2000)

At least 8 of every 10 automobile searches carried out by state troopers on the New Jersey Turnpike over most of the decade were conducted on vehicles driven by blacks and Hispanics, state documents have revealed.

Federal Inquiry Finds Racial Profiling in Street Searches (headline from the *New York Times,* October 5, 2000)

Prosecutors told the city that their [statistical] analysis concluded that blacks and Hispanics in [New York City] were disproportionately singled out in the searches, and that the imbalance could not be explained by the fact that the city's minority neighborhoods typically had higher crime rates.

In diversity training he conducts nationwide and in communications with his own officers, Deputy Chief Ondre Berry (Reno, Nevada, Police Department) advises: "When contemplating stopping a motorist, ask yourself 'Is there a *possibility* that I may be making an assumption about this driver based on race? Am I moving from my own personal "data" and making a leap of extraction about this vehicle or about this person?' Officers need to recognize that this is a possibility." Berry further advises, "Do not take race into account when deciding who to stop. Use your good policing skills. Again, if you are normal, you have unbalanced views about people who are different from you" (Berry, 2000).

In his book entitled *The Fifth Discipline Fieldbook: Strategies and Tools for Building a Learning Organization,* the management specialist Peter M. Senge and his coauthors (1994) provide a clear and simple model called the *Ladder of Inference,* which illuminates most people's typical patterns (and flaws) of thinking. In intensive nationwide training conducted by Senge, police and other corporate executives are able to apply this model to issues and challenges in their own organizations. The model gives some insight into what may be going on in officers' minds as they stop blacks, Latinos, and other groups disproportionately. Thus the model has implications for helping officers better understand their actions vis-à-vis racial profiling. What is happening when law enforcement officials make stops based on race? Some have a biased belief system that results in the observation and collection of certain "data" to reinforce their belief system. Meanings are added to make sense of the observations. (For example, officers may notice people who are black and brown more and stop them more because of biased beliefs about them.) They make assumptions based on their own personal meanings and use these assumptions to fill in for missing data ("this motorist is carrying drugs on him"). They draw conclusions based on their beliefs and then take action—that is, they decide to stop African American and Hispanic motorists much more frequently than they stop whites. These thought processes take place very quickly, almost simultaneously, and most individuals are not aware that they go on constantly.

It is natural for people to substitute assumptions for what they may not know, but in the case of racial profiling, this is a very dangerous proposition. One African American citizen (who prefers to remain anonymous) said, "I am upper middle class, go out to nice restaurants, have coffee with my wife in the morning, kiss my children goodbye every day, hold an excellent job . . . but feel like I am seen as a criminal on the road. I have been stopped two times this year for extremely petty reasons (one had to do with a license plate light being out) and with no ultimate results for the officer."

Officers have to recognize when they are converting their biases into "facts" and when their assumptions substitute for real data. The disproportionate stopping of minorities must stop. No one of any race should have to fear being stopped by police while driving purely on the basis of skin color.

Professional Police Traffic Stops

The reason for every stop a law enforcement official makes must be legally defensible. Professionalism in police stops involves an integrated strategy on the part of the police organization. Major Grady Carrick, a Florida Highway Patrol Troop Commander in northeast Florida, gives the following advice:

> To implement professional police traffic stops, agencies must adopt a three-dimensional approach. Organizational policy, officer training, and data collection represent the essential ingredients of a comprehensive agency strategy. (Carrick, 2000, p. 8)

The following are key points from each of the previously noted areas (Carrick, 2000):

> *Organizational or agency policy:* Agencies must develop a well-structured policy concerning professional traffic stops, outlining the conduct of officers and the prohibition of discriminatory practices. Leaders must bring the message personally to employees, as well as to the public. Managers, supervisors, and the entire workforce must embrace and employ the policy.
>
> *Officer training:* Agencies . . . can infuse [a component on racial profiling] into an existing program. . . . [W]orkshop discussions on the issue of racial profiling will elevate the level of information and institutional knowledge about the problem. . . .

Nationally, the Police Officer Standards and Training Commission should evaluate the topic for inclusion in current diversity training programs required for all officers. . . . [D]iscussion of racial profiling is appropriate for both entry-level and in-service officer training. Agencies may want to consult local chapters of [community group organizations] to obtain accounts and examples for use in training programs.

A number of jurisdictions across the country, including San Diego, California, San Jose, California, Houston, Texas, and many others, have begun to track traffic stops. As of November 2000, at least five states had outlawed the practice of racial profiling at the suggestion of Janet Reno (Carrick, 2000, p. 9). Two states, Connecticut and North Carolina, had enacted legislation that required record keeping of police stops (Carrick, 2000). Many departments still resist record keeping; nevertheless, some state and federal lawmakers continue to express their views regarding the need for more widespread legislation.

The San Diego, California, Police Department was the first department to study racial profiling voluntarily ("S.D. Police Found to Stop Black and Latino Drivers Most," *New York Times,* October 1, 2000) and was commended by Attorney General Janet Reno for taking action in the area of data collection. The San Diego Police Department, under the direction of Chief David Bejaranjo, began keeping records of stops and searches in January 2000, after community leaders raised concerns about police practices. In addition, according to Sergeant Robert Lewis, special assistant to Chief Bejaranjo and liaison to San Diego's African American community, the San Diego Police Department took additional steps in its efforts to end racial profiling. The department brought in outside consultants and community groups to analyze the numbers from the data collection on stops and to solicit additional input on what the numbers mean. These groups included representatives from the National Association for the Advancement of Colored People (NAACP), the Urban League, the American Civil Liberties Union (ACLU), the Latino Unity Coalition, and Pan Pacific Asian representatives. The police department listened to their input and planned to implement the suggestions in subsequent phases of its project. Under the direction of former San Diego police chief Jerry Sanders (since 1990), the San Diego Police Department has made community-based policing a priority. Clearly, this partnership with ethnically and racially diverse community groups has been beneficial in the department's efforts to investigate and solve the problems associated with allegations of racial profiling.

According to the International Association of Chiefs of Police (IACP), departments should look at as many models as possible before they decide to select one that would meet their needs. The Highway Safety Committee believes, however, that there are core elements that must be included in policies guiding professional traffic stops. These include:

Definitions of "profiling" and "reasonable suspicion"
A clear statement that race or ethnicity alone cannot constitute a reason for a traffic stop, unless, it is related to a specific, detailed description pertaining to a specific crime
A requirement that all persons be treated with the utmost courtesy in traffic stops
Provision for adequate training and supervisory oversight

As a beginning point for officer training, the Highway Safety Committee and the National Highway Traffic Safety administration have completed a curriculum on Professional Traffic Stops. This curriculum may be obtained by contacting governor's highway safety representatives or IACP's Division of State and Provincial Police. (Ibid. p. 3)

COMMUNITY-BASED POLICING

Community-based policing is one of several terms that police agencies across the nation are using to refer to working partnerships with communities. (See Chapters 14 and 15 for further discussion of community-based policing.) A few of the more commonly used terms are *problem-oriented policing (POP), community policing (CP), neighborhood-oriented policing (NOP), community-oriented policing (COP),* and *innovative neighborhood-oriented policing (INOP).* The concept of and practices associated with community-based or community-oriented policing are central to any discussion on minority groups and immigrant populations. The legislative basis of what became known as Community Oriented Policing Services (COPS, Title 1 of the Violent Crime Control and Law Enforcement Act of 1994) listed four specific goals intended to change the level and practice of policing in the United States. The first two goals link directly to our discussion of police interaction and professionalism with community members, including those from diverse racial, cultural, ethnic, religious, and lifestyle backgrounds. These two goals are as follows (National Institute of Justice, 2000):

1. To increase the number of officers deployed in American communities
2. To foster problem solving and interaction with communities by police officers

A great deal of literature is available to law enforcement agencies on community-based policing. (See references at the ends of Chapters 1, 14, and 15). Community-based policing depends on a strong partnership with the various communities that make up a city or jurisdiction. The partnership ensures dialogue and provides the mechanism by which a police department is aware of current relevant issues in the community. The following description of a police department without a community-based approach, while dated, is a graphic example of how world events and the influx of refugees (which dramatically alters demographics) have to be monitored in a community-based partnership format.

Consider the case of a medium-sized police department in southern California that exemplifies the problems associated with not using community-based policing. Neither the management of the department nor the city was aware that the ethnic community had been changing significantly. Only two years after dramatic events began happening did patrol officers start to pay attention to the changes, most of which had occurred suddenly following the fall of Saigon in 1975. After the withdrawal of American forces from Vietnam, the United States changed its immigration policy to relocate peoples in jeopardy from Southeast

Asia. Police officers were performing their "crime fighter" role, but because there was no partnership with the community, there was no reason or incentive to monitor and report the changes they were noticing. This particular community, therefore, was not prepared for the increase in racial disputes and violence on the streets and in the schools, nor was it prepared for increasing needs in government, infrastructures, and social services. Former Captain Stan Knee of the Garden Grove Police Department, in a 1987 interview, observed that officers spent five times longer answering calls involving Vietnamese citizens than those in the Anglo community because of language and cultural differences. Officer and management frustrations resulted. Community-based policing would have had a plan in place for that neighborhood transition. Why? Because the department (including all local government institutions) and the neighborhoods would have been working together closely.

Community-based policing allows for collaboration with the community. As Deputy Chief Ondre Berry (2000) says, "We don't know the community as well as the community does." Community-based policing represents a more democratic style of policing. It allows for openness and dialogue. The police department is not cut off or insulated from the community (Skolnick, 1999). Community-based policing has developed a momentum in recent years and is a contributing factor to the decrease in crime in certain areas. Deputy Chief Ondre Berry shared the following firsthand account of how the implementation of community-based policing in his community (Reno, Nevada) was the definitive factor in the decrease in gang-related activities, including homicide.

> Deputy Chief Berry spoke of the alarming homicide rates in Reno, Nevada, in 1992, which included the deaths of two Hispanic children—a 13-year-old girl killed at a soccer game and a 3-year-old boy, both victims of Hispanic gang-related shootings. The dissension between the community and the police department was growing rapidly. The police department had no choice but to address the homicide rate in the community from an enforcement point of view; the community's needs were to address basic issues of survival and quality of life. Deputy Chief Berry's dedication to the community resulted in the ultimate collaborative effort in community-based policing. Berry, with the help of the ethnic communities as well as the community at large, brought together representatives from the police department (and especially the gang task units), officials from the school districts, government, and nonprofit sectors of the community, and business representatives. Together they devised a plan for combating gang activity in Reno. The community had a strong voice; the police department valued and listened to community members' input. As a result of the collaboration, the police-community partnership created the Gang Alternative Partnership Center, which includes (1) gyms open until 1 A.M., (2) officers helping to coach basketball teams consisting of gang members, (3) drill teams and after-school programs, (4) community assistance to youth in the finding of jobs, and (5) organized tattoo removal available to gang members. In addition, the community and the police directed nonprofit organizations (such as United Way) in the channeling of funds to provide programs for youth. The police department also increased its gang units.

According to Deputy Chief Berry, because of the successful collaboration of police department and community, lives have been saved. Since 1995 there have been one or two gang-related shootings. Drive-by shootings went down from an average of 140 shots-fired calls a month to an average of 20 calls per month. Gangs are still present in the city, but activity has decreased in Reno.

The Police Executive Research Forum (PERF) concluded in a 1992 report that community policing had become the fastest-growing movement in policing in decades, both in theory and in practice. The PERF research looked for commonalities among the various community policing programs and research on the subject. The forum discovered five different perspectives on community policing within agencies across the nation:

1. *Deployment perspective:* Placing officers in closer proximity to members of the community and thereby improve their knowledge of the area in which they work.
2. *Community revitalization perspective:* Focusing on preventing deterioration of neighborhoods by police paying closer attention to fear-inducing characteristics of neighborhoods.
3. *Problem-solving perspective:* Maintaining that the most critical element of community policing is the problem-solving efforts in which the police and community (residents, other government agencies, and private businesses) participate.
4. *Customer perspective:* Developing proactive mechanisms for determining the needs of the public relative to the police function; the approach uses routine surveys of citizen and advisory groups to accomplish this goal.
5. *Legitimacy perspective:* Attempting, via community policing, for officers to be more equitable in their relationships with the minority community.

Such perspectives require opening a dialogue between the police and diverse community groups so that groups can identify their peacekeeping concerns and the police can respond to them. Departments typically mix varieties of community policing perspectives; however, the common thread within all approaches is that the police assist the community in policing and protecting itself. To do so, the police must engage the community in the task of policing. The police are actually dependent on a relationship and partnership (some call it "building bridges") with the community to perform these tasks. The community identifies problems with the encouragement, direction, and participation of the police.

SUMMARY

Dramatic changes in the ethnic and racial makeup of the population have created new challenges at all levels of police work. Willingness to gain cultural information about the new communities that they serve will ultimately benefit officers in their interactions with people of different backgrounds. Officers' knowledge of cultural differences, coupled with an ability to demonstrate respect for those differences, can result in increased rapport and effective communication with people from various ethnic and racial backgrounds. Trust in many ethnic communities has to be earned because of the cultural "baggage" that community members bring to their relationships with the police. Members of the law enforcement profession have to examine their words, behaviors, and actions to evaluate whether they are conveying professionalism and respect to all people, regardless of their race, culture, religion, or ethnic background. Law enforcement agencies must be free of all expressions of prejudice on the part of their officers and civilian employees. Finally, law enforcement agencies in partnership and collaboration with communities are likely to experience decreased crime rates and increased trust and cooperation with citizens of all backgrounds.

EIGHT TIPS FOR IMPROVING LAW ENFORCEMENT IN MULTICULTURAL COMMUNITIES*

- Make positive contact with community group members from diverse backgrounds. Don't let them see you only when something negative has happened.
- Allow the public to see you as much as possible in a nonenforcement role.
- Make a conscious effort in your mind, en route to every situation, to treat all segments of society objectively and fairly.
- Remember that *all* groups have some bad, some average, and some good people within them.
- Go out of your way to be personable and friendly with minority-group members. Remember, many don't expect it.
- Don't appear uncomfortable with or avoid discussing racial and ethnic issues with other officers and citizens.
- Take responsibility for patiently educating citizens and the public about the role of the officer and about standard operating procedures in law enforcement. Remember that citizens often do not understand "police culture."
- Don't be afraid to be a change agent in your organization when it comes to improving cross-cultural relations within your department and between police and community. It may not be a popular thing to do, but it is the right thing to do.

"Remember the history of law enforcement with all groups and ask yourself the question, Am I part of the past, or a part of the future?"

DISCUSSION QUESTIONS AND ISSUES*

1. *Views on the Multicultural Society.* The following viewpoints regarding our increasingly multicultural population reflect varying levels of tolerance, understanding, and acceptance. Discuss these points of view and their implications for law enforcement:

   - Diversity is acceptable if there is not too much of it, but the way things are going today, it is hard to absorb and it just may result in our destruction.
   - They are here now and they need to do things our way.
   - To advance in our diverse society, we need to accept and respect our differences rather than maintaining the myth of the melting pot.

*Tips and quote are from Deputy Chief Ondra Berry, Reno, Nevada Police Department.
*See instructor's Manual accompanying this text for additional activities, role-play activities, questionnaires, and projects related to the content of this chapter.

2. ***Police Work and Ethnicity.*** In a 1988 study entitled *Policing Multi-Ethnic Neighborhoods* Alpert and Dunham say that ethnicity complicates every police procedure. In your experience, do race, culture, and ethnicity complicate police procedures and interactions? Explain why or why not.

3. ***Dealing with Illegal Immigrants.*** Does the police department in which you work have a policy regarding undocumented immigrants? Are officers instructed not to inquire into their status unless a crime has been committed? How do you think police officers should deal with illegal immigrants?

4. ***Mini Case Study 1.*** Reread, then discuss.

   ### Driving under the Influence?

   (a) Has this issue (kava drink and its use among Pacific Islanders) been identified as an issue or problem in your jurisdiction? If so, what has the prosecuting attorney said about dealing with these cases?

   (b) What would the officer's liability be if he released the driver and the erratic driving continued?

5. ***Mini Case Study 2.*** Reread, then discuss.

   ### A Tragic Case of Cross-Cultural Misinterpretation

   (a) Do you think this case would have proceeded differently if all the authorities involved understood the cultural tradition of the medical practice ("coin rubbing") that caused the bruising? Explain your answer.

   (b) Discuss whether you think Southeast Asian refugees should give up this medical practice because it can be misinterpreted.

6. ***Mini Case Study 3.*** Reread, then discuss.

   ### Latino Values as a Factor in Sentencing

   (a) Discuss whether culture should play any part in influencing the sentencing of a criminal convicted of violent crimes such as murder and rape. Was the lighter verdict in this case justified? Explain your answer.

   (b) According to Superior Court Judge Katz, culture influenced the sentencing in this case. In your opinion, if the husband involved were not Latino, would the sentence have been the same?

7. ***Prejudice and Discrimination in Police Work.*** In your own words, define prejudice and discrimination. Give examples of (a) discrimination in society in general, (b) discrimination against police officers, and (c) discrimination toward minorities by police officers.

8. ***Community-Based Policing.*** Why is community-based policing (CBP) in minority, ethnic, and immigrant communities especially crucial to the success of law enforcement in any given city? Discuss the two cases presented in this section (i.e., the case of the police department without CBP in place [at the time of the fall of Saigon] and the case of the police department whose CBP efforts resulted in a dramatic decline of the homicide rate in the city). What lessons can you extract from these two examples that may be applicable to your jurisdiction?

   Note: Chapters 14 and 15 contain further information and discussion questions on community-based policing.

REFERENCES

ALPERT, G. P., AND R. G. DUNHAM. (1988). *Policing Multi-Ethnic Neighborhoods: The Miami Study and Findings for Law Enforcement in the United States.* Westport, Conn.: Greenwood Press.

ANDERSON, MICHELLE. (1993, April). "A License to Abuse: The Impact of Conditional Status on Female Immigrants," *Yale Law Journal, 102,* 1401.

BARLOW, H. D. (2000). *Criminal Justice in America.* Upper Saddle River, N.J.: Prentice-Hall.

BERRY, ONDRA. (2000, December 8). Deputy Chief, Reno, Nevada, Police Department, personal communication.

BERRY-WILKINSON, ALISON. (1993). "Be Careful What You Say When . . . ," *Labor Beat, 5* (1), 16.

CARRICK, GRADY. (2000, November). "Professional Police Traffic Stops: Strategies to Address Racial Profiling in Perspective," *FBI Law Enforcement Bulletin,* 8–10.

Coalition for Immigrant and Refugee Rights, 1991 Survey.

COFFEY, ALAN, EDWARD ELDEFONSON AND WALTER HARTINGER. (1982). *Human Relations: Law Enforcement in a Changing Community,* 3rd ed. Englewood Cliffs, N.J.: Prentice-Hall.

The Convention on the Elimination of all Forms of Racial Discrimination: Initial Report of the United States of America to the United Nations Committee on the Elimination of Racial Discrimination, September 2000. http://www.state.gov/www/global/human_rights/cerd_report/cerd_intro.html.

Council of Economic Advisors for the President's Initiative on Race. (1998, September). "Indicators of Social and Economic Well-Being by Race and Hispanic Origin," in *Changing America: Crime and Criminal Justice.* (Chapter 7). http://www.whitehouse.gov/Initiatives/OneAmerica/cevent.html.

FERNANDEZ, DONYA. (2000, December 20). Language Rights attorney for the Language Rights Project, Employment Law Center/Legal Aid Society, San Francisco, California, personal communication.

HALL, EDWARD T. (1959). *The Silent Language.* Greenwich, Conn.: Fawcett.

HANDLIN, OSCAR. (1975). *Out of Many: A Study Guide to Cultural Pluralism in the United States.* Anti-Defamation League of B'nai B'rith, published through Brown & Williamson Tobacco Corporation.

HARRIS, DAVID. (2000, March 30). Written testimony for the Hearing on Racial Profiling within Law Enforcement Agencies, United States Senate Subcommittee on the Constitution, Federalism, and Property Rights.

HARRIS, P. R. (1994). *High Performance Leadership: HRD Strategies for the New Work Culture.* Amherst, Mass.: Human Resource Development Press.

HUNTER, R. D., P. D. MAYHALL, AND T. BARKER. (2000). *Police Community Relations and the Administration of Justice.* Upper Saddle River, N.J.: Prentice-Hall.

Immigration and Naturalization Service, Office of Policy and Planning. (2000, October 31). *Monthly Statistical Report, September 2000 FY Year End Report.* Washington, D.C.: U.S. government Printing Office.

JANG, DEEANA, C. KLEIN, AND L. ORLOFF. (1995, Summer). "With No Place to Turn: Improving Advocacy for Battered Immigrant Women," *Family Law Quarterly, 29,* (2), 313.

KATZ, LAWRENCE. (2000, December). Residing judge, Juvenile Court of Contra Costa (California) County, personal communication.

KENNEDY, JOHN F. (1986). *A Nation of Immigrants.* New York: Harper & Row.

LEWIS, ROBERT. (2000, December). Sergeant, San Diego, California, Police Department, personal communication.

LIPSCOMB, WENDELL. (1993, January). Psychiatrist, personal communication.

MILLER, CHAR. (2000, December). Professor of History, Trinity College, San Antonio, Texas, personal communication.

National Institute of Justice. (2000, August). *The COPS Program after 4 Years: National Evaluation,* by Jeffrey A. Roth and Joseph F. Ryan. Washington, D.C.: U.S. Department of Justice.

National Office of Samoan Affairs. (1984). *Samoan Family Care, Child Abuse, and Neglect Prevention: A Service Provider Handbook.* Grant 90CA923-01. San Francisco: National Center on Child Abuse and Neglect.

OLIVER, W. M. (2001). *Community Oriented Policing: A Systematic Approach to Policing.* Upper Saddle River, N.J.: Prentice-Hall.

One America in the 21st Century: Forging a New Future, Executive Summary, Advisory Board to the President's Initiative on Race, September 1998, http//www.whitehouse.gov/Initiatives/OneAmerica/cevent.html.

ORLOFF, LESLYE. (2000, July 20). Director, NOW Legal Defense and Education Fund Immigrant Women Program, addressing the House Judiciary Subcommittee on Immigration Claims on H.R. 3083.

PEAK, K. J., AND R. W. GLENSOR. (1997). *Community Policing and Problem Solving: Strategies and Practices.* Upper Saddle River, N.J.: Prentice-Hall.

Police Chief Magazine

Police Executive Research Forum. (1992). *Revisiting Community Policing: A New Typology.* Washington, D.C.: Police Executive Research Forum.

Public Policy Institute. (2000, July). "Research Brief," *Ethnicity, Neighborhoods, and California Politics, 38.*

RAWLINS, GARY H. (1992, October 8). "Africans Came 200 Years Earlier," *USA Today,* p. 2a.

RODRIGUEZ, R. (1995, May–June). "Evaluation of the MCN Domestic Violence Assessment Form and Pilot Prevalence Study," *Clinical Supplement of the Migrant Clinicians Network,* 1–2.

RUHLY, SHARON.(1976). *Orientations to Intercultural Communication: Modules in Speech Communication* (p. 4). Chicago: Science Research Associates.

SENGE, PETER M., ART KLEINER, CHARLOTTE ROBERTS, RICK ROSS, AND BRYAN SMITH. (1994). *The Fifth Discipline Fieldbook: Strategies and Tools for Building a Learning Organization.* New York: Doubleday/Currency.

SHERMAN, SPENCER. (1986). "When Cultures Collide," *California Lawyer,* 6, (1), 33.

SKOLNICK, JEROME H. (1999). *On Democratic Policing.* Washington D.C.: Police Foundation.

STEVENS, D. J. (2001). *Case Studies in Community Policing.* Upper Saddle River, N.J.: Prentice-Hall.

TROJANOWICZ, ROBERT, AND BONNIE BUCQUEOUX. (1990). *Community Policing: A Contemporary Perspective.* Lansing: Michigan State University: Cincinnati, Ohio: Anderson Publishing.

TROJANOWICZ, ROBERT, AND DAVID CARTER. (1990). "The Changing Face of America," *FBI Law Enforcement Bulletin, 59,* 6–12.

U.S. Bureau of the Census. (1997). *Demographic State of the Nation: 1997.* Washington, D.C.: U.S. Government Printing Office.

ZANGWILL, ISRAEL. (1908). *The Melting Pot: Drama in Four Acts.* New York: Macmillan.

2

THE CHANGING LAW ENFORCEMENT AGENCY:

A Microcosm of Society

OVERVIEW

The ethnic, racial, gender, and lifestyle composition of law enforcement agencies is changing in the United States. In this chapter we address the increasingly pluralistic workforce and provide examples of racism and cultural insensitivity within the law enforcement agency. We present suggestions for defusing racially and culturally rooted conflicts and address issues related to women, gays, and lesbians in law enforcement. The chapter ends with recommendations for all employees who work within a diverse workforce and particularly emphasizes the role of the chief executive.

COMMENTARY

The changing law enforcement environment, both internal and external, is strikingly evident in todays diverse society:

> The Federal Bureau of Investigation and the Drug Enforcement Administration are grappling with charges of discrimination in their ranks—charges that culminated recently in a meeting at FBI headquarters in Washington between Director William S. Sessions and the bureau's 56 field office heads to discuss discrimination. ("FBI, DEA Nearer to Accord with Minority Agents," *Washington Post,* April 30, 1991, p. 3)

> San Rafael—A San Francisco woman is suing [the city of] San Anselmo for allegedly forcing her out of her job as a police officer because she is a lesbian. In a civil suit in Marin [she said] . . . her supervisor repeatedly harassed her and that other officers made deprecating remarks about women and homosexuals. ("Ex-Police Officer Sues over Alleged Gay Bias," *San Francisco Chronicle,* December 31, 1992, p. A-3)

Last week they celebrated gay pride day at the CIA. The most stuffy and insular of all government institutions, the intelligence community routed out gay employees in the 1950s on the theory that they could easily be blackmailed and therefore pose a security risk. But last week, gay Central Intelligence Agency employees and a busload of employees from the National Security Agency gathered at CIA headquarters in Virginia for the gay pride event, and even the director of the CIA showed up. ("America Accepting Gays Easier," *Contra Costa Times,* June 17, 2000, p. A27.)

Eight current or former Secret Service agents who are black charged . . . that top officials are dragging their feet on ridding the agency of deep-rooted racial discrimination, which they said has also infected Vice President Al Gore's protective detail. ("8 Agents Accuse Secret Service of Racial Bias," *Contra Costa Times,* August 31, 2000, p. A22)

INTRODUCTION

In Chapter 1, we presented the evolution of multicultural communities and the demographic changes that the United States has experienced in recent decades. The most notable demographic changes mentioned involve the increases in racial, ethnic, and immigrant populations in our country. Diversity is becoming so commonplace in communities that terms such as *majority group* and *minority group* are almost obsolete. There has been a negative reaction to the term "minority." Foes of the term find it is not just outmoded, but offensive. The term leaves non-whites feeling diminished—almost second class. The word carries overtones of "inferiority and inequity." The word, technically, is used to describe numerical designations, but over the years, it has come to have much larger implications. The range of reactions to these changes found in society as a whole is no different from the range within law enforcement agencies. Members of police communities across the country have demonstrated both tolerance of and resistance toward the changing society and workforce. Some officers dislike the multicultural workforce and the involvement of women in policing. They may resent diversity because of their own personal prejudices or biases. This resentment is due in part to perceived or actual advantages others receive when competing for law enforcement positions. In addition, because of past incompetent affirmative action hiring (i.e., management rushed to fill quotas but did not focus on competence), some officers perceive that affirmative action means the lowering of standards. Indeed, where standards have been lowered, everyone suffers, especially less qualified employees hired because of affirmative action. (This issue is discussed further in Chapter 3.) Officers must understand that affirmative action policies do not advocate the hiring of incompetent people, even if officers know of specific cases in which that has happened. No officer wants to work with an incompetent coworker, especially in life-threatening situations. In law enforcement agencies that have faced such problems, officers have become extremely critical of affirmative action hiring. Chief executives and managers must find ways to address this issue; peer relationships can suffer greatly because of perceptions about affirmative action hiring. Personnel must receive guarantees from their management that standards will not be lowered and that competence is the key criterion for hiring.

Leading positively and valuing the diversity within an agency are the keys to meeting the challenge of policing multicultural communities. As discussed in

Chapter 1, racial and ethnic tensions still exist in the law enforcement community. Agency personnel must first address the conflicts in their own organizations before dealing with community racial and ethnic problems. For example, in the commentary section of this chapter there is reference to the accusations of discrimination by eight black Secret Service agents. In the article quoted, the journalist continued: "But the Secret Service is in complete denial and [it is] stonewalling us." Some agents reported racial harassment and a hostile work environment. Others said they were "routinely denied" the opportunity to take management training courses that were necessary for promotion. These allegations must be addressed on a timely basis or they fester and result in lawsuits, court injunctions, and unhappy employees who do not remain with the organization.

Action or inaction of police departments is crucial to resolution of social problems that manifest themselves in law enforcement agencies. Across the United States the national press has reported numerous cases in which inaction or the wrong action was taken. Whether they like it or not, police officers are primary role models for citizens and are judged by a higher standard of behavior than are others. While supervision of police officers is important to ensure a higher standard of behavior is maintained, no supervision of officers working with the public, no matter how thorough and conscientious, will keep some officers from violating policies; there simply are too many police officers and too few supervisors. Thus, it is important that police officers have integrity and a stable set of core moral virtues. These virtues must include the ability to be professional in the general goals of protection and service to a diverse public.

As stated in Chapter 1, those concerned with peacekeeping and enforcement must accept the realities of a diverse society, as well as the heterogeneity in their workforce. The irony is that the peacekeepers sworn to uphold laws pertaining to acts of bias sometimes themselves become perpetrators, even with their own peers. If police departments are to be representative of the populations served, police executives must effect changes. These changes have to do with the treatment of peers as well as recruitment, selection, and promotion of employees who have traditionally been underrepresented in law enforcement. The argument (Chapter 1) that the United States has never really been a melting pot, applies also to the law enforcement community. In some cases relationships within the law enforcement workplace, especially as diversity increases, are characterized by disrespect and tension. Although many in the police subculture would argue that membership implies brotherhood (and therefore belonging), this membership has traditionally excluded certain groups in both subtle and obvious ways.

CHANGING WORKFORCE

As microcosms of their communities, law enforcement agencies increasingly include among their personnel more women and ethnic and racial minorities. Although such groups are far from achieving parity in most agencies in the United States, advances have been made (see Chapter 3). In many regions of the country, today's law enforcement workforce differs greatly from those of the past; the profound shift in demographics has resulted in notable changes in law enforcement.

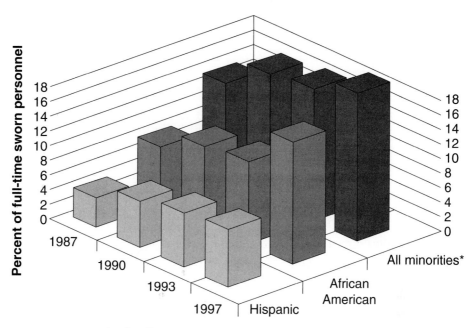

Exhibit 2.1 Minority sheriff's officers. *Source:* U.S. Department of Justice office of Justice Programs, Bureau of Justice Statistics, February 2000 NCJ 173428 Washington D.C. *Includes African Americans, Pacific Islanders, and American Indians.

Law Enforcement Diversity: A Microcosm of Society

The Bureau of Justice Statistics February 2000 Law Enforcement Management and Administrative Statistics (LEMAS) report established the overall percentage of racial and ethnic minority-group representation among full-time sworn personnel nation-wide as of 1997. The percentage of change for the three-year period between 1993 and 1997, as obtained by comparison of the LEMAS reports, was as follows:

- Local racial and ethnic minority police officers increased from 19.1 percent in 1993 to 21.5 percent in 1997.
- Racial and ethnic minority sheriffs' deputies increased from 16.9 percent in 1993 to 19 percent in 1997.

With increases came a corresponding reduction in the number of white officers and deputies in law enforcement workforces. Although the number of white males decreased, the number of white females in the workforce increased. Exhibits 2.1 and 2.2 provide more details on the percentages by ethnic and racial groups as of 1997 in state, local, and sheriffs' departments.

Some major law enforcement agencies have achieved parity in terms of the percentage of diverse groups in their workforce compared to the percentage in the community; most have not. Law enforcement is still a predominantly white male occupation, and there must be an expansion of efforts in the recruitment, hiring, and promotion of women and people of other races and ethnicities nationwide. This issue is discussed further in Chapter 3.

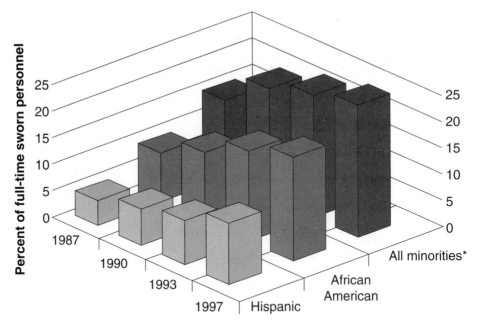

Exhibit 2.2   Minority local police officers. *Includes African Americans, Pacific Islanders, and American Indians. *Source:* U.S. Department of Justice, Office of Justice Programs, Bureau of Justice Statistics, February 2000 NCJ 173429. Washington D.C.

Measuring Responsiveness to Diversity.

A manual produced by the Canadian Association of Chiefs of Police includes a 10-question checklist and scoring method for law enforcement organizations to determine how responsive they are in adapting to diversity. It is reproduced here (Exhibit 2.3) for use in rating your own agency.

ETHNIC AND RACIAL ISSUES WITHIN THE WORKFORCE

Racism

Racism within law enforcement agencies has been documented for decades. An African American history display at the New York Police Academy in October 1992 contained the following written account of the experiences of one of the first black officers in the New York Police Department:

> Seven years before the adoption of the charter creating New York City, Brooklyn, then an independent city, hired the first black policeman. Wiley G. Overton was sworn in March 6, 1891. . . . His first tour of duty was spent in civilian clothing because fellow officers breaking with tradition refused to furnish him with a temporary uniform. . . . Officers in his section refused to sleep in the same room with him. . . . The officers in the precinct ignored him and spoke only if it was necessary in the line of duty.

The New York Police Department is not alone. Racism can occur in police departments regardless of size or region. The Dallas police strike in 1992, with its racial

---

Exhibit 2.3   How responsive is your organization?

Circle and count the number of initiatives that your police service has undertaken. See how you rate.

( )   1. Are members of ethnic/cultural communities participating in your community and crime prevention programs?

( )   2. Do your programs provide for community input into the development and implementation of local policing programs?

( )   3. Does your organization have a race relations policy that is integrated into your overall mission?

( )   4. Do your patrol officers use foot patrols in areas of high concentrations of ethnic minorities?

( )   5. Do you sue translators or interpreters from within your police department or from local immigrant service agencies or ethnic community organizations in your contacts with linguistic minorities?

( )   6. Are your ads and brochures multilingual, and do they depict a multicultural community?

( )   7. Do you have a recruitment campaign that actively targets ethnic and visible minorities?

( )   8. Have your hiring and promotional practices been evaluated to see if they recognize and value knowledge and skills related to community pricing, especially with ethnic/cultural communities?

( )   9. Have your in-service training programs dealt with the issue of diversity?

( )   10. Have your officers participated in programs in multicultural or race relations training for trainers?

Scoring:

0–3,   Don't panic. The fact that you did the checklist shows that you are interested. Start small, but start today!

4–6,   Good start. You are part of a community-based policing movement. You are beginning to tackle some of the issues that face police services in a multicultural environment.

7–9,   Well done. It is obvious that you understand and value the benefits of ethnoculturally sensitive and community-based policing. You're on the right track, keep up the good work!

10,   Congratulations. Your challenge is to maintain the momentum and evaluate the effectiveness of your initiatives.

Source: Canadian Association of Chiefs of Police. (1992). *Police Race Relations: Raising Your Effectiveness in Today's Diverse Neighborhoods through Community Policing.* Place de Ville, Tower B, 112 Kent St., Suite 1908, Ottawa, Ontario K1P 5P2, Canada.

---

overtones, polarized the department—cop versus cop. The *New Jersey Daily News* in 1993 had bold headlines: "Racism on the Job: Black N.J. Troopers Charge Harassment, Bias, and Discrimination" (*New York Daily News,* April 22, 1993, p. C–3). In May 2000, the federal government concluded that there was sufficient evidence of civil rights violations within the Los Angeles Police Department (LAPD) to file a so-called pattern and practice discrimination suit. The LAPD faced the possibility of intervention by the federal government. The department was warned to make changes in police training and procedures to avoid a lawsuit. Similar accusations could be heard in Pittsburgh, Pennsylvania, Steubenville, Ohio, New Jersey, and other communities across the nation in reaction to accusations of racial profiling in traffic stops and police brutality directed toward persons of color. Unfortunately, racism has been an issue in many communities for decades. As long as racism exists in society, the potential exists for police agencies to reflect these attitudes.

We spoke with several officers from different states about racism in their departments. Those interviewed requested that their names not be included, because they felt they might face repercussions. One African American officer recalled almost coming to blows with a white officer who used a racial slur against him; the use of such slurs was commonplace for the white officer and his friends. A Cuban American officer recounted the story of a nonresisting Latino suspect who was caught in the commission of a minor crime and beaten by the white arresting officers, who used racial epithets. One major city in Massachusetts suspended a deputy superintendent of police for using the word *nigger* directed toward one of his own officers. An African American officer in a large city in Florida was fired after using racial epithets against other blacks in violation of a strict citywide policy. In this particular case, the African American officer's conduct was reported by another officer at the scene. In yet another city, an African American officer was overheard telling a white prisoner, "Wait until you get to central booking and the niggers get a hold of you."

City and state police and county sheriffs are not the only ones facing problems with racism. Between 1985 and 1991, within the Federal Bureau of Investigation (FBI) a total of three agents and eight managers were disciplined for racial harassment of a former agent who is African American. In August 1991 the chairperson of the U.S. Commission on Civil Rights called for an investigation into what he described as pervasive race discrimination against black service personnel and civilian employees in the armed forces. According to newspaper accounts, the charges ran counter to the widespread view among sociologists and others that the U.S. military is relatively free from the racial tensions that divide the rest of society (*New York Times,* August 24, 1991, p. A–12). An article in the *New York Times* in 1999 indicated many in the military still face discrimination and overt racism. (Steven Holmes, "Cohen Calls for Review of Racism in Military," *New York Times,* November 23, 1999, p. A1).

Defusing Racially and Culturally Rooted Conflicts

Racism exists within our law enforcement organizations; police are not immune to social ills. One of the greatest challenges of society and for police officers is dealing with their own racism. The first step in addressing the problem is for police department personnel, on all levels, to admit that racism exists rather than denying it. One reads an account, for example, of an African American police officer, off duty or on plain-clothes assignments, who is an instant suspect in the eyes of some white officers. If this occurs in one city or county, it can occur in another. The police researcher David Shipler, after two years of interviews across the country, maintained that he encountered very few black officers (including those out of uniform) who had not been "hassled by white cops." He was quick to point out, however, that not every white police officer is a bigot and not every police force a bastion of racism; in fact, some agencies have made great strides in improving race relations.

Shipler, advocated that law enforcement should combat and defuse racism by using the U.S. Army model developed during a time of extreme racial tension in the military in the early 1970s (*New York Times,* May 26, 1992, p. A–17). Obviously, no model of training will bring guaranteed success and alleviate all acts of prejudice and racism. However, professional groups can build on each other's attempts, especially when these have proven to be fairly successful. Shipler agrees that police officers are not identical to soldiers, because the former have constant contact with the public (where they see the worst) and must use personal judgment in dangerous and ambiguous situations. Nevertheless, he suggests that some military approaches are adaptable to law enforcement. According to Shipler, the basic framework for combating and defusing racism in the military has been

- *Command commitment:* The person at the top sets the tone all the way down to the bottom. Performance reports document any bigoted or discriminatory behavior. A record of racial slurs and discriminatory acts can derail a military career, and the same is true in law enforcement
- *Training of advisers:* Military personnel are trained at the Defense Equal Opportunity Management Institute in Florida as equal opportunity advisers. The advisers are assigned to military units with direct access to commanders. They conduct local courses to train all members of the unit on race relations
- *Complaints and monitoring:* The advisers mentioned provide one channel for specific complaints of racial and gender discrimination, but they also drop in on units unannounced and sound out the troops on their attitudes. Surveys are conducted and informal discussions are held to lessen racial tensions.

Sondra Thiederman (1991), cultural diversity consultant and author, provides 9 tips that will help organizational managers or leaders identify and resolve conflicts that arise because of cultural (not only racial) differences in the workplace. She says that the following guidelines are applicable no matter which cultures, races, religions, or lifestyles are involved:

1. Give each party the opportunity to voice his or her concerns without interruption.
2. Attempt to obtain agreement on what the problem is by asking questions of each party to find out specifically what is upsetting each person.
3. During this process, stay in control and keep employees on the subject of the central issue.
4. Establish whether the issue is indeed rooted in cultural differences by determining

   - If the parties are from different cultures or subcultures.
   - If the key issue represents an important value in each person's culture.
   - How each person is expected to behave in his or her culture as it pertains to this issue.
   - If the issue is emotionally charged for one or both of the parties.
   - If similar conflicts arise repeatedly and in different contexts.

5. Summarize the cultural (racial, religious, or lifestyle) differences that you uncover.
6. State the negative outcomes that will result if the situation is not resolved (be specific).
7. State the positive outcomes that will result if the situation is resolved (be specific).
8. Negotiate terms by allowing those involved to come up with the solutions.
9. Provide positive reinforcement as soon as the situation improves.

Thiederman's approach is based on conflict resolution and crisis intervention techniques training that many police and correctional officers receive in either their academy or in-service training. Police department command must encourage the use of conflict resolution techniques by officers of all backgrounds as a way of handling issues prior to their becoming flash points. With professionalism and patience, conflict resolution techniques used to reduce racial and ethnic problems will work within both the workforce and neighborhoods.

John Sullivan and Henry DeGeneste, in July 1997, in an article for *Fresh Perspectives* (a Police Executive Research Forum publication) wrote:

> Police play a pivotal role in the life of communities. As the most visible branch of civil government, police agencies are called on to mitigate and resolve conflict among both groups and individuals. This intimate relationship with conflict resolution and management is a natural extension of the primary police duty to preserve the public peace and prevent crime. The recent focus on community policing and problem solving strengthens these traditional police roles, highlighting the importance of police interaction with the diverse communities they serve. Communities, however, are not static collections of people. Rather, communities are dynamic and constantly changing. The ethnic, social and class composition of nations and individual communities shifts over time.

As a result of allegations of racism against it, the Alameda, California, Police Department developed a series of general orders as one approach to remedy the problem. Violation of the department general orders (DGOs) carries progressive disciplinary ramifications up to and including termination. The general orders deal with control of prejudicial conduct based on race, religion, ethnicity, disability, sex, age, or sexual orientation and are as follows:

1. *Code of ethics:* commits to personal suppression of prejudice, animosities, malice, and ill will, as well as respect for the constitutional rights of all persons.
2. *DGOs 80-1:* Specifically addresses discrimination and racial remarks and requires courtesy and respect for all persons. It states: "Discrimination or racism in any form shall never be tolerated."
3. *DGO 80-1:* Requires impartiality toward all persons and guarantees equal protection under the law. Prohibits exhibition of partiality due to race, creed, or influence.
4. *DGO 90-3:* Deals with harassment in the workplace based on race, religion, color, national origin, ancestry, disability, marital status, sex, age, or sexual preference. Used by permission of Chief Robert Shields, 1993

The Alameda Police Department also produced the following as an in-service training guide and a posted announcement within the agency:

Alameda Police Department Mortal Sins

1. Racism, racial slurs, racial discrimination
2. Sexism, offensive sexual remarks, sexual harassment, sexual discrimination
3. Discrimination or harassment for sexual orientation
4. Religious discrimination
5. Untruthfulness and falsifications
6. Unnecessary or excessive force

7. Use of illegal drugs
8. Violations of the law

This department sent a clear message to its employees that its leaders will not tolerate discriminatory behavior. The same department adapted a San Diego Police Department attitude assessment survey instrument on perceptions regarding contact with the multicultural community and workforce. The survey instrument is reproduced in Appendix A.

Police Fraternal Organizations

Police fraternal, religious, and ethnic organizations offer members social activities, counseling, career development, resources, and networking opportunities with persons of common heritage, background, or experience. The New York Police Department, for example, has many clubs, societies, and associations to address the needs of its pluralistic organization. The Irish are represented by the Emerald Society, African Americans by the Guardians Association, Christian officers by Police Officers for Christ, those of Asian or Pacific Islander heritage (which includes Chinese, Japanese, Korean, Filipino, and Asian Indian officers) by the Asian Jade Society, Italian officers by the Columbia Association, and so on. The police subculture can be a stressful environment, so it is only natural that persons different from the majority workforce members seek emotional comfort zones with those of similar background. Membership in these groups provides emotional sanctuary from the stereotypes, hostility, indifference, ignorance, or naïveté that members encounter within their organizations and communities.

Occasionally, one hears of criticism within a department or by the public that such organizations actually highlight the differences between groups of people. At a 1992 National Organization of Black Law Enforcement Executives (NOBLE) conference, a white female (nonattendee) asked the meaning of the acronym NOBLE. When given the answer, she asked: "Is it ethical for blacks to have their own organization? Could whites have an organization called 'The National Organization of White Law Enforcement Executives' without being referred to as racists? Why can't the multicultural, social, and professional organizations that already exist satisfy the needs of everyone?"

The woman's concern was brought up directly with one of the conference participants, Sergeant Thomas Hall, an African American, who at the time was a Virginia state trooper. Sergeant Hall (1992) explained:

> In America, we need independent black institutions . . . to foster cultural pride, and have a place where we can go and feel comfortable. We cannot express ourselves in society. We cannot assimilate in society. We cannot even assimilate like some Hispanic groups can because of their complexions. I can't assimilate on a bus. As soon as I step on the bus, you are going to realize there is a black guy on the bus. I can't assimilate in a police organization . . . so without these black institutions, I cannot survive. We all have survival mechanisms. I have cultural needs and I have to be around people that share my needs and frustrations. I cannot do that in organizations that are predominantly white. The whites don't suffer from the racial pressures and tensions that I suffer from. So how can they [mostly white organizations] meet my interests and needs. It is impossible.

Hall (now chief of police at a university in Virginia) stressed that African American law enforcement organizations provide him with a network of persons with similar interests, concerns, and background.

The racial, ethnic, religious, and lifestyle organizations within law enforcement are not meant to divide but, rather, to give support to groups that traditionally were not accepted in law enforcement fully and had no power in the organization. Yet the sentiment expressed by the white female who inquired into the meaning of NOBLE is a common sentiment among some police officers. Police command officers and supervisors must not ignore this debate (whether expressed or not). They must address the issues underlying the need for the support groups within the department. They must also ensure dialogue and shared activities between all formalized groups within the organization. All officers must hear from the officers' of different ethnic, racial, and lifestyle perspectives what benefit they receive from membership in the groups. Officers must be willing to discuss ways to guard against divisiveness, either real or perceived, within their agencies.

Assignments Based on Diversity

There has been limited research on the assumption that an increase in the proportions of any underrepresented group in a police agency would have a positive effect in the community. Some believe that an increase in Hispanic, African American, or Asian officers in a neighborhood of the same race or ethnicity would improve police–community relations. One can speculate that there would be a more sensitive response of "like folks" who are aware of needs and issues of "their kind." In fact, historically, immigrants (Irish, Italians, and Germans) were hired by police departments because they could communicate and operate more effectively than could nonimmigrant officers in neighborhoods with immigrants.

Although citizens appreciate having officers of their own color or national origin work their area, this deployment strategy may result in unfairness. Studies have concluded that this practice can result in a career path for minorities that may be a very different path than that of white officers in agencies that follow this practice (Benson, 1992; Ross, Snortum, and Beyers, 1982; Wells, 1987). For example, instead of receiving specialized assignments in traffic, investigations, Special Weapons and Tactics (SWAT) team, and so on, the minority officer who is working effectively in the minority community may have an extended tour of duty in that function. In addition, the area to which this officer is assigned is often a tougher, high-crime area, which means that he or she is exposed more frequently to violence.

Officers of the same background as the predominant ethnicity or race in the neighborhood do not necessarily make the best crime fighters or problem solvers there. Not all ethnically diverse officers may have the skills or desire to work with their own cultural or racial group. Assignments based on diversity alone, therefore, are generally unfair and may be a disservice to both the officer and the neighborhood. Officers should not be restricted to work in specific areas based on the notion that police–community relations will improve automatically. In addition, it cannot be assumed that an officer of the same background as the citizens will always show sensitivity to their particular needs.

Ron Hampton, a Washington, D.C., peace officer and executive director of the National Black Police Officers Association, illustrated this point at a 1992 NOBLE conference when he discussed the reasons why a new African American recruit wanted to work the black areas of Washington, D.C. The recruit said that he could tell people of his own race what to do and could not always do so in predominantly white neighborhoods. Hampton (1992) noted that the young recruit "called people from his neighborhood 'maggots.' " (Hampton, 1992). Hampton made the point that supervisors must hold subordinates accountable for their conduct, and the chief executive must make it known that inappropriate behavior will be disciplined no matter what the neighborhood. We present this example here also to illustrate how some officers may have internalized the hatred society has directed toward them and, consequently, they are not automatically the most effective officers in certain neighborhoods.

When Chief Burgreen was the top executive of the San Diego Police Department, he, like many other law enforcement managers, did not deploy officers according to color or ethnicity. Deployment was based on the best fit for the neighborhood and was related to an officer's competence and capabilities. However, Chief Burgreen had four community relations sergeants, one acting as a liaison for each major group in the city: Hispanic, African American, Asian, and gays and lesbians. He describes these sergeants as his "eyes and ears" for what is going on in the various communities. Some cities use cultural affairs committees made up of people from diverse groups in the community and the officers who provide them service.

WOMEN IN LAW ENFORCEMENT

Historically, women have always been part of the general workforce in American society, although usually in jobs that fulfilled traditional female employment roles, as nurses, secretaries, schoolteachers, waitresses, and flight attendants, to name a few. In 1845 New York City hired its first police "matron." In 1888 Massachusetts and New York passed legislation requiring communities with a population over 20,000 to hire police matrons to care for female prisoners. According to More (1992), during the first half of the nineteenth century a number of police practices were challenged, thus allowing for the initial entry of women into the police field. In 1922 the International Association of Chiefs of Police passed a resolution supporting the use of policewomen.

Barriers to female entry into the police field, however, included separate entrance requirements, limits on the number of women who could be employed, and lower pay (More, 1992). Women police officers were given duties that did not allow or require them to work street patrol. Assignments and roles were limited to positions such as juvenile delinquency and truancy prevention, child abuse, crimes against women, and custodial functions (Bell, 1982). In 1972 the passage of the Equal Employment Opportunity (EEO) Act applied to state and local governments the provisions of Title VII of the Civil Rights Act of 1964. The EEO Act prohibited employment discrimination on the basis of race, color, religion, sex, or national origin. Selection procedures, criteria, and standards were changed or eliminated and/or made "job related." The law played an important role in opening up police departments to women. Adoption of affirmative action policies, along with court orders and injunctions also played a role in bringing more women into law enforcement.

The first major movement of women into the general workforce occurred during World War II. With men off to war, women entered the workforce in large numbers and successfully occupied many nontraditional employment roles. After the war, 30 percent of all women continued working outside the home (*Business Week,* September 19, 1991, p. 112). By 1990 almost 55 percent of women in the United States worked outside the home. It was predicted that by 2000, that number would be as high as 75 percent (Naisbitt and Aburdene, 1986).

Considering how long organized police departments have existed in the United States, women have entered relatively late into sworn law enforcement positions within them. It was not until the early 1970s that women were assigned to patrol duties in some departments. This delay was due, in part, to role perceptions. The predominant belief that law enforcement agencies function to exercise authority and use force is accompanied by the idea that women are not capable of performing the necessary functions.

A 1986 Police Foundation study reported the following findings: "In those agencies under court order to increase the representation of women and minorities, women made up 10.1 percent of the sworn personnel in 1986; in those with voluntary affirmative action policies, women made up 8.3 percent of the personnel; and, in those without affirmative action plans, women constituted only 6.1 percent of the personnel" (Martin, 1990, p. 1).

The February 2000 Law Enforcement Management and Administrative Statistics (LEMAS) report, issued by the U.S. Department of Justice, established the overall percentage change of sworn women in local and sheriffs' departments nationwide for the three-year period from 1993 to 1997 as follows:

- Local women police officers increased from 8.8 percent in 1993 to 10.0 percent in 1997
- Women sheriffs' deputies increased from 14.6 percent in 1993 to 15.6 percent in 1997

Researchers in the late 1980s made various predictions of the numbers of women expected to be in law enforcement professions by the turn of the century. They ranged from 47 to 55 percent of the workforce, but those predictions never materialized.

McCoy (1992) conducted enlightening research useful to law enforcement executives. He addressed one primary topic and four related subissues (p. 64):

Primary Topic: What organizational structure will support a positive work environment for policewomen by 2001?

Conclusion: The research suggests that the majority of policing executives have not created an organizational culture that values the diversity of women within law enforcement. An organizational structure that will support a positive work environment for policewomen is one that values the complex role and competing interests that policewomen face within both societal and workplace environments. An organizational culture that does not view women as an intrusion into the male-dominated profession of law enforcement must be developed.

Subissue 1: How will increasing the number of women in law enforcement affect the organizational culture?

Conclusion: The research indicates that the personal traits women bring to law enforcement will foster a greater service-oriented approach to the organizational culture and that increased numbers of women within law enforcement will provide a more flexible approach to the policing ranks.

Subissue 2: How will job assignments and methods be affected by the increasing employment of women in law enforcement?

Conclusion: Police agencies will have to explore a restructuring of traditional work methods. Such options as job sharing and flextime will have to be considered to assist women officers in balancing family responsibilities and career development.

Subissue 3: What kind of support programs should be provided for women in law enforcement?

Conclusion: Women in policing need support programs to assist in family responsibilities, including child care, and the development of mentoring and network programs, as well as specific programs for women to discuss gender-related issues to reduce unnecessary stress. Department wide diversity and awareness training programs should include issues of women in law enforcement.

Subissue 4: How will legal mandates affect the organizational structure?

Conclusion: Legal actions have driven the work environment for women in policing.

McCoy's study concluded that legal mandates may continue to drive change of the organizational structure until police executives take a proactive leadership role to support a positive work environment for women.

McCoy made the following recommendations:

- A committed chief executive must create a positive work environment for policewomen by establishing it as a priority in his or her organizational mission and values statement and through policies and procedures.
- Agencies must provide awareness training valuing the diversity of the workforce to all members of the organization.
- To maintain a positive work environment, employees must be held accountable for actions that are harmful to any segment of the workforce.
- Problems within the organizational structure that inhibit a positive work environment for women must be acknowledged and corrected.
- Agencies must develop and employ mechanisms that allow women to express concerns without spotlighting gender.
- Agencies must demonstrate their support of a positive work environment for women by actively providing opportunities for career development.

In November 1998 the International Association of Chiefs of Police (IACP) released the results of a study it had commissioned entitled **The Future of Women in Policing.** The stated purpose of the survey was to query IACP members on their perspectives and opinions about the following issues:

- Status and roles of women in policing
- Recruitment and selection of women officers
- Supporting and mentoring women officers
- Training and supervision as correlates of tenure, success, and promotion of women officers

- Attrition and resignation of women officers
- Gender discrimination and sexual harassment
- Whether a glass ceiling exists as a barrier to promotions
- Future directions for women in policing

The study confirmed that although the number of women in law enforcement is growing and women are progressing through the ranks the following are also true:

- There are fewer women than men in policing
- Women officers still face bias from male officers
- Many departments lack strategies for recruiting women
- Women officers may face gender discrimination and a glass ceiling that inhibits promotion
- Sexual harassment still occurs in many departments
- Although the need is great, there are very few mentoring programs for women officers

The integration of women into policing has led many departments to grapple with gender issues such as sexual harassment and discrimination, family leave, and maternity policies.

Gender Issues

Research on gender issues confronting women in law enforcement focus on discrimination and sexual harassment, role barriers, the "brotherhood," a double standard, and career versus family.

Discrimination and Sexual Harassment.   Although sexual harassment exists in both private and public sectors, we believe it is particularly problematic in law enforcement—an occupation that is still mostly male. The predominantly male makeup and macho image of law enforcement lead to problems of sexual harassment in the workplace. Harassment on the basis of sex is a violation of Section 703 of Title VII of the Civil Rights Act (29CFR Section 1604.11[a][1]) and is defined as unwelcome or unsolicited sexual advances, requests for sexual favors, and other verbal or physical conduct of a sexual nature when

1. Submission to such conduct is made either explicitly, or implicitly, a term or condition of an individual's employment; or
2. Submission to, or rejection of, such conduct by an individual is used as the basis for employment decisions affecting such individual; or
3. Such conduct has the purpose, or effect of unreasonably interfering with an individual's work performance or creating an intimidating, hostile, or offensive working environment

The majority of women officers interviewed for this book (who requested that their names not be used) said they had been sexually harassed in the workplace. Most indicated that when they were exposed to offensive behavior by male officers, they remained quiet for fear of negative male backlash. Sexual harassment occurs at all levels of an organization and is not limited to male harassment of women. Women, too, can be offenders when they initiate sexual jokes or innuendoes and use provocative language with men. This kind of behavior usually results in men coun-tering in a similar fashion, which contributes to and escalates the problem. In these instances, women must be held accountable. The questions of what is offensive and where the line should be drawn are frequently the central issues and must be ad-dressed. Rather than simply stating, "We don't have a harassment problem here," command officers must first model acceptable behavior and then set very clear guidelines for what constitutes acceptable behavior.

When harassment takes place, the results for the employees involved can be devastating in terms of their careers, the internal environment of the organization, and the public image. The importance of training all law enforcement employees (sworn and nonsworn) on the issues of sexual harassment cannot be stressed enough.

In response to increased sexual harassment complaints and lawsuits in law en-forcement, training and policies against harassment have also expanded. With training and awareness, sexual harassment is expected to decrease in the law enforcement work-force as the once male-dominated occupation makes its transition to mixed-gender, multiethnic, and multilifestyle organizations—a microcosm of the society served. Dis-crimination and sexual harassment training should not only deal with legal and liabil-ity issues but also address deep-seated attitudes about differences based on sex.

Role Barriers.   Barriers based on gender have diminished, both in the gen-eral population and within law enforcement. For example, ideas about protection differ by gender—who protects whom? In American society, women may protect children, but it has been more socially acceptable and traditional for men to protect women. In the act of protecting, the protectors become dominant and the protected become subordinate. This gender role perception takes time to break down, espe-cially in the law enforcement and corrections workforce. Many veteran police and correctional officers have difficulty with the transition as women come into the dan-gerous, male-dominated occupations that men felt required "male" strength and abilities. The result has been described as a clash between cultures—the once male-dominated workforce and one in which women are becoming integral parts of a new organizational environment. Veteran male police or correctional officers, socially conditioned to protect women, often feel that in addition to working with inmates or violent persons on the streets, they have the added responsibility of protecting the women officers with whom they work. These feelings, attitudes, and perceptions have made men and women in law enforcement positions uncomfortable with each other. Women sometimes feel patronized, overprotected, or merely tolerated rather than appreciated and respected for their work.

It appears that many in the new generation of male officers are more willing to accept women in law enforcement. In our numerous interviews with veteran offi-cers we found that, with few exceptions, women were generally accepted by men, but the acceptance was related to how well a specific woman performed her duties. Those who favored women in law enforcement recognized that even some men were not suited for such an occupation.

The Christopher Commission, assigned to investigate the LAPD in the wake of the Rodney King beating, offered numerous conclusions and recommendations pertaining to critical issues within the department. One of its conclusions was that women officers are better equipped to peacefully resolve situations of potential violence. None of the 120 LAPD officers who were most frequently charged with excessive use of force were women. (Definitive conclusions regarding women and the absence of excessive force will need to be supported by thorough research.) The commission also observed that although female officers were performing effectively, they were still not fully accepted as part of the workforce on an equal basis (Independent Commission on the Los Angeles Police Department, 1991). To overcome barriers to women in law enforcement, departments, mentors, and trainers would need to take action, including

- Increased training focusing on physical conditioning and self-defense
- The use of role playing to prepare for violent confrontation
- More rigorous supervision of backup officers
- Sensitivity training to modify the male-oriented environment of the police department
- Commitment (to eradicating gender bias) by top management
- Affirmative action programs with formal goals and guidelines (where legal)

The Brotherhood. Women who are accepted into the "brotherhood" of police or correctional officers have generally had to "become one of the guys." (Refer to Chapter 5 for more information on how language used in the brotherhood excludes women.) However, a woman who tries to act like one of the guys on the street or in a jail or prison is considered too hard, too coldhearted, or too unemotional and may be criticized by peers and supervisors. Karen Kimball, the women's coordinator in the LAPD, says that she has seen some " 'Jane Waynes' in the department who swagger, spit and are so aggressive they make many testosterone-charged men seem tame" (*Los Angeles Times*, June 5, 1993, p. A-12).

If she is too feminine or not sufficiently aggressive, men will not take her seriously and she will not do well in either police or correctional work. Women are confronted with a dilemma: They must be aggressive enough to do the job but feminine enough to be acceptable to male peers and must also be able to take different approaches to problems. Pat Ellis, a police officer with the Lothian and Borders Police, headquartered in Edinburgh, Scotland, was a 26-year veteran of the force as of September 2000. She says attitudes toward women in policing are the same in Great Britain as in the United States. She said:

> I had to work hard at being as good or better than my male counterparts on a daily basis. I also made sure I maintained my feminine side by always looking feminine. Hair done, makeup, perfume. She said I know a lot of males are really put off by women who not only act like men, but look like them.

Different approaches mean that women will use communication skills (verbal and nonverbal) in situations in which men might resort to force. Women should not feel compelled to behave like men in the workplace. When women do, the results can be counterproductive and can even result in disciplinary action. To succeed, women have to stay within narrow bands of acceptable behavior and exhibit only certain traditionally masculine and feminine qualities. Walking this fine line is difficult. This phenomenon is not unique to law enforcement. An article on a woman ironworker reported that "today's female ironworkers are still pioneers. . . . [N]o matter how skilled she becomes, she's got to prove herself over and over again. 'What it is, is attitude,' [one woman ironworker] says. 'I know that I'm on male-dominated home turf' " (*Contra Costa Times,* October 11, 2000, p. A3).

A Double Standard. Interviews of women officers showed clearly that the majority felt they had to perform better just to be measured as being equal to male officers—a double standard. These women spoke of how they imposed pressures on themselves to perform up to or exceed the expectations of their male peers. (Note that minority employees often express the same sentiment.) One woman officer explained that many women were using a community policing philosophy long before it became the practice of their agency. She mentioned that when she tried to do problem solving, she was criticized in her evaluations. Her supervisor rated her negatively for "trying too hard to find solutions to complainants' problems" and said she "spends too much time on calls explaining procedures" and "gets too involved" (Jones, 1993). The more senior women interviewed indicated that as their careers progressed, their confidence increased and the pressures and stress lessened.

Career versus Family. Women in law enforcement are faced with another dilemma—trying to raise a family and have a successful career, two goals that are difficult to combine. Women, especially single parents, who had children when they entered law enforcement frequently find that they have difficulty balancing their commitments to family and work. If they had children after entering the occupation, they may be confronted with difficult maternity-leave policies. In both cases, women often have a sense of guilt, stress, and frustration in trying to both do well in a job and maintain a family. As an International Association of Chiefs of Police 1998 study indicated, this is one of the top reasons for women leaving the profession. Progressive criminal law enforcement organizations have innovative work schedules, child care programs, mentoring and support groups, and a positive work atmosphere for women. Such programs benefit all employees within the organization. Today, men are taking a more active role in parenting and family; therefore, child care, creative work schedules, and even maternity leave should be of importance to them as well.

Mentor and Support Programs

A national study of women in law enforcement concluded that policewomen have a significantly higher rate of divorce than do male officers and have a lower rate of marriage as a group than the national female rate (Pogrebin, 1986). Research also revealed that although both male and female officers were affected by burnout, females were associated with higher levels of emotional burnout, while males showed higher levels of depersonalizing citizens (Johnson, 1991). As already mentioned, issues of child care, maternity leave, family responsibilities, flexible work schedules, job sharing, mentoring and support programs, and promotional opportunities are all important to woman peace officers and must be addressed adequately by law enforcement agencies. If not, frustration and stress result. Many of these issues are seen as barriers to women and their ability to work and advance in law enforcement. As a result, women's performance and attitudes can be enhanced if they have access to support and mentoring programs.

Why are mentors important? Marrujo and Kleiner (1992) found that "women who had one or more mentors reported greater job success and job satisfaction than women who did not have a mentor" (page 13). A mentor is described as an experienced, productive supervisor or manager (usually 8 to 10 years older than the employee) who relates well to a less experienced employee and facilitates his or her personal development for the benefit of both the individual and the organization. Usually, mentoring occurs in a one-on-one coaching context over a period of time through suggestions, advice, and support on the job. Several associations provide an organized voice for the interests of women in policing: the International Association of Women Police (IAWP), the National Association of Women Law Enforcement Executives (NAWLEE), and the National Center for Women and Policing (NCWP). The NAWLEE focuses on helping women to strengthen their leadership roles in policing, while the NCWP focuses on growth and leadership. However, these organizations cannot take the place of departmental, in-house mentoring programs for women. (Mentors and networking are discussed in more detail in Chapter 15.)

It is crucial that law enforcement managers recognize the differences between men and women employees and embrace the talents both contribute. Old traditions, beliefs, and attitudes can frequently surface, especially during times of stress. Although progress has been made, changing men's attitudes toward women in law enforcement is a slow process, and women, too, must develop confidence. As older male supervisors, managers, and executives retire, their male replacements will be younger men who are more accustomed to working with women. Research on police performance has clearly shown that male and female peace officers are comparable in their performance and that the public perceives women as equally effective. The only exception mentioned in some studies is the handling of violent or confrontational situations, when the physical strength of women to subdue the suspect was questioned (Cordner and Hale, 1992). However, with the " less authoritarian, more open style of women, they are less likely to trigger showdowns" (*Los Angeles Times,* June 5, 1993, p. A–1). Progress has been made in recent years. Women are now working street patrol assignments in almost all agencies, regardless of department size. Women also have nontraditional job assignments such as participating in special weapons and tactics teams, bomb units, hostage negotiations units, training, motorcycle traffic enforcement, and community relations. Thus, opportunities for women in law enforcement careers have grown and will continue to do so.

GAYS AND LESBIANS IN LAW ENFORCEMENT

The varied and complex issues related to the increased involvement of gays and lesbians in law enforcement are exemplified in the following newspaper accounts:

> In a precedent-setting case, a Florida jury ruled March 9 1992 in favor of a deputy fired because he is gay. The case . . . will set the stage for a landmark ruling on the privacy rights of gays. ("Fired Florida Gay Deputy Wins Major Gay Rights Case," *Frontiers,* March 27, 1992)

Milwaukee—Homosexuals are actively being recruited by the city's Police and Fire Commission as police officer candidates. . . . It is estimated that nearly 200 gay or lesbian officers are on the Milwaukee Police Department. The department has more than 1,900 officers. ("Milwaukee Police Recruiting Gays," *Bay Area Reporter,* June 18, 1992, p. 18)

The San Diego County Sheriff's Department announced Thursday that it will officially forbid discrimination or harassment against lesbians and gay men based on sexual orientation, settling a suit brought by a lesbian graduate of a recent department training academy. ("San Diego Sheriff Academy Graduate Settles Suit," *Los Angeles Times,* December 4, 1992, p. B–1)

An appellate court in Texas on February 10 [1993] affirmed a lower court ruling that struck down the state's sodomy law, while barring the City of Dallas and its police department from using it to reject lesbian and gay applicants. ("Texas Sodomy Law Ruled Unconstitutional," *Frontiers,* March 12, 1993, p. 19)

Evolution of Gays and Lesbians into Law Enforcement Occupations

Although still a silent minority in most police and sheriffs' departments, some gay and lesbian officers are no longer willing to conceal their sexual orientation. In law enforcement agencies on both coasts gay and lesbian officers have been "coming out of the closet" and feeling comfortable about it while remaining secure in their jobs. As late as 1992, an FBI agent of 20 years was fired when he revealed his homosexuality (*60 Minutes* report, September 13, 1991). As of 1993 most law enforcement agencies still did not knowingly hire or retain homosexuals. In 1993 and 1994 several federal class action lawsuits challenged employment barriers for gays and lesbians in sensitive federal law enforcement agencies. The issue for the federal government was whether discrimination against homosexuals might have a basis related to security considerations. For example, whether a homosexual agent could avoid being blackmailed or compromised on an investigation was in question.

Many states still use sodomy laws to disqualify law enforcement candidates who are openly or are discovered to be homosexual during a background investigation. In those states, agencies use the laws to indicate that homosexuals' propensity to violate the law due to their orientation makes them unsuitable as officers.

The issues related to hiring, retaining, and promoting homosexual officers or agents must be addressed proactively. If they are not, the result will be increases in litigation to enforce or legislate rights and proper treatment of gays and lesbians in the law enforcement workforce.

In Los Angeles, for example, a gay sergeant was awarded $770,000 for wrongful discharge and was offered reinstatement. LAPD Sergeant Mitchell Grobeson (now an author) claimed in a 1988 lawsuit that years of harassment forced him to resign. As a result of the settlement, the city council of Los Angeles also promised to adopt new provisions that would make discrimination against gays and lesbians grounds for dismissal from employment. This 1993 settlement also involved two other LAPD officers, who joined the case because of harassment by fellow officers. Sergeant Grobeson was the first openly gay officer in the LAPD and the first police officer in the nation to successfully force a police agency to adopt anti-discrimination policies and procedures to protect gay and lesbian employees. In August 2000 an independent study of the Los Angeles Police Department was completed; The

Hartmann Report specifically addressed the treatment of gays and lesbians within the department and within the city of Los Angeles.

Those issuing the Hartmann Report reviewed 28 discrimination complaint files that alleged discrimination or harassment related to sexual orientation. They found that the city of Los Angeles failed to conduct any investigation in over half of those complaints. As for the LAPD's compliance with the terms of the original 1993 settlement agreement, the report concluded:

> The department originally at issue in the . . . litigation . . . is unable to say accurately whether it has conformed with the . . . Agreement requirements because the department, supported by the City Attorney, refused to give us the documents and the access necessary to make that determination.

The report cited repeated instances in which the LAPD purposely misreported or concealed information that might have revealed the department's lack of compliance with the terms of the agreement, as well as occurrences of homophobic discrimination and harassment. In conclusion, the Hartmann investigators provided over 100 recommendations to bring the LAPD into compliance with the original agreement to end antihomosexual behaviors and actions within the department.

Forced changes are usually uncomfortable and can be costly for all involved. Chiefs who have encouraged gays and lesbians to apply to their departments understand that they cannot discriminate or restrict opportunities to these applicants. They are keenly aware that to be effective, departments must represent the diverse communities they serve. Many top executives are reviewing their policies and procedures to ensure that neither they nor the organizations with which they are affiliated discriminate against homosexuals.

The Controversy

Some police officers see homosexuals as only extremist militant types who publicly display their sexuality in offensive or socially unacceptable ways. This is a stereotype; the majority of heterosexuals do not draw attention to their sexual preference, and neither do most homosexuals.

Law enforcement researchers report that morale has not dropped in urban police departments that have adopted nondiscrimination statutes and actively recruit homosexual officers. The San Francisco Police Department was among the first major agencies to take such steps. San Francisco Police Chief Anthony Ribera wrote General Colin Powell, chairman of the Joint Chiefs of Staff, to express concern over Powell's opposition to lifting the military ban on homosexuals in the services. In his letter he declared:

> In 1979, before the first openly gay and lesbian officer entered our department, I had doubts about the propriety of hiring gays as police officers. . . . Today the San Francisco Police Department has approximately 85 openly gay and lesbian officers. Their performance, professional conduct and loyalty to the department has been exemplary. (*Contra Costa Times*, January 30, 1993).

In 2000, the San Francisco Police Department had 24 openly gay male officers and 150 open lesbians employed out of approximately 2,200 sworn personnel (1,523 men and 677 women).

Concerns about homosexuals in the military or law enforcement include beliefs that gay soldiers or police officers will walk hand in hand, dance together at clubs, make passes at nongay colleagues, and display aspects of their private lives (as well as seek benefits for gay marriages). These arguments for bans are not based in reality, however, since the majority of gays in the military and the criminal justice system are as work oriented as their heterosexual colleagues. They do not wish to provoke anyone in the system; rather, like the majority of other officers, homosexual officers want to accomplish their missions, make the rank, work special assignments, and avoid harassment. Homosexual officers are no different from others in wanting to support the disciplinary processes, and they believe that any inappropriate conduct should be handled with proper discipline.

According to a University of California at Santa Barbara study completed in 2000, Australia's 1992 decision to allow gays and lesbians to serve openly in its armed forces "has had no negative impact on military readiness" (Center for the Study of Sexual Minorities in the Military, University of California at Santa Barbara). The study confirmed similar results regarding homosexuals serving openly in Israeli and Canadian armed forces. After extensive interviews with soldiers, Defense Ministry officials, and academics, the report determined that, despite initial fears, ending the ban was not detrimental to recruitment, troop cohesion, or combat effectiveness. It concluded that "the integration of openly gay soldiers since 1992 had proceeded with ease and had virtually no widespread impact." In fact, the investigators reported that many senior Australian military commanders believed the policy change to have created "greater equity and effective working relationships within the ranks." (Since Britain ended its ban in 2000, the United States and Turkey are the only members of the North Atlantic Treaty Organization [NATO] that still ban open homosexuals from serving in their armed forces.)

Differences in Treatment of Gay versus Lesbian Officers

Many law enforcement professionals have voiced opinions that a double standard exists with respect to the way gay and lesbian officers are viewed in police work, which relates to the "macho" requirements of police work. The traditional male dominance of the profession has made it difficult for many male officers to accept that women are equally able to perform the same tasks they do. They view their work as an occupation for only the "strongest and the toughest." Male officers' self-esteem can be threatened by women's ability to do "their" job. (This issue is discussed further in the earlier section "Women in Law Enforcement.")

In reference to gays and lesbians, this phenomenon seems to apply very differently, according to Grobeson. Many officers are more accepting of lesbian officers, particularly those who are not openly homosexual, than they are of heterosexual women. They, like Chief Gates (*60 Minutes,* September 13, 1991), may believe that because of hormonal differences, lesbian women have men's strength. Officers fear that heterosexual (and therefore more feminine) women cannot be trusted to provide backup and are more willing to rely on lesbian officers, whom they stereotype as being macho and athletic. According to Grobeson, there is still much discrimination directed toward women who break the cultural mores and choose to be open or apparent about their sexual orientation. Yet there is a double standard for treatment of gay and lesbian officers.

Grobeson asserts that homosexual men are relegated to the least desirable status of any minority group in terms of acceptance in police culture. Homophobic jokes and nicknames, for example, are still prevalent locker room banter, whereas racial epithets have been mostly eliminated. One stereotype characterizes effeminate men as unworthy of trust as partners. This view biases heterosexual officers, despite the fact that many homosexual officers are military combat veterans with awards and accolades for bravery, heroism, and service under fire. For example, many homosexual officers in New York and San Francisco have received medals for their valor (see *CYBERSOCKET,* September–October 2000). Officers even thought to be homosexuals are teased, belittled, or openly harassed with little or no intervention from supervisors or managers. Some newly hired homosexual officers have reported that they believe it is important to stay "in the closet" until they have proven to their peers and supervisors that they are effective officers.

Many gay officers identify more easily with their fellow officers than they do with members of the gay community. Even in 2000 many gays were not accepting of law enforcement and viewed it as society's arm of social control. With many law enforcement officers still hostile and untrusting of gays, homosexual officers must choose a side, particularly when it comes to the issue of vice enforcement. Therefore homosexual officers are often accepted by neither the gay community nor their peers.

The Transition

Problems will inevitably surface within the police organization as gay and lesbian officers "come out of the closet." Many organizations and employees will be hesitant to welcome such a major change.

Because of the small number of open homosexuals in law enforcement, there are no policies dealing specifically with inappropriate displays of sexuality; obviously, discipline would be applied equally to both homosexual and heterosexual officers who behave inappropriately. Among gay law enforcement officers, however, there is a strong desire to conform to the norms of the organization and to prove their worth as members of that organization. Homosexual officers seldom engage in behaviors that would challenge those norms or shock or offend fellow officers.

Officers thought to be or who are openly homosexual may encounter discriminatory treatment and/or hostility because of other employees' negative stereotypes and attitudes. People without proper education on acquired immunodeficiency syndrome (AIDS) may also be afraid of AIDS transmission. Because of this fear, gay men may have an even more difficult time in assimilating into departments than other minorities, women or lesbians. In interviews conducted for this book, some heterosexual officers stated that they did not view gay males as being "masculine" enough for reliable backup in dangerous situations. Patrol officers must trust their partners.

Gay and lesbian officers are often placed in a position of having to prove themselves on the job. This may be through a physical confrontation with an arrestee or a test including confidential information regarding personal conduct of patrol officers. As open gay or lesbian officers are recruited and hired, the comfort level within the organization may be altered. Many officers will resist the change unless measures are taken to allay their fears. Individual and group prejudices and assumptions, for example, will be challenged. The organizations should have both written policies to assist homosexual officers' transition into the department and operational plans to promote employee acceptance of these officers.

These challenges of law enforcement must be addressed in a timely manner. If they are not, agencies will be ill prepared to deal with the complex, controversial issues involved and with other officers' attitudes surrounding these issues.

Evolution of "Uncle Toms" Homosexual Officers

Within law enforcement, there has been a progression of the acceptance of non-Caucasian, nonmale, and nonheterosexual officers. Many law enforcement agencies, especially those in states that have overturned sodomy laws, have advanced beyond policies that openly tout that "homosexuality is incompatible with law enforcement" (Grobeson, 2000). The first outcome in accepting homosexual officers has been identical to that experienced by the outcome associated with accepting African American officers. When blacks were first hired by police agencies, other members of the African American community referred to them as "Uncle Toms" and "Oreos," alluding to their internal "whiteness" despite their skin color. They were viewed as traitors to their own communities, as they were seen as assisting the oppressors in "keeping the black man down."

Interestingly, in law enforcement agencies that have experienced gay officers coming out, administrators have often decided to co-opt them, according to Grobeson. The newly "out" officers are brought into administrative positions by department heads to assist in maintaining the status quo. He indicates that although officers are used as public relations entities in dealing with the gay community, they are usually not allowed to engage the community in any meaningful political manner. They often have to fulfill a variety of other duties not typically assigned to officers of their status. These officers, often given the title of "liaison officers," provide interviews with gay and lesbian media outlets, stating unequivocally that there is no discrimination within their agencies. These officers are not allowed to engage in proactive recruitment activities or to be spokespersons for homosexual causes. Instead, their duties involve appearing in public relations booths or tables at gay and lesbian community events. Liaison officers can be used effectively, but only when supported by the management to interact freely with the community. In turn, management must be receptive to the feedback, both positive and negative, that these liaison officers can provide.

Support Groups for Homosexual Officers

Gays and lesbians benefit from support groups and peer counselors in their own or neighboring police agencies. In the early 1980s, openly gay and lesbian officers formed networks of support within the San Francisco Sheriff's Department. In the late 1980s, the San Francisco and New York City Police Departments, along with other agencies, assisted homosexual officers in forming support groups. In the early 1990s, chapters of the Golden State Peace Officers Association (founded in San Francisco) and the Gay Officers Action League (founded in New York) were established in southern California to assist homosexual officers. In addition to networking, the groups give public presentations and provide mentoring and support for their members. These groups may also be necessary for heterosexual employees who promote or defend the rights of homosexual officers.

Policies against Discrimination and Harassment

Unfortunately, there have been many incidents in which gay and lesbian officers have been subjected to discrimination or harassment by fellow officers. A few examples follow:

- A 10-year veteran sergeant with the California Highway Patrol filed a complaint when someone urinated on his clothes, shoes, and bulletproof vest inside his locker. He received a $1.5 million judgment including $17,500 in personal damages against two CHP officers who referred to the sergeant as a "fag, queer, and faggot." ("Gay Officer's $1.5M Harassment Award Stands," *Daily Journal,* September 29, 1995, and November 5, 1997.)
- In June 1999, a former Long Island, New York, police officer was awarded $380,000 by a federal jury for antigay harassment. A superior had threatened the officer with a knife, telling him, "I kill queers. All faggots deserve to die." This verdict was perhaps the first time in the nation that a police agency was held liable for antigay harassment. ("Gay Officer Wins Harassment Suit," *Daily Journal,* July 15, 1999.)
- A New York police officer filed a suit accusing his fellow officers of placing posters throughout the city announcing his sexual orientation and also for attacking him in the presence of supervisors, physically forcing him inside his locker. (*ABC News 20/20,* April 16, 1999.)
- An Indiana sheriff's deputy filed a suit claiming he was forced to resign after someone outed him as a cross-dresser. He was served with a memo by his captain advising him that an internal investigation was being conducted: "The possible policy violations relate to your making public your transgender lifestyle, how that admitted lifestyle affects your ability to perform your duties as a deputy sheriff and to interact with your co-workers and the public perception of any apparent endorsement by the Sheriff's Office of such a lifestyle." The deputy was married for 25 years and served for 20 years as an Army paratrooper. ("Dressed Down Indiana Deputy Files Suit After Being Fired Due to His Transgender Lifestyle," *Frontiers,* November 10, 2000.)

The chief executive must establish departmental policies and regulations regarding gay and lesbian officers. These policies must clearly state that discrimination, harassment, or failure to assist fellow gay and lesbian officers is unacceptable and will result in severe discipline. The chief executive must obtain the support of his or her supervisors and managers to ensure that the intent of these rules, policies, and procedures is clear and that all employees adhere to these policies and regulations. All employees must be held accountable, and those who do not support these antidiscrimination laws will not be promoted or transferred to special assignments. Evaluation of employees should reflect how supportive they are of departmental policy that protects homosexual officers. Department executives must be aware that homosexual officers might not report victimization by other employees. An independent investigation conducted in late 2000 determined that within the LAPD, 64 percent of gay and lesbian employees interviewed stated they would fear retaliation if they made a departmental complaint against another officer for discrimination or harassment ("LAPD Confidential Anti-Gay Cover Up," *fab!* Newspaper, October 13, 2000).

If the state does not have one, the city, county, or law enforcement agency should adopt an antidiscrimination policy with regards to homosexuals in the workplace. As of October 2000, 11 states had extended civil rights protection to homosexuals. City or county administration officials must support and possibly even champion such legislation. The policy should establish that

- Sexual orientation is not a hindrance in hiring, retention, or promotion.
- Hiring is based solely on merit as long as the individual meets objective standards of employment.
- Hiring is done not on a quota basis but on the basis of the identical job-related standards and criteria for all individuals.

Managers must routinely check to ensure that this policy is being carried out as intended.

Training on Gay, Lesbian, and Transgender Issues

Cultural awareness programs that train department personnel on diversity in communities and the workforce must also educate employees on gay, lesbian, and transgender issues. The training should address and show the falsehoods of stereotypes and myths. It must cover legal rights, including a discussion of statutes and departmental policies of nondiscrimination and subsequent penalties. These penalties include liability for acts of harassment and discrimination. Often, involving openly gay officers (from other agencies, if necessary) in these training programs provides the best outcome. Ideally, this training will enable employees to know the gay or lesbian officer as a human being. It can help reduce personal prejudices and false assumptions and thus hopefully change officers' behavior. This type of training furthers the ideal of respect for all people. A secondary benefit of this training is the decreased likelihood of personnel complaints and lawsuits by homosexual employees or community members against a city, county, or individual officer.

For a nondiscrimination policy to be implemented effectively, managers must provide regular and ongoing training at all levels of their department (see curricula in Instructor's Manual). This nondiscrimination policy must be articulated clearly, communicated effectively, and enforced consistently. Because homophobic attitudes are present among the rank and file, and because sensitivity training and similar programs usually provoke resentment rather than tolerance, the emphasis on training is most successful when it focuses on strict standards of professional conduct and behavior (RAND's National Defense Research Institute, 1993).

Most training conducted by law enforcement agencies is nonthreatening sensitivity training. Many officers outside of the entry-level, recruit academy are disdainful of such training. In addition, such training does little to promote change in behaviors that discriminate against gay and lesbian community members and officers.

On the other hand, a few agencies have provided cultural diversity training, which is much more confrontational but not abrasive. This training challenges officers' current attitudes without being condescending. In measuring officers' attitudes, beliefs, feelings, and knowledge, this second type of training has been shown to have a positive impact. The training uses simulated situations in which officers deal with partners who are gay. Managers and supervisors are required to handle situations in which a fellow officer is being harassed for perceived homosexuality. Management must be firmly committed to disciplining officers who behave in a discriminatory manner. Such presentations are most successful when conducted by gay officers who are experienced diversity trainers. It is not suggested, however, that the trainers will be qualified or successful merely because of their sexual orientation.

It is recommended that the training include discussion panels made up of local gay and lesbian community members, business owners, service providers, community groups, and gay youth and gay youth service providers. For supervisors and managers, additional panels comprising attorneys, including municipal attorneys who prosecute hate crimes and who specialize in defense work dealing with gay arrestees, HIV issues, and sexual orientation employment discrimination, should be provided.

Successful training programs about gay, lesbian and transgendered (see glossary) issues have been completed at the San Francisco, Alameda, and Sacramento Police Departments and the Santa Clara Sheriff's Department. The San Francisco, California Police Department is a good source of information about transgendered people. San Francisco probably has the largest population of transgendered residents with an estimated 15,000 to 18,000 people. The city has become the place for transgendered people from all over the world. ("S.F.'s Transgendered Gain Visibility, Rights, a Civic Voice," *Contra Costa Times,* February 25, 2001, p. A33.) For more information on conducting diversity training, refer to Chapter 4 of this text. The Instructor's Manual available for this textbook offers suggestions for a cultural diversity training program that includes gay, lesbian, bisexual, and transgender awareness.

Police officers are the protectors of individuals in a diverse society that includes gay and lesbian people. Although we recognize that police officers are human and entitled to their own personal beliefs, they cannot display biased behavior or engage in discriminatory actions. Police officers who are prejudiced against homosexuals must still uphold the rights of homosexuals. When prejudice or bias results in an overt discriminatory act, these officers must be appropriately punished for harassment. Officers cannot remain silent if they witness a discriminatory act or homophobic crime committed by fellow employees. Those same officers also must maintain a good working relationship with peers who may be homosexual. Police officers represent the entire community. Any act they commit while on duty (or off) can bring dishonor not only to them but also to their agency, the community they serve, and the entire profession of law enforcement. Repercussions of an act of discrimination could be the "shot heard 'round the world," as happened in the Rodney King case.

Most managers and supervisors need to change their leadership style to meet the challenges and requirements of a culturally diverse society and workforce. Management experts suggest that modern leaders must have two important traits: vision and the ability to communicate that vision to others. The challenge for managers and supervisors is to communicate visions and values to others who are from different ethnic, racial, religious, or lifestyle backgrounds within the workforce and the community.

THE CHIEF EXECUTIVE

The chief law enforcement executive should follow specific guidelines to meet the challenge of policing a multicultural and multiracial community. As emphasized previously, he or she must first effectively manage the diversity within his or her own organization. Progressive law enforcement executives are aware that before employees can be asked to value diversity in the community, it must be clear that diversity within the organization is valued. Managing diversity in the law enforcement workplace is therefore of high priority.

Executive leadership and team building are crucial to managing a diverse workforce and establishing good minority–community relations. The chief executive must take the lead in this endeavor by

- Demonstrating commitment
- Developing strategic, implementation, and transition management plans
- Managing organizational change
- Developing police–community partnerships (community-based policing)
- Providing new leadership models

Demonstrate Commitment

The organization must adopt and implement policies that demonstrate a commitment to policing a diverse society. Policies must be developed with input from all levels of the organization and community representatives. Valuing diversity and treating all persons with respect must be the imperative first from the chief executive. His or her personal leadership and commitment are viewed as keystones to implementing policies and awareness training within the organization and to successfully building a bridge to the community. One of the first steps is the development of a "macro" mission statement for the organization that elaborates the philosophy, values, vision, and goals of the department to foster good relationships with a diverse workforce and community. All policies and practices of the department must be reviewed to see how they may affect women, members of diverse ethnic and racial groups, and gays and lesbians on the force. Recruitment, hiring, and promotional practices must be reviewed to ensure that there are no institutional barriers to different groups in an agency. The chief executive stresses, via mission and values statements, that the agency will not tolerate discrimination, abuse, or crimes motivated by hate against protected classes within the community or within the agency itself. The policy statements would also include references to discrimination or bias based on physical disability, gender, or age.

The executive must use every opportunity to speak out publicly on the value of diversity and to make certain that people inside and outside the organization know that upholding those ideals is a high priority. He or she actively promotes policies and programs related to improved community relations and uses marketing skills to sell the program, both internally and externally. Internal marketing is accomplished by involving senior management and the police association in the development of the policies and action plans. The chief or sheriff uses this opportunity to gain support for the policies by demonstrating the value of having community support in terms of the department's effectiveness and officer safety. External marketing is accomplished by involving representatives of community-based organizations in the process.

Police leaders institute policies that develop positive multicultural beliefs and attitudes even as early as the selection process. During background interviews, polygraphs, and psychological exams, candidates for law enforcement employment must be carefully screened. The questions and processes help determine candidates' attitudes and beliefs and, at the same time, make them aware of the agency's strong commitment to a multicultural workforce.

Develop Strategic, Implementation, and Transition Management Plans

Textbooks and courses that teach strategic, implementation, and transition management planning are available to law enforcement leaders. The techniques, although not difficult, are quite involved and are not the focus of this book. Such techniques and methodologies are planning tools, providing the road map that the organization uses to implement programs and to guide the agency through change. An essential component is the action plans that identify specific goals and objectives. Action plans include budgets and timetables and establish accountability—who is to accomplish what by when. Multiple action plans involving the improvement of police–community relations in a diverse society would be necessary to cover such varied components as policy and procedures changes; affirmative action recruitment (where legal), hiring, and promotions; cultural awareness training (see Chapter 4); and community involvement (i.e., community-based policing).

Manage Organizational Change

The department leadership is responsible for managing change processes and action plans. This is an integral part of implementation and transition management, as discussed previously. The chief executive must ensure that any new policies, procedures, and training result in increased employee responsive and awareness of the diversity in their community and within the organization's workforce. He or she must require that management staff continually monitor progress on all programs and strategies to improve police–community relations. Additionally, the chief must ensure that all employees are committed to those ideals. Managers and supervisors need to ensure application of these established philosophies and policies of the department, and they must lead by example. When intentional aberrations of the system are discovered, retraining and discipline should be quick and effective. Employees (especially patrol officers) must be rewarded and recognized for their ability to work with and within a multicultural community. The reward systems for employees, especially first- and second-line supervisors, would recognize those who foster positive relations with individuals of different gender, ethnicity, or race both within and outside the organization. As we have illustrated, the chief executive, management staff, and supervisors are role models and must set the tone for the sort of behavior and actions they expect of employees.

Develop Police–Community Partnerships

Progressive police organizations have adopted community-based policing as one response strategy to meet the needs and challenges of a pluralistic workforce and society. The establishment of community partnerships is a very important aspect of meeting the challenges. For example, a cultural awareness training component will not be as effective if police–community partnerships are not developed, utilized, and maintained. The chief executive establishes and maintains ongoing communications with all segments of the community. Open lines of communication are best established by community-based policing (discussed in detail in Chapters 1 and 15).

Provide New Leadership Models

In the past all methods or models of management and organizational behavior were based on implicit assumptions of a homogeneous, white male workforce. Even bestsellers such as *The One-Minute Manager* and *In Search of Excellence* that continue to be useful management tools are based on that traditional assumption. Managers must learn to value diversity and overcome personal and organizational barriers to effective leadership, such as stereotypes, myths, unwritten rules, and codes (one of those being that the organizational role model is a white male). New models of leadership must be incorporated into law enforcement organizations to manage the multicultural and multiracial workforce.

Jamieson and O'Mara (1991) address the topic of motivating and working with a diverse workforce, explaining that the leader must move beyond traditional management styles and approaches. They indicate that the modern manager must move from the traditional one-size-fits-all management style to a "flex-management" model. They describe flex-management as not just another program or quick fix but one that is "based on the need to individualize the way we manage, accommodating differences and providing choices wherever possible" (p. 31). The flex-management model they envision involves three components:

1. *Policies:* Published rules that guide the organization
2. *Systems:* Human resources tools, processes, and procedures
3. *Practices:* Day-to-day activities

The model is based on four strategies: matching people to jobs, managing and rewarding performance, informing and involving people, and supporting lifestyle and life needs. Five key management skills are required of the modern manager to use this model successfully:

1. Empowering others
2. Valuing diversity
3. Communicating responsibly
4. Developing others
5. Working for change

Good leaders not only acknowledge their own ethnocentrism but also understand the cultural values and biases of the people with whom they work. Consequently, such leaders can empower, value, and communicate more effectively with all employees. Developing others involves mentoring and coaching skills, important tools for modern managers. To communicate responsibly leaders must understand the diverse workforce from a social and cultural context and flexibly utilize a variety of verbal and nonverbal communication strategies with employees. Modern leaders are also familiar with conflict mediation in cross-cultural disputes.

Jamieson and O'Mara (1991) explain that to establish a flex-management model, managers must follow a six-step plan of action that includes:

1. Defining the organization's diversity
2. Understanding the organization's workforce values and needs
3. Describing the desired future state
4. Analyzing the present state
5. Planning and managing transitions
6. Evaluating results

They contend that to be leaders in the new workforce, most managers will have to "unlearn practices rooted in old mindsets, change the way their organization operates, shift organizational culture, revamp policies, create new structures, and redesign human resource systems" (p. 25).

The vocabulary of the future involves leading employees rather than simply managing them. Hammond and Kleiner (1992) wrote about the distinction between the two:

> One of the first things companies must look at in multicultural environments is the leadership vs. management issue. Leadership, in contrast to management, deals with values, ethics, perspective, vision, creativity and common humanity. Leadership is a step beyond management; it is at the heart of any unit in any organization. Leadership lies with those who believe in the mission and through action, attitude, and attention pass this on to those who have to sustain the mission and accomplish the individual tasks. People want to be led, not managed; and the more diverse the working population becomes the more leadership is needed.

Hammond and Kleiner explain that in a multicultural and multiracial society and workforce, "the genius of leadership" is

- Learning about and understanding the needs of the diverse people you want to serve—not boss, not control—but serve
- Creating and articulating a corporate mission and vision that your workers can get excited about, participate in, and be a part of
- Behaving in a manner that shows respect to and value for all individual workers and their unique contributions to the whole. Those you can't value, you can't lead (p. 13).

Management, to build positive relationships and show respect for a pluralistic workforce, needs to be aware of differences, treat all employees fairly (and not necessarily in identical ways), and lead. The differing needs and values of a diverse workforce require flexibility by organizations and their leaders. Modern leaders of organizations recognize not only that different employees have different needs but also that these needs change over time. The goal of law enforcement leaders is to bridge cultural and racial gaps within their organizations.

SUMMARY

Officers who traditionally worked in predominately white male workforces must learn to work with increasing numbers of women, blacks, Hispanics, Asians, and others within our diverse society. In this chapter we have suggested that to be effective in this new environment, officers must have a knowledge of conflict resolution techniques to reduce racial and ethnic problems.

The chapter focused on concerns and issues of members of underrepresented ethnically and racially diverse groups as well as women and homosexuals in law enforcement. The importance of support and mentoring programs for women and diverse groups was stressed. Such programs help them make transitions into organizations, cope with stress, and meet their workplace challenges more effectively.

In the chapter we provided suggestions for law enforcement executives whose jurisdictions are pluralistic and whose workforces are diverse. Law enforcement leaders must be committed to setting an organizational tone that does not permit bigoted or discriminatory acts and must act swiftly against those who violate these policies. They must monitor and deal quickly with complaints both within their workforce and from the public they serve.

DISCUSSION QUESTIONS AND ISSUES*

1. *Measuring Responsiveness to Diversity.*   Using the check-off and scoring sheet (Exhibit 2.3), determine how responsive your police department has been to the diversity of the jurisdiction it serves. If you are not affiliated with an agency, choose a city or county police department and interview a command officer to determine the answers and arrive at a score. Discuss with the command officer what initiatives his or her department intends to undertake to address the issues of community diversity.

2. *Defusing Racially and Culturally Rooted Conflicts.*   What training does the police academy in your region provide on defusing racially and culturally rooted conflicts? What training of this type does your local city or county law enforcement agency provide to officers? What community (public and private) agencies are available as referrals or for mediation of such conflicts? Discuss what training should be provided to police officers to defuse, mediate, and resolve racially and culturally rooted conflicts. Discuss what approaches a law enforcement agency should utilize.

3. *Women in Law Enforcement.*   How many women officers are there in your local city or county law enforcement agency? How many of those women are in supervisory or management positions? Are any of the women assigned to nontraditional roles such as special weapons and tactics teams, motorcycle enforcement, bomb units, hostage negotiations, or community relations? Have there been incidents of sexual harassment of women employees? If so, how were the cases resolved? Has the agency you are examining implemented any programs to increase the employment of women, such as flextime, child care, mentoring, awareness training, or career development? Discuss your findings in a group setting.

*See Instructor's Manual accompanying this text for additional activities, role-play activities, questionnaires, and projects related to the content of this chapter.

4. ***Diversity in Law Enforcement.***   Comment on the diversity in your local city or county law enforcement agency. What is the breakdown in your agency's hierarchy? For example, who holds supervisory or management positions? Have there been reported acts of discrimination against people of diverse backgrounds? Has the agency you are examining implemented any programs to increase the employment of minorities? Discuss your findings in a group setting.

REFERENCES

BELL, DANIEL. (1982). "Policewomen: Myths and Reality," *Journal of Police Science and Administration, 10* (1), 112.

BENSON, KATY. (1992, August). "Black and White on Blue," *Police,* 167.

BLANCHARD, KENNETH H., AND SPENCER JOHNSON. (1983). *The One-Minute Manager.* Berkeley Publishing Group.

CORDNER, GARY, AND DONNA HALE. (1992). "Women in Policing," in *What Works in Policing: Operations and Administration Examined.* pp. 125–142. Cincinnati, Ohio: Anderson Publishing.

DEGENESTE, HENRY I. AND JOHN SULLIVAN (1997). Policing a Multicultural Community. Fresh Perspectives: A police Executive Research Forum Publication. Washington D.C.

GROBESON, MITCHELL (2000, November). Sergeant-Retired, Los Angeles Police Department, California, personal communications.

HALL, THOMAS. (1992, October) Sergeant Virginia State Troopers personal communication.

HAMMOND, TERESA, AND BRIAN KLEINER. (1992)."Managing Multicultural Work Environments," *Equal Opportunities International,* 11 (2).

HAMPTON, RON (1992, September 27–29). "Unfinished Business: Racial and Ethnic Issues Facing Law Enforcement II," paper presented at a conference sponsored by the National Organization of Black Law Enforcement Executives and the Police Executive Research Forum, Reno, Nevada.

HARTMANN REPORT (2000, August). City of Los Angeles Police Department Study.

Independent Commission on the Los Angeles Police Department. (1991). Summary: Racism and Bias (pp.7–8). Los Angeles: Independent Commission.

International Associated of Chiefs of Police (1998). The Future of Women in Policing: *Mandates for Action.* Washington, D.C.JAMIESON, DAVID, AND JULIE O'MARA. (1991). *Managing Workforce 2000: Gaining the Diversity Advantage.* San Francisco: Jossey-Bass.

JOHNSON, L. (1991). "Job Strain among Police Officers: Gender Comparisons," *Police Studies,* 14 (1), 12–16.

JONES, SUSAN. (1993, February). Sergeant, Concord, California, Police Department, personal communication.

MARRUJO, ROBERT, AND BRIAN KLEINER. (1992). "Why Women Fail to Get to the Top," *Equal Opportunities International,* 11 (4), 1.

MARTIN, SUSAN. (1990, September). *The Status of Women in Policing.* Washington, D.C. Police Foundation.

MCCOY, DANIEL. (1992, June). "The Future Organizational Environment for Women in Law Enforcement," California Command College Class XIV, Peace Officer Standards and Training, Sacramento, Calif.

MCMAHON, BROOK. (1990, June). "How Will the Role of Law Enforcement Change by the Year 2000 as It Deals with Suspected or Openly Gay Police Officers?" California Command College Class X, Peace Officer Standards and Training, Sacramento, Calif.

MORE, HARRY. (1992). *Male-Dominated Police Culture: Reducing the Gender Gap,* (pp.113–137). Cincinnati, Ohio: Anderson Publishing.

NAISBITT, JOHN, AND PATRICIA ABURDENE. (1986). *Reinventing the Corporation* (p.243). New York: Warner

PETERS, THOMAS J., AND ROBERT H. WATERMAN. (1984). *In Search of Excellence.* Warner Books, Inc.

POGREBIN, MARK. (1986, April–June). "The Changing Role of Women: Female Police Officers' Occupational Problems," *Police Journal,* 59 (2), 131.

RAND's National Defense Research Institute. (1993). *Sexual Orientation and U.S. Military Personnel.* Policy, Options and Assessment Rand Institute Santa Monica, California

ROSS, RUTH, JOHN SNORTUM, AND JOHN BEYERS. (1982). "Public Priorities and Police Policy in a Bicultural Community," *Police Studies,* 5 (1) 18–30.

THEIDERMAN, SONDRA. (1991). *Bridging Cultural Barriers for Corporate Success.* San Francisco, California. Jossey-Bass Inc.

SHEILDS, ROBERT (1993, February). Chief of Police, Alameda, California, Police Department, personal communications.

University of California at Santa Barbara (2000). Center for the Study of Sexual Minorities in the Military.

WATTS, P. (1989). "Breaking into the Old-Boy Network," *Executive Female Magazine,* 12 (32), pp.12–14

WELLS, JAMES. (1987). *Crime and the Administration of Criminal Justice,* "A Common Destiny: Blacks and American Society," in (pp.491–97).

3

MULTICULTURAL REPRESENTATION IN LAW ENFORCEMENT:

Recruitment, Retention, and Promotion

OVERVIEW

In this chapter we discuss the current recruitment crisis and the probability that recruitment will be an ongoing challenge for law enforcement agencies. A brief historical perspective of women and minorities in law enforcement is provided, including a profile of their numbers in state and local agencies across the country. We discuss reasons for recruitment difficulties and offer strategies for success. The retention and promotion of minorities and women are addressed in the final section of the chapter.

COMMENTARY

The following quotes draw attention to the recruitment crisis for law enforcement occupations and illustrate the importance of recruitment, hiring, and promotion of women and minorities.

> According to Trojanowicz and Carter, "By 2010, more than one third of all American children will be black, Hispanic, or Asian." The Caucasian majority of today will become a minority within America in less than 100 years. Obviously, this change in society will have a tremendous impact on the recruiting process of the future. (Osborn, 1992, p. 21)

In what is described as the most comprehensive analysis of women in policing, authorities say women remain grossly under-represented in the ranks; they are routine targets of gender bias and sexual harassment; and they have largely been unable to punch through a virtually bullet-proof glass ceiling. ("Female Cops: Nation's Policewomen Are Facing a Bullet-Proof Glass Ceiling," *USA Today*, November 24, 1998, p. 1)

In the harsh battleground over jobs, college education and access to the promotion ladder, the issues of quotas and racial preferences can come to dominate, if not supersede, the national struggle to achieve equity in the workplace and on the college campus. Take, for example, the core of city government: the police and fire departments. In many communities well into the 1960's, these departments were white male enclaves, controlled by such European ethnic groups as Irish, Italian and Polish Americans. (Edsall, 1991.)

The state [California] prison system, facing a staffing shortage triggered by a booming economy and new early retirement plan, is devoting $1 million to a new recruiting effort. The Department of Corrections projects it will need 1,300 new guards this year, while the youth authority will need about 480 officers for each of the next three years. . . . . Both departments are caught between an applicant shortage on one end and an increase in retirements on the other. ("Prison System Recruits Hard for Employees," *Contra Costa Times*, October 2, 2000, p. 2A).

INTRODUCTION

Our society is becoming more and more diverse. In California, demographers predict that by 2005 there will be no single racial or ethnic group constituting the majority. That trend is occurring in some major U.S. cities as well. Some demographers say that in the future every group will be a minority.

To recruit and retain a representative staff and provide effective services, therefore, law enforcement executives must have a clear understanding of their community and their own workforce. The recruitment and retention of qualified employees, and especially of women, blacks, Asians, Hispanics, and other diverse groups, have become a concern and a priority of law enforcement agencies nationwide. Many agencies are having difficulty finding qualified applicants, resulting in a general recruitment crisis. The recruitment pool of eligible and qualified candidates is diminishing. The crisis is multidimensional and is discussed in detail in this chapter.

RECRUITMENT OF A DIVERSE WORKFORCE

The recruitment of women and members of diverse groups has been a concern and a priority of law enforcement agencies nationwide for a few decades. This is not a new issue in the history of U.S. law enforcement. A President's Crime Commission Report in 1967 recommended that more minorities be hired and that they receive opportunities for advancement. Soon after the Watts riot in Los Angeles, the 1968 Kerner Commission Report identified the underrepresentation of blacks in law enforcement as a serious problem. The report recommended improved hiring and promoting policies and procedures for minorities. The Kerner Commission also concluded that racism among whites in communities and within law enforcement organizations was a dominant factor leading to civil disorder. The Warren Christopher Commission report on the Los Angeles Police Department, released soon after the 1992 riots following the first Rodney King trial, cited the problems of racism and bias within the LAPD. The commission recommended, among other things, improved hiring and promotions processes that would benefit all groups.

Profile of Local, County, and State Law Enforcement Agencies

What is the overall composition of law enforcement agencies across the United States? The U.S. Department of Justice collects information on law enforcement agencies and produces a report every three years profiling the demographic makeup of departments in the United States. According to the Law Enforcement Management and Administrative Statistics (LEMAS) report in 2000, there were 18,760 publicly funded state, county, and local law enforcement agencies operating in the United States. As of June 1997, these agencies employed a total of 940,275 full-time employees, 695,378 of whom were sworn officers. LEMAS reports established the percentages of women, blacks, Hispanics, and other racial and ethnic minorities within local and county law enforcement agencies for 1987, 1990, 1993, and 1997 (see Exhibit 3.1). These numbers show that women and minorities are not yet represented to any great degree in the law enforcement workforce, although some progress has been made.

Exhibit 3.1 Percentage of women and minorities in local and sheriffs' departments, 1987–1997.

LEMAS Reports	1987	1990	1993	1997
Women				
Local police	7.6%	8.1%	8.8%	10.0%
Sheriffs' departments	12.6%	15.4%	14.6%	15.6%
All racial and ethnic minorities				
Local police	14.8%	17.5%	19.1%	21.5%
Sheriffs' departments	13.0%	5.4%	16.9%	19.0%
Black officers				
Local police	9.3%	0.5%	11.3%	11.7%
Sheriffs' departments	8.3%	9.8%	10.0%	11.8%
Hispanic officers				
Local police	4.5%	5.2%	6.2%	7.8%
Sheriffs' departments	4.3%	4.7%	5.8%	5.8%

Note: Regarding sheriffs' departments, the 2000 LEMAS report indicates that of the estimated 174,674 full-time sworn personnel employed, about 16 percent were women. The percentage of female officers varied slightly across population sizes, ranging from about 20 percent in jurisdictions with a population of 500,000 to 999,999 to about 12 percent in jurisdictions with a population of under 25,000. The report indicates that in 1997, 19 percent of full-time sheriffs' officers were members of a racial or ethnic minority, with higher percentages in jurisdictions with a population of 500,000 or more.

Regarding local police departments, the 2000 LEMAS report indicates that of the estimated 420,152 full-time sworn personnel employed, 10 percent were women. The percentage of female officers was highest in departments serving a population of 1 million or more (16 percent), followed by those serving a population of 250,000 to 999,999 (14 percent). Women comprised just 3 percent of the workforce in jurisdictions with fewer than 2,500 residents. According to the report, just over a fifth (21.5 percent of full-time local police were members of a racial or ethnic minority. Minority officers comprised more than a third of the total in jurisdictions with 500,000 or more residents.

Recruitment Crisis

Gordon Bowers, who teaches justice administration courses, predicted the following in 1990:

> There is a crisis developing in recruitment that will change law enforcement as it is known today. For each year over the next decade, the number of new police officers needed and the minimum qualifications will be raised, but both the number and percentage of high school graduates in the normal age range of police applicants will decrease. The shortage of qualified applicants may be so severe that some departments will be dissolved. (Bowers, 1990, p. 64)

The situation in 2000 confirmed Gordon Bowers's prediction of a shortage of applicants for police departments and a struggle for departments to maintain authorized strength. A number of factors have contributed to the reduction of the once substantial law enforcement applicant pool. One explanation is offered by the futurists Cetron, Rocha, and Luckins (1988). They predicted that "the percentage of the population between 16 and 24 years old [would] shrink from 30 percent of the labor force in 1985 to 16 percent in the year 2000" (p. 64) and that "during the next decade, white men will account for only one in four new workers" (p. 34). Therefore, the field of law enforcement is attempting to recruit from an applicant pool that is not only shrinking but also expected to be dominated by minorities and women. An additional reason for fewer numbers of applicants within the typical age range eligible for careers as peace officers is that millions of young people between the ages of 15 and 29 are arrested each year for crimes that disqualify them for police work.

Then, during the late 1990s and in 2000, the United States experienced the lowest unemployment rate in decades because of a robust economy. There were plenty of jobs, and the number of applicants for law enforcement positions was substantially lower than in the past. Compounding this problem was the negative impact of highly publicized scandals involving police in major cities—New York, Los Angeles, and Philadelphia, to name a few. These scandals, it is suggested, "tarnished the image" of law enforcement work ("A Law Enforcement Shortage. Area Agencies Scramble for Recruits," *Contra Costa Times,* May 1, 2000, p. A1). At the same time, departments were not fully staffed because many employees who had been hired in the police expansion wave of the 1960s and 1970s were retiring. From New York to Los Angeles, recruiters are now trying to lure experienced officers away from other agencies with various promises of benefits to working for their departments. The effort was compared to the National Football League (NFL) draft, in which everyone is looking for qualified candidates. And many law enforcement agencies have generous retirement packages, meaning that those eligible are leaving at a younger age and the problem will not just disappear.

Law enforcement competes with private industry for this reduced pool of qualified and eligible applicants, especially for blacks, Hispanics, Asians, women, and people of diverse ethnic and racial origins, resulting in an even smaller pool of applicants for police agencies. The U.S. Department of Labor reported in October 2000 that unemployment was at a 30-year low of 3.9 percent; it was an employee's market, and those seeking jobs could be very selective. Many jobs in private industry, especially high-tech jobs, come with high salaries, stock options, signing bonuses, company cars, and year-end bonuses. Public-sector employers have difficulty competing with such incentives. Another factor in recruitment difficulties in 2000 was court decisions (and pretrial settlements) against such companies as Coke, Texaco, and Wall Street's Smith Barney in race bias lawsuits. U.S. firms scrambled to recruit and promote talented candidates of both genders and from diverse groups. Many large companies, aware that the populations within their recruitment areas were diversifying, knew that their employee demographics had to match those of the world outside or they would be subject to lawsuits and/or criticism. This is particularly true of companies that sell products or services to the public. Their recruitment efforts, therefore, focused on women and members of diverse groups. The wide-open market also made for transitory employees, causing employee retention problems for employers, especially of trained persons. The lack of a qualified pool of applicants is a problem of special concern to small police departments, which simply do not have the resources for extensive recruiting efforts.

At one point a decline in minority employment in the United States was cause for concern. During the 1980s and early 1990s a recession forced some cities and counties to lay off or fire employees. The downsizing of departments through layoffs most often affects those hired last. Women and those of diverse ethnic and racial groups, often the last hired, were usually the first fired or laid off. Also, many of those laid off secured jobs in non–law enforcement occupations. Some experts speculated that the decrease in numbers might also have been due to "covert institutional racism that, among other things, blocks career advancement"; and that those employees became disgruntled and left (Walker, 1989, p. 21). Clearly, more research is needed to explore the degree to which institutional racism may have led to a decline in the number of employees from diverse backgrounds.

Therefore, gains made in terms of a multicultural workforce, including women, were lost. Substantial efforts to recruit nonwhites followed as economic conditions improved. Law enforcement is still a predominantly white male occupation. Although there has been some improvement in multicultural recruitment, more must be done for departments to reflect the makeup of their local communities.

Law Enforcement Recruitment Difficulties

Cultural Diversity at Work, a newsletter addressing multicultural issues, presented a list of the 10 most frequent causes of the failure to attract and retain high-level minority and female employees in its September 1993 issue (Micari, 1993). Following is a brief synopsis of those most pertinent to law enforcement:

1. *Senior management is not sending the "diversity message" down the lines.* Senior management does not always demonstrate commitment in the form of value statements and policies emphasizing the importance of a diverse workforce.

2. *Informal networking channels are closed to outsiders.* Women and minorities often experience discomfort within the traditional all-white, all-male informal career networks, including extracurricular activities. For example, some women police officers are uncomfortable participating in police association activities that involve recreational gambling, fishing, sports activities, or the roughhousing that can take place at meetings.

3. *In-house recruiters are looking in the wrong places.* Recruiters must use different methods and resources than those they have traditionally used to find diverse candidates.

4. *Differences in life experience are not taken into account.* Some applicants, both women and minorities, will have had life experiences that differ from those of the traditional job candidate. For example, the latter has typically had some college experience, with a high grade point average, and is often single (and thus does not have the many responsibilities associated with marriage and children). On the other hand, many minority job candidates have had to work through school and are married and may have children. Therefore, their grade point averages may have suffered.

5. *Negative judgments are made based on personality or communications differences.* Although not everybody's style reflects cultural, racial, or gender characteristics, there are distinct differences in communication style and personality between women and minorities and traditional white-male job applicants. Communication style differences are especially apparent when English is the applicant's second language. Generally speaking, women are not as assertive as men in communication. Sometimes these factors can affect the outcome of a preemployment interview and become barriers to a job offer.

6. *The candidate is not introduced to people who are like him or her.* It is important that the candidate or new hire meet people of the same gender, race, or ethnicity within the agency. A mentor or support group may be crucial to a successful transition into the organization.

7. *Organizations are not able or willing to take the time to do a thorough search.* Recruitment specialists indicate that searches for qualified minority and women candidates take four to six weeks longer than others. These searches take commitment, resources, and time.

8. *Early identification is missing from the recruitment program.* Programs that move students into the proper fields of study early on and that provide the education required for the job are essential. Examples of these programs include internships, scholarships, and police programs (e.g., police athletic league) that bring future job candidates into contact with the organization.

The Police Executive Research Forum (PERF) created a nationwide task force to address the issue of decreasing numbers of qualified police applicants. Some of the findings of the task force, which completed its study in 1987, are as follows:

1. *Identification of recruiting problems.* The problems most frequently reported were a decreasing number of qualified applicants; the inability to offer competitive compensation; and difficulty in recruiting Asians, blacks, Hispanics, and other minorities. Those responding to the survey who perceived a decline in the number of qualified applicants attributed it to a lack of education, the use of drugs, and limited life experience.

2. *In which testing areas are police officer candidates most likely to fail?* The top three in rank order were the written test, background investigation, and polygraph.

Bowers (1990) concluded that law enforcement agencies will have to utilize alternatives to the traditional applicant pool to secure qualified candidates. He suggests that it is possible to develop a recruitment strategy that would target people not usually recruited (where such strategies are legal). Bowers defined the "alternative applicant pool" as those people who are qualified but who have no current intention of pursuing law enforcement as a career. An applicant's age is another criterion that law enforcement agencies need to reexamine. Older physically fit applicants looking for a second career can bring wisdom, maturity, and other skills to the occupation. Police academies are now emphasizing moral decision making and minimizing physical factors. Also, despite history and tradition, applicants should not always have to start in patrol assignments. Agencies employing community policing could hire well-qualified personnel to perform specific types of police work that do not require them to be "crime fighters." Veteran police officers, however, may resent and reject this idea, and attitudes would have to change for this concept to be implemented.

Recruitment Strategies

With regard to building a diverse workforce, recruitment strategies used in the past will not be sufficient and will not provide agencies with high-quality applicants. In fact, a study commissioned by the International Association of Chiefs of Police and completed in 1998, *The Future of Women in Policing: Mandates for Action,* discovered that "unfocused, random recruiting is unlikely to attract diversity. Targeted programs are more likely to do so." The study determined that approximately one in four departments (26 percent) have had policies and strategies in place to recruit women. Also, larger departments are about three times more likely to actively recruit female applicants than are smaller ones. Agencies with the most success in recruiting women have had specific goals, objectives, and timetables in place; these policies must be established at the top level of the organization. At the same time, management must commit to not lowering standards for the sake of numbers and deadlines. The philosophy and procedures required are discussed in the following sections.

Commitment. Law enforcement chief executives must commit to hiring, promoting, and retaining women and employees of diverse backgrounds who are representative of the community's population. This genuine commitment must be demonstrated both inside and outside the organization. Internally, chief executives should develop policies and procedures that emphasize the importance of a diverse workforce. Affirmative action programs (where legal) will not work in a vacuum. Chief executives must integrate the values that promote diversity and affirmative action into every aspect of the agency, from its mission statement to its roll-call training. Externally, police executives should publicly delineate the specific hiring and promotion goals of the department to the community through both formal (e.g., media) and informal (e.g., community-based policing, networking with organizations representing the diverse groups) methods. Although chief executives promote the philosophy, policies, and procedures, committed staff who are sensitive to the needs for affirmative hiring and promotions carry them out. Executives should also build partnerships with personnel officials so that decisions clearly reflect the affirmative action goals of the department.

Although chiefs may be genuine in their efforts to champion diversity and affirmative action hiring, care must be taken. They must make sure that their policies and procedures do not violate Title VII of the Civil Rights Act of 1964. Also, states that have enacted laws that prohibit affirmative action hiring programs and the targeting of "protected classes" (e.g., California's Proposition 209, passed in 1996 and discussed later in this chapter) must adhere to these regulations. A knowledgeable personnel department or legal staff should review policies and procedures prior to implementation.

Planning. Action plans should be developed that commit the objectives, goals, budget, accountability, and timetables for the recruitment campaign to paper. Demographic data should form one of the foundations for the plans, which must take into account the current political, social, and economic conditions of the department and the community.

Resources. Adequate resources, including money, personnel, and equipment, must be made available to the recruitment effort. Financial constraints challenge almost every organization's recruitment campaign. The economic condition of a particular city or county is an important factor when budgeting for recruitment. The size or financial constraints of an agency may necessitate less expensive—and perhaps more innovative—approaches. For example, many small law enforcement jurisdictions can combine to implement regional testing. One large county on the West Coast successfully formed a consortium of agencies and implemented regional testing three times per month for law enforcement candidates. To participate, each agency pays into an account based on the population of its jurisdiction. Alternatively, each agency can pay according to how many applicants it hired from the list. The pooled money is then used for recruitment advertising (e.g., billboards, radio, television, newspapers) and the initial testing processes (e.g., reading, writing, and agility tests, including proctors). The eligibility list is provided to each of the participating agencies, which then continue the screening process for applicants in whom they have interest. Police agencies should not see others as adversaries with respect to recruiting. By combining their efforts, they may be able to

- Save money (consolidate resources)
- Develop a larger pool of applicants
- Become more competitive with private industry and other public agencies
- Test more often
- Reduce the time it takes from application to hire

In terms of recruiting a diverse workforce, the second benefit listed—developing a larger pool of applicants—is central to reaching beyond the traditional applicant pool. Law enforcement agencies, in taking advantage of the Internet's global coverage, can post position openings in the hopes of recruiting individuals with a wide variety of backgrounds and skills.

Selection and Training of Recruiters. A recruiter is an ambassador for the department and must be selected carefully. Full-time recruiters are a luxury most often found only in large agencies. The benefit of a full-time recruiter program is that usually the employees in this assignment have received some training in marketing techniques. They have no other responsibilities or assignments and can therefore focus on what they do and do it well. They develop the contacts, resources, and skills to be effective. Whether full-time, part-time, or assigned on an as-needed basis, the following criteria should be considered when selecting recruiters:

- Commitment to the goal of recruiting
- Belief in a philosophy that values diversity
- Ability to work well in a community policing environment
- Belief in and ability to market a product: law enforcement as a career
- Comfort with people of all backgrounds and ability to communicate this comfort
- Ability to discuss the importance of entire community representation in police work and the advantages to the department without sounding patronizing

Recruiters must be provided resources (e.g., budget and equipment) and must have established guidelines. They must be highly trained with respect to their role, market research methods, public relations, and cultural awareness. They must also understand, appreciate, and be dedicated to organizational values and ethics.

The California Commission on Peace Officer Standards and Training (POST) developed a 24-hour course entitled "Techniques and Methods of Recruitment." For information about this course, contact California POST at (916) 227-2820. Some other state POST commissions have also developed such courses. Progressive large agencies (or a consortium of agencies) could develop an in-house course patterned after these POST recruitment training courses.

Agencies that cannot afford the luxury of their own recruiters should develop incentive programs to encourage officers to recruit bilingual whites, women, and ethnically and racially diverse candidates, informally, while on or off duty. One possible incentive program would give officers overtime credit for each person in those categories they recruit who makes the eligibility list, additional credit if that same applicant is hired, and additional credit for each stage the new officer passes until the probation period ends. For example, the San Jose, California, Police Department has a Recruiting Incentive Program. The program authorizes an award to any department member (not assigned to the personnel unit), whether sworn or nonsworn, of up to 20 hours compensatory time for recruiting a lateral police officer. Department members can also receive an additional 40 hours of compensatory time for recruiting a lateral who is bilingual or from a protected class. The department defines a protected class member as African American, Asian, Hispanic, Native American, Filipino, or female. Qualifying languages for bilingual are Spanish, Vietnamese, Chinese (Mandarin or Cantonese), Cambodian, Korean, and Filipino (Tagalog or Ilocano). The time is awarded in increments at a straight-time rate based on the following phases of employment:

- Hire date (20 hours)
- Completes the field training officer (FTO) program (20 hours)
- Completes probation (20 hours)

A member of the San Jose Police Department can also receive up to 20 hours of compensatory time for recruiting an entry-level applicant. An additional 20 hours is provided if an applicant is bilingual or from a protected class. The increments are as follows:

- Hire date (10 hours)
- Graduates from the academy (10 hours)
- Completes the Field Training Officer (FTO) program (10 hours)
- Completes probation (10 hours)

Another agency awards $250 to employees who recruit applicants (of any racial or ethnic origin) who are hired, complete all phases of the background process, and start the academy. The same department awards $250 to employees who recruit lateral police officer candidates once they complete all phases of the background process, are hired, and report for duty. When these recruits make it through probation, employees receive $250 as an additional incentive. Encouraging all department members to be involved in the recruitment effort, including the promotion of law enforcement as a career, is usually effective. To be competitive in recruiting employees, especially minorities and women, agencies must offer perks just as corporations do. Also, high-tech videos and the Internet are important recruitment tools.

Portland, Oregon, hired a professional recruiter from outside the department for a period of time, which yielded some positive results. As of August 2000, women made up a little over 16 percent (169) of a total sworn workforce of 1,056, a higher percentage than in other agencies its size nationwide. Portland is one of a few departments that require entry-level candidates with no previous law enforcement experience to have a four-year college degree, a requirement that limits the number of eligible candidates. Lateral applicants are required to have an associate of arts degree or its equivalent number of units. Pittsburgh, Pennsylvania, is one of the nation's most diverse police departments, with women making up 25 percent of its force. Much of its success in this regard is due to a federal court order that required Pittsburgh to hire one white woman, one black man, and one black woman for every white man hired between 1976 and 1992. Police executives point to Albuquerque, New Mexico, as a potential model for other departments regarding recruitment. Between 1995 and 1998, female recruits increased from 8 percent in academy classes to 25 percent. As of December 2000, women made up 11.6 percent of the department (1 African American, 43 Hispanics, and 57 Whites). Men comprised 88.3 percent of the department (6 Asians, 16 African Americans, 274 Hispanics, and 6 Native Americans). Ethnic minorities comprised 39.6 percent of the department, whereas ethnic minorities made up 22 percent of the general population. The department has done well in the recruitment of women and people from diverse backgrounds. The Police Departments of Miami Beach, Florida (28 percent female) and Madison, Wisconsin (22 percent female) might also be contacted for recruitment ideas since each had a high percentage of female officers as of 1998. These departments must have successful programs they will share with other agencies. Certainly, city and county affirmative action plans of the 1980s and 1990s played a significant role in police employment trends in agencies across the nation. Many of these plans were the result of court orders, but some were voluntary.

We acknowledge that there may be some controversial and even legal aspects to recruitment efforts that target women and ethnically and racially diverse candidates or provide incentives for recruiting them. In California, Proposition 209, which outlawed governmental discrimination and preferences based on race, sex, color, ethnicity, or national origin, was passed in 1996. There had been 25 years of experiments with affirmative action in California. The controversial proposition was delayed by a challenge in federal court. In September 2000, however, justices of the California Supreme Court largely affirmed that the proposition is legal. The justices also placed strict limits on employers regarding the types of outreach programs they can legally use to recruit employees; any outreach program that gives minorities and women a competitive advantage is a violation of Proposition 209. Agencies need to decide what strategies are legal and appropriate within their states.

The Supreme Court in March of 2001 cast doubt on the future of affirmative action across the nation as it agreed to hear a white contractor's challenge to federal programs that give an edge to minority-owned businesses. The case, to be heard in the fall of 2001, will test whether race can ever be used as a plus factor for awarding government contracts to such companies. The argument that affirmative action preferences for racial and ethnic minorities are unconstitutional is yet to be decided, but the trend appears to be the elimination of preferences. Only time will tell what impact the elimination of affirmative action, if it occurs, will have upon the recruitment of a diverse law enforcement workforce. At the University of California, Berkeley where the affirmative action practice of using race and ethnicity as a factor in admissions for years was eliminated, reports years later was that it did not result in a reduction of admissions of black, Latino, or Asian students.

The controversial practice of even tracking race is considered divisive by some. Ward Connerly, an African American University of California regent who championed the end of affirmative action in California, says that the practice is divisive, especially in California where no race holds a majority and people increasingly consider themselves multiracial. ("Connerly Starts Push to End Tracking Race," *Contra Costa Times*, March 27, 2001, pp. A1, A12.) Opponents to eliminating race tracking argue that collecting such data is crucial to preventing discrimination and allocating state resources.

Most recruitment programs, wherein applicants are solicited to apply for a career in law enforcement (excluding those who "walk in" already interested), involve innovative techniques to reach out to targeted groups (in states where this approach is legal). They also involve police managers who are outspoken in support of recruiting a diverse workforce. Aggressive recruitment efforts must be followed up immediately by a streamlined system to handle the new flow. If they are not brought into the system quickly, good recruits usually accept other employment. Successful programs vary by community. If recruitment efforts result in a large enough pool of qualified applicants, the pool will contain persons of all backgrounds.

There is also a need to be creative and flexible to build a pluralistic workforce. For example, the former chief of police of San Jose, California, Louis Cobarruviaz, was asked the following question by an Asian Indian whose religion was Sikh: If he were hired into the department, would he be permitted to wear his turban representing the Sikh religion? The chief told him yes, as long as it was blue and as long as the department could place its official emblem on it. Many tradition-bound executives might tell him to seek another job.

In December 1992 the federal Equal Opportunity Employment Commission ruled that an Orthodox Jewish postal worker could wear a yarmulke, or skullcap, rather than a postal service cap while delivering mail, despite the opposition of his supervisors. In law enforcement, strict dress codes have been part of the tradition for generations; strict codes may sometimes have to be broken to accommodate a multicultural workforce.

Satisfaction Level for Employees. The first step before outreach recruitment can take place is to look inward. Are any members, sworn or nonsworn, experiencing any emotional pain or suffering because of their race, ethnicity, nationality, gender, or sexual orientation? A department offering careers to these employees cannot have internal problems, either real or perceived, related to racism or discrimination. The department must resolve any such internal problems before meaningful recruitment can occur.

If the environment of the organization is hostile, it is difficult to make progress in hiring, retaining, and promoting a diverse workforce. (See Appendix A, a survey that can help your department determine the overall environment with regard to employees.) Managers must talk with all members of their workforce on a regular basis to find out if any issues are disturbing them. Managers must then demonstrate that they are taking steps to alleviate the source of discomfort for the employee, whether it involves modifying practices or discussing behavior with other employees.

The field training program for new recruits should be reviewed and evaluated to ensure that new officers are not being arbitrarily eliminated or subjected to prejudice or discrimination. By the time a recruit has reached this stage of training, much has been invested in the new officer; every effort should be made to see that he or she completes the program successfully. Negligent retention, however, is a liability to an organization. When it is well documented that a trainee is not suitable for retention, release from employment is usually the best recourse regardless of race, ethnicity, lifestyle, or gender.

Role models and mentoring programs should be established to give recruits and junior officers the opportunity to receive support and important information from senior officers of the same race, ethnicity, and gender. However, many successful programs include role models of different backgrounds than the recruits.

Community Involvement. A pluralistic community must have some involvement early in the recruitment effort of candidates for police work. Representatives from different ethnic and racial backgrounds should be involved in initial meetings to plan a recruitment campaign. They can assist in determining the best marketing methods for the groups they represent and can help by personally contacting potential candidates. They should be provided with recruitment information (e.g., brochures and posters) that they can disseminate at religious institutions, civic and social organizations, schools, and cultural events. Community-based policing also offers the best opportunity for peace officers to put messages out regarding agency recruiting.

Community leaders representing the diversity of the community should also be involved in the selection process, including sitting on oral boards for applicants (regardless of applicants' backgrounds). The San Francisco Police Department utilizes community leaders in all the processes mentioned. Many progressive agencies have encouraged their officers to join community-based organizations, in which they interact with community members and are able to involve the group in recruitment efforts for the department.

RETENTION AND PROMOTION OF A DIVERSE WORKFORCE

Recruiting officers who reflect the pluralism of the community is one important challenge of law enforcement agencies. Retention and promotion are equally important. Retention of any employee is usually the result of good work on the part of the employee and a positive environment wherein all employees are treated with dignity and respect by every member of the workforce. Retention is most likely in organizations that meet the basic needs of employees and that offer reasonable opportunities for career development. Employees who are provided opportunities to rotate through various assignments within the organization and have career development opportunities are more inclined to remain than those without such opportunities. In fact, once an agency earns a reputation for fairness, talented men and women of all ethnicities and races will seek out that agency and will remain with the agency longer.

The lack of promotions of protected classes and women to supervisor and command ranks has been cited as a severe problem in policing for at least three decades by scholars and police researchers. Authors and advocates for the promotion of women have used the term *glass ceiling* to describe an unacknowledged barrier that inhibits those officers from reaching ranks above entry level. The Glass Ceiling Commission, a federal bipartisan group studying diversity in the workplace (1994–1995), discovered that the glass ceiling has not been broken to any significant extent in most organizations, including law enforcement agencies. A 1997 study by the National Center for Women in Policing determined that in 100 of the largest law enforcement agencies in the country, women held 7.4 percent of top command positions and 8.8 percent of supervisory positions. Such low numbers are of concern.

Although women are making gains, they still constitute only a minuscule proportion of police managers. Marrujo and Kleiner (1992) reached conclusions about women in the corporate world that are applicable to women in law enforcement:

> Women are faced with the dilemma of fighting traditional values that have been ingrained into male executives running today's corporations. These executives were raised since birth to believe that the man is responsible for being the breadwinner, whereas the woman is to stay at home and raise the family. Unfortunately, these stereotypes and attitudes that these male executives possess blind their business judgement and inhibit competent and talented women from making it to the top. These men believe women will eventually quit their careers to raise a family; therefore, they view women as uncommitted to their careers (p. 1).

One could speculate that some law enforcement executives hold these same attitudes and beliefs, which keep women from obtaining important promotions. Watts (1989) has written that a woman must learn certain executive qualities to fit into male-dominated corporate ranks: "She has to be a risk taker but consistently outstanding; she has to be tough but not macho; she has to be ambitious without expecting equal treatment; and she has to take responsibility while still being able to follow others' advice." The qualities necessary for women in business are also important for women aspiring to rank within the criminal justice system.

In 1998 a comprehensive analysis of women in policing was published by the International Association of Chiefs of Police. The study, which involved surveys of 800 police departments, highlighted the following major points: (1) women remain grossly underrepresented in the ranks, (2) they are routine targets of gender bias and sexual harassment, and (3) they have largely been unable to punch through a virtually "bullet-proof glass ceiling." Other findings were as follows:

- Nearly 20 percent of the departments had no female officers at all.
- About 12 percent of the nation's nearly 600,000 police officers were women (a number that has not increased appreciably in nearly a decade).
- Approximately 91 percent of departments reported having no women in policy-making positions.
- Of the nation's 17,000 police departments, only 123 had female police chiefs or top executives.
- Nearly 10 percent of the departments listed gender bias among the reasons that women were not promoted.
- Women won more than one-third of the lawsuits in which they accused police departments with gender bias or sexual harassment during the period of time studied.

The report also noted that 28 percent of agencies reported that it is somewhat difficult to retain women officers; however, 24 percent said the same thing about men.

On the other hand, Penny Harrington, a former Portland, Oregon, police chief who now directs the National Center for Women in Policing in Los Angeles said, "I don't think things are getting worse, I think they're getting better." She also commented, "This younger generation is more apt to speak out about it than the first groups of women who were just interested in surviving" ("Bias Still Handcuffing Female Police Officers," *Contra Costa Times,* April 18, 1998, p. A1). Unfortunately, too often when they do speak out, and, especially if they sue the department, they face retaliation. Women who have complained or sued have reported retaliatory verbal abuse, petty reprimands from supervisors and managers, dead-end assignments, and, in some cases, no backup on patrol.

Police executives and city or county managers cannot afford to minimize the consequences of poor retention and inadequate promotional opportunities for women and ethnically diverse groups. Some departments have done very well in recruiting and hiring women, but, for reasons that have yet to be studied, women have left departments more quickly than men. "You can imagine that there is a level of frustration here," says Susan Riseling, president of the National Association of Women Law Enforcement Executives. "Until we figure out what drives women away from this business, we're not going to see any progress" ("Female Cops, Nation's Policewomen are Facing a Bullet-Proof Glass Ceiling. Survey: Women Muscled Out by Bias, Harassment," *USA Today,* November 24, 1998). A 1998 study by the International Association of Chiefs of Police found that about 60 percent of the women who leave work do so between their second and fifth year on the job. The reasons vary, but family pressures are the most frequently cited cause. The report recommended fairer screening procedures, tougher sexual harassment policies, and sustained drives designed to attract women and keep them on the job.

Failure to promote qualified candidates representative of the diverse populations agencies serve, including women, can result in continued distrust of the police by the communities. Underrepresentation within police departments also aggravates tensions between the police and the community. Some scholars and criminal justice experts argue that underrepresentation at all levels within law enforcement agencies hurts the image of the department in the eyes of the community (Walker, 1989).

Within organizations, women and others of diverse backgrounds are frustrated when promotional opportunities seem more available to white males than to them. The disenchantment that often accompanies frustration frequently leads to low productivity and morale, early burnout, and resignation because opportunities appear better elsewhere. Lack of attention to equal opportunity promoting practices at some law enforcement agencies has resulted in court-ordered promotions. Court orders have a negative impact on a department's operations and relationships, both internally and externally, and often lead to distrust and dissatisfaction.

Court findings show reverse bias as well: "With affirmative action under fresh scrutiny, the Supreme Court . . . left intact two court victories by white men who said they were victims of reverse discrimination" ("Supreme Court Allows Findings of Reverse Bias," *Contra Costa Times,* April 18, 1995, p. 1A). In a similar court verdict

> Three white workers win discrimination case. A jury awarded three white men more than $4 million after finding that the men endured racial discrimination while employed with the police department at Fresno State University [California]. Their claim was that the university gave preferential treatment to African-Americans over whites. ("Three White Workers Win Discrimination Case," *Contra Costa Times,* August 13, 2000, p. A3)

Proposition 209 in California ended affirmative action hiring and promotional practices for the most part.

A study by Lanham (1993) found that police professionals, civic leaders, POST consultants, community groups, and educators believed

> that their respective police departments' administrators were progressive in hiring ethnic minorities, but felt that most of the same administrators were hesitant and almost resistant toward achieving ethnic diversity within their own police command ranks. Some stated that they have heard the explanation from several police administrators that minority recruitment is a relatively new issue and more time is needed to promote officers through the ranks. However, this explanation was viewed as implausible or, at best, inaccurate since the Civil Rights Act, Affirmative Action, and the Equal Opportunity Act all are over 20 years old. It was felt that it should take less than 20 years to recruit, train, and promote ethnic minorities into the police command ranks. (Lanham, 1993)

Affirmative action and consent decrees have been only moderately successful in achieving parity in the hiring of women and individuals from ethnically diverse backgrounds. There has been even less success with promotions of these groups to command ranks. In fact, studies have found that affirmative action has produced uneven results by race, gender, and occupation across the nation. In October 1998 a federal judge ended the 19 years of court-supervised integration of the San Francisco Police Department and no officers objected. In this case, the results were impressive—an increase in the numbers of officers with diverse backgrounds from 14 to 37 percent and in female officers from 4 to 15 percent. The figures did not meet the decree's long-term goals, but lawyers involved said they believed the city is committed to diversifying the department completely.

An unfortunate problem that can be associated with the promotion of women and nonwhites is a stigma about qualifications: "Are they qualified for the job or are they products of affirmative action?" Peers may subtly or even explicitly express to each other that the promotion did not result because of competence, and the promoted candidate may feel that his or her success is not based entirely on qualifications. Consequently, employees may experience strained relationships and lowered morale. There is no denying the potential for a strong negative internal reaction in an organization when court orders have mandated promotions. Some white employees feel anger or frustration with consent decrees or affirmative action–based promotions. Clearly, preventive work must be done to avoid the problems described.

A transition is taking place as police continue to move from the strong, male-dominated (and predominantly white) police departments and culture of the past. Most law enforcement observers agree that with the shift to community policing, women can thrive. Departments are looking for people who are community related and who have good interpersonal skills, and they are finding increasingly that women meet these qualifications. Those seeking additional information about multicultural recruitment, retention, and promotion might examine the book *The New Leaders: Leadership Diversity in America,* by Ann M. Morrison (1987). Morrison examines the experiences of a number of U.S.-based private and public organizations to identify practices that obstruct and those that encourage the advancement of white women and people of color into executive ranks. She discusses the country's best practices for promoting white women and people of color and offers a step-by-step action plan for creating diversity strategies that achieve measurable results.

SUMMARY

Affirmative recruitment, hiring, and promotions will remain important issues in law enforcement for a long time. Too many of the issues of equity and diversity have not been resolved in the law enforcement workplace, by the courts, or even in the legislative and executive branches of the U.S. government. The number of persons available and qualified for entry-level jobs will continue to decrease; more employers, both public and private, will be vying for the best candidates.

With changes in the hiring, screening, and promotional policies and practices of law enforcement agencies come an unprecedented opportunity to build a future in which differences are valued and respected in our communities and our workforces. Progressive law enforcement executives must strive to secure the most qualified persons to serve the public. To do so, they must not only be committed to the challenges of affirmative hiring (where legal) but also be capable of educating and selling their workforce on the legitimate reasons, both legal and ethical, for such efforts.

In this chapter we presented effective strategies to implement changes and successful programs of recruitment and promotion of a diverse workforce. Law enforcement will have to use innovative and sophisticated marketing techniques and advertising campaigns to reach the population of desired potential applicants. Community and law enforcement officials should remember that serving multicultural and multiracial neighborhoods can never be the sole responsibility of workforce members from diverse ethnic and racial groups. In most jurisdictions, their limited numbers make this level of responsibility unrealistic. All staff should be prepared to understand and relate to diverse groups in a professional and sensitive manner, whether the persons contacted are perpetrators, victims, or witnesses.

Although it contributes to better police–community relations, improvement in protected class representation in law enforcement and other criminal justice professions will not in and of itself resolve misunderstandings. Increased numbers of diverse staff members provide only the possibility of improved dialogue, cooperation, and problem solving within both the organization and the community the organization serves.

DISCUSSION QUESTIONS AND ISSUES

1. ***Institutional Racism in Law Enforcement.*** Law enforcement agencies typically operate under the pretense that all their members are one color and that the uniform or job makes everyone brothers or sisters. Many members of diverse ethnic and racial groups, particularly African American, do not agree that they are consistently treated with respect and believe that there is institutional racism in law enforcement. Caucasians clearly dominate the command ranks of law enforcement agencies. Discuss with other students in your class whether you believe that this disparity is the result of subtle forms of institutional racism or actual conscious efforts on the part of the persons empowered to make decisions. Consider whether tests and promotional processes give unfair advantage to white applicants and whether they discriminate against department employees of other races and ethnicities. Do officers from diverse groups discriminate against members of other, different cultures?

2. ***Employment of a Diverse Workforce and Police Practices.*** How has the employment of a diverse workforce affected police practices in your city or county? Is there evidence that significant changes in the ethnic or racial composition of the department alter official police policy? Can the same be said of gay and lesbian employment? Does employment of protected classes have any significant effect on the informal police subculture and, in turn, police performance? Provide examples to support your conclusions.

REFERENCES

BOWERS, GORDON A. (1990). "Avoiding the Recruitment Crisis," *Journal of California Law Enforcement, 24* (2), 64.

CETRON, MARVIN J., Wanda Rocha, and Rebecca Luckins. (1988, July–August). "Into the 21st Century: Long-Term Trends Affecting the United States," *The Futurist,* 64.

DETTWEILER, JOSH. (1993, September). "Women and Minorities in Professional Training Programs: The Ins and Outs of Higher Education," *Cultural Diversity at Work, 6* (1), 3.

EDSALL, THOMAS B. (1991, January 15). "Racial Preferences Produce Change, Controversy," *Washington Post.*

GOLDSTEIN, HERMAN. (1977). *Policing a Free Society* (Chapter 10). Washington, D.C.: U.S. Department of Justice Law Enforcement Assistance Administration.

GUYOT, DOROTHY. (1977). "Bending Granite: Attempts to Change the Rank Structure of American Police Departments," *Journal of Police Science and Administration, 3,* 253–284.

International Association of Chiefs of Police (1998). The Future of Women in Policing: Mandates for Action. Washington, D.C.

LANHAM, MICHAEL. (1993, January). "Achieving Ethnic Diversity in the Police Command Ranks by the Year 2001." California Command College Class XV, Peace Officer Standards and Training, Sacramento, Calif.

MARRUJO, ROBERT AND BRIAN KLEINER (1992). "Why Women Fail to Get to the Top," Equal Opportunities International, Vol. II, No. 4.

MICARI, MARINA. (1993, September). "Recruiters of Minorities and Women Speak Out: Why Companies Lose Candidates," *Cultural Diversity at Work, 6* (1), 1.

MORRISON, ANN M. (1987). *The New Leaders: Leadership Diversity in America.* San Francisco: Jossey-Bass.

OSBORN, RALPH. (1992, June). "Police Recruitment: Today's Standard—Tomorrow's Challenge," *FBI Law Enforcement Bulletin,* Washington, D.C. 21.

Police Executive Research Forum (1987). Nationwide Task Force Study on Recruitment. Washington, D.C.

U.S. Department of Labor: Glass Ceiling Commission Reports (1994-5). Washington, D.C.

WALKER, SAMUEL J. (1989). "Employment of Black and Hispanic Police Officers 1983–1988: A Follow-Up Study." Occasional paper 89-1, Center for Applied Urban Research, University of Nebraska, Omaha.WATTS, P. (1989). "Breaking Into the Old-Boy Network," Executive Female, Vol. 12, (No. 32).

WATTS, P. (1989). "Breaking into the Old-Boy Network," Executive Female, Vol. 12, (No. 32).

PART TWO

Training in Cultural Understanding for Law Enforcement

4 PREPARATION AND IMPLEMENTATION OF CULTURAL AWARENESS TRAINING
5 CROSS-CULTURAL COMMUNICATION FOR LAW ENFORCEMENT

In Part Two we present readers with information on cultural awareness training and cross-cultural communication in law enforcement. Chapter 4 is of particular significance to both police executives and managers, as well as officers who provide instruction in cultural awareness or diversity programs. The chapter provides examples of successful police cultural awareness training program designs, methods of implementation, and guidelines for chief executives and trainers. We discuss officer resistance to such training and point out the need to explore reasons for it. The reader will find useful information on the selection of external consultants, along with key training phases and issues that cultural awareness curriculum should reflect. We emphasize the role of the chief executive, who must demonstrate strong support for the training and develop action plans, in addition to implementing courses. The chapter summary includes a review of suggestions for both cultural awareness instructors and training participants. The Instructor's Manual contains useful additional resources for cultural awareness programs.

Chapter 5 provides practical information highlighting the dynamics of cross-cultural communication in law enforcement. We present typical styles of communication that people may display when they are uncomfortable with cross-cultural contact. The chapter includes a discussion of the special problems involved when officers must communicate with citizens who have limited facility with the English language. In addition, it emphasizes sensitivity to nonverbal differences across cultures and to some of the communication issues that arise between men and women in law enforcement agencies. We present skills and techniques for officers to apply in situations of cross-cultural contact.

The following appendixes correspond to chapter content in Part Two:

Appendix A   Multicultural Community and Workforce: Attitude Assessment Survey
Appendix B   Cultural Diversity Survey: Needs Assessment
Appendix C   Listing of Consultants and Resources
Appendix D   Self-Assessment of Communication Skills in Law Enforcement

4

PREPARATION AND IMPLEMENTATION OF CULTURAL AWARENESS TRAINING

OVERVIEW

Every human resources program in criminal justice should have a substantial component that deals with culture and its impact on human behavior, both lawful and deviant. In this chapter we describe assumptions related to cross-cultural understanding that must be examined before cultural awareness training can be effective. We then present designs and methods of cultural awareness training for police officers and provide guidelines for chief executives and for those who implement courses. Information is included on the selection of cultural awareness trainers, instructors, and consultants.

COMMENTARY

The importance of cultural awareness training for law enforcement employees is highlighted in the following quotations:

> Law enforcement professionals need to develop cultural empathy. They need to put themselves in other people's cultural shoes to understand what motivates their behavior. By understanding internal cultures, they can usually explain why situations develop the way they do. And if they know their own internal cultures, they also know the reasons behind their reactions and realize why they may feel out of control. Law enforcement officers should remember that racial and cultural perceptions affect attitudes and motivate behavior. (Weaver, 1992, p. 2)

> The "police subculture" has a tendency to be very opinionated and sometimes prejudicial in its dealings with others. This prejudice is often subconsciously directed at anyone who is not a "cop." The goal of any human relations training should be to raise the police department's awareness of the needs of its particular community as a whole, encompassing the needs of the minority and ethnic community. (Kusunoki and Rivera, 1985, p. 32)

Many Southern California police chiefs, expressing disbelief at the Rodney G. King verdicts, say they will diligently move forward with sensitivity training and community outreach programs that have been cornerstones of reform since the case erupted 14 months ago. . . . As a result, many organizations have turned to new training techniques, scrutinized policies for reviewing brutality complaints and encouraged officers to loosen up and build stronger bridges to neighborhoods.
("Police Chiefs Examine New Training Policy," *Los Angeles Times,* May 3, 1992, p. B-7)

Diversity is emerging as one of the most serious issues in the workplace today, yet most employers are not prepared to deal with it, nor are their managers. Many managers grew up having little contact with other cultures. They are actually "culturally deprived," and their graduate school texts did not cover the kinds of situations that arise in today's multicultural settings. (Copeland, 1990, p. 16)

INTRODUCTION

Throughout U.S. history, ethnic and racial minority groups and government have clashed; periodically, violence accompanied these clashes (as we witnessed in the late 1960s, early 1970s, and 1992). The public, scholars, and independent study commissions paid considerable attention to the causes of the strife, and much of the focus centered on law enforcement procedures and training. Some agencies reacted by implementing or revising community and human relations training; a few instituted "sensitivity" classes using outside facilitators.

It appears, however, that law enforcement did not accomplish much more than that, especially following those earlier years of conflict. The emphasis on community relations skills in law enforcement academies and in-service courses never materialized to any great degree. Many promising programs soon faded, giving the mistaken impression that such training was no longer needed.

Private organizations, governmental agencies, textbooks, and educators or trainers use various terms to describe such training: *human relations, cultural diversity, cultural awareness,* and *sensitivity training.* Community relations training, traditionally provided for many law enforcement officers in academies or in-service courses since the 1970s, is somewhat similar to the cultural awareness training taking place today. Police–community relations "seeks to involve the citizen *actively* in determining what (and how) police services will be provided to the community and in establishing ongoing mechanisms for resolving problems of mutual interest to the community and the police (Mayhall, 1985, p. 43). Community relations is thus the process by which community members and police work together to identify and resolve problems that have caused or might cause difficulties between them. Public relations would include all activities engaged in by the police to develop or maintain a favorable public image.

Human relations is a rather ambiguous term that applies to the interaction of people. It can mean everything from a study of organizational behavior and productivity of its employees to the positive relationship skills an officer uses to provide services to the community. Human relations is an all-encompassing term and includes cross-cultural and race relations.

The term *sensitivity training,* used in the 1970s, had a negative connotation for many law enforcement practitioners. Some officers resented and criticized what they referred to as "touchy-feely" training. "As police work in increasingly diverse communities, their academies are emphasizing recognition of ethnic customs. Officers say they want practical advice, not 'touchy-feely' lessons" ("Cultural Sensitivity On The Beat," *Los Angeles Times,* January 10, 2000, p. A1). "Sometimes, traditional sensitivity classes have also provided a forum for representatives of minority communities to vent their frustrations by berating the officers for their alleged insensitivity. No wonder police officers cringe when they hear the words 'sensitivity training' " (Torres, 1992, p. 8). Even some supervisors, managers, and instructors did not take the training seriously. The nature of the training was delicate, and officers were unaccustomed to being confronted with police–minority group issues. Some officers approached the training with the attitude that citizens, not police officers, needed training on such subjects as violence reduction, respect for the police, and the law.

During training classes officers felt uncomfortable dealing with issues of bias, prejudice, and racism. Officers, whose primary training and tools were law enforcement (laws and procedures) and officer safety (crime fighter methods), were forced to sit through human relations and sensitivity skills courses that made many uneasy. They were particularly uncomfortable discussing their own feelings and attitudes on such topics as race relations and immigration issues. Dr. David Barlow, faculty member in the criminal justice program at the University of Wisconsin–Milwaukee, observed that the key buzzword—*sensitivity*—alienated officers in those 1970s courses and made them defensive. He elaborated:

> " 'Sensitivity' is inherently accusatory, because the assumption is that officers are insensitive. The very concept of sensitivity runs counter to the image which many police officers hold of their role in society—as enforcers of the law. Police officers generally do not respond well to courses designed to give special treatment to minority cultures or to promote affirmative action." (Barlow, 1992)

According to Barlow, officers maintain that their job is to enforce the law uniformly and that, in their perception, they do so without regard to race, religion, ethnic background, sexual orientation, age, disability, or gender. For this reason it is important that the focus of training not be on any one group. Cultural awareness training must be presented as a universal issue that provides officers with skills to deal more effectively with all segments of the population served.

Members of certain groups still confront discrimination, violence, and prejudice—sometimes at the hands of the police. While few law enforcement professionals today would dispute the important role that training plays in improving relationships between police officers and the community, there are two other significant factors. It is crucial that law enforcement agencies have policies in place describing penalties for employees who violate the rights of citizens. Managers and supervisors must vigorously enforce these policies. The education of law enforcement officers is a vital component of any training approach that aims to reduce incidents of hate and bias toward a large and increasingly diverse ethnic and racial population. The education and training must start with understanding people, their cultures, ethnicities, religions, races, and lifestyles. In today's multicultural society, cultural understanding on the part of officers contributes to police professionalism.

Law enforcement practitioners must embrace the idea that to be professionals, they need to understand and appreciate the diversity in their communities.

CULTURAL AWARENESS AND CULTURAL DIVERSITY TRAINING

What Is Cultural Awareness? Assumptions and Resistance

Cultural awareness is the understanding that an individual has about different cultures. The term is often expanded to include race, religion, gender, age, physical disability, and gay and lesbian issues. We use the terms *cultural awareness* and *cultural diversity* interchangeably.

In terms of officers' receptivity to cultural awareness training, a number of assumptions and areas of resistance must be explored. Instructors must understand that they will encounter resistance to the training by some course participants. Gary Weaver, a professor of international and intercultural communications in the School of International Service at American University, Washington, D.C., indicates that instructors must consider four assumptions, in particular, to understand the mind-set of law enforcement students (Weaver, 1975, p. 377).

Assumption 1: As society and the workforce become more diverse, differences become less important.   Weaver maintains that simply mixing people will not cause conflict to disappear or resolve misunderstandings. Quite the contrary: as differences become more apparent, hostilities can actually increase among culturally diverse persons and groups. Individuals who associate only with those who share the same basic values, beliefs, and behaviors take their culture for granted. When those persons interact with people from different cultures, they see contrasts and make comparisons and therefore become more aware of their own culture. The best way to learn about other cultures, therefore, is to leave your own and enter another.

Some police cultural awareness training programs require recruits or veteran officers to spend time with members of minority communities in their environment. Two agencies with these types of programs are the Fresno, California, Police Department and the San Bernardino County, California, Sheriff's Department.

Assumption 2: "We're all the same" in the American melting pot.   Weaver postulates that the notion that "we are all the same" is a spin-off of the melting pot hypothesis or myth. Those offering this hypothesis (also discussed in Chapter 1) would argue that America is a nation of immigrants who came from all parts of the world and threw their cultures into the American melting pot. By doing so, and through their own individual efforts, they advanced economically. However, Weaver and others suggest that this notion is exaggerated, as "all cultures did not melt into the pot equally."

> What many immigrants found could be described as a cultural cookie cutter—a white, male, Protestant, Anglo-Saxon mold. Those who could fit in the mold more easily advanced in the socioeconomic system. The Irish, Italians, and Poles could get rid of their accents, change their names, and blend into the dominant white community. But, African Americans, American Indians, and Latinos couldn't change the color of their

skin or the texture of their hair to fit the mold. They were identifiably different. (Weaver, 1975, p. 377)

Weaver also tells us:

Along these same lines, all cultural, racial, and gender differences do not disappear when someone dons a uniform. Even though law enforcement asserts that everyone is the same when wearing blue, it becomes practically impossible to deny the diversity that shows itself in the ranks. *What law enforcement needs to do is to accept and to manage this diversity.* In the long run, this only strengthens law enforcement organizations. [emphasis added] (p. 379)

An African American state trooper in Virginia described his experience of being assigned to a coal miners' strike in southwest Virginia. All the coal miners could pick him out easily because he was the only black trooper there. He told of difficulties, in general, of assimilating in society and within the law enforcement workplace because of his color (Hall, 1992). In Alameda, California, a black police officer described his frustration when a citizen called his dispatcher saying that a police car had been stolen because a black was driving it. He was in uniform at the time.

Assumption 3: It's just a matter of communication and common sense.   According to Weaver, 90 percent of the messages that people send are not communicated verbally but by posture, facial expressions, gestures, and eye contact (or lack thereof). Examples would include misinterpretation of the lack of eye contact; the reaction by some cultures to gesturing with the palm or fingers up; and the lack of facial expression, giving the appearance of being uncooperative or uncaring. These nonverbal messages can vary across cultures. Nonverbal communication is not taught in any culture. How, then, are people of different cultures supposed to understand each other, especially police officers? It is not just a matter of communication or using common sense when interacting with people from different cultures.

Assumption 4: Conflict is conflict, regardless of the culture.   Among members of certain ethnic groups, words and gestures are sometimes for effect and not intent. In some cultures, inflammatory or "fighting" words are used to get attention and communicate feeling, whereas in the mainstream American culture, those same actions and words would demonstrate a threat. (Examples are provided in Chapters 5 and 7.)

Police officers must understand these types of differences to be effective in their interactions with people of other cultures and races. Understanding different communication styles across cultures, particularly in conflict situations, for example, can help officers know how to defuse tension and confrontation.

As society and the law enforcement workforce become more diverse, the ability to manage cultural diversity becomes essential. The law enforcement community needs to weave cross-cultural awareness into all aspects of training.

Why Cultural Awareness Training?

An overview.   At no time has the need for cultural understanding and ethnic and race relations been more important than now, in the twenty-first century. Media headlines, especially during the late 1980s and 1990s, continually showed that racism, hate violence, cultural misunderstandings, community tensions, and conflict were major problems in the United States. "The triggering event that ignited national interest in the adoption of cultural diversity training for police officers in the early 1990's was the videotaped police beating of Rodney King. The series of events connected to the beating radically challenged policing strategies throughout the country. Police were motivated to demonstrate their sincerity in the area of improving police-minority relations" (Barlow, 2000, p. 113). The Rodney King incident was followed by other traumatic events: in New York, a Haitian immigrant, Abner Louima, was beaten and tortured in a police station bathroom; Amadou Diallo, an African immigrant, was shot 19 times by police in New York; there was a Los Angeles Police scandal within the Ramparts Division, in which rogue officers of the elite antigang unit were implicated in everything from bank robbery and drug dealing to shooting an unarmed man and framing him for attempted murder; Louisville, Kentucky, was torn apart by a brouhaha sparked by police killing of an unarmed black youth; and in Chicago, Illinois, in June 1999, in two separate events the same night, two different African Americans were shot and killed by police. (One of the African Americans, Bobby Russ, a football player, was shot by an African American officer, but being of the same race was no protection from citizen charges of racism by the police.)

Because of such events over the past two decades, there has been continual and increased demand for improved police–community relations from the public and from government. The problem can no longer be ignored or addressed in a haphazard, short-term, or unilateral manner. Incidents originally simple in nature cannot be allowed to escalate because of ethnic, racial, or cultural misunderstanding or hostility. It is no longer a matter of agencies doing the minimum to protect themselves and reduce liability exposure. It is time for all law enforcement employees to work with and understand the pluralistic society they serve. The broad goals of cultural awareness training contribute to this understanding. In a successful training program, officers gain the following understanding:

- The need to protect themselves by responding with control and in a professional manner
- Insight into various cultures and subcultures and ways to be more effective in providing services to all "customers"
- The impact of diversity on interdependent relationships and the development of skills for communicating with those who are different
- The ramifications of demographic and sociological changes on law enforcement
- The influence of perceptions, culture, and prejudices on behavior
- Information about public and private agencies providing assistance to needy members of the community, such as immigrants and the poor
- The reduction of citizen complaints, lawsuits, agency–customer friction, negative media, and liability
- Officer safety skills
- Conflict resolution techniques and effective verbal and nonverbal behaviors that will promote positive interpersonal relations
- The benefits of developing a positive perception of law enforcement in the communities they serve
- Cross-cultural knowledge and skills as part of "real" police work

Cultural awareness training will effectively prepare academy students and officers to confront sensitive issues and interact more positively with fellow officers and the people they serve. For example, a police supervisor in a records bureau, excited about the productivity of one of his Vietnamese office clerks, acknowledged her and thanked her profusely in front of her coworkers. He assumed that she would appreciate his overt praise. In fact, she felt that he overdid it as he went on and on with his compliments. She was so uncomfortable with the attention that she called in sick for one day. She later confided that she felt that her peers would think that she was trying to rise up faster than them in the organization. Her main concern had to do with breaking harmony in her interpersonal relations with her coworkers. Not all Vietnamese employees would react in this way, of course, but this response was culturally based. Another example involved an officer working a case involving a female Middle Eastern crime victim. The officer continually patted the victim on the back and placed his arm around the victim, intending to demonstrate sensitivity and empathy, just as he was taught in recruit school. The Arab female hated being touched and became distant and uncooperative. No strange male in her culture would ever touch her. Thus, in these cross-cultural interactions, the "standard" ways of motivating and showing concern were counterproductive.

The complex problems arising in diverse neighborhoods where officers work also demand that they think differently about their law enforcement role. Officers must understand the importance of their role as sensitive and caring agents of the people they serve, not just as crime fighters who travel from one call to another. (Police officer role and image are discussed further in Chapter 15.) The ultimate goal of cultural awareness training is for law enforcement personnel to become more comfortable with and understanding of diverse ethnicities, races, religions, and cultures. With officers' increased comfort comes the ability to establish rapport and help put other people at ease. Each improved interaction with citizens slowly leads to overall improved police–community relations. Further, cross-cultural communication skills enhance officer safety. Knowledge of words, gestures, and labels offensive to particular groups is the first step in controlling one's use of them. Responding positively to an individual's cultural style of communicating and knowing not to imitate that style (discussed further in Chapter 5) can contribute to the successful defusing of potential confrontation. The application of cultural knowledge on the streets must be treated as real police work.

There are cultural customs which require police officers to use discretion on if to arrest or not; district attorneys to use discretion on if to charge; or courts the latitude to be lenient if the immigrant is convicted. If they understand the cultural issues and the offense is not so egregious, police departments, prosecutors, and courts have some latitude and can use discretion. Using discretion, when warranted, can help each part of the criminal justice system do the job and minimize tension and conflicts with different ethnic and racial communities. What is considered reasonable varies from culture to culture. For example, eating pigs or dogs or cows in some countries is reasonable while in others it is not. We have to be flexible in how we view some cultural practices. Some customs cross the line, however. For example, female circumcision, a ritual practiced in some African countries, is illegal in the United States. There have been cases in the United States where this tradition by immigrant parents has resulted in arrest and prosecution. In Massachusetts, a couple were indicted in June of 1999 on charges of mutilating the genitals of their 3-year-old daughter. (*LA Times*, January 10, 2000, p. A12). The Hmong tribal tradition in Laos of "marriage by capture," when practiced in the United States, is treated in most cases as a kidnapping and rape. While this is true, the officers involved in the case should have an understanding of the Hmong tradition which dictates that the girl feign resistance, but if the prospective groom does not take her to his home and consummate the union, he is considered too weak to be a husband.

Law enforcement is not alone in the need to gain *cultural competence*. The term has become a buzzword in many professions, including in many medical circles, especially in communities with diverse populations. Doctors and health care workers are increasingly having to learn about patients from more than a dozen different cultures, each with a different set of beliefs, customs, and needs. Traditional caregiving is not always enough anymore, and the same is true of providing law enforcement services to a community.

Perspective.   As mentioned previously, there has been a dramatic increase in the range of courses and training materials developed by public agencies (including criminal justice) to address issues of community diversity. Private organizations and individuals are also attending to race relations, diversity in the workforce and community, prejudice, and discrimination. Currently a wide variety of courses are taught on these subjects in each state. Interested readers can contact their state's Peace Officer Standards and Training unit for course information.

In many U.S. cities, agencies scrutinized their policies and procedures following the King case and similar police-related incidents that followed. Departments modified how brutality complaints were handled and tightened up supervision of their officers. Some agencies encouraged their officers to "loosen up" and build stronger bridges to the neighborhoods—a task compatible with a community-policing philosophy. Other agencies introduced their officers to "verbal judo" (see Chapter 5) and other methods of communication leading to nonconfrontational ways of handling escalating situations.

Some departments have experimented with the installation of video cameras in patrol cars, intended to protect both the officers and the citizens they pull over. Other agencies have installed cameras in areas of their departments, such as in booking rooms, jails, and interview rooms, where suspect and officer contacts were potentially violent. However, most agencies have turned to a reexamination of police training with the goal of restoring public confidence in law enforcement and improving the morale of officers.

The June 1988 issue of *Crime Control Digest* contained a study that found that "training is the best way to reduce police–citizen violence" (p. 17). The Police Foundation in 1989 completed a study on police training and also concluded that courses can reduce the possibility of confrontation for police officers. According to this study, the right training improves an officer's ability to defuse possible violence. The National Organization of Black Law Enforcement Executives (NOBLE) made cultural awareness training for police officers a primary focus in 1993 and developed a series of national and regional conferences that included exemplary programs to address the emerging cultural issues facing law enforcement. NOBLE and the Police Executive Research Forum (PERF), along with many other organizations, including the American Civil Liberties Union (ACLU) and the National Rainbow Coalition, supported human relations and cultural awareness training because such training fit well with their support for community or problem-oriented policing. These organizations and law enforcement professionals view community- or problem-oriented policing and cultural diversity awareness training as strategies that can make a difference. The goal is to make law enforcement, which includes federal, state, and local police, more responsive to the diversity in the communities they serve. Law enforcement executives will also see an added advantage of such programs and training in the reduction of complaints and lawsuits due to police brutality, misconduct, and abrasiveness.

Cultural awareness training contains components that deal directly with face-to-face interaction with citizens and therefore can be linked to conflict resolution training. Awareness of the importance of training should be a call to action by police executives, training certification commissions, and legislatures in every state. Proper training can increase officers' ability to reduce tensions in their interactions with citizens.

Police executives must carefully choose the type of training their officers will receive. Some diversity training programs in the private and public sectors have been conducted by confrontational trainers who accuse employees of bigotry or pit them against each other on issues or discussions of stereotypes. Executives, both private and public, have assumed that training sessions led by diversity trainers are adequate to address the issue. Barlow, Blakemore, and Padgett (1995) indicate that there are problems with hiring consultant trainers who use "canned" programs:

> The production, distribution, and marketing of cultural diversity awareness training programs for police officers has become a profit-oriented business. Frequently this training is done in a routinized manner that results in "canned" programs. It is the contention of the authors that when these so-called "canned" programs attempt to transfer "known" blocks of information about specific groups or present standardized communications formats for selected populations, the meaningful purpose of the training is lost. . . . The authors contend that to avoid the pitfalls of the "canned" program, it is necessary to develop a dynamic training that focuses on process and not content. (p. 71)

The processes to achieve meaningful training will be discussed later in this chapter.

Neither training nor education is a panacea for correcting the ills that exist within society or law enforcement. Training is only a part of what should be a holistic approach to problem solving. Too often, when a police officer has deviated from acceptable behavior, a lack of training is blamed or is used to "correct" the problem. However, effective supervision and management, backed by policies that identify penalties for behavior violations, are also integral parts of providing direction and exerting control over employees. There are limits to what training can achieve; even less can be accomplished if the training program's objectives and approaches are not integrated with the values, philosophy, and mission of the law enforcement organization.

Cultural training for the criminal justice community (especially for police officers) can be informative, interesting, and pragmatic. Officers are more receptive to training when it helps them do their job better such as interviewing witnesses, suspects or victims. When the training will help them defuse a potentially violent situation and make them safer working the street. When they are shown how understanding different cultures can help them in their job, then they're very interested and receptive. The case for including cultural training as part of officers' professional development is summed up best by Weaver (1992):

> Because of naive assumptions, the criminal justice community seldom views cross-cultural awareness and training as vital. Yet, as society and the law enforcement workforce become more diverse, the ability to manage cultural diversity becomes essential. Those agencies that do not proactively develop cultural knowledge and skills fail to serve the needs of their communities. More importantly, however, they lose the opportunity to increase the effectiveness of their officers. Unfortunately, cross-cultural training in law enforcement often occurs after an incident involving cross-cultural conflict takes place. If provided, this training can be characterized as a quick fix, a once-in-a-lifetime happening, when in reality it should be an ongoing process of developing awareness, knowledge, and skills. (p. 6)

Cultural awareness and diversity training must be ongoing and interwoven into the fabric of every agency training venture, but especially in the basic academy program. Large law enforcement agencies with in-house training staff and training academies must increase trainer diversity. Agencies that use qualified women and diverse trainers in teaching defensive tactics, pursuit driving, physical fitness, and firearms courses, to name a few, can do a great deal to change attitudes positively within the white male–dominated law enforcement culture.

What is to be gained by an organization that introduces cultural awareness training? David Tullin, president of Tullin DiversiTeam Associates, has identified 24 reasons for making such a human resources development investment. Those that have particular significance for law enforcement agencies include the following:

- More problems are solved as cooperation increases and lawsuits decrease.
- The working environment becomes more positive and safer, with less conflict.
- Managers become more effective in leading a diverse workforce, thus allowing them to focus on other activities.
- Employees become more tolerant and motivated as morale improves.
- Performance becomes the focus of success, and more suitable job assignments and evaluations result.
- Client or community relations improve as more information is shared.
- Personnel become more committed to professional growth, and better mentoring and coaching emphasize potential and performance.

Other Training Applications

Professor Gary Weaver stresses that there is another reason to provide training to police officers on cultural awareness: police hostage negotiating teams can directly apply cultural knowledge.

> The response teams to hostage situations must be trained on how culture impacts their work. It is increasingly common for hostage takers to be culturally different than the negotiator and vice versa. For example, in some cultures, no serious negotiation is taking place until there is a display of emotion which indicates sincerity. This is often the case in many Hispanic cultures. To most Anglo-Americans, the meaning of this

emotional outburst is anger and lack of control. While Hispanics may think that negotiations are just beginning to be down to brass tacks, Anglo-Americans might believe
they are breaking down. The meanings given to messages could be completely different to someone from another culture. (Weaver, 2000)

Weaver postulates that during a crisis situation involving hostage negotiations,
team members are unlikely to take culture into account unless they have been
trained. They must act quickly and decisively under enormous emotional pressure.
Weaver stresses that at these times, negotiators "tend to use (their) 'rule-of-thumb'
to size up the situation, which means [they] look at it through the lens of their own
experience." He explains that when the crisis involves people from another culture,
negotiators must try to put themselves into others' cultural and psychological shoes.
He indicates that possessing these skills could prevent negotiations from breaking
down and might allow crises to be resolved without use of force.

DESIGN AND EVALUATION OF CULTURAL TRAINING

To be most effective, cultural awareness training must be agency and community
specific and must encompass all aspects of multicultural relations, both internal and
external to the organization. It is vital that the instructor create a positive learning
environment to maximize officers' receptivity to the training.

Agency- and Community-Specific Training

In a 1991 article the cultural awareness trainer Joyce St. George advocated that
course design must:

- *Be multidimensional:* Students must learn via such courses to assess what they encounter
  from several perspectives—organizational, community, and legal—to allow the totality
  of the circumstances encountered to be considered.
- *Be relevant:* Training programs must be structured to satisfy the specific interests and
  needs of the audience and the community. Needs, goals, demographic and cultural
  information, and issues participants currently face should be specific to the training
  audience.
- *Be behavior based:* The course should focus on how students express their attitudes
  through their actions and behaviors, which are governable and can be legally and de-
  partmentally controlled.
- *Be empathetic:* The program must ask students to empathize with the feelings and concerns of minority community members, but it should also address the feelings and concerns of students.
- *Be practical:* Programs must offer officers practical ways to assess and confront human
  dynamics—the tools students will need to handle persons from diverse backgrounds
  and lifestyles.
- *Allow for controversy:* Courses on such topics often stir up controversy among students.
  The program design must allow students to openly question the materials presented,
  especially if they are being asked to evaluate their own beliefs and behavior.
- *Be experiential:* The use of exercises (e.g., role-playing activities, game playing) in a controlled workshop environment is important. This training medium allows students time

to practice and/or refine their communication, conflict management, and confrontation skills. Participants practice using the culture-specific information they have received while following appropriate officer safety procedures.

- *Provide follow-up supports:* Organizations should implement follow-up training on an ongoing basis through briefings and the like.
- *Identify potentially hostile employees:* Trainers conducting these programs should identify employees who are aggressive or adversarial toward members of diverse groups. Employees who might be a threat to good community relations should be identified. They should receive additional training and be made aware of the potential for discipline if their behavior is unacceptable.

Barlow, Blakemore, and Padgett (1995) identified nine key principles of the role of training in promoting policing in a manner that is culturally sensitive, responsive, interactive, and dynamic. Trainers following these principles will encourage learning as a process rather than a static approach to learning. The principles are as follows:

1. Encourage an atmosphere that helps officers to begin a process of understanding and appreciating diversity.
2. Encourage behavioral changes and not attitudinal adjustments; attitudes are not likely to be altered in limited training blocks.
3. Promote the development of a set of process-oriented skills that officers can use to assess their level of cultural competence and to increase it through independent action.
4. Discourage the promotion of stereotypes.
5. Promote the perspective that different does not directly equate to deficient.
6. Focus on the issues of the training participants and provide a thorough question-and-answer period as part of the training.
7. Link the training to other relevant issues that law enforcement officials and officers face, including community policing, safety, legal liability, and law enforcement effectiveness.
8. Discuss issues that promote the development of new insights for participants.
9. Encourage the analysis of the agency's capacity for being culturally competent.

Trainers should refer to Barlow and colleagues' comprehensive publications (see references at the end of this chapter) as guidelines for preparing police diversity training sessions.

Training Delivery Methods

Training in multicultural policing should be a continuous and natural extension of community policing. The training emphasizes human relations skills, which most officers already understand as being necessary. Cultural awareness instructors and facilitators should utilize a mixture of teaching approaches and strategies, such as combining lectures (academics) with skills development and self-appraisal techniques (simulations, role-playing, group exercises). Critical incident case studies, experiential assignments, and some cross-cultural films are highly useful.

The Multicultural Law Enforcement Instructor's Manual that accompanies this text is particularly useful for instructors and facilitators of cultural awareness programs because it contains detailed information and resources for conducting such courses. Free or low-cost resources for teaching tolerance are also available from the Southern Poverty Law Center (www.splcenter.org). The organization began the Teaching Tolerance Project in 1991 in response to an alarming increase in hate crimes among youth. A number of other guideline handbooks are available for teaching about hate crime. Excellent materials for instructors are available from the National Organization of Black Law Enforcement Executives (908 Pennsylvania Ave., SE, Washington, D.C., 20003). One example is *Hate Crime: A Police Perspective Training Manual*, published in 1991.

Training Format

In this section we outline steps to accomplish before any training program can take place. Your particular agency may require more steps initially.

- Develop a mission statement incorporating the chief executive officer's vision, values, and philosophy concerning police–community relations and cultural diversity awareness.
- Research what and how other agencies and academies are teaching cultural awareness, including who is providing the instruction.
- Appoint a cultural awareness training facilitator. With the approval of organization management, this person selects the cultural awareness trainers from within the organization or agency. The facilitator might also hire a cross-cultural communications specialist or consultant in the field of cultural awareness training from outside the organization.
- Design training needs assessment form and disseminate to all personnel within the department. Analyze training needs based on results of assessment survey form. Involve members of the various ethnic and racial communities to assist in program design. (Appendix B contains examples of needs assessment forms.)
- Select community-based organization representatives of the various cultural, racial, and ethnic groups to assist in program design. Include police–community relations topics. Get as much input as you can from the community.
- Develop and implement program using the following suggested format or phases.

First phase: The relationship between cultural awareness and police professionalism. After an overview of topics are presented, the trainer provides the rationale for such training. The objective is to emphasize that knowledge of diversity and good police–community relations is both professional and practical. It is important to emphasize that the knowledge and skills gained will improve officers' effectiveness in working with diverse communities, as well as enhance officer safety and reduce complaints and lawsuits. The instructor's objective during the first phase is to motivate the course participants to want to learn. Only an effective, prepared instructor is capable of accomplishing this objective. Many instructors' experience has shown that achieving this objective is best facilitated by small-group discussion and exercises.

The class can be divided into groups and requested to list the reasons why cultural diversity (police–community relations, human relations) awareness and skills training is important to the participants. The groups come back together, and the spokesperson for each records his or her list on flip charts at the front of the room. Discussion is generated by the instructor on those items that reinforce the training objective. If an instructor does not successfully convey the importance of the training, officers may remain skeptical throughout the sessions.

Second phase: Recognizing personal prejudices.   One of the most difficult and sensitive aspects of the training course deals with participants' awareness and acceptance of their own personal prejudices and biases. Once students have awareness, the instructor can develop participants' understanding of how those prejudices and biases affect behavior—their own as well as that of others. This instruction should take place through a brief lecture, small-group exercise, and open class discussions when the small groups report back to the entire class. Police participants resent and react negatively to confrontational instructional approaches; this method must be avoided. The instructor and/or facilitator must be highly skilled and sensitive in this aspect of training and demonstrate the relevance of performance skills to the participants. That is, the instructor must approach the material from a practical perspective rather than a moralistic one and must especially avoid a preaching manner.

Third phase: Police–community relations.   The block of instruction on police–community relations is critical to the success of the training. It involves the instructor and community members, who can provide participants with current information on and a historical overview of minority community perceptions about the police. Some instructors may have the ability to lecture on what community perceptions are, but if they do so, they must not alienate the class. Some courses have effectively used minority community members to discuss culture- or race-specific information, but this approach must be closely monitored and controlled. The same is true of classes on the gay and lesbian community. Community member presenters must be carefully selected. Many community people are unable to handle the defensiveness of police officers during cultural awareness training classes. Some do not understand police behavior and tactics. The community member selected should work with the police trainer or facilitator in the development of his or her lesson plan so that there are no surprises.

Outsiders must receive guidance so they will become familiar with the precise goals and objectives of the training before they participate. Understanding the goals will ensure that their involvement contributes to, rather than detracts from, the overall intent of the training and curriculum. A healthy discussion of issues between police and spokespersons from the ethnic and racial communities is useful; however, the intimidation of officers is nonproductive. Instructors representing ethnic or racial communities who are hostile toward police will alienate the audience and should therefore not be part of the training. This forum is not an opportunity for community representatives to vent their frustrations by berating officers for alleged insensitivity in officers or the department as a whole. Community members who have had negative experiences with the police may not be able to transcend their feelings. Representatives of community-based organizations who want to assist will avoid confrontation and can provide valuable interaction and discussion on relevant topics. They must be prepared for officers to be direct, critical, and even confrontational if the officers feel even slightly attacked. If this forum is used, the training facilitator is encouraged to have ongoing meetings with the community-based presenters to ensure that the goals and objectives of the course are being met. Modifications of presentations are appropriate if problems are identified in evaluations or trainer observations.

Fourth phase: Interpersonal relations skills training.   The fourth phase of training deals with the development or review of interpersonal relations skills that can help the participant reduce tension and conflict in their interaction with community members. The goal is to improve students' verbal and nonverbal communications skills. The approach is based on the idea that students learn how their behavior affects feelings and, in turn, the behavior and response of persons with whom they come in contact. Through brief lectures, role-playing exercises (videotaped with discussion), and other individual or group exercises, participants can learn how to appropriately control their own verbal and nonverbal behavior, thereby influencing the responses they receive. The training can cover such subjects as barriers to effective communications, conflict resolution skills, the power of words (e.g., slurs, abusive, racial), and problem solving. Most participants will actually be eager to receive tools for the job—those immediate and practical skills that will help them deal more effectively and safely with minority community members.

Cultural awareness training courses involve imparting a great deal of information and skills to participants in a short period of time. To ensure learning and maximum retention, the instructor or facilitator, in addition to using a variety of proven teaching methods, must provide the class with several basic principles to remember at the end of each session. The basic principles should be related directly to their job assignment. The instructor may use computer-generated presentations, overheads, or flip charts to summarize the key points learned. The best approach to cultural awareness training is to link it to other curricula, such as officer safety and legal updates.

Training Evaluation

Cultural awareness courses must be evaluated on an ongoing basis to ensure that learning objectives are being met. Some trainers survey participants before training to assess their knowledge of the subject and then after each class to assess how much information was gained. This type of survey also helps the facilitator or instructor evaluate change in students. If participants are required to evaluate the training six months after the course is completed, such a survey could be designed to determine how the information learned has been applied to job performance in the real world of the work environment. Other evaluation alternatives may include

- Community survey before and after training
- Random follow-up survey by phone to victims, witnesses, and even suspects who have come into contact with employees who have received the training
- An analysis of citizen complaints of all types against the agency or organization before and after the training
- Outgoing examination of and course critique by all participants

EXTERNAL CONSULTANTS AND TRAINERS

According to Dr. George Simons (1991), most consultants hired by organizations follow a four-stage pattern:

1. *Needs assessment:* The consultant, depending on the size and scope of the task, may conduct meetings and interviews or initiate an extensive in-depth assessment with instrumentation designed for the situation or circumstances in which the organi-

zation operates. The consultant may also be able to assist the organization leader with the "internal selling" of the project.

2. *Project design and pilot:* In collaboration with his or her clients, the consultant produces a design or sequence of events and activities that are aimed at achieving the results that the needs assessment has found critical. The design is customized to meet the needs of the organization and is normally tested in a "pilot" program with a limited group of people to determine whether the results desired can actually be achieved by the proposed design. The pilot program process may be repeated until the program is fine-tuned and ready for full presentation. Packaged programs should be chosen carefully to ensure that the material meets the training objectives and needs of the organization (We discourage the use of most packaged programs.)

3. *Implementation, program delivery, and administration.* The tested program is then put into service by either organizational trainers or the consultant or consultant team. Consultants can also train organization trainers and evaluate the results for the agency employing them.

4. *Evaluation and follow-up.* The consultant can also assist in the design and implementation of a training evaluation program.

Consultant Selection

According to Simons, organizations frequently do not know how to select a consultant and wonder whether the firm selected should include minority persons. He believes that in a very mixed target population, it may be useful, at least at the outset or for longer-term programs, to employ a team that is at once visibly diverse and able to model working together successfully. According to Simons, the decision whether to use internal or external consultants is usually dictated by two factors: (1) the resources of the organization and (2) the balance between objectivity toward the issues and the need for familiarity with the organization. To minimize the risks associated with hiring a consultant, Simons provides the following tips:

- Know roughly what objectives the organization intends to address through use of the training consultant.
- Interview thoroughly from a wide selection of candidates or services.
- Expect to pay for these services, including the expenses of the interviewing process.
- Watch how the potential consultant or team interacts with the diverse population of your interviewing team or your organization.
- Make sure that the candidate sees the relationship of diversity to the big picture of the organization and the community in which it operates.

There are many diversity or cross-cultural consultants throughout the United States. There are also organizations, such as the National Coalition Building Institute (NCBI), with 35 chapters in the United States, Canada, England, and Northern Ireland. According to the *Law and Order Journal,* this organization has been successful in creating and teaching effective prejudice reduction models for police departments. The Internet is an excellent source for locating cultural awareness training consultants and resources. We cannot stress enough the importance of selecting a consultant who understands the law enforcement profession, officers and the nature of their work. Prior experience working with law enforcement agencies is important.

LAW ENFORCEMENT AGENCY MODELS FOR CULTURAL TRAINING

Within the United States, various law enforcement agencies in many states have developed their own diversity training for their employees. The amount and scope of training vary considerably. In California, legislation passed in 1993 required all police academies to provide a minimum of 24 hours of cultural diversity and discrimination training. This is administered by the Commission on Peace Officer Standards and Training. The Los Angeles Police Department's academy has steadily increased the amount of cultural diversity training during the past decade such that as of the year 2000, it is almost 100 hours. Long Beach, California requires every officer to complete a three-day course that culminates at the Simon Wiesenthal Center. The Monterey Park, California Police Department, in addition to officer training, offers an 11 week citizens academy for immigrants that includes what to do if they are victims of crime; how to file a report against a police officer; and how to use the 911 system.

The California Peace Officer Standards and Training (POST) offers an eight-hour course for executives. The executive attending learns the following:

- Leadership role as an agent of change
- Managing organizational diversity
- Development of agency cultural awareness policy, value, and vision statements
- Selection criteria for cultural awareness facilitators
- Evaluation considerations for the entire training program

If a chief of police wants to send a staff member to the facilitator training course, he or she must have first attended the executive course. The executive also attends the first day of the train-the-trainer class to develop an agency training protocol with the course facilitator. This involvement emphasizes the importance of the training and the facilitator position. During that first day, the chief receives an overview of the goals of cultural awareness training and makes a pledge to support the program actively. He or she is provided with specific examples of how cultural training is beneficial and models that can be modified and implemented at the agency.

Another California POST course for the agency's cultural awareness facilitator ("train the trainer") consists of two modules and lasts 48 hours. The first learning unit, in a classroom setting, covers the skills and knowledge needed to

- Understand the elements of culture, effective communications, and perceptions
- Perform an agency assessment using evaluation techniques
- Inventory the community
- Select and train community training mentors
- Design and implement a cultural awareness training plan that is customized to the local agency and community using effective instructional strategies and resources

During the final days of the classroom segment of the course, students apply what they learned by actually developing a needs assessment for their agencies and a cultural awareness training plan. The second phase of training takes place at the agency and in the community, where the cultural awareness facilitator

- Conducts an agency and community assessment
- Selects and trains a community training mentor
- Designs a cultural awareness training plan that is customized to the local agency and community

More information is available from the State of California Commission on Peace Officer Standards and Training (916-227-3909).

ADMINISTRATIVE GUIDELINES FOR CULTURAL AWARENESS TRAINING

The Chief Executive

The key to successful diversity training in any police agency is executive leadership, which provides clearly stated cultural awareness goals. Two important steps, as they pertain to training, involve, on the part of the executive, demonstration of commitment and development of an action plan.

Demonstrating commitment.   Commitment to cultural awareness training by the chief executive and the senior staff of an organization is crucial. They must be role models through attendance in training sessions and proactive leaders in all matters concerning diversity in the workforce and community. The chief's personal leadership is viewed as the keystone to successful training. Demonstrating commitment is accomplished in part via policy and practices (discussed in Chapter 2) in which the chief develops an overarching mission statement about his or her philosophy, values, vision, and goals pertaining to diversity. The chief also develops a more specific mission statement prior to the initiation of diversity training. For example, the following is an example of such a statement, in the form of a memorandum, from a chief executive to employees preceding training: "The demographics in our various jurisdictions are changing rapidly. To counter that change positively we have embarked on a new era of cultural awareness training for all sworn ranks. Our goals are to develop awareness and facilitate understanding in each of you as you deal with persons from different cultures. The end result will be an increased level of service to all citizens" (Harman, 1992).

The chief executive must ensure continued commitment to ongoing training by making it a mandate for recruits, in-service officers (including supervisors, managers, and executives), and nonsworn support staff. To be effective, cultural awareness training cannot be a one-time-only event but, rather, must be a continuous educational effort. The chief has to repeatedly set a positive tone for training if positive change is to take place in the organization. This commitment then gets translated to better police–community relations.

Developing an action plan.   Action plans are part of strategic, implementation, and transition management planning. An action plan for cultural awareness training identifies the specific goals and objectives and includes a budget, accountability, and a timetable. Another essential element of designing cultural awareness training programs (part of the action plan) is involvement of community leaders in the planning and, where appropriate, the implementation. One strategy could involve the formation of a cultural awareness committee (CAC) with both internal and external membership. The CAC assists the law enforcement agency in the development of a survey instrument that could provide useful input from employees and/or the community in the design of a cultural awareness training program. The CAC also reviews and evaluates the cultural awareness training course and makes recommendations for improvement. In addition, the CAC helps to identify the unique needs of each community or neighborhood that should be addressed in the training. An example of an internal survey is contained in Appendix B.

Cultural Awareness Trainer or Facilitator Selection

The selection of an in-service trainer or facilitator is crucial to the success of cultural awareness training programs. Successful programs have involved the chief executive appointing one person within the organization to be the cultural awareness facilitator. Smaller agencies sometimes form a consortium of departments, and one facilitator is selected, usually from the largest, to perform the required functions. The facilitator must be respected and have credibility with the organizations and be a good role model for the philosophies and values that will be taught. The facilitator must be trained on how to assess the agency and community; to select and train trainers, including community mentors; and to design an agency training plan. The facilitator may also be one of the cultural awareness trainers.

The selection of the trainer should be based on effective communication and good interpersonal skills. The trainer must be highly committed to the subject and be a good role model for the philosophies and values that he or she is going to teach (i.e., the value of diversity). A trainer or facilitator who is not dedicated to the subject or is a novice can cause more damage and create more dissension than existed before the cultural awareness training. Therefore, according to Sandra Glosser, an effective trainer or facilitator must possess several competencies and attributes:

Self-awareness: The trainer understands how personal belief systems and values may affect others. He or she is comfortable discussing diversity issues and encourages questions, comments, and challenges.

Commitment to diversity: An effective trainer does not demonstrate cultural sensitivity just on training days but regularly "walks the talk."

Expertise in the subject: An effective trainer understands the goals and objectives of valuing differences and knows how to communicate this information to an audience.

Facilitation skills: An effective trainer knows how to keep an audience awake and involved. He or she is adept at preparing and delivering training curricula, listening, assessing group dynamics, and using conflict resolution skills to defuse hostility.

Glosser also outlines common mistakes cross-cultural or diversity trainers make:

- Telling attendees that they should not be prejudiced
- Allowing "white male bashing" to take place
- Focusing on differences instead of commonalities
- Using too many gimmicks
- Implementing techniques that emphasize negative stereotypes
- Embarrassing trainees by using them as examples of stereotypes

- Moving through the material so quickly that they do not break through attendees' resistance to the training (Glosser, 1997)

The facilitator may use a combination of approaches: trainers from inside the organization, community mentors, presenters, and or private consulting firms specializing in cultural awareness training. Some agencies have effectively used police employees from other law enforcement agencies of different ethnic, racial, religious, and/or lifestyle backgrounds in discussion groups. These employees have credibility with police officers and are especially effective when they discuss their own experiences with discrimination and bias directed at them.

Academy instructors and departmental in-service trainers must attend technical courses to develop their teaching skills. A few states have developed a certified train-the-trainer course for cultural awareness facilitators. The facilitator then trains instructors on the specifics of cultural awareness training. The instructors must earn the respect and gain the credibility of their audience. More detailed instructions for trainers and facilitators are contained in the Multicultural Law Enforcement Instructor's Manual.

Tips for the Course Participant

The course participant needs to understand the expectations of the trainer and the program. The participant

- Must be able to express himself or herself openly and freely in front of a group and not be afraid to do so
- Can offer constructive criticism of the information being taught
- Should keep an open mind and be willing to learn about other cultures, races, religions, and lifestyles
- Should make an effort to learn about the community and neighborhoods in which he or she works
- Must make a positive effort to build an understanding of the diverse members of the community and workforce
- Will be open to learning about interpersonal and cross-cultural communications skills that contribute to effectiveness
- Will not take remarks by trainers or community presenters personally
- Will share factual knowledge and experiences about his or her own culture, race, religion, or lifestyle if appropriate
- Will accept that one purpose of training is to make his or her job safer

SUMMARY

Education that helps familiarize officers with ethnic and cultural groups in their community is a high priority for law enforcement. Police officers can effectively address a community's needs only if they understand the cultural traditions, mores, and values of that community. This understanding is essential to awareness on the beat and to formulating collaborative problem-solving activities that are an integral part of community-oriented policing.

In this chapter we have dealt with cultural awareness training for law enforcement agencies in multiethnic and multiracial communities. The guidelines provided are equally effective in classes covering sexual orientation issues. The information will provide both the law enforcement executive and the trainer strategies and program ideas on awareness training that can be implemented in agencies of any size and in any community. We have stressed that executives must take a leadership role in the development of community partnerships and the training of employees who are culturally aware and effective. Executives must look to policy and training to encourage their agency to meet the unique community-oriented challenges of the twenty-first century. Agencies that certify state law enforcement training academies (e.g., POST) must take the lead in developing cultural awareness course guidelines and train-the-trainer classes. They must standardize and certify the core elements of cultural awareness training not only for police academies but also for advanced officer, supervisory, and executive-level courses.

Effective training models concentrate on cultural education, communications skills, interpersonal skills with minority-group members, and conflict resolution techniques. To be successful, courses must be designed to fit participant and community needs.

DISCUSSION QUESTIONS AND ISSUES*

1. *Personal Action Plan.* Complete a short- and long-term personal goals summary that makes use of concepts learned during cultural awareness training and explain how you will apply them at work.

2. *Instructors.* You are a cultural awareness trainer. What skills have you learned that will assist you in teaching others about prejudice reduction on the part of your audience? Make a list of teaching methods that you would utilize to teach about prejudice, bias, and their effects on behavior. How can prejudice be revealed in a nonthreatening way in a training course?

3. *Training Goals and Objectives.* You have been selected as the training facilitator for your agency. Make a prioritized outline of the steps and processes that you will need to complete to design and implement a cultural awareness training course. After the course is planned, make a to-do list of things that must be accomplished three weeks before, one week before, and after the program.

4. *Chief Executive Officer.* You intend to implement cultural awareness training at your agency. List the steps you will need to take to ensure that an effective training course is prepared, implemented, and accepted. How will you determine what cultural and racial groups to include and discuss in the training sessions? How will you budget for the training? How will you remove patrol officers from their beats for the training sessions and still provide the level of services required for your community?

5. *Course Evaluation.* You are the cultural awareness trainer or facilitator. Make a list of the various methods you might employ to evaluate the effectiveness of the training class that is implemented at your agency or in your academy.

*See Instructor's Manual accompanying this text for additional activities, role-play activities, questionnaires, and projects related to the content of this chapter.

REFERENCES

BARLOW, DAVID. (1992, October 2–4). "Cultural Sensitivity Revisited," paper presented at the NOBLE/PERF/Reno Police Department Conference, Reno, Nev., and at the Academy of Criminal Justice Sciences Meetings, Pittsburgh, Pa.

BARLOW, DAVID, JEROME BLAKEMORE, AND DEBORAH PADGETT. (1995). "From the Classroom to the Community: Introducing Process in Police Diversity Training," *Police Studies, 18*(1), 71.

BARLOW, DAVID AND MELISSA H. BARLOW. (2000). *Police in a Multicultural Society - An American Story.* Waveland Press, Inc., Prospect Heights, Illinois.

COPELAND, LENNIE. (1990, January). "Learning to Manage a Multicultural Workforce," *California Police Recorder, Law and Order,* 16.

GLOSSER, SANDRA. (1997, September–October). "Community Policing Exchange. Community Solutions: The Nuts and Bolts of Valuing Differences Training."

HALL, W. THOMAS. (1992, September 29). Virginia state trooper, personal communication.

HARMAN, PAUL. (1992, June). "Cultural Diversity Training for the Future." California Police Officers Standards and Training Command College, Sacramento, Calif. (Order 14-0274).

HIMELFARB, FRUM. (1991). "A Training Strategy for Policing in a Multicultural Society," *Police Chief, 5B* (11), 53–55.

KUSUNOKI, GARY, AND HECTOR RIVERA. (1985, July). "The Need for Human Relations Training in Law Enforcement," *Police Chief,* 32.

MOLDEN, JACK. (1992, March). "The FTO as Evaluator, Part III: Evaluator Attitude and Bias," *Law and Order,* 21.

MAYHALL, PAMELA. (1985). *Police Community Relations and the Administration of Justice.* Prentice Hall, New Jersey.

National Organization of Black Law Enforcement Executives. (1991). *Hate Crime: A Police Perspective Training Manual.* Washington, D.C.

SIMONS, GEORGE F. (1991). *Diversity: Where Do I Go for Help? A Guide to Understanding, Selecting, and Using Diversity Services and Tools.* George Simons International. Santa Cruz, Calif.

ST. GEORGE, JOYCE. (1991, November 30). " 'Sensitivity' Training Needs Rethinking," *Law Enforcement News, 7,* (347), 8–12.

TORRES, JANE. (1989). "Can Training Reduce Police/Citizen Violence?" *Trainer.* 21–23.

TORRES, JANE. (1992, August). "Making Sensitivity Training Work," *The Police Chief,* 8.

TULLIN, DAVID. (1992). Tullin DiversiTeam Associates.

WEAVER, GARY. (1975, March). "American Identity Movements: A Cross-Cultural Confrontation," *Intellect,* 377–380.

WEAVER, GARY. (1992, September). "Law Enforcement in a Culturally Diverse Society," *FBI Law Enforcment Bulletin, 2,* 1–7.

WEAVER, GARY. (2000, November). Professor of International and Intercultural Communications in the School of International Service at American University, Washington, D.C., personal communication.

5

CROSS-CULTURAL COMMUNICATION FOR LAW ENFORCEMENT

OVERVIEW

This chapter begins with an overview of specific issues that law enforcement officials face with regard to communication in a diverse environment. We discuss several common reactions that people have when communicating with people from different backgrounds, including defensiveness, overidentification, denial of biases, and the creation of "we–they" attitudes. The next section provides information on language barriers and gives examples of police departments' efforts to work with populations with limited English-language skills. Then we discuss commonly held attitudes about nonnative English speakers and explain the challenges involved in second-language acquisition. The section on language barriers and law enforcement ends with a list of tips for communicating in situations in which English is an individual's second language. We then present information on key issues and skills required for interviewing and gathering data, particularly across cultures. The next section covers cross-cultural nonverbal differences, emphasizing areas of contrast of which officers should be aware. The final section presents male–female communication issues, particularly within law enforcement agencies.

COMMENTARY

The challenge of communication across cultures for law enforcement personnel is multifaceted. Officers not only have to consider how communicating with populations with limited English skills affects their day-to-day work but also deal with the changing culture within their agencies and the sensitivities required in a multicultural workforce.

> For the first few months of being here, I was always tired from speaking the language. I had to strain my ears all day long and all my nerves were bothered. It was hard work to make people understand my broken English and to listen to them. Sometimes, I just could not

anymore and I just stopped speaking English. Sometimes I had to pretend I understood what they said and why they were laughing. But inside I felt very depressed. I am an adult and my language sounded worse than a child's. Sometimes it was better not to say anything at all. (Interview with Vietnamese police officer [northern California department]; 1993).

Language barriers can lead to serious problems for non-English speakers. . . . In one case, a man was in jail for agreeing that he molested his daughter. It turned out that the man had agreed that his drinking *bothered* his daughters. In Spanish, the word for bother, or annoy, is "molestar." After this was explained [by the court interpreter], the man was released. ("Helping People Who Lack English," (Contra Costa [Calif.]) *Sunday Times*, September 19, 1999, p. A-32).

One night last January, Oakland resident "Anita C." was severely beaten by her husband. She called the police, who came, took a statement from her husband and told her to go back to bed. They didn't talk to her, they didn't make an arrest, they didn't try to ask, 'Do you want to press charges?' said . . . her attorney. She is so fearful now. Anita's complaint was ignored because she speaks little or no English. ("Speaking English—Language Barrier Between Police, Crime Victims—Traumatic Situation for Crime Victims," *San Francisco Chronicle*, July 20, 1992, p. 1).

The Nigerian [cab driver] then ignores the [officer's] command to "step back." Most likely, this doesn't make any sense to him because, in his eyes, he is not even close to the officer. The social distance for conversation in Nigeria is much closer than in the United States. For Nigerians, it may be less than 15 inches, whereas 2 feet represents a comfortable conversation zone for Americans.

In Nigeria . . . people often show respect and humility by averting their eyes. While the officer sees the cabbie defiantly "babbling to the ground," the Nigerian believes he is sending a message of respect and humility. Most likely, the cab driver is not even aware of [what is perceived to be] wild gestures, high-pitched tone of voice, or rapid speech. But the officer believes him to be "out of control," "unstable," and probably "dangerous." (Weaver, 1992, p. 4).

You have to go along with the kind of kidding and ribbing that the guys participate in; otherwise, you are not one of them. If you say that you are offended by their crass jokes and vulgar speech, then you are ostracized from the group. I have often felt that in the squad room men have purposely controlled themselves because of my presence, because I have spoken up. But what I've done to them is make them act one way because of my presence as a woman. Then they call me a prude or spread the word that I'm keeping track of all their remarks for the basis of a sexual harassment suit down the road. I have no interest in doing that. I simply want to be a competent police officer in a professional working environment. (Comments by a woman police officer made at a Women's Peace Officer Association conference, Concord, Calif., July 18, 1992).

Nothing about avoiding discrimination requires compromising officer safety. . . . However, you should also remember that the misunderstandings and escalations which can be created by insensitive or discriminatory acts and words are also threats to your safety and your career advancement. (Los Angeles Sheriff's Department's explanation of its cultural awareness training in the academy).

CROSS-CULTURAL COMMUNICATION IN THE LAW ENFORCEMENT CONTEXT

To understand the need for skillful communication with members of culturally and ethnically diverse groups, including women, officers should recognize some of the

---

Exhibit 5.1   Key areas for officers to consider: cross-cultural communication.

- Officers have traditionally used styles of communication and language that at one time were considered acceptable. Now, because of diverse groups within the police agency and within our cities, the unspoken rules about appropriate and inappropriate communication are changing.
- For officers, communication can be tense in crises and culturally unfamiliar environments.
- Officers' perceptions of a cultural group may be skewed by the populations they encounter.
- Officers' communication will be enhanced when they are aware of
  1. Perceptions
  2. Cultural filters
  3. Possible biases and stereotypes
- Through communication, officers have tremendous power to influence the behavior and responses of the citizens they contact. A lack of knowledge of the dynamics of cross-cultural communication will diminish this power.
- Improved communication with all citizens will also result in *safer* interactions for officers.

---

special characteristics of cross-cultural communication in the law enforcement context (Exhibit 5.1). To best protect and serve communities made up of individuals from many different racial and cultural backgrounds, officers as peacekeepers, crime fighters, and law enforcement representatives need to look beyond the "mechanics" of policing and examine what takes place in the process of cross-cultural communication. Communication, in general, is a challenge because it is "both hero and villain—it transfers information, meets people's needs, and gets things done, but far too often it also distorts messages, develops frustration, and renders people and organizations ineffective" (Harris and Moran, 1991, p. 31). Why does communication pose this much of a challenge? Talking to others, making one's points, and giving explanations should not be so difficult. Every communication act involves a message, a sender, and a receiver; given that any two human beings are fundamentally different, there will always be a psychological distance between the two involved (even if they have the same cultural background). Professional police officers have learned ways of bridging the gap, or psychological distance, between the two very different worlds of sender and receiver. In instances of *cross-cultural communication* (which includes cross-racial and cross-ethnic interactions), in which the sender and receiver are from different cultures, officers have an even greater gap to try to bridge. Cultural influences affecting communication style potentially contribute to misunderstanding, and the "baggage" that goes along with the role of police for some citizens can set people up for communication breakdown and conflict.

CROSS-CULTURAL COMMUNICATION ATTEMPTS

It is usually much easier to interact with people who are like you than to communicate with those who are different. Communication can be strained and unnatural when there is no apparent common ground. The "people are people everywhere" argument and "just treat everyone with respect" advice both fall short when one learns that there are basic differences, especially in the area of values, that influence behavior and communication. Some police officers feel that an understanding of cross-cultural communication is unnecessary if respect is shown to every person. Yet many people, including some officers, have had limited contact with people from different backgrounds; this lack of understanding can be obvious when certain types of statements are made or certain behaviors are exhibited. In the next few sections we exemplify typical ways people attempt to accommodate or react to cultural or racial differences and how they may cover up their discomfort in communication across cultures.

Using Language or Language Style to Become Just Like One of "Them"

Black officer to a white officer: "Hey, what kind of arrest did you have?"
        White officer: "Well, man. I saw this bro and he was trying to jive me. . . ."

Officer Darryl McAllister, an African American from the Hayward, California, Police Department, used the preceding example in a cultural diversity workshop in response to the question: What do you never want other officers to say to you as an African American officer? His pet peeve was hearing other officers trying to imitate him in speech and trying to act like a "brother." He explained that this type of imitative language was insincere and phony. The artificiality made him feel as if people were going overboard to show just how comfortable they were with black people (when, in fact, they may not have been). He said that he did not feel that this style of imitation was necessarily racist (although in some instances it could be) but that it conveyed an attitude to him that people were uncomfortable with his "blackness."

Similarly, officers attempting to establish rapport with citizens should not pretend to have too much familiarity with the language and culture or use words selectively to demonstrate how "cool" they are (e.g., using "senor" with Spanish-speaking people, calling an African American "my man," or referring to a Native American as "chief"). People of one cultural background may find themselves in situations in which an entire crowd or family is using a particular dialect or slang. If the officer lapses into the manner of speaking of the group, he or she will likely appear to be mocking that style. Ultimately, the officer should be sincere and natural. "Faking" another style of communication can have extremely negative results.

Walking on Eggshells

When in the presence of people from different cultural backgrounds, some find that they have a tendency to work hard not to offend. Consequently, they are not able to be themselves or do what they would normally do. In a cultural diversity training workshop for employees of a city government, one white participant explained that he normally has no problem being direct when solicitors come to the door trying to sell something or ask for a donation to a cause. His normal response would be to say,

---

Exhibit 5.2 Key areas for officers to consider: Self-Awareness.

- Self-awareness about one's early life experiences that helped to shape perceptions, filters, and assumptions about people
- Self-awareness about how one feels toward someone who is "different"
- Management of assumptions and discomfort in dealing with people who are different (e.g., do we try to deny that differences exist and laugh differences away, or imitate "them" in order to appear comfortable?)
- Ability to be authentic in communication with others while modifying communication style, when necessary

Note: The Instructor's Manual contains discussion questions and role-play activities on this aspect of communication.

"I'm not interested," and then he would promptly shut the door. He explained, however, that when a black solicitor comes to the door, he almost never rudely cuts him or her off, and most of the time he ends up making a donation to whatever cause is being promoted. His inability to be himself and communicate directly stems from his concern about appearing to be racist. It is not within the scope of this subsection to analyze this behavior in depth but simply to bring into awareness some typical patterns of reactions in cross-cultural and cross-racial encounters. A person must attempt to recognize his or her tendencies to reach the goal of communicating in a sincere and *authentic* manner with people of all backgrounds (Exhibit 5.2).

"Some of My Best Friends Are . . ."

In an attempt to show how tolerant and experienced they are with members of minority groups, many people often feel the need to demonstrate their tolerance strongly by saying things such as "I'm not prejudiced" or "I have friends who are members of your group" or "I know people . . .," or, worse, "I once knew someone who was also [for example] Jewish/Asian/African American." Although the intention may be to break down barriers and establish rapport, these types of statements often sound patronizing. To a member of a culturally or racially different group, this type of comment comes across as extremely naive. In fact, many people would understand such a comment as signifying that the speaker actually does have prejudices toward a particular group. Minority-group members would question a non-member's need to make a reference to others of the same background when there is no context for doing so. These types of remarks indicate that the speaker is probably isolated from members of the particular group. Yet the person making a statement such as, "I know someone who is [for example] Asian" is trying to establish something in common with the other person and may even go into detail about the other person he or she knows. As one Jewish woman reported in a cross-cultural awareness session, "Just because a person I meet is uncomfortable meeting Jews or has very little experience with Jews doesn't mean that I want to hear about the one Jewish person he met 10 years ago while traveling on a plane to New York!"

"You People," or the We–They Distinction

Some may say "I'd like to get to know you people better" or "You people have made some amazing contributions." The usage of "You people" may be another signal of prejudice or divisiveness in one's mind. When someone decides that a particular group is unlike his or her own group (i.e., not part of "my people"), that person makes a simplistic division of all people into two groups: "we" and "they." (Chapter 1 introduces this concept.) Often, accompanying this division is the attribution of positive traits to "us" and negative traits to "them." Members of the "other group" (the out-group) are described in negative and stereotypical terms (e.g., "They are lazy," "They are criminals," "They are aggressive") rather than neutral terms that describe cultural or ethnic generalities (e.g., "They have a tradition of valuing education" or "They have a communication style that is more formal than that of most Americans"). The phenomenon of stereotyping makes it very difficult for people to communicate with each other effectively because they do not perceive others accurately. By attributing negative qualities to another group, a person creates myths about the superiority of his or her own group. Cultural and racial put-downs are often attempts to make people feel better about themselves. (This issue is discussed further in Part Five, in the context of police officer self-image.)

"You Stopped Me Because I'm . . .," or Accusations of Racial Profiling

There are three types of situations in which an officer may hear the accusation: "You stopped me because I'm [black, Mexican, and so forth]." The first situation is when citizens from a neighborhood with people predominantly from one culture are suspicious of *any* person in their neighborhood from another background. Thus they may call 911 reporting a "suspicious character" and may even add such statements as "I think he has a gun" when there is no basis for such an accusation. In this situation the police officer must understand the extreme humiliation and anger citizens feel when they are the object of racist perceptions. Once the officer determines that there is no reason to arrest the citizen, it is most appropriate for the officer to apologize for having made the stop and to explain that department policy requires that officers are obliged to investigate all calls.

Indeed, there are many incidents all over the country in which citizens call a police department to report a "suspicious character" just because he or she does not happen to fit the description of the majority of the residents in that area. Since there is a history of stopping minorities for reasons that are less than legitimate, the officer must go out of his or her way to show respect to the innocent citizen who does not know why he or she has been stopped and is caught totally off guard. Many people reported to be "suspicious" for merely being of a different race would appreciate an officer's making a final comment, such as "I hope this kind of racism ends soon within our community" or "It's too bad there are still people in our community who are so ignorant." Comments such as these, said with sincerity, may very well get back to the community and contribute to improved future interactions with members of the police department. Of course, some people who are stopped will not appreciate any attempt that the officer makes to explain why the stop was made.

Nevertheless, many citizens will react favorably to an officer's understanding of their feelings.

A second situation in which an officer may hear, "You stopped me because I'm . . ." may occur not because of any racist intentions of the officer but rather as a "reflex response" of the citizen (in other words, it has no bearing in reality). Many people have been stopped without reason in the past (or know people who have) and are carrying this baggage into each encounter with an officer. One police officer explained: "I don't consider myself prejudiced. I consider myself a fair person, but let me tell you what happens almost every time I stop a black in City X. The first words I hear from them are 'You stopped me because I'm black.' That's bugging the hell out of me because that's not why I stopped them. I stopped them because they violated the traffic code. It's really bothering me and I'm about to explode."

Officers accused of racially motivated stops truly need to remain professional and not escalate a potential conflict or create a confrontation. Law enforcement officials should not only try to communicate their professionalism, both verbally and nonverbally, but also try to strengthen their self-control. According to Dan Martin, former police officer and justice administration chairperson of Diablo Valley College (Pleasant Hill, California), who himself is African American, the best formula in dealing with these types of remarks from citizens is to work on your own reactions and stress level. His response to the police officer who made the previous remark was, "If you work in City X or any other city for that matter, you could be told on a daily basis, 'You stopped me because I'm black.' You have to develop a method whereby you don't internalize these things. You have to ignore these comments. People are reacting to you as a symbol and are taking their frustrations out on you" (Martin, 1992). This response assumes no racial profiling has taken place.

Let's assume that the officer did not stop a person because of his or her ethnicity or race and that the officer is therefore not abusing his or her power. George Thompson (1992), founder and president of the Verbal Judo Institute, Inc., believes that in these situations, people bring up race and ethnicity to throw the officer off guard. According to Thompson (who is white and a former English professor and police officer), the more professional an officer is, the less likely he or she will let this type of statement become a problem. Newer officers, especially, can be thrown off by such allegations of racism when, in fact, they are simply upholding the law and keeping the peace as they have been trained to do. Thompson advocates using "verbal deflectors" when citizens make such remarks as "You stopped me because I'm . . ." He recommends responses such as "I appreciate that, but . . . [e.g., you were going 55 miles in a 25-mile zone]," or "I hear what you're saying, but . . . you just broke the law." The characteristics of "verbal deflectors" are (1) they are readily available to the lips, (2) they are nonjudgmental, and (3) they can be said quickly. Contrary to what Martin advocates, Thompson believes that statements from citizens should *not* be ignored because silence or no response can make people even more furious than they already are (because they were stopped).

> Pay attention to what citizens say, but deflect their anger. You are not paid to argue with citizens. You are paid to keep the peace. If you use tactical language and focus every word you say so that it relates to your purpose, then you will sound more professional. The minute you start using words as defensive weapons, you lose power and endanger

your safety. If you "springboard" over their arguments, and remain calm, controlled, and nonjudgmental, you will gain voluntary compliance most of the time. The results of this professional communication are that (1) you feel good, (2) you disempower the citizen, and (3) you control them in the streets (and in courts and in the media). Never take anything personally. (Thompson,1992).

Thompson adds that an officer should talk Friday night the way he or she wants to be quoted Monday morning in front of a jury. Finally, he emphatically asserts: "There's no one in America who can pull me into an argument." Thompson noted that since the Rodney King beating, many more officers in his classes have been wanting help in improving their responses to citizens.

The third and final situation in which an officer may hear "You stopped me because I'm [black, Latino, and so forth]" is when the citizen is correct and, indeed, racial profiling is taking place. (Racial profiling is discussed in depth in Chapters 1 and 7.) Police department personnel are not immune from the racism that still exists in our society. Reflecting biased attitudes outside the law enforcement agency, some officers use their positions of power to assert authority in ways that cannot be tolerated. Here we are not only referring to the white officer who subjugates citizens from different backgrounds but also, for example, to an African American officer who has internalized the racism of the dominant society and may actually treat fellow group members unjustly. Alternatively, this abuse of power could take place between, for example, a black or Latino officer and a white citizen.

Officers must consider the reasons a citizen may say "You stopped me because I'm . . . " and respond accordingly. The situations described call for different responses on the part of the officer (i.e., citizens call in because of racist perceptions and the "suspicious character" is innocent; the citizen stopped is simply "hassling" the officer, and may or may not have been unjustly stopped in the past; and the citizen making the accusation toward the officer is correct). The officer would do well, in all three situations, to remember the quote included in the final section of Chapter 1: *"Remember the history of law enforcement with all groups and ask yourself the question, Am I part of the past, or a part of the future?"* (Berry, 2000).

LANGUAGE BARRIERS AND LAW ENFORCEMENT

Nationwide, changing demographics have resulted in the need for law enforcement to deal increasingly with a multicultural population lacking good English skills or fluency. From limited English speakers who report crimes to crime suspects and victims, there are no absolute assurances that officers will understand them. Officers are justifiably frustrated by language barriers and find it difficult to do their jobs the way they have been trained to do them. On a "good day" some officers make a point to modify their English so that they will be better understood; on a stressful day, many officers are frustrated at having to slow down and listen more patiently. Some law enforcement officers are noticeably impatient when they deal with nonnative English speakers. Citizens who do not speak English know when police are not listening to their side of the story. As a result, a citizen with a language barrier is not successful at communicating even the minimum amount of necessary information. Perhaps most difficult is the situation in which a person with limited English skills is traumatized, further affecting the victim's ability to speak English. Officers need to be aware of the potential for inadvertent discrimination based on a citizen's language background, which could fall under "language and national origin discrimination" (Fernandez, 2000).

Important Memo For Sworn Personnel

Occasionally, officers will encounter drivers that deserve a reexamination by the DMV under the authority of section 21061(a). Please note that section only refers to actual driving indicators based on specific evidence of incapacity—nothing else. Any notes on citations or reexamination notices (DMV for DS 427) regarding a perceived *inability to speak* English would be inappropriate and possibly construed as language and national origin discrimination.

From California Vehicle Code

12805. Refusal to issue or renew driver's license: mandatory grounds

(d) Who is *unable to read and understand simple English used in highway traffic and directional signs* . . . (*Source: The Insider*, the official weekly publication of the San Jose [California] Police Department, no. 39, October 22, 1998.)

Clearly, the more bilingual officers a department has, the more efficient and effective the contact. Many agencies subsidize foreign-language training for their personnel or seek recruits with multiple-language skills. When the resources are not available for such programs, however, there can be serious and sometimes tragic consequences. Non-English-speaking citizens may not understand why they are being arrested or searched. They may not know their rights if they are unfamiliar with the legal system, as is the case with many recently arrived immigrants and refugees. Using the wrong translator can mislead officers, so much so that a victim and his or her translator may give two completely different versions of a story—for example, using the friend of a suspected child abuser to translate the allegations of the child who has been abused.

In some cases there is no sensitivity when it comes to language obstacles. For example, within a largely Spanish-speaking area in Los Angeles, a deputy, according to witnesses, asked a Hispanic male to get out of his car. The man answered in Spanish, "I'm handicapped," and he reached down to pull his left leg out of the car. The deputy apparently believed that the man was reaching for a weapon and, consequently, "struck him on the head with the butt of his gun" (The Troubled LA County Sheriff's Department, *Los Angeles Times*, July 21, 1992, p. A–18). Insensitivity to language differences was also involved in the case of an officer who had been called to the scene of an accident in which a third-grade girl had died almost immediately after having been struck by a car that leaped a curb and hurled the girl 60 feet through the air. When the police investigator arrived, he tried to ascertain what had happened: "[The police officer] shouted out if anyone had seen what had occurred. No one responded because they had not actually been witnesses. The officer in apparent disgust and derision then remarked, 'Why don't any of you speak English?'" (Ogawa, 1990).

Sensitivity to the difficulties of those who do not speak English is in order, but that is only a partial solution to the problem. In attempting to cope with the problem of non-English-speaking citizens, suspects, and criminals, many departments have not only increased the number of bilingual officers in their forces but have also begun to utilize translation services such as "Language Line Services," which provides translation services in almost 150 languages 24 hours a day. The 911 emergency line has interpreters 24 hours a day for some languages. Having access to translation services and referrals is a first step in addressing the challenge of communication with those who speak no or limited English, but this is not a long-term solution. Having bilingual officers or nonsworn personnel, however, constitutes a more direct method of addressing the problem. Many departments across the country offer language classes on the job with tuition reimbursement for classes and extra pay for second-language proficiency. The California Highway Patrol , in 1996, added a 90-hour basic Spanish class to the curriculum for the basic officer academy. The Redwood City, California, Police Department also mandated the successful completion of a Spanish course while on the job (Miller, 1996). Police department training personnel are encouraged to look for classes specially designed for law enforcement. If they do not exist, a few selected officers and language educators should form a partnership so that officers can guide language teachers in the development of police-specific second-language curricula (i.e., to meet the specialized needs of officers on the street). In *Policing a Multicultural Community,* DeGeneste and Sullivan write:

> Since a degree of ethnic or racial distrust is undoubtedly the result of frustration stemming from language and communication difficulties, enhanced language training during initial entry-level police academies, with subsequent refresher courses throughout an officer's career, should be strongly considered. [And, on a practical level] developing language skills for a police agency can be a costly undertaking. Initial training would extend the length of academy training, leading to additional costs for instructors, training space and course development. Agencies in large urban areas would need to craft curricula for multiple languages (for example, Spanish, Mandarin, Cantonese, etc.). Refresher training would require replacing officers while they receive updated, or perhaps even initial instruction in a new language if demographic shifts warrant. Limiting these costs requires close monitoring of demographic trends to match language skills with community needs. (DeGeneste and Sullivan, 1997, p. 17).

Increasing bilingual hires is the most practical direction in which to go; in addition these officers often have a better understanding of the communities they serve. Some community-based police programs use trained community volunteers to assist them in situations in which English is not spoken. When translation is not available, officers have no choice but to rely on English. In doing so, the tips listed in Exhibit 5.3 on modifying one's language will be helpful.

ATTITUDES TOWARD NON- OR LIMITED-ENGLISH SPEAKERS

Most officers are aware that a citizen with few or no English skills is not necessarily an illegal immigrant. However, sometimes officers have seen English difficulties as a

---

Exhibit 5.3 Tips for communicating when English is a second language.

1. Speak slowly and enunciate clearly.
2. Face the person and speak directly even when using a translator.
3. Avoid concentrated eye contact if the other speaker is not making direct eye contact.
4. Do not use jargon, slang, idioms, or reduced forms (e.g., "gonna," "gotta," "wanna," "couldja").
5. Avoid complex verb tenses (e.g., "If I would have known, I might have been able to provide assistance.").
6. Repeat key issues and questions in different ways.
7. Avoid asking questions that can be answered by "yes" or "no"; rather, ask questions so that the answer can show understanding.
8. Use short, simple sentences; pause between sentences.
9. Use visual cues such as gestures, demonstrations, and brief written phrases.
10. Use active rather than passive verbs (e.g., "I expect your attention" [active] rather than "Your attention is expected" [passive].
11. Have materials duplicated in bilingual format.
12. Pause frequently and give breaks. Monitor your speed when you speak.
13. Use only one idea per sentence.
14. Respect the silence that nonnative English speakers need to formulate their sentences and translate them in their minds.
15. Check comprehension by having the other speaker repeat material or instructions, and summarize frequently.
16. Encourage and provide positive feedback on the person's ability to communicate.
17. Listen even more attentively than you do when communicating with a native speaker of English.
18. Be patient. Every first generation of immigrants struggles with the acquisition of English.
19. Do not speak louder. It will not help.

---

sign that a person is an illegal immigrant and the consequences have been unfortunate. Donya Fernandez (2000), Language Rights attorney, cited the case of a Spanish speaker with extremely limited English skills whom police turned over to the Immigration and Naturalization Services (INS). The INS held him for 48 hours, despite the fact that the man was a U.S. citizen who was born in the United States but had spent most of his life in Mexico.

Citizens' constant use of a second language and the accompanying frustrations for officers can be overwhelming. In general, whether the society at large (or police as a microcosm of society) is concerned about a particular group's use of their native language seems to be directly related to the population size of that group. For example, when large groups of Cubans or Puerto Ricans speak Spanish, there is often a higher level of anxiety among the dominant white population than when a few Armenians speak their native language. Virtually every immigrant group is said to resist learning English, yet the pattern of language acquisition among the generations of immigrants follows a predictable course. Members of the second and third generations of an immigrant family almost always become fluent in English, while many of the first-generation immigrants (the grandparents and the parents) struggle, sometimes partly learning English and sometimes not learning it at all. Many immigrants, however, are extremely motivated to learn English and become productive members of society. In urban areas, access to English classes is often limited (e.g., there have been known to be four- and five-year waiting lists for English programs at Los Angeles community colleges). Newcomers are fully aware that without English, they will never be able to integrate into the society.

Nevertheless, some people (including established immigrants) have a tendency to overgeneralize their observations about newcomers. It is true that some people do not want to learn English, and even some middle-class U.S.-born Americans do not make efforts to improve their language abilities. How often does one hear that high school graduates who are native English speakers have not learned to write or speak well? Here laziness or lack of high-quality education (or both) may have contributed to this aspect of illiteracy. In fairness, all groups have a percentage of lazy people, but sometimes people tend to stereotype others. Although not all first-generation immigrants learn English, there is a great deal of mythology around the "masses" of immigrants who hold on to their native language.

The native language for an immigrant family is the language of communication for that family. It is not uncommon to hear comments such as, "They'll never learn English if they insist on speaking their native tongues at home." Imagine having been away from your family all day and coming home and interacting in a foreign language. Is it reasonable to expect that one could express affection, resolve conflicts, show anger, and simply relax in another language? Language is an integral part of a person's identity. During the initial months and even years of communicating in a second language, a person does not truly feel like himself or herself. Initially, one often has a feeling of play acting or taking on another identity when communicating in a second language.

From a physiological point of view, speaking a foreign language can be fatiguing. As a child, when speaking one's own native language, one uses a set of muscles to articulate the sounds of a given language. Changing to another language, particularly as an adult, requires the use of an entirely new set of muscles. This causes mental strain and facial tension, which can result in a person "shutting down"—the result being an inability to communicate in English (or whatever the new language is). It is no wonder that in the multicultural workforce, clusters of people from different ethnic groups can be seen having lunch together, taking breaks together, and so on. Simply put, it is more relaxing to be able to speak one's own language than to struggle with a new one all day.

Sometimes police officers say: "I know they speak English because they speak it among themselves (i.e., when the group is culturally mixed). The minute I'm on the scene, it's 'No speak English.' Why do they have to play dumb? What do they think I am—stupid?" It would be naive to say that this situation does not occur. There will always be some people who try to deceive others and use or not use English to their own advantage. However, there may be other reasons that people "feign" not knowing English. Several factors affect an immigrant's ability to use English at any given moment. A few of these, in particular, are of special significance to law enforcement officers. Generally speaking, an immigrant's ability to express himself or herself in English is best when that person is comfortable with the officer. So the more intimidating an officer is, the higher the likelihood that anxiety will affect the speaker's ability in English. Language breakdown is one of the first signs that a person is ill at ease and stressed to the point of not being able to cooperate and communicate. It is in the officer's best interest to increase the comfort level of the citizen, whether a victim, a suspect, or simply a person requiring help. Language breakdown in a person who is otherwise fairly conversationally competent in English can also occur as a result of illness, intoxication, fatigue, and trauma.

Finally, officers must realize that their attitudes about immigrants and nonnative English speakers, whether positive or negative, may very well affect their interaction with them. This is especially true when an officer is under pressure and negative attitudes are more likely to surface in communication.

INTERVIEWING AND DATA-GATHERING SKILLS

Interviewing and data-gathering skills form the basic techniques for communication and intervention work with multicultural populations. For the officer, the key issues in any interviewing and data-gathering situation are as follows:

- Bringing structure and control to the immediate situation
- Establishing interpersonal relationships with the parties involved to gain trust and rapport for continual work
- Gaining information about the problems and situations that require the presence of the law enforcement officer
- Giving information about the workings of the law enforcement guidelines, resources, and assistance available
- Providing action and interventions, as needed
- Bolstering and supporting the different parties' abilities and skills to solve current and future problems on their own

Listed in Exhibit 5.4 are helpful guidelines for providing and receiving better information in a multicultural context.

In the area of data gathering and interviewing, the officer in a multicultural law enforcement and peacekeeping situation cannot assume that his or her key motivators and values are the same as those of the other parties involved. Recognizing such differences in motivation and values will result in greater effectiveness. For example, the values of saving face and preserving one's own honor as well as the honor of one's family are extremely strong motivators and values for many people from Asian, Latin American, and Mediterranean cultures. An Asian gang expert from the Oakland, California, Police Department illustrated this value system with the case of a niece who had been chosen by the police to translate for her aunt, who had been raped. The values of honor and face-saving prevented the aunt from telling the police all the details of the crime of which she was the victim. Her initial story, told to the police through her niece's translation, contained very few of the facts or details of the crime. Later, through a second translator who was not a family member, the rape victim gave all the necessary information. Precious time had been lost, but the victim explained that she could not have revealed the true story in front of her niece because she would have shamed her family.

Exhibit 5.4   Interviewing and Data Gathering in a Multicultural Context.

1. Be knowledgeable about who is likely to have information. Ask questions to identify the head of a family or respected community leaders.

2. Consider that some cultural groups have more of a need than others for rapport and trust building before they are willing to share information. Do not consider the time it takes to establish rapport a waste of time. For some, this may be a necessary step.

3. Provide background and context for your questions, information, and requests. Cultural minorities differ in their need for "contextual information" (i.e., background information) before getting down to the issues or business at hand. Remain patient with those who want to go into more detail than you think is necessary.

4. Expect answers to be formulated and expressed in culturally different ways. Some people tend to be *linear* in their answers (i.e., giving one point of information at a time in a chronological order), some present information in a *zigzag* fashion (i.e., they digress frequently), and others tend to present information in a *circular* style (i.e., they may appear to be talking in circles). And, of course, there are individual differences in ways of presenting information, as well as cultural differences.

5. It is important to speak simply, but do not make the mistake of using simple or "pigeon" English. Remember, people's comprehension skills are usually better than their speaking skills.

6. "Yes" does not always mean "yes"; do not mistake a courteous answer for the facts or the truth.

7. Remember that maintaining a good rapport is just as important as coming to the point and getting work done quickly. Slow down!

8. Silence is a form of speech; do not interrupt it. Give people time to express themselves by respecting their silence.

Exhibit 5.5 lists key values or motivators for police officers. In any given situation, these values may be at odds with what motivates the victim, suspect, or ordinary citizen of any background. However, when the officer and citizen are from totally different backgrounds, additional cultural or racial variables may also be in conflict.

Finally, when interviewing and data gathering in the area of hate incidents and crimes (as well as threats [phone calls, letters] targeted at individuals of particular backgrounds), the officer's need for control and structure may have to encompass possible hysterical or at least highly emotional reactions from other people of the same background. In the officer's attempt to be in control of the situation, he or she must consider that there will also be a community needing reassurance. For example, an officer will need to be willing to respond sensitively to heightened anxiety on the part of group members and not downplay their fears. Interviewing and data gathering may therefore last much longer when the officer is required to deal with multiple community members and widespread fears.

NONVERBAL COMMUNICATION

Up until this point in the chapter we have discussed verbal communication across cultures and its relevance to the law enforcement context. Consider the following

---

Exhibit 5.5 Key values or motivators in law enforcement.

1. Survival or injury avoidance
2. Control and structure
3. Respect and authority
4. Use of professional skills
5. Upholding laws and principles
6. Avoiding conflict and tensions
7. Harmony and peacekeeping
8. Conflict resolution and problem solving
9. Self-respect and self-esteem

---

examples of reactions to *nonverbal* differences across cultures and their implications for day-to-day police work:

> He didn't look at me once. I know he's guilty. Never trust a person who doesn't look you in the eye.
>
> —*American police officer*
>
> Americans seem cold. They seem to get upset when you stand close to them.
>
> —*Jordanian teacher*

In the first example, if an officer uses norms of eye contact as understood by most Americans, he or she could make an incorrect judgment about someone who avoids eye contact. In the second example, an officer's comfortable distance for safety might be violated because of a cultural standard defining acceptable conversational distance. The comments demonstrate how people can misinterpret nonverbal communication when it is culturally different from their own. Misinterpretation can happen with two people from the same background, but it is more likely when there are cultural differences. Universal emotions such as happiness, fear, and sadness are expressed in similar nonverbal ways throughout the world. However, nonverbal variations across cultures can cause confusion.

Take the example of the way people express sadness and grief. In many cultures, such as Arabic and Iranian cultures, people express grief openly and out loud. In contrast, in other parts of the world (e.g., in China and Japan), people are generally more subdued or even silent in their expressions of grief. In Asian cultures, the general belief is that it is unacceptable to show emotion openly (whether sadness, happiness, or pain). Without this cultural knowledge, in observing a person who did not openly express grief, for example, one might come to the conclusion that he or she is not in emotional distress (Levine and Adelman, 1992). This would be an incorrect and ethnocentric interpretation based on one's own culture.

The expression of friendship is another example of how cultural groups differ in their nonverbal behavior. Feelings of friendship exist everywhere, but their expression varies. It is acceptable for men to embrace and kiss each other (in Saudi Arabia and Russia, for example) and for women to hold hands (in China, Korea,

Egypt, and other countries). Russian gymnasts of the same sex have been seen on television kissing each other on the lips; this is apparently an acceptable gesture in their culture and does not imply that they are gay or lesbian. What is considered "normal" behavior in one culture may be viewed as "abnormal" or unusual in another.

The following areas of nonverbal communication have variations across cultures; the degree to which a person displays the nonverbal differences depends on how Westernized the person has become. Note that some people who are very Westernized in their thinking may still display traditional forms of nonverbal communication simply because they are unaware that the differences exist.

1. *Gestures:* A few American gestures are offensive in other cultures. For example, the OK gesture is obscene in Latin America, the good luck gesture is offensive in parts of Vietnam, and the "come here" gesture (beckoning people to come with the palm up) is very insulting in most of Asia and Latin America (Levine and Adelman, 1992).

2. *Body position:* A police sergeant relaxing at his desk with his feet up, baring the soles of his shoes, would most likely offend a Saudi Arabian or Thai (and other groups as well) coming into the office. To show one's foot in many cultures is insulting because the foot is considered the dirtiest part of the body. This would also apply to an officer who makes physical contact with the foot when, for example, someone is lying on the ground.

3. *Facial expressions:* Not all facial expressions mean the same thing across cultures. The smile is a great source of confusion for many people in law enforcement when they encounter people from Asian, especially Southeast Asian, cultures. A smile or giggle can cover up pain, humiliation, and embarrassment. Some women (e.g., Japanese, Vietnamese) cover up their mouths when they smile or giggle. Upon hearing something sad, a Vietnamese person may smile. Similarly, an officer may need to communicate something that causes a loss of face to a person, resulting in the person smiling. This smile does not mean that the person is trying to be a "smart aleck"; it is simply a culturally conditioned response.

4. *Eye contact:* In many parts of the world, eye contact is avoided with authority figures. In parts of India, for example, a father would discipline his child by saying, "Don't look me in the eye when I'm speaking to you"; an American parent would say, "Look me in the eye when I'm speaking to you." To maintain direct eye contact with a police officer in some cultures would be disrespectful.

   Direct eye contact with some citizens can also be perceived as threatening to that citizen. Chad Borstein, a security officer in a large store in San Jose, California, offered the example of officers looking directly at Latino/Hispanic young people suspected of stealing items from the store. On a number of occasions, the officers' direct eye contact was met with a physical reaction (i.e., the young person attempting to punch the officer). Borstein explained that the Latino/Hispanic individual mistook the eye contact as confrontation and a challenge for a fight.

5. *Facial expressiveness:* People in law enforcement have to be able to "read faces" in certain situations to be able to assess situations correctly. The degree to which people show emotions on their faces depends, in large part, on their cultural background. Whereas Latin Americans, Mediterraneans, Arabs, Israelis, and African Americans tend to show emotions facially, other groups, such as many of the Asian cultural groups, tend to be less facially expressive and less emotive. An officer may thus incorrectly assume that a person is not being cooperative or would not make a good witness.

Exhibit 5.6 Nonverbal communication: key points for law enforcement.

1. Body language and nonverbal messages can override an officer's verbal content in high-stress and crisis situations. For example, the officer's statement that he or she is there to help may be contradicted by a body posture of discomfort and uncertainty in culturally unfamiliar households.

2. For people of different ethnic backgrounds, stress, confusion, and uncertainty can also communicate unintended messages. For example, an Asian may remain silent and look nervous and anxious at the scene of a crime. He or she may appear to many as being "uncooperative" when in fact this person may have every intention of helping the officer.

3. For people with limited English skills, the nonverbal aspects of communication become even more important. Correct gestures and nonverbal cues help the nonnative English speaker in understanding the verbal messages.

4. It is important for officers to learn about and avoid offensive gestures and cultural taboos. However, immigrants and international visitors are quick to forgive and to overlook gestures and actions made out of forgetfulness and ignorance. Officers should realize, too, that in time, newcomers usually learn many of the nonverbal mannerisms with which officers are more familiar. Nevertheless, learning about offensive gestures can help officers avoid interpersonal offenses.

Note: Each of the culture-specific chapters (Chapters 6 through 10) contains information about nonverbal characteristics of particular groups.

---

6. *Physical distance:* All people unconsciously keep a comfortable distance around them when communicating with others, resulting in invisible walls that keep people far enough away. Police officers are perhaps more aware than others of the distance they keep from people in order to remain safe. When someone violates this space, a person often feels threatened and backs away or, in the case of an officer, begins to think about protective measures. Although personality and context also determine interpersonal distance, cultural background comes into play. In general, Latin Americans and Middle Easterners are more comfortable at closer distances than are northern Europeans, Asians, or the majority of Americans. An officer should not necessarily feel threatened, for example, if approached by an Iranian or a Greek in a manner that feels uncomfortably close. While maintaining a safe distance, the officer should also consider cultural background.

For the law enforcement professional, nonverbal communication constitutes a major role in all aspects of peacekeeping and enforcement. For multicultural populations, it is even more important that the officer be aware of the variety of nuances and differences that may exist from one group to another. Clearly, studies show that up to 50 percent of interpersonal communication is understood because of the nonverbal "body language" aspects of the speaker. Moreover, in many cultures, as is true for many ethnic minorities in the United States, greater weight and belief are placed on the visual and nonverbal aspects of communication (Exhibits 5.6 and 5.7).

Officers must be authentic in their communication with people from various backgrounds. When learning about both verbal and nonverbal characteristics across cultures, officers do not need to feel that they must communicate differently each time they are in contact with someone of a different background. However,

---

Exhibit 5.7   Key questions concerning nonverbal communication across cultures.

- When is touch appropriate and inappropriate?
- What is the comfortable physical distance between people in interactions?
- What is considered proper eye contact? What do eye contact and lack of eye contact mean to the people involved?
- What cultural variety is there in facial expressions? For example, does nodding and smiling mean the same in all cultures? If someone appears to be expressionless, does that mean he or she is uncooperative?
- What are appropriate and inappropriate gestures for a particular cultural group?
- Is the person in transition from one culture to another and therefore lacking the knowledge of nonverbal communication with which the officer is familiar?

---

understanding that there are variations in communication style will help the officer interpret people's motives and attitudes more accurately and, overall, assess situations without a cultural bias.

MALE–FEMALE COMMUNICATION IN LAW ENFORCEMENT

With the changing workforce, including increasing numbers of women in traditionally male professions, many new challenges in the area of male–female communication are presenting themselves. Within law enforcement, in particular, a strong camaraderie characterizes the relationships mainly among the male members of a police force, although, in some cases, women are part of this camaraderie. Women allowed into what has been termed the "brotherhood" have generally had to "become one of the guys" to gain acceptance into a historically male-dominated profession. (The subject of women in law enforcement is also addressed in Chapter 2.)

Camaraderie results when a group is united because of a common goal or purpose; the glue cementing the camaraderie is the easy communication among its members. The extracurricular interests of the members of the group, the topics selected for conversation, and the jokes that people tell all contribute to the cohesion or tightness of police department members. In some departments, women find that they or other women are the object of jokes about sexual topics or that there are simply numerous references to sex. Because certain departments within cities have consisted mostly of men, they have not had to consider the inclusion of women on an equal basis and have not had to examine their own communication with each other.

Young women who are new to a department feel that they must tolerate certain behaviors to be accepted. A female sheriff participating in a 1992 Women's Peace Officer Association (WPOA) conference in Concord, California, said that on a daily basis she confronts vulgar language and sexual references in the jail where she works. Her list was long: "I am extremely bothered about the communication of the men where I work. Without mincing words, I'll tell you—at the county jail, officers are very degrading to women. . . . They sometimes make fun of rape victims, they are rude and lewd to female inmates, and they are constantly trying to get me to join into the 'fun.' A woman is referred to as a 'dyke,' a 'cunt,' a 'douche bag,' a 'whore,' a 'hooker,' a 'bitch,' and I'm sure I could come up with more. The guys don't call me those names, but they use them all the time referring to other women." This sheriff also noted that she did not experience the disrespectful verbal behavior in one-to-one situations with male deputies, only when they were in a group. She wondered out loud, "What happens to men when they group with each other? Why the change?"

It is not only the male grouping phenomenon that produces this type of rough, vulgar, and sexist language. One study of a large urban police department conducted for California Law Enforcement Command College documented inappropriate communications from patrol cars' two-way radios and computers. The language on the official system was often unprofessional—rough, vulgar, offensive, racist, and sexist. Obviously, both discipline and training were needed in this agency.

Certainly, not all men behave and talk in offensive ways, but the phenomenon is frequent enough that women in traditionally male work environments mention this issue repeatedly. Some women join in conversations that make them uneasy, but they do not let on that their working environment is uncomfortable and actually affecting their morale and productivity. Other women seem to be comfortable with the sexual comments of their male counterparts and may not object to the use of certain terms that other women find patronizing (e.g., "honey," "doll," "babe"). However, the percentage of women who fall into this category may very well be decreasing. Through sexual harassment policies, both women and men have learned that, for some, sexual innuendoes and patronizing terms can contribute to a hostile working environment.

In male-dominated institutions, vocations, and professions, women find that speaking out against this type of talk and joking creates discomfort for them and puts them in a double bind. A female police officer at a workshop on discrimination in the workplace said she felt that women's choices regarding communication with fellow male officers were limited. She explained that when a woman objects or speaks up, she risks earning a reputation or label that is hard to shed. If she remains quiet, she must tolerate a lot of verbal abuse and compromise her professionalism. This particular police officer decided to speak up in her own department, and, indeed, she earned a reputation as a troublemaker. In fact, she had no interest in going any further than complaining to her supervisor but nevertheless was accused of preparing for a lawsuit. She explained that a lawsuit was the farthest thing from her mind and that all she wanted was professional respect.

Some women who have objected to certain mannerisms of their male counterparts' communication say that when they come into a room or office, the men stop talking. The result is that the communication that normally functions to hold a group together is strained and tense. The ultimate result is that the workplace becomes segregated by gender. When shut out from a conversation, many women feel excluded and disempowered; in turn, many men feel resentful about having to modify their style of communication.

Exhibit 5.8 Inclusive workplace communication.

- Use terms that are inclusive rather than exclusive.

Examples: "police *officer*," "chair*person*," "*commendations*" (instead of the informal "atta boys")

- Avoid using terms or words that many women feel diminish their professional status.
Examples: "chick," "babe"

- Avoid using terms or words that devalue groups of women or stereotype them.

Example: Referring to women officers as "dykes"

- Avoid sexist jokes, even if you think they are not offensive. (*Someone is bound to be offended; the same applies to racist jokes.*)

- Avoid using terms that negatively spotlight or set women apart from men.

Examples: "For a woman cop, she did a good job" (implying that this is the exception rather than the rule) (also applies to references about other cultural groups: "He's Latino, but he works hard." "He's black, but he's really skilled.")

Women in traditionally male work environments such as police and fire departments find that they are sometimes put in a position of having to trade their professional identity for their personal one. A woman officer who proudly tells her sergeant about the arrest she made may be stunned when he, totally out of context, compliments the way she has been keeping in shape and tells her how good she looks in her uniform. This is not to say that compliments are never acceptable. But in this context, the woman is relating as a professional and desires reciprocal professional treatment. Men and women often ask, "Where do I draw the line? When does a comment become harassment?" In terms of the legal definition of sexual harassment, when comments are uninvited and unwelcome (as made clear by the harassee, whether male or female), the perpetrator of the comments must be reasonable enough to stop making them. It is not within the scope of this chapter to detail sexual harassment and all its legal implications; however, it should be noted that everyone has his or her own limits. (See Chapter 2 for additional information on this subject.) What is harassment to one may be appreciated by another. When communicating across genders, each party must be sensitive to what the other party considers acceptable or insulting (see Exhibit 5.8). It is also the responsibility of the individual who has been offended, whether male or female, to make it clear that certain types of remarks are offensive.

SUMMARY

In cross-cultural communication in law enforcement, officers' own filters and perceptions influence the assessment of each situation and the reactions the officers choose to exhibit. Each officer has unique "blind spots" and emotional "buttons" that may negatively affect the communication. To explore one's own skills in this regard, the reader is urged to undertake a self-evaluation by filling out the Communications Inventory (in Appendix D of this text).

Officers must keep in mind that rapport building is related to trust for many persons of different backgrounds. The more trust officers earn with members of ethnic communities, the more helpful these group members will be when officers need cooperation and information. To improve communication across cultures, it is essential that people in law enforcement understand the overall style of communication of different groups, including the special challenges facing men and women in the profession.

Finally, we would like to reiterate two points made earlier in this chapter regarding police officer communication:

- Officers have traditionally used styles of communication and language that at one time were considered acceptable, not only within the police agency but with citizens as well. Because of cultural diversity in the population and the accompanying need to respect all individuals, the unspoken rules about what is appropriate have changed dramatically.

- Through communication, officers have tremendous power to influence the behavior and responses of the citizens with whom they contact. This is true of all citizens, regardless of background. A lack of knowledge of the cross-cultural aspects of communication will diminish that power with people whose backgrounds differ from that of the officer.

DISCUSSION QUESTIONS AND ISSUES*

1. *The Origins of Stereotypes.* In this chapter, we argue that officers need to recognize how their early experiences in life and later adult experiences shape their perceptions and "filters" about people from groups different from their own. What do you remember learning about various ethnic and racial groups when you were young? Did you grow up in an environment of tolerance or did you hear statements such as "That's the way they are . . . " or "You've got to be careful with those people . . . " or "They are lazy [or dishonest, etc.]? Also discuss your experiences as an adult with different groups and how those experiences may be affecting your perceptions.

2. *Police Officer Interaction with Limited-English Speakers.* The following dialogue illustrates a typical interaction between a police officer and a nonnative speaker of English, in this case a Vietnamese man. Judging from the English that the Vietnamese is speaking, how would you rate the officer's use of English? Analyze this interaction by being specific as to how the officer can improve.

Situation: An officer pulls a car over, gets out of the car, and approaches the driver. The driver, who is Vietnamese, says, in poor English, "What happen? Why you stop me?"

Officer: I pulled you over because you ran a red light.

Citizen: (No response)

Officer: This is a traffic violation. (Receives no feedback). Do you understand?

Citizen: (Nodding) Yeh, I understand.

Officer: I'm going to have to issue you a traffic citation.

Citizen: (Staring at officer)

Officer: Where's your driver's license?

Citizen: License? Just a minute. (Leans over to open glove compartment, but finds nothing. He gets out of car and goes to trunk.)

*See Instructor's Manual accompanying this text for additional activities, role-play activities, questionnaires, and projects related to the content of this chapter.

Officer: (Irritated and slightly nervous) HEY! (In a loud voice) What's going on here? I asked to see your driver's license. Are you the registered owner of this car?

Citizen: Yeh. I go get my license.

Officer: (Speaking much louder) Wait a minute. Don't you understand? Are you not the owner of this car? Do you even have a license?

Citizen: Wait. (Finds license in trunk and produces it for officer)

Officer: OK. Would you mind getting back into the car now?

Citizen: (Does nothing) Yeah, I understand.

Officer: (Pointing to the front seat) Back into the car!

Citizen: (Does as told)

Note: The officer could make improvements in at least four areas: (1) choice of words, (2) manner of asking questions, (3) use of idioms (there are at least two or three that could be changed to simple English), and (4) tone and attitude.

3. ***Police Officers' "Hot Buttons."*** Discuss how citizens (e.g., suspects, victims, complainants) affect your reactions in communication. Specifically, what words and attitudes do they use that break down your attempts to be professional? What emotionally laden language "sets you off"?

4. ***Professional Communication with Citizens.*** After you have discussed what affects your communication negatively (question 3), role-play with fellow officers situations in which you respond professionally to abuses you hear. (Refer back to the section on verbal judo if you need suggestions.)

5. ***Racially Derogatory Remarks.*** In late 1992, Marge Schott, the 61-year-old owner of the Cincinnati Reds, was accused of making racist remarks over a period of years; she was accused of allegedly calling two Reds outfielders her "million dollar niggers" and admitted to keeping a swastika armband in her desk drawer. She also told the *New York Times* that Hitler was "good" but that he went too far. One of the issues related to her racially and culturally insensitive remarks was that her comments were made in front of other people, but that no one said anything to her or objected. Some felt that she should have been confronted.

   Answer the following questions as accurately as you can. If you were with friends in a social gathering and one friend made an off-color remark similar to those of Mrs. Schott, what would you do? If you think that you would say something, what would it be? If you know that you would not say anything, does this mean that you condone the behavior? Would things change if the remarks were made in the law enforcement agency or you overheard officers on the streets making such remarks? Explain your answer.

6. ***Cultural Observations.*** Make a list of your observations for each of the cultural groups with which you have had a substantial amount of contact. After you make your list, try to find someone from that culture with whom you can discuss your observations.

   (a) Display of emotions and expressions of feelings

   (b) Communication style: loud, soft, direct, indirect

   (c) Expressions of appreciation; conventions of courtesy (i.e., forms of politeness)

   (d) Need (or lack thereof) for privacy

   (e) Gestures, facial expressions, and body movements

   (f) Eye contact

   (g) Touching

   (h) Interpersonal space (conversational distance)

   (i) Taboo topics in conversation

   (j) Response to authority

7. ***Discomfort with Unfamiliar Groups.*** Try to recall a situation in which you found yourself in a culturally unfamiliar environment (e.g., responding to a call in an ethnically different

household or being the only minority person of your background among a group of people from another cultural or ethnic group). How much discomfort, if any, did you experience? If the situation was uncomfortable, did it affect your communication effectiveness or professionalism?

8. ***Accusations of Racially or Ethnically Motivated Stops.*** Have you encountered, "You stopped me because I'm [any ethnic group]?" If so, how did you handle the situation? How effectively do you think you responded?

REFERENCES

BERRY, ONDRA. (2000, December 8). Deputy Chief, Reno, Nevada, Police Department, personal communication.

BERRY-WILKINSON, ALISON. (1992, July 18). "Confronting Discrimination in the Workplace," paper presented at a meeting of the Women's Peace Officer Association (WPOA), Concord, Calif.

DEGENESTE, HENRY I., AND JOHN D. SULLIVAN. (1997, July). "Policing a Multicultural Community," *Fresh Perspectives: A Police Executive Research Forum Publication.* p. 7.

FERNANDEZ, DONYA. (2000, December 20). Language Rights attorney for the Language Rights Project, Employment Law Center/Legal Aid Society, San Francisco, Calif., personal communication.

HARRIS, PHILIP R. (1989). *High Performance Leadership.* Carmel, Ind.: Scott Foresman.

HARRIS, PHILIP R., AND ROBERT T. MORAN. (1991). *Managing Cultural Differences: High Performance Strategies for a New World of Business.* Houston, Texas: Gulf.

LEVINE, DEENA, AND MARA ADELMAN. (1992). *Beyond Language: Cross-Cultural Communication,* rev. ed., Englewood Cliffs, N.J.: Prentice-Hall.

MARTIN, DAN. (1992). Former police officer and Justice Administration chair, Diablo Valley College. Pleasant Hill, Calif.

MILLER, SCOTT. (1996, July). "Communicating Effectively with Non-English Speaking Customer Populations in Mid-Size California Cities by the Year 2005." California Command College Class XXII, Peace Officer Standards and Training, Sacramento, Calif.

OGAWA, BRIAN. (1990). *Color of Justice: Culturally Sensitive Treatment of Minority Crime Victims* (pp. 5–6.) Sacramento, Calif.: Office of Criminal Justice Planning.

THOMPSON, GEORGE. (1983). *Verbal Judo: Words as Force Option.* Staten Island, N.Y.: The Verbal Judo Institute, Inc.

THOMPSON, GEORGE. (1992, July 1). President of Verbal Judo Institute, Westcliffe, Colo. (1-800-448-1042, verbal judo @rmi.net), personal communication.

THOMPSON, GEORGE. (1997). *Verbal Judo: Redirecting Behavior with Words.* Staten Island, N.Y.: Verbal Judo Institute, Inc.

THOMPSON, GEORGE, AND JERRY B. JENKINS. (1983). *Verbal Judo: The Gentle Art of Persuasion,* Staten Island, N.Y.: Verbal Judo Institute, Inc.

WEAVER, GARY. (1992, September). "Law Enforcement in a Culturally Diverse Society," *FBI Law Enforcement Bulletin,* 4.

PART THREE

Cultural Specifics for Law Enforcement

6 LAW ENFORCEMENT CONTACT WITH ASIAN/PACIFIC AMERICANS
7 LAW ENFORCEMENT CONTACT WITH AFRICAN AMERICANS
8 LAW ENFORCEMENT CONTACT WITH LATINO/HISPANIC AMERICANS
9 LAW ENFORCEMENT CONTACT WITH ARAB AMERICANS AND OTHER MIDDLE
    EASTERN GROUPS
10 LAW ENFORCEMENT CONTACT WITH AMERICAN INDIANS

Part Three presents information on Asian/Pacific, African American, Latino/Hispanic, Middle Eastern, and American Indian cultural backgrounds with regard to the needs of law enforcement representatives. We selected these groups (as opposed to other groups not described in this book) for one or more of the following reasons: (1) the group is a relatively large ethnic or racial group in the United States, (2) the traditional culture of the group differs widely from that of mainstream American culture, or (3) typically or historically there have been problems between the particular group and law enforcement officials.

In these culture-specific chapters, general information is presented on the following areas: historical background, demographics, and diversity within the cultural group. Following the introductory information, we present specific details relevant to law enforcement in the following areas: communication styles (both verbal and nonverbal), group identification terms, offensive labels, stereotypes, and family structure. Each chapter ends with key concerns for officers related to the particular cultural group and a summary of recommendations for law enforcement officials.

Important note: In this section's presentation of specific cultural and racial groups, we would like to reference the section "The Overlap of Race and Ethnicity" in Chapter 1 (pages 8–9). This is to remind readers that individuals in our multicultural population do not always easily fall into neat categories of only one race or culture. There can be an overlap of race and ethnicity, as in the example of a black Latino. Our categorization of different groups is a convenient way of presenting information; we do not wish to imply that there can be no overlap among the group categories.

6

LAW ENFORCEMENT CONTACT WITH ASIAN/PACIFIC AMERICANS

OVERVIEW

This chapter provides specific ethnic and cultural information on Asian Americans and Pacific Islanders. The label *Asian Americans/Pacific Islanders* encompasses over 32 different ethnic and cultural groups. For ease of use, we will use the shortened version *Asian/Pacific Americans* to refer to members of these ethnic groupings. We first define this very diverse group and then present a historical overview, focusing on the relationship between law enforcement personnel and citizens. We present demographics and elements of diversity among Asian/Pacific Americans as well as issues related to ethnic and cultural identity. Aspects of the Asian/Pacific American family are discussed including myths and stereotypes, assimilation and acculturation processes, the extended family and community, gender roles, generational differences, and adolescent and youth issues. The section "Cultural Influences on Communication" discusses the subtle aspects of nonverbal and indirect communications peace officers often find troublesome. The closing section presents several key issues for law enforcement: underreporting of crimes, differential treatment, increasing Asian/Pacific American community police services, increasing the number of Asian/Pacific peace officers, and the rise in crimes within the Asian/Pacific community. Finally, we review recommendations for improved communication and relationships between law enforcement personnel and Asian/Pacific American communities.

COMMENTARY

For many Asian/Pacific American groups, especially those who have recently immigrated into the United States, the law enforcement system seems to be a mystery and not understandable. As such, Asian/Pacific Americans may find it difficult to cooperate and to participate fully with law enforcement officers.

> 'To the Vietnamese immigrant, our law enforcement system doesn't seem to serve his community well. In Vietnam, if you are arrested, then the work of the attorney is to prove that you are innocent. You remain locked up in jail until your innocence is proven. In the United States, a suspect who is arrested is released upon posting bail, usually within 24 hours. To the Vietnamese immigrant, it would seem that if you have the money, you can *buy* your way out of jail!' (Vietnamese community advocate's comments about a local merchant's reluctance to cooperate with the police)

Many law enforcement officers have difficulty understanding the diversity of customs, activities, behaviors, and values within the different Asian/Pacific American groups. They do not know where to go to get such cultural information without the fear of offending. Yet this cultural knowledge is vital to understanding and to effective peacekeeping in any Asian/Pacific American community.

> For some of the Asian groups, you just hear things that you're not sure about, but there's no one you can turn to to ask sometimes. For example, in our work, we hear that Sikhs always carry a sword or knife on their person (which they carry as a religious object), so is it insensitive to confiscate it? We also hear that if it is drawn, they must also draw blood—true or false? Moreover, what is the thing to do with their turbans? Would it be an insult to pat-search a turban while it's on the person's head? (Police officer's comments in a cultural awareness training session)

INTRODUCTION

For the past four decades, the Asian/Pacific American population has experienced the largest proportional increases of any ethnic minority population in the United States (over 100 percent growth for the decades from 1960 to 1990 and at least 55 percent growth for the decade from 1990 to 2000). The population growth can be attributed to (1) higher immigration from the Pacific Rim countries, (2) greater longevity, (3) higher birth rates, and (4) immigrants admitted for special skills and expertise for work in high-technology industries in the United States. Growth in major urban areas has been particularly striking, as is seen in San Francisco, New York City, Los Angeles, San Jose, San Diego, Boston, Denver, Chicago, Seattle, Houston, Philadelphia, and Phoenix. Growth in the population as a whole is most dramatically reflected in terms of increased numbers of Asian/Pacific Americans in politics, community leadership, business, education, and public service areas. Law enforcement contact with Asian/Pacific people has increased because of their greater presence in communities.

ASIAN/PACIFIC AMERICAN DEFINED

The term *Asian/Pacific Americans* is actually a contraction of two terms, *Asian Americans* and *Pacific Islander peoples*. Although used throughout this chapter, *Asian/Pacific*

Americans is, in fact, a convenient summary label for a very heterogeneous group. There certainly is not universal acceptance of this labeling convention, but for practical purposes it has been adopted frequently, with occasional variations (e.g., Asian and Pacific Americans, Asian Americans/Pacific Islanders, Asians and Pacific Islanders). It represents the self-designation preferred by many Asian and Pacific people in the United States, particularly in preference to the more dated (and, to some, offensive) term *Orientals*. The U.S. government and other governmental jurisdictions usually use "Asian Americans/Pacific Islanders" to refer to members within any of the 32 or more groups comprising this category.

At least 32 distinct ethnic and cultural groups might meaningfully be listed under this designation: (1) Bangladeshi, (2) Belauan (formerly Palauan), (3) Bhutanese, (4) Chamorro (Guamanian), (5) Chinese, (6) Fijian, (7) Hawaiian, (8) Hmong, (9) Indian (Asian, South Asian, or East Indian), (10) Indonesian, (11) Japanese, (12) Cambodian, (13) Korean, (14) Laotian, (15) Malaysian, (16) Marshallese (of the Marshall Islands, to include Majuro, Ebeye, and Kwajalein), (17) Micronesia (to include Kosrae, Ponape, Truk, and Yap), (18) Myanmarese (formerly Burmese), (19) Nepalese, (20) Okinawan, (21) Pakistani, (22) Pilipino (preferred spelling of Filipino), (23) Saipan Carolinian (or Carolinian, from the Commonwealth of the Northern Marianas), (24) Samoan, (25) Singaporian, (26) Sri Lankan (formerly Ceylonese), (27) Tahitian, (28) Taiwanese, (29) Tibetan, (30) Tongan, (31) Thai, and (32) Vietnamese. Although there are marked differences between the 32 groups listed, individuals within any of the 32 groups may also differ in a vast number of ways.

From the viewpoint of law enforcement, it is important to recognize some of the differences that may cut across or be common to all Asian/Pacific ethnic groups—for example, (1) area of residence in the United States, (2) comfort and competence with the English language, (3) generational status in the United States (first, second, third generation, and so forth), (4) degree of acculturation and assimilation, (5) education (number of years outside and inside the United States), (6) native and other languages spoken and/or written, (7) age (what is documented on paper and what may be the real age), (8) degree of identification with the home country and/or region of self or parents' origin, (9) family composition and extent of family dispersion in the United States and globally, (10) extent of identification with local, national, and global Asian/Pacific sociopolitical issues, (11) participation and degree to which the individual is embedded in the ethnic community network, (12) religious beliefs and cultural value orientation, (13) economic status and financial standing, (14) sensitivity to ethnic and cultural experiences and perceptions as an Asian/Pacific person in the United States, and (15) identification with issues, concerns, and problems shared by other ethnoracial groups (e.g., racial profiling and other discrimination issues voiced by African American, Latino/Hispanic Americans).

It should be noted that the definition itself of the Asian/Pacific group points to and embodies an ever-emerging ethnic mosaic of diverse constituencies. Groups are added and removed based on self-definition and needs for self-choice. In our definition, we have not added immigrants or refugees from the relatively recently formed Central Asian nations of Kazakhstan, Kyrgyzstan, Tajikistan, Turkmenistan, and Uzbekistan (all were republics of the Soviet Union before that country dissolved at the end of 1991) because of the self-choice issue. Clearly the pooling of separate Asian and Pacific Islander groups under the label of Asian/Pacific Americans emerged, in part, out of the necessity to have a larger collective whole when a larger numerical count may make a difference (especially in political and community areas). Merging these 32 ethnic groups into a collective entity allowed for sufficiently large numbers for meaningful representation in the community and other arenas.

Other Key Definitions

Since a large proportion of Asian/Pacific Americans whom law enforcement officers may encounter are born outside the United States, it is important to understand some of the key differences that relate to immigration status. One key difference is that found for Asian/Pacific Americans who are considered refugees and those who are considered immigrants at the time they enter the United States. Some of the between-group hostilities (within the Asian/Pacific community and among other ethnic minority communities) have been a result of not understanding what is implied by the refugee status in the United States.

Refugees are sponsored into the United States under the authority of the U.S. government. Although many ethnic groups have come in under the sponsorship of the federal government with refugee or emigre status, the largest numbers have been from Southeast Asia as a result of the past upheaval brought on by the Vietnam War. Refugees, since they are sponsored into the United States by the government, are expected to utilize public support services fully (welfare, English-as-a-second-language [ESL]) programs, educational tuition, job training programs, and case management, etc.). It is part of being a "good refugee" to participate fully, and oftentimes case managers are assigned refugee families to ensure that family members are fully utilizing all services provided. Such participation in public programs also creates dependency and learned helplessness that result from having others help or interfere with what many could have done for themselves.

Immigrants enter into the United States under the direct sponsorship of individuals' families. The federal government establishes that immigrants are allowed to enter the United States only if their families can completely support or establish work for the individual. In fact, one criterion for being able to attain permanent residence status (a "green card") is that the immigrant will not become a burden to the government, which means that participation in any publicly funded program may jeopardize that individual's chances for attaining permanent residence status. (Thus, immigrants try very hard to avoid getting involved in public or community programs and services.) In contrast to the refugee, being a "good immigrant" means avoiding any participation in public service programs.

TYPOLOGY OF ASIAN/PACIFIC AMERICANS

As we look at Asian/Pacific American individuals, families, and communities, we have developed a seven-part typology that will be useful in understanding and in summarizing some of the differences between individuals within this group (see Exhibit 6.1).

Exhibit 6.1 Typology of Asian/Pacific Americans.

Type I	Asian/Pacific recently arrived immigrant or refugee (less than five years in the United States, with major life experiences in Asia or the Pacific Islands)
Type II	Asian/Pacific immigrant and refugee (five or more years in the United States, with major life experiences in Asia or the Pacific Islands)
Type III	Asian/Pacific American (second generation; offspring of immigrant or refugee)
Type IV	Asian/Pacific Immigrant (major life experiences in the United States)
Type V	Asian/Pacific American (third or later generations in the United States)
Type VI	Asian/Pacific national (anticipates return to Asia or to the Pacific Islands, to include visitors and tourists)
Type VII	Asian/Pacific national (global workplace and residence)

Our typology suggests that as law enforcement and public safety organizations prepare and train their personnel to work with Asian/Pacific American communities, a focus on the key differences within each of the typological groups would be most effective. We will come back to this typology in a later section to discuss how the motivational components within each of the groupings can affect the way Asian/Pacific American persons may respond in law enforcement situations.

HISTORICAL INFORMATION

The first Asians to arrive in the United States in sizable numbers were the Chinese in the 1840s to work on the plantations in Hawaii. Then, in the 1850s, they immigrated to work in the gold mines in California and later on the transcontinental railroad. Of course, the native populations of the Pacific Island areas (e.g., Samoans, Hawaiians, Guamanians, Fijians) were there before the establishment of the 13 colonies of the United States. The Chinese were followed in the late 1800s and early 1900s by the Japanese and the Pilipinos (and in smaller numbers by the Koreans and South Asian Indians). Large numbers of Asian Indians (nearly 500,000) entered the United States as a result of congressional action in 1946 for "persons of races indigenous to India" to have the right of naturalization. Most immigrants in these earlier years were men, and most worked as laborers and at other domestic and menial jobs. Until the change of the immigration laws in 1965, the number of Asians and Pacific Islander peoples immigrating into the United States was severely restricted (families often had to wait over a decade or more before members of a family could be reunited). With the change in the immigration laws, large numbers of immigrants from the Pacific Rim came to the United States from Hong Kong, Taiwan, China, Japan, Korea, South Asia (e.g., India, Ceylon, Bangladesh), the Philippines, and Southeast Asia (e.g., Vietnam, Thailand, Singapore, Cambodia, Malaysia). After the Vietnam War, large numbers of Southeast Asian refugees were admitted in the late 1970s and early 1980s. The need for engineering and scientific expertise and skills by high-technology and Internet companies resulted in many Asian/Pacific immigrants (under special work visas) immigrating in the late 1990s and early 2000s.

Law Enforcement Interactions with Asian/Pacific Americans: Law Enforcement as Not User-Friendly

Asian/Pacific Americans have found the passage and enforcement of "anti-Asian" federal, state, and local laws to be more hostile and discriminatory than some of the racially motivated community incidents they have experienced. Early experiences of Asians and Pacific Islanders were centered on the majority population wanting to keep them out of the United States and putting tremendous barriers in the way of those who were already here. It was the role of law enforcement agencies and officers to be the vehicle to carry out these laws against Asian/Pacific American immigrants. From the beginning, the interactions of Asian/Pacific Americans with law enforcement officials were fraught with conflicts, difficulties, and mixed messages.

Anti-Asian Federal, State, and Local Laws

Almost all of our federal immigration laws were written such that their enforcement made Asian newcomers feel unwelcomed and unwanted. Following the large influx of Chinese in the 1850s to work in the gold mines and on the railroad, many Americans were resentful of the Chinese for their willingness to work long hours for low wages. With mounting public pressure, the Chinese Exclusion Act of 1882 banned the immigration of Chinese laborers for 10 years, and subsequent amendments extended this ban indefinitely. Because of this ban and because the Chinese population in the United States was primarily male, the Chinese population in the United States dropped from 105,465 in 1880 to 61,639 in 1920 (Takaki, 1989). Since the Chinese Exclusion Act only applied to Chinese, Japanese immigration started around 1870 to Hawaii, with larger numbers to the mainland in the 1890s to work as laborers and in domestic jobs on the farms on the West Coast. Similar to the Chinese, public pressure to restrict Japanese immigration ensued. In the case of the Japanese, the Japanese Government did not want a "loss of face" or of international prestige through having its people "banned" from immigrating to the United States. Rather, the "Gentleman's Agreement" was negotiated with President Theodore Roosevelt in 1907 which resulted in the Japanese Government voluntarily restricting the immigration of Japanese laborers to the United States. Family members of Japanese already in the United States, however, were allowed to enter. Under the Gentleman's Agreement, large numbers of "picture brides" began entering into the United States resulting in a large increase in Japanese American populations—25,000 in 1900 to 127,000 in 1940 (Daniels, 1988). Subsequent laws banned or prevented immigration from the Asiatic countries: The Immigration Act of 1917 banned immigration from all counties in the Pacific Rim except for the Philippines (a U.S. territory). The Immigration Act of 1924 restricted migration from all countries to two percent of the countries' national origin population living in the United States in 1890. This "two percent" restriction was not changed until 1965. Moreover, it was not until 1952 that most Asian immigrants were eligible to become naturalized citizens of the United States, and therefore, the right to vote (African Americans and American Indians were able to become citizens long before Asian/Pacific Americans were given the same rights).

While Pilipinos* have been immigrating to the United States since the early 1900s, large numbers of Pilipino laborers began entering in the 1920s because of the need for unskilled laborers (and because of the unavailability of Chinese and Japanese immigrants who were restricted entry by law). Similar to previous Asian groups, Pilipino immigration was soon to be limited to a quota of 50 immigrants per year with the passage of The Tydings-McDuffie Act of 1934. Moreover, Congressional resolutions in 1935 reflected clear anti-Pilipino sentiment by providing free, one-way passage for Pilipinos to return to the Philippines with the agreement that they not return to the United States.

Anti-Asian immigration laws were finally repealed starting with the removal of the Chinese Exclusion Act in 1943. Other laws were repealed to allow immigration of Asians and Pacific Islanders, but the process was slow. It was not until 1965 that amendments to the McCarran-Walter Act opened the way for Asian immigrants to enter in larger numbers (a fixed quota of 20,000 per country, as opposed to 2 percent of the country's national origin population living in the United States in 1890). The 1965 amendment also established the "fifth preference" category, which allowed highly skilled workers needed by the United States to enter this country. Because of the preference for highly skilled workers, a second major wave of immigrants from Hong Kong, Taiwan, India, Korea, the Philippines, Japan, Singapore, and other Asiatic countries entered in the mid-1960s. With the upheaval in Southeast Asia and the Vietnam War, the third major wave of close to 1 million refugees and immigrants arrived in the United States from these affected Southeast Asian countries starting in the mid-1970s and lasting to the early 1980s (Special Services for Groups, 1983). Most recently, the need for and opportunities in high-technology, engineering, and scientific skills and expertise in the computer, software, and Internet industries have led to an additional influx of immigrants from India, Pakistan, Singapore, Korea, China (including Hong Kong), Taiwan, and other Asiatic countries in the mid-1990s and early 2000s.

Although many immigrant groups (e.g., Italians, Jews, Poles) have been the target of discrimination, bigotry, and prejudice, Asian/Pacific Americans, like African Americans, have experienced extensive legal discrimination, hindering their ability to participate fully as Americans. This discrimination has gravely affected their well-being and quality of life. Some states had laws that prohibited intermarriage between Asians and whites. State and local laws imposed restrictive conditions and taxes specifically on Asian businesses and individuals. State courts were equally biased; for example, in the case of *People v. Hall* heard in the California Supreme Court in 1854, Hall, a white defendant, had been convicted of murdering a Chinese man on the basis of testimony provided by one white and three Chinese witnesses. The California Supreme Court threw out Hall's conviction on the basis that state law prohibited blacks, mulattos, or Indians from testifying in favor of or against whites in court. The court's decision read:

> Indian as commonly used refers only to the North American Indian, yet in the days of Columbus all shores washed by Chinese waters were called the Indies. In the second

---

Preferred spelling for Filipinos.

place the word "white" necessarily excludes all other races than Caucasian; and in the third place, even if this were not so, I would decide against the testimony of Chinese on the grounds of public policy. (California Supreme Court: *People v. Hall*) People v. George W. Hall(California Supreme Court, October, 1854)

This section of anti–Asian/Pacific American laws and sentiments cannot close without noting that Japanese Americans are the only immigrant group of Americans in the history of the American people who have been routed out of their homes and interned without due process. President Roosevelt's Executive Order 9066 resulted in the evacuation and incarceration of 100,000 Japanese Americans in 1942. For Asian/Pacific Americans, the internment of Japanese Americans represents how quickly anti-Asian sentiments can result in incarceration and punishment by law, even if no one was convicted of a crime. Moreover, stereotypes and bigotry against Asian/Pacific Americans are not only issues of the past, as is illustrated in the following:

> Bruce Yamashita, a Japanese American born in Hawaii, had decided to join the U.S. Marine Corp after earning his law degree from Georgetown University. Prior to entering law school, Yamashita had many accomplishments including serving as his high school's student body president and as an elected delegate to the Hawaii State Constitution Convention. Bruce Yamashita was admitted to the Marine Corp's Officer Candidate School (OCS), and throughout his 10 weeks of training, was the target of steady, vicious, and stereotypic ethnic and racial harassment with remarks like "kamikaze man" and "go back to your country." Upon his completion of the 10-week OCS and passing all of his written examinations, Bruce Yamashita was discharged for "leadership failure" and was not allowed to serve in the United States Marine Corp. (Schmitt, 1992) (1992, November 20) Marines Find Racial Disparity in Officer Programs. (The New York Times, p. A8)

DEMOGRAPHICS: DIVERSITY AMONG ASIAN/PACIFIC AMERICANS

As we noted in the section defining Asian/Pacific Americans, this is an extremely heterogeneous population comprised of many different ethnic and cultural groups, generational differences within the United States, educational and socioeconomic diversity, and many other background and life experience differences. Asian/Pacific Americans currently number about 11.3 million and represent approximately 3.7 percent of the U.S. population. As stated, the Asian/Pacific American population more than doubled with each census from 1970 to 1990 (1.5 million in 1970, 3.5 million in 1980, and 7.3 million in 1990) and increased by 55 percent from 1990 to 2000 (11.3 million in 2000). While greater longevity and higher birth rates contribute to this population increase, the major contributor to the growth of the Asian/Pacific American population is immigration from the Pacific Rim countries. Since the 1970s, Asian/Pacific American immigration has made up over 40 percent of all immigration to the United States (U.S. Bureau of the Census, 1990). As is evident in Exhibit 6.2, Chinese are the largest group, with 22.6 percent of the total Asian/Pacific American population. Pilipinos are close behind, with 19.3 percent of this population; in the next decade, Pilipinos will be the largest Asian/Pacific American

Exhibit 6.2 1990 Asian/Pacific American population by groups.*

ASIAN/PACIFIC AMERICAN GROUPS	PERCENTAGE OF TOTAL
Chinese	22.6
Pilipino	19.3
Japanese	11.6
Asian Indian	11.2
Korean	11.0
Vietnamese	8.4
Laotian	2.0
Thai	1.3
Cambodian	2.0
Hmong	1.2
Pakistani	—
Indonesian	—
All other groups	—
All Asian/Pacific Americans	100.0

Source: U.S. Census Bureau, Racial Statistics Division. U.S. Bureau of The Census (1990). We the Asian and Pacific Island Americans current population reports, Washington, D.C. U.S. Gov't Printing Office, Table 7, p. 11
*Information available as book goes into press.

group in the United States. Japanese, Asian Indians, and Koreans each comprise approximately 11 percent of the Asian/Pacific American population. Vietnamese Americans constitute 8.4 percent, and all other Asian/Pacific American groups account for 6.5 percent of this population.

For law enforcement officers, the key Asian/Pacific American groups to understand would be the six largest groups: Chinese, Pilipino, Japanese, Asian Indian, Korean, and Vietnamese (considering, in addition, local community trends and unique qualities of the community's populations). Knowledge of the growing trends among this Asian/Pacific American population would also be important for officer recruitment and other human resource considerations. Current Asian/Pacific Americans involved in professional law enforcement careers are largely Japanese, Chinese, and Korean Americans. To plan for the changing Asian/Pacific American population base, it is critical to recruit and develop officers from the Pilipino, Vietnamese, and Asian Indian communities.

As noted in Exhibit 6.3, the vast majority of Asian/Pacific Americans are not born in the United States. Most of the Japanese, Pilipinos, Cambodians, and Indonesians reside in the western states. Chinese, Koreans, Vietnamese, Laotians, and Thais are fairly widely distributed in the large urban areas of the United States. Most of the Asian Indians and Pakistanis live in the eastern states. Minnesota and Fresno, California, have the largest Hmong populations in the country. Proficiency in the English language varies within groups: groups that have immigrated most recently (Southeast Asians) have the largest percentage of those not able to speak English well.

Law enforcement and peace officers, depending on their jurisdictions, can use Exhibit 6.3 to determine what additional languages and skills training might be appropriate in their work with Asian/Pacific American communities.

Exhibit 6.3   1990 Asian/Pacific American population by three key demographic characteristics.*

ASIAN/PACIFIC AMERICAN GROUP	PERCENTAGE NOT U.S.-BORN	PERCENTAGE WHO DO NOT SPEAK ENGLISH WELL	PERCENTAGE IN THE WEST
Chinese	63.3	23.0	52.7
Pilipino	64.7	6.0	68.8
Japanese	28.4	9.0	80.3
Asian Indian	70.4	5.0	19.2
Korean	81.9	24.0	42.9
Vietnamese	90.5	38.0	46.2
Laotian	93.7	69.0	45.7
Thai	82.1	12.0	43.0
Cambodian	93.9	59.0	55.6
Hmong	90.5	63.0	37.4
Pakistani	85.1	10.0	23.5
Indonesian	83.4	6.0	56.2
All Asian/Pacific Americans	62.1	15.0	56.4

Source: U.S. Commission on Civil Rights, 1992.
*Information available as book goes into press.

Exhibit 6.4   Key motivating perspectives in understanding Asian/Pacific American groups.

Surviving	Asian/Pacific most recent immigrant or refugee (less than five years in the United States with major life (experiences in Asia or the Pacific Islands)
Preserving	Asian/Pacific immigrant or refugee (five or more years in the United States with major life experiences in Asia or the Pacific Islands)
Adjusting	Asian/Pacific American (second generation; offspring of immigrant or refugee)
Changing	Asian/Pacific immigrant (major life experiences in the United States)
Choosing	Asian/Pacific American (third or later generations in the United States)
Maintaining	Asian/Pacific national (anticipates return to Asia or to the Pacific Islands)
Expanding	Asian/Pacific national (global workplace and residence)

ASIAN/PACIFIC AMERICANS' KEY MOTIVATING PERSPECTIVES

Earlier in this chapter, we provided a typology for viewing Asian/Pacific Americans. We provide in Exhibit 6.4 the same typology and have appended to it the key motivating perspectives for members in each group. By understanding some of these key motivating perspectives, law enforcement officers might be better able to understand the behaviors exhibited by citizens from these groupings.

For example, the key to understanding the behavior of the most recent immigrants and refugee group (Asian/Pacific Refugee Type I) is to recall that members are in a survival mode (see Exhibit 6.4). Many members from this category may remember that law enforcement and police officers in their country of origin were corrupt, aligned with a repressive government and the military, and subjected to bribes by those who were more affluent. All activities tend to be guided by this perspective to survive, to get through. This perspective also makes sense in terms of the traumatic ordeals faced by refugees (as revealed by their past memories) in their journeys to the United States. Encounters with law enforcement personnel by these people usually involve saying and doing anything to discontinue the contact because of possible fears of personal harm (e.g., not speaking English, not having any identification, "Yes, I will cooperate!").

> Mr. Pok and Mr. Nguyen came in as part of the "boat people" in 1979. Although both of them are in their early thirties, because of their size and informal dress, they look much younger. Both worked as building maintenance personnel for one of the high-technology companies on the West Coast. One evening as they were driving home following their work at approximately 1:30 A.M., Mr. Pok and Mr. Nguyen found themselves pulled over by two police cars. Two officers approached their car and requested that they step outside. The officers were responding to a call about two young Asian males, driving a light-colored car, involved in an armed robbery of a nearby convenience store. Mr. Pok's and Mr. Nguyen's car was light-colored. When the officers asked both individuals to take a kneeling position while the officers conducted a search and verified DMV information, Mr. Pok fell to the ground and pleaded at the feet of one of the officers, "Please don't kill me!" It was Mr. Nguyen who finally explained that the kneeling position is the "execution position," and Mr. Pok saw many individuals executed that way in his escape from Cambodia. (Example cited by community organizer) Center for Southeast Asian Refugees Resettlement (CSEARR), San Francisco, California.

With regard to Asian/Pacific immigrants (Type II), understanding their behaviors should focus on preserving their home culture as the motivating perspective. Since the majority of their life experiences occurred in Asia or the Pacific Islands, members are trying to preserve much of the values and traditions of their culture as it was alive and operating. Many Asian businesspersons and investors in the United States are included in this category. Much intergenerational conflict between grandparents or parents and youths occurs within this group. Members are inclined to keep to their ethnic communities (e.g., Little Saigons, Chinatowns, Koreatowns, Japantowns, Manilatowns) and have as little to do with law enforcement as possible. Many remember that the police have not served them well in the past (e.g., immigration laws, Japanese internment).

> Police officers in a West Coast city were confused and wondered if a local "private bar" frequented by Japanese and Korean businessmen was a front for prostitution. They noticed that the bar had many Asian female "hostesses" and that companies paid hundreds of dollars per bottle for the liquor served to guests (when the off-the-shelf price of these liquors was one-fifth of what the bar charged). Only after much exchange between members of the local Asian/Pacific American community and the community relations police officers was the understanding made that these "private bars" allowed many immigrant businesspersons to feel at home in this culture. Among their own peers and in keeping with their own customs and cultural practices, they were comfortable, and no prostitution nor any other illegal activities were involved. (Police officer's anecdote in a cultural awareness training session)

Asian/Pacific Americans (second generation, Type III) tend to be who we picture when we hear the term *Asian American*. Those of the second generation work very hard at being assimilated into the mainstream, adjusting and changing to be a part of mainstream America. Oftentimes, the expectations of second-generation parents are high; parents will sacrifice so that their offsprings will "make it" in their lifetime. Members may interact primarily with non-Asians and take on many of the values and norms of the mainstream society. This group may be considered "marginal" by some in that, try as each person may to become like the mainstream ("become white"), others may still consider them Asian. Many from this group try to minimize their contact with law enforcement personnel and agencies primarily because of the immigration and other experiences relayed to them by their parents' generation. Individuals of the second generation were born in the United States before the mid-1960s and may have had relatives (or parents) who entered the United States by using false papers. Fears of disclosure of such illegal entries have prevented many Asian/Pacific Americans from cooperating with peace officers and with other human and social service agencies and programs.

The Asian/Pacific immigrant (Type IV), whose major life experience is in the United States, focuses much of the member's energies on changes (through assimilation or acculturation) that have to be made to succeed. Although these individuals have tended to continue to value the cultural and ethnic elements of their former homeland, most know that changes are necessary. Members of this group reflect the socioeconomic standings of the different waves in which each entered into the United States. For example, individuals who entered as part of the first wave of laborers and domestic workers (primarily Chinese and Japanese, with some Pilipinos, Koreans, and Asian Indians) represent one grouping. Others entered more as part of the second wave of immigration as Foreign students and/or under the "fifth preference" as professional skilled workers. Asian/Pacific immigrants (Type IV) who are designated as entering the United States under "fifth preference" are those who checked the fifth category on the Immigration and Nationalization Service form indicating that the reason for immigration into the United States was that the person has a professional skill in short supply in the United States and that it would be in the best interest of the United States to allow that person to enter. This group consists of educated, professional individuals (e.g., the largest numbers of foreign-trained medical doctors an psychiatrists in the United States are from India, the Philippines, and Korea [President's Commission on Mental Health, 1978]). Since the fall of Saigon in 1975 and the beginning of the immigration of Southeast Asians into the United States, this third wave has included over 1 million Asian/Pacific immigrants who suffered great trauma in their escape; many are young adults today. For members of this group, reactions to law enforcement officials vary depending on their wave of immigration and socioeconomic experiences. For law enforcement officers, it is critical to understand the differences among the immigrant groups (i.e., do not confuse the professional Asian/Pacific immigrant with one of the other groups).

The Asian/Pacific American (third or later generation, Type V) category includes individuals who are more able to choose which aspects of the old culture to keep and of the new culture to accept. The focus is on choosing activities, values, norms, and lifestyles that blend the best of Asian/Pacific and American cultures. The importance of being bicultural is a unique aspect of this group. Many may no longer have as much skill with their native language and may rely on English as their primary or only language (thus an individual can be bicultural and not bilingual). Contact by members of this group with law enforcement personnel may not be any different than contact with other Americans.

For the last two categories, Asian/Pacific nationals, we make a key distinction between those who plan to return to their own country following a work assignment in the United States (Type VI) and those whose work is truly global, in that individuals may have several residences in different parts of the world (Type VII). Those in the former category (Type VI, on a U.S. work assignment that may last five to seven years) are working to maintain their home-base cultural orientation and experiences, knowing that when the work assignment is over, they will go back to their home country again. Because they mean to maintain the native culture, many individuals of this group may be inadequately prepared to understand many of the laws and practices of the United States. For members of this group, being able to stay in the United States to complete their assignments is of key importance. Oftentimes, individuals may not be aware of the differences between "minor" violations (e.g., minor traffic violations, small claims) and "major" violations and crimes. Let's look at the following example:

> Mr. Sato is a manager assigned to oversee a technical department in a joint United States–Japan automobile plant in the Midwest. One evening, while driving home from a late night at the plant, Mr. Sato did not see a stop sign and went right through it on a nonbusy intersection. A police officer in a patrol car saw the violation and pulled Mr. Sato over. The interaction puzzled the police officer, since Mr. Sato seemed very cooperative but kept asking the officer "to forgive him and to please let him go!" After much discussion and explanation, it was discovered that Mr. Sato thought that the officer would have to confiscate his passport because of the stop-sign violation (something that is done in many Asiatic countries) and that he might be "kicked out" of the country and, thus, be unable to complete his work assignment. On clearing up this misconception, Mr. Sato accepted the traffic citation "with appreciation."

For the second group of Asian/Pacific nationals (Type VII), the key focus on these individuals is their ability to "expand" their actions and behaviors effectively into different global environments. These individuals see themselves as being able to adapt in a variety of global environments; many may speak three or more languages (including English). Individuals within this group pride themselves in knowing about the different laws, norms, values, and practices of the countries they encounter. Law enforcement personnel would find this group equally able to understand and to follow the laws and practices of a given community as well.

LABELS AND TERMS

As we noted earlier, the term *Asian/Pacific Americans* is a convenient summarizing label used to refer to a heterogeneous group of people. The key to understanding which terms to use is based on the principle of self-designation and self-preference. Asian and Pacific Islander people are sensitive about the issue because up until the 1960 census the population was relegated to the "Other" category. With the ethnic pride movement and ethnic minority studies movement in the late 1960s, people of Asian and Pacific Islands descent began to designate self-preferred terms for group reference. The terms were chosen over the previous term *Oriental,* which many Asian/Pacific Americans consider to be offensive. *Oriental* is considered offensive because it symbolizes to many the past references, injustices, and stereotypes of Asian and Pacific people. It was also a term designated by the West (i.e., the Occident, the Western Hemisphere) for Asian people and reminds many Asian/Pacific Americans about the colonial mentality of foreign policies and its effects on the Pacific Rim countries.

In federal and other governmental designations (e.g., the census), the label used is "Asian American/Pacific Islanders." Although very few Asian/Pacific Americans refer to themselves as such, the governmental designation is used in laws and regulations and in most reports and publications. For individuals within any of the groups, often the more specific names for the groups are preferred (e.g., Chinese, Japanese, Vietnamese, Pakistani, Hawaiian). Some individuals may prefer that the term *American* be part of their designation (e.g., Korean American, Pilipino American). For law enforcement officers, the best term to refer to an individual is the term he or she prefers to be called. It is perfectly acceptable to ask an individual what ethnic or cultural group(s) he or she identifies with and what he or she prefers to be called.

The use of slurs such as "Jap," "Chink," "Gook," "Chinaman," "Flip," and other derogatory ethnic slang terms is never acceptable in crime fighting and peacekeeping, no matter how provoked an officer may be. Other stereotypic terms, including "Chinese fire drill," "DWO (*Driving While Oriental*)," "Fu Man Chu mustache," "Kamikaze kid," "yellow cur," "yellow peril," "Bruce Lee Kung Fu type," "slant-eyed," "Vietnamese bar girl," and "dragon lady" do not convey the kinds of professionalism and respect for community diversity important to law enforcement and peacekeeping and need to be avoided in law enforcement work. Officers hearing these words used in their own departments (or with peers or citizens) should provide immediate helpful feedback about such terms to those who use them. Officers who may out of habit routinely use these terms may find themselves (or their superiors) in the embarrassing situation (on the 6:00 o'clock news) of explaining to offended citizens and communities why the term was used and that they had intended no prejudice.

MYTHS AND STEREOTYPES

Knowledge of and sensitivity to Asian/Pacific Americans' concerns, diversity, historical background, and life experiences will facilitate the crime-fighting and peacekeeping mission of peace officers. It is important to have an understanding about some of the myths, environmental messages, and stereotypes of Asian/Pacific Americans that contribute to the prejudice, discrimination, and bias they encounter. Many Americans do not have much experience with the diversity of Asian/Pacific American groups and learn about these groups only through stereotypes, often perpetuated by movies and the media. Stereotypic views of Asian/Pacific Americans reduce this group to simplistic, one-dimensional characters whom many people lump into one stereotypic group. Oftentimes, the complexities of the diverse Asian/Pacific American groups in terms of language, history, customs, cultures, religions, and life experiences become confusing and threatening, and it is easier to deal with stereotypes of these groups. Nonetheless, it is important for law enforcement officers to be aware of the different stereotypes of Asian/Pacific Americans, because the key to effectiveness with any ethnic or racial group is not complete elimination of myths and stereotypes about these groups but rather awareness of these stereotypes and management of our behaviors when the stereotypes are not true of the person with whom we are dealing.

Some of the stereotypes that have affected Asian/Pacific Americans in law enforcement include the following:

1. *Viewing Asian/Pacific Americans as "all alike."* That is, because there are many similarities in names, physical features, and behaviors, many law enforcement officers may make comments about their inability to tell people apart or to deal with them in stereotypic group fashion (e.g., they are *all* "inscrutable," involved in gangs, etc.). Cultural awareness training and sensitivity will allow the officer the skills and knowledge to avoid a mistake like the following:

In Florida, Mr. Nguyen Ngoc Tieu, a Vietnamese defendant, was charged with murder and was awaiting trial at the county jail. At the time of the trial, Mr. Nguyen Hen Van, also of Vietnamese descent, was in jail charged with theft and was mistakenly transported to stand trial for murder. During the two days of the trial, no one had noticed the difference, even though the defendant had continuously protested that he was the wrong person. Two testifying witnesses in the murder trial even identified the mistaken defendant as the murderer, and even the defense attorney (who previously had interviewed the alleged murderer two weeks ago) did not recognize that the wrong person was on trial. It was finally through the recognition of someone viewing the trial in the courtroom that called the court's attention to the fact that the wrong Mr. Nguyen was on trial and that a mistrial was declared. (*Seattle Times,* 1985)

2. *Viewing Asian/Pacific Americans as successful, "model minorities" or worst yet, as a "super minority."* Some hold the stereotype that Asian/Pacific Americans are "all" successful, and this stereotype is further reinforced by the media (Ramirez, 1986). Such stereotypes have resulted in intergroup hostilities and hate crimes directed toward Asian/Pacific Americans and have served to mask true differences and diversity among the various Asian and Pacific Islander groups. Clearly no groups of people are "all successful" or "all criminals." Nonetheless, the "success" and the "model minority" stereotypes have affected Asian/Pacific Americans negatively. For example, because of their implied success, law enforcement organizations may not spend the time to recruit Asian/Pacific American individuals for law enforcement careers (assuming that they are more interested in other areas such as education and business pursuits). This stereotype also hides the existence of real discrimination for those who are successful, as seen in glass ceilings in promotional and developmental opportunities, for example. The success stereotype has resulted in violence and crimes against Asian/Pacific persons:

The murder of Vincent Chin, and the subsequent inability of the court system to bring the murderers to justice, is now a well-known case among Asian/Pacific American communities. The perpetrators in this case, Ronald Ebens and Michael Nitz, were two white automobile factory workers who blamed Vincent Chin (a Chinese American) for the success of the *Japanese* automobile industry that was, in turn, blamed for taking away

American jobs in the automobile factory. (Takaki, 1989b) Takaki, 1989b. Takaki R. (1989b). "Who Killed Vincent Chin," in G. Yun (ed.) A Look Beyond the Model Minority Image: Critical Issues in Asian America, p. 23–29, New York: Minority Rights Group

3. *Perceiving Asian/Pacific Americans as "foreigners" and not a part of the diversity mosaic of America.* It is not unusual for Asian/Pacific Americans to be asked by a stranger, "What country are you from?" or "How long have you been in the United States?" The implication conveyed by these questions is that the Asian/Pacific American is a foreigner and therefore could not possibly be an American. This perception of Asian/Pacific Americans as foreigners has resulted in consequences such as the internment of Japanese Americans in the United States during World War II (while, at the same time, the most decorated World War II unit [fighting in Europe] was the U.S. Army 442nd Division, consisting entirely of Asian/Pacific Americans, the majority of whom were Japanese Americans). Stereotypes of Asian/Pacific Americans as being foreign have resulted in serious consequences to Asian/Pacific Americans:

Hate-motivated killings have claimed eight Asian American lives in the past two years. In the latest incident, three Asian Americans, a Jewish American and an African American were killed in Pittsburgh on April 28. These hate-motivated killings have had a devastating effect on a broad cross-section of Asian Americans across the U.S., in part because the ethnic backgrounds of the victims have been so diverse, including South Asian, Filipino, Japanese, Korean, Vietnamese and Chinese. This horrible loss of life was for no other apparent reason than the color of the victims' skin and often their perceived immigrant status. It is an unprecedented number of hate killings of Asians since monitoring of such incidents began in the 1980s by the National Asian Pacific American Legal Consortium.

Further, the government's concerted campaign against Los Alamos National Laboratory scientist Wen Ho Lee has especially stirred the Chinese American community. While his guilt or innocence is certainly open to inquiry, community leaders are united in the view that Lee has not received due process, may not receive a fair trial and that his incarceration in solitary confinement and without bail is an abuse of human rights.

Asian Americans have long borne the stereotype of the perpetual foreigner—the unwelcome immigrant or the disloyal or distrusted foreign agent. Japanese Americans bore the brunt of this during World War II as 120,000 were interned. Filipino World War II veterans have never received proper recognition and benefits for fighting bravely under U.S. command. When the 1996 campaign finance scandal implicated a handful of Asian Americans, thousands were investigated or stigmatized without cause. The recent hate crime wave and treatment of scientists are reminders of this ugly past. (Kwoh, 2000)

From a law enforcement perspective, many hate crimes against Asian/Pacific Americans are related to the stereotype of the group as "foreigners" and not as "Americans."

4. *Misunderstanding Asian/Pacific cultural differences and practices and viewing differences stereotypically as a threat to other Americans.* The more than 32 Asian/Pacific American groups encompass great differences in life experiences, languages, backgrounds, and cultures. It is easy to make mistakes and draw incorrect conclusions because of such cultural differences. Certainly, when one lacks information about any group, it is natural to draw conclusions based upon our own filtering system, stereotypes, and assumptions. Most of the time, these incorrect assumptions and

stereotypes are corrected by favorable contact and actual interpersonal relationships with Asian/Pacific American people. From a law enforcement perspective, the thrust of community policing, as well as cultural awareness training is to provide the opportunities to modify stereotypes and to provide opportunities to learn about ethnic communities. Law enforcement agencies, however, have to intervene in situations in which individuals and/or groups view Asian/Pacific American cultural differences as perceived "threats" to themselves: On January 17, 1989, Patrick Edward Purdy entered the school yard at Cleveland Elementary School in Stockton, California firing an AK47 assault rifle. In the ensuing few minutes of fire, Purdy had killed five Southeast Asian children and wounded 30 other children. He then turned the rifle on himself and killed himself. More than 60% of the children at this school were Southeast Asians. The California Attorney General's Report noted that, "It appears highly probable that Purdy deliberately chose Cleveland Elementary School as the location for his murderous assault in substantial part because it was heavily populated by Southeast Asian children. His frequent resentful comments about Southeast Asians indicated a particular animosity against them." (Mathews & Lait, 1989)

The misunderstanding of cultural differences that leads to stereotypic conclusions about Asian/Pacific Americans' behaviors has resulted in law enforcement involvement between Asian/Pacific American communities and other ethnic and racial minority groups, including (1) the Korean American and African American conflicts in the Los Angeles riots following the Rodney King verdict, (2) disputes among Vietnamese and Hispanic fishermen in Florida, and (3) the Flatbush boycott incident described in the following:

> While there are many conflicting stories to this incident, it is clear that aspects of cultural stereotyping and misunderstanding of cultural differences led to a more than a year conflict between Korean Americans and Blacks in Flatbush, Brooklyn, New York with much involvement by law enforcement, city, state Federal, and community parties. Specifically, on January 18, 1990, Ghislaine Felissaint, a Haitian American resident of Flatbush was shopping for a few small items at the Red Apple store, owned by Korean Americans. While the details are not clear about the ensuing altercation at the cash register, both the Black community and the Asian/Pacific American community began to be involved in a year long conflict which eventually resulted in the closing of two Korean American stores in the area. One of the reasons mentioned for the inability of the police to help solve this conflict was the lack of any police officers with the ability to speak Creole, French or Korean, at the time of the incident, to interview witnesses. (Kandel, 1991)

THE ASIAN/PACIFIC AMERICAN FAMILY

Obviously, with over 32 different cultural groups under the label of Asian/Pacific Americans, we find great differences in how families operate within the various subgroups. We would like to share some common characteristics to describe Asian/Pacific American families that might be of value in crime fighting and community peacekeeping. Asian/Pacific American families generally exhibit very strong ties among extended family members. It is not unusual for three to four generations of the same family to live under one roof. Moreover, the extended family can even have an ongoing relationship network that spans great geographic distance. For example, family members (all of whom consider themselves as one family) can be engaged in extensive communications and activities with members in the same family in the United States, Canada, Hong Kong, and Vietnam, all simultaneously. It is not uncommon for an officer to come into contact with members of the extended Asian/Pacific American family in the course of servicing these communities. One key to the success of law enforcement officers in working with an extended family network is the knowledge of how best to contact an Asian/Pacific American family and which family member to speak to for information, help, and referral.

Culture Shock and the Asian/Pacific American Family

Because the traditional cultures of Asia and the Pacific Islands are so very different from that of the United States, many Asian/Pacific American families (whether refugees, immigrants, businesspersons, students, or tourists) experience some degree of culture shock when they enter and reside in the United States. Culture shock results not only from differences in values and traditions but also from differences in urbanization, industrialization, and modernization from technology that may be different from that in their homeland. Peace officers need to be aware that Asian/Pacific Americans may cope with their culture shock by becoming "clannish" (e.g., Chinatowns, Koreatowns). Other survival mechanisms include avoiding contact and interaction with those who are different (including police officers).

The Role of the Man and the Woman in an Asian/Pacific American Family

In most Asian/Pacific American families, relationship and communication patterns tend to be quite hierarchical, with the father as the identified head of the household. Although many decisions and activities may appear to be determined by the father, other individuals may come into the picture. Generally, if there are grandparents in the household, the father would still act as the spokesperson for the family, but he would consult the grandparents, wife, and others regarding any major decision. As such, it may be important in any kind of law enforcement contact that requires a decision and/or choice to allow the parties time to discuss issues in, as much as feasible, a "private" manner. Self-control and keeping things within the family are key values for Asian/Pacific Americans. Officers thus may find that there is more control in a situation by allowing the Asian/Pacific American to come to the same conclusion and to exercise his or her own self-choice (which may be the same as what the officer would want the parties to do anyway). For example, the officer can explain an arrest situation to the father of a family member, and instead of saying directly to the family member to be arrested that he or she has to leave with the officer, the officer can allow the father to suggest to the family member that he or she leave with the officer. What may appear to be a minor consideration in this case can result in a higher degree of persuasion, control, and cooperation by all parties concerned. The importance of self-control for Asian/Pacific Americans is illustrated by the differences used in the late 1960s and early 1970s to stop the "skyjacking" of airlines:

> Americans and Western countries had used more "external" control methods to stop skyjackers. That is, external approaches including using metal detectors, scanning luggage, and psychological profiles by gate agents were used by an "external" party to

prevent a potential skyjacker from taking an airplane. Francis Hsu, a Chinese American anthropologist, noted that in Japan, use was made of more "internal," self-control approaches. For example, at the entry gate to the airplane was posted a large sign that read, "If you try to steal this airplane, you may *disgrace* your family!" This self-control approach was aimed at having the Asian person think about his or her own behavior and stop a negative behavior before it had to be stopped by someone externally. (Hsu, Frances Personal Communication)

Although there are no clear-cut rules as to whether one goes to the male head of the household or to the female head to make a law enforcement inquiry, the general rule of thumb is that one would not go too wrong by starting with the father. It should be noted that for most Asian/Pacific American families, the role of the mother in discipline and in decision making is very important. While the household may appear to be "ruled" by the father, the mother's role in finances, discipline, education, operations, and decision making is major.

Children, Adolescents, and Youths

Most Asian/Pacific American families involve at least two or more individuals within the same household working outside of the home. Thus, if young children are present, there is a high reliance on either family members or others to help care for them while the parents are at work. It is not uncommon for older children to care for younger children within a household. Moreover, latchkey children within an Asian/Pacific American home are common, especially for families that cannot afford external child care. In recent immigrant and refugee families, Asian/Pacific American children have a special role in being the intermediaries between parents and the external community because of the ability of the younger individuals to learn English and the American ways of doing things. Children often serve as translators and interpreters for peace officers in their communication and relations with Asian/Pacific American families involving recent immigrants and refugees. In such situations, it is suggested that the officer review the role expected of the youthful member of the family, how sensitive an area the translated content is to the different family members, and the consequences if the content is incorrectly translated. (For example, asking a juvenile to translate to his or her parents who speak no English that the juvenile had been involved in a sexual abuse situation at the school may result in significant omission and/or changed content because of the embarrassment caused to the juvenile and possibly to the parents.) In all cases, when a child is acting as a translator, the officer should direct all verbal and nonverbal communication to the parents (as one would normally do without a translator). Otherwise, the parents may view the officer's lack of attention to them as an insult.

Asian/Pacific American Family Violence

Given the Asian/Pacific American cultural factors to keep family issues within the family and to use self-help and personal effort strategies, reports of and research studies on family violence (e.g., spousal physical abuse, child abuse, sexual abuse) by Asian/Pacific American are, at best, incomplete. The few reported studies seem to indicate significant and emerging problems with family violence within the

Asian/Pacific American community. Song (1996), in his interview of 150 Korean immigrant women from the Chicago area, found that 60 percent of those sampled reported being battered, with 37 percent of those battered at least once a month. Abraham (2000), in her survey of community-based women's service organizations, found that over 1,000 south Asian women sought help for abuse and family violence. Anecdotal reports for the Chinese (K. Chin, 1994), Pilipino (Cimmarusti, 1996), Cambodian (Frye & D'Avanzo, 1994), Vietnamese (Kibria, 1993), and other Asian/Pacific American groups indicate that family violence within these Asian/Pacific American communities has been underestimated and underreported. Song (1996) noted that most of the abused women used self-help efforts to keep the problem within the home (e.g., fought back physically and verbally, ignored the battering or did nothing, stared at the abusing person), and 70 percent of the battered women indicated that they did not know about community services that could have helped them. The role of peace officers in detecting, assessing, and intervening in family violence situations within Asian/Pacific American communities is a critical one given this emerging area of needs and problem areas. The sensitivity of the peace officer to the cultural influences and patterns of communication (as noted in the next section) will be critical in the effective gathering of initial information and subsequent referral and interventions with Asian/Pacific American families involved in domestic violence and other issues of abuse.

CULTURAL INFLUENCES ON COMMUNICATION: VERBAL AND NONVERBAL STYLES OF ASIAN/PACIFIC AMERICANS

We do not wish to create any kind of stereotypes, but there are key features of Asian/Pacific American verbal and nonverbal communication styles that necessitate explanation. Misunderstanding resulting from style differences can result in perceptions of poor community services from police agencies, conflicts resulting from such misunderstandings, and safety and control issues for peace officers.

1. *It is important that officers take the time to get information from witnesses, victims, and suspects even if the individuals have limitations to their English speaking abilities.* The use of officers who may speak different Asian/Pacific dialects or languages, translators, and language bank resources will help. Often Asian/Pacific Americans have not been helped in crime-fighting and peacekeeping situations because officers could not or did not take information from individuals who could not speak English well.

Huang Jin Bao, a Chinese American who could read English but did not speak it well was being given a ticket for double parking. He tried to explain himself to the officer but was unsuccessful. While he sat in the car and waited for the ticket, the officer came back with two tickets for Huang, the original ticket for double parking, and another ticket. The officer left, but he also walked away with Huang's driver's license. When Huang followed the officer and asked for his driver's license back, the officer handcuffed him, pushed him around, and arrested him. Huang Jin Bao was charged with traffic violations, harassing a police officer, and resisting arrest. ("Huang Jin Bao Update—*Centre Daily News* Interview Reveals More Details," *New York Nichibei*, April 9, 1987).

2. *Asian/Pacific Americans tend to hold a more "family" and/or "group" orientation.* As such, the lack of the use of *I* statements and/or self-reference should not be evaluated as not being straightforward or as being evasive about oneself or one's relationships. The officer may be concerned because an Asian/Pacific American may wish to use the pronoun *we* when the situation may call for a personal observation involving an *I* statement. For example, in a traffic accident, the Asian/Pacific American may describe what he or she saw by saying "We saw . . ." Such group statements to mean what the individual saw are consistent with the family and group orientation of Asian/Pacific Americans.

3. *The officer must be aware that for many Asian/Pacific Americans, it is considered to be rude, impolite, and to involve a "loss of face" to directly say no to an authority figure such as a peace officer.* Peace officers need to understand the following possibilities when an answer of yes is heard from an Asian/Pacific American. It can mean (1) "Yes, I heard what you said (but I may or may not agree with you)," (2) "Yes, I understand what you said (but I may or may not do what I understand)," (3) "Yes, I can see this is important for you (but I may not agree with you on this)," or (4) "Yes, I agree (and will do what you said)." Because the context of the communication and the nonverbal aspects of the message are equally meaningful, it is vital for law enforcement officers to be sure of the yes answers received, as well as other language nuances from Asian/Pacific Americans. Two examples might be illustrative: (1) If an Asian/Pacific American says that he or she will "try his or her best to attend," this generally means that he or she will not be there, especially for more voluntary events and situations such as community neighborhood safety meetings. (2) If an Asian/Pacific national says in response to a question "It is possible," this generally means do not wait for the event to happen. Such communications, as noted previously, may be more applicable to some Asian/Pacific Americans than others, but sensitivity on the part of law enforcement officers to these language nuances will facilitate communication. Specific rules for interacting with each Asian/Pacific American group are not necessary, but officers should have a general understanding of language and cultural styles. In a communication situation in which the response of yes may be ambiguous, it is suggested that law enforcement officers rephrase the question so that the requested outcome action and understanding are demonstrated in the verbal response.

Ambiguous Response

Officer: "I need you to show up in court on Tuesday. Do you understand?"

Asian witness: "Yes!"

Rephrasing of Questions to Show Understanding and Outcome

Officer: "What are you going to do on Tuesday?"

Asian witness: "I will be in court on Tuesday. I must go there."

4. *Asian/Pacific Americans tend to be "high context" in communication style.* This means that the officer needs to provide both interpersonal and situational contexts for effective communications. Context for Asian/Pacific Americans means that members of the community know the officers in the community. Community members may have had previously working relationships with the officer (e.g., crime prevention meetings, police athletic league, etc.). Moreover, other members of the community may help to provide information and context for police cooperation based on past relationships. Context also means providing explanations and education to Asian/Pacific Americans about procedures, laws, etc. before asking them questions and/or requesting their participation in an activity. By providing background information and by establishing prior relationships with Asian/Pacific American communities, the Asian/Pacific American individual has a context for cooperating with law enforcement agencies and officers.

5. *Be aware of nonverbal and other cultural nuances that may detract from the effective communication of the officer.* Many Asian/Pacific Americans find it uncomfortable and, sometimes, inappropriate to maintain eye contact with authority figures like police officers. It is considered in many Asian/Pacific American cultures to be disrespectful if there is eye contact with someone who is of higher status, position, importance, or authority. As such, many Asian/Pacific Americans may look down on the ground and/or avert their eyes from gazing at a police officer. The officer should not automatically read this nonverbal behavior as indicating a lack of trust or as a dishonest response. Likewise, for the police officer, he or she should be aware of possible nonverbal gestures and actions that may detract from his or her professional roles (e.g., gesturing with the curled index finger for a person to come forward in a manner that might be used only for servants in that person's home culture).

6. *Asian/Pacific Americans may not display their emotionality in the same way that the officer expects.* The central thesis guiding Asian/Pacific Americans is the Confucian notion of "walking the middle road." This means that extremes—too much or too little of anything are not good. As such, Asian/Pacific Americans tend to moderate their display of positive and/or negative emotion. Often, in crisis situations, nonverbal displays of emotions are controlled to the point that the affect of the Asian/Pacific American appears "flat." Under such circumstances, the officer needs to correctly understand and interpret such displays of emotion appropriately. For example, just because the parent of a murder victim does not appear emotionally shaken by an officer's report does not mean that the person is not experiencing a severe emotional crisis.

KEY ISSUES IN LAW ENFORCEMENT

Underreporting of Crimes

Asian/Pacific Americans, because of their past experiences with some law enforcement agencies (e.g., anti-Asian immigration laws, health and sanitation code violations in restaurants, as well as perceived unresponsiveness by police), are reluctant to report crimes and may not seek police assistance and help. Many Asian/Pacific Americans remember how police in their home countries have brutalized and violated them and others (e.g., in Southeast Asian and other Asian countries). Crimes that occur within a family's home (e.g., home invasion, family violence) or within the confines of a small family business (e.g., robbery of a Chinese restaurant) often go unreported unless these crimes are connected to larger criminal activities, as in the example that follows.

> A grand jury has indicted three Chinese nationals accused of traveling to Western New York last month to burglarize the Lancaster home of a man whose family owns a local Chinese restaurant. Law enforcement officials said Wednesday they were investigating allegations that the three are part of an organized-crime outfit that has been targeting the operators of Chinese restaurants. . . . Lin's family owns a local Chinese restaurant, and law enforcement officials said they believe the robbery may be tied to other recent robberies targeting the owners of Chinese restaurants. (Herbeck, 2000)

Many immigrants and refugees are simply not knowledgeable about the legal system of the United States and therefore avoid any contact with law enforcement personnel. Outreach and community policing perspectives will enhance the contact and relationship with Asian/Pacific American communities in the underreporting of crimes.

Differential Treatment

The U.S. Commission on Civil Rights (1992) highlighted several areas in which Asian/Pacific Americans may have received different treatment in police services as a result of their culture or ethnic heritage. Incidents reported included police misconduct and harassment. The commission reported the following two cases as examples:

> On June 1, 1991, a young Italian American man who had recently moved to Revere, Massachusetts was murdered. Witnesses said that he was brutally beaten and stabbed repeatedly by a group of Asian men. The Revere Police Department, which has no Asian American police officers and has no access to interpreters, was unable to solve the case and apprehend the murderers quickly and came under increasing criticism from the victim's family.

> On July 1, in an attempt to force information about the murder to the surface, a team of 40 Revere police officers, along with representatives of the Immigration and Naturalization Service, made a 2-hour sweep through a Cambodian neighborhood in search of persons with outstanding warrants and possible illegal aliens. "We wanted to break open the case," said one of the police officers involved in the sweep. The Cambodian Americans living in Revere were frightened and angered by the police sweep. (U.S. Commission on Civil Rights, 1992)

> In September, 1987, a Korean student was stopped in Manhattan, New York for a traffic violation he committed while on his bicycle. According to a newspaper account, witnesses saw him being forced off his bicycle onto the ground by the police, who proceeded to beat his head against the pavement. The student was then arrested for traffic violations, disorderly conduct, and obstructing governmental administration. The witnesses followed the student to the police station, where, they claim, the police made a reference to the student's "Asian nose." (U.S. Commission on Civil Rights, 1992) Ibid.

Increasing Asian/Pacific American Community Police Services

James Chin (1987), an officer with the Los Angeles Police Department Airport Police Bureau, describes the benefits and improved police–community relationships that resulted from a storefront outreach effort to better service the Asian/Pacific American neighborhood in the Korean area of Los Angeles (a second storefront has been established in the Chinese area as well). Although this example is from the mid-1980s, it is a clear and simple illustration of steps that can be taken to reach out to communities:

> The Los Angeles Police Department has two storefronts serving Asian/Pacific Islander communities, one located in a Korean neighborhood; the other in a Chinese neighborhood. Both storefronts are the results of organized community demands for such operations and subsequent donations from individuals and organizations within the community who helped provide space and needed materials. The store-

fronts are staffed by a police officer and a bilingual community person whose salary is paid by community donations and the police department. (J. Chin, 1987, pp. 52–60)

Another outreach approach is the use of Asian/Pacific American bilingual community service officers (CSOs), nonsworn officers with badges and uniforms who serve the Southeast Asian communities in San Diego, California. The CSOs provide many of the supportive services available from the police department by using bilingual nonsworn personnel.

Increasing Asian/Pacific American Peace Officers

There is a noticeable underrepresentation of Asian/Pacific Americans in federal, state, and local law enforcement positions, although the number of Asian/Pacific Americans as peace officers and in law enforcement has increased in the past decade. The small number of Asian/Pacific American officers has hampered many departments in neighborhoods with large Asian/Pacific American populations in effectively serving those communities with appropriate role models and bicultural expertise. A variety of reasons exist for such underrepresentation, including (1) history of law enforcement relationships with Asian/Pacific American communities, (2) interests of Asian/Pacific Americans in law enforcement careers, (3) image of law enforcement personnel in Asian/Pacific American communities, (4) lack of knowledge about the different careers and pathways in law enforcement, (5) concern with and fear of background checks, physical requirements, and the application process, and (6) limited number of role models and advocates for law enforcement careers for Asian/Pacific Americans.

Crimes within Asian/Pacific American Communities

Many crimes committed in Asian/Pacific American communities are perpetrated by others within the same group, particularly among Asian/Pacific refugee and Asian/Pacific immigrant groups. Law enforcement officials have often found it difficult to get cooperation from refugee and immigrant victims of extortion, home robbery, burglary, theft, blackmail, and other crimes against persons. In part, the lack of cooperation stems from a fear of retaliation by the criminal, who is within the Asian/Pacific American community. Other concerns of Asian/Pacific American victims include (1) the perceived level of responsiveness of the peacekeeping officers and agencies, (2) lack of familiarity with and trust in police services, (3) perceived level of effectiveness of law enforcement agencies, and (4) prior stereotypes and images of law enforcement agencies as discriminatory (e.g., immigration laws) and unresponsive to crimes against Asian/Pacific Americans. Recent Asian/Pacific American refugees and immigrants are often prime targets, in part because of their distrust of most institutions (e.g., banks, police departments, hospitals). As a result, they are more inclined to hide and store cash and other valuables in the home. A key challenge for police agencies is to educate this group and to work cooperatively with Asian/Pacific Americans to reduce the crimes within these communities.

SUMMARY OF RECOMMENDATIONS FOR LAW ENFORCEMENT

As a result of the early immigration laws and other discriminatory treatment received by Asian/Pacific Americans in the United States, the experiences of Asian/Pacific Americans with law enforcement officials had been fraught with conflicts, difficulties, and mixed messages. Officers should realize that some Asian/Pacific Americans may still remember this history and carry with them stereotypes of police services as something to be feared and avoided. Law enforcement officials may need to go out of their way to establish trust and to win cooperation in order to effectively accomplish their goals to serve and protect Asian/Pacific Americans.

The label *Asian Americans/Pacific Islanders* encompasses over 32 very diverse ethnic and cultural groups. Law enforcement officials need to be aware of the differences between the 32 diverse ethnic groups (e.g., different cultural and language groups) as well as the differences that may result from the individual life experiences within any one of the 32 groups (e.g., generational differences). Since a key stereotype of concern for Asian/Pacific Americans is that they are regarded by mainstream Americans as very much alike, it is important that peace officers not make such errors in their interactions with Asian/Pacific Americans.

There is tremendous diversity among Asian/Pacific Americans, and one way to understand individuals within these communities is to look at some of the motivating forces that might affect decisions by Asian/Pacific American citizens. Earlier in this chapter we provided a seven-part typology that will assist officers in viewing some of these motivational bases.

Although there are many ethnicities, cultures, and languages among the 32 or more groups within Asian/Pacific American communities, one way to understand the impact of their immigration and life experiences is by learning the motivational determinants of individuals within different generational and immigrant groups.

The self-preferred term for referring to Asian/Pacific Americans varies with contexts, groups, and experiences of the individual. Law enforcement officials need to be aware of terms that are unacceptable and derogatory and terms that are currently used. When in doubt, officers have to learn to become comfortable in asking Asian/Pacific Americans which term they prefer. Officers are advised to provide helpful feedback to their peers when offensive terms, labels, and/or actions are used with Asian/Pacific Americans. Such feedback will help reduce the risk of misunderstanding and improve the working relationships between officers and Asian/Pacific American communities. Moreover, it will help enhance the professional image of the department for those communities.

Many Asian/Pacific Americans are concerned with their ability to communicate clearly, and this is of particular concern among Asian/Pacific Americans who are immigrants and refugees. Peace officers need to take the time and be aware that bilingual individuals and nonnative English speakers want to communicate effectively with them. Maintaining contact, providing extra time, using translators, and being patient with speakers will allow Asian/Pacific Americans to communicate their concerns.

Cultural differences in verbal and nonverbal communication often result in misinterpretation of the message and of behaviors. Officers need to be aware of nonverbal aspects of Asian/Pacific Americans in their communication style, including eye contact, touch, gestures, and affect (show of emotions). Verbal aspects such as accent, limited vocabulary, and incorrect grammar may give officers the impression that an Asian/Pacific American individual is not understanding what is communicated. It is important to remember that the English listening and comprehension skills of Asian/Pacific American immigrants and refugees are usually better than their speaking skills.

Asian/Pacific Americans, because of their past experiences with law enforcement agencies, along with their own concerns about privacy, self-help, and other factors, are reluctant to report crimes and may not seek police assistance and help. Law enforcement departments and officials need to build relationships and working partnerships with Asian/Pacific American communities. Relationship building is often helped by outreach efforts such as community storefront offices, bilingual officers, and participation of officers in community activities.

DISCUSSION QUESTIONS AND ISSUES

1. *Law Enforcement as Not User-Friendly.*   Under the historical information section of this chapter, we noted that many anti–Asian/Pacific American laws and events may leave Asian/Pacific Americans with the view that law enforcement agencies are not user-friendly. What are the implications of this view for law enforcement? What are ways to improve such possible negative points of view?

2. *Diversity among Asian/Pacific Americans.*   As noted earlier in this chapter, the Asian/Pacific American category comprises over 32 diverse ethnic and cultural groups. Which groups are you most likely to encounter in crime fighting and peacekeeping in your work? Which groups do you anticipate encountering in your future work?

3. *How Asian/Pacific American Groups Differ.*   A typology for understanding motives for some of the behaviors of Asian/Pacific American people (in terms of their generational and immigration status in the United States) was provided. How might you apply this typology to better understand an Asian/Pacific American refugee involved in a moving traffic violation? An Asian/Pacific American immigrant involved as a victim of a house robbery? An Asian/Pacific national involved as a victim of a burglary? Southeast Asian youths involved in possible gang activities?

4. *Choice of Terms.*   The term *Asian Americans and Pacific Islanders* is used in many publications and by many people to refer to members of the more than 32 diverse groups included in this category. How might you find out which is the best term to refer to an individual if ethnic and cultural information of this kind is necessary?

5. *Offensive Terms and Labels.*   We strongly urge that offensive terms such as Chinks, Gooks, and Flips not be used in law enforcement work at any time. Give three practical reasons for this perspective.

6. *Effects of Myths and Stereotypes.*   Myths and stereotypes about Asian/Pacific Americans have greatly affected this group. What are some of the Asian/Pacific American stereotypes that you have heard of or have encountered? What effects would these

stereotypes have on Asian/Pacific Americans? What are ways to manage these stereotypes in law enforcement?

7. ***Verbal and Nonverbal Variations among Cultures.***   How do you think that the information in this chapter about verbal and nonverbal communication styles can help officers in their approach to Asian/Pacific American citizens? When you can understand the cultural components of the style and behaviors, does this help you to become more sensitive and objective about your reactions? Provide some examples of rephrasing questions in such a way that they elicit responses to show understanding and intended actions on the part of Asian/Pacific Americans.

8. ***Self-Monitoring and Avoidance of Law Enforcement.***   Why do you think many Asian/Pacific Americans keep to their own communities and express the desire for self-monitoring and within-community resolution of their problems? When are such efforts desirable? When are they ineffective? How can police agencies be of greater service to Asian/Pacific American communities in this regard?

REFERENCES

ABRAHAM, M. (2000). *Speaking the Unspeakable: Marital Violence against South Asian Immigrant Women in the United States.* New Brunswick, N.J.: Rutgers University Press.

ANCHETA, A. N. (1998). *Race, Rights, and the Asian American Experience.* New Brunswick, N.J.: Rutgers University Press.

BARKAN, E. R. (1992). *Asian and Pacific Islander Migration to the United States: A Model of New Global Patterns.* Westport, Conn.: Greenwood Press.

CHANG, R. S. (1999). *Disoriented: Asian Americans, Law, and the Nation-State.* New York: New York University Press.

CHIN, J. (1987). "Crime and the Asian American Community: The Los Angeles Response to Koreatown," *Journal of California Law Enforcement, 19,* 52–60.

CHIN, K. (1994). "Out-of-Town Brides: International Marriage and Wife Abuse among Chinese Immigrants," *Journal of Comparative Family Studies, 25,* 53–69.

CIMMARUSTI, R. A. (1996). "Exploring Aspects of Filipino-American Families," *Journal of Marital and Family Therapy, 22,* 205–217.

DANIELS, R. (1988). *Asian America: Chinese and Japanese in the United States since 1850.* Seattle: University of Washington Press.

DU, P. L. (1996). *The Dream Shattered: Vietnamese Gangs in America.* Boston: Northeastern University Press.

EFFRON, S. (1989, September). "Racial Slaying Prompts Fear, Anger in Raleigh," *Greensboro News and Record.*

FRYE, B. A., AND C. D. D'AVANZO. (1994). "Cultural Themes in Family Stress and Violence among Cambodian Refugee Women in the Inner City," *Advances in Nursing Science, 16,* 64–77.

GOLDSTEIN, L. (1990, May 8). "Split between Blacks, Koreans Widens in N.Y. Court," *Washington Post.*

HERBECK, D. (2000, July 6). "Asian Organized-Crime Ties Eyed in Lancaster Robbery," *Buffalo News.*

KALAVAR, J. M. (1998). *The Asian Indian Elderly in America.* New York: Garland.

KANDEL, B. (1991, January 4). "Tensions Ease Year after NYC Grocery Boycott," *USA Today.* p. A8

KEMPSKY, N. (1989, October). *"A Report to Attorney General John K. Van de Kamp on Patrick Edward Purdy and the Cleveland School Killings"* State of California Attorney General's Office. Sacramento, California.

KIBRIA, N. (1993). *Family Tightrope: The Changing Lives of Vietnamese Americans.* Princeton, N.J.: Princeton University Press.

KWOH, S. (2000, May 28). "Asians Battle Rights Abuses—in the U.S.," *Los Angeles Times.* p. M8

LEE, L. C., AND ZANE, N. W. S. (1998). *Handbook of Asian American Psychology.* Thousand Oaks, Calif.: Sage Publications.

LEE, S. J. (1996). *Unraveling the "Model Minority" Stereotype: Listening to Asian American Youths.* New York: Teachers College Press.

MATHEWS, J., AND M. LAIT. (1989, January 18). "Rifleman Slays Five at School: 19 Pupils, Teacher Shot in California; Assailant Kills Self," *Washington Post.* p. A1

NG, F. (1998a). *Asian American Family Life and Community.* New York: Garland.

NG, F. (1998b). *The History and Immigration of Asian Americans.* New York: Garland.

President's Commission on Mental Health. (1978). *Report of the Special Population Subpanel on Mental Health of Asian/Pacific Americans.* Vol. 3. Washington, D.C.: U.S. Government Printing Office.

RAMIREZ, A. (1986, November 24). "America's Super Minority," *Fortune.*

SCHMITT, E. (1992, November 20). "Marines Find Racial Disparity in Officer Programs," *New York Times. p.A8*

SONG, Y. I. (1996). *Battered Women in Korean Immigrant Families*. New York: Garland.

Special Services for Groups. (1983). *Bridging Cultures: Southeast Asian Refugees in America*. Los Angeles: Special Services for Groups.

TAKAKI, R. (1989a). *Strangers from a Different Shore: A History of Asian Americans*. Boston: Little, Brown.

TAKAKI, R. (1989b). "Who Killed Vincent Chin?" in G. Yun (ed.), *A Look Beyond the Model Minority Image: Critical Issues in Asian America*. New York: Minority Rights Group. pp. 23–29.

TUAN, M. (1998). *Forever Foreigners or Honorary White? The Asian Ethnic Experience Today*. New Brunswick, N.J.: Rutgers University Press.

U.S. Bureau of the Census. (1990). *United States Population Estimates by Age, Sex, Race, and Hispanic Origin: 1980 to 1988* (Current Population Reports, Series P-25, No. 1045.) Washington, D.C.: U.S. Government Printing Office.

U.S. Commission on Civil Rights. (1992). *Civil Rights Issues Facing Asian Americans in the 1990s*. Washington, D.C.: U.S. Government Printing Office.

WOO, D. (2000). *Glass Ceiling and Asian Americans: The New Face of Workplace Barriers*. Walnut Creek, California: AltaMira Press.

7

LAW ENFORCEMENT CONTACT WITH AFRICAN AMERICANS

OVERVIEW

This chapter provides specific cultural and historical information on African Americans that both directly and indirectly affects the relationship between law enforcement officials and citizens. It presents information about demographics and diversity among African Americans, as well as issues related to cultural and racial identity. Following the background information is a section on group identification terms and a discussion of myths and stereotypes. Aspects of the family are discussed, including the extended family, gender roles, single-mother families, and adolescents. A section on cultural influences on communication deals with African American vernacular English; nonverbal and verbal communication, including emotionalism; and fighting words, threats, and aggressive behavior. The closing section presents several key concerns for law enforcement, including information on differential treatment, racial profiling, perceptions of and reactions to legal authority, excessive force and brutality, police interaction in poor urban communities, the needs of the inner city, and issues related to women. The summary of the chapter reviews recommendations for improved communication and relationships between law enforcement officials and African Americans.

COMMENTARY

The history of intimidation of African Americans by police continues to affect the dynamics of law enforcement in some black communities today.

> There is no point in telling blacks to observe the law. . . . It has almost always been used against them. (Senator Robert Kennedy, after visiting the scene of the Watts Riot, 1965)
> We must learn to live together as brothers or perish together as fools. (Martin Luther King, 1964)
> If . . . inclusion of African Americans and other minorities in policing and in the broader society [is] continued, then community policing might finally realize a vision

of police departments as organizations that protect the lives, property, and rights of all citizens in a fair and effective way. (Williams and Murphy, 1990)

Law enforcement should move away from thinking only about the inner city when "African American" comes to mind. African Americans are more sophisticated [than 10 or 20 years ago]; they understand societal rules and community resources, including complaint procedures when it comes to law enforcement actions. Their expectations for law enforcement professionalism have risen significantly. (Berry, 2000)

African Americans today are not as intolerant of injustice as they once had to be and have higher expectations of law enforcement than they did in the past. Community leaders expect to become involved with law enforcement agencies in community-based policing formats and understand that police professionals have no choice but to listen to them as one voice in the community. In Chapter 1, we presented an example of the San Diego Police Department, whose leaders collaborated with African Americans and other community members (Latinos, Asians) to interpret racial profiling data and to deal jointly with the problem. This example is not intended to gloss over the reality that law enforcement still has much progress to make in relations with the African American community, but it illustrates that a shift is beginning to take place between law enforcement and some segments of the African American population.

AFRICAN AMERICAN CULTURE

Americans of all races often gloss over the cultural differences between white and black Americans because of the overwhelming problems associated with the racial aspects of black–white relations. The effects of slavery and discrimination on the black experience in America are not to be downplayed, but, in addition, African American culture must also be considered. African American culture is in part influenced by African culture and is significantly different from white culture. Many police executives have come to recognize that when there is an influx of immigrants from a particular part of the world, their officers are better equipped to establish trust, good communication, and mutual cooperation if they have some basic understanding of the group's cultural background. However, the cultural differences of African Americans are rarely considered, even though they can cause serious communication problems between citizens and police officers. Failing to recognize the distinctiveness of black culture, language, and communication patterns can lead to misunderstandings, conflict, and even confrontation. In addition, understanding the history of African Americans (which is related to the culture) is especially important for law enforcement officials as they work toward improving relations and changing individual and community perceptions.

HISTORICAL INFORMATION

The majority of African Americans, or blacks (the terms are used interchangeably), in the United States trace their roots to West Africa. They were torn from their cultures of origin between the seventeenth and nineteenth centuries, when they were brought here as slaves. Blacks represent the only migrants to come to the Americas (North and South) against their will. Blacks from Africa were literally kidnap victims, kidnapped by Europeans and purchased as captives by Yankee traders. This factor makes African Americans, as a group, very different from immigrants, who chose to come to the United States to better their lives, and from refugees, who fled their homelands to escape religious or political persecution.

The very word *slave* carries the connotation of an "inferior" being; slaves were counted as three-fifths of a person during census taking. Most slave owners inwardly understood that treating people as animals to be owned, worked, and sold was immoral, but they wanted to think of themselves as good, religious, and moral people; hence they had to convince themselves that their slaves were not really human, but a lower form of life. They focused on racial differences (e.g., skin color, hair texture) as "proof" that black people were not really people after all. Racism began, then, as an airtight alibi for a horrifying injustice. The notion of the slave (and, by extension, any African American) as less than human has created great psychological and social problems for succeeding generations of both black and white citizens. Slavery led to a system of inferior housing, schools, health care, and jobs for black people that persists to this day.

The institution of slavery formally ended in 1863, but the racist ideas born of slavery have persisted. These ideas continue to leave deep scars on many African Americans. Today, particularly in the lower socioeconomic classes, many blacks continue to suffer from the psychological heritage of slavery, as well as from active, current discrimination that still prevents them from realizing the American dream.

Until recently, the history that many Americans learned presented a distorted, incomplete picture of black family life (emphasizing breakdown) during the slave era, which had crippling effects on families for generations afterward. This version of history never examined the moral strength of the slaves or the community solidarity and family loyalty that arose after emancipation. Undoubtedly, these strengths have positively affected the rebuilding of the African American community.

> According to almost all witnesses, the roads of the South were clogged in 1865 [after emancipation] with Black men and women searching for long-lost wives, husbands, children, brothers and sisters. The in-gathering continued for several years and began in most communities with mass marriage ceremonies that legalized the slave vows. This was a voluntary process for husbands and wives who were free to renounce slave vows and search for new mates. Significantly, most freedmen, some of them 80 and 90 years old, decided to remain with their old mates, thereby giving irrefutable testimony on the meaning of their love. (Bennett, 1989)

Despite slave owners' attempts to destroy black family life, some slaves did manage to form lasting families headed by a mother and a father, and many slave couples enjoyed long marriages. Although white slave masters would often do everything possible to pull families apart (including the forced "breeding" and the selling of slaves), there is evidence that slaves maintained their family connections as best they could and produced stable units with admirable values. According to the U.S. historian Char Miller (2000), "Despite the fact that slavery tore apart many families, blacks maintained links, loves, and relationships just as anyone else would under these circumstances."

A more accurate version of history counters the impression that all slave families were so helpless that they were always torn apart and could never reestablish themselves, as well as that their social relationships were chaotic and amoral. The resolve of large numbers of blacks to rebuild their families and communities as soon as they were freed reveals an impressive determination in a people who survived one of the most brutal forms of servitude that humankind has seen. African American survival and, consequently, African American contributions to American society deserve a high level of respect and testify to the great strength of a people. It is not within the scope of this chapter to discuss African American contributions to society. Frequently the perceptions of some people in law enforcement are conditioned by their exposure to the black underclass, for whom crime is a way of life.

Law Enforcement Interaction with African Americans: Historical Baggage

In the United States during the late seventeenth and eighteenth centuries, following slave uprisings in a number of colonies, colonists created strict laws to contain the slaves. Even minor offenses were punished harshly. These laws set a negative tone between law enforcement and blacks. American police were called on to form "slave patrols" and to enforce racially biased laws (Williams and Murphy, 1990). In many areas of the country, police were expected to continue enforcing deeply biased, discriminatory laws (including those setting curfews for blacks and barring blacks from many facilities and activities). Today, segments of the African American population, especially those in the lower socioeconomic classes, continue to struggle with "historical baggage" related to interactions with law enforcement. "The fact that the legal order not only countenanced but sustained slavery, segregation and discrimination for most of our Nation's history—and the fact that the police were bound to uphold that order—set a pattern for police behavior and attitudes toward black communities that has persisted until the present day. That pattern includes the idea that blacks have fewer civil rights, that the task of the police is to keep them under control, and that the police have little responsibility for protecting them from crime within their communities" (Williams and Murphy, 1990).

Most police officers have had some exposure to the historical precedents of poor relationships between police and minority communities. The damages of the past require that we make a greater effort today with groups such as African Americans, for whom contact with law enforcement has long been problematic.

DEMOGRAPHICS: DIVERSITY AMONG AFRICAN AMERICANS

Currently, blacks comprise 12 percent of the population of the United States, with approximately 34 million people. (Population by Race and Hispanic Origin, 2000, U.S. Bureau of the Census). (Refer to Chapter 1, in the section "The Overlap of Race, Culture, and Ethnicity," for information about individuals who do not fit "neatly" into one demographic category, such as black.) Until the past few decades, the vast majority lived in the South. Between 1940 and 1970, over 1.5 million blacks migrated initially to the northern United States and then to the West Coast, largely seeking better job opportunities. Since 1980 the percentage of blacks living in inner cities has remained steady (approximately 56 percent of the black population). However, the percentage of blacks living in suburban areas has increased since 1980. At that time, 21.2 percent lived in the suburbs; by 1994 the percentage had increased to 30.2 percent (Frey, 1998). The rural black population has decreased, and the shifting flow has contributed to the increase in numbers in suburban areas. (Some rural blacks may migrate directly into the inner city, whereas others may move to more suburban areas; the pattern of flow is not actually known.) Urban cores experience cycles of repopulation, mainly by blacks, Hispanics, and various new immigrant groups. The most vivid example is the city of Detroit, where approximately 60 percent of the population is black; most whites and immigrant groups have settled in the outlying areas. Similarly, other cities, such as Washington, D.C., St. Louis, Chicago, and Cleveland, are populated mainly by blacks and new immigrants, creating layers of tension where diverse groups with conflicting values and customs suddenly find themselves crowded into the same urban neighborhoods.

Between 1970 and 1980 3.5 million blacks and Hispanics moved to cities that had been abandoned by more than 3 million white residents (Lohman, 1977). These population shifts have created "two Americas." One America is the world of the suburbs, where schools, recreational facilities, and community resources are good. The other is the inner city, where many African Americans (as well as Latinos and other diverse groups) have poor access to educational and job opportunities and where living conditions are often more similar to those of cities in the developing world than to those of America's comfortable suburban environment.

Although many African Americans are in the lower socioeconomic classes, blacks are represented in all the classes, from the extremely poor to the extremely affluent, and have moved increasingly into the middle class. As with all ethnic groups, significant class-related differences among blacks affect values and behavior. Poor and rich blacks have little more in common socioeconomically than do poor and rich whites. (Later in this chapter we discuss stereotyping of all blacks based on the black underclass.) However, color, more so than class, often determines how the larger society reacts to and treats blacks. Therefore, the racial (as opposed to cultural) experience of many African Americans in the United States is similar, regardless of an individual's level of prosperity or education.

The cultural diversity that exists among African Americans is related to a variety of factors. Over the past 400 years, black families have come from many different countries (e.g., Jamaica, Trinidad, Belize, Haiti, Puerto Rico). By far, the largest group has origins in Africa. In addition, there are cultural differences among African Americans related to the region of the country from which they came. As with whites, there are southern and northern characteristics, as well as urban and rural characteristics.

Religious backgrounds vary, but the majority of American-born blacks are Protestant, and many are specifically Baptist. The first black-run, black-controlled denomination in the country was the African Methodist Episcopal Church (which was created because churches in the North and South either banned blacks or required them to sit apart from whites). In addition, some blacks belong to the Black Muslim religion, including the Nation of Islam and American Muslim Mission. (The term *Black Muslim* is often used but is rejected by some members of the religion.) There are also sizable and fast-growing black populations among Seventh-Day Adventists, Jehovah's Witnesses, and Pentecostals (especially among Spanish-speaking blacks); among blacks of Caribbean origin, Santeria, Candomble, Voudun, and similar sects blending Catholic and West African (mainly Yoruba) beliefs and rituals are common. Rastafarianism has spread far beyond its native Jamaica to become an influential religious movement among immigrants from many other English-speaking Caribbean nations.

ISSUES OF IDENTITY

In the 1960s and 1970s the civil rights and Black Pride movements marked a new direction in black identity. The civil rights movement opened many barriers to educational and employment opportunities and to active political involvement. Some adults marched in the civil rights movement knowing that they themselves might never benefit directly from civil rights advances; they hoped that their efforts in the struggle would improve the lives of their children. The middle-class youths who attended community churches and black colleges became the leaders in the movement for equal rights (McAdoo, 1992).

Many blacks (both American-born and Caribbean-born), inspired by a growing sense of community identification and increased pride in racial identity, have become determined to learn more about Africa. Despite the great differences in culture between African Americans and Africans, blacks throughout the Western Hemisphere are discovering that they can take pride in the richness of their African heritage, including its high ethical values and community cohesiveness. Examples of African culture that have influenced American black culture or are held in high esteem by many African Americans include the following (A. Walker, 1982):

- Cooperative interdependence among and between people (contrasted with Western individualism)
- Partnership with nature and with the spirit world reflected in the approach to ecology and in communication with the spirit world (closer to Native American beliefs)
- Balance and harmony among all living things, reflected in the placing of human relations as a priority value (contrasted with the Western view of achievement and "doing" as taking priority over the nurturing of human relations)
- Joy and celebration in life itself
- Time as a spiral, focused on "now" (contrasted with the Western view of time as "money" and time running away from us)
- Focus on the group and not on the individual
- Giving of self to community
- Renewed interest in respecting elders

The combination of the Black Pride movement of the 1960s and 1970s and the more current focus on cultural roots has freed many African Americans from the "slave mentality" that continued to haunt the African American culture long after emancipation. A new pride in race and heritage has, for some, replaced the sense of inferiority fostered by white racial supremacist attitudes.

GROUP IDENTIFICATION TERMS

Several ethnic groups, in a positive evolution of their identity and pride, have initiated name changes for their group, including African Americans. Although it can be confusing, this shift shows growth and a desire for groups to name themselves rather than be named by the dominant society. Until fairly recently, the most widely accepted term was *black,* which replaced *Negro* (which, in turn, replaced *colored people*). *Negro* has been out of use for at least two decades, although some older blacks still use the term (as do some younger African Americans among themselves). To many, the term *Negro* symbolizes what the African American became under slavery. The replacement of *Negro* with *black* came to symbolize racial pride. (The exception to the use of *Negro* and *colored* is in titles such as United Negro College and National Association for the Advancement of Colored People [NAACP].) *African American,* a term preferred by many, focuses on positive historical and cultural roots rather than race or skin color.

In the 1990s the usage of the term *African American* grew in popularity. (It is the equivalent of, for example, *Italian American* and *Polish American.*) Many believe that the word *black* is no more appropriate in describing skin color than is *white.* Yet some Americans who are black do not identify with the label "African American" because it does not fully represent their background, which may be Caribbean or Haitian; they may not identify with the "African" part at all. In the 1980s and early 1990s, the term *people of color* was briefly popular, but this catchall phrase has limited use for police officers. Indeed, there is much historically based controversy associated with broad, collective terms that attempt to summarily categorize people.

Use of the words *"nigger," "boy,"* or *"coon"* is never acceptable at any time, especially in crime fighting and peacekeeping, no matter how provoked an officer may be. (Although black youths may use "nigger" to refer to each other, the word is absolutely taboo for outsiders—especially outsiders wearing badges.) Police who do not like to be called "pigs" can certainly relate to a person's feelings about being called "gorilla." Officers hearing these types of labels used in their own departments, even when they are not being used to address somebody directly, should remind their peers of the lack of professionalism and prejudice that those terms convey. Officers who fall into the habit of using these words in what they think are harmless situations may find that they are unable to control themselves during more volatile situations with citizens.

MYTHS AND STEREOTYPES

Many of the impressions that people in a society (and, consequently, in law enforcement) form about African Americans come from their exposure to or contact with the criminal element, usually representing one component of America's underclass. Here the phenomenon of stereotyping is at much at work as it is when citizens see all police officers as repressive and capable of brutality. Police officers know that they will face consequences nationwide when there is publicity about an instance of police brutality against blacks or reports of racial profiling.

The white majority's view of blacks reflects the same problem. Those who are prejudiced may feel that their racism is justified whenever a crime involving an African American makes the evening news. A suburban African American mother addressing a community forum on racism pointed out: "Every time I hear that there has been a murder or a rape, I pray that it is not a black who committed the crime. The minute the media reports that a black person is responsible for a crime, all of us suffer. When something negative happens, I am no longer seen as an individual with the same values and hopes as my white neighbors. I become a symbol, and [even] more so my husband and sons become feared. People treat us with caution and politeness, but inside we know that their stereotypes of the worst criminal element of blacks have become activated."

A disproportionately high crime rate among young black males does not justify sweeping statements about all African Americans. Certainly, 34 million African Americans cannot be judged by a statistic about the criminal element. Unfortunately for the vast majority of the African American population, some whites do base their image of all blacks largely on the actions, including criminal behavior, of the black members of America's underclass. It is well known that women clutch their purses harder when they see a black man approaching. Similarly, officers have been known to stop blacks and question them simply for not "looking like they belong" to a certain neighborhood. (This issue is discussed and further illustrated later in this chapter.) Many people, including whites and Asians, harbor unreasonable fears about black people. Having never had a black friend or acquaintance, they feed such fears instead of reaching out to meet or get to know people who look different from them.

African Americans have to contend with many myths and stereotypes that are central to a prejudiced person's thinking. For example, one myth, related to "raw and uncontrolled sex," leads people to believe that blacks have no morals, easily surrender to their "instincts," and cannot practice self-restraint (Bennett, 1989). This type of thinking gives some people a sense of moral superiority over blacks for what they perceive to be black sexual habits. In a nationwide survey on sex practices of married couples, including adultery, it was found that blacks are no more likely than (or, expressed differently, precisely as likely as) whites to commit adultery. White sexuality never became a racial issue during the interlude of highly publicized "wife swapping" among middle- and upper-class suburbanites or during the 1960s and 1970s, when many young people (e.g., white "hippies" in the 1960s and whites on the singles-bar scene a few years later) were sexually promiscuous. Although these practices were often criticized, the white racial element was ignored.

For African Americans race has historically been connected to sexuality in ways that it never has been for whites. This is another legacy of slavery and of the self-justifying racist thinking that arose from that institution. Many slave owners routinely and brutally raped their female slaves (often even before puberty) and forced their healthiest slaves to couple and breed regardless of the slaves' own attachments and

Exhibit 7.1 Are people viewed in equal terms?

BLACK MALE	WHITE MALE
Arrogant	Confident
Chip on shoulder	Self-assured
Aggressive	Assertive
Dominant personality	Natural leader
Violence prone	Wayward
Naturally gifted	Smart
Sexual prowess	Sexual experimimentation

preferences. (The fact that many African Americans' genetic backgrounds are part Caucasian is testimony to the slave owners' violation of slave girls and women.) While using slaves to indulge their desires, white slave owners convinced themselves that Africans had no morals and would couple indiscriminately like animals if left to do so. Like the myth of black inferiority, the white view of black sexuality was shaped by the need of slave owners to find an excuse for their cruel and unjust behavior.

CROSS-RACIAL PERCEPTIONS IN LAW ENFORCEMENT

Prejudice, lack of contact, and ignorance lend themselves to groups' developing perceptions about the other that are often based on biased beliefs. Unfortunately, perceptions function as reality for the individuals and groups who hold them; perceptions are seen as the truth, regardless of whether they are the truth. Exhibit 7.1 illustrates differing perceptions that some members of the dominant society have toward black and white males. In this case, the media and popular literature have contributed to the differing perceptions.

What about perceptions that African Americans have developed of police officers' actions? Because of a history of prejudice and discrimination toward blacks, police officers have sometimes used techniques that create negative views of law enforcement among many African Americans. Although most officers no longer exhibit racist actions, the perceptions remain.

The description of perceptions as listed in Exhibit 7.2 were presented to northern California police officers in the early 1990s by Al DeWitt, then vice president of the Alameda, California, chapter of the NAACP. According to DeWitt, over time, African Americans have formed perceptions about police behavior that often lead to a lack of trust, riots, and race problems. Improving and preventing racial misperceptions will take time and effort on the part of officers, but will inevitably benefit those in law enforcement by way of increased cooperation and officer safety.

THE BLACK FAMILY

African American families generally enjoy very strong ties among extended family members, especially among women. Female relatives often substitute for each other

Exhibit 7.2   Perceptions of police officers' actions by some blacks.

POLICE ACTION	BLACK PERCEPTION
Being stopped in or expelled from so-called white neighborhoods	Whites want blacks to "stay in their place."
Immediately suspecting and reacting to blacks without distinction between a drug dealer and a plainclothes police officer	Police view black skin itself as probable cause.
Using reasonable force, beatings, adding charges	When stopped, blacks must be submissive or else.
Negative attitudes, jokes, body language, talking down to people	Officers are racists.
Quick trigger, takedowns, accidental shootings	Bad attitudes will come out under stress.
Slow response, low priority, low apprehension rate	Black-on-black crime is not important.
Techniques of enforcing local restrictions and white political interests	Police are the strong arm for the status quo.
Police sticking together, right or wrong	We-against-them mentality; they stick together, so we have to stick together.

in filling family roles; for example, a grandmother or aunt may raise a child if the mother is unable to do so. Sometimes several different family groups may share one house. When there is a problem (e.g., an incident that has brought an officer to the house), extended family members are likely to be present and want to help. An officer may observe a number of uncles, aunts, brothers, sisters, partners, and friends who are loosely attached to the black household. Enlisting the aid of any of these household members (no matter what the relationship) can be beneficial.

The Role of the Man and the Woman

One widespread myth is that black culture is matriarchal, with one or more women heading the typical household. Historically, African American women have played a crucial role in the family, because of repeated attempts to break down black manhood (Bennett, 1989). However, in a true matriarchy (female-ruled society), women control property and economic activities. This is not generally true of black America, but outsiders often assume that black women are always the heads of households. In the 1960s and 1970s, for instance, the media stereotyped the black mother as loud and domineering, clearly the boss. In addition, black women have, in a sense, been considered less of a threat to the status quo than have black men, and consequently have been able to be more assertive in public (Odom, 1992). Historically, in contacts with law enforcement, a black man may feel that, unlike a black woman, he risks arrest or at least mistreatment if he "talks back."

Black fathers, regardless of their income, usually view themselves as heads of their households (Hines and Franklin, 1982); thus, any major decisions regarding the family generally include the father's participation. It is insulting to the father when, with both parents present, officers automatically focus on the mother. It does not necessarily follow that if the mother is assertive the father is passive or indifferent, and a father's silence does not always indicate agreement. It is always worthwhile to get his view of the situation (Shusta, 1986).

The Single Mother

Feeding the stereotype of the female-headed black household is the absence of fathers in many urban black homes. In 1965 about 25 percent of black families nationally were headed by women. Between 1970 and 1997, births to single black women increased by 93 percent, and 69.1 percent of black births were to single women (National Center for Health Statistics, 1996, 1998). Police observed that in some urban core areas (particularly in housing projects) in 2000, it was not uncommon to find nearly 90 percent of black women living alone with children.

Single mothers, particularly in inner cities, do not always receive the respect they are due; outsiders may be critical of the way these women live—or the way they think these women live. Single mothers are often stereotyped by officers who doubt their own effectiveness in the urban black community. For instance, an unmarried mother on welfare who has just had a fight with her boyfriend should receive the same professional courtesy that a married suburban mother is likely to receive from an officer. In practice, this is not always the case. Some officers may mistakenly speak to the single black mother as if she were promiscuous, or treat her callously as though "She's seen it all and done it all; therefore, it does not matter how I [the officer] treat her." A complaint frequently heard in the . . . black community by black women is that non-black people, especially white men, treat the black woman poorly. This means that they feel comfortable using profanity in the woman's presence and treat [her] with little respect" (Odom, 1992).

Deputy Chief Berry (2000) offers advice regarding relations between the peace officer and the single black mother. He advises officers to go out of their way to establish rapport and trust. Following are his suggestions for assisting single mothers:

- Offer extra assistance to poor mothers on welfare.
- Try to get the children into organized social, recreational, or therapeutic programs.
- Show warmth to the children (e.g., touch them).
- Offer the children something special, such as toy badges or other police souvenirs.
- Give your business card to the mothers to show that you are available for further contact.
- Make follow-up visits when there are not problems so that the mothers and children can associate the officer with good times.
- Carefully explain to the mothers their rights.
- Use the same discretion you might use with another minor's first petty offense (e.g., shoplifting), simply by bringing the child home and talking with the mother and child, rather than sending the child into the juvenile corrections system.

All of these actions will help single black mothers (and their children) see that you can be trusted and that you are there to help. "Since you are dealing with history, you have to knock down barriers and work harder with this group than with any other group" (Berry, 2000).

Children, Adolescents, and Youths

Since there are so many homes, especially in the inner city, in which the father is absent, young boys in their middle childhood years (ages 7 to 11) are at real risk, and school is often where serious behavior problems show up. According to Berry, many single mothers unwittingly place their young sons in the position of "father," giving them the message that they have to take care of the family. These young children can get the mistaken impression that they are the heads of the household, and in school situations, they may try to control the teacher—who is often female and often white. Berry observed that many young boys are placed in special education programs because they have been belligerent and domineering with the teacher. What these boys lack is an older male role model who can help them to grow into the appropriate behavior. Officers who refer these children to agencies that can provide such role models (even if only on a limited-time basis) will gain the trust and respect of families and the community. Eventually, they will win more cooperation from community members.

Among older black male children, especially in inner cities, statistics indicate a disproportionately high crime rate, stemming from the difficult economic conditions of their lives. Officers have to remind themselves that the majority of black teenagers, regardless of economic condition, are law-abiding citizens (Shusta, 2000). Perfectly responsible black teens and young adults report being stopped on a regular basis by officers when they are in predominantly "white neighborhoods" (including those where they happen to live). A 19-year-old African American male living in an upper-middle-class suburban neighborhood in Fremont, California, reported that he was stopped and questioned four times in two weeks by different officers. On one occasion, the conversation went this way:

Officer: "What are you doing here?"
Teen: "I'm jogging, sir."
Officer: "Why are you in this neighborhood?"
Teen: "I live here, sir."
Officer: "Where?"
Teen: "Over there, in that big house on the hill."
Officer: "Can you prove that? Show me your I.D."

On another occasion, when he was jogging, a different officer stopped him and asked (referring to the very expensive jogging shoes he was wearing), "Where did you get those shoes?" When the boy answered that he had bought them, the next question was "Where do you live?" When the teen answered "In that large house on the hill," the officer apologized and went on his way. (Racial profiling is discussed later in this chapter.)

LANGUAGE AND COMMUNICATION

Racial conflicts between black and nonblack citizens can cover up cultural differences that until recently have been largely ignored or minimized. Yet many would acknowledge that cultural differences between, for example, a white officer and a Vietnamese citizen could potentially affect their ability to communicate as well as their perceptions of each other. Similarly, culture comes into play when looking at patterns of language and communication among many African Americans.

African American Vernacular English

"The use of what has been called black language does not represent any pathology in blacks. . . . The beginning of racial understanding is the acceptance that difference is just what it is: different, not inferior. And equality does not mean sameness" (Weber, 1991). There are many varieties of English that are not "substandard," "deficient," or "impoverished" versions of the language. Instead, they often have a complete and consistent set of grammatical rules and may represent the rich cultures of the groups that use them. For example, Asian Indians speak a variety of English somewhat unfamiliar to Americans, and the British speak numerous dialects of British English, each of them containing distinctive grammatical structures and vocabulary not used by Americans. Similarly, some African Americans speak a variety of English that historically has been labeled as substandard because of a lack of understanding of its origins.

Many African Americans use (or have used at least some of the time) what has been called "black English" or, more recently, "African American vernacular English," which we will refer to here as AAVE (Fillmore, 1997) at least some of the time. Although some African Americans speak this variety of English, many enjoy the flexibility and expressiveness of speaking AAVE among peers and switch to "standard English" when the situation calls for it (e.g., at work, in interviews, with white friends).

Most language and dialect researchers accept the notion that AAVE (which some linguists call "Ebonics") is a dialect with its own rules of grammar and structure (Labov, 1972). To many white people, AAVE merely sounds "southern." However, the presence of some of the same grammatical structures—spoken in a wholly different accent—throughout the English-speaking Caribbean (as far south as Trinidad, 8 miles north of Venezuela) points to an earlier, African origin for the grammar. Linguists have done years of research on the origins of AAVE and now believe that it developed from the grammatical structures common to several West African tribal languages. Following are some examples:

AAVE: You lookin good.
Standard English: You look good right now.
AAVE: You be looking good.
Standard English: You usually look good.

That is, the presence of the word *be* indicates a general condition and not something related only to the present. Apparently, some West African languages have grammatical structures expressing these same concepts of time. Nonetheless, many people cling to an unscientific (and racist) view of language varieties of African Americans.

> One [view] says that there was African influence in the development of the language and the other . . . says there was not. Those who reject African influence believe that the African arrived in the United States and tried to speak English. And [according to this first view], because he lacked certain intellectual and physical attributes, he failed. This hypothesis makes no attempt to examine the . . . structures of West African languages to see if there are any similarities. . . . [W]hen the German said zis instead of this, America understood. But, when the African said dis [instead of this], no one considered the fact that [the sound] *th* may not exist in African languages. (Weber, 1991)

Slaves developed black English to overcome the differences in their tribal languages and communicate with one another and with their English-speaking slave masters. They also developed a type of "code language" so that they could speak and not be understood by their slave owners.

Many people still assume that AAVE is "bad" English, and they display their contempt nonverbally, either facially or through an impatient tone of voice. They may interrupt and finish the speaker's sentences for him or her, as though that person were unable to speak for himself or herself. Acceptance of another person's variety of English can go a long way toward establishing rapport. People interacting with blacks who do not use standard English should realize that blacks are not making random "mistakes" when they speak and that they are not necessarily speaking badly. In fact, verbal skill is a highly prized value in most African-based cultures.

Finally, in attempting to establish trust and rebuild relations with a people who historically have not been able to trust the police, white officers should not try to imitate black accents, dialects, and styles of speaking. Imitation can be very insulting and may give blacks the impression that they are being ridiculed—or that the officer is seriously uncomfortable with them. (This issue was elaborated on in Chapter 5.) Officers should not try to fake a style that is culturally different from their own. Being authentic and sincere when communicating with all citizens, while remaining aware and accepting of differences, is the key to beginning to build better relationships with citizens.

Nonverbal Communication: Style and Stance

Black social scientists have been studying aspects of black nonverbal communication, which have often been misunderstood by people in positions of authority. Richard Majors, a psychologist at the University of Wisconsin, termed a certain stance and posturing as the "cool pose," which is demonstrated by many young black men from the inner city. "While the cool pose is often misread by teachers, principals and police officers as an attitude of defiance, psychologists who have studied it say it is a way for black youths to maintain a sense of integrity and suppress rage at being blocked from usual routes to esteem and success" (Goleman, 1992).

Majors explains that while the "cool pose" is not found among the majority of black men, it is commonly seen among inner-city youth as a "tactic for . . . survival to cope with such rejections as storekeepers who refuse to buzz them into a locked shop." The goal of the pose is to give the appearance of being in control. However, a storekeeper, a passerby, or a police officer may perceive this stance as threatening, so a negative dynamic enters the interaction (e.g., the officer seeing the "cool pose" feels threatened and then becomes more authoritarian in response). This form of nonverbal communication may include certain movements and postures designed to emphasize the youth's masculinity. The pose involves a certain way of walking, standing, talking, and remaining aloof facially. The pose, writes Majors, is a way of saying, "[I'm] strong and proud, despite [my] status in American society" (Goleman, 1992).

A Harvard Medical School psychiatrist, Dr. Possaint, points out that because so many inner-city male youths have no male role models in their families, they feel a need to display their manliness (Goleman, 1992). Problems occur when others read their nonverbal language as a sign of irresponsibility, apathy, defiance, and/or laziness. With the knowledge that for some black youths, the "cool pose" is not intended to be a personal threat, officers should be less on the defensive (and, consequently, less on the offensive) when observing this style.

In a *20/20* broadcast entitled "Presumed Guilty" (ABC News, November 6, 1992), the mother of an African American premed student referred to style and communication: "They don't have to be doing anything but being who they are, and that's young black men, with a rhythm in their walk and an attitude about who they are, and expressing their pride and culture by the clothes they choose to wear." This young man had been stopped on numerous occasions for no apparent reason. (This subject is discussed in the section "Differential Treatment" later in this chapter.)

Verbal Expressiveness and Emotionalism

The linguist and sociologist Thomas Kochman has devoted his professional life to studying differences in black and white culture that contribute to misunderstandings and misperceptions. Chicago's African American mayor Harold Washington passed out copies of Kochman's book *Black and White Styles in Conflict* (1981) to the city hall press corps because he believed that he was seriously misunderstood by the whites of the city. According to Kochman, "If a person doesn't know the difference in cultures, that's ignorance. But if a person knows the difference and still says that mainstream culture is best, that 'white is right,' then you've got racism."

Kochman explains in *Black and White Styles in Conflict* (which is still used widely) that blacks and whites have different perspectives and approaches to many issues, including conversation, public speaking, and power. This notion is supported in the following advice to police officers: "Don't get nuts when you encounter an African American who is louder and more emotional than you are. Watch the voice patterns and the tone. Blacks can sound militant [even when they are not]. Blacks have been taught (i.e., socialized) to be outwardly and openly emotional. Sometimes we are emotional first and then calm down and become more rationale*" (Berry, 2000). Berry went on to say that often whites are rational at first but express more emotion as they lose control. This cultural difference has obvious implications for overall communication, including how to approach and react to angry citizens.

Kochman explains that many "whites [are] able practitioners of self-restraint [and] this practice has an inhibiting effect on their ability to be spontaneously self-assertive." (This description would apply to many Asians as well and, perhaps for some, to an even greater degree.) He continues: "the level of energy and spiritual intensity that blacks generate is one that they can manage comfortably but whites can only manage with effort."(Ibid) The problems in interaction come about because neither race understands that there is a cultural difference between them. Kochman states: "Blacks do not initially see this relative mismatch, because they believe that their normal animated style is not disabling to whites. . . . Whites are wor-

---

*Recommended reading: *Verbal Judo: The Gentle Art of Persuasion* and *Verbal Judo: Words as a Force Option,* both by Dr. George Thompson, 1983.

ried that blacks cannot sustain such intense levels of interaction without losing self-control* because that degree of "letting go" of emotions for a white would signify a lack of control. In other words, a white person or an Asian, unaware of the acceptability in black culture of expressing intense emotion (including rage), may not be able to imagine expressing such intense emotion without losing control. The white or Asian may feel threatened, convinced that the ventilation of such hostility will surely lead to a physical confrontation.

Although racism is also a factor for some in communication breakdowns, differing conventions of speech contribute in ways that are not always apparent. In several cultural awareness training sessions, police officers have reported that neighbors (non–African Americans) who overheard highly emotional discussions (among African Americans) called to report fights. When the police arrived on the scene of the "fight," the so-called guilty parties responded that they were not fighting, just talking. While continuing to respond to all calls, officers can be aware of different perceptions of what constitutes a fight. Although they can never make any automatic assumptions, an awareness of style can affect the way they approach the citizen.

Berry (2000) illustrated how a white police officer can let his or her own cultural interpretations of black anger and emotionalism influence judgment. He spoke of a fellow officer who made the statement: "Once they [blacks] took me on, I wanted to take control." This officer, working in a predominantly black area for a three-month period, made 120 stops and 42 arrests (mainly petty offenses such as prowling and failure to identify). He then worked in a predominantly white area for the same period and made 122 stops and only 6 arrests. The officer went on to say, "One group will do what I ask; the other will ask questions and challenge me." His need to "take control" over people whom he perceived to be out of control was so extreme that it resulted in a lawsuit against him. His perception of the level of threat involved was much higher in the black community than in the white. One of the factors involved was, undoubtedly, this officer's inability to deal with being "taken on." If he had used communication skills to defuse citizens' anger rather than escalate it, he might have been able to work situations around to his advantage rather than creating confrontations. Listening professionally, instead of engaging in shouting matches with citizens of other backgrounds, can require a great deal of self-control, but it usually brings better results. (Once again, George Thompson of the Verbal Judo Institute reminds officers, "You are not paid to argue." See Chapter 5.)

Threats and Aggressive Behavior

Kochman, who has conducted cultural awareness training nationwide (for both police departments and corporations) asks the question, "When does a fight begin?" Many whites, he notes, believe that "fighting" has already begun when it is "obvious" that there will be violence ("when violence is imminent"). Therefore, to whites, a fight begins as soon as the shouting starts. According to whites, then, the fight has begun whenever a certain intensity of anger is shown, along with an exchange of insults. If threats are also spoken, many whites would agree that violence will surely result.

Kochman explains that although verbal confrontation and threats may indeed be a prelude to a fight for blacks, many blacks have a clear boundary between their fighting words and their physical actions. Kochman argues that fighting does not begin until one person does something physically provocative: "If two guys are talking loudly and then one or the other starts to reduce the distance between them, that's a sign, because it's important to get in the first blow. Or if a guy puts his hand in his pocket, and that's not a movement he usually makes, then you watch for that—he might be reaching for a knife. But if they're just talking—it doesn't matter how loud it gets—then you got nothing to worry about" (Allen Harris, quoted in Kochman, 1981).*

Of course, officers who are trained to think about officer safety might have a problem accepting this dismissal ("then you got nothing to worry about"). Similarly, a threat in today's society, in which anyone may be carrying semiautomatic weapons, may be just that—a very real threat that will be carried out. Officers must always take threats seriously. However, sometimes cultural differences are at work and extreme anger can be expressed without accompanying physical violence. When this is the case, an officer can actually escalate hostilities with an approach and communication style that demonstrates a lack of understanding toward culturally or racially different modes of expression.

KEY ISSUES IN LAW ENFORCEMENT

Differential Treatment

A national study by the National Institute of Justice, titled "Police Attitudes toward Abuse of Authority," found race to be a divisive issue for American police. In particular, black and non black officers had significantly different views about the effect of a citizen's race and socioeconomic status on the likelihood of police abuse of authority. (Weisburd and Greenspan, 2000)

"I am not prejudiced. I treat all citizens fairly." Police officers around the country make these kinds of statements daily. Some officer's actions support their claims, but explicit utterances of this type usually signal prejudice. In the wake of many publicized allegations of differential treatment of African Americans (and other groups), officers with prejudices have to face them and recognize when the prejudices result in action:

My partner and I several years ago went to an all white night club. He found cocaine on this white couple. He poured it out and didn't make an arrest. Later we were at an all black nightclub. He found marijuana on one individual and arrested him. I was shocked, but I didn't say anything at the time because I was fairly new to the department. He had told me on two occasions that he "enjoyed" working with black officers and "has no difficulty" with the black community. (anonymous African American police officer)

In an ABC *20/20* television segment entitled "Presumed Guilty," an undercover investigation set out to answer the question "Are black men being singled out by police and pulled over even when they're doing nothing wrong?" This program was aired in 1992, before the term *racial profiling* came into existence. Many officers deny that they are doing this and register the counterclaim (heard repeatedly in cultural awareness training sessions), "They're always saying that I'm stopping them because they're black when, in fact, I've pulled them over because they have violated the law." African American parents continue to complain that their teenage and young adult children are pulled over or stopped as pedestrians and questioned when they have violated no laws. How are these two viewpoints reconciled? How can perceptions be so far apart?

The truth most likely lies between the categorical denial of some police officers and the statement, "We're always being stopped only because we're black." Undoubtedly, there are police procedures of which citizens are unaware, and they do not see all the other people an officer stops in a typical day. However, citizens are not getting paid to be professional, truthful, or even reasonable with officers. Some officers believe they are doing "good policing" when they stop citizens they feel might be guilty of a crime. However, this "feel" for who may be guilty can actually be a reflection of a bias or assumptions that substitute for real data. Observing and selecting "guilty-looking" motorists can be the result of unconscious biased thinking. (Refer to Chapter 1 for an explanation of the "Ladder of Inference" with respect to racial profiling.)

In a discussion of drug arrests among blacks, a high-ranking African American officer in a Southern California department made the following statement:

> When officers go out to make arrests, they'll go immediately into the inner city where they can find the "lowest hanging fruit." What I mean is . . . blacks are easy to identify; in the inner city they're standing out on the street and it's natural for officers to be suspicious and try to do their drug arrests there. But we all know that alcohol abuse is rampant among white kids and if we go to just about any campus, we'll find drugs. But that's not where officers first gravitate to. Whites don't stand on street corners, but they're still using drugs and alcohol pretty heavily.

Racial Profiling in the African American Community

> An ordinary commuter turns the key in the ignition, glances in the rear view mirror, and pulls away from the curb. Rounding the corner, his slightly worn tires slip on a fresh layer of light rain. He executes a perfect "California rolling stop" at an intersection and enters the freeway, accelerating to a comfortable 70 mph for the cruise into downtown. Our commuter just violated the traffic code at least four times, just as we all do each time we get behind the wheel. But if our commuter is a person of color, there's a good chance he won't make it to work without being pulled over for "driving while black or brown." (Hills and Trapp, 2000)*

Although *20/20's* "Presumed Guilty" was made in 1992, we know that the phenomenon of racial profiling (a term not yet used when the program was made) has always existed in America. In the program, the reporters cite the case of Al Joyner, Olympic track and field athlete, who at the time said he "refused to drive the streets of L.A. for fear of the police." He was stopped because it was believed that he was driving a stolen car. Joyner was asked to walk with his hands behind his head when he noticed about five or six police cars "out there, and all of them in their gun position with their guns out on me." Joyner was instructed to get on his knees while his license plate was being checked. When the officers discovered that the car was registered in his wife's name (Griffith-Joyner) they realized their mistake and let Joyner

Exhibit 7.3   *"What Would You Do if You Saw This Man Riding a Bike Through Your Neighborhood?"*
(*Source: Sonoma Index Tribune,* June 12, 1992, p. A-13; reprinted with permission)

go. Joyner then drove less than two blocks before he was stopped again by the same group of officers. This time he was told that he was a suspect in a hit and run: The officers were looking for "a burgundy RX7; a black man with a baseball cap." Joyner explained to the *20/20* reporters: "I didn't have an RX7, but I am black with a baseball cap." This was one of the early widely publicized cases of racial profiling.

Officers in cultural awareness training have said they have been surprised when suburban middle-class blacks express as much anger and outrage about differential treatment, including racial profiling, as do poorer blacks in inner-city areas. Many middle- and upper-class parents whose children have experienced the types of stops described are likely to be even less forgiving: Stops like these are painful indications, despite much hard-won social and economic success, that race prevails for some as the defining characteristic.

Consider the case of Antoine Bigirimana, an immigrant from Africa, educated in Europe and owner of a northern California software company. In the early 1990s Bigirimana was one of only six African American residents in the small town of Sonoma. He was the victim of racial profiling not as a motorist but as a bicyclist. He paid $1,500 to buy a full-page ad telling others in his town of his experiences with the police (see Exhibit 7.3, reproduced from his town's newspaper). In the article under the picture, Bigirimana explained that he was stopped for not having a bicycle license (he was riding his bicycle because his car was not working) and because police thought he was riding a stolen bicycle. He could not understand the pattern of stops and arrests that he was experiencing (this incident took place before the term *racial profiling* was coined). In the newspaper ad, he created mug shots from photos of himself and titled the ad: *What would you do if you saw this man riding a bike through your neighborhood?* His intention was to raise awareness in a humorous way of the treatment he had been receiving because of racial stereotypes. He felt that he must have fit a profile because he was stopped on a regular basis and, among other things, was accused of stealing a bicycle. After two days of searching for records indicating that Mr. Bigirimana had bought the bicycle, police were able to verify that the merchandise was not stolen. He concluded the explanation in his ad with the following:

> I am not a thief. It says so on a piece of paper the police gave me. I do not have a criminal record. . . . Some of my friends say that any Black person is automatically considered a thief, a violent person, possibly a drug addict or a drug dealer. They ought to know, they are all white. I do not believe any of this; however I do not understand why all of these things are happening to me on a regular basis. If you know me, please call the Sonoma Police Department and let them know that I AM NOT A CROOK. (*Sonoma Index Tribune,* June 12, 1992, p. A-13)

One of the positive results of this publicity was the formation of a cultural awareness committee consisting of police officers and citizens of Sonoma who began, for the first time, to address local racial and cultural concerns. In recent years, the department has oriented itself according to the philosophy of community policing and maintains an active working relationship with the community. As we now know from the huge number of racial profiling cases that have been publicized since the late 1990s, officers and police departments would benefit from forward thinking and professional behavior rather than waiting for an incident (or incidents) that eventually force them into acting properly with citizens.

Racial profiling is not limited to police officers and stops of motorists or bicyclists. The case of Yvette Bradley at Newark International Airport (April 1999) is a widely publicized example in the context of searches and U.S. Customs. Upon returning from Jamaica with her sister Yvette Bradley, an African American advertising professional with SpikeDDB (a partnership between Spike Lee and DDB), was singled out to be strip-searched for no reason immediately apparent to Ms. Bradley. Prior to the search, Ms. Bradley had observed "that during the search selection process, a disproportionately large percentage of black women were singled out for searches, while nearly all the white passengers were allowed to continue on their way" (Bradley, 1999). Ms. Bradley filed a complaint with the customs officer in charge; the investigation revealed that she had been strip-searched (by a female officer) because of the designer hat she was wearing (i.e., drugs could have been hidden in it). The search was a degrading and highly invasive physical probe, which did not yield any drugs or contrabands. Despite the reason given for the search, according to Ms. Bradley's testimony, none of the officers involved ever asked her to remove her hat, nor did they examine it. Her sister, who was wearing a baseball hat, was also sent through to the secondary search area. But apparently the group of white college-aged men nearby (all wearing baseball caps) were not asked to be searched. In Ms. Bradley's words:

> I felt completely degraded, and, worst of all, helpless. My pride, self-respect, and dignity were trampled on. I think that if I had been a blonde, blue-eyed white woman under the same circumstances this would not have happened to me. . . . My body and my civil liberties were violated because I am a black woman. (Bradley, 1999)

According to Hills and Trapp (2000), the U.S. Customs Service's own figures show that the "hit rates" for drugs and contrabands searches for people of color were actually lower than for whites, despite figures showing that over 43 percent of those searched were from minority groups. According to the Policy News and Information

Services (Issues Library: Civil rights, April 2000), Representative John Lewis (Georgia) formally petitioned the Treasury Department to investigate alleged racial and gender biases by U.S. Customs officers at airports in the United States. Specifically, the petition surfaced as "lawsuits related to the filing of strip search allegations, including a class action law suit in Chicago by close to 100 women increased"(Daily Briefings: SpeakOut.Com April 10, 2000) www.speakout.com/Content/DailyBriefings/2552/). Law enforcement agents throughout the criminal justice system need to recognize that racial profiling is a reality. Although many stops are justified (and the citizen may be unaware of the reasons involved), stops or searches reflecting racial profiling represent one of the most persistent legacies of institutional and individual racism.

Reactions to and Perceptions of Authority

As a response to a series of racial events in California that received national and international attention in the 1990s, including the beating of black motorist Rodney King in 1991, race riots in Los Angeles in 1992, and the trial of O. J. Simpson in 1995, the Public Policy Institute of California asked two social scientists to begin a study on ethnic reactions to legal authority (Huo and Tyler, 2000). Following are three of the major findings of the study (in which 1,500 residents of Los Angeles and Oakland, California, were questioned):

1. Compared to whites, African Americans and Latinos report lower levels of satisfaction with interactions with legal authorities. They also report less willingness than whites to comply with the directives of the authorities they deal with. This pattern of difference between minorities and whites was especially apparent among those who reported interactions with the police compared to those who reported interactions with authorities in court.

2. Much of the difference between minorities and whites in their reactions to legal authorities can be accounted for by differences in their perceptions of how fairly or unfairly they were treated. When asked whether the legal authorities involved in their encounters used fair procedures to make decisions, African Americans and Latinos reported experiencing less procedural fairness than did whites.

3. The perception of fair treatment and positive outcomes was the most important factor in forming reactions to encounters with the police and courts. It was more important than the concerns about the outcomes people received from legal authorities. This pattern held up across different situations and ethnic groups. (Huo and Tyler, 2000)

African Americans and Latinos are still reporting more negative treatment from legal authorities than are whites. These perceptions by minorities are significant in that they relate directly to compliance rates with authority among members of minority groups (Huo and Tyler, 2000). The study indicated that all groups were equally satisfied with their experiences in the court and that, as a result, there was compliance with court directives. However, African Americans and Latinos were less willing to comply with directives from police. The findings in this study were similar to those from the Milwaukee Domestic Violence Experiment conducted in 1997. In that study, African Americans and Latinos perceived that "legal authorities treated them with less procedural fairness than they do whites" (Paternoster et al., 1997).*

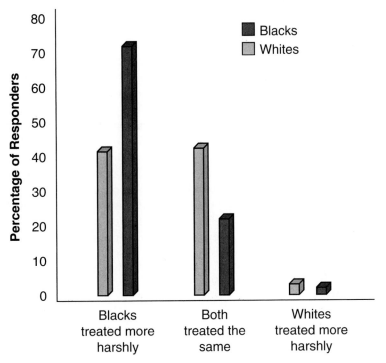

Exhibit 7.4   Perceptions by whites and blacks of treatments by the criminal justice system.
Source: Gallup Poll. The Gallup Organization. 1997. The Gallup Poll Social Audit. Black/White Relations in the United States.

The results of both these studies suggest that "group differences in perceived procedural fairness may lead to group differences in compliance with legal directives" (Huo and Tyler, 2000).

According to a 1997 Gallup poll, "a large percentage of the population, both black and white, perceive that blacks are treated more harshly by the criminal justice system than whites, although blacks are more likely than whites to have this view (72 percent of blacks compared with 44 percent of whites). Forty-six percent of whites perceived that the criminal justice system treats whites and blacks the same, compared with only 23 percent of blacks." (See Exhibit 7.4.)

Excessive Force and Brutality

Patrolling the mean streets can be a dangerous and dehumanizing task for police officers. Drawing the line between necessary force and deliberate brutality is perhaps the toughest part of the job. . . . A career of confronting the vicious, conscienceless criminal-enemy frays the nerves. . . . (Morrow, 1991)*

*In Chapter 14, readers may read the specific details of these two tragic cases in the history of law enforcement. This section also includes corresponding learning activities for law enforcement officers.

The case of Rodney King in 1992 brought public attention to the serious problems of excessive force and brutality in American policing. Blacks and other racial and ethnic groups have long maintained that police brutality was a problem, but until the early 1990s (when several cases were highly publicized), many whites either did not believe or closed their eyes to this reality. Nearly a decade after the Rodney King event, in 1999, Americans and citizens worldwide witnessed two more incidents of brutality against black Americans,* Abner Louima, a Haitian immigrant, and Amadou Diallo, an immigrant from Guinea. The majority of officers around the nation do not use excessive force, but police brutality is not yet a thing of the past.

Controlling racist behavior based on biases and prejudices must be a priority training issue in all departments across the country. (Chapter 1 deals with prejudices and biases.) Police departments need to address an officer's buildup of stress as frequently and as seriously as, for example, self-defense issues. Finally, individual officers must remember that even though abusive behavior from citizens constitutes one of the worst aspects of the job, they must maintain their professionalism.

Law Enforcement Interaction with Poor Urban Black Communities

Many police officers feel that they are putting their lives in danger when they go into certain black communities, particularly those in urban areas where poverty and crime go hand in hand. As a result, some segments of the black community believe police are not protecting them, and are extremely fearful of "black-on-black" crime. The increase in the number of citizens' weapons in urban areas, including increased self-protective weaponry, contributes to defensive reactions among both police officers and citizens. A vicious cycle escalates and reinforces hostilities. Police are often expected to solve the social ills of society but have neither the resources nor the training to deal with problems that are rooted in historical, social, political, and economic factors. Blacks and police officers are often frustrated with each other and barriers seem insurmountable. Although the following quote comes from a source in the early 1970s, the dynamic described is still operative:

> Many policemen find themselves on the alert for the slightest sign of disrespect. One author has shown [McNamara] that the police [officer] is often prepared to coerce respect and will use force if he feels his position is being challenged. Likewise, the attitudes and emotions of the black citizen may be similar when confronted with a police [officer]. Intervention by police is often seen as an infringement on the blacks' rights and as oppression by the white population. Consequently many blacks are on the alert for the slightest sign of disrespect that might be displayed by the police [officer]. (Cross and Renner, 1974)

Cross and Renner go on to explain that fear of belittlement and fear of danger operate for both the black citizen and the officer, and these fears cause both sides to misinterpret what might otherwise be nonthreatening behavior. The problem often arises not from the reality of the situation but from mutual fears. In some parts of the country, this is as true now as it was in the mid-1970s when the article cited was written.

Social scientists have been studying the problems of inner-city young men, in particular, because this group is most endangered. Consider the following statistics*:

- Homicide victimization rates for blacks have been at least five times those of whites for the past half century, sometimes reaching more than 10 times the white rate. In 1996 blacks had the highest victimization rates at 29.8 percent, compared to Hispanics (12.4 percent), American Indians (9.8 percent), and non-Hispanic whites and Asians (3.5 percent and 4.6 percent, respectively).
- Black males have by far the highest homicide victimization rate (123.1 per 100,000 population), followed by Hispanics (48.9), American Indians (26), and non-Hispanic whites (6.4).
- Regarding prison rates, black admissions increased more than fivefold between 1970 and 1995.
- In 1994, blacks represented 43 percent of arrests, 54 percent of convictions, and 59 percent of prison admissions for violent crime. Compared with whites, blacks were more likely to be convicted if arrested and more likely to be imprisoned if convicted. (Council of Economic Advisors, 1998)

Regarding the final statistic (i.e., the high rate of arrests, convictions, and prison admissions for violent crimes in 1994), the report reads: "Discriminatory behavior on the part of police and elsewhere in the criminal justice system may contribute to blacks' high representation in arrests, convictions, and prison admissions" (Council of Economic Advisors, 1998).

Black Women and Police

It is beyond the scope of this book to delve into the specific issues and attitudes of black women toward police and authority. However, one area is worthy of attention. Results from a Gallup Poll of over 2,000 respondents (Gallup Poll Release, December 1999) indicated that between one-quarter and one-third of black women polled did not perceive fair treatment from police. Although the results of this poll reflect overall interracial conflict with law enforcement, the crime of rape and how it is treated are particularly notable. Many black women perceive (sometimes correctly) that law enforcement has not always considered the rape of a black woman to be as serious as the rape of a white woman, either legally or psychologically. Some black women perceive that their assailants are less likely to be tried and convicted. Perceptions by African American women are indeed supported by research (Wriggins, 1983; Wyatt, 1992). According to some social scientists, "There is reason to believe some African American women may be convinced that rape is not treated any differently today than it was in the past" (Wyatt, 1992).*

Law enforcement officials alone cannot solve social ills but should realize that African Americans in disadvantaged communities desperately need excellent police protection. The perception that whites in middle-class communities are better served by the police forces naturally reinforces existing antipolice attitudes among the lower class.

---

*Additional statistics regarding hate crimes and African Americans can be found in Chapter 11.

Addressing the Needs of the Inner City

"Black-on-black crime seems to be tolerated and even accepted as inevitable" (*USA Today,* April 24, 1991). This statement, made by an African American chief of police in 1991, is as true today as it was a decade ago. African Americans and other racial and ethnic groups have criticized law enforcement for underpolicing in the inner city, but progress has been made to improve relations between police and community members. Currently more African American officers and police executives are influencing and changing policy that directly affects police–black relations. Many departments (although by no means all) have put into writing strict rules regarding the use of excessive force, discourtesy, racial slurs, and aggressive patrol techniques. Police management in some areas is beginning to understand why many people in urban black communities believe they receive unequal police services.

SUMMARY OF RECOMMENDATIONS FOR LAW ENFORCEMENT

The experience of slavery and racism as well as cultural differences have shaped African American culture. Patterns of culture and communication among black Americans differ from those among white Americans. In face-to-face communication, officers should not ignore or downplay these differences.

For many African Americans, particularly those in the lower socioeconomic classes, the history of slavery and later discrimination continue to leave psychological scars. Law enforcement officials, in particular, represent a system that has oppressed African Americans and other minorities. To protect and serve in many African American communities across the nation necessarily means that officers will need to go out of their way to establish trust and win cooperation.

There is tremendous diversity among African Americans, including socioeconomic status, religion, region of the country (rural or urban area), and country of origin. Color and race, however, often determine how the larger society will react to and treat African Americans. Therefore, the racial (as opposed to the cultural) experience of many African Americans is similar.

The changing terms that African Americans have used to refer to themselves reflect stages of racial and cultural growth, as well as empowerment. Officers should respect the terms that African Americans prefer to use. *Negro* and *colored* are no longer used and have been replaced by *black* in many police communications. However, in speech, many people prefer the term *African American.* Officers can learn to become comfortable asking a citizen which term he or she prefers if there is a need to refer to ethnicity in the conversation. Officers are advised to stop each other when they hear offensive terms being used. Doing so not only contributes to making a department free of overt prejudices but also helps the individual officer to practice control when he or she is faced with volatile citizens. An officer in the habit of using offensive terms may not be able to restrain himself or herself in public situations. Therefore, peer monitoring will ultimately be of benefit to the department.

African Americans react as negatively to stereotypes that they hear about themselves as officers do when they hear such statements as "Police officers are biased against blacks" and "All police officers are capable of brutality." Many of the stereotypes about African Americans stem from ignorance and the impression people receive from the criminal element. Law enforcement officers, in particular, must be sensitive to how their own perceptions of African Americans are formed. The disproportionately high crime rate among African American males does not justify sweeping statements about the majority of African Americans, who are law-abiding citizens.

The predominance of households headed by women, particularly in the inner city, coupled with the myth of a black matriarchy has created situations in which officers have dismissed the importance of the father. Despite common myths and stereotypes regarding black women, officers should always approach both parents to get both versions of the story and to consider their opinions in decision making. If the father is ignored or not given much attention, he will likely be offended.

Young African American males, in particular, and their parents (of all socioeconomic levels) feel a sense of outrage and injustice when officers stop them for no apparent reason. Officers will destroy any possibility of establishing trust (and later winning cooperation) by stopping youths (and others) because it "looks like they don't belong in a given neighborhood." Every time an instance of this nature occurs, police—community and police—youth relations suffer.

The use of African American varieties of English does not represent any pathology or deficiency and is not a combination of random errors but rather reflects patterns of grammar from some West African languages. Many people have strong biases against this variety of spoken English. Officers should take care not to convey a lack of acceptance through disapproving facial expressions, a negative tone of voice, or a tendency to interrupt or finish the sentences for the other person. When it comes to "black English" or an accent, police should not fake it to be accepted by the group. People will immediately pick up on this lack of sincerity, which in and of itself can create hostility.

People in positions of authority have often misunderstood aspects of black nonverbal communication, including what has been termed the "cool pose." Police officers may interpret certain ways of standing, walking, and dressing as defiant. This can create defensive reactions on the part of the police officer. In many cases, the police officer need not take this behavior personally or feel threatened.

Cultural differences in verbal communication can result in complete misinterpretation. Officers should not necessarily equate an African American's expression of rage and verbal threats with a loss of control that leads automatically to violence. Within cultural norms, it can be acceptable to be very expressive and emotional in speech. This is in contrast to an unspoken white mainstream norm, which discourages the open and free expression of emotion, especially anger.

Racial profiling, excessive force, and brutality still exist in policing in the United States. When acts of bias, brutality, and injustice occur, everyone suffers, including officers and entire police departments. Every officer should be on the lookout for unchecked biases within themselves and others that could result in inappropriate language or force with citizens of all backgrounds. They should be aware of their own levels of stress and frustration and have the means and support to release tension before it breaks loose in the streets.

A dynamic exists between some officers and African Americans, particularly in poor urban areas, whereby both the officer and the citizen are on the alert for the slightest sign of disrespect. The fear that both the citizen and the officer experience can interfere with what may actually be a nonthreatening situation. The police officer can be the one to break the cycle of fear by softening his or her verbal and nonverbal approach.

In areas populated by African Americans and other racial and immigrant groups all over the United States, there is a need for increased and more effective police protection. Bridging the gap that has separated police from African Americans involves radical changes in attitudes toward police–community relations. Together with changes in management, even the individual officer can help by making greater efforts to have positive contact with African Americans. The task of establishing rapport with African Americans at all levels of society is challenging because of what the officer represents in terms of past discrimination. Turning this image around involves a commitment on the part of the officer to break with deeply embedded stereotypes and to have as a goal respect and professionalism in every encounter.

DISCUSSION QUESTIONS AND ISSUES*

1. ***Racism: Effects on Blacks and Whites.*** Under "Historical Information" in this chapter, we suggest African American slavery has created great psychological and social problems for blacks and whites of later generations. How is this true for both races? What are the implications for law enforcement?

2. ***Offensive Terms.*** We advise refraining from using such offensive terms as "nigger" at all times, even where there are no African Americans present. Give two practical reasons for this advice.

3. ***"Cool Pose" and the Use of Threats.*** How do you think the information in this chapter about threats, emotional expression (including rage), and the "cool pose" can help officers in their approach to citizens? Describe or role-play how an officer would communicate if he or she did not feel threatened by such behavior, then describe or role-play how an officer might approach and interact with the citizen if he or she was threatened by the behavior.

4. ***Inner Cities: Officers' and Citizens' Reactions.*** Near the end of the chapter, we mention the vicious cycle created in urban areas, especially where citizens have become increasingly armed (with highly sophisticated weapons) and officers, consequently, have to take more self-protective measures. Each views the other with fear and animosity and approaches the other with extreme defensiveness. Obviously, there is no simple answer to this widely occurring phenomenon, and police cannot solve the ills of society. Discuss your observations of the way officers cope with the stresses of these potentially life-threatening situations and how the coping or lack thereof affects rela-

*See Instructor's Manual accompanying this text for additional activities, role-play activities, questionnaires, and projects related to the content of this chapter.

tions with African Americans and other minorities. What type of support do police officers need to handle this aspect of their job? Do you think police departments are doing their job in providing the support needed?

5. ***When Officers Try to Make a Difference.*** Many young African American children, especially in housing projects in inner cities, live without a father in the household. This means that they do not have a second authority figure as a role model and are thus deprived of an important source of adult support. No one can take the place of a missing parent, but there are small and large things a police officer can do to at least make an impression in the life of a child. Compile a list of actions officers can take to demonstrate their caring of children in these environments. Include in your first list every gesture, no matter how small; your second list can include a realistic list of what action can be taken given the resources available. Select someone to compile both sets of suggestions (the realistic and ideal suggestions). Post these lists as reminders of how officers can attempt to make a difference in their communities not only with African American children but with other children as well.

6. ***Racial Profiling.*** Every criminal justice student, policy academy student, and law enforcement representative needs to look closely at instances of racial profiling, study them, and learn from previous officers' mistakes. Discuss the following two incidents of racial profiling, using the questions that follow each incident as guidelines for your discussion.

A student from Liberia attending college in North Carolina was driving along I-95 in Maryland when he was pulled over by state police who said he wasn't wearing a seatbelt. The officers detained him and his two passengers for two hours as they searched the car for illegal drugs, weapons, or other contraband. Finding nothing, they proceeded to dismantle the car and removed part of the door panel, a seat panel, and part of the sunroof. Again finding nothing, the officers in the end handed the man a screwdriver as they left the scene saying, "You're going to need this." (Rice, 1999)

Questions to discuss: First, describe in detail all the potential negative consequences from this police incident. What else do we need to know about this incident to reach a decision as to whether the stop was legitimate or related to racial profiling? For example, would we want to know the following?

- Time of day (could the trooper have seen that the driver was not wearing a seat belt)?
- Does the state police administration encourage stops on I-95 of individuals and vehicles that fit the profile of drug runners?

What other information would you want to know? Officers usually ask for permission or consent to search a vehicle they stop when probable cause does not exist for a search. Do you think the officers requested a voluntary consent to search this vehicle? Was the length of the detention reasonable? Was it disrespectful and unwarranted to leave the student to replace his vehicle parts? If you are a police officer, could you justify this sort of traffic stop to your supervisor, department, or community or in your own conscience?

An African American police officer was pulled over while driving an unmarked car in the city of Carmel, Indiana. The man was wearing a uniform at the time, but he was not wearing a hat, which would have identified him as a police officer. According to a complaint filed with the ACLU, the trooper who pulled the man over appeared "shocked and surprised" Then the man got out of his car. The trooper explained that he had stopped the man because he had three antennas on the rear of his car. (Rice, 1999)

Questions to discuss: Do you feel that the officer who pulled over a colleague was guilty of racial profiling? Do you think the officer was being honest when he said that the reason for the stop was the multiple antennas? Can you think of any law violated by having multiple antennas or why this would make the stopping officer suspicious of the vehicle or occupant? What else must we know about the incident to reach a decision about the appropriateness of the traffic stop? For example, would time of day be a factor? Location?

REFERENCES

BENNETT, LERONE, JR. (1989, November). "The 10 Biggest Myths about the Black Family," *Ebony.*

BERRY, ONDRE. (2000, December). Deputy Chief, Reno, Nevada, Police Department, personal communication.

BRADLEY, YVETTE. (1999). Statement given to the American Civil Liberties Union Freedom Network News.www.acluors/news/1999/BradleyState.htm

Council of Economic Advisors. (1998, September). "Changing America: Indicators of Social and Economic Well-Being by Race and Hispanic Origin." In *Crime and Criminal Justice.*, pp. 50–59 Council of Economic Advisors for the President's Initiative on Race, National Center for Health Statistics, Bureau of Justice Statistics. Washington, D.C.

CROSS, STAN, AND EDWARD RENNER. (1974). "An Interaction Analysis of Police-Black Relations," *Journal of Police Science Administration, 2* (1),

FILLMORE, CHARLES J. (1997, January). *A Linguist Looks at the Ebonics Debate.* Washington, D.C.: Center for Applied Linguistics.

FREY, WILLIAM H. (1998, June–July). "New Demographic Divide in the US: Immigrant and Domestic 'Migrant Magnets,'," *Public Perspective, 9* (4),

GALLUP, POLL. (Release December 1999). "Attitudes of Black Women Towards Police and Authority"

GETMAN, K. (1984). "Sexual Control in the Slaveholding South: The Implementation and Maintenance of a Racial Caste System," *Harvard Women's Law Review, 7,* pp. 5–7

GOLEMAN, DANIEL. (1992, April 21). "Black Scientists Study the 'Pose' of the Inner City," *New York Times.*

HILLS, LINDA, AND RANDA TRAPP. (2000, October). "Beyond the Mythology of Racial Profiling," *San Diego Union.* October 13, 2000 www.aclu.sandiego.org/racialprofiling/html

HINES, PAULETTE MOORE, AND NANCY-BOYD FRANKLIN. (1982). "Black Families." In Ethnicity and Family Therapy. M. McGoldrick et al. (Eds.), New York: Guilford Press.

HUO, YUEN J., AND TOM R. TYLER. (2000). *How Different Ethnic Groups React to Legal Authority.* Public Policy Institute of California. San Francisco, California

KOCHMAN, THOMAS. (1981). *Black and White Styles in Conflict.* Chicago: University of Chicago Press.

LABOV, WILLIAM. (1972). *Sociolinguistic Patterns.* Philadelphia: University of Pennsylvania Press.

LOHMAN, D. L. (1977). "Race Tension and Conflict." In N. A. Watson (Ed.), *Police and the Changing Community.* Washington, D.C.: International Association of Chiefs of Police.

McADOO, HARRIET PIPES. (1992). "Upward Mobility and Parenting in Middle Income Families." In *African American Psychology.* Newbury Park, Calif.: Sage Publications, pp. 59–86

MILLER, CHAR. (2000, December). U. S. historian, personal communication.

MORROW, LANCE. (1991, April 1). "Rough Justice," *Time,* 16–17.

National Center for Health Statistics. (1996). Report of Final Natality Statistics (Series 21, no. 53).

National Center for Health Statistics. (1998). Division of Data Services, Hyattsville, MD. Monthly Vital Statistics Report, (Vol. 46, no. 11).

ODOM, STEVE. (1992, November 5). Sergeant, Berkeley, California, Police Department, personal communication.

PATERNOSTER, R. AND R. BACHMAN, R. BRAME, AND L. W. SHERMAN. (1997). "Do Fair Procedures Matter?" The Effect of Procedural Justice on Spouse Assault," *Law and Society Review, 31,* pp. 163–204

RICE, GEORGE. (1999). *People and Possibilities. Racial Profiling: Prejudice or Protocol?* Horizon. www.horizonmag.org/b/Racial-profiling. asp 12/15/00

SHUSTA, ROBERT. (1986). *Cultural Issues Manual* (p. 5). Concord, Calif.: Concord Police Department.

SHUSTA, ROBERT. (2000, December). Retired captain, personal communication.

SMITHERMAN, GENEVA. (1972). *Talkin' and Testifyin'* (p. 2). Boston: Houghton Mifflin.

THOMPSON, GEORGE. (1983). Verbal Judo: The Gentle Art of Persuasion. Verbal Judo Ins. Inc Staten Island, NY.

THOMPSON, GEORGE. (1983). Verbal Judo: Words as Force. Verbal Judo Institute Inc. (Verbal Judo @rmi.net)

TYLER, T. R., R. J. BOECKMANN, H. J. SMITH, AND Y. J. HUO. (1997). *Social Justice in a Diverse Society.* Boulder, Colo.: Westview Press.

U.S. Bureau of the Census (2000). *Population by Race and Hispanic Origin.* Washington, D.C.: U.S. Government Printing Office.

WALKER, ANNA. (1982). "Black American Cultures." In *California Cultural Awareness Resource Guide.* pp. 93–123 Compiled by: Cultural Awareness Training Project San Francisco: Chinatown Resources Development Center.

WALKER, SAMUEL. (1992). *The Police in America.* New York: McGraw-Hill.

WEBER, SHIRLEY N. (1991). "The Need to Be: The Socio-Cultural Significance of Black Language." Larry Samovar and Richard Porter (Eds.) *Intercultural Communication: A Reader* (4th ed.) Belmont, Calif.: Wadsworth Press. pp. 244–253

WEISBURD, DAVID, AND ROSANN GREENSPAN. (2000, May). "Police Attitudes toward Abuse of Authority: Findings from a National Study," *National Institute of Justice Research in Brief.* pp. 1–15

WILLIAMS, HUBERT, AND PATRICK MURPHY. (1990, January). *The Evolving Strategy of Police: A Minority View.* Washington, D.C.: National Institute of Justice, U.S. Department of Justice; Cambridge, Mass.: Program in Criminal Justice Policy and Management, Harvard University.

Wriggens, J. (1983). "Rape, Racism, and the Law," *Harvard Women's Law Journal, 6,* 103–141.

WYATT, G. E. (1992). "The Sociocultural Context of African American and White Women's Rape," *Journal of Social Issues, 48,* 77–91.

8

LAW ENFORCEMENT CONTACT WITH LATINO/HISPANIC AMERICANS

OVERVIEW

This chapter provides specific ethnic and cultural information on Latino/Hispanic Americans. The label *Latino/Hispanic Americans* encompasses over 25 different ethnic and cultural groups from Central and South America and the Caribbean. For ease of use, we will use the term *Latino/Hispanic Americans* to refer to members of these ethnic groupings. We first define this highly diverse group and then provide a historical overview that will contribute to readers' understanding of the relationship between law enforcement personnel and citizens. We present demographics and elements of diversity among Latino/Hispanic Americans, as well as issues related to ethnic and cultural identity: myths and stereotypes, the extended family and community, gender roles, generational differences, and adolescent and youth issues. The section "Cultural Influences on Communication" introduces the subtle aspects of nonverbal and indirect communications law enforcement personnel often find troublesome. We present, in the closing section, several key issues for law enforcement: underreporting of crimes, victimization, differential treatment, racial profiling of Latino/Hispanic Americans, attitudes toward crime and safety, exposure to environmental risks and job hazards, and increasing community services to the community and peace officers from the community. Finally, we review recommendations for improved communication and relationships between law enforcement personnel and members of Latino/Hispanic American communities.

COMMENTARY

In this chapter, we refer to Latino/Hispanic Americans more in terms of the similarities shared across groups than in terms of the differences. Certainly, there are great differences in terms of culture, values, and behaviors. A first concern by many law enforcement officers is how to refer to the different groups comprising Latino/Hispanic Americans.

> The term *Hispanic* means so many different things to so many different people. To the typical American, stereotypes of poverty, illegal aliens, laborers, and uneducated come to mind. For those who are part of the so-called Hispanic group, there is really no agreement as to what we want to be called: Is it Latino, Hispanic, or the people from the specific countries of origin like Mexican, Puerto Rican, Cuban, Salvadorean, Colombian, Dominican, Nicaraguan, Chilean, Argentinean, Brazilian, and other South and Central Americans? (Latino/Hispanic American community organizer-Personal Communication)

Law enforcement officers are called to respond to concerns or complaints by community members against Latino/Hispanic Americans. Often, such complaints are made by individuals who do not understand the Latino/Hispanic American community. Moreover, law enforcement officers, in response to community members' concerns and complaints, see only one side of a diverse group of people. As is evident by the two quotes that follow, the Latino/Hispanic American community reflects the full range of economic and cultural diversity.

> Every day, we get complaints from parents, merchants, commuters, etc. wanting the police to do something about the "Mexicans" and other "Latino/Hispanic" types waiting to be picked up for a job around the freeway on-ramps. They stand there for hours waiting for a *patron*, a boss, to drive up and employ them for a day, a week, or a few hours. It's a community issue, yet the police are expected to solve it. We can ask them to disband and move on, but all that would do is to have them move around the corner. (Police officer's anecdote told at a cultural awareness training session-Confidential Communication)

> It's unfortunate that for the average American, the stereotypes of Latino/Hispanic Americans include the characteristics of poor, uneducated immigrants, and perhaps of illegal status. What's missing from the picture are the vast numbers of us who are successful in business, university-educated, community leaders, and active in shaping the political future of our country. (Business owner's comment at a Hispanic Chambers of Commerce Conference in Denver, Colorado)

INTRODUCTION

Latino/Hispanic Americans are the fastest growing cultural group in the United States in terms of numbers of people. Between the 1990 and 2000 censuses, the population increased by 45 percent from 22.4 million in 1990 to 32.5 million in 2000. Growth in all urban and rural areas of the United States has been striking. The population growth can be attributed to (1) higher birthrates; (2) higher immigration from Mexico, Central and South America, and the Caribbean; (3) greater longevity, since this is a relatively young population; and (4) larger numbers of subgroups being incorporated into the Latino/Hispanic American grouping.

LATINO/HISPANIC AMERICANS DEFINED

Hispanic is a generic term referring to all Spanish-surname and Spanish-speaking people who reside in the United States and in Puerto Rico (a U.S. territory). *Latino* is generally the preferred label on the West Coast, parts of the East Coast, and the Southeast and is a Spanish word to indicate a person of Latin American origins (and to correctly reflect the gender-specific nature of the term: *Latino,* for men, and *Latina,* for women). *Hispanic* is generally preferred on the East Coast, primarily by the Puerto Rican, Dominican, and Cuban communities (although the members within each of these communities may prefer the specific term referring to their country of heritage). *Hispanic* is also the official term used in federal, state, and local governmental writings and for demographic references (in 1976, Congress passed Public Law 94-311, called the Roybal Resolution, which required the inclusion of a self-identification question on Spanish origin or descent in government surveys and censuses). Objections to the use of the term *Hispanic* include the following: (1) *Hispanic* is not derived from any culture or place (i.e., there is no such place as "Hispania") and (2) the term was primarily invented for use by the U.S. Census Bureau. Sometimes, the term *Spanish speaking/Spanish surnamed* may be used to recognize the fact that a large number of Latino/Hispanic Americans may not speak Spanish (thus *Spanish surnamed*). *La Raza* is another term used, primarily on the West Coast and in the Southwest, to refer to all peoples of the Western Hemisphere who share a cultural, historical, political, and social legacy of the Spanish and Portuguese colonists and the Native Indian and African people; it has its origins with the notions of the political struggles and the mixing of the races, *el mestizaje. Chicano* is another term that grew out of the ethnic pride and ethnic studies movement in the late 1960s and refers to Mexican Americans (used primarily on the West Coast, in the Southwest, and in the Midwest and in college communities that have an ethnic studies curriculum).

The definition of Latino/Hispanic is considered by many to be a "megalabel" that does not fit well with members included in the group. This view is illustrated in the following two examples:

> One version of this objection argues against all existing ethnic names, and particularly "Hispanic" or "Latinos/Latinas," because these labels have had connotations among the general population. They create a negative perception of those named and tend to perpetuate their disadvantageous situation in society. To call someone Hispanic or Latino/Latina, like calling someone negro or colored, carries with it all sorts of negative baggage, demeaning the person and harming him or her in diverse ways. (Gracia, 2000)

> Younger people in some cities, especially, find Hispanic archaic, if not downright offensive, much as "Negro" displeased a previous generation of blacks and African-Americans. They say it recalls the colonization by Spain and Portugal and ignores the Indian and African roots of many people it describes. Yet others, including business and political leaders, dismiss "Latino" as a fad. Still others use the terms Hispanic and Latino interchangeably. (Gonzalez, 1992) Section 4, p. 6

HISTORICAL INFORMATION

The historical background of Latino/Hispanic Americans provides key factors that affect their interactions and understanding of law enforcement and peacekeeping personnel. Clearly, this brief historical and sociopolitical overview can only highlight some of the commonalities and diversity of cultural experiences of Latino/Hispanic Americans. The largest numbers under the Latino/Hispanic groupings in the United States are from Mexico, Puerto Rico, and Cuba. Our historical review will focus primarily on these larger Latino/Hispanic communities.

Under the declaration of Manifest Destiny, the United States began in the 1800s the expansionist policy of annexing vast territories to the south, north, and west. As Lopez y Rivas (1973) noted, the United States viewed itself as a people chosen by "Providence" to form a larger union through conquest, purchase, and annexation. With the purchase (or annexation) of the Louisiana Territories in 1803, Florida in 1819, Texas in 1845, and the Northwest Territories (Oregon, Washington, Idaho, Wyoming, and Montana) in 1846, it was inevitable that conflict would occur with Mexico. The resulting Mexican-American War ended in 1848 with the signing of the Treaty of Guadalupe Hidalgo, in which Mexico received $15 million from the United States for the land that is now Texas, New Mexico, Arizona, and California, with more than 100,000 Mexican people living in those areas. As is obvious from this portion of history, it makes little sense for many Mexican Americans to be stereotyped as "illegal aliens," especially since more than a million Mexican Americans (some of whom are U.S. citizens and some of whom are not) can trace their ancestry back to families living in the southwestern United States in the mid-1800s (Fernandex, 1970). Moreover, for Latino/Hispanic Americans (especially Mexican Americans), the boundaries between the United States and Mexico are seen as artificial:

> The geographic, ecological, and cultural blending of the Southwest with Mexico is perceived as a continuing unity of people whose claim to the Southwest is rooted in the land itself. (Montiel, 1978)

While one-third of Mexican Americans can trace their ancestry to families living in the United States in the mid-1800s, the majority of this group migrated into the United States after 1910 because of the economic and political changes that occurred as a result of the Mexican Revolution.

Puerto Rico was under the domination of Spain until 1897, at which time it was allowed the establishment of a local government. The United States invaded Puerto Rico and annexed it as part of the Spanish-American War (along with Cuba, the Philippines, and Guam) in 1898. Although Cuba (in 1902) and the Philippines (in 1949) were given their independence, Puerto Rico remained a territory of the United States. In 1900 the U.S. Congress passed the Foraker Act, which allowed the president to appoint a governor, to provide an Executive Council consisting of 11 presidential appointees (of which only 5 had to be Puerto Rican), and to elect locally a 35-member Chamber of Delegates. In reality, the territory was run by the president-appointed governor and the Executive Council. The Jones Act of 1917 made Puerto Ricans citizens of the United States. It was not until 1948 that Puerto Rico elected its first governor, Luis Munoz Marin. In 1952 Puerto Rico was given Commonwealth status, and Spanish was allowed to be the language of instruction in the schools again (with English taught as the second language).

Following World War II, large numbers of Puerto Ricans began migrating into the United States. With citizenship status, Puerto Ricans could travel easily and settled in areas on the East Coast, primarily New York City (in part because of the availability of jobs and affordable apartments). The estimated number of Puerto Ricans in the United States is 2 million on the mainland and 3.9 million on the island (Ramos-McKay, Comas-Diaz, and Rivera, 1988).

Cubans immigrated into the United States in three waves. The first wave occurred between 1959 and 1965 and consisted of primarily white, middle-class or upper-class Cubans who were relatively well educated and had business and financial resources. The federal government's Cuban Refugee Program, Cuban Student Loan Program, and Cuban Small Business Administration Loan Program were established to help this first wave of Cuban immigrants achieve a successful settlement (Bernal and Estrada, 1985). The second wave of Cuban immigrants occurred between 1965 and 1973. This second wave resulted from the opening of the Port of Camarioca, which allowed all who wished to leave Cuba to exit. Those who left as part of the second wave were more often of the working class and lower middle class, primarily white adult men and women. The third wave of immigrants leaving Cuba from Mariel occurred from the summer of 1980 to early 1982. This third wave was the largest (about 125,000 were boat-lifted to the United States) and consisted primarily of working-class persons more reflective than previous waves of the Cuban population as a whole. Most immigrated into the United States with hopes for better economic opportunities. Within this group of *Marielito* were many antisocial, criminal, and mentally ill persons released by Fidel Castro and included in the boat lift (Gavzer, 1993).

In addition to the three major groups that have immigrated to the United States from Mexico, Puerto Rico, and Cuba are immigrants from the 21 countries of South and Central America and the Caribbean. Arrival of these immigrants for political, economic, and social reasons began in the early 1980s and has added to the diversity of Latino/Hispanic American communities in the United States. Total numbers of some groups, such as the Dominicans, a rapidly growing group on the East Coast, are difficult to determine because of their undocumented entry status in the United States.

DEMOGRAPHICS: DIVERSITY AMONG LATINO/HISPANIC AMERICANS

As is evident from the historical background provided, Latino/Hispanic Americans are a very heterogeneous population composed of many different cultural groups with significant generational, educational, and socioeconomic differences, varying relocation experiences, and many other life experience differences. Although the Spanish language may provide a common thread to most Latino/Hispanic Americans, there are cultural and national differences in the terms and expressions used, including nonverbal nuances. Moreover, the language of Brazil is Portuguese, not Spanish, and thus the language connection for Brazilian Latino/Hispanic Americans is unique. The Latino/Hispanic American population numbers about 32.5 million and represents 11.8 percent of the U.S. population (not including the 3.9 million people who live in Puerto Rico). The numerical growth of the Latino/Hispanic American population is the fastest, with more than 10 million people added to the U.S. population between the 1990 and 2000 censuses. About 85 percent of Latino/Hispanic Americans trace their roots to Mexico, Puerto Rico, and Cuba, while the remaining 15 percent are from the other countries of Central and South America, the Caribbean, and Spain (Gonzalez, 1992).

Latino/Hispanic Americans are concentrated in five states: California (33 percent), Texas (18 percent) , New York (9 percent), Florida (7 percent), and Illinois (4 percent). Some of the key demographics information about this population includes the following (the implications of the demographic information that follows are presented in the "Key Issues in Law Enforcement" section):

1. *Age:* The Latino/Hispanic American population tends to be younger than the general U.S. population. The median age is 26.4 years, in contrast to 34.9 for the rest of America.

2. *Size of household:* The average Latino/Hispanic household consists of 3.5 people, which is nearly one person more for every Latino/Hispanic household than that for other U.S. households, which average 2.6 persons per household.

3. *Birthrate:* Latino/Hispanic Americans have a higher birthrate than the general U.S. population. The Latino/Hispanic American birthrate per 1,000 is 104.8, in comparison to 65.4 for the rest of America.

4. *Purchasing power:* The estimated purchasing power of Latino/Hispanic Americans in the United States is $383 billion (Rodriguez, 2000).

5. *Urban households:* About 88 percent of all Latino/Hispanic Americans live in metropolitan areas, making this group the most highly urbanized population in the United States. For example, Latino/Hispanic Americans constitute noted percentages of the population for the following large cities: El Paso (74 percent), Corpus Christi (57 percent), San Antonio (52 percent), Fresno (41 percent), Seattle-Tacoma (40 percent), Los Angeles (38 percent), Albuquerque (38 percent), Miami-Ft. Lauderdale (37 percent), Tucson (27 percent), San Diego (25 percent), Austin (24 percent) and San Francisco/Oakland (19 percent) (Hornor, 1999).

6. *Language:* Latino/Hispanic American self-identification is most strongly demonstrated in the use and knowledge of Spanish. The Spanish language is oftentimes the single most important cultural aspect retained by Latino/Hispanic Americans. The Hispanic Monitor, based on research by Yankelovich Clancy Shulman and Market Development, Inc., summarized its findings relative to Spanish spoken at home in Latino/Hispanic American households (see Exhibit 8.1).

Exhibit 8.1 Language spoken at home by Latino/Hispanic Americans.

LANGUAGE SPOKEN AT HOME	TOTAL (%)	BORN IN THE U.S. (%)	BORN OUTSIDE THE U.S. (%)
Spanish dominant	56	18	78
Spanish and English equally	23	35	16
English dominant	21	47	6

As might be expected, with the large number of Latino/Hispanic Americans born in the United States, English will soon be the dominant language as this population moves into successive future generations.

LABELS AND TERMS

As noted earlier, the term *Latino/Hispanic American* is a convenient summarizing label to achieve some degree of agreement in referring to a very heterogeneous group of people. Similar to the case of Asian/Pacific Americans, the key to understanding which terms to use is based on the principle of self-preference. As Cisneros noted in Gonzalez (1992):

> "To say Latino is to say you come to my culture in a manner of respect," said Sandra Cisneros, the author of "Women Hollering Creek: And Other Stories," who refuses to have her writing included in any anthology that uses the word Hispanic. "To say Hispanic means you're so colonized you don't even know for yourself or someone who named you never bothered to ask what you call yourself. It's a repulsive slave name." (Gonzales, 1992 Sec. 4., p. 6)

Although many Latino/Hispanic Americans may not hold as strong a point of view as Cisneros, sensitivity is warranted in use of the term *Hispanic* with the Latino/Hispanic American community. For those who have origins in the Caribbean (e.g., Puerto Rican, Cuban, Dominican), the term *Latino* may be equally problematic for self-designation and self-identification.

In federal and other governmental designations, the label used is *Hispanic*. Although only some refer to themselves as such, the governmental designation is used in laws, programs, and regulations and in most reports and publications. For individuals within any of the groups, often the more specific names for the groups are preferred (e.g., Mexican, Puerto Rican, Cuban, Dominican, Argentinean, Salvadorean). Some individuals may prefer that the term *American* be part of their designation (e.g., Mexican American). For law enforcement officers, the best term to use in referring to individuals is the term they prefer to be called. It is perfectly acceptable to ask individuals what they prefer to be called.

The use of slurs like, "wetback," "Mex," "Spic," "Greaser" or other derogatory ethnic slang terms are never acceptable in crime fighting and peacekeeping, no matter how provoked an officer may be. Other stereotypic terms like, "Illegal," "New York Rican," "Macho man," "Latin lover," "Lupe the Virgin," and "Low Rider" do not convey the kinds of professionalism and respect for community diversity important to law enforcement and peacekeeping, and need to be avoided in law enforcement work. Officers hearing these (or other similar) words used in their own departments (or with peers or citizens) should provide immediate feedback about the inappropriate use of such terms to the other officer. Officers who may out of habit routinely use these terms may find themselves (or their superiors) in the *embarrassing situation* of explaining to offended citizens and communities why the term was used and how they had intended no bias, stereotype, nor prejudice.

Exhibit 8.2 Typology of Latino/Hispanic Americans

Type I	Latino/Hispanic Recently Arrived Immigrant or Refugee (Less than Three Years in the U.S. with Major Life Experiences in Mexico, the Caribbean, South and Central America)
Type II	Latino/Hispanic Immigrant and Refugee—(Three or More Years in the U.S. with Major Life Experiences in Mexico, the Caribbean, South and Central America)
Type III	Latino/Hispanic American (2nd Generation-Offspring of Immigrant or Refugee)
Type IV	Latino/Hispanic Immigrant—(Major Life Experiences in the U.S.)
Type V	Latino/Hispanic American (3rd or Longer Generations in the U.S.)
Type VI	Latino/Hispanic National (Anticipates Return to Mexico, the Caribbean, South and Central America, to include Visitors and Tourists)
Type VII	Latino/Hispanic multinational (global work place and residence)

TYPOLOGY OF LATINO/HISPANIC AMERICANS

Similar to our typology for Asian/Pacific American individuals, families, and communities, we have developed a seven-part typology that may be useful in understanding and in summarizing some of the differences between individuals within this Latino/Hispanic American group (see Exhibit 8.2).

Our typology suggests that as law enforcement and public safety organizations prepare and train their personnel to work with Latino/Hispanic American communities, a focus on the key differences within each of the typological groups would be most effective. Please refer to Chapter 6 for examples (with Asian and Pacific Americans) on the use of this typology to discuss how the motivational components within each of the groupings could affect the way Latino/Hispanic American persons may respond in a law enforcement situation.

MYTHS AND STEREOTYPES

Knowledge and sensitivity to Latino/Hispanic Americans' concerns, diversity, historical background, and life experiences will facilitate the crime-fighting and peace-keeping mission of law enforcement officers. It is important to have an understanding about some of the myths and stereotypes of Latino/Hispanic Americans that contribute to the prejudice, discrimination, and bias this population encounters. Many law enforcement officers do not have much experience with the diversity of Latino/Hispanic American groups and learn about these groups only through stereotypes, often perpetuated by movies and through the very limited contact involved in their law enforcement duties. Stereotypic views of Latino/Hispanic Americans reduce this group to simplistic, one-dimensional characters and have led many Americans to lump members of these diverse groups into one stereotypic group, "Mexicans." It is important for law enforcement officers to be aware of the different stereotypes of Latino/Hispanic Americans, because the key to effectiveness with any ethnic or racial group is not that we completely eliminate myths and stereotypes about these groups but that we are aware of these stereotypes and can monitor our thinking and our behaviors when the stereotypes are not true of the person we are dealing with.

Some of the stereotypes that have affected Latino/Hispanic Americans in law enforcement include the following:

1. *Viewing Latino/Hispanic Americans as "illegal aliens."* Although many may argue over the number of Latino/Hispanic illegal and undocumented immigrants (see Ferriss, 1993), the vast majority of Latino/Hispanic Americans do not fall into this stereotype (i.e., the vast majority of Latino/Hispanic Americans in the United States are U.S. citizens or legal residents). The issues of illegal aliens and undocumented immigrants are complex ones (see Chapter 1), but cultural awareness and sensitivity will allow officers the knowledge to avoid an offensive situation by acting on the stereotype of Latino/Hispanic Americans as illegal immigrants. The following illustrates this point:

   Juan Vasquez* worked in the maintenance department of one of the larger downtown hotels in southern California. While at work on his day shift, all "immigrant members" of his maintenance department were asked to go to personnel. When he had arrived, he found himself (and others) questioned by several officers of the Immigration and Nationalization Services (INS), asking for identifications and "papers." Juan was asked if he was an illegal and undocumented alien. He explained that he was a fourth-generation Mexican American, that he was born and grew up in Arizona, and that his family had lived for several generations in Arizona and Colorado. When Juan was asked for proof of citizenship and/or permanent residency, he told the officers that he had a driver's license and car insurance papers. He further explained that he had grown children in college and one was even pursuing a master's degree. While the INS officers were finally satisfied with his explanations, Juan felt very insulted and offended by the assumption made that he was an illegal alien and not a United States citizen. (Latino/Hispanic American Personal Communication confidential)

   The October 1989 issue of *Badge 911* provides an example of the kinds of blatant discrimination and stereotyping of Latino/Hispanic Americans present. Exhibit 8.3 shows a memorandum displayed on the wall of a sheriff's station.

2. *Viewing Latino/Hispanic Americans as lazy and as poor workers.* This is a stereotype that has been perpetuated in the workplace. Moreover, this stereotype of Latino/Hispanic Americans is often extended to include being a "party people." A workplace law enforcement example illustrates this stereotype:

   A flyer was sent out through interdepartmental mail announcing the retirement party for Sergeant Juan Gomez. The flyer showed a man (with sergeant's stripes) dressed in traditional Mexican garb (sombrero, serape, sandals, etc.) sleeping under a large shade tree. While Sergeant Gomez did not appear offended by the stereotype, a Latina nonsworn departmental employee was deeply offended by this flyer and requested that it not be used to announce a party by the organization. The people planning the event said that she was being "overly sensitive" and ignored her request. (Police officer's anecdote told at a cultural awareness training session)

   It is difficult to understand why some continue to hold this stereotype or what factors continue to perpetuate it (given what we know about the Latino/Hispanic American workforce in the United States and globally). Harbrecht, Smith, and Baker (1993) noted that the Mexican workers (in Mexico) comprise a smart, motivated, and highly productive workforce and "a potent new economic force to be reckoned with." Latino/Hispanic American community advocates make the argument that it is

---

*not the real name

Exhibit 8.3 Example of memorandum containing stereotypes about Latino/Hispanic Americans.

To: All sworn personnel
      Sheriff's station

From: _____ Administrative Sgt.
        _____ Sherriff's station

Please inventory your assigned patrol vehicles for aliens.

The City of _____ has been generous enough to see that each vehicle is equipped with three (one tall, two short), and they should be alpha-numerically designated per your unit number, i.e., 495-a, -b, and-c.

Please check your vehicle and make sure all three aliens are present and properly numbered. They should also be fully equipped with baseball caps and plastic shopping bags.

In addition, these aliens are to be carried only in your vehicle's trunk, under no circumstances are they to be put in the console or glove compartment.

Thank you,

Note: As of October 8, 1989, this official memo from a sergeant was hanging on the briefing board at the Sheriff's Station. Information has it that this type of unprofessional communication is commonplace. Another example of this type of practice is a so-called "Mexican Day," where deputies are instructed to stop all vehicles with "Mexican-looking" people (and for no other reason).
It is very unfortunate to hear that this type of activity exists and apparently is not only condoned but is initiated by some members of the supervisory staff.

difficult to imagine anyone being labeled as "lazy" or "poor workers" if they are willing to work as laborers from dawn to dusk in the migrant farm fields, day in and day out, year after year. Moreover, comparisons of the labor force participation rate for all persons 16 years old and over showed virtually no differences between Latino/Hispanic Americans (67.9 percent) and all other ethnic and racial groups (67.1 percent) working into today's labor force (Hornor, 1999).

3. *Perceiving Latino/Hispanic Americans as uneducated and uninterested in educational pursuits.* Prior to 1948 many Latino/Hispanic American children were denied access to the educational system available to others and instead were relegated to "Mexican" schools. A challenge in the U.S. Courts on segregated schools allowed Latino/Hispanic children access to the "regular" school system (see *Mendez v. Westminster School District*, 1945, and *Delgado v. Bastrop Independent School District*, 1948). This stereotype of "uneducated" relates to how Latino/Hispanic officers may be *inappropriately* stereotyped and seen in terms of being able to learn and to achieve in law enforcement and other professional training in peacekeeping.

4. *Viewing Latino/Hispanic Americans as dishonest and untrustworthy.* Clearly, this stereotype would affect professionals in law enforcement and peacekeeping. Cultural understanding would allow the following shopkeeper (and peace officers as

well) to avoid insulting situations such as the following:

Angel Llano, a New York native of Hispanic descent who works for the State of California and lives in a Northern California city, wrote in complaining about a local video store that fingerprints only male Latinos among its new customers. (A subsequent review of 200 membership cards found 11 with fingerprints—all those of men with Hispanic surnames.) (Mandel, 1993)

5. *Seeing Latino/Hispanic American young males as gang members and drug dealers.* Some hold the stereotype, especially among young males in inner cities, that Latino/Hispanic Americans are gang members and drug dealers. Latino/Hispanic cultures are group oriented, and people from young to old tend to congregate as groups rather than as individuals or couples. "Hanging out" as a group tends to be the preferred mode of socialization. However, given the stereotype of Latino/Hispanic American young males as being gang members, it is easy to perceive five young Latino/Hispanic males walking together as constituting "a gang." Such stereotypes have resulted in suspicion, hostility, and prejudice toward Latino/Hispanic Americans and have served to justify improper treatment (e.g., routine traffic stops) and poor services (e.g., in restaurants and stores). Such stereotypes can be perpetuated by the television media (as illustrated in the following account) and can lead law enforcement officers to associate Latino/Hispanic Americans with criminal activity.

A "Law & Order" episode about violence during New York's Puerto Rican Day parade provoked angry complaints from Hispanic groups and a promise from NBC never to air the hour again. The episode that aired depicted a parade day rampage by Puerto Rican youths in which women are molested and one is killed. A Brazilian youth is shown convicted in the death. NBC made the decision after a meeting in New York with Hispanic representatives, including Manuel Mirabal, head of the National Puerto Rican Coalition, and Maria Roman, parade president. . . . Mirabal said the drama distorted a real occurrence on parade day last year in which groups of men sexually assaulted women in Central Park. The attacks occurred after, not during, the parade and the majority of those arrested were not Latino, Mirabal said. "Every Puerto Rican shown in that show was portrayed negatively as a criminal, as a delinquent, as someone who abuses women," he said in a telephone interview from New York. Such depictions reflect negatively on all Hispanics because many viewers fail to distinguish between different groups, he said. (Elber, 2001)

6. *Assuming that all Latino/Hispanic Americans speak Spanish.* As noted earlier in the chapter, 21 percent of Latino/Hispanic Americans reported that their families speak predominately English in the home. Many Latino/Hispanic Americans have been in the United States for six generations or more and English is the only language they speak and write. George Perez is a Latino/Hispanic American cultural awareness trainer for many law enforcement, emergency service, and other public service organizations. As one of the outstanding trainers in his field, he is not surprised by the frequently heard stereotypic comment of, "You speak English so well, without an accent. How did you do it?" His reply would usually be, "It's the only language I know! I'm a fifth generation Latino/Hispanic American. I grew up in northern California and received my bachelor's and master's degree in the field that I teach."

THE LATINO/HISPANIC AMERICAN FAMILY

Obviously, with over 25 different cultural groups that make up the Latino/ Hispanic American category, many differences exist among the groups in this collective. We would like to address some family characteristics that many of the different cultural groups share; Understanding the importance of family for Latino/Hispanic Americans might be of value in community peacekeeping and crime fighting. *La familia* is perhaps one of the most significant considerations in working and communicating with Latino/Hispanic Americans. (In places where we use the Spanish term, we have done so to indicate the additional cultural meanings encompassed in a term such as *La familia* that is not captured in the English term *the family*.) The Latino/Hispanic American family is most clearly characterized by bonds of interdependence, unity, and loyalty and includes nuclear and extended family members, as well as networks of neighbors, friends, and community members. Primary importance is given to the history of the family, which is firmly rooted in the set of obligations tied to both the past and the future. In considering the different loyalty bonds, the parent–child relationship emerges as primary, with all children owing *respecto* to parents (*respecto* connotes additional cultural meanings than in the English term *respect*). Traditionally, the role of the father has been that of the disciplinarian, decision maker, and leader of the household. The father's word is the law, and he is not to be questioned. The father will tend to focus his attention on the economic and well-being issues of the family and less the social and emotional issues. The mother, on the other hand, is seen as balancing the father's role through her role in providing for the emotional and expressive issues of the family. Extended family members such as grandmothers, aunts and uncles, and godparents (*compadrazgo*) may supplement the mother's emotional support. In the Latino/Hispanic American family, the older son is traditionally the secondary decision maker to the father and the principal inheritor (*primogenito*) of the family. Because of the central nature of the Latino/Hispanic American family, it is common for police officers to come into contact with members of nuclear and extended families in the course of working with the Latino/Hispanic American community. One key to the success of law enforcement officers in working with the Latino/Hispanic American extended network is the knowledge of how best to communicate in the family context and with whom to speak for information, observations, and questions.

THE ROLE OF THE MAN AND THE WOMAN IN A LATINO/HISPANIC AMERICAN FAMILY

In many Latino/Hispanic American families, the relationship and communication patterns are hierarchical, with the father as the identified head of the household and deserving of high respect. When it comes to family well-being, economic issues, and discipline, the father may appear to be the decision maker; however, many other individuals may come into the picture. Generally, if there are grandparents in the household, the father may consult them, as well as his wife, on major decisions. For law enforcement matters, it may be of great importance for officers to provide the father and the family some privacy, as much as possible, to discuss key issues and situations. With central values such as *respecto* (respect) and *machismo* (see later explanation) in the Latino/Hispanic American culture, it is critical for the father and other family members to demonstrate control in family situations. In this way, law enforcement officers may find they have more control in a situation by allowing citizens to think through a decision, come to the same conclusion as the officers, and exercise self-control in behaving in the best interests of all parties concerned. In the training videotape *Common Ground,* by the Orange County Sheriff's Department (1990), several examples are provided

1. In a vignette in which the father of the family had to be arrested, the officers responded to the father's concern about being handcuffed in the presence of his children. The arresting officers were willing to wait until the father had left the house and gotten into the car before handcuffing the father (provided that he was willing to go peacefully).
2. In the scenario in which neighbors had complained about the noise of a wedding party and officers were dispatched to disband the party, the officer in charge allowed the father to tell everyone that the party was over and to bid his guests farewell (instead of the officers closing down the party).

Within the Latino/Hispanic American family, the sex roles are clearly defined; boys and girls are taught from childhood two different codes of behavior (Comas-Diaz & Griffith, 1988). Traditional sex roles can be discussed in the context of the two codes of gender-related behaviors: *machismo* and *marianismo. Machismo* literally means maleness, manliness, and virility. Within the Latino/Hispanic American cultural context, *machismo* means that the male is responsible for the well-being and honor of the family and is in the provider role. *Machismo* is also associated with having power over women, as well as responsibility for guarding and protecting them. Boys are seen as strong by nature and do not need the protection required by girls, who are seen as weak by nature.

Women are socialized into the role of *marianismo,* based on the beliefs about the Virgin Mary, in which women are considered spiritually superior to men and therefore able to endure all suffering inflicted by men (Stevens, 1973). Women are expected to be self-sacrificing in favor of their husbands and children. Within the context of the Latino/Hispanic American family, the role of the woman is in the home as the caretaker of children and the homemaker. In the current U.S. context, the traditional gender roles of women and men in the Latino/Hispanic American community have undergone much change and have resulted in key conflicts since women have begun to work, earn money, and have some of the financial independence men have (e.g., they can go out and socialize with others outside of the family).

Although there are no clear-cut rules as to whether officers should go to the male head of the household or to the female family member, law enforcement officers would probably be more correct to address the father first in law enforcement inquiries. Consistent with the cultural values of *machismo* and *marianismo,* the Latino/Hispanic American household appears to be run by the father; however, in actual practice, the mother's role in discipline, education, finance, and decision making is also central.

Children, Adolescents, and Youths

Within the Latino/Hispanic American family, the ideal child is obedient and respectful of his or her parents and other elders. Adults may at times talk in front of the children as if they are not present and as if the children cannot understand the adults' conversations. Children are taught *respecto* (respect), which dictates the appropriate behavior toward all authority figures, older people, parents, relatives, and others. If children are disrespectful, they are punished and scolded. In many traditional families, it is considered appropriate for parents (and for relatives) to discipline a disrespectful and misbehaving child physically.

In Latino/Hispanic American households, there is a high reliance on family members (older children and other adults) to help care for younger children. Both parents of a Latino/Hispanic American family often work. As such, it is not uncommon for Latino/Hispanic American families to have latchkey children or have children cared for by older children in the neighborhood. As in other communities in which English is the second language, Latino/Hispanic American children have a special role in being the intermediaries for their parents on external community matters because of the ability of the younger individuals to learn English and American ways of doing things. Children often serve as translators and interpreters for peace officers in their communication and relations with Latino/Hispanic American families involved in legal matters, immigration concerns, and community resources. Although the use of children and family members as translators is viewed as professionally and culturally inappropriate, oftentimes it is the only means available to the law enforcement officer. In such situations, it is suggested that the officer review what role is expected of the youthful member of the family. The officer needs to see how sensitive a topic might be for different family members. Moreover, the consequence of an incorrect translation needs to be evaluated (e.g., asking a juvenile to translate to his or her parents who speak no English that the juvenile has been involved in drinking and riding in a stolen vehicle may result in significantly changed content because of the embarrassment and fear of punishment by the juvenile and possibly a sense of shame or embarrassment to the parents). In all cases, when a child is acting as a translator for parents, the officer should direct all verbal and nonverbal communication to the parents. Otherwise, the parents may view the officer's lack of attention to them as an insult. Such sensitivity by the peace officer is particularly important for Latino/Hispanic Americans because of the cultural value of *personalismo*, which emphasizes the importance of the personal quality of any interaction. This cultural concept implies that relationships occur between particular individuals as persons, not as representatives of institutions (e.g., law enforcement) or merely as individuals performing a role (e.g., as a person who enforces the law).

Cross-National Family Issues

In Exhibit 8.2, we provide a typology of the Latino/Hispanic American to identify the different immigration and migration patterns within Latino/Hispanic

American communities. This typology can also be used to understand the family, personal, and political issues involved in the interaction of Latino/Hispanic Americans crossing several types. For example, the Latino/Hispanic American (third generation or later; Type V) category consists of individuals who desire to choose which aspects of the old culture to keep and which of the new culture to accept. The focus is on choosing activities, values, norms, and lifestyles that blend the best of that which is Latino/Hispanic and that which is American. The importance of being bicultural is a unique aspect of this group. However, much conflict may occur when there are family conflicts that involve cross-national and value differences of being American and being bicultural, as was illustrated in the custody case of nine-year-old Elian Gonzalez (Lewis, 2000). In this particular case, Elian Gonzalez had escaped from Cuba with his mother, and, because of the hazardous trip, the mother died at sea. Elian's relatives in Miami took the boy into their home; however, Elian's father, a Cuban national, fought to regain legal custody of his son and to return him to Cuba. As illustrated by the case, today's law enforcement personnel may often have to intervene in such family and domestic disputes as well as in cross-national political situations involved in community peacekeeping assignments.

CULTURAL INFLUENCES ON COMMUNICATION: VERBAL AND NONVERBAL STYLES OF LATINO/HISPANIC AMERICANS

Although we do not wish to create stereotypes of any kind, key features of Latino/Hispanic American verbal and nonverbal communication styles necessitate explanation. Misunderstanding resulting from style differences can result in perceptions of poor community services from police agencies, conflicts resulting from such misunderstandings, and safety and control issues for the peace officer.

1. *Latino/Hispanic Americans' high cultural value for* la familia *results in a very strong family and group orientation.* As such, officers should not view the frequently seen behavior of "eye checking" with other family members before answering and the lack of the use of *I* statements and/or self-reference as Latino/Hispanic Americans not being straightforward about themselves or their relationships. The officer may be concerned because a Latino/Hispanic American witness may wish to use the pronoun *we* when the situation may call for a personal observation involving an *I* statement. For example, a Latino/Hispanic American family member who witnessed a store robbery may first nonverbally check with other family members before talking and then describe what he or she saw. Such verbal and nonverbal behavior is consistent with the family and group orientation of Latino/Hispanic Americans.

2. *Speaking Spanish to others in the presence of a law enforcement officer even though the officer had requested responses in English should not automatically be interpreted as an insult or as attempts to hide information from the officer.* In times of stress, those who speak English as a second language will automatically revert to their first and native language. In a law enforcement situation, many individuals may find themselves under stress and may speak Spanish, which is the more comfortable language for them. Moreover, speaking Spanish gives the citizen a greater range of expression (to discuss things with other speakers and family members) and thus provides

more useful and clearer information to law enforcement personnel about critical events.

3. *It is important for officers to take the time to get information from witnesses, victims, and suspects even if the individuals have limited skills in speaking English (the use of officers who speak Spanish, translators, and language bank resources will help).* Often Latino/Hispanic Americans have not been helped in crime-fighting and peacekeeping situations because officers could not or did not take information from nonnative English speakers.

4. *Although Latino/Hispanic Americans may show respect to law enforcement officers because of police authority, they do not necessarily trust the officers or the organization. Respeto* is extended to elders and those who are in authority. This respect is noted in the Spanish language, in which respect is shown by the use of *Usted* (the formal *you*) rather than *tu* (the informal *you*). Showing respect, however, does not ensure trust. The cultural value of *confianza* (or trust) takes some time to develop. Like many from ethnic minority communities, Latino/Hispanic Americans have experienced some degree of prejudice and discrimination from the majority community, and citizens with such experiences need time to develop trust with law enforcement officers, who are identified as being a part of the majority community.

5. *The cultural value of* personalismo *emphasizes the importance of the person involved in any interaction.* Latino/Hispanic Americans take into strong consideration not only the content of any communication but also the context and relationship of the communicator. This means that it is important for the officer to provide information about why questions are asked, who is the person asking the question (i.e., information about the officer), and how the information will be used in the context for effective communications. Additionally, context for Latino/Hispanic Americans means taking some time to find out, as well as to self-disclose, some background information (e.g., living in the same neighborhood, having similar concerns about crime). Additional context such as providing explanations and information to Latino/Hispanic Americans about procedures, laws, and so forth before asking them questions or requesting their help will ease the work of the officer. By providing background information and establishing prior relationships with community members, law enforcement agencies and officers set a context for cooperation with Latino/Hispanic American individuals.

6. *Officers should be cognizant of nonverbal and other cultural nuances that may detract from effective communication.* Many Latino/Hispanic Americans, especially younger individuals, find it uncomfortable and sometimes inappropriate to maintain eye contact with authority figures such as police officers. Strong eye contact with someone who is of higher position, importance, or authority is considered a lack of *respecto* in Latin/Hispanic American cultures. As such, many citizens from this background may deflect their eyes from gazing at police officers. It is important that officers not automatically read this nonverbal behavior as indicative of a lack of trust or as a dishonest response.

7. *Latino/Hispanic Americans may exhibit behaviors that appear to be evasive, such as claiming not to have any identification or by saying that they do not speak English.* In many of the native countries from which some Latino/Hispanic Americans have emigrated, the police and law enforcement agencies are aligned with a politically repressive government. The work of the police and of law enforcement in those countries is not one of public service. Therefore, many Latino/Hispanic Americans may have similar "fear" reactions to law enforcement officers in the United States. It is suggested that officers take the time to explain the need for identification and the importance of acknowledging comprehension and cooperation.

Carlos and his family had escaped from one of the South American countries where he saw the police serving as part of the politically repressive force upon his community. He was aware of the role of some of the police as members of the "death squad." He and his family were admitted to the United States and given political asylum and lived in southern California. Although he speaks fluent English and Spanish and has been in the United States for over five years, he relates how on one occasion when he was pulled over by the police (for a broken taillight) he automatically had this fear reaction and had the thought of saying to the officer, "No habla English" in the hope of avoiding any further contact. (Latino/Hispanic American trainer's anecdote told in a police cultural awareness training course)

KEY ISSUES IN LAW ENFORCEMENT

Under-Reporting of Crimes

Latino/Hispanic Americans, because of their past experiences with some law enforcement agencies in their countries of origin (e.g., as part of the repressive military force in their native country, as well as perceived "unresponsiveness" by police) are reluctant to report crimes and may not seek police assistance and help. Many people bring with them memories of how police in their home countries have brutalized and violated them and others (e.g., as members of the "death squad"). Moreover, there is the perception among many that the police, no matter how "good" they are, will not be able to reduce crime in the Latino/Hispanic American neighborhoods (Carter, 1983). Many immigrants and refugees are just not knowledgeable about the legal system of the United States and avoid any contact with law enforcement personnel. Outreach and community policing perspectives will enhance the contact and relationship with Latino/Hispanic American communities and may help alleviate the underreporting of crimes. As Carter (1983) noted in his study in Texas, 98.8% of the Latino/Hispanic American respondents cited inadequate police protection as the reason for their fear of crime.

Victimization

The Bureau of Justice Statistics published the report, "Criminal Victimization in the United States, 1997." Following are some key conclusions from the ongoing study of persons age 12 or older, interviewed twice a year in about 50,000 households:

1. Latino/Hispanic Americans experienced higher rates of victimization from violent crime than all other populations. For every 1,000 Latino/Hispanic Americans age 12 and over, there were 16.2 aggravated assaults and 7.3 robberies (as compared to 11.6 aggravated assaults and 4.3 robberies for all other populations).

2. Latino/Hispanic Americans suffered a higher rate of household crimes (e.g., burglary, household larceny, motor vehicle theft) than all other populations. In the 1994 Bureau of Justice Statistics study, there was an annual average of 425.5 household victimizations per 1,000 households headed by a Latino/Hispanic American, as compared to 307.6 crimes per 1,000 households for all other populations.

3. The street was the most common place for violent crimes to occur: 45 percent of the robberies of Latino/Hispanic Americans occurred on city streets (Bastian, 1990). As such, the higher victimization rate can be partly explained by some of the individual and environmental characteristics of Latino/Hispanic Americans— that is, a younger, poorer population concentrated in large urban areas.

4. Latino/Hispanic American victims of violent crime were more likely to be accosted by a stranger (65 percent) than were African American victims (54 percent) or Caucasian (white) victims (58 percent). Latino/Hispanic American and African American victims were more likely to face an offender with a weapon (57 percent for each group) than were Caucasian victims (43 percent) (Bastian, 1990).

A teenager covered with 18 tattoos, including swastikas and white supremacist symbols, has confessed that he left his Queens home before 5 on a Sunday morning and traveled 50 miles to a Long Island town to attack two day laborers because they were Mexican, the police said today. The teenager, Ryan Wagner, a 19-year-old construction worker who lives with his parents in Maspeth, was arraigned today in Islip on two counts of attempted murder and two counts of aggravated harassment in the Sept. 17 attack, in which the police say he used a knife. He was held without bail at the Suffolk County jail in Riverhead. The two laborers said that two white men, posing as contractors promising work, had picked them up in a car in Farmingville and driven them to an abandoned factory in Shirley, where they were attacked but managed to escape. . . . In a confession on Tuesday, the police said, Mr. Wagner said he was simply doing what the other suspect wanted him to do. "What we gather from his confession was, the motive was in fact to go out and attack Mexicans," said Detective Sgt. Robert Reecks, commanding officer of the bias crimes unit. "We cannot say they are tied to any organization, or they were hired by anybody, or they were prompted to do this by any particular group." (Kelley, 2000) p. B.5

Differential Treatment

In Bastian's (1990) study, Latino/Hispanic Americans gave as one of the reasons for not reporting victimizations to the police that "the police would not do anything." Among nonreporting Latino/Hispanic American and African American victims of robbery, personal theft, and household crimes, similar percentages said that they did not call the police or other law enforcement agencies because they felt that the police would think the incident unimportant or would do little to respond. Clearly, outreach and community efforts are needed to change this stereotype. Many of the crimes within Latino/Hispanic American communities are perpetrated by others within the same group; however, for this community, a greater number of violent crimes are committed by strangers (65 percent). Law enforcement officials have often found it difficult to get cooperation from Latino/Hispanic American crime victims. In part, the fear of the Latino/Hispanic American person in these cases relates to the retaliatory possibilities of the criminal within his or her own community. Other concerns of the Latino/Hispanic American victim include (1) the perceived nonresponsiveness of the peacekeeping officers and agencies, (2) lack of familiarity with and trust in police services, (3) perceived lack of effectiveness of the law enforcement agencies, and (4) stereotypes and images of law enforcement agencies as discriminatory. A key challenge for police agencies is to educate this group and to work cooperatively with the communities to reduce crime.

Racial Profiling of Latino/Hispanic Americans

As noted in Chapters 1 and 7, the issue of racial profiling, a major problem and concern for African Americans, is also a problem for Latino/Hispanic Americans. They believe that the determining factor in whether peace officers exercise their discretion to stop a vehicle driven by a Latino/Hispanic American has to do with the driver's race and ethnicity. According to Hills and Trapp (2000), "Every study of racial profiling shows that, contrary to popular belief, people of color are not more likely to carry drugs or other contraband in their vehicles than whites. In Maryland, the percentage of black and white drivers carrying contraband was statistically identical. The U.S. Customs Service's own figures show that while over 43 percent of those searched were minorities, the 'hit rates' for these searches were actually lower for people of color than for whites." In a study by the San Diego Police Department (Hills and Trapp, 2000), African Americans and Latino/Hispanic Americans were stopped more often than would be expected given their numbers in the local population; that is, 40 percent of those stopped and 60 percent of those searched were African Americans and Latino/Hispanic Americans, whereas both groups together only represent 28 percent of the driving population. The following New Jersey racial profiling case illustrates the issues for Latino/Hispanic Americans:

> The Star-Ledger of Newark reported that the state was close to agreeing to a nearly $13 million settlement with the four black and Hispanic men from New York City whose van was stopped on the turnpike in April 1998 by Troopers John Hogan and James Kenna. Three of the men were wounded when the troopers opened fire on the vehicle, firing 11 shots, while the men were inside. The four have sued the state, charging, among other things, that the shootings were unjustified, that they had been victims of racial profiling and that the state had condoned the practice of singling out minority drivers for traffic stops. When the van with the four men inside accidentally began backing up toward the troopers, the troopers opened fire. The four men were basketball players on their way to professional tryouts in North Carolina, and their claim for damages against the state rests in part on their contention that the shooting disrupted, and may have ended, their playing careers. The Star-Ledger reported that the state had agreed to have the four men divide $12.9 million in a settlement. The state is engaged in a complicated and contentious criminal case it filed against Troopers Kenna and Hogan, and the state's lawyers have expressed an eagerness to want the civil case out of the way before the outcome of the criminal case is known. . . . [A] New Jersey appeals court reinstated the criminal charges against the two troopers, overruling a lower-court judge who had dismissed the charges. Mr. Kenna is now charged with attempted murder and aggravated assault and Mr. Hogan with aggravated assault. (Peterson, 2001) p. B.S

Attitudes toward Crime and Safety

The National Opinion Survey on Crime and Justice conducted in 1996 (Hornor, 1999) provided some key differences on attitudes toward crime and safety by Latino/Hispanic American respondents when compared to all other respondents:

> 1. Approximately 32.5 percent of Latino/Hispanic Americans worried "very frequently" about getting murdered as compared to 10.6 percent of all other race and ethnic groups.
>
>   When dusk comes, the streets empty and the *esquineros* hurry to the homes they share with 15, 20 and sometimes 30 others to drink beer and eat supper. The *esquineros*—the men of the corner—used to walk home alone from the corners where they gather each morning to be hired out for yardwork or other day jobs. Now they walk in groups. At one house, where the Guatemalans live, the door is punctured with bullet holes; a white man recently drove by and unloaded a pistol. . . . Up until now, the culture divide of the suburbs has been more a cold war than a hot one, an uneasy peace with periodic clashes over public issues like limits

on the number of boarders allowed in a house or a proposal in Suffolk County to sue the Immigration and Naturalization Service to more stringently enforce immigration laws. But when two Hispanic immigrants seeking work were lured to an abandoned building on Sunday and attacked by two white men wielding a knife, a crowbar and a shovel, the assault was a sobering reminder of the lives of the unwanted strangers. The divide plays out in towns like Brewster, Mount Kisco and Yonkers, N.Y., and Freehold, N.J. . . . . There are plenty of jobs in this tree-lined hamlet in central Long Island that is home to 15,000 residents and acres of blacktop and strip malls. Mostly they are menial jobs like cleaning pools and landscaping, and like a quarter of all jobs in the United States, they pay about $8 an hour. The Latinos have come in great numbers over the past four years to take the jobs locals are unwilling or unable to do. Most are here illegally, and it is their illegal status that most irritates local residents. The people taunt each other. Some Americans picket the Latinos every Saturday as they stand on the corners waiting for work. The *esquineros* have become schooled in the ways of America. They picket back. And after the ambush of the two workers, more than 500 of the illegal immigrants took to the streets demanding their civil rights. (LeDuff, 2000) p. 1

2. About 29.5 percent of Latino/Hispanic Americans worried "very frequently" about getting beaten up, knifed, or shot as compared to 12.5 percent of all other race and ethnic groups.

3. Approximately 40.0 percent of Latino/Hispanic Americans worried "very frequently" about oneself or someone in one's family getting sexually assaulted as compared to 18.1 percent of all other race and ethnic groups.

4. About 47.4 percent of Latino/Hispanic Americans worried "very frequently" about their home being burglarized as compared to 20.4 percent of all other race and ethnic groups.

As noted, a key challenge for police agencies is to educate this group, work cooperatively with the communities, and provide police services to reduce crime and the fears associated with crime victimization within these communities. Unfortunately, some Latino/Hispanic Americans may fear the police as much as they fear crime and criminals:

Latino New Yorkers are almost as fearful of the police as they are of becoming crime victims, according to an annual poll released yesterday by the Hispanic Federation. While seven in 10 Hispanics worry about becoming crime victims, nearly six in 10 also fear becoming victims of police brutality, the poll found. "It's a very interesting finding," said Doug Muzzio, a Baruch College pollster who assisted in the eighth annual survey by the federation, an alliance of 60 nonprofit health and human service agencies. "It's a very nuanced view. It's not simplistic." Muzzio said some of the negative view Hispanics have of cops has been influenced by media coverage of such recent cases as the police shooting deaths of Amadou Diallo and Patrick Dorismond and the torture of Abner Louima. But also contributing to Hispanics' dim view of cops is "direct experience" with brutal or disrespectful officers, Muzzio said. "They are experiencing these stops and searches," he said. (Lombardi, 2000)

Exposure to Environmental Risk and Job Hazards

Morales and Bonilla (1993) noted that in the state of California, where Latino/Hispanic Americans are approximately one-third of the population, Latino/Hispanic Americans live in the most polluted neighborhoods and work in the most hazardous jobs. For example, in Oakland, California, 24 percent of whites and 69 percent of Latino/Hispanic Americans live in communities with hazardous waste sites; in Los

Angeles, the percentages are 35 percent for whites and 60 percent for Latino/Hispanic Americans. In addition to Latino/Hispanic American communities' concern regarding crime and violence are the concerns for the safety of their homes and their exposure to environmental hazards and risks. Such concerns add to the role of law enforcement and peace officers within Latino/Hispanic American communities. In addition, as is illustrated in the following case, some job risks are related to stereotypic and oppressive actions of the employer:

> W. R. Grace & Company said yesterday that it would pay $850,000 to settle a lawsuit in which the United States Equal Employment Opportunity Commission charged managers at a Maryland food-processing plant with egregious sexual harassment of 22 female workers from Central America. The Commission said four plant managers and two non-supervisors had engaged in systematic harassment that included exposing themselves, demanding oral sex and touching workers' breasts, buttocks and genital areas. Commission officials said that the harassment had lasted four years and that there had been one case of rape. "This stuff was pretty bad, and it seemed to be pervasive, all over this large plant," said Regina Andrew, one of the lawyers at the Commission's Baltimore office who handled what became a class-action lawsuit. "This was one of the worst sexual harassment cases we've seen." The Commission said numerous women at the plant in Laurel, MD., were given menial or difficult work assignments after they rejected the managers' sexual demands. (Greenhouse, 2000)

Law enforcement professionals need to be alert to environmental (including workplace) exploitation of Latino/Hispanic Americans and to be particularly sensitive to the fear many immigrants have in reporting crimes to the police.

Increasing Latino/Hispanic American Community Police Services

Chin (1987), a police officer with the Los Angeles Police Department (Airport Police Bureau), describes the benefits and improved relationships as a result of a storefront outreach effort to provide better service for ethnic neighborhoods of Los Angeles (see Chapter 6). Such strategies would be equally appropriate for Latino/Hispanic American neighborhoods given the high concentration of the population in inner cities. The outreach approach of using bilingual community service officers (CSOs) who are nonsworn officers (i.e., they hold badges and wear uniforms) to serve the ethnic communities in San Diego, California, provides yet another viable model for the Latino/Hispanic American community as a whole. The CSOs provide many of the informational, referral, educational, and crime-reporting services available through the police department. The use of bilingual CSOs increases the effectiveness of law enforcement in Spanish-speaking communities. As many officers will attest, Spanish-language training is not always effective:

> "Crash courses are a waste of time," says Stephen Hrehus, Brighton Beach's Russian-speaking officer, who learned his Russian as a child. "It's like college Spanish. All I remember from my college Spanish is, *'Las montanas en Mexico son bonitas'*—the mountains in Mexico are pretty. All that in six weeks! In six weeks, you are not going to be able to learn much of anything." (Taft, 1982)

The willingness of law enforcement officers to use Spanish phrases in their interactions with Latino/Hispanic Americans is very useful even if the officers have not attained Spanish-language fluency. The use of everyday greetings and courteous phrases in Spanish indicates officers' respect and positive attitude and is seen favorably by members of the Latino/Hispanic American community. (See Chapter 5 for a discussion of language training in police departments.)

> The changing demographics of the United States make it more important than ever for police to get to know a minority community, Pittsburgh police Lt. Rashelle Brackney told about 40 law enforcement officers yesterday. In this country, the Hispanic population is outpacing the general population by 5 percent to 8 percent while Asians are doing so at twice that rate, she said. . . . The 40 police chiefs, state troopers and representatives from the state attorney general's office and fish and game commissions involved in the discussion were participants in "Police and Minority Community Relations" in Washington, PA. The symposium was an outgrowth of Gov. Ridge's Alliance for Community and Law Enforcement Relations, a task force he commissioned in 1996 to study police relations statewide, and to bridge the gap that has developed between minorities and police. Members of the Chiefs of Police Association and the alliance, along with representatives of minority groups, law enforcement and the criminal justice system and educators, developed the curriculum for the symposium. (Taylor, 2000)

Increasing the Number of Latino/Hispanic American Peace Officers

Latino/Hispanic Americans are significantly underrepresented in federal, state, and local law enforcement positions. Police departments' attempts to effectively serve states, cities, and community neighborhoods with large Latino/Hispanic American populations have been hampered by the small number of Latino/Hispanic American officers. A variety of reasons exist for such underrepresentation, including (1) history of law enforcement stereotypes and relationships with Latino/Hispanic American communities; (2) interests of Latino/Hispanic Americans with respect to law enforcement careers; (3) image of law enforcement personnel in Latino/Hispanic American communities; (4) lack of knowledge about the different careers and pathways in law enforcement; (5) concern with and fear of background checks and immigration status, physical requirements, and the application process; (6) ineffective and misdirected law enforcement recruitment and outreach efforts in the Latino/Hispanic American community; and (7) lack of role models and advocates for law enforcement careers for Latino/Hispanic Americans.

> When John Garcia, a senior law enforcement executive, was traveling through some of the Latino/Hispanic American neighborhoods to do some research on how law enforcement agencies might better serve the community, he was constantly receiving comments from Latino/Hispanic American community residents like, "You must be very rich to be a police chief." "You must have been very famous to be a police captain." "Are you really a police chief? I've never seen anyone like you before." (Latino/Hispanic American law enforcement executive's anecdote in a cultural awareness seminar in southern California)

Clearly, role models are needed to help clarify to the community what is required for a career in law enforcement.

SUMMARY OF RECOMMENDATIONS FOR LAW ENFORCEMENT

The experience of Latino/Hispanic Americans with law enforcement officers in the United States has been complicated (1) by the perceptions of Latino/Hispanic Americans regarding the enforcement of immigration laws against illegal aliens and by the discriminatory treatment received by Latino/Hispanic Americans in the United States and (2) by community conflicts, as well as perceptions of police ineffectiveness and unresponsiveness. Officers should realize that some citizens may still remember this history and carry with them stereotypes of police services as something to be feared and avoided. Law enforcement officials need to go out of their way to establish trust, to provide outreach efforts, and to win cooperation in order to effectively accomplish their goals to serve and protect Latino/Hispanic Americans. Building partnerships focused on community collaboration in the fight against crime is important.

The label *Latino/Hispanic Americans* encompasses over 25 very diverse ethnic, cultural, and regional groups from North, Central, and South America. Law enforcement officials need to be aware of the differences between the diverse groups (e.g., nationality, native cultural and regional differences and perceptions, and language dialects), as well as the within-group differences that may result from individual life experiences (e.g., sociopolitical turmoils). Since key stereotypes of Latino/Hispanic Americans are regarded by mainstream Americans as more negative than positive, it is important that peace officers make a special effort to extend respect and dignity to this community of very proud people with a culturally rich heritage.

The preferred term for referring to Latino/Hispanic Americans varies with the contexts, groups, and experiences of Latino/Hispanic American individuals. Law enforcement officials need to be aware of terms that are unacceptable and derogatory and terms that are currently used. When in doubt, officers have to learn to become comfortable in asking citizens which terms they prefer. Officers are advised to provide helpful feedback to their peers whenever offensive terms, slurs, labels, and/or actions are used with Latino/Hispanic Americans. Such feedback will help reduce the risk of misunderstanding and improve the working relationships of officers with Latino/Hispanic American communities. Additionally, it will help enhance the professional image of the department for those communities.

Many Latino/Hispanic Americans are concerned with their ability to communicate clearly and about possible reprisal from the police, as associated with the role of law enforcement in more politically repressive countries. Peace officers need to take the time and be aware that bilingual and nonnative English speakers want to communicate effectively with them. Maintaining contact, providing extra time, using translators, and being patient with speakers encourage citizens to communicate their concerns.

Cultural differences in verbal and nonverbal communication often result in misinterpretation of the message and of behaviors. Officers need to be aware of nonverbal aspects of some Latino/Hispanic Americans in their communication styles, such as eye contact, touch, gestures, and emotionality. Verbal aspects such as accent, mixing English with Spanish, limited vocabulary, and incorrect grammar may give the officer the impression that the individual does not understand what is communicated. As in all cases when English is the second language, it is important to remember that listening and comprehension skills with English are usually better than speaking skills.

Latino/Hispanic Americans, because of their past experiences with law enforcement agencies, along with their own concerns about privacy, self-help, and other factors, are reluctant to report crimes and may not seek police assistance and help. It is important for law enforcement departments and officials to build relationships and working partnerships with Latino/Hispanic American communities. This is helped by outreach efforts such as community offices, bilingual officers, and participation of officers in community activities.

Latino/Hispanic Americans tend to hold a severe, punishment-oriented perception of law enforcement and corrections (Carter, 1983). That is, citizens have strong authoritarian views and an equally strong sense of "rightness" and of punishing the criminal. Because of this perspective, members from this community may view law enforcement as more severe than it really is. It is important for law enforcement departments and officials to be aware that some Latino/Hispanic Americans may perceive that law enforcement is more severe and punitive than they actually are.

DISCUSSION QUESTIONS AND ISSUES

1. *Latino/Hispanic Americans Viewing Law Enforcement as Not Sensitive.* In the historical information section of this chapter, we noted many associations made about immigration law enforcement and events that may leave Latino/Hispanic Americans with the view that law enforcement agencies are not "sensitive, effective, and responsive." What are ways to improve such possible negative points of view?

2. *Diversity among Latino/Hispanic Americans.* Latino/Hispanic Americans consist of over 25 diverse regional, national, ethnic, and cultural groups. Which groups are you most likely to encounter in crime fighting and peacekeeping in your work? Which groups do you anticipate encountering in your future work?

3. *Choice of Terms.* Use of the terms *Latino, Hispanic, Chicano, Mexican, La Raza, Puerto Rican,* and so forth is confusing for many people. How might you find out which term to use when referring to an individual if ethnic and cultural information of this kind is necessary? What would you do if the term you use seems to engender a negative reaction?

4. *Offensive Terms and Labels.* Offensive terms such as "Wetbacks," "Illegals," and "Spics" should not be used in law enforcement work at any time. Give three practical reasons for this perspective. How would you go about helping other officers who use these terms in the course of their work?

5. *Effects of Myths and Stereotypes.* Myths and stereotypes about Latino/Hispanic Americans have affected this group greatly. What are some of the Latino/Hispanic American stereotypes that you have heard of or have encountered? What effect might these stereotypes have on Latino/Hispanic Americans? What are ways to manage these stereotypes in law

enforcement? In what ways can you help an officer who uses stereotypes about Latino/Hispanic Americans?

6. ***Verbal and Nonverbal Variations among Cultures.*** How do you think the information in this chapter about verbal and nonverbal communication styles can help officers in their approach to Latino/Hispanic American citizens? When you can understand the cultural components of the style and behaviors, does this help you to become more sensitive and objective about your reactions? In what ways might you use your understanding about Latino/Hispanic American family dynamics in law enforcement?

7. ***Avoidance of Law Enforcement and Underreporting of Crimes.*** Why do you think that many Latino/Hispanic Americans keep to their own communities and underreport crimes of violence? When are such efforts desirable? When are they ineffective? How can police agencies be of greater service to Latino/Hispanic American communities in this regard?

8. ***The Future of Latino/Hispanic Americans and Law Enforcement.*** The Latino/Hispanic American population is the fastest growing segment in the U.S. population. What implications do you see for law enforcement in terms of services, language, recruitment, and training?

REFERENCES

BASTIAN, L. D. (1990). *Hispanic victims* (NCJ-120507). Bureau of Justice Statistics, U.S. Department of Justice. Washington, D.C.

BEAN, F. D., AND M. TIENDA. (1987). *The Hispanic Population of the United States.* New York: Russell Sage Foundation.

BERNAL, G., AND A. ESTRADA. (1985). "Cuban Refugee and Minority Experiences: A Book Review," *Hispanic Journal of Behavioral Sciences, 7,* 105–128.

BERNAL, G., AND M. GUTIERREZ. (1988). "Cubans." In L. Comas-Diaz and E. E. H. Griffith (Eds.), *Cross-Cultural Mental Health.* New York: Wiley. pp. 233–261.

CARTER, D. L. (1983). "Hispanic Interaction with the Criminal Justice System in Texas: Experiences, Attitudes, and Perceptions," *Journal of Criminal Justice, 11,* 213–227.

CHIN, J. (1987). "Crime and Asian American Community: The Los Angeles Response to Korea town," *Journal of California Law Enforcement, 19,* pp. 52–60.

COMAS-DIAZ, L., AND E. E. H. GRIFFITH (Eds.). (1988). *Cross-Cultural Mental Health.* New York: Wiley.

ELBER, L. (2001, January 25). "NBC Apologizes for 'Law & Order' Episode That Offended Some Hispanics," *Associated Press.*

FERNANDEX, L. F. (1970). *A Forgotten American.* New York: B'nai B'rith.

FERRISS, S. (1993, March 21). "Racists or Realists? All over California, Forces Are Being Mustered against Undocumented Immigrants," *San Francisco Examiner.*

GAVZER, G. (1993, March 21). "Held without Hope." *Parade.*

GONZALEZ, D. (1992, November 15). "What's the Problem with 'Hispanic'? Just Ask a 'Latino,' " *New York Times.* Section 4, p. 6.

GRACIA, J. J. E. (2000). *Hispanic/Latino Identity: A Philosophical Perspective.* Malden, Mass: Blackwell Publications.

GREENHOUSE, S. (2000, June 2). "Companies Pay $1 Million in Harassment Suit," *New York Times.* p. A12.

HARBRECHT, D., G. SMITH, AND S. BAKER. (1993, April 19). "The Mexican Worker," *Business Week.* p. 84.

HILL, L., AND R. TRAPP. (2000, October 29). "African Americans and Latinos in a San Diego Study," *San Diego Union-Tribune.* p. B11.

Hispanic Monitor. (1991). *Segmenting the Hispanic Market.* New York: Yankelovich, Clancy Shulman and Market Development, Inc.

HORNOR, L. L. (Ed.). (1999). *Hispanic Americans: A Statistical Sourcebook—1999 Edition.* Palo Alto, Calif.: Information Publications.

KELLEY, T. (2000, October 12). "Suspect Admits Attacking Immigrant," *New York Times.* p. B5.

LEDUFF, C. (2000, September 24). "For Migrants, Hard Work in Hostile Suburbs," *New York Times.* p. 1.

LEWIS, A. (2000, April 29). "Abroad at Home: Elian and the Law," *New York Times.* p. A13.

LOMBARDI, F. (2000, June 24). "Most Hispanics Fear Cops: Poll Finds Concern about NYPD Brutality and Bigotry," *New York Daily News.* p. 8.

LOPEZ Y RIVAS, G. (1973). *The Chicanos.* New York: Monthly Review Press.

MANDEL, B. (1993, January 24). "Black Man's Ad Is the Talk of the Town," *San Francisco Examiner.*

MARTINEZ, C., JR. (1988). "Mexican-Americans." In L. Comas-Diaz and E. E. H. Griffith (Eds.), *Cross-Cultural Mental Health.* New York: Wiley. pp. 182–203.

MONTIEL, M. (1978). *Hispanic Families: Critical Issues for Policy and Programs in Human Services.* Washington, D.C.: COSSMHO, Coalition of Spanish Speaking Mental Health Organizations.

MORALES, R., AND F. BONILLA (Eds.). (1993). *Latinos in a Changing U.S. Economy.* Newbury Park, Calif.: Sage Publications.

Orange County Sheriff's Department. (1990). *Common Ground* (videotape by the Orange County Sheriff's Department). Santa Ana, Calif.: Author.

PETERSON, I. (2001, January 26). "Settlement Is Said to Be Near in Case of Turnpike Shooting," *New York Times.* p. B5.

RAMOS-MCKAY, J. M., L. COMAS-DIAZ, AND L. A. RIVERA. (1988). "Puerto Ricans." In L. Comas-Diaz, and E. E. H. Griffith (Eds.), *Cross-Cultural Mental Health.* New York: Wiley. pp. 204–232.

RODRIGUEZ, C. E. (2000). *Changing Race: Latinos, the Census, and the History of Ethnicity in the United States.* New York: New York University Press.

STEVENS, E. (1973). "Machismo and Marianismo," *Transaction-Society, 10*(6), 57–63.

TAFT, P. B., JR. (1982, July). "Policing the New Immigrant Ghettos," *Police Magazine.*

TAYLOR, L. G. (2000, March 1). "Police Get Crash Course in Minority Relations," *Pittsburgh Post-Gazette.* p. B4.

9

LAW ENFORCEMENT CONTACT WITH ARAB AMERICANS AND OTHER MIDDLE EASTERN GROUPS

OVERVIEW

This chapter provides specific cultural information on the largest group of Middle Easterners to settle in the United States, Arab Americans. We begin with an explanation of the scope of the term *Middle Easterner* as it is used in this chapter and provide information briefly on non-Arab Middle Eastern groups. This is followed by a summary of the two major waves of Arab immigration to the United States. The chapter presents demographics, information on the diversity among Arab Americans, and information on basic Arab values and beliefs. The background information leads into a discussion of commonly held stereotypes of Arabs. A brief presentation of some aspects of the Islamic religion is included, because a substantial percentage of Arab newcomers to the United States are Muslim. Elements of family life, including the role of the head of the household and issues related to children and Americanization, are presented. The next section describes various cultural practices and characteristics, including greetings, approach, touching, hospitality, verbal and nonverbal communication, gestures, emotional expressiveness, and general points about English-language usage. The final section describes several key concerns for law enforcement, including information on perceptions of police, women and modesty, Arab store owners in urban areas, and hate crimes against Arab Americans. The chapter summary offers recommendations for improved communication and relationships between law enforcement personnel and Arab American communities.

COMMENTARY

Middle Easterners come to the United States for numerous reasons: to gain an education and begin a career, to escape an unstable political situation in their country of origin, and to invest in commercial enterprises, with the goal of gaining legal entry into the country. People in law enforcement have contact with Middle Easterners from a number of different countries. They would benefit from a rudimentary knowledge of world events related to Middle Easterners and should be aware of stereotypes that others hold of Middle Easterners. Attitudes toward Middle Easterners in this country and geopolitical events in the Middle East can have implications for law enforcement.

> If you're riding in a cab in New York and you glance at the name of the cabdriver on the license in front of you, it might be something like Issa Mohammed (an Arab name) or Igall Nidam (an Israeli name). You don't have to stretch your imagination too far to envisage them, facing one another across enemy lines in the Sinai Desert or across the banks of the Suez Canal. Why are they here driving cabs in New York? The answer is simple. There is instability in the Middle East and the future is uncertain. (Abou-Saif, 1990, p. xiii)

Established Americans of Arab origin are sometimes treated as if they have just come from the Middle East and may be potential terrorists. Stereotypes, which have long been imprinted in people's minds, can have an impact on Middle Easterners, whether they are second- or third-generation immigrants or recent refugees, receiving less than welcome treatment.

> Some believe that Arab- and Muslim-Americans are more prone to violence, that all of them are wealthy oil sheiks or irrational religious fanatics. . . . Improbable crude stereotypes persist; Arab-Americans report being asked if people in their native countries ride camels and wander in the desert. ("Arabs and Muslims Brace for Post-Bombing Backlash: Groups Still Victimized by Crude Stereotypes," *Baltimore Sun*, September 6, 1998, p. 5C)

MIDDLE EASTERNERS DEFINED

Among the general population there is considerable confusion as to who Middle Easterners are and, specifically, who Arabs are. Although commonly thought of as Arabs, Iranians and Turks are not Arabs. Many people assume that all Muslims* are Arabs and vice versa. In fact, many Arabs are also Christians, and the world's Muslim population is actually composed of dozens of ethnic groups.

What all Arabs have in common is the Arabic language, even though spoken Arabic differs from country to country (e.g., Algerian Arabic is different from Jordanian Arabic). The following countries constitute the Middle East, and all except three are Arab countries:

- Aden
- Bahrain
- Egypt
- Iran (non-Arab country)
- Iraq
- Israel (non-Arab country)

---

*Also spelled *Moslem,* but *Muslim* is preferred.

- Jordan
- Kuwait
- Lebanon
- Oman
- Palestinian National Authority*
- Qatar
- Saudi Arabia
- Syria
- Turkey (non-Arab country)
- United Arab Emirates
- Yemen

Other Arab countries are not in the Middle East (e.g., Algeria, Tunisia, Morocco, Libya) but the majority population shares a common language and religion (Islam) with people in the Arabic countries of the Middle East. In this chapter, we cover primarily information on refugees and immigrants from Arab countries in the Middle East, because they constitute the majority of Middle Eastern newcomers who bring cultural differences and special issues requiring clarification for law enforcement. We only briefly mention issues related to the established Arab American community (i.e., people who began arriving in the United States in the late nineteenth century). Following is a brief description of the population from the three non-Arab countries.

Iranians and Turks

Iranians use the Arabic script in their writing but speak Farsi (Persian), not Arabic. Turks speak Turkish, although some minority groups in Turkey speak Kurdish, Arabic, and Greek. More than 99.8 percent of Iranians and Turks are Muslim, which is the most common religion among people in many other Middle Eastern countries (Central Intelligence World Factbook, 2000). However, many Iranians in the United States are Jewish and Bahai; both groups are minorities in Iran. Of the Muslim population in Iran, the majority belong to the Shi'ah sect of Islam, which is the state religion. Persians are the largest ethnic group in Iran, making up about 50 percent of the population (Central Intelligence World Factbook, 2000), but there are other ethnic populations, including Kurds, Arabs, Turkmen, Armenians, and Assyrians (among others), most of whom are represented in the United States. During the Iranian hostage crisis in 1979, many Iranians in the United States were targets of hate crimes and anti-Iranian sentiment; the same attitudes prevailed against other Middle Easterners (Arabs) and Asian Indians, who were mistakenly labeled Iranian. Iranians and Turks are not Arabs, but they share some cultural values (extended family and emphasis on pride, dignity, and honor) with those in the traditional Arab world. Many Iranian Americans and Turkish Americans came to the United States in the 1970s and were from upper-class, professional groups such as doctors, lawyers, and

*The Palestine National Authority is the name used for the political entity created in the Gaza Strip and the West Bank under the 1993 Oslo Peace Accords (as of January 2001).

engineers. Of the Iranian immigrant population in the United States, many are Jewish Iranians who left Iran after the fall of the Shah. In the United States, there are large Iranian Jewish populations in the San Francisco Bay Area, Los Angeles, and New York. Also, one can find populations of Muslim Iranians in major U.S. cities, such as New York, Chicago, and Los Angeles.

Israelis

Israel is the only country in the Middle East in which the majority of the population is not Muslim. Approximately 20 percent of the population in Israel is made up of Arabs (both Christian and Muslim); 80 percent of the Israeli population is Jewish (Central Intelligence World Factbook, 2000), with the Jewish population divided into two main groups: Ashkenazim and Sephardim. The Ashkenazim are descended from members of the Jewish communities of Central and Eastern Europe. The majority of American Jews are Ashkenazim, and currently the majority of Israeli Jews are Sephardim, having come originally from Spain, other Mediterranean countries, and the Arabic countries of the Middle East. Israeli immigrants in the United States may be either Ashkenazic or Sephardic, and their physical appearance does not indicate ethnicity. An Israeli may look like an American Jew, a Christian, or a Muslim Arab (or none of these).

Most Israeli Arabs who live within the borders of Israel are Palestinians whose families stayed in Israel after the Arab-Israeli war in 1948, when Israel became a nation. The Six-Day War in 1967 resulted in Israel occupying lands that formerly belonged to Egypt, Syria, and Jordan, but where the majority of the population was Palestinian. Thus until the signing of the 1993 Oslo Peace Accord between Israel and the Palestine Liberation Organization (PLO), Israel occupied territories with a population of approximately 1 million Palestinians. The Palestinian–Israeli situation in the Middle East has created a great deal of hostility on both sides. In fall 2000, failure to reach a negotiated settlement agreement required by the Oslo Peace Accords of 1993 resulted in a period of increased hostilities. The tension continues and may have implications for law enforcement officials in the United States, especially in communities with large populations of Jews and Arabs or Israelis and Palestinians (e.g., Los Angeles, New York, Chicago). Police should also know whether individuals and groups with extremist views operate out of their cities.

Public events such as Israeli Independence Day celebrations and Israeli or Palestinian political rallies have the potential for confrontation, although the majority of these events have been peaceful. Police presence is required at such events, but, as with other situations, excessive police presence can escalate hostilities. Law enforcement officials need to be well informed about current events in the Middle East, because conflicts there often have a ripple effect across the world. The monitoring of world events and community trends (discussed in Chapter 12) will help police officers take a preventive posture that can help to avoid confrontation between various Middle Eastern ethnic groups in the United States.

HISTORICAL INFORMATION

Although many recent Middle Eastern immigrants and refugees in the United States have come for political reasons, some Arab Americans left their country of origin for other reasons. There have been two major waves of Arabic immigrants to the United States. The first wave came between 1880 and World War II, largely from Syria and what is known today as Lebanon (at the time these areas were part of the Turkish Ottoman Empire). Of the immigrants who settled during this wave, approximately 90 percent were Christian. Many people came to further themselves economically (and thus were immigrants and not refugees forced to leave their countries), but some young men wanted to avoid serving in the military in the Ottoman Empire (Naff, 1993). A substantial percentage of these immigrants were farmers and artisans who became involved in the business of peddling their goods to farmers and moved from town to town.

Naff (1993) has recorded several conversations with older immigrants in which they have recounted their early experiences with and perceptions of American police at the time they were newly arrived immigrants. She explains that because Arabs competed with local, native-born merchants, there were calls to the police requesting that Arab peddlers be sent away. Naff heard several accounts in which Arab immigrants reported that they had positive views toward the American police. One immigrant from Syria said that he appreciated the way police treated him in the United States and that in his own country, the police (i.e., the Turkish military police) would have beaten him; there was no civilian police force at the time. This immigrant was impressed with the hospitality of the police; a police officer actually let him sleep in the jail (Naff, 1993). In the way of crime statistics, not much is reported, partly because in the Arabic immigrant community, people took care of their own. When there was a crime, the tendency would have been to cover it up.

In sharp contrast to the characteristics and motivation of the first wave of immigrants, the second wave of Arabic immigrants to the United States, beginning after World War II, came in large part as students and professionals because of economic instability and political unrest at home. As a result, these groups brought a "political consciousness unknown to earlier immigrants" (Zogby, 1993). The largest group of second-wave immigrants is made up of Palestinians, many of whom came around 1948, the time of the partition of Palestine, which resulted in Israel's independence. In the 1970s, after the Six-Day War between Israel and Egypt, Syria, and Jordan, another large influx of Palestinians came to the United States. In the 1980s a large group of Lebanese came as a result of the civil war in Lebanon. Yemenis have continued to come throughout the century; Syrians and Iraqis have made the United States their home since the 1950s and 1960s because of political instability in their countries (Zogby, 1990). Thus these second-wave immigrants came largely because of political turmoil and have been instrumental in changing the nature of the Arab American community in the United States.

The most dramatic example of how Arab immigration has affected a U.S. city is the Detroit area in Michigan. Arabs began to arrive there in the late nineteenth century, but the first huge influx was between 1900 and 1924, when the auto indus-try attracted immigrants from all over the world (Woodruff, 1991). The Detroit–Dearborn area has the largest Arab community in the United States, with Arab Americans constituting about one-fourth of the population in Dearborn.

DEMOGRAPHICS

Immigrants from all over the Arabic world continue to settle in the United States. For example, in 1996 approximately 40,000 immigrants (combined total) were admitted to the United States from Iran, Iraq, Israel, Jordan, Kuwait, Lebanon, Qatar, Saudi Arabia, Syria, Turkey, and the United Arab Emirates (Department of Justice, 1997).

There are approximately 3 million Americans of Arabic ancestry in the United States, constituting approximately 1 percent of the total population. The communities with the largest Arab American populations are Detroit, Chicago, New York, and Boston. California, Texas, and Ohio have a number of smaller Arab American communities. Between 1986 and 1996 Iran was the leading Middle Eastern nation in terms of number of immigrants to the United States (Department of Justice, 1997).

DIFFERENCES AND SIMILARITIES

Differences

There is great diversity among Arab American groups. Understanding this diversity will assist officers in not categorizing Arabs as one homogeneous group and will encourage people to move away from stereotypical thinking. Arabs from the Middle East come from at least 13 different countries, many of which are vastly different from each other. The governments of the Arabic countries also differ, ranging from monarchies to military governments to socialist republics (Nydell, 1987). Arab visitors such as foreign students, tourists, businesspeople, and diplomats to the United States from the Gulf states (e.g., Saudi Arabia, Qatar, Oman, Bahrain, United Arab Emirates) are typically wealthy, but their Jordanian, Lebanese, and Palestinian brethren do not generally bring great wealth to the United States—in fact, many are extremely poor. Another area of difference is clothing. In several Middle Eastern countries, many older men wear headdresses, but they are less common among men who are younger and who have more education. Similarly, younger women in the Middle East may abandon head coverings and long dresses that cover them from head to toe. Yet traditional families even in the United States may insist that their daughters and wives dress modestly (discussed later in this chapter).

The younger generation of Arabs, much to the disappointment of the parents and grandparents, may display entirely different behavior from what is expected of them (as is typical in most immigrant and refugee groups). In addition, as with other immigrant groups, some Arab Americans who have been in the United States for generations are completely assimilated into the American culture. They may not identify with their roots. Others who have been here just as long consciously try to keep their Arabic traditions alive and pass them on to their children. Officers should not treat established Arab Americans as if they are newcomers.

Some broad differences among Arab American groups are associated with social class and economic status. Although many Arab Americans who come to the United States are educated professionals, some are from rural areas (e.g., peasants from southern Lebanon, West Bank Palestinians, Yemenis) who differ in outlook and receptiveness to modernization. On the other hand, despite traditional values, many newcomers are modern in outlook. Many people have a stereotypical image of the Arab woman, yet the following description certainly illustrates that not all women of Arabic descent adhere to the image. John Zogby, president of John Zogby Group International, describes many modern Arab women who defy the stereotype: "Among the upper-class, educated Palestinian population here, you can find many women who are vocal and outspoken. You might see the young husbands wheeling the babies around in strollers while the women are discussing world events"(Zogby, 1993).

On the other hand, certain Arab governments (e.g., Saudi Arabia) place restrictions on women mandating that women not mix with men, always wear a veil, and never travel alone or drive a car (*New York Times International*, February 7, 1993, p. Y7). Thus women from less restrictive Arab countries (e.g., Egypt and Jordan) might exhibit very different behavior from those whose governments grant them fewer freedoms. Nevertheless, women in traditional Muslim families from any country typically have limited contact with men outside their family and wear traditional dress. Some implications of these traditions as they relate to Arab women and male police officers in the United States are discussed later in this chapter.

It is important to look at people's motivation for coming to the United States to help avoid stereotypical thinking. Mohamed Berro, an Arab American police officer of the Dearborn, Michigan, Police Department distinguishes between immigrants (who have "few problems adjusting to the United States") and refugees. He explains that refugees, having been forced to leave their country of origin, believe they are here temporarily because they are waiting for a conflict to end. As a result, they are usually more hesitant to change and may pose a greater challenge for police officers (Berro, 1992).

Similarities

Despite differences among Arab Americans in socioeconomic status, levels of traditionalism, or motivation for coming to the United States, law enforcement officials should understand some common values and beliefs associated with Arab culture in order to establish rapport and trust. Readers will recognize that some of the information that follows does not apply only to the Arab culture. At the same time, the following explains deeply held beliefs that many Arab Americans would agree are key to understanding traditional Arab culture.

Basic Arab Values

Following are some basic Arab values:

1. "A person's dignity, honor and reputation are of paramount importance and no effort should be spared to protect them, especially one's honor" (Nydell, 1987). Traditional Arab society upholds honor; the degree to which an Arab can lose face and be shamed publicly is foreign to the average Westerner. Officers recognize that dignity and respect should be shown to all individuals, but citizens from cultures emphasizing shame, loss of face, and honor (e.g., Middle Eastern, Asian, Latin American) may react even more severely to loss of dignity and respect than do other individuals. (Keep in mind that "shame" cultures have sanctioned extreme punishments for loss of face and honor—for example, death if a woman has sexual intercourse before marriage.)

2. "Loyalty to one's family takes precedence over other personal needs" (Nydell, 1987). A person is completely intertwined with his or her family; protection and privacy in a traditional Arab family often overrides relationships with other people. Members of Arab families tend to avoid disagreements and disputes in front of others.

3. Communication should be courteous and hospitable. Harmony between individuals is emphasized. Too much directness and candor can be interpreted as extremely impolite. From a traditional Arab view, it may not be appropriate for a person to give totally honest responses if they result in a loss of face, especially for self or family members (this may not apply to many established Arab Americans). From this perspective, "adjusting" the truth (not lying) is acceptable because it furthers the goals of honor and face-saving. Most Westerners have difficulty understanding this aspect of cross-cultural communication and may be critical of it. Certainly, officers will not accept an "adjusted truth" because of cultural ideals having to do with shame and saving face. However, an officer may get nowhere pointing out a person's "lies" directly when the statements are not perceived by the person as such. The officer would be well advised to work around the issue of the "half-truths" rather than insisting on proving the citizen is a liar.

STEREOTYPES

> The Arab world has long been perceived in the West in terms of negative stereotypes, which have been transferred to Americans of Arab descent. . . . Briefly put, Arabs are nearly universally portrayed as ruthless terrorists, greedy rich sheiks, religious fanatics, belly dancers or in other simplistic and negative images. When these stereotypes are coupled with the growing centrality of the Middle East in world politics and the increased political visibility of Arab-Americans, one result is that our community becomes more susceptible to hate crimes. (American–Arab Anti-Discrimination Committee, 1992).

The Western media have been largely responsible for representing Arabs in a less than human way. When one hears the word *Arab,* several images come to mind: (1) wealthy sheik (despite the class distinctions in the Middle East [as elsewhere] between a wealthy Gulf Arab sheik and a poor Palestinian or Lebanese individual); (2) violent terrorist (the majority of Arabs worldwide want peace and do not see terrorism as an acceptable means for achieving peace); (3) sensuous harem owner or man with many wives (harems are rare, and, for the most part, polygamy [having more than one wife] has been abolished in the Arab world); and (4) ignorant, illiterate, and backward (Arab contributions to civilization have been great in the areas of mathematics, astronomy, medicine, architecture, geography, and language, among others, but this is not widely known in the West) (Macron, 1989).

As with all distorted information on ethnic groups, it is important to understand how stereotypes interfere with a true understanding of a people. Laurence Michalak, cultural anthropologist and former director of the Center for Middle Eastern Studies at the University of California, Berkeley, points out: "When we consider the Western image of the Arab—Ali Baba, Sinbad the Sailor, the thief of Baghdad, the slave merchant, the harem dancer, and so on—we have to admit that, at least in the case of Arabs, fiction is stranger than truth. . . . The Arab stereotype, while it teaches us very little about the Arabs, teaches us a good deal about ourselves and about mechanisms of prejudice" (Michalak, 1988).

Movies and Television

Some of the most offensive types of stereotyping of Arabs can be seen in children's television programs, in which Arabs are portrayed as evil and foolish. In Michalak's publication *Cruel and Unusual,* he mentions cartoons that include Arab villains, or "troublemakers who look vaguely Middle Eastern—swarthy, with a turban and curling mustache" (Michalak, 1988, p. 7). He recalls that even *Sesame Street,* a program noted for its sensitivity and respect toward people of all backgrounds, illustrated the word *danger* by using an Arab figure. Michalak points out further that via movies and television programs, Americans (and Westerners, in general) have "mass produced and marketed a negative stereotype." Indeed, images of terrorists, sheiks, harems, and thieves are prevalent in films that include Arabs.

A May 1997 Knight-Ridder poll by Princeton Survey Research asked 1,314 longtime Americans how they viewed recent immigrant groups and how they felt these groups were portrayed in the media. Nearly one-third of those polled gave unfavorable opinions of Middle Easterners and nearly half of the same group thought that Middle Easterners were negatively portrayed in TV shows, movies, and books. (The two other groups rated more negatively were Cubans and Mexicans.)

Because many Americans do not know Arabs personally, media images become embedded in people's minds. A film involving the abduction of a child to Jordan (*Desperate Rescue*) can subtly influence decision makers in cases involving custody and Muslim and Arabic fathers, especially where the wives are non-Arabic and non-Muslim. Yet according to the State Department (Child Custody Division, statistics from July 1992), nearly five times as many children were abducted to the United Kingdom as were abducted to Jordan. Apparently, although abduction to Arabic countries does occur and is a matter for concern, it is not as common as abduction to Europe. In 1998 the film *The Siege* was released and received extremely negative reactions from Islamic groups. The film was said to have linked Islam to terrorism and showed Muslim Americans being rounded up and placed in internment camps. "Whenever Hollywood productions and TV series portray terrorism or violence, it always has to be an Arab. They seem to think it is our monopoly" (comment by the president of the American–Arab Anti-Discrimination Committee, as reported in "Film's Portrayal of Muslims Troubling to Islamic Groups," *Boston Globe,* November 8, 1998).

Operation Abscam: The Government's Stereotype

Finally, it is worth noting that the U.S. government used a common stereotype of Arabs (that of the wealthy Arabic sheik) in an official capacity to try to stop white-collar crime and corruption. "Operation Abscam" ("Ab" for Abdul, the name used in the sting), which began in 1978, involved dressing up two Federal Bureau of Investigation (FBI) agents as rich oil barons in order to entrap politicians. Because the media have succeeded in portraying Arabs as terrorists or rich sheiks, the politicians fell into the trap, which involved the "sheiks" discussing Arab investments with the lawmakers. If the politicians had been more aware of Arabic culture and the distinctions between Arabic groups, they would not have fallen for the sting. For example, one of the "sheiks" was from Oman, a Gulf state. In Oman, a rich man is not known as a "sheik" and may only be referred to as "Sayeed," which simply means "Mr." or "Sir" (Shaheen, 1988, p. 1). The other so-called sheik was from Lebanon. In Lebanon, however, there are no sheiks and there is no oil.

Eight members of Congress were entrapped in the FBI bribery sting. Although law enforcement officials have been known to disguise themselves to make arrests (e.g., drug dealers and pimps), there are several issues to be aware of with regard to "Abscam." Despite the "success" of the law enforcement operation, the message sent to both Arabs and non-Arabs around the world was that of acceptance of one Arab stereotype, "a dehumanizing caricature that purposely widens the communications gap between their culture and ours" (Shaheen, 1988, p. 5). Twenty-four Congress members called on the FBI to publicly apologize to the Arab community in this country and to Arabs worldwide, saying: "We find this insensitive choice of ethnicity to be abrasive in spirit and intent, to perpetuate an unjust stereotype and to nurture an already firmly established prejudice" (p. 4).

Many people might respond by saying that the operation was one big joke and should not be taken seriously. However, whenever stereotypes are promoted, people's prejudice becomes more established and they become more convinced of the truth of their stereotypical beliefs. When a stereotype is promoted by a government agency, people believe that there is all the more reason to hold on to their stereotypical thinking.

Arabs, especially Muslims, in addition to being perceived as wealthy sheiks, are simultaneously labeled as illiterate and terrorists. Muslims have been described as "backward" and primitive by people who consider the West and Christianity to be the standard by which all other cultures should be evaluated (once again, ethnocentrism is operating). These stereotypes that many Westerners have mistakenly formed of Arabs in general have extended to Arab Americans (even those who have been here for generations): "Although there are around three million Arab Americans . . . our image has long been distorted and defamed. A great part of the distortion stems from American perceptions of Arabs of the Middle East, an image which suffers from a historic bias in Western culture which has treated the Middle Easterner as 'Other'" (Jabara, no date). The stereotype with the greatest implications for law enforcement is that of the Arab as "terrorist." This issue is discussed later in this chapter in the section titled "Key Issues in Law Enforcement."

ISLAMIC RELIGION

Misunderstanding between Americans and Arabs or Arab Americans can often be traced, in part, to religious differences and a lack of tolerance of these differences. Islam is practiced by the majority of Middle Eastern newcomers to the United States, as well as by many African Americans. Many Arab Americans (especially those from the first wave of Arab immigration) are Christian, however, and prefer that others do not assume they are Muslim simply because they are Arabs.

By and large, most Americans do not understand what Islam is and, because of stereotyping, wrongly associate Muslims with terrorists or fanatics. Many but by no means all Arabic Muslims in the United States are deeply religious and have held on to the traditional aspects of their religion, which are also intertwined with their way of life. Islam means submission to the will of God, and for traditional religious Muslims, the will of God (or fate) is a central concept. The religion has been called "Mohammadanism," which is an incorrect name for the religion because it suggests that Muslims worship Muhammad rather than God (Allah). It is believed that Allah's final message to man was revealed to the prophet Muhammad. *Allah* is the Arabic word for God and is used by both Arab Muslims and Arab Christians.

The Koran and the Pillars of Islam

The Koran is the Islamic holy book and is regarded as the word of God (Allah). There are five pillars of Islam, or central guidelines that form the framework of the religion:

- Profession of faith in Allah (God)
- Prayer five times daily
- Alms giving (concern for the needy)
- Fasting during the month of Ramadan (sunrise to sunset)
- Pilgrimage to Mecca (in Saudi Arabia) at least once in each person's lifetime

There are several points where law enforcement officials can respect a Muslim's need to practice his or her religion. The need to express one's faith in God and to be respected for it is one area. Normally, people pray together as congregations in mosques, the Islamic equivalent of a church or synagogue. However, people can pray individually if a congregation is not present. Religious Muslims in jails, for example, will continue to pray five times a day and should not be ridiculed or prevented from doing so. Prayer five times a day is a pillar of Islam, and strict Muslims will want to uphold this command no matter where they are. Call to prayer takes place at the following times:

- One hour before sunrise
- At noon
- Midafternoon
- Sunset
- Ninety minutes after sunset

Taboos in the Mosque

Police officers convey respect to Muslim communities if they avoid entering a mosque and interrupting prayers (except in emergencies). Religion is so vital in Arab life that law enforcement officials should always show respect for any Islamic customs and beliefs. Thus, other than in emergency situations, officers are advised to

- Avoid entering a mosque, or certainly the prayer room of a mosque, during prayers
- Never step on a prayer mat
- Never place the Koran on the floor or put anything on top of it
- Avoid walking in front of people who are praying
- Speak softly as you would in a church or synagogue
- Dress conservatively (both men and women are required to dress conservatively—shorts are not appropriate)
- Invite a person out of a prayer room to question him

Proper protocol in a mosque requires that people remove their shoes before entering, but this must be left to the officer's discretion; officer safety comes before consideration of differences.

Ramadan: The Holy Month

One of the holiest periods in the Islamic religion is the celebration of Ramadan, which lasts for one month. There is no fixed date because like the Jewish and Chinese calendars, the Islamic calendar is based on the lunar cycle and dates vary from year to year. During the month of Ramadan, Muslims do not eat, drink, or smoke from sunrise to sunset. The purpose of fasting during Ramadan is to "train one in self-discipline, subdue the passions, and give [people] . . . a sense of unity with all Moslems" (Devine and Braganti, 1991, p. 28). On the twenty-ninth night of Ramadan, when there is a new moon, the holiday is officially over. The final fast is broken and for up to three days people celebrate with a feast and other activities. On the last night of Ramadan, Muslim families pray in the mosque.

For Muslims, Ramadan is as important and holy as Christmas is for Christians; Muslims appreciate it when others (who are not Muslim) recognize the holiday's importance. One city with a sizable Arab American population put up festive lights in its business district during Ramadan as a gesture of acceptance and appreciation of the diversity that the Arab Americans bring to the city. The Arab American community reacted favorably to this symbolic gesture. Meanwhile, in the same city, at the end of Ramadan, while many families were in the mosque, police ticketed hundreds of cars that were parked in store parking lots across from the mosque, even though according to some Arab American citizens, the stores were closed. When people came out of the mosque and saw all the tickets, the mood of the holiday naturally was spoiled. The perception from the Arab American citizens was that "They don't want to understand us, they don't know how we feel, and they don't know what's important to us." (Readers will have a chance at the end of the chapter to analyze this situation from an enforcement and community relations point of view and discuss whether the situation could have been prevented.)

Knowledge of Religious Practices

Knowledge of religious practices, including what is considered holy, will help officers avoid creating problems and conflicts. A belief in the Islamic religion that may occasionally arise in the course of police work will illustrate this point. In a suburb of San Francisco, California, a group of police officers and Muslims (from Tunisia, an Arab country in North Africa) were close to violence when, in a morgue, police entered to try to get a hair sample from a person who had just been killed in a car accident. Apparently, the body had already been blessed by an Iman (a religious leader) and, according to the religion, any further contact would have been a defilement of the body since the body had already been sanctified and was ready for burial. The police officers were merely doing what they needed to do to complete their investigation and were unaware of this taboo. This, together with a language barrier, created an extremely confusing and confrontative situation in which officers lost necessary control. In this case they needed to explain what had to be done and communicate their needs in the form of a request for permission to handle a body that had already been sanctified. If the citizens had not granted permission, the police would then have had to decide how to proceed. Most members of the Arab American community would comply with the wishes of police officers. As in many other situations involving police–citizen communication, the initial approach sets the tone for the entire interaction.

FAMILY STRUCTURE

Arab Americans typically have close-knit families in which family members have a strong sense of loyalty and fulfill obligations to all members, including extended family (aunts, uncles, cousins, grandparents). Traditionally minded families also believe strongly in the family's honor, and members try to avoid any behavior that will bring shame or disgrace to the family. The operating unit for Arab Americans (and this may be less true for people who have been in the United States for generations) is not the individual but the family. Thus if a person behaves inappropriately, the entire family is disgraced. Similarly, if a family member is assaulted (in the Arab world), there would be some type of retribution. Three characteristics of the Arabic family will affect police officers' interactions with family members:

- Extended family members are often as close as the nuclear family (mother, father, children) and are not seen as secondary family members. If there is a police issue, officers can expect that many members of the family will become involved in the matter. Although officers might perceive this as interference, from an Arabic cultural perspective, it is merely involvement and concern. The numbers of people involved are not meant to overwhelm an officer.
- Family loyalty and protection are seen as some of the highest values of family life. Therefore, shaming, ridiculing, insulting, or criticizing family members, especially in public, can have serious consequences.
- Newer Arab American refugees or immigrants may be reluctant to accept police assistance. Because families are tightly knit, they can also be closed units in which members prefer to keep private matters or conflicts to themselves. As a result, officers will have to work harder at establishing rapport if they want to gain cooperation.

There is an important point of contact between all three of these characteristics and law enforcement interaction with members of Arab American families. Berro and Jabour (1992) explain: "When we respond to a call at a home, the police car is like a magnet. Every family member comes out of the house and everyone wants to talk at once. It can be an overwhelming sensation for an officer who doesn't understand this background."

A police officer who is not trained in understanding and responding appropriately and professionally to cultural differences could alienate the family by (1) not respecting the interest and involvement of the family members and (2) attempting to gain control of the communication in an authoritarian and offensive manner. The consequences may be that he or she would have difficulty establishing the rapport needed to gain information about the conflict at hand and would then not be trusted or respected. To do the job effectively, law enforcement officials must respect Arab family values, along with communication style differences (the latter will be discussed shortly).

Head of the Household

As in most cultures with a traditional family structure, the man in the Arab home is overtly the head of the household and his role and influence are strong. The wife has a great deal of influence, too, but it is often restricted to private situations. An Arab woman does not always defer to her husband in private as she would in public (Nydell, 1987). As mentioned earlier in the chapter, many women have broken out of the traditional mold and tend to be more vocal, outspoken, and assertive than their mothers or grandmothers. Traditionally, in many Arab countries, some fathers maintain their status by being strict disciplinarians and demanding absolute respect, thus creating some degree of fear among children and even among wives. Once again, Arab Americans born and raised in this country have, for the most part, adopted middle-class American styles of child raising whereby children participate in some of the decision making and are as respected as each adult member would be. In addition, as with changing roles among all kinds of families in the United States, the father as traditional head of the household and the mother as having "second-class" status is not prevalent among established Arab Americans in the United States. Wife abuse and child abuse are not considered respectable by educated Arab Americans, but the practice still occurs, just as it does in mainstream American society (particularly, but not exclusively, among people in lower socioeconomic classes).

In traditional Arabic society, men exert influence and power publicly. Westerners may view this power negatively but it is important to caution against misinterpreting a husband's or father's behavior as merely control (Shabbas, 1984). He, and other male figures of importance, can be employed in securing the compliance of the family in important matters. The husband or father can be a natural ally of authorities. Officers would be well advised to work with both the father and the mother, for example, in matters where children are involved. On family matters the woman frequently is the authority, even if she seems to defer to her husband. Communicating with the woman, even if indirectly, while still respecting the father's need to maintain his public status will win respect from both the man and the woman.

Children and Americanization

Americanization, the process of adopting American behaviors, attitudes, and beliefs, has always been an issue with refugees and immigrants and their children. Typically, children are better able than their parents to learn a language and pick up the nuances of a culture. In addition, peer influence and pressure in American society begin to overshadow parental control, especially beginning in the preteen years. Arab children, who are sacred to and cherished by their parents, face an extremely difficult cultural gap with their parents if they reach a stage where they are more American than Arabic. Children in Arabic families are taught to be respectful in front of parents and to be conscious of family honor. Parents do not consider Americanized behavior, in general, to be respectful or worthy of pride. When children exhibit certain behaviors that bring shame to the family, discipline can indeed be harsh.

In extreme and infrequent cases, shame to the family can result in violent crimes against the children. Officer Berro and Sergeant Jabour (1992) of the Dearborn, Michigan, Police Department described three cases involving homicide. In one case, parents were having a discussion about how Americanized their children should become. In another, a father shot his daughter because she had a boyfriend (Arab women are not allowed to associate freely with men before marriage and are expected to remain virgins). Finally, the third case involved a brother who shot his sister when she returned late from a New Year's party. These cases do not suggest that violent crime, in the Arabic cultural context, is an appropriate response. Mental problems or drugs and alcohol accompany most violent acts. However, when a child's (especially a girl's) Americanized behavior involves what is seen as sexual misconduct, the family's reputation is ruined. When this happens, all members of the family suffer.

There is very little an officer can do to change the attitudes of parents who oppose their children's Americanized behavior. However, if an officer responding to calls notices that a family has become dysfunctional because of children's Americanized behavior, social services intervention or referrals may be appropriate. If a family is already at the point of needing police assistance in problems involving children and their parents, then, more likely than not, they need other types of assistance as well. At the same time, newer immigrants and refugees will not necessarily be open to social services interventions, especially if the social workers do not speak Arabic.

CULTURAL PRACTICES

As with all other immigrant groups, the degree to which Arab Americans preserve their cultural practices varies. The following descriptions of everyday behavior do not apply equally to all Arab Americans, and they do not necessarily apply only to newcomers. Immigrants may preserve traditions and practices long after they come to a new country by conscious choice or sometimes because they are unaware of their cultural behavior (i.e., it is not in their conscious awareness).

Greetings, Approach, and Touching

Most recent Arab American newcomers expect to be addressed with a title and their last name (Mr. _____; Miss _____), although in many Arab countries people are addressed formally by Mr. or Mrs. and a first name. Most Arabic women do not change their names after they are married or divorced. They therefore may not understand the distinction between a "maiden" name and a "married" name. The usual practice is to keep their father's last name for life (Boller, 1992).

Many Arab Americans who have retained their traditional customs shake hands and then place their right hand on their chest near the heart. This is a sign of sincerity and warmth. In the Middle East, Americans are advised to do the same if they observe this gesture (Devine and Braganti, 1991). Officers can decide whether they are comfortable using this gesture; most people would not expect it from an officer, but some might appreciate the gesture as long as the officer was able to convey sincerity. Generally, when Arabs from the Middle East shake hands, they do not shake hands briefly and firmly. (The expression "He shakes hands like a dead fish" does not apply to other cultural groups.) Arabs (but not assimilated Arab Americans) tend to hold hands longer than other Americans and shake hands more lightly. Older children are taught to shake hands with adults as a sign of respect. Many Arabs would appreciate an officer shaking hands with their older children. With a recent immigrant or refugee Arabic woman, it is generally not appropriate to shake hands unless she extends her hand first. This guideline would definitely apply to women who wear head coverings.

Many Arabs of the same sex greet each other by kissing on the cheek. Two Saudi Arabian men, for example, may greet each other by kissing on both cheeks a number of times. This practice does not suggest homosexuality, but rather is a common form of greeting. Public touching of the opposite sex is forbidden in the traditional Arabic world, and officers should make every effort not to touch Arabic women, even casually (discussed further under "Key Issues in Law Enforcement").

Police officers should be aware that some Arab American citizens (e.g., Lebanese) who are new to the United States may react to a police officer's approach in an unexpected way. For example, an officer who has just asked a person to give his license may find that this person will then get out of his car in order to be able to talk to the officer. From the person's perspective, he or she is simply trying to be courteous (since this is done in the home country). An officer, always conscious of safety issues, may simply have to explain that in the United States, officers require citizens to remain in their cars.

Hospitality

"Hospitality is a byword among [Arabs], whatever their station in life. As a guest in their homes you will be treated to the kindest and most lavish consideration. When they say, as they often do, 'My home is your home,' they mean it" (Salah Said, as quoted in Nydell, 1987, p. 58). Hospitality in the Arab culture is not an option; it is more an obligation or duty. In some parts of the Arab world, if you thank someone for their hospitality, they may answer with a common expression meaning "Don't thank me. It's my duty." (Here the word *duty* has a more positive than negative connotation.) Officers should understand how deeply ingrained the need to be hospitable is and not misinterpret this behavior for something it is not. When officers enter a home or a business owner's shop or office, an Arab American may very well offer coffee and something to eat. This is not to be mistaken for a bribe and, from the Arabic perspective, carries no negative connotations. According to Berro and Jabour (1992), most people would be offended if you did not accept their offers of hospitality. However, given police regulations, you may have to decline. If this is the case, Berro and Jabour advise that officers decline graciously. On the other hand, if the decision to accept the Arab American's hospitality depends on the officer's discretion, accepting can also be good for police–citizen relations. The period of time spent socializing and extending one's hospitality gives the person a chance to get to know and see if he or she can trust the other person. Business is not usually conducted among strangers. Obviously, on an emergency call, there is no time for such hospitality. However, with the move toward increasing community-based police organizations, officers may find that they are involved in more situations in which they may decide to accept small gestures of hospitality, if within departmental policy.

Verbal and Nonverbal Communication

Arabs in general are very warm and expressive people, both verbally and nonverbally, and appreciate it when others extend warmth to them. Americans without cultural knowledge of Arabs have sometimes misinterpreted the behavior of Arab Americans simply because of their own ethnocentrism (i.e., the tendency to judge others by one's own cultural standards and norms).

Conversational distance.   The acceptable conversational distance between two people is often influenced by culture. Officers are very aware of safety issues and keep a certain distance from people when communicating with them. Generally, officers like to stand about an arm's length or farther from citizens to avoid possible assaults on their person. This distance is similar to how far apart most Americans stand when in conversation. Cultures subtly influence the permissible distance between two people. When the distance is "violated," a person can feel threatened (either consciously or unconsciously). Many, but not all, Arabs, especially if they are new to the country, tend to have a closer acceptable conversational distance with each other than do other Americans. In Arab culture, it is not considered offensive to "feel a person's breath." Yet many Americans, unfamiliar with this intimacy in regular conversation, have misinterpreted the closeness. While still conscious of safety, law enforcement officers can keep in mind that the closer than "normal" (i.e., "normal" for the officer) speaking distance does not necessarily constitute a threat.

Devine and Braganti (1991) offer advice to American travelers in the Middle East; the advice is also applicable to police officers in the United States, especially when communicating with recent immigrants and refugees. Their advice includes the following: "Don't back away when an Arab stands very close while speaking to you. He won't be more than two feet away. Arabs constantly stare into other people's eyes, watching the pupils for an indication of the other person's response [i.e., dilated pupils mean a positive response]. However, foreign men [non-Arabs] should never stare directly into a woman's eyes, either in speaking to her or passing her on the street. He should avert his eyes or keep his eyes on the ground."

Gestures. The gestures Arabs from some countries use are distinctly different from those familiar to non-Arabic Americans. In a section titled "Customs and Manners in the Arab World," Devine and Braganti (1991, p. 13) describe some commonly used gestures among Arabs:

- "What does it mean? or What are you saying? Hold up the right hand and twist it as if you were screwing in a light bulb one turn.
- Wait a minute. Hold all fingers and thumb touching with the palm up.
- No. This can be signaled in one of three ways: moving the head back slightly and raising the eyebrows, moving the head back and raising the chin, or moving the head back and clicking with the tongue.
- Go away. Hold the right hand out with the palm down, and move it as if pushing something away from you.
- Never. A forceful never is signaled by holding the right forefinger up and moving it from left to right quickly and repeatedly."

As with many other cultural groups, pointing a finger directly at someone is considered rude.

Emotional expressiveness.

When I came to my brother's house to see what the problem was [i.e., with the police], I asked, 'What the hell is going on?' I held my hands out and talked with my hands as I always do. I repeated myself and continued to gesture with my hands. Later [i.e., at a trial] the police officer said that the Arab woman was yelling and screaming and acting wild, waving her arms and inciting observers to riot by her actions.*

The Arab American involved in the preceding situation explained that Arab women, in particular, are very emotional and that police sometimes see this emotionalism as a threat. She explained that on seeing a family member in trouble, it would be most usual and natural for a woman to put her hands to her face and say something like "Oh, my God" frequently and in a loud voice. While other Americans can react this same way, it is worth pointing out that in mainstream American culture, there is a tendency to subdue one's emotions and not to get "out of control." What some Americans consider to be "out of control," Arabs (like Mexicans, Greeks, Israelis, and Iranians, among other groups) consider to be perfectly "normal" behavior. In fact, the lack of emotionalism Arabs observe among mainstream Americans can be misinterpreted as lack of interest or involvement.

Although a communication style characteristic never applies to all people in a cultural group (and we have seen that there is a great deal of diversity among Arab Americans), there are group traits that apply to many people. Arabs, especially the

*The names of individuals and departments have been omitted even though permission has been granted to quote. The purpose of including these incidents is not to put undue attention on any one department or individual but rather to provide education on police professionalism in interethnic relations.

first generation of relatively recent newcomers, tend to display emotions when talking. Unlike many people in Far East Asian cultures (e.g., Japanese and Korean), Arabs do not believe that the expression of emotion is a sign of immaturity or a lack of control. Arabs, like other Mediterranean groups, such as Israelis and Greeks, tend to shout when they are excited or angry and are very animated in their communication. They may repeatedly insert expressions into their speech such as "I swear by God." This is simply a cultural mannerism.

Westerners, however, tend to judge this communication style negatively. To a Westerner, the emotionalism, repetition, and emphasis on certain statements can give the impression that the person is not telling the truth or is exaggerating for effect. An officer unfamiliar with these cultural mannerisms may feel overwhelmed, especially when involved with an entire group of people. The officer would do well to determine the spokesperson for the group but refrain from showing impatience or irritation at this culturally different style. The following comment was made by an Arab American community member (who prefers not to be identified) about police reactions to Arab Americans:

> Police see Arab emotionalism as a threat. They see the involvement of our large families in police incidents as a threat. They don't need to feel overwhelmed by us and try to contain our reactions. We will cooperate with them, but they need to show us that they don't view us as backward and ignorant people who are inferior just because we are different and because we express ourselves in a more emotional way than they do.

Swearing, the use of obscenities, and insults. Officers working in Arab American communities should know that for Arabs, words are extremely powerful. Whether consciously or unconsciously, some believe that words can affect the course of events and can bring misfortune (Nydell, 1987). If an officer displays a lack of professionalism by swearing at an Arab (even words such as *damn*), it will be nearly impossible to repair the damage.

In one case of documented police harassment of several Arab Americans (names have been omitted to avoid singling out this department), witnesses attest to officers' saying, "Mother-f_____ Arabs, we're going to teach you. Go back home!" One of the Arab American citizens involved in the case reported that officers treated him like an animal and were very insulting by asking questions in a demeaning tone such as, "Do you speak English? Do you read English?" (The man was a highly educated professional who had been in the United States for several years.) In asking him about his place of employment (he worked at an Arab American organization), the man reported that they referred to his place of employment as "the Arab Islamic shit or crap? What is that?"

Officers who understand professionalism are aware that this type of language and interaction is insulting to all persons. By using obscenities and insults, especially related to ethnic background, officers risk never being able to establish trust with the ethnic community. This lack of trust can translate into not being able to secure cooperation when needed. Even a few officers exhibiting this type of behavior can damage the reputation of an entire department for a long time.

English-language problems. If time allows, before asking the question "Do you speak English?" officers should try and assess whether the Arab American is a recent arrival or an established citizen who might react negatively to the question. A heavy accent does not necessarily mean that a person is unable to speak English (although that can be the case). Specific communication skills can be used with non-native English speakers (see Chapter 5), including Arab Americans. Officers should proceed slowly and nonaggressively with questioning and, wherever possible, ask open-ended questions. An officer's patience and willingness to take extra time will be beneficial in the long run.

KEY ISSUES IN LAW ENFORCEMENT

Perceptions of and Relationships with Police

It is not possible to generalize about how all Arab Americans perceive the police. As mentioned earlier, Arab immigrants who came in the late nineteenth century through World War II had the Turkish military police with whom to compare to the American police. Their experiences, then, in the United States were largely positive and they were cooperative with police. Since the majority of Arab Americans today are from that wave of immigrants, it is fair to say that a large part of the Arab American community respects the police. On the other hand, some immigrants, such as Jordanians and Palestinians, do not understand the American system and have an ingrained fear of police because of political problems in their own region of the world (Zogby, 1993). Since they distrust government, they are more likely to reject help from the police, and this puts them at a decided disadvantage in that they can more easily become victims. Their fear, in combination with the interdependence and helpfulness that characterizes the extended family, results in families not wanting assistance from the police. Thus police encounter some families that would prefer to handle conflict themselves even though police intervention is clearly needed. Some recent immigrants and refugees feel that it is dishonorable to have to go outside the family (e.g., to police and social services providers) to get help, and, if given a choice, they would choose not to embarrass themselves and their families in this manner.

In the Arab world of the Middle East, there are major differences in the institution of policing and the manner in which citizens are required to behave with police. In Saudi Arabia there is more of a fear of police than in some other countries because the punishments are stricter. For example, someone who is caught stealing repeatedly will have a hand removed. A Saudi Arabian woman caught shoplifting in a San Francisco Bay Area 7-Eleven store begged a police officer on her knees not to make the arrest because she feared being sent back to Saudi Arabia and did not know what would happen to her there. As it turned out, the officer did let her go since this was her first offense. He felt that he had some discretion in this case and decided to consider the woman's cultural background and circumstances. When it comes to interpreting cultural influences on police incidents and crimes, especially those of a lesser nature, each officer has to decide for himself or herself. (This aspect of law enforcement is discussed in Chapter 1.)

Women and Modesty

In the traditional Muslim world, women do not socialize freely with men and are required to dress modestly. However, the everyday practices in various Arabic countries differ greatly. In some countries, such as Lebanon, Jordan, and Egypt, women dress more in the manner of people in the West, whereas in countries such as Saudi Arabia, strict rules are maintained (e.g., the "morals police" tap women on the ankles with a long stick if their dresses are too short.)

Modesty for a traditional Arab Muslim woman may include the need to cover her head so that men will not see her hair. In some traditional Islamic societies, a man must not see a woman's hair, and officers should understand that asking a woman to remove a head covering (e.g., for the purpose of searching her or getting a photo identification) is analogous to asking her to expose a private part of her body. Officers Berro and Jabour (1992), who are Arab Americans, advise officers to approach this matter sensitively: "Don't overpower the woman, intimidate her, or grab her head cover. Ask her to go into a private room and have her remove it or get a female officer to help with the procedure."

American officers may have difficulty understanding the violation that a traditional Arabic woman feels when her head covering is taken away forcibly. Even if a woman is arrested for something like disorderly conduct, she will be offended by any aggressive move on the part of the officer to remove her head cover. When police procedures require that a head cover be removed, the officers should explain the procedure and offer some kind of an apology to show empathy. Having dealt with this same issue, the Immigration and Naturalization Service (INS) modified its regulations in the following way: "Every applicant . . . shall clearly show a three-quarter profile view of the features of the applicant with the head bare (unless the applicant is wearing a headdress as required by a religious order of which he or she is a member)" (INS Regulation 8 C.F.R. 331.1[a], 1992). Thus INS officials photograph Muslim women with their head coverings on. Because police departments deal with safety issues (such as concealed weapons), they may not have the liberty to accommodate this particular cultural difference in the same way as the INS was able to do. The matter of women and head coverings must be handled with extreme sensitivity.

Arab Grocers and Liquor Store Owners

> The ransacking of a North Richmond [California] liquor store reflects . . . tension between Middle Eastern store owners and their black customers. . . . It's a rift that has pitted Middle Eastern store owners, many of whom shun alcohol for religious reasons but sell it, against some of their black customers who believe money is being made off of the misery of alcohol. "I don't want to be a racist . . . but the Arab people are coming into the black community and they're not putting anything back into it," said a Richmond resident. (Richmond rift deepens over liquor-sales issues (*Contra Costa Times,* January 9, 1993, p. 10A)

These types of comments can be heard across the United States where there are Arab grocers and liquor store owners in low-income areas (e.g., Detroit, Cleveland). The dynamics between Arab store owners and African Americans are similar to those between Koreans and African Americans in inner cities. The non-Arab often views the Arab as having money and exploiting the local residents for economic gain. James Zogby explains that this perception is reinforced because one rarely sees a non-Arab working in an Arab-owned store. The local resident, according to Zogby (director of the Arab-American Institute) does not understand that Arabs, for the most part, are political refugees (e.g., Palestinians) and have come to the United States for a better life. When they first arrive, the only work that they can do is operate small, marginal businesses. Most of the small Arab-run grocery stores or liquor stores are family-operated businesses managed by two brothers or a father and two sons, for example. It would not be economically possible for them to hire outside their family (the situation is similar to Korean family-run businesses) (Zogby, 1993). Police officers, in the midst of the conflicts between store owners and local residents, can attempt to explain the position of the refugees, but, of course, the explanation by itself cannot take care of the problem. Many poor American-born citizens harbor a great deal of animosity toward immigrants and refugees because of scarce resources.

Alcohol is forbidden in the Muslim religion, yet Arab liquor store owners sell it to their customers. There has been a debate in the Arab American community as to whether Muslim immigrants and refugees should go into this type of business. The majority of newcomers have very limited choices. Members of other ethnic groups have owned many of the mom-and-pop stores throughout the years and now some are asking: "Where did all these Arabs come from, and why is it all they want to do is sell alcohol to black folks?" (Richmond rift deepens over liquor-sales issue (*Contra Costa Times,* January 9, 1993, p. 10A). Some Arab liquor store owners, however, do set limits as to whom they will sell liquor. One Arab American store owner in Richmond, California, explained, "Just this morning, I refused to sell wine to a lady and her husband with food stamps. I said, 'I'm not going to do it,' and she said, 'Oh you dumb Arab, we're going to come back and blow up the whole store' " (Richmond rift deepens over liquor-sales issue (*Contra Costa Times,* January 9, 1993, p. 10A). (Ibid)

There is another dimension to the problem of Arab store owners in inner cities. Many inner-city residents (Arab Americans and African Americans included) do not feel that law enforcement officials take the needs of the inner city as seriously as they do problems elsewhere. A pattern has emerged in the Arab American community whereby Arab American store owners feel that they have to take on problems of crime in their stores themselves (Zogby, 1993). If an Arab store owner is robbed and receives nonsupportive or harsh treatment by the police, he feels that he has to defend himself and his store alone. In some cases, Arab store owners have assaulted shoplifters in their stores, potentially putting themselves at risk of becoming victims. Like other minority-group members, some Arab shop owners in the inner city have given up on the police. Police officers cannot solve the social ills that plague the inner city, but at a minimum they need to instill the confidence that they will be as supportive as possible when dealing with the crimes that immigrant and refugee store owners experience.

Hate Crimes against Arab Americans

In Chapters 11 to 13, hate crimes are discussed fully. The following explanation deals only with the stereotyping and scapegoating of Arabs that often takes place

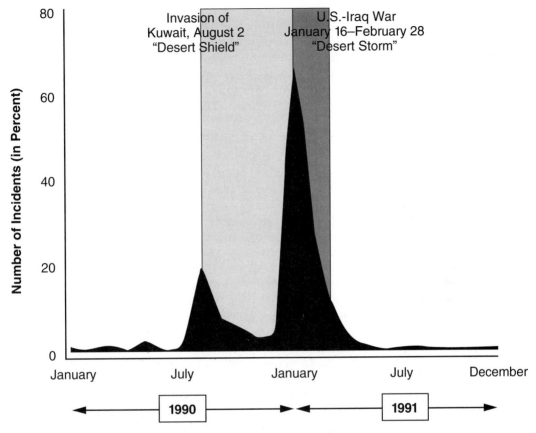

Exhibit 9.1 Influence of the changing political crisis on hate crime incidents against Arabs in the United States in 1990 and 1991. *Source:* American–Arab Anti-Discrimination Committee, 1992.

when a crisis in the Arab world involves Americans. Arab Americans have a special need for protection during times of political tensions in the Middle East. "The number of racial incidents suffered by Arab Americans increased threefold in 1991 as the Persian Gulf War raged," the Arab–American Anti-Discrimination Committee (1992) reported. Exhibit 9.1 shows only the reported crimes; According to the Arab–American Anti-Discrimination Committee, many cases do not come to their attention because victims fear additional violence against them.

Throughout 1991, violence against individual Arab Americans escalated more than ever before. The crisis in the Gulf began in August 1990 with Desert Shield and climaxed in January 1991 when the United States went to war with Iraq. Throughout this period, the number of hate crimes directed toward Arab Americans increased, with the largest number of attacks occurring during the first few weeks following the onset of hostilities. The American–Arab Anti-Discrimination Committee published the "1991 Report on Anti-Arab Hate Crimes." The opening paragraph reads: "Significantly, a dramatic increase was recorded in acts involving physical violence such as arson, bombings, and physical assaults as Arab-Americans again became convenient scapegoats for a small minority of individuals seeking to vent their fears and frustrations by intimidating, harassing, and carrying out acts of violence against others. In short, Arab-Americans proved to be the domestic casualties of the war" (American-Arab Anti-Discrimination Committee, 1992). Even though the majority of Arab Americans supported President George Bush's decision to invade Iraq some people viewed all Arab Americans as "the enemy."

The "Terrorist" Stereotype

Adding to an anti-Arab feeling during the Gulf War was the FBI announcement to conduct investigations (extensive interviewing) in the Arab American community to gather information about domestic terrorism (*Washington Times,* January 9, 1991, p. A–5). At least a few of the interviews took place with officers of local police departments such as in Los Angeles, where one Arab American described the visit of an FBI agent "unannounced, unexpected and accompanied by a member of the Los Angeles Police Department's anti-terrorist squad" (*New York Times National,* January 12, 1991). FBI agents interviewed at least 200 prominent Americans of Arab descent and offended them by their very insinuation that because of their identity, they must know of Arab terrorists in the United States.

In a letter to President George Bush (January 9, 1993), Albert Mokhiber, former president of the American–Arab Anti-Discrimination Committee stated, "To assume that Arab Americans as a community have special knowledge about potential acts of terrorism in the United States is offensive. Such an assumption is a throwback to the dark days of our national history with the Japanese Internment camps during World War II." Mokhiber pointed out that Arab Americans are not known to be terrorists but, rather, have been victims of terrorism and hate crimes. Arab American leaders acknowledged their appreciation that FBI agents investigated hate crimes against community members during the Gulf crisis. However, according to Mokhiber, the FBI's investigations to locate terrorists "gave the appearance that the Arab American community is 'suspect' . . . and will allow others . . . justification for their continued suspicion and acts of violence against us." James Zogby (1993), referring to the FBI procedure and the general description of the Arab American community, pointed out, "Most of the Arab American community is assimilated and identifies themselves as Americans."

A most convincing example of the persistence of discrimination against Arabs and the stereotypical view of them as terrorists occurred after the Oklahoma City bombing in April 1995. Immediately following the bombing, many journalists and political leaders said that the tragedy appeared to be the work of Muslim terrorists. This was the initial conclusion without any evidence to support it; they were obviously proved wrong with the arrest and conviction of Timothy J. McVeigh. The paranoia that led to the hasty conclusion of Arab involvement in the bombing gave way to Arab bashing, including many hate calls to Arabs. The scapegoating against Arabs spread across the country like wild fire.

> Terror in Oklahoma City; U.S. Muslims Feel Sting of Accusations; Harassment: Talk of a Middle East Link Led to Epithets against Ethnic Community. But Arrest of Midwesterner has spurred a Collective Sigh of Relief.

It was as if we were accomplices to what happened in Oklahoma City, while all we wanted to do was unite with other Americans in the healing process, said Salam Al-Marayati of the Muslim Public Affairs Council. . . . The Islamic Center had logged about a dozen harassment phone calls since [the bombing]. . . . "Baby killers" . . . What are you Muslims doing now? You should all be run out of town. . . . You animals." Muslim leaders said they understand that the involvement of Muslim terrorists in the bombing two years ago [in 1993] of the World Trade Center in New York helps explain why the rage of so many was suddenly directed at them. . . . USC Professor Richard Hrair Dekmejian, who has taught courses on terrorism and studied Islamic fundamentalism, said the backlash is nothing new. . . . "This is not the first time in American history when this has happened. Every time there is some type of violence in the United States, immediately we tend to look at the Middle East and blame the Islamic extremists." (*Los Angeles Times*, April 22, 1995, p. A22)

The 1996 crash of TWA flight 800 in New York also led to scapegoating of Arabs. Following are reactions from the Arab community: There are lessons for Americans in both the bombing of the Oklahoma City building and the crash of TWA flight 800—neither incident turned out to be what many Americans assumed. Clearly, law enforcement officials must monitor world and community events to be prepared for potential backlash against Arab Americans.

SUMMARY OF RECOMMENDATIONS FOR LAW ENFORCEMENT

Officers should keep in mind several basic Arabic cultural values when interacting with Arab American citizens:

- "A person's dignity, honor, and reputation are of paramount importance and no effort should be spared to protect them, especially one's honor" (Nydell, 1987).
- "Loyalty to one's family takes precedence over [other needs]"; thus an individual is completely intertwined with his or her family (Nydell, 1987).
- Communication should be courteous and hospitable; honor and face-saving govern interpersonal interactions and relationships.

Arab Americans have been wrongly characterized and stereotyped by the media; as with all stereotypes, this has affected people's thinking on Arab Americans. Officers should be aware of stereotypes that may influence their judgments. Common stereotypes of Arabs include that they are illiterate and backward, that the women are passive and uneducated, and that they are thiefs and terrorists.

Officers can demonstrate to Muslim Arabs a respect for their culture and religion by (1) respecting the times when people pray (five times a day); (2) maintaining courteous behavior in mosques, such as not stepping on prayer mats, not walking in front of people praying, and speaking softly; and (3) working out solutions with community members regarding religious celebrations (e.g., parking problems, noise).

The basic unit for Arab Americans, especially recent arrivals and traditional families, is not the individual but the family (including the extended family). If a family member is involved in a police incident, officers should expect that other family members will become actively involved. Officers should not automatically assume that this involvement is an attempt to interfere with police affairs. The traditional Arabic family is used to working out conflicts themselves; this is further reason for all members to become involved.

Traditionally and outwardly, the father is the head of the household, and much of the conversation should be directed toward him. Officers should, however, keep in mind the following. Many Arab women are outspoken and vocal. Officers should not dismiss their input simply because men may appear to be, at least publicly, the ones with the power. Traditional Arab women who do not freely communicate with men may have difficulty expressing themselves to a male police officer. In their own families, however, they are often the real decision makers. Officers may consider various ways of getting information (e.g., the use of a female translator, female police officer, or indirect and open-ended questions).

Officers should consider a number of specific cultural practices and taboos when communicating with Arab Americans who have preserved a traditional lifestyle. (The following points do not apply to the majority of Arab Americans who have been in the United States for generations.) Officers should avoid even casually touching women and should be respectful of the need some Arab women have to be modest. They should never point the soles of their shoes or feet at a person. Officers can expect Arab Americans to extend hospitality by offering coffee or food (which is not a bribe, from their cultural perspective). Arab Americans may stand closer to each other than other Americans do when talking. This is not meant to be threatening; it is largely unconscious and reflects a cultural preference for closer interpersonal interaction.

There are cultural differences in communication style that can affect officers' judgments and reactions. Becoming highly emotional (verbally and nonverbally) and speaking loudly is not looked down on in the Arab world. Officers who may have a different manner of communication should not express irritation at this culturally different style. Nor should they necessarily determine that the people involved are being disrespectful. Developing patience with culturally different styles of communication is a key cross-cultural skill. When a person speaks with an accent, it does not necessarily mean that he or she is not fluent in English or is illiterate. Many highly educated Arab Americans speak English fluently but with an accent and would be insulted if they were treated as if they were not educated.

In areas with Arab American grocers and liquor store owners as well as poor residents, there is great potential for conflict. Arab American grocers and liquor store owners need to be able to depend on local police services. Many do not feel that they have the protection they need. Police officers may be in positions to explain to other residents why Arab American store owners do not usually hire people from the community. Explanations will not resolve the conflicts, but at least officers can attempt to make some people understand the economic realities of life for refugees and immigrants.

During crises in the Middle East, Arab Americans become targets of prejudice and racism. Police departments need to monitor communities and keep informed of world events so that Arab American communities have more protection during times when they may be vulnerable to hate crimes.

DISCUSSION QUESTIONS AND ISSUES*

1. ***Police–Ethnic Community Relations.*** From the section titled "Islamic Religion," recall the incident that took place at the end of the holy month of Ramadan, when officers ticketed many cars parked across the street from the mosque. According to community people, the stores adjacent to the parking lots were closed and although parking was technically for customers only, the Arab Americans did not anticipate a problem with utilizing the parking lot after hours. From a community relations point of view, the mass ticketing created some very negative feelings and a collective perception that "They [the police] don't respect us and don't want to understand us." What is your opinion on the way things were handled? Do you have any suggestions as to how this situation could have been prevented? Comment on what both the community and the police could have done to prevent the problem.

2. ***Who Is the Head of the Household?*** The stated head of the household in most traditional Arabic families is the father, although the mother actually has a great deal of power within the family. Although in public many Arabic women defer decision making to their husbands, a police officer should not discount what the woman might have to offer in various police-related situations. How can the police officer, while respecting the status of the father, still acknowledge the mother and get her input?

3. ***Nonverbal Variations across Cultures.*** When Arab Americans greet each other, they sometimes shake hands and then place their right hand on their chest near their heart. This is a sign of sincerity. In your opinion, should officers greet Arab Americans using this gesture if a person greets them in this way? What are the pros and cons of using the gesture?

4. ***Hospitality toward Officers: A Cultural Gesture.*** Hospitality is a virtue in Arabic culture and also functions to help people get to know (and see if they can trust) others with whom they are interacting. Given this cultural emphasis on being hospitable, what should an officer do if offered a cup of coffee and something to eat? If an officer has to decline the hospitality, how can he or she do so politely? Should department policy regarding the acceptance of hospitality be reexamined in light of this cultural tendency? Would your answer be different for departments that have adopted a community-based policing philosophy?

5. ***"But It's the Custom in My Country."*** In January 1991, the Associated Press reported that a Stockton, California, man originally from Jordan was arrested for investigation of "selling his daughter into slavery" because he allegedly accepted $25,000 for her arranged marriage. After police officers had taken the girl to a shelter, a police lieutenant reported that the father protested that "he was within his rights to arrange his daughter's marriage for a price. The father contacted us and quite upset, explained it was the custom in his country and is perfectly acceptable. Of course, we explained that you can't do that in this country. It is slavery. . . . The father then went to the shelter [where the daughter was] and was arrested after creating a disturbance." If you were investigating this case, how would you proceed? How might you assess the validity of what the father was saying? If you found out that the act was indeed "perfectly acceptable" in his country, how would you explain practices in the United States? Comment on the statement that the lieutenant made ("It is slavery."). From the perspective of needing cooperation from this man, what type of approach should be taken?

*See Instructor's Manual accompanying this text for additional activities, role-play activities, questionnaires, and projects related to the content of this chapter.

6. ***Officer Discretion: To Let Her Go?*** In the section on the perceptions of police, we mention an incident involving a Saudi Arabian woman who was caught shoplifting in a 7-Eleven. She begged the officer to let her go because she feared being sent home, where she would receive a harsh punishment (typically, in Saudi Arabia, a person's hand is cut off if he or she steals). The officer decided that since this was her first offense, he would let her go. What is your reaction to the officer's decision? What would you have done?

REFERENCES

ABOU-SAIF, LAILA. (1990). *A Woman's Journey into the Heart of the Arab World.* New York: Charles Scribner's Sons.

American–Arab Anti-Discrimination Committee. (1992, February). *1991 Report on Anti-Arab Hate Crimes: Political and Hate Violence against Arab-Americans.* Washington, D.C.: Author.

Arab American Institute. (2000, February). *Arab-Americans: Issues, Attitudes, Views.* Zogby, International and Arab American Institute. Washington, D.C.

BERRO, MOHAMED, AND MARK JABOUR. (1992, December 5). Officer and sergeant, Dearborn, Michigan, Police Department, personal communication.

BOLLER, PHILIP J., JR. (1992, March). "A Name Is Just a Name—Or Is It?" *FBI Law Enforcement Bulletin,* Central Intelligence World Factbook, 2000. Department of Justice, (1997, October). *1996 Statistical Yearbook of the Immigration and Naturalization Service.* Washington, D.C.: Author.

DEVINE, ELIZABETH, AND NANCY L. BRAGANTI. (1991). *The Traveler's Guide to Middle Eastern and North African Customs and Manners.* New York: St. Martin's Press.

JABARA, ABDEEN. (no date). "Time for a Change." In *The Arab Image in American Film and Television.* Washington, D.C.: American–Arab Anti-Discrimination Committee.

MACRON, MARY. (1989). *Arab Contributions to Civilization.* Washington, D.C.: American–Arab Anti-Discrimination Committee.

MICHALAK, LAURENCE. (1988). *Cruel and Unusual: Negative Images of Arabs in American Popular Culture.* Washington, D.C.: American–Arab Anti-Discrimination Committee.

NAFF, ALIXA. (1993, January 25). Middle Eastern social and political historian, personal communication.

NYDELL, MARGARET K. (1987). *Understanding Arabs: A Guide for Westerners.* Yarmouth, Maine: Intercultural Press.

SHABBAS, AUDREY. (1984). *Cultural Clues for Social Service Case Workers and Special Educators* (unpublished monograph). Berkeley, Calif.: Arab World and Islamic Resources and School Services.

SHAHEEN, JACK. (1988). *Abscam: Arabiaphobia in America.* Washington D.C.: American–Arab Anti-Discrimination Committee.

SULEIMAN, MICHAEL W. (Ed.). (2000). *Arabs in America: Building a New Future.* Philadelphia: Temple University Press.

WOODRUFF, DAVID. (1991, February 4). "Letter from Detroit: Where the Mid-East meets the Midwest—uneasily," *Business Week,* 30A.

Zogby International Study. (2000). *Arab Americans: Protecting Rights at Home and Promoting a Just Peace Abroad.* Washington, D.C. Arab American Institute. Available at: www.aaiusa.org

ZOGBY, JAMES. (1993, January 25). Director of the Arab American Institute, personal communication. Washington, D.C.

10

LAW ENFORCEMENT CONTACT WITH AMERICAN INDIANS

OVERVIEW

This chapter provides specific cultural information on American Indians, including aspects of their history that both directly and indirectly can affect relationships with law enforcement officials. It presents information about American Indian identity and group identification terms and explains briefly the tribal system, reservations, American Indian mobility, and family structure. It addresses the diversity that exists among American Indian groups and includes a description of cultural differences and similarities found among various Indian groups. We point out labels, terms, and stereotypical statements that are offensive to Indians. The closing section outlines several key concerns for law enforcement, including information on perceptions of police, police jurisdiction problems, peyote, medicine bags, trespassing, violation of Indian sacred places, and problems related to fishing rights. In the summary of the chapter, we provide a review of recommendations for improved communication and relationships between law enforcement personnel and members of American Indian communities.

COMMENTARY

"It's just a bunch of Indians—let them go!" This quote is excerpted from an interview with retired Chief Jim Cox (1992), a Comanche Indian and former chief of police of the Midwest City Police Department, Oklahoma, discussed in an interview the subject of officers' biased and prejudicial treatment of Indians. He described an incident during his youth in Oklahoma when he was riding with other American Indian teenagers in an old Nash automobile. Police officers stopped the car and discovered that the teens had been drinking. Instead of taking the appropriate action, which would have been to arrest the young people or at least call their parents to pick them up, the officers let them go. Former Chief Cox recalls to this day hearing one of the officers tell the other that Indians were not worth the time or bother: "It's just a bunch of Indians—let them go!" Cox interpreted this statement to mean that if they killed themselves, it did not matter because they were just Indians. This impression remained with him even after he became a police officer more than 35 years ago.

> When an officer contacts an Indian person, there is often 500 years of frustration built up. . . . Officers should be aware of the "baggage" that they bring to the encounter. (Rivera, 1992).

> What treaty that the whites have kept has the red man broken? Not one. What treaty that the white man ever made with us have they kept? Not one. When I was a boy the Sioux owned the world; the sun rose and set on their land; they sent ten thousand men to battle. Who slew [the warriors]? Where are our lands? Who owns them? What white man can say I ever stole his land. . . ? Yet, they say I am a thief. What white woman, however lonely, was ever captive or insulted by me? Yet they say I am a bad Indian. What white man has ever seen me drunk? Who has ever seen me . . . abuse my children? What law have I broken? Is it wicked for me because my skin is red? (Sitting Bull [Lakota],in *The Spirit of Crazy Horse,* quoted in Matthiessen, 1992)

In this chapter, the terms *American Indian, Native American,* and *Indian* are used interchangeably.

HISTORICAL INFORMATION AND BACKGROUND

Recorded history disputes the origins of the first "Indians" in America. Some researchers claim they arrived from Asia more than 40,000 years ago; others claim they originated in the Americas. In either case, despite their long history in North America and their status as the first "Americans," traditional U.S. history books did not mention their existence except in relation to the European conquests, beginning with Christopher Columbus in 1492. The view of native peoples as either nonexistent or simply insignificant reflects an ethnocentric (in this case, a Eurocentric) perspective on history. Even the word *Indian* is not a term that native Americans originally used to designate their tribes or communities. Because Columbus did not know that North and South America existed, he thought he had reached the Indies (which then included India, China, the East Indies, and Japan). In fact, he arrived in what is now called the West Indies (in the Caribbean), and he called the people he met Indians (*Los Indios*). Eventually, this became the name for all indigenous peoples in the Americas. However, before white settlers came to North and South America, almost every Indian tribe had its own name, and, despite some shared cultural values, native Americans did not see themselves as one collective group or call themselves Indians. Most tribes continue to refer to themselves in their own languages as "The People," "The Allies," or "The Friends." Some of the terms whites use for various tribes are not even authentic names for these tribes. For example, the label *Sioux,* which means enemy or snake, was originally a term given to that group by an enemy tribe and then adopted by French traders. In many cases, a tribe's real name is not necessarily the name commonly used.

Today in public schools across the country, some educators are only beginning to discuss the nature of much of the contact with Native Americans in early American history. Traditionally, rather than being presented as part of the American people's common legacy, Native American cultural heritage has been presented as bits of colorful exotica. Genocide, or the killing of entire tribes, is not a chapter in U.S. history on which people have wanted to focus. The reality is that Euro-American and Indian relations have been characterized by hostility, contempt, and brutality. Euro-Americans have generally treated native peoples as less than human or as "savages" and have ignored or crushed the rich Native American cultures. For this reason, many American Indians who identify culturally with this group do not share in the celebrations of Thanksgiving or Christopher Columbus Day. To say that Columbus discovered America implies that Native Americans were not considered "human enough" to be of significance. Ignoring the existence of the Native Americans before 1492 constitutes only one aspect of ethnocentrism. American Indians' experience with the "white man" has largely been one of exploitation, violence, and forced relocation. This historical background has shaped many Native American views of Euro-Americans and their culture. Although most people in the United States have a sense that Native Americans were not treated with dignity in U.S. history, many are not aware of the extent of the current abuse directed toward them. This oversight may result because this group is a small and traditionally forgotten minority in the United States. (Native Americans, including Alaska Natives, constitute approximately 1 percent of the overall population.)

It would not be accurate to say that no progress at all has been made in United States with respect to the awareness and rights of our nation's first Americans. On November 6, 2000, President Clinton renewed his commitment to tribal sovereignty by issuing an executive order on consultation with tribal governments. The purpose of the order is "to establish meaningful consultation and collaboration with tribal officials in the development of federal policies having tribal implications, to strengthen the administration's government-to-government relationship to tribes, and to reduce the imposition of unfounded mandates by ensuring that all Executive departments and agencies consult with tribes and respect tribal sovereignty as they develop policies on issues that impact Indian communities" (Legix Social and General Update, November 9, 2000). The 2000 executive order includes:

> The Administration's goal of strengthening the United States government-to-government relationship with tribes
>
> The [requirement] that the federal government grant tribal governments the maximum administrative discretion possible with respect to federal statutes administered by tribal governments
>
> The [prohibition] of agencies from promulgating any regulation that has tribal implications and that imposes direct substantial cost that preempts tribal law unless the agency first consults with tribal officials early in the process of developing the regulation. (www.legix.com)

Despite the progress made on the records in Washington, D.C., many Native Americans do not see how this "progress" has affected their daily lives. Indians have among the highest school dropout rates and unemployment rates of all the ethnic and racial groups. As for protection from the federal government, American Indians continue to fight legal battles over the retention of Indian lands and other rights previously guaranteed by U.S. treaties. They still feel abused by a system of government that has violated many treaties with natives. The federal government has disregarded rights guaranteed in the form of binding treaties.

The U.S. government has not always acted in good faith toward its Native American citizens, breaching many treaties. Consequently, individuals and tribes are reluctant to trust the words of the government or people representing the system. Whether they are aware of it or not, law enforcement agents encounter this baggage in interactions with Native Americans. The police officer historically has been a rigidly authoritarian part of governmental control that has affected nearly every aspect of an Indian's life, especially on reservations. Often, officers (like most citizens) have only a limited understanding of how the government, including the criminal justice system, caused massive suffering by not allowing Indians to preserve their cultures, identities, languages, sacred sites, rituals, and lands. Because of this history, officers have a responsibility to educate themselves about the history of the treatment of Indian peoples in order to deal with them effectively and fairly today. Law enforcement officers must understand Indian communities and put forth extra effort to establish rapport; doing so will increase the possibility of success at winning cooperation and respect from people who never before had reason to trust representatives of government.

THE QUESTION OF AMERICAN INDIAN IDENTITY

Law enforcement officials may find themselves confused as to who is an American Indian. Individuals may claim to have "Indian blood," but tribes have their own criteria for determining tribal membership. Because the determination of tribal membership is a fundamental attribute of tribal sovereignty, the federal government generally defers to tribes' own determinations when establishing eligibility criteria under special Indian entitlement programs. However, for historical and political reasons, a number of Indian tribes are not currently recognized by the federal government. Members of such tribes, although Indian, are not necessarily eligible for special benefits under federal Indian programs. On the other hand, fraud in this area is quite rampant, with people falsely claiming Indian ancestry to take unfair advantage of governmental benefits and other perceived opportunities.

Officers may find themselves in situations in which an individual claims to be Indian when he or she is not. If officers have any doubt, they should inquire as to what tribe the person belongs to and then contact the tribal headquarters to verify that person's identity. Every tribe has its own authority and administration, the members of which will be able to answer questions of this nature. By verifying information with tribal authorities rather than making personal determinations of "Indian-ness," officers will help create a good rapport between tribal members and law enforcement officials (LaVelle, 1993).

According to estimates in 2000, there were approximately 2.3 million American Indians and Alaska Natives living in the United States (U.S. Bureau of the Census 2000). However, there is a great deal of numerical misinformation because of the lack of a method for verifying the accuracy of people's claims to be Native American.

The term *Native American* came into popularity in the 1960s and referred to groups served by the Bureau of Indian Affairs (BIA), including American Indians and natives of Alaska. Later, the term under certain federal legislation began to include natives of Hawaii. (*Native American,* however, has never been accepted by all Indian groups and is rarely used on reservations.) Natives of Alaska, such as Eskimos and Aleuts, are separate groups and prefer the term *Alaska Native.* To know by what terms individuals or tribes prefer to be called, officers should listen to the names they use for themselves rather than try to guess which one is "correct."

In the area of mislabeling, some Native Americans have Spanish first or last names (because of intermarriage) and may "look" Hispanic or Latino (e.g., the Hopis). Identification can be difficult for officers, so they should not assume that a person is Latino just because of name or appearance. Many Native Americans do not want to be grouped with Latinos because (1) they are not Latinos, (2) they may resent the fact that some Latinos deny their Indian ancestry and instead identify only with the Spanish part of their heritage, and (3) many tribes have a history of warfare with the mestizo populations of Mexico. As an aside, the majority population in Mexico, Central America, and South America is of "Indian" ancestry. However, they adopted or were given Spanish names by the Conquistadores (conquerors). Many Hispanics in U.S. border communities are really of Indian, not Spanish, heritage, or they may be a mixture of the two.

TRIBES, RESERVATIONS, AND MOBILITY OF NATIVE AMERICANS

In the United States, according to the BIA figures in the mid-1990s, there were over 550 federally recognized tribes (some of which use *tribe* and *nation* interchangeably), including native groups of Alaskans such as Aleuts. Federal recognition means that a legal relationship exists between the tribe and the federal government. Many tribes still do not benefit from federally recognized status. Some may be state recognized and or in the process of seeking federal recognition, while others may not seek recognition at all. The issue of the increasing rivalry among some Indian groups seeking recognition is reflected in the sentiment that some Indian tribes are pitted against each other over government benefits and resources.

An Indian reservation is land that a tribe has reserved for its exclusive use through the course of treaty making. It may be on ancestral lands or simply the only land available when tribes were forced to give up their own territories through federal treaties. A reservation is also land that the federal government holds in trust for the use of an Indian tribe. The BIA estimated in the mid-1990s that about 1.2 million Indians were living on approximately 300 reservations (exact figures are difficult to obtain). The largest of the reservations is the Navajo reservation (and trust lands), which extends into three states. Since reservations are self-governing, most have tribal police. (The issue of jurisdiction is presented later in this chapter.) Indians are not forced to stay on reservations, but many who leave have a strong desire to remain in touch with and be nourished by their culture on the reservations. For this reason and because of the culture shock experienced in urban life, many return to reservations (LaVelle, 1993).

In general, the Indian population is characterized by constant movement between the reservation and the city, and sometimes relocation from city to city. In urban areas, when officers have contact with an Indian, they will not necessarily know how acculturated to city life that individual is. In rural areas it is easier for officers to get to know the culture of a particular tribe. In the city, the tribal background may be less important than the fact that the person is an American Indian.

Since the early 1980s, more than half of the Native American population has lived outside of reservation communities; many have left to pursue educational and employment opportunities, as life on some of the reservations can be very bleak. Although a large number return home to the reservations to participate in family activities and tribal ceremonies, many attempt to remake their lives in urban areas. A percentage of Indians do make adjustments to mainstream educational and occupational life, but the numbers are still disproportionately low.

DIFFERENCES AND SIMILARITIES AMONG NATIVE AMERICANS

As with other culturally or ethnically defined categories of people (e.g., Asian, African American) it would be a mistake to lump all Native Americans together and to assume that they are homogeneous. For example, in Arizona alone, one finds a number of different tribes with varying traditions: there are Hopis in the northeast, Pimas and Papagos in the south, and Yuman groups in the west. All descend from people who came to what is now called Arizona. The relative "newcomers" are the Navajos and Apaches, who arrived about 1,000 years ago. These six tribes represent differences in culture, and each group has its own history and life experiences.

Broadly speaking, in the United States, one finds distinct cultural groups among Native Americans in Alaska, Arizona, California, the central plains (Kansas and Nebraska), the Dakotas, the eastern seaboard, the Great Lakes area, the Gulf Coast states (Florida, Alabama, Mississippi, Louisiana, and Texas), the lower plateau (Nevada, Utah, and Colorado), Montana, Wyoming, New Mexico, North Carolina, Oklahoma, and the Northwest (Washington, Oregon, and Idaho). Every tribe has evolved its own sets of traditions and beliefs, and each sees itself as distinct from other tribes, despite some significant broad similarities. (It is beyond the scope of this book to delve deeply into differences among tribes.)

Similarities among Native Americans

It is possible to talk about general characteristics of Native American groups without negating the fact of their diversity. The cultural characteristics described in the following section will not apply to all such Americans, but rather to many who are traditionally "Indian" in their orientation to life. Although officers should be aware of tribal differences, they should also understand that there is a strong cultural link among the many worlds and tribes of Native Americans and their Indian counterparts throughout the American continent.

Philosophy toward the Earth and the Universe

"The most striking difference between . . . Indian and Western man is the manner in which each views his role in the universe. The prevailing non-Indian view is that man is superior to all other forms of life and that the universe is his to be used as he sees fit.. . . [A]n attitude justified as the mastery of nature for the benefit of man" characterizes Western man's philosophy (Bahti, 1982). Through this contrast with Western philosophy (i.e., that people have the capacity to alter nature) readers can gain insight into the values and philosophies common to virtually all *identifying* Native Americans. Although each Indian tribe or nation is unique, there is a common set of values and beliefs involving the earth and the universe, resulting in a deep respect for nature and "mother earth." According to American Indian philosophy, the earth is sacred and is a living entity. By spiritual involvement with the earth, nature, and the universe, individuals bind themselves to their environment. Indians do not see themselves as superior to all else (e.g., animals, plants) but rather as part of all of creation. Through religious ceremonies and rituals, Indians are able to transcend themselves such that they are in harmony with the universe and connected to nature.

The inclination of some people who do not understand this philosophy would be to dismiss it as primitive and even backward. The costumes, rituals, ceremonies, and dances are often thought of as colorful but strange. Yet from an Indian perspective, "It is a tragedy indeed that Western man in his headlong quest for Holy Progress could not have paused long enough to learn this basic truth—one which he is now being forced to recognize (with the spoilage of the earth), much to his surprise and dismay. Ever anxious to teach 'backward' people, he is ever reluctant to learn from them" (Bahti, 1982). Many non-Indians now embrace certain Native American beliefs regarding the environment; what people once thought of as "primitive" is now seen as essential in the preservation of our environment.

An Indian Prayer

Oh our Mother the earth, Oh our Father the sky,
Your children are we, and with tired backs
We bring you the gifts you love.
Then weave for us a garment of brightness . . .
May the fringes be the falling rain.
May the border be the standing rainbow.
That we may walk fittingly where birds sing . . . and where grass is green, Oh our mother earth, Oh our father sky. (Author unknown)

When law enforcement officers make contact with people who are in the midst of celebrating or praying, whether on reservations or in communities, it is vitally important to be as respectful as possible. They must refrain from conveying an air of superiority and ethnocentrism, an attitude that the rituals are primitive. American Indian prayers, rituals, and ceremonies represent ancient beliefs and philosophies, many of which have to do with the preservation of and harmony with the earth. Officers should, at all costs, try to avoid interrupting prayers and sacred ceremonies, just as one would avoid interrupting church services. (Officers should also be aware that taking photographs during ceremonies would constitute an interruption and is forbidden. In general, officers should seek permission before taking photos of Indians; this is true for Navajos, Hopis, and many other groups.)

Acculturation to Mainstream Society

Significant differences exist among the cultures, languages, history, and socioeconomic status of Native American tribes, communities, and individuals. Nevertheless, in a national study on suicide and ethnicity in the United States, the Committee on Cultural Psychiatry (1989) concluded that there is still "a definitive pattern of self-destructive behavior which can be generalized to all [Indian] groups." However, it cannot be overstressed that many of the psychosocial problems that some Indians experience in mainstream society do not result from their own weaknesses or deficiencies. The cause of the problems dates back to the way the U.S. government has handled and regulated Indian life. The dominant society in no way affirmed the cultural identity of Indians; thus many Indians have internalized the oppression they experienced from the outside world. Furthermore, many young people feel the stresses of living between two cultural worlds. They are not fully part of the traditional Indian world (as celebrated on the reservation or in a community that honors traditions) and they are not fully adapted to the dominant American culture. People who are caught between two cultures and are successful in neither run the risk of contributing to family breakdown, often becoming depressed, alcoholic, and suicidal. The most recent statistics from the Pan-American Health Organization (Demographics and Health Risk Indicator, 2000) indicate that the suicide rate for American Indian males, ages 15 to 24 years, was one-third higher than the rate for white youths. Alcoholism is the leading health and social problem of American Indians; 75 percent of the deaths of people under age 45 years can be attributed to alcohol use (e.g., unintentional injury). Interestingly, according to the Committee on Cultural Psychiatry (1989), Indian groups that have remained tightly identified with their culture because of isolation from the mainstream culture and strong ties to indigenous lands do not exhibit the type of behavior described. Tribes exemplifying healthier attitudes toward their identities and a lower suicide rate include the southwestern Pueblos and the Navajo.

Despite the persistence of many social problems, some progress has been made with respect to education and political participation. Law enforcement officials must not hold on to the stereotype of American Indians as being uneducated. The population attending colleges and rising to high positions in education, entertainment, sports, and industry is increasing. Many people are now working on revitalizing Native American culture rather than letting it die. This emphasis on culture has resulted in the movement of Pan-Indianism, in which American Indians across the United States are celebrating their cultural heritage, while organizing politically. The National Congress of American Indians (NCAI) specifically deals with political and social issues that arise among Native Americans nationally. For example, in 1999 the NCAI condemned the use of sports team mascots using Native American and native cultural terms (e.g., Redskins). The NCAI is the oldest, largest, and most representative Indian organization devoted to promoting and protecting the rights of American Indians and Alaska Natives.

An American Indian culture, in which members of tribes or communities with very different traditions are identifying as a group by following certain practices associated with Indians, has been developing nationally (Brown, 1992)—for example, (1) males wearing long hair (long hair is a sign of a free man, not a slave); (2) the use of the sacred pipe (i.e., the pipestone pipe, sometimes referred to as the peace pipe); and (3) participation in sweat lodges, purification rituals, and the sacred sun dance for purification. Not every tribe practices these rituals, but they are becoming symbols of a growing movement reflecting American Indian pride. However, not all Indians view the Pan-Indian movement positively; some believe there is a strong possibility of misusing a tradition or diluting the meaning of a ritual. In *A Short History of Pan-Indianism,* Flattery (1997) provides a brief synopsis of the movement:

> Pan-Indianism involves the process of synthesizing the collective spiritual reality and traditional wisdom of more than one Native American Nation. [It] is a non-violent liberation philosophy with roots in Native American [philosophies]. The Pan-Indian movement serves to stabilize Indian youth . . . and to provide a way of practicing Native American spirituality [in order to] . . . stimulate the next generation to remain Indian . . . . ; [It] is open to all peoples.

Organizers of the Pan-Indian movement are devoted to helping educate and bring Native Americans back to their roots. Many younger people feel alienated when it comes to their native identity. Following is a quote from a Native American officer in a southern California police department who wishes to remain anonymous: "I know very little about my roots. My mother and grandmother were denied the opportunity to learn about their culture [forced assimilation], and nothing was passed on. I feel empty and have intense anger toward those who held the power to decide that certain traditions were not worth preserving. Forced denial of our ethnicity has resulted in extremely high alcohol and suicide rates as a collective response."

LANGUAGE AND COMMUNICATION

It is possible to make some generalizations about the way a group of people communicate, even when there is great diversity within the group. The following sections contain information about nonverbal and verbal aspects of communication as well as tips for law enforcement officers interacting with Native Americans. We describe patterns of communication and behavior as exhibited by some American Indians who are traditional in their outlook. However, no description of communication traits would ever apply to everyone within a group, especially a group that is so diverse.

Openness and Self-Disclosure

In early encounters, many Native Americans approach people and respond with caution. Too much openness is to be avoided, as is disclosing personal and family problems. This often means that the officer has to work harder at establishing rapport and gaining trust. In the American mainstream culture, appearing friendly and open is highly valued (especially in certain regions, such as on the West Coast and in the South). Because different modes of behavior are expected and accepted, the non-Indian may view the Indian as aloof and reserved. The Indian perception can be that the Euro-American person, because of excessive openness, is superficial and thus untrustworthy. Mainstream American culture encourages speaking out and open expression of opinions, while American Indian culture does not.

Silence and Interruptions

The ability to remain quiet, to be still, and to observe is highly valued in Native American culture; consequently, silence is truly a virtue. (In mainstream American culture, it is said that "silence is golden," but this is probably more of an expression of an ideal than a description of reality.) Indians are taught to study and assess situations and only act or participate when they are properly prepared. Indians tend not to act impulsively for fear of appearing foolish or bringing shame to themselves or to their family (Los Angeles Police Department Cross-Cultural Awareness tapes, 1992). When law enforcement officials contact Native Americans, they may mistake this reticence to talk as sullenness or lack of cooperation. The behavior must not be misinterpreted or taken personally. A cultural trait must be understood as just that (i.e., a behavior, action, or attitude that is not intended to be a personal insult). Officers must also consider that interrupting an Indian when he or she speaks is seen as very aggressive and should be avoided whenever possible.

Talking and Questions

Native Americans do not see talking just to fill the silence as important. The small talk observed in mainstream society (e.g., "Hi. How are you? How was your weekend?") is traditionally not required by Native Americans. Words are considered powerful and are therefore chosen carefully. This respect for speech may result in a situation in which Native Americans retreat and appear to be withdrawn if someone is dominating the conversation. When law enforcement officials question Native Americans who exhibit these tendencies (i.e., not being prone to talkativeness), they should not press aggressively for answers. (Aggressive behavior, both verbal and physical, is traditionally looked down on.) Questions should be open-ended, and officers should be willing to respect the silence and time it may take to find out the needed information.

Nonverbal Communication: Eye Contact and Touching

People often note that American Indians avoid making direct eye contact. Although this is true for some tribes, it is not true of all. To know whether this characteristic applies, officers can simply watch for this signal (i.e., avoidance of eye contact) and follow the lead of the citizen. In this section we explain the phenomenon of avoidance of eye contact from the perspective of groups that do adhere to this behavior. Some Indian tribes believe that looking directly into someone's eyes for a prolonged period is disrespectful (just as pointing at someone is considered impolite). The

Lakota tribe, for example, believes that direct eye contact is an affront or an invasion of privacy (Mehl, 1990). Navajo tribe members have a tendency to stare at each
other when they want to direct their anger at someone. An Indian who adheres to
the unspoken rules about eye contact may appear to be shifty and evasive. Officers
and other law enforcement officials must not automatically judge a person as guilty
or suspicious simply because that person is not maintaining direct eye contact. To
put a person at ease, officers can decrease eye contact if it appears to be inhibiting
the Native American citizen. Avoidance of eye contact with officers can also convey
the message that the officers are using an approach that is too forceful and demanding. Where such norms about eye contact avoidance apply, and if an officer
has to look at a person's eyes, it would help to warn the person (e.g., "I'm going to
have to check your eyes").

With regard to their sense of space, most Native Americans are not comfortable
being touched by strangers, whether a pat on the back or an arm around the shoul-
der. Officers should either avoid touching or limit contact to a brief handshake. (Married Native American couples do not tend to show affection in public.) Additionally,
people should avoid crowding or standing too close. Many Indian relations with
strangers are more formal than those of the mainstream culture; therefore, officers
might be viewed as overly aggressive if they do not maintain a proper distance.

Language

Some Native Americans speak one or more Indian languages. English, for many, is
a second language. Those who do not speak English well may be inhibited from
speaking for fear of "losing face" because of their lack of language ability. In addition, because of a tendency to speak quietly and nonforcefully, law enforcement
agents will need patience and extra time; interaction must not be rushed. Native
Americans who struggle in speaking English need to spend more time translating
from their own language to English when formulating a response (this is true of all
second-language speakers who are not yet fluent). As with all other languages, English words or concepts do not always translate exactly into the various Indian languages. Indian languages are rich and express concepts reflecting particular views
of the world. Officers must show the utmost respect when Native Americans speak
their own language, keeping in mind that Indians have a long history of forced assimilation into Anglo society (including, among other things, denial of the right to
speak their native languages).

Offensive Terms, Labels, and Stereotypes

In an interview, retired chief of police Jim Cox, a Comanche Indian, described situations in which insensitive police officers told Indian jokes or used derogatory terms
in his presence. He stated that he is proud of his heritage and is offended by commonly held stereotypes. Use of racial slurs (toward any group) is never acceptable in
crime fighting and peacekeeping, no matter how provoked an officer may be. Officers hearing disrespectful terms and stereotypes about Native Americans (and other
groups) should educate fellow officers as to the lack of professionalism and respect
for community diversity that such terms convey.

A number of words are offensive to Native Americans: *chief* (a leader who has reached this rank is highly honored), *squaw* (extremely offensive), *buck, redskin, Indian "brave,"* and *skins* (some young Indians may refer to themselves as "skins" but would be offended by others using the term). In addition, the use of Indian tribal names or references as mascots for sports teams has been highly objectionable.

Other terms used to refer to Native Americans are apple (a slightly dated term referring to a highly assimilated Indian: "red" on the outside and "white" on the inside) and "the people" (commonly used by some groups of Indians to refer to themselves). In some regions of the country, a reservation is called a "rez" by Indians; for example, in Oklahoma (where there is only one reservation), the term *reservation* is negative and the term *community* is used instead (Brown, 1992). It is also patronizing when non-Indians use certain kinship terms, such as "grandfather" when talking to an older man, even though other Indians may be using that term themselves.

Until recently, most public school children held the stereotypical picture of an Indian as a wild, savage, and primitive person. In textbooks and other history books recounting Native American history, Indians were said to "massacre" whites, whereas whites simply "fought" or "battled" the Indians (Harris and Moran, 1991). Other common stereotypes or stereotypical statements highly resented are as follows:

> "All Indians are drunks" (despite a large percentage of alcohol-related arrests, not all Indians have a problem with liquor). Furthermore, the argument has been put forth that whites introduced "fire water" (alcohol) to Indians as a means of weakening them.
>
> "You can't trust an Indian."
>
> "Those damn Indians" (as if they are simply a nuisance).
>
> "The only good Indian is a dead one" (a remark that can be traced back to a statement made by a U.S. general in 1869). (Harris and Moran, 1991).

Indians find it offensive when non-Indians make claims (which may or may not be true) about their Indian ancestry: "I'm part Indian. My great-grandfather was Cherokee [for example]." Although this may be an attempt to establish rapport, it rings of "Some of my best friends are Indians . . ." (i.e., trying to prove that one does not have any prejudice).

> [People] should not assume affinity [with American Indians] based on novels, movies, a vacation trip, or an interest in silver jewelry. These are among the most offensive, commonly made errors when non-Indians first encounter an American Indian person or family. Another is a confidential revelation that there is an Indian "Princess" in the family tree—tribe unknown, identity unclear, but a bit of glamour in the family myths. The intent may be to show positive bonding. . ., but to the Indian they reveal stereotypical thinking. (Attneave, 1982)

FAMILY-RELATED ISSUES

Respect for Elders

"Nothing will anger Indians more than seeing their grandmother or grandfather being spoken to belligerently or being ordered around with disrespect. [If that happens], that's a firecracker situation right there" (Rivera, 1992). Unlike mainstream Americans, Indians value aging because of the respect they have for wisdom and experience. People do not feel that they have to cover up signs of aging, because this phase of life is highly revered. The elders of a tribe or the older people in Native American communities must be shown the utmost respect by people in law enforcement. This includes acknowledging their presence in a home visit, even if they are not directly related in the police matter at hand. In some tribes (e.g., the Cherokee) the grandmother often has the most power in the household and is the primary decision maker. It is advisable for people in law enforcement to include the elders in discussions where they can give their advice or perspective on a situation. The elders are generally respected for their ability to enforce good behavior within the family and tribe.

It should also be noted, however, that because of assimilation or personal preference among some Native Americans, the elders in any given household may tend to avoid interfering with a married couple's problems. And although the elders are respected to a higher degree than in mainstream culture, they may withdraw in some situations where there is police contact, letting the younger family members deal with the problem. If in doubt, it is advisable to begin the contact more formally, deferring to the elders initially. Then officers can observe how the elders participate and if the younger family members include them.

Extended Family and Kinship Ties

In mainstream society, people usually think of and see themselves first as individuals and only after that may (or may not) identify with their families or various communities and groups with which they are affiliated. In traditional Native American culture, a person's primary identity is related to his or her family and tribe. Some law enforcement agents may be in positions to make referrals when there is a problem with an individual (e.g., an adolescent) in a family. A referral for counseling for that person only may be culturally alienating for two reasons: (1) Western counseling or therapy is a foreign way to treat problems and (2) the person is an integral part of a group in which strong bonds and interdependence are emphasized (Mehl, 1990).

Unfortunately, today, family and tribal cohesiveness has lessened because of forced assimilation, extreme levels of poverty, and lack of education and employment. However, many Native Americans still have large networks of relatives in close proximity with each other. It is not uncommon for children to be raised by someone other than their father or mother (e.g., grandmother, aunts). When law enforcement officials enter an Indian's home and, for example, ask to speak to the parents of a child, they may actually end up talking to someone who is not the biological mother or father. Officers must understand that in Native American culture various other relatives can function exactly as a mother or father would in the mainstream culture. This does not mean that Indian "natural" parents are necessarily being lazy about their child-rearing duties, even when the child is physically living with another relative (and may be raised by several relatives throughout childhood). The intensely close family and tribal bonds allow for this type of child raising. Officers must not assume that something is abnormal with this type of arrangement or that the parents are neglecting their children.

Interestingly, one Lakota Indian who became a psychiatrist found the traditional mainstream way of raising children odd. Referring to mothers in the 1950s, he said, "I could never understand how mothers could have their babies and then raise them alone and stay in boxes [i.e., their houses] all day!"

Children and Separation from Parents

It is crucial that police officers working with Native Americans understand the importance of not separating children from family members, if at all possible. Many families in urban areas and on reservations have memories of or have heard from elder family members stories involving the federal government's systematic removal of Indian children from their homes and placement in boarding schools often hundreds of miles away. This policy, which included education for the children that stripped them of their language and culture, was implemented in the late nineteenth century. According to Ogawa (1990), "Until 1974, the Bureau of Indian Affairs (BIA) was operating 75 boarding schools with more than 30,000 children enrolled."

Although for many families, the severe trauma of children being forcibly separated from parents took place years ago, the aftereffects still linger (Rivera, 1992). In the early twentieth century there was a famous case in which Hopi Indian fathers were sentenced to years in high-security prisons and were subject to the fullest persecution. Their crime was hiding their children from BIA officials because they did not want the children to be taken by the BIA boarding schools. By hiding the children, the Hopi fathers violated federal law. This case is still talked about today (Rivera, 1992). The memory of a "uniform coming to take away a child" is an image some Indians can conjure up easily and one that greatly affects interactions with law enforcement officers.

Since Native American parents can be very protective of their children, officers would be well advised to let parents know about any action that needs to be taken with their children. Law enforcement officials can establish good rapport with Indian families if they treat the children well.

KEY ISSUES IN LAW ENFORCEMENT

Perception of Police

The general distrust of police by Native Americans stems from a history of bad relations with "the system" (federal, state, and local governments). In their view, officers represent a system that has not supported Indian rights and their tribes or communities. Most Native American contact with the police is negative. Thus many Native Americans (like other groups) have not had a chance to build a relationship of trust and cooperation with people in law enforcement.

Jurisdiction

Jurisdiction on tribal lands can cause a great deal of friction between tribal and civilian law enforcement, particularly on reservations where the lines of jurisdiction are not clear. Jurisdiction of the tribal police may be limited, but the non-Indian is not always subject to Indian tribal law. Some tribes have decriminalized their codes and taken on civil codes of law (e.g., for basic misdemeanors, civil fines may go to the tribal court), yet still conduct a trial (of the non-Indian) in a tribal court. Who has authority and who has responsibility can be an ambiguous area in tribal and civilian law enforcement (Setter, 2000). Police officers are put into an unusual situation when it comes to enforcing the law among Indians. They may make an arrest on area that is considered to be Indian land (on which tribal police have jurisdiction). The land may be adjacent to non-Indian land, sometimes forming checkerboard patterns of jurisdiction. In the case of an Indian reservation (on which tribal police may have authority), civil law enforcement agencies sometimes have difficulty knowing where their jurisdiction begins and ends. With the multijurisdictional agreements that many tribes have signed with local and state officials, civil police officers may have the right to enter reservations to continue business. For example, a criminal can be apprehended by a civil police officer on a reservation (Brown, 1992b).

It is expected and desired (because it does not always happen) that civil law enforcement agents inform tribal police or tribal authorities when entering a reservation. Going onto reservation land without prior notice and contacting a suspect or witness directly is an insult to the authority of the tribal police (Willie, 1992). In other words, civil police should see themselves as partners with tribal police. Obviously, in dangerous or emergency situations, expediency may prevent civil authorities from conferring with the tribal police. Where possible, it is essential that the authority of the reservation be respected. As we mentioned, on some reservations, it may not be clear who has jurisdiction and it becomes all the more necessary to establish trusting relations. On reservations, as elsewhere, police officers must refrain from using abusive language or mannerisms.

Levels of cooperation and attitudes toward civil and tribal law enforcement partnerships differ from area to area. The Sac and Fox nation (originally from the Midwest) is an example of a tribe that initiated a relationship with civil law enforcement that resulted in a cooperative approach to law enforcement. The cross deputization that resulted from the Sac and Fox nation's efforts enables both sets of officers (from the tribal and civil police) to make arrests in each other's jurisdiction without being sued. Similarly, certain police departments, including Albuquerque, New Mexico, have gone out of their way to work out relationships with local Indian tribes. If there is a will to work cooperatively, police departments and Indian tribal departments can be of tremendous benefit to each other. Initiating this type of effort means, for both Indians and non-Indians, putting aside history and transcending stereotypes.

Furthermore, individual officers should be sensitive to their own potentially condescending attitudes toward tribal police and tribal law.

> American Indians have struggled to retain as much of their own culture and tradition within tribal police operations as possible. Within the very limited jurisdiction in which tribal police have been allowed to exercise their tribal police powers, American Indians have struggled to incorporate tribal laws and procedures. Dominant white authorities are reluctant to allow Indian police agencies to have power over their own when whites do not control the law and procedures of that agency. (Barlow, 2000)

According to Deloria and Lytle, in *American Indians, American Justice* (quoted in Barlow, 2000),

> The tribal police continue to play an important role in resolving criminal cases on reservations. They are usually the ones who discover the crime, conduct initial interviews, know the personalities and circumstances involved, and provide continued assistance throughout the case. Their recommendations are well respected by the federal government.

Police Stops

When Indians drive large, poorly maintained cars (and especially when there are several Indians in a car together), they will be stopped simply because they are perceived as suspicious and because negative stereotypes are operating. We know that the phenomenon of profiling exists with other racial and ethnic groups (see Chapters 1 and 7 for an extensive discussion of this issue). Similarly, negative biases against Indians are strong and have persisted for generations. A group of Indians in an old, run-down car should not signal anything but a group of friends driving around together. When there is not a legitimate reason to stop a car, the next step is for officers to check their stereotypes of who they think a criminal is. Like members of other groups, Indians have repeatedly reported being stopped for no reason; this racial profiling obviously adds to their distrust of police.

Peyote

Many states in the United States have specific laws exempting the traditional, religious use of peyote by American Indians from those states' drug enforcement laws. Following is a definition of peyote:

> Peyote is a small turnip-shaped, spineless cactus [containing] nine alkaloid substances, part of which, mainly mescaline, are hallucinogenic in nature; that is, they induce dreams or visions. Reactions to peyote seem to vary with the social situation in which it is used. In some it may merely cause nausea; believers may experience optic, olfactory and auditory sensations. Under ideal conditions color visions may be experienced and peyote may be "heard" singing or speaking. The effects wear off within twenty-four hours and leave no ill aftereffects. Peyote is non-habit forming. (Bahti, 1982)

Various uses have been associated with peyote: (1) a charm for hunting, (2) medicine, (3) an aid to predict weather, (4) an object to help find things that are lost (the belief being that peyote can reveal the location of the lost object through peyote-induced visions; peyote was even used to help locate the enemy in warfare), and (5) an object to be carried for protection. People have faith in peyote as a powerful symbol and revere its presence.

Peyote is carried in small bags or pouches, and these can be "ruined" if touched.* Police officers may need to confiscate peyote, but they can do it in a way

---

*Native Americans from many tribes across the country wear small bags referred to as medicine bags that are considered extremely sacred. The medicine bags do not carry drugs or peyote but hold symbols from nature (e.g., corn pollen, cedar, sage, bark of a tree) that are believed to have certain powers. Law enforcement officers should handle these (if it becomes necessary) as they would handle any sacred symbol from their own religion. Ripping into the bags would be an act of desecration. The powerful medicine contained in the bags is often blessed and therefore must be treated in a respectful manner.

that will cause the least amount of upset. It is far better to ask the Native American politely to remove the bag in which the peyote is contained rather than forcing it away from him or her.

In a 1990 freedom of religion case, the Supreme Court dealt a severe blow to traditional American Indians when it ruled that state governments could have greater leeway in outlawing certain religious practices. The ruling involved ritual use of peyote by some American Indians who follow the practices of the Native American Church (NAC). Until that time, the U.S. government allowed for the religious use of peyote among Native Americans based on the Bill of Right's free exercise of religion guarantee; in other words, peyote use was generally illegal, except in connection with bona fide American Indian religious rituals.

From a law enforcement perspective, if drugs are illegal, no group should be exempt, and indeed, officers have to uphold the law. From a civil rights perspective, religious freedom applies to all groups and no group should be singled out for disproportionately burdensome treatment. The historical legal and illegal status of peyote is complex. There have been many attempts to prohibit the use of peyote on the federal level, and many states passed laws outlawing its use. However, several states modified such prohibitions to allow traditional American Indians to continue using peyote as a sacrament. Moreover, in some states, such as Arizona, antipeyote laws have been declared unconstitutional by state courts insofar as they burden the religious practice of American Indians. Following is an example of how one state, Arizona, revised its original statutes (see A) with respect to the use of peyote (see B for the revision):

Arizona Revised Statutes State Law 13-3402(**B**). Possession and sale of peyote; classification

A. A person who knowingly possesses, sells, transfers or offers to sell or transfer peyote is guilty of a class 6 felony.

B. In a prosecution for violation of this section, it is a defense that the peyote is being used or is intended for use: 1. In connection with the bona fide practice of a religious belief, and 2. As an integral part of a religious exercise, and 3. In a manner not dangerous to public health, safety or morals.

This historic ambiguity on the state level, together with the 1990 ruling on the federal level, causes confusion and resentment on the part of many Native Americans. In 1993 Congress passed legislation preempting state law that would protect numerous Indian ceremonies and ritual practices, including the traditional use of peyote by American Indians in bona fide religious ceremonies (Native American Free Exercise of Religion Act, 1993). (Officers are advised to become familiar with the Native American Free Exercise of Religion Act of 1993, including its 1994 amendments.) The act was passed based on the following findings (partial listing):

Some Indian people have used the peyote cactus in religious ceremonies for sacramental and healing purposes for many generations, and such uses have been significant in perpetuating Indian tribes and culture by promoting and strengthening the unique cultural cohesiveness of Indian tribes;

While numerous states have enacted a variety of laws which protect the ceremonial use of peyote by Indians, many others have not, and this lack of uniformity has created hardships for Indian people who participate in such ceremonies;

The traditional ceremonial use by Indians of the peyote cactus is integral to a way of life that plays a significant role in combating the scourge of alcohol and drug abuse among some Indian people;

The United States has a unique and special historic trust responsibility for the protection and preservation of Indian tribes and cultures, and the duty to protect the continuing cultural cohesiveness and integrity of Indian tribes and cultures;

Existing Federal and State laws, regulations and judicial decisions are inadequate to fully protect the ongoing traditional uses of the peyote cactus in Indian ceremonies. [*Note:* "Existing" refers to laws (and so forth) prior to the passing of this act.] (Title II— Traditional Use of Peyote; Sec. 201 Findings) www.Council fire.com.referral 12.20.00

The use of peyote outside the Native American Church (established in 1918) is forbidden and regarded by church members as sacrilegious. If individuals are using peyote under the guise of religion, however, they are breaking the law. Within the NAC, there are very specific rules and rituals pertaining to its sacramental use. Establishing respectful communication with the leaders of the NAC would assist officers in determining whether peyote was being abused in certain circumstances.

This revised statute was referenced in the highly publicized case of the removal and confiscation of 11,323 plants from the home of Leonard Mercado in Pinal County, Arizona, an active member of the Native American Church. For bona fide members of the Native American Church, this type of act (which had happened earlier in 1995 with the removal of 700 plants) is essentially religious desecration.

Law enforcement officials should understand the importance and place of peyote in the culture from a Native American point of view. It is not our intent to recommend a particular course of action with regard to enforcement or lack thereof. If they understand the use of peyote from an Indian perspective, officers will communicate an attitude that shows respect for an ancient ritual that some researchers say dates back 10,000 years. Police officers who burst into a meeting or ceremony where peyote is being used (often along with prayers and drumming) and aggressively make arrests will find it very difficult to establish trust and rapport with the community. When peyote is an issue, officers must recognize their own ethnocentrism (i.e., unconsciously viewing other cultures or cultural practices as primitive, abnormal, or inferior). Appreciating the fact that cultures are acquired (i.e., they are not passed on through the genes) includes the realization that "If I had been born in another culture, I might be doing things similar to those being done by the majority of other people in the culture." With this attitude in mind, it is easier to remain respectful of differences. Law enforcement personnel working in communities where peyote use is an issue should anticipate the problems that will occur and should discuss the issue with members of the Indian community. Officers must also understand the law and their agency policies on enforcement.

Historically, the federal government actively tried to suppress and change Native American cultures, from condemning traditional marriage practices as being "loose and barbaric" to condemning Indians' "long-time tendency . . . to give too much time to dances, powwows, celebrations, and general festive occasions" (1992 Report of the Commissioner of Indian Affairs). The commissioner wrote in 1923: "To correct this practice a letter was widely circulated among the Indians. . . that they shorten somewhat the length of these gatherings and omit from them use of harmful drugs [peyote], intoxicants, gambling and degrading ceremonials." This explanation is given to illustrate to people in law enforcement that their peyote arrests symbolize official acts of condemning cultural practices. The banning of peyote was and has been viewed by Native American groups as a failure of the Bill of Rights to truly guarantee the freedom to practice one's religion.

Trespassing and Sacred Lands

In a number of states, traditional Indian harvest areas or sacred burial and religious sites are now on federal, state, and especially private lands. Indians continue to go to these areas just as their ancestors did to collect resources or to pray. The point of concern for law enforcement involves conflicts occurring between the ranchers, farmers, and homeowners on what Indians consider their holy ground. How officers react to allegations of Indians' trespassing determines whether there will be an escalated confrontation (Rivera, 1992). When there is a dispute, officers will alienate Indians by choosing an authoritarian and aggressive method of handling the problem (e.g., "You're going to get off this land right now"). Alternatively, they could show some empathy, and the Native American may very well be more supportive of the officers' efforts to resolve the immediate conflict. If there is no immediate resolution, officers can, at a minimum, prevent an escalation of hostilities.

Since police officers cannot solve this complex and very old problem, the only tool available is the ability to communicate sensitively and listen well. "The officer is put between a rock and a hard place. If the officer is sensitive, he could try to speak to the landowner and describe the situation, although often the landowners don't care about the history (claiming, 'It's my land now'). However, there have been some people who have been sensitive to the needs of the Native Americans and who have worked out agreements" (Rivera, 1992).

In California, Native Americans have initiated their own Indian Gathering Policy Act. When this problem arises in other jurisdictions (i.e., in other states), people might consider contacting the state of California (Assistant Director of Advisory Councils and Concessions, Office of the Director, California State Parks, Sacramento, California) and use its model as a point of negotiation for trying to resolve the conflict.

Native American Sites: Use Desecration, and Looting

The Native American Free Exercise of Religion Act of 1993 (Senate Bill 1021, introduced to the 103rd Congress), Title I, Protection of Sacred Sites, gives tribal authority over Native American religious sites on Indian lands:

> (a) **Right of Tribe—** All Federal or federally assisted undertakings on Indian lands which may result in changes in the character or use of a Native American religious site or which may have an impact on access to a Native American religious site shall, unless requested otherwise by the Indian tribe on whose lands the undertakings will take place, be conducted in conformance with the laws or customs of the tribe.
>
> (b)...

(c) **Protection by Tribes**— Indian tribes may regulate and protect Native American religious sites located on Indian lands.

Beyond use or undertaking of religious sites by the federal government or any governmental agency is the history of desecration and looting of sacred sites and objects. Most often, the looting has been done to make a profit on Native American articles and artifacts. Native Americans witness vandalism on their archeological sites, but often without any criminal prosecution.

Even more degrading to Native Americans is the taking of human remains (skulls and bones) from Indian reservations and public lands. Officers in certain parts of the country may enter non-Indian homes and see such remains "displayed" as souvenirs of a trip into Indian country. The Native American Grave Protection and Repatriation Act (NAGPRA) passed by Congress and signed by President George Bush Sr. resulted as a response to such criminal acts. If officers see any human remains, they must investigate whether foul play might have been involved. Officers should contact state agencies established to enforce laws that protect Indian relics (e.g., in California, the Native American Heritage Commissions) to determine how to proceed in such situations.

Fishing

"If you ever want to get into a fight, go into a local bar [e.g., in parts of Washington State] and start talking about fishing rights. The fishing issue is a totally hot issue" (Rivera, 1992).

> The wording of the treaties [i.e., with regard to the fishing rights of Native Americans] is clear and unequivocal in English as well as in the language of the specific tribes concerned. For example, the treaty with Indians of the Northwest regarding fishing rights on the rivers gives these rights to the Indians "for as long as the rivers shall flow." The rivers in the Northwest are still flowing, and the Indians are still struggling with the state of Washington about the state's violations of the treaty's terms, even on Indian property. (Social Work: Association of Social Workers, 1972, p. 76.)

Indians in 2000 continue to say, "We have treaties with the government allowing us to fish here." Commercial and sports fishermen, on the forefront of trying to prevent Native Americans from exercising their treaty rights, claim that Indians are destroying the industry. For the Indians, this is one way they can provide sustenance to their families and earn extra money for themselves or their tribes to make it through the year. (For 150 years, there has been no industry on many, if not most, of the reservations.) Once again, officers on the front line will be unable to solve a problem that has been raging for generations. Officers' actions, in part, depend on the sensitivity of their departments' chief executives. Admittedly, commanders are in a difficult position. They are caught between the state fish and game industry and the people trying to enforce federal treaties. Nevertheless, they can communicate to officers the need for cultural sensitivity in their way of approaching and communicating with Native Americans. The alternative could be deadly, as at least one situation illustrated when, in northern California, peace officers with flack jackets and automatic weapons resorted to pursuing Native Americans with shotguns up and down the river (Rivera, 1992).

There are many complex dimensions to cases involving Native Americans "breaking the law" when, at the same time, the federal government is not honoring its treaties with them. Native Americans are frustrated by what they see as blatant violations of their rights. The history of the government's lack of loyalty to its American Indian citizens has caused great pain for this cultural group. Clearly, sensitivity and understanding on the part of officers are required. Officers need patience and tact, remembering that history has defined many aspects of the current relationships between law enforcement and American Indians. Being forceful and displaying anger will alienate Native Americans and will not result in the cooperation needed to solve issues that arise.

SUMMARY OF RECOMMENDATIONS FOR LAW ENFORCEMENT

Those who are entrusted with keeping the peace in rural areas, in cities, or on Indian reservations should exhibit respect and professionalism when interacting with Native American peoples, who have traditionally been disrespected by governmental authority. It is important to remember that the U.S. government has violated many treaties with American Indians and that their basic rights as Americans have repeatedly been denied. Officers should understand the initial resistance to their efforts to establish rapport and goodwill and not take it personally. They can make an effort to get to know the community in their particular area and make positive contact with American Indian organizations and individuals. This behavior will be unexpected and will result in more cooperation.

The younger, more environmentally conscious generations of Americans have adopted much valuable ideology from the culture of America's original peoples. Officers should convey a respect for Native American values. They are not alienating or "un-American," and many believe that those very values of preservation are necessary for our environmental survival.

Indians have been victims of forced assimilation whereby their languages, religions, and cultures have been suppressed. The negative effects have stayed with generations of Indians. The point of contact between a law enforcement professional and an American Indian can often involve issues related to poor adjustment to urban life. While the law must be upheld, officers must consider the conditions that led some Native Americans toward, for example, alcoholism and unemployment. Having empathy for the conditions that led to a person's current circumstances need not make someone any less effective in his or her line of duty.

Preferred mainstream American ways of communication often run counter to American Indian styles of communication. When trying to build rapport with citizens who are Indians, officers should not take advantage of the American Indian just because he or she may be silent, appear passive, or not be fluent in English. Officers should also avoid interrupting Indian people when they are speaking; it is seen as aggressive and rude.

Many American Indians who favor traditional styles of communication will tend toward closed behavior and slow rapport building with strangers (this is a cultural trait for some and does not mean the person is aloof or hostile), silent and highly observant behavior (which does not imply a lack of cooperation), withdrawal if the method of questioning is too aggressive (time, patience, and silence will assist officers in getting the responses they need), and indirect eye contact for members of some but not all tribes (officers' penetrating or intense eye contact may result in intimidating the person and, consequently, in his or her withdrawal).

The terms *chief, redskin, buck, squaw, braves,* and *skins* are offensive when used by a non-Indian. (Sometimes younger Indians may use some of the terms themselves [e.g., "skins"], but this does not make it acceptable for others to use the terms.) If officers need to refer to the cultural group, they can ask those with whom they are in contact whether they prefer the term *Indian, Native American,* or another tribal name. Officers' sensitivity to these labels can contribute to establishing a good rapport. If asking seems inappropriate, officers can listen carefully to how the individuals refer to each other.

The extended family is close knit and interdependent among Native American peoples. Officers should keep in mind the following:

- Be respectful and deferential to elders.
- The elders should be asked for their opinion or even advice, where applicable, because they are often major decision makers in the family.
- If there are problems with a child, consider other adults, besides the mother and father, who may also be responsible for child raising.
- Whenever possible, do not separate children from parents. This can bring back memories of times when children were forcibly taken from their parents and sent to Christian mission schools or government boarding schools far from their homes.

With regard to key issues of law enforcement and contact with American Indians, particularly sensitive areas include use of peyote, allegations of trespassing, violations of sacred sites, fishing, and jurisdiction. All these areas involve matters in which Indians feel they have been deprived of their rights: in the case of peyote, the right to religious expression; in the case of trespassing, the right to honor their ancestors (e.g., when visiting burial grounds); and in the case of fishing, the ability to exercise their rights as guaranteed by treaties made with the U.S. government.

Many American Indians feel that they are abused by a system of government that is neither honest nor respectful of their culture. Many believe the government degrades the land on which all people depend. To a large extent, Indian rights are still ignored because members of the dominant society do not always uphold the laws made to protect Indians. This background makes relationships and interactions between law enforcement officials and Indians especially difficult. For this reason, law enforcement officials need to go out of their way to demonstrate that they are fair, given the complexities of history and current law. In addition, chief executives and command staff of police departments have a special responsibility to provide an accurate education to officers on American Indian cultural groups (with an emphasis on government–tribal relations) and to address the special needs and concerns of American Indian peoples.

DISCUSSION QUESTIONS AND ISSUES*

1. *Popular Stereotypes.* What are some commonly held stereotypes of Native Americans? What is your personal experience with Native Americans that might counter these stereotypes? How have people in law enforcement been influenced by popular stereotypes of Native Americans?

2. *Recommendations for Effective Contact.* If you have had contact with Native Americans, what recommendations would you give others regarding effective communication, rapport building, and cultural knowledge that would be beneficial for officers?

3. *The Government's Broken Promises to American Indians.* The famous Lakota chief Sitting Bull spoke on behalf of many Indians when he said of white Americans: "They made us many promises . . . but they never kept but one: They promised to take our land, and they took it." There was a time when many acres of land in what we now call the United States were sacred to Native American tribes. Therefore, today many of us are living on, building on, and, in some cases, destroying the remains of Indian lands where people's roots run deep. Given this situation, how would you deal with the problem of an Indian "trespassing" on someone's land when he or she claims to be visiting an ancestral burial ground, for example? What could you say or do so as not to totally alienate the Native American and thereby risk losing trust and cooperation?

4. *Jurisdiction.* What are law enforcement agents supposed to do in situations in which the state law is in conflict with a federal law that has been based on treaties with Native Americans signed by the federal government? How can officers who are on the front lines win the respect and cooperation of Native Americans when they are asked to enforce something that goes against the treaty rights of the Indians? A special unit was established by the San Diego Sheriff's Department to patrol Native American reservations, which were (in 1991) overrun from the outside by drugs and violence. Federal Public Law 280 transferred criminal jurisdiction and enforcement on reservations to some states. Research law enforcement jurisdiction issues and tribal lands in your region or state (if applicable); note where there are still unresolved areas or areas of dispute.

REFERENCES

Social Work: Association of Social Workers. (1972). *Ethnicity and Social Work, 17* (3).

ATTNEAVE, CAROLYN. (1982). "American Indians and Alaska Native Families: Emigrants in Their Own Homeland." In M. McGoldrick et al. (eds.), *Ethnicity and Family Therapy.* New York: Guilford Press. pp. 55-83

BAHTI, TOM. (1982). *Southwestern Indian Ceremonials.* Las Vegas, Nev.: KC Publications.

BARLOW, DAVID. (2000). *Criminal Justice in America.* Upper Saddle River, N.J.: Prentice-Hall.

BROWN, DONALD. (Ed.). (1992a). *Crossroads Oklahoma: The Ethnic Experience in Oklahoma.* Stillwater, Okla.: Crossroads Oklahoma Project.

BROWN, DONALD (1992b, August 13). Professor of sociology and specialist in Native American communities, Oklahoma State University, personal communication.

Bureau of Indian Affairs (2000). Answers to Frequently Asked Questions, Section AI-3 [www.doi.gov/bia/aitoday/q_and_a.html]. 12/19/00.

Committee on Cultural Psychiatry, Group for the Advancement of Psychiatry. (1989). *Suicide and Ethnicity in the United States.* New York: Brunner/Mazel.

COX, JIM. (1992, December 18). Former chief of police, Midwest City, Okla., personal communication.

Demographics and Health Risk Indicator. (2000) Pan American Health Organization.

*See Instructor's Manual that accompanies this text for additional activities, role-play activities, questionnaires, and projects related to the content of this chapter.

FLATTERY, ELAINE. (1997). *A Short History of Pan-Indianism.* Available at: nativenet.uthsca.edu

FORBES, JACK. (1982). *Native Americans of California and Nevada.* Happy Camp, Calif.: Naturegraph Publishers.

HARRIS, PHILIP R., AND ROBERT T. MORAN. (1991). *Managing Cultural Differences: High Performance Strategies for a New World of Business.* Houston, Texas: Gulf Publishing Company.

LAVELLE, JOHN. (1993, September 24). Executive director and cofounder of the former Center for the Spirit, San Francisco, Calif., personal communication.

Legix. (2000). Native American lobbying firm specializing in issues involving housing, tribal justice, sovereignty, education, economic development, and gaming. Legix Social and General Update, Nov. 9, 2000 (www.legix.com).

LOCKLEAR, HERBERT H. (1972). "American Indian Myths." *Journal of the National Association of Social Workers, 17* (3), pp. 72–80.

MATTHIESSEN, PETER. (1992). *The Spirit of Crazy Horse.* New York: Penguin Books.

MEHL, LEWIS. (1990). *Creativity and Madness.* Paper presented at a meeting sponsored by the American Institute of Medical Education, Santa Fe, N.M.

Native American Free Exercise of Religion Act of 1993, Senate Bill 1021 Introduced to 103rd Congress, May 25, 1993, by Mr. Inouye (D, HI); eventually passed as the American Indian Religious Freedom Act Amendments of 1994.

OGAWA, BRIAN. (1990). *Color of Justice: Culturally Sensitive Treatment of Minority Crime Victims.* Sacramento, Calif.: Office of the Governor, State of California, Office of Criminal Justice Planning.

REDHORSE, J., A. SHATTUCK, AND F. HOFFMAN. (Eds.). (1981). *The American Indian Family: Strengths and Stresses.* Isleta, N. M. American Indian Research and Development and Associates.

Report of the Commissioner of Indian Affairs. (1992) Bureau of Indian Affairs, Washington, D.C.

RIVERA, JOSE. (1992, September 11). California State peace officer, personal communication.

SETTER, DREW. (2000, December). Lobbyist, Legix Company, personal communication.

U.S. Bureau of the Census, Population Trends by race and Hispanic Origin (2000). Washington, D.C. October, 2000.

WILLIE, ANDREW. (1992, August 11). Bureau of Indian Affairs law enforcement, Ponga City, Okla., personal communication.

PART FOUR

Response Strategies for Crimes Motivated by Hate/Bias

11 HATE/BIAS CRIMES: INSIGHTS AND RESPONSE STRATEGIES
12 HATE/BIAS CRIMES: REPORTING AND TRACKING
13 HATE/BIAS CRIMES: INVESTIGATIONS, CONTROL, AND VICTIMOLOGY

Part Four provides a detailed explanation of strategies for preventing, controlling, reporting, tracking, and investigating crimes that are based on hate or bias because of the victim's race, ethnicity, religion, or sexual orientation. Criminal cases of these types have come to be known as bias crimes, or hate crimes; noncriminal cases are referred to as incidents. Some agencies refer to these acts as civil rights violations. The chapters that follow contain policies, practices, and procedures for responding to these types of crimes or incidents. We recognize that others, such as women, the elderly, and the disabled, are sometimes victimized. However, in this book we focus only on hate crimes and incidents wherein the motivation was related to the victim's race, ethnicity, religion, or sexual orientation. The recommended policies, training, practices, and procedures outlined are currently in operation, and many law enforcement agencies across the nation are in the process of adopting them. Many of the policies and procedures are based on studies and recommendations by the U.S. Department of Justice, Community Relations Service. The Commission on Peace Officer Standards and Training, found in all states of the nation, has been another major source of materials.

Unfortunately, statistical data useful in analyzing trends of hate violence have been lacking except in a very few states and in some progressive departments. Part Four outlines methods used to collect data on such crimes and/or incidents. The following three chapters provide a framework for peace officers, students, and law enforcement agencies interested in developing sensitive and workable programs for handling these crimes and incidents in the community and in the law enforcement workplace. The type of policing and peace-keeping reviewed in this unit is a civilizing process that will contribute to multicultural coexistence and cooperation. All law enforcement professionals must have a good working knowledge of all the guidelines that follow.

11

HATE/BIAS CRIMES:

Insights and Response Strategies

OVERVIEW

This chapter focuses on the hate/bias crime problem. First we discuss the scope of the problem, including historical perspectives and examples. We stress that the law enforcement professional must be aware of discrimination and hate crimes toward immigrants and people from different ethnic, racial, lifestyle, and religious backgrounds. We present some aspects of urban dynamics as they relate to the economy, hate violence, and move-in violence. The focus of hate crimes in this chapter is on Jews, gays, and lesbians.* The chapter highlights the need for law enforcement officials to treat hate violence with the same concern as heinous crimes such as rape and sexual assault. It presents information on special statutes that provide for increased penalties for the perpetrator and specific response strategies within the criminal justice system. We also include model response and management strategies and policies to be used when hate/bias crimes occur. We present future trends that provide the law enforcement practitioner with potential consequences if society does not establish control of this insidious problem. The chapter considers the need for the community (religious institutions, schools, public agencies, private organizations, and neighborhood residents) to deal with the problem cooperatively because the challenge of hate crimes is not solely a law enforcement issue.

---

*Information about hate crimes toward other groups can be found in the culture-specific chapters (Chapters 6–10).

COMMENTARY

Violence motivated by racial, religious, ethnic, or sexual orientation hatred has existed for generations in the United States and all over the world, and it seems to be on the rise. Law enforcement must address this problem.

> The institute estimates that a full 10 percent of the U.S. population is annually victimized by some form of ethnoviolence. That translates to more than 25 million victims this year [1991]! (National Institute against Prejudice Violence, 1992, p. 2)

> But what happens when people of different origins, speaking different languages and professing different religions, inhabit the same locality and live under the same political sovereignty? Ethnic and racial conflict—far more than ideological conflict—is the explosive problem of our times. (Schlesinger, 1991, p. 27)

> Law enforcement officials, police officers, and prosecutors are essential in efforts to respond to and prevent hate violence, but often they are not trained to handle situations involving violence motivated by bigotry. Lack of training produces inadequate and inappropriate responses that exacerbate community tensions. Law enforcement basic academies, field training programs, and advanced officer and management courses should include training on cultural differences and hate crimes. (California Attorney General's Commission on Racial, Ethnic, Religious, and Minority Violence, 1986, p. 51) We can conclude that our environment contributes to our behavior. No social scientist would disagree. The issue becomes determining what social conditions contribute most to our behavior and to what degree "they" are responsible. Numerous studies show that the reduced space and increased stress of urban life give rise to increased incidence of violence. Economic levels have also been shown as paralleling the incidence of violence. (Fritsche, 1992, p. 13)

HISTORICAL PERSPECTIVES

Although civilization and technology have progressed, it does not appear that human behavior has evolved. Since the beginning of time people have gathered into tribes or groups with those of similar color, speech, and background for reasons of safety and commonality. Since that beginning, groups of people have been suspicious of others who are different from them. From such suspicions and discomfort about the new neighbor came conflict, crimes, and even killings between the existing majority and the new minority interlopers; the territorial imperative to protect oneself from the "alien" became entrenched.

However, as civilization continued to progress, intermingling resulted in diverse mixtures of people in many countries. In the past half-century, with advances in communications and transportation, cross-border migration of ideas, travelers, and even settlements increased. Locals became less ethnocentric and less afraid of new arrivals and thought more in terms of the human family. But suddenly in the process of creating a world culture and a "global village" mind-set, the world witnessed the breakup of superpowers and nation-states. The movement was then toward more local autonomy and separatism, often along the lines of ethnicity and religious fundamentalism: Canada split into conflict between its Anglo and French citizens, the Soviet Union crumbled and broke into separate republics, former central European satellite countries squabbled over borders and ancient rivalries flared, and Germany broke down the Berlin Wall in 1989 (but experienced violence between neo-Nazis and those against their racist politics and actions). In Yugoslavia, ethnocentricism and the reversion to tribalism ended in civil wars among the former states, with Serbs, Croats, and Bosnians and Christians and Muslims engaged in wholesale slaughter of one another. By the end of 1992, 14,000 people had died in the former Yugoslavia, where so-called ethnic cleansing took place to oust members of other ethnic groups from targeted areas. Street violence erupted in London in 1993 as riot police fought to keep more than 15,000 antiracism marchers away from an office of a racist political party that advocates expelling immigrants and Jews from England.

In 1994 the International Red Cross estimated that tens of thousands of Tutsis of Rwanda were murdered in what many referred to as mass genocide carried out by Hutu extremists. They used state resources and authority to incite–or force–tens of thousands of Rwandans to slaughter more than half a million people, three quarters of the Tutsi of Rwanda. (PBS Online, 1999).

In Kosovo, a southern province of the Federal Republic of Yugoslavia, issues at the center of fighting went back nearly two decades and there were years of reported atrocities between Serbs and ethnic Albanians. The Serbs were against the Albanians, who made up 90 percent of Kosovo's population. The ethnic Albanians of Kosovo share the ethnic background of the people of neighboring Albania and speak the Albanian language. They are largely Muslim, while Serbs are generally Eastern Orthodox Christians. The Serbs were struggling to maintain control over Kosovo for cultural reasons since the territory has a significant role in Serbian history. Tensions built up between 1996 and 1998 until government-sponsored violence against Albanian civilians escalated. Reports of mass murders of Albanians under the government leadership of Slobodan Milosevic shocked the world. The North Atlantic Treaty Organization (NATO), led by the United States, stepped in and, after months of unsuccessful attempts to restore peace, in March, 1999, launched an air campaign that lasted 78 days. Serbia finally agreed to sign a UN-approved peace agreement with NATO on June 9 and the area was divided up under the supervision of peacekeepers.

Other conflicts occurred in the late 1990s and continued into the twenty-first century, such as the tragic events that took place in East Timor, a tiny half island occupied by Indonesia. In addition to the fatalities, tens of thousands of people fled from their homes to refugee camps controlled by the military. Even UN peacekeepers were victims of the violence.

Ancient animosities peoples have toward each other in Asia, Latin America, and Europe may be brought with them as they relocate in North America. For example, Armenians, Turks, and Greeks in the United States keep alive ancient dislikes and distrusts; in 2000 anti-Semitic incidents in America took place, reflecting the turmoil in the Middle East between Israel and the Palestinians; and Serbs and ethnic Albanians living in the United States maintain their hatred due to events in Kosovo. Following the conflict in Bosnia between Serbs and Croatians, the Saint Sava

Serbian Church in Phoenix, Arizona, in 1996 was vandalized with extensive graffiti espousing hate for the Serbs. The offenders were never brought to justice, but the evidence pointed to Croatian men carrying into the present hatred from historical events in Europe during World War II. Instead of newcomers adapting to their new opportunities and moving beyond past cultural biases and old country hatreds, the hatreds and sometimes criminal acts simply get transplanted.

Thus, in the United States, the so-called melting-pot society struggles not only with inhumanity toward new immigrants but also with the imported hatreds and racism of those new immigrants. Elie Wiesel, Nobel Peace Prize winner, in a February 1992 interview at a Peace Prize Forum, said racism, fanaticism, and anti-Semitism are on the rise in many nations, including the United States.

Practitioners in law enforcement must have some perspective on both the global and local situation when it comes to hatred and bias within the population they serve. Peacekeepers must be trained to counteract hate crimes and violence, as well as to learn to cope with their inhumane impact. The importance of local law enforcement officials' monitoring of such world events is discussed in Chapter 12. This is a major undertaking as we begin the twenty-first century because the United Nations is currently involved actively in peacekeeping efforts in 15 different countries.

THE HATE/BIAS CRIME PROBLEM

Introduction

Crimes motivated by hate in the United States have occurred for generations. Most of the immigrant groups that have come to America, including the Irish, Italian, Chinese, Polish, and Arabic, to name a few, have been victimized. Although they are indigenous peoples, Native Americans have not been immune to hate crimes. Racists targeted as victims African slaves, who were brought to the United States between 1619 and 1850. The descendents of slaves continue to be victims of bias, discrimination, and crimes motivated by hate. This segment of the chapter addresses only crimes motivated by hate wherein the victims are Jewish or homosexuals. Issues related to racial and ethnic groups are discussed in the culture-specific chapters (Chapters 6 through 10).

An unprecedented upward spiral of crimes motivated by hate began in the 1990s. Whether there was an actual increase or simply new documentation procedures is not known. In either case, the figures are disconcerting. History has shown that increasing diversity has led to intergroup conflict in countries throughout the world. This fact requires police to seriously consider their role in moderating complex intergroup relationships in the communities they serve. Consider the perspective offered by *Los Angeles Times* journalist Robin Wright:

> The world's now dizzying array of ethnic hot spots—at least four dozen at last count— starkly illustrate how, of all the features of the post–Cold War world, the most consistently troubling are turning out to be the tribal hatreds that divide humankind by race, faith and nationality. (Wright, 1993, p. A1)

Wright indicates that fewer than 10 percent of the world's 191 nations are still ethnically or racially homogeneous. Fueled by widespread migration and cultural intermixing, "there are now between 7,000 and 8,000 linguistic, ethnic or religious minorities in the world. This mass migration is focused on cities. Its sheer magnitude in an increasingly complex and crowded world makes classes and conflict a virtually unavoidable consequence of modern urban life." (Wright, 1993, p. A13). Wright identified four key factors that contribute to intergroup conflict: migration, power quest, insecurity, and limited resources. According to Wright (1993),

> In the aftermath of migration, individuals or groups seeking power often exploit ethnic, religious and cultural differences. This drive for personal power and individual gain is characterized as a "power quest." Similarly, the transition that accompanies migration contributes to uncertainty, which can fuel ethnic and religious passions or rivalry. Coping with change, many people seek refuge within "their" group. When combined with limited resources, this heightened sense of group consciousness can exacerbate ethnic/cultural tensions. This economic dimension is critical and must be recognized by community police. (p. A13)

Racial and ethnic groups, already frustrated with their poor economic situation, are more prone to resentment and intolerance of actual or perceived discrimination, especially when the police are suspect. The combination is often the triggering event for a riot.

The U.S. Attorney General's Commission on Racial, Ethnic, Religious, and Minority Violence (1986) has adopted a comprehensive definition of a hate/bias crime:

> Any act of intimidation, harassment, physical force or threat of physical force directed against any person, or family, or their property or advocate, motivated either in whole or in part, by hostility to their real or perceived race, ethnic background, national origin, religious belief, sex, age, disability, or sexual orientation, with the intention of causing fear or intimidation, or to deter the free exercise or enjoyment of any rights or privileges secured by the Constitution or the laws of the United States or of the State of California whether or not performed under the color of law. (p. 5)

Victims of hate/bias crimes are particularly sensitive and unsettled because they feel powerless to alter the situation since they cannot change their racial, ethnic, or religious background. Furthermore, the individual involved is not the only victim, because often an entire group of citizens is affected due to fear. A physical attack on a person because of race, religion, ethnic background, or sexual orientation is a particularly insidious form of violent behavior. Verbal assaults on persons because of others' perceptions of their "differences" are equally distressing to both the victim and society. And, unfortunately, these kinds of incidents can also occur in the law enforcement workplace among coworkers. Treating such occurrences seriously in law enforcement sends a message to community members that the local police agency will protect them. Doing the same within the law enforcement organization sends a vitally important message to all employees.

The criminal justice system, and especially local law enforcement agencies, will become the focus of criticism if attacks are not investigated, resolved, and prosecuted promptly and effectively. A hate/bias crime can send shock waves through the ethnic or racial community at which the act was aimed. These acts create danger, frustration, concern, and anxiety in our communities.

A 1993 study by Northeastern University determined that a large number of hate crime perpetrators are youthful thrill seekers: 60 percent of offenders committed crimes for the thrill associated with the victimization. The second most common group responsible for hate crimes is reactive offenders who feel that they are answering an attack by their victims. The least common perpetrators, according to the report, are hard-core fanatics who are driven by racial or religious ideology or ethnic bigotry. These individuals are often members of or potential recruits for extremist organizations. Some perpetrators of hate crimes live on the U.S. borders and are petrified by what they consider to be "brown hordes" of Mexicans, Cubans, and Haitians who enter the United States both legally and illegally. They feel that if they cease their militant rhetoric and violence toward these immigrants that the country will be inundated with them. "Mexicans are the largest immigrant group in the country, accounting for 27 percent of foreign born. Their visibility makes them a magnet for anti-immigrant sentiment. Mexicans being the most numerous are taking the heat" ("Clinton seeks race dialogue, rhetoric needs to match deeds, say advocates," *Contra Costa Times,* June 15, 1997, p. A9). There are also many racists living near Native American reservations whose aim of violence is to challenge the few remaining treaty rights granted to native people.

Despite the abundance of rhetoric deploring acts of bigotry and hate violence, few communities have utilized a holistic approach to the problem. Typically, efforts to prevent and respond to such crimes by local agencies have not been coordinated. Indeed, there are many effective programs that deal with a particular aspect of bigotry or hate in a specific setting; however, few models weave efforts to prevent hate violence into the fabric of the community. Community awareness of hate violence grew rapidly in the United States during the late 1980s and 1990s. Many states commissioned special task forces to recommend ways to control such violence, and new legislation was passed.

Hate crimes are the most extreme and dangerous manifestations of racism. Law enforcement professionals, including neighborhood police officers (the best sources of intelligence information), must be aware of the scope of the hate/bias crime problem from both historical and contemporary perspectives.

The U.S. Commission on Civil Rights, Intimidation, and Violence (1990) identified several factors that contribute to racial intimidation and violence, including the following:

- Racial integration of neighborhoods, leading to "move-in violence" (explained later in the chapter)
- Deep-seated racial hatred played on by organized hate groups
- Economic competition among racial and ethnic groups
- Insensitive media coverage of minority groups
- Poor police response to hate crimes

According to a study titled "When Hate Comes to Town: Preventing and Intervening in Community Hate Crime" (Corporate, 1989), hate violence can be attributed to

- A growing pattern of economic prejudice built on the stereotype that minorities are making economic gains that threaten the economic and social well-being of whites

- The unprecedented numbers of Latin American and Asian immigrants moving into neighborhoods, which were unprepared for the social, economic, political, and criminal justice system consequences of multicultural living
- The higher visibility of gay men, often seen as "easy targets" unable to fight back, combined with the increasing national fear of acquired immuno deficiency syndrome (AIDS)
- The lack of social preparedness of most young people when plunged into a multicultural school environment

The Scope of Hate Crimes Nationally

The psychocultural origin of hate crimes stems from human nature itself. To hate means to dislike passionately or intensely—to have an extreme aversion or hostility toward another person, idea, or object. Hate can have a benign manifestation, such as when one hates evil, or bad weather, or certain foods, or an abnormal expression when it becomes obsessive or is wrongly directed at someone who has done no harm. People can be culturally conditioned to hate those who are different from them because of their places of origin, looks, beliefs, or preferences. As the song in the musical *South Pacific* reminds us, "we have to be taught to hate and fear. We have to be taught from year to year."

A comparison of Federal Bureau of Investigation (FBI) hate crime statistics covering the period 1991 through 1998 offers some insights into the problem (see Exhibit 11.1). It must be pointed out, however, that the collection of hate incident and crime data is voluntary and only commenced in 1991. It is also true that not all law enforcement agencies collect or submit hate crime data to the Bureau of Justice Statistics. Making comparisons between years, therefore, will not clearly identify trends. Statistics covering the same period were also collected on the offenders' reported motivation (see Exhibit 11.2). A study of the data contained in the exhibits tells us that of the 7,775 total incidents in 1998, 4,321 (58 percent) were motivated by racial bias, 1,390 (16 percent) by religious bias, 1260 (16 percent) by sexual orientation bias, and 754 (10 percent) by ethnicity or national-origin bias. The statistics also show that African Americans are the most frequent targets of hate crime by a factor of three to one. Tracking hate crimes, which have typically been underreported, did not begin in earnest until the 1990s. The Internet continues to expand into every corner of our culture; in 1999 electronic mail emerged as a favorite vehicle for purveyors of hate and recruiters of new, young hate group members.

Urban Dynamics Theories

The relationships among the clustering of new immigrant groups, the economy, move-in violence, and hate/bias incidents and crimes in cities are well documented. It is important that readers understand that hate incidents and crimes often do not occur in a vacuum but are rather part of a larger social and economic interchange.

Clustering and target zone theory. Studies have shown that initially new immigrants tend to locate or cluster where people of their own ethnic and racial background are already established. They tend to congregate in the same areas of the country or within the city to be near relatives or friends; to have assistance

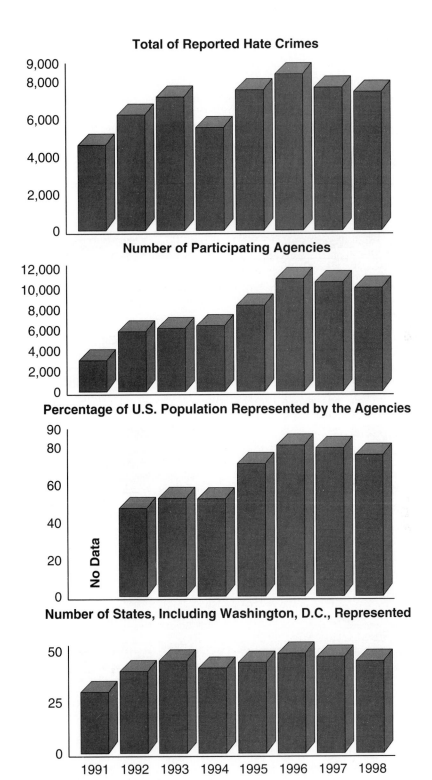

Total of Reported Hate Crimes

Number of Participating Agencies

Percentage of U.S. Population Represented by the Agencies

No Data

Number of States, Including Washington, D.C., Represented

1991 1992 1993 1994 1995 1996 1997 1998

Exhibit 11.1 Investigation of hate crimes (1991–1998).
Source: Federal Bureau of Investigation. U.S. Department of Justice Office of Justice Programs Bureau of Justice Statistics Washington, D.C.

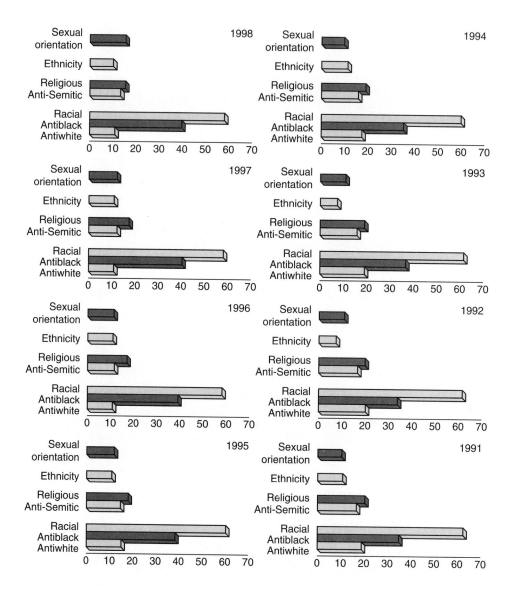

Exhibit 11.2 Reported motivation of offenders (values are the percentage of offenses).
Source: Anti-Defamation League, from data collected by the Department of Justice, Federal Bureau of Investigation. Anti-Defamation League of B'nai B'rith National Office. New York, New York.

in finding housing and jobs and in coping with language barriers; and to find the security of a familiar religion and social institutions. One study on new immigrant grouping was completed by Steven Wallace (1987) for the University of California, San Francisco. He stated that, generally,

> for the first generation or two, ethnic communities are helpful because they provide a sense of continuity for immigrants while easing subsequent generations into American values and society. . . . The existence of an ethnic or immigrant community is obvious evidence that a group has not assimilated. A community represents a place where immigrants are able to associate with others like themselves. An immigrant community provides a safe place to engage in these activities that deviate from dominant norms such as speaking a language other than English, honoring "foreign" symbols of pride, and exhibiting other non-Anglo behavior. Commonly located in low-rent districts, ethnic communities are functionally found where members can afford to live while they work at low wage jobs. (Wallace, 1987, pp. 88–89)

Wallace indicates that the rewards of better education and jobs come with assimilation into mainstream society. Some groups of immigrants can be seen as "temporary inhabitants" of the inner city; they work toward and achieve their goal of moving into the suburbs as they improve their economic situation. As they gain wealth and education, they acquire the same economic and educational advantages as long-time Americans (Wallace, 1992). The past two decades have also seen changes for the black population, with over 30 percent of blacks now living in suburban areas in the United States as compared to 21.2 percent in 1980 (U.S. Bureau of the Census, 1980, 1990, 1994).

Ron Martinelli (a criminologist and former San Jose, California, police officer) discusses a theory called target zoning, or, as termed by sociologists, the concentric zone theory, shown in Exhibit 11.3. This model of urban ecology explains in simple terms what takes place when new ethnic minorities settle in an existing core area (inner city) that is often already economically depressed. These core areas are typically where low-socioeconomic-class whites, blacks, Hispanics, and established immigrants have settled because housing is cheap (or government subsidized), employment or welfare services are available, and there is some degree of comfort from living with people of one's own race or culture. (These areas are often impoverished ghettos, with substandard, older housing, and they are frequently overcrowded, with high incidents of social conflict and crime, including drug and gang activity.) As new immigrants and members of racial and cultural groups move into the core area, they come into conflict with existing members of that community—a phenomenon that has been going on for generations. The newcomer and the established community member compete for housing, jobs, financial resources (e.g., welfare, food stamps), and education. When there is a collapse of affordable health services, lack of affordable housing, and reductions in benefits (cuts in social programs by federal and state authorities), as occurred in the 1990s, conflicts intensify among racial and ethnic groups. These circumstances magnify, and incidents of discrimination, bias, and hate violence increase (Shusta, 1987). Those established want to move out, not just to improve their lot but to escape the conflict. Thus they move to the next ring out in the concentric circles. The whole process is then repeated as those in the next circle move to outer circles. The result in many cases is "move-in violence," discussed later in this chapter. Similar processes have also been observed at the scale of entire states. States such as Texas, New York, and California have been targets for large-scale immigration for several decades. More recently,

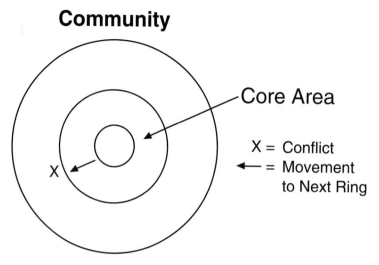

Exhibit 11.3
Source: California Peace Officer Standards and Training Command College Independent Study:
A Model Plan for California Cities Experiencing Multicultural Impact by Robert Shusta, 1987.

a counterflow has been observed wherein native-born white families exit these states to neighboring states, such as Arizona, Oregon, and Nevada (Frey, 1998). This process can be seen as analogous to white migration to the suburbs, but on a much larger geographic scale.

The concentric zone theory, while it works well to describe some cities, does not describe others. For example, in the past 25 years, "urban renewal" has further complicated the theory as inner-city slums have been flattened and expensive condos, shopping centers, or civic center projects have been built in their places. Thus one sees a small but important return from the suburbs to areas to which the concentric zone theory would predict only poor immigrants would move. For example, the south-central area of Los Angeles, which is thought to be populated predominately by poor blacks, is actually now half Latino immigrant. This area of comparatively low-cost housing is where most recent immigrants settled. On the other hand, Iranian immigrants, who are mostly businesspeople and professionals, are heavily concentrated in west Los Angeles, which is an expensive housing market. Many from Hong Kong who have moderate means are settling in Monterey Park, a middle-class community that is now heavily Chinese.

The economy and hate violence. Poor economic times contribute greatly to hate violence (Wynn, 1987). In many areas of the country, when major industries such as steel and auto manufacturing have downturns, go out of business, or relocate, the likelihood of economic distress among low-skilled and unskilled workers increases. Scapegoating and blaming often result when blue-collar jobs are unavailable. The distress that accompanies unemployment and rising prices is often directed toward immigrants and minorities and manifests itself in harassment and violence. A harmful tendency seems to exist within some people wherein they must blame others for their own misfortune or society's failings. Thus the frequency and intensity of such acts are shown to increase when the economy deteriorates.

Sociologists indicate that hate frequently stems from being deprived or having one's needs unsatisfied; so the poor can despise the rich, the uneducated ridicule the intellectual, and the established ghetto inhabitant can hate the new immigrant or refugee who moves into the area. Social scientists argue that the government definition of poverty does not measure the real depths or the changes taking place in inner cities (not only has the number of ghetto poor increased but so has the severity of economic deprivation among them). Ghetto poverty and concentrations of large numbers of a diverse population in one area often lead to conflict in these neighborhoods. The stresses of urban life, especially in inner cities, give rise to increased incidents of violence, especially in depressed economic conditions and reduced space.

Move-in violence. *Move-in violence* can occur when people of one ethnicity or race move into a residence or open a business in a neighborhood composed of people from a different race or ethnicity. It can also take place when the new resident is of the same ethnicity or race—for example, a Cuban moving into a Mexican neighborhood or a Caribbean black moving into an African American community. Changing community diversity and demographics can have a significant impact on the community because of hostility and hatred based on perceived and real group differences. However, the presence of new migrants or immigrants in a racially or ethnically different neighborhood does not automatically result in intergroup conflict or violence.

Historically, most cases of violence have involved black, Hispanic, or Asian victims who locate housing or businesses in previously all-white suburbs or neighborhoods. Whites have not been the sole perpetrators, however, and have also been victims. For example, in Worcester, Massachusetts (1999), and in Sacramento, California (2000), Russian immigrants moved into nonwhite neighborhoods and community conflict occurred. New residents or business owners have moved into areas that are primarily black, Hispanic, or Asian and experienced friction with the original residents. According to the U.S. Community Relations Service, there have been cases of Hispanic migration or immigration into communities that had been governed for many years by black leaders. In these new mixed communities, for example, Hispanic/Latino community members have perceived that their concerns are being ignored (e.g., in the Los Angeles area around Lakewood, Watts, and Pomona) (Borgquist, 2000).

New immigrants can meet with resentment, biased treatment, and criminal victimization, especially if they appear to be different from the established community into which they move (the new neighborhood can be dominated by any racial population). Whether we are talking about the Irish, the Somalis, the Vietnamese, or the Cubans, intergroup tension and hatred are as common today as in past centuries. Crimes directed at persons perceived as different and new to a neighborhood typically range from threats and vandalism to arson and fire bombings. Historically, most cases have involved racist whites attacking their victims out of a desire to preserve racial segregation in their communities. This trend still exists today, but with the changing demographics of the twenty-first century, we see perpetrators of crimes and victims from many different groups. According to Daryl Borgquist (2000), Media Affairs Officer for the U.S. Community Relations Service, Washington, D.C.,

> White-on-black bias crime [of the] 1960s and 1970s does not reflect the dramatic demographic changes in the country. The case work at the Community Relations Service has changed dramatically since the 1960s. Asian immigration has accounted for almost

half of all U.S. immigration since the late 1960s, meaning that many Asians have settled in communities which never had Asians or only had a few. Cities such as Los Angeles, Houston, New York, and Washington, D.C. (including Prince Georges County, Maryland), to name a few, have had a number of incidents of conflict between Korean grocers or market owners and the black communities in which their stores are located. For example, there has been a protest of a Korean store in D.C. that was firebombed in December of 2000. In Los Angeles, the Korean community was armed and formed a "security group" to protect their stores from violence in the black community.

Researchers and hate/bias enforcement officials have found that neighborhood integration, competition for jobs and services, and issues involving "turf" create the primary scenario for hate crimes (McDevitt, 1989; Southern Poverty Law Center, 1987). Social scientists and scholars from other disciplines have referred to "turf" as "the territorial imperative." Since the beginning of time, the drive to preserve and gain territory has characterized people's need to protect what they believe is their own (i.e., land, area, or family). A relatively homogeneous group feels threatened by the invasion of "others," whether they are refugees, job seekers, or immigrants in search of a better way of life. Suspicion, hostility, and even violence toward the "stranger" describe human tendencies, especially in bad economic times.

Jack McDevitt (1989) of Northeastern University's Center for Applied Social Research in Boston, Massachusetts, also found that over a five-year period, the majority of confirmed bias crime cases in Boston had to do with the victim being in a neighborhood where he or she "did not belong." The territorial imperative ("this is my turf") dictates the violent actions of those with deep-seated, xenophobic prejudices. A study conducted by the New York State Governor's Task Force on Bias-Related Crime in 1988 reported that "young people in communities with exclusionary housing patterns often view themselves as guardians of the invisible walls that mark their community, and actively seek to drive away 'intruders' who are 'invading' their 'turf.'" p. 13 (The subject of gangs and turf wars is beyond the scope of this book.) Again, no one group has a monopoly on hate crimes: perpetrators of such offenses come from every racial, ethnic, and religious background. In summary, Borgquist (2000) advises officers to

- Be sensitive to changing demographics
- Help new groups assimilate or work into the community
- Use human relations commissions
- Use police advisory groups to help department chiefs and district commanders know what is happening among new residents.

Philadelphia Police Department conflict prevention/resolution unit.   The city of Philadelphia tested a way to prevent move-in violence in 1986 by utilizing a newly created police unit, which still exists, called the Conflict Prevention and Resolution (CPR) Team. The unit trains officers to investigate and prevent racial incidents. They work in partnership with detective personnel and other law enforcement officials to conduct a complete and thorough investigation of all hate-related incidents and crimes. Their goal is to maintain a proactive posture in the enforcement of Pennsylvania's Ethnic Intimidation Statute (a law that deals with hate crimes) by investigating hate incidents that are motivated by a victim's race, color, religion, national origin, or sexual orientation. They also develop awareness and prevention educational programs that address bias crime, racism, and other forms of bigotry.

One of the most successful proactive programs undertaken by this unit is the Pre-Move Survey. The program involves officers of CPR performing a door-to-door canvas in the neighborhood to communicate with the "majority" population prior to a "minority" family assuming residence. The program is predicated on the premise that potential conflict can be averted when persons residing in a community see that the police are interested in the welfare and rights of new neighbors. The survey gauges the sentiment of the established residents toward the ethnic or racial group in question. It also alerts the local police district hierarchy of the potential for trouble in a given location. This proactive approach gives notice to potential antagonists that the police department and city government are aware of the situation and will not tolerate any criminality perpetrated against the new neighbors. The sources of information for the CPR unit about the possibility of a minority moving into a neighborhood with a different ethnic or racial majority are the Human Relations Commission, realtors, social services agencies, politicians, public servants, and other police officers. Certainly, many neighborhoods have been integrated without the unit's assistance and without incident. However, the Philadelphia Police Department is proud of the fact that there has never been an ethnically motivated criminal act perpetrated against the new neighbors when the CPR unit has performed this procedure prior to the move-in. Philadelphia police officials do not claim that racial relations are significantly better because of the CPR unit, but they feel that their outreach approach has contributed to the reduction of racial violence in their city. The department has printed pocket guide cards to assist patrol officers and supervisors in explaining the ethnic intimidation laws to neighborhood residents. It has also produced and displayed multilingual posters within the community to explain CPR's functions and responsibilities.

VICTIMS OF HATE CRIMES

Targets of Hate Crimes

According to statistics collected by the Justice Department, more hate crime targets race, often black, than ethnicity, religion, or sexual orientation. Of the 7,755 hate crime incidents reported in 1998, 55.7 percent were due to race, 9.7 percent to ethnicity, 17.9 percent to religion, and 16.2 percent to sexual orientation. Of the racially motivated crimes, 2,901 incidents, or 67.1 percent, were directed at blacks, and whites were targets of 791 incidents, or 18.3 percent. The statistics reflect that three out of every five hate crimes were motivated by race and blacks were the targets in two out of three of the racial attacks. That same year, 87 percent of white victims were killed by white people. The report reflects that 94 percent of the nation's black murder victims were killed by black assailants that year. Hate crimes targeting ethnicity, primarily Hispanic, were 9.7 percent of the total hate crime incidents in 1998. Of the reported 754 incidents, 482, or 63.9 percent, were directed at Hispanics. The National Asian Pacific American Legal Consortium (NAPALC) indicated in a June 2000 report that the organization has noticed an unprecedented increase in the numbers of Asians killed each year since 1980, when they commenced collecting statistics. The NAPALC said that these hate-motivated killings have had a devastating effect on a broad cross section of Asian Americans across the United States; the ethnic backgrounds of the victims have been diverse, including South Asian, Philipino, Japanese, Korean, Vietnamese, and Chinese. "This horrible loss of life was for no apparent reason than the color of the victims' skin and often their perceived immigrant status" ("Asians Battle Rights Abuse in U.S.," *Contra Costa Times,* June 4, 2000, p. A15).

There are many examples of hate crimes that have victimized blacks, Asians, and Hispanics. Clearly, such hate goes back for many generations. One of the most recent cases of extreme hate violence, however, occurred near Jasper, Texas. On June 7, 1998, three white men, two with links to racist groups, dragged James Byrd, a 49-year-old African American, to his death by a chain bound around his ankles and connected to a pickup truck. He was dragged for two miles and his body ripped apart. Two of the perpetrators were sentenced to death and one life in prison without possibility of parole. Crimes and acts of hate serve as frightening reminders to vulnerable citizens that they may not take safety for granted. Collectively, they begin to develop a mentality that hate crimes can take place anywhere—in streets, in neighborhoods, at workplaces, and even in their homes.

JEWS AND ANTI-SEMITISM

Jews

Jews belong to a religious and cultural group, although they have sometimes been incorrectly labeled as constituting a separate racial group. Jews have experienced discrimination, persecution, and violence throughout history because their religious beliefs and practices set them apart from the majority. Even when they were totally assimilated (i.e., integrated into society), as was true in Germany early in the twentieth century, they were still not accepted as full citizens and eventually experienced the ultimate hate crime—genocide. The term *anti-Semitism* means "against Semites," which literally includes Jews and Arabs. Popular use of this term, however, refers to anti-Jewish sentiment.

European anti-Semitism had religious origins: Jews did not accept Jesus Christ as the son of God and were considered betrayers and even killers of Christ. This accusation gave rise to religious anti-Semitism and what others saw as justification for anti-Jewish acts. In the past three decades, there have been great strides by religious leaders to eliminate centuries of prejudice. For example, a 1965 Roman Catholic decree (the *Nastra Aetate*) stated that the church did not hold Jews responsible for the death of Christ. The decree, written by the Second Vatican Council under the leadership of the pope, encouraged people to abandon blaming Jews and instead work for stronger links between the religions and increased understanding. Despite some progress in ecumenical relations, there are still individuals who, 2000 years after the birth of Christ, believe that Jews today are responsible for Christ's death.

Of more recent origin is another type of anti-Semitism, which falls under what some would label as anti-Zionism (i.e., against the establishment of the state of Israel as a homeland for Jews). Although politically oriented, this type of anti-Semitism still makes references to "the Jews" and equates "Jews" with the suppression of the Palestinian people. Finally, racially based anti-Semitism originated in nineteenth-century pre-Nazi ideology, which claimed that Jews were an inferior race. In their attempts to eliminate the Jewish "race," the Nazis considered people "unpure" if one grandparent or even great-grandparent in their family was Jewish. Anti-Semitism is ancient in roots and worldwide in scope, with religious, political, and racial origins.

Prevalence of Anti-Semitic Crimes

The total reported number of anti-Semitic incidents documented by the Anti-Defamation League (ADL) decreased 4 percent between 1998 (1,611) and 1999 (1,547) (refer to Exhibit 11.4). Of those incidents, 868 were reports of harassment (down 3 percent, from 896, in 1998) and 679 were acts of vandalism (down 5 percent, from 715, in 1998). The number of anti-Semitic incidents reported to the ADL in 1999 was the lowest since 1989. However, some of the most violent episodes of anti-Semitic activities took place the summer of 1999. First, three Sacramento, California, synagogues were set afire, causing an estimated $1 million damage. (The Sacramento arsonists' explicit intent was to target the Jewish community, and they made their intentions known by distributing anti-Semitic fliers.) Then, a hate group activist went on a racially motivated shooting spree, killing two people and seriously injuring eight others in Indiana and Illinois, including six Jews leaving their synagogue. Finally, in Los Angeles, a man walked into a Jewish day care center and shot five people and later shot and killed a Philipino American postal worker. According to the FBI's 1998 annual report on hate crimes, more than 77.8 percent of all such acts perpetrated on the basis of religion were directed against Jews and Jewish religious institutions. According to David Lehrer, executive director of the Anti-Defamation League in Los Angeles,

> the Anti-Defamation League had been monitoring anti-Semitic hate crimes for more than 20 years, and the number over the past several years has been steadily declining, although there have been occasional up-ticks. Our concerns focus mainly on the increased virulence of the individual acts that are being committed. The hate incidents of 15 and 20 years ago tended to be swastika daubings, cross-burnings and inflammatory graffiti that outrage and hurt a community. Of late, the hate crimes tend to be more violent, more intense and reflective of more than casual racial or religious animus. (ADL report, 1999) p. 3

Lehrer said that the numbers of hate groups and members are stagnant or dwindling. He contends that they have no potential of being a serious political force or of galvanizing American public opinion. He also maintains that the threat posed by these groups is one of isolated violence, not of a meaningful political movement.

The five states reporting the most anti-Semitic incidents in 1999, continuing a longtime trend, were New York (352), California (275), New Jersey (226), Massachusetts (111), and Florida (88). Together, these states (with the largest Jewish populations and thus the most targets) accounted for 1,054 of the 1,547 incidents reported (68 percent). New York, California, and Massachusetts showed increases and New Jersey and Florida showed decreases in the number of reported incidents (Anti-Defamation League, 1999).

Anti-Semitic groups and individuals.   Several different types of groups in the United States have exhibited anti-Semitic attitudes, and some of the most extreme groups have committed hate crimes against Jews. The most glaringly anti-Semitic

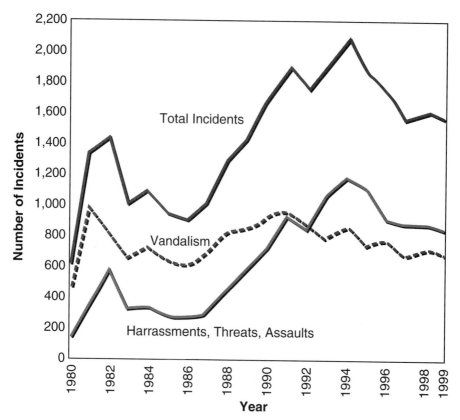

Exhibit 11.4 Anti-Semitic incidents.
Source: Anti Defamation League.

organizations are white supremacist groups, such as the Ku Klux Klan (KKK), the Aryan Nation, White Aryan Resistance (WAR), the Order, the Posse Comitatus, the Covenant and the Sword, the Arm of the Lord, and neo-Nazi skinheads (discussed further in Chapter 12). These groups tend to hate all who are different from them but focus a great deal of attention on blacks and Jews. In addition, those who are vehemently pro-Arab and anti-Israel may exhibit strong anti-Jewish attitudes; however, it is not common for anti-Zionist attitudes to result in acts of violence against Jews in the United States (although there have been terrorist acts against Jews in Europe). Some messianic individuals who believe that Armageddon (the end of the world) is imminent have been known to threaten Jews by phone or mail, but rarely have these threats been carried out. These people believe that Jews need to repent and see themselves as instruments of God, connected to the coming of the end of the world. Additionally, Jewish Americans, like Arab Americans, can become targets during Middle Eastern crises, such as the Gulf War or after a terrorist attack takes place.

Finally, in times of recession, Jews are often blamed for the economic decline, and the notion of Jewish "influence" provides a convenient scapegoat (i.e., it is said that the Jews control the media, the banks, and even the world economy). It is not within the scope of this section to delve into these myths, but we point out that there is widespread harmful misinformation about Jews that anti-Semites continue to spread.

Jewish Community Concerns

Around the holiest days of the Jewish year (Rosh Hashanah and Yom Kippur, occurring in the early fall), there can also be heightened anxiety among some community members regarding security. Indeed, many synagogues hire extra security during times of worship over this 10-day holiday period. Acts of defilement can occur in synagogues and other Jewish institutions at random times as well. Acts of defilement and manifestations of prejudice bring back painful memories for Jews who experienced violent expressions of anti-Semitism in other countries, especially those who lived through the Holocaust; some of the memories and fears have been passed on to subsequent generations. At the same time, some people may overreact to an insensitive remark that stems from ignorance on the part of the speaker rather then malicious anti-Semitism. Some people may not understand that a swastika painted by teenagers on a building does not necessarily precede any acts of anti-Jewish violence. Yet a swastika almost always evokes a fearful reaction among many Jewish community members because of the historical significance of the symbol.

Police officers must understand that different segments of the Jewish community feel vulnerable to anti-Semitism, and therefore officers are advised to listen to and take seriously Jews' expressions of concern and fear. At the same time, they need to explain to citizens that sometimes acts of vandalism are isolated and are not targeted at any group in particular (e.g., many skinheads or "thugs" are unhappy with their lot in life and tend to hate everyone). Finally, officers who take reports from citizens should reassure them that their local law enforcement agency views hate crimes and incidents seriously and that extra protection will be provided if the need arises.

What law enforcement can do. By discussing the concerns and fears of some Jewish community members, we do not imply that all Jewish citizens are overly concerned for their safety. In fact, a large percentage of American Jews do not even identify as Jews and do not share a collective or community consciousness with other Jews. At the other extreme are people who interpret events or remarks as anti-Semitic rather than as ignorance or insensitivity. Whatever the case, police officers should be aware that anti-Semitism has a long and active history, and, even if some fears appear to be exaggerated, they have a basis in reality.

Officers can take some steps to establish rapport and provide protection in Jewish communities when the need arises:

1. When an officer hears of an act that can be classified as a hate crime toward Jews, it should be investigated, tracked, and dealt with as such. Dismissing acts of anti-Semitism as petty crime will result in a lack of trust on the part of the community.
2. When hate crimes and incidents are perpetrated against other groups in the community (e.g., gay, African American, Asian American groups), officers should alert Jewish community leaders immediately. Their institutions may be the next targets.
3. Officers should be aware of groups and individuals who distribute hate literature on people's doorsteps. Publications such as *Racial Loyalty,* for example, target Jews and "people of color" and accuse Jews of poisoning the population. A book published by the same organization, *On the Brink of a Bloody Racial War,* has been left on

many Jews' doorsteps. Even if no violence occurs, the recipients of such hate literature become very fearful.

4. In cooperation with local organizations (e.g., Jewish Community Relations Council, ADL), officers can provide information (through joint meetings) on ways that community individuals can heighten the security of Jewish institutions (e.g., information on nonbreakable glass, lighting of facilities in evenings).

5. Law enforcement officials should be familiar with the dates of the Jewish calendar, especially when the High Holidays (Rosh Hashanah and Yom Kippur) occur. Some people are concerned about safety and protection during events at which large groups of Jews congregate.

6. Finally, officers may contact a Jewish umbrella organization in the community to assist them in helping to send necessary messages to local Jewish institutions and places of worship. Two organizations in particular are worth noting: the national JCRC and the ADL. The JCRC has representative organizations in almost every major city in the United States. This organization, the regional ADL organizations, and the Jewish Federations can be of great assistance to law enforcement in disseminating information to members of the Jewish community.

Because of their history, some Jews expect anti-Semitic incidents, and the reality is that there are still anti-Semites in our society. According to Riva Gambert (former associate director of the JCRC of the Greater East Bay, October, 1993), whether the act was simply insensitive or whether it was indeed a hate crime, the officer still has to be responsive to the generated fears and community concerns. An officer's ability to calm fears as well as to investigate threats thoroughly will result in strong relations between law enforcement officials and Jewish community members.

GAY AND LESBIAN VICTIMIZATION

Most of the discussion in this chapter, until now, has centered on race, ethnic background, and religion in regard to hate/bias crimes and incidents. The motivation behind gay and lesbian hate crimes and incidents is unique because they target a group due to sexual orientation or gender identity, unlike any other community group. Gay and lesbian crimes and incidents are seriously underreported and deserving of attention. The National Gay and Lesbian Task Force (NGLTF) defines antigay and antilesbian violence as "any violence directed against persons because they are gay or lesbian, or perceived to be so. It is motivated by irrational fear and by the perception that gay people are easy targets, unable to fight back, or unwilling to risk exposure by reporting crimes against them to authorities" (Berrill, 1986). The definition has now been expanded to include bisexual and transgender persons. Within the past 5 years, hate crimes against people whose appearances differ from what might be expected by their birth gender (including transvestites and transsexuals) have dramatically increased within the United States, both in number and in ferocity.

Prevalence of Homophobic Crimes

Every year in the United States, thousands of lesbians, gay men, bisexuals, and transgender people are verbally harassed, beaten, raped, and murdered because of their sexual orientation or gender identity. These types of crimes are increasing in the United States. "Racism and homophobia are byproducts of a society that does not value diversity," said Kerry Lobel, executive director of the NGLTF. He continued: "A climate exists in our country that devalues people of color as well as gay, lesbian, bisexual and transgender people. Racism and homophobia are symptoms of the same disease and the disease is named intolerance" (*News + Views* [National Gay and Lesbian Task Force publication], March 24, 2000). p. 2

Hate violence against gay, lesbian, bisexual, and transgender (GLBT) people has increased dramatically over the past decade. In 1998, 2,252 anti-GLBT incidents were reported in the United States. According to the NGLTF, anti-GLBT attacks are also among the most violent bias crimes. GLBT murder victims are more likely than heterosexual victims to die brutal deaths characterized by dismemberment, multiple stabbing, and severe bludgeoning, and their killers are less likely to be caught, according to a 1994 study by the National Coalition of Anti-Violence Programs. And many assaults against GLBT persons are not reported. A NGLTF study in 1992 revealed that the percentage of gay and lesbian hate crime victims who did not report these crimes to the police ranged from 76 to 82 percent.

Impact of Hate Crimes on Gay and Lesbian Victims

A hate-motivated attack is a psychological as well as a physical assault. For many gay and lesbian people, it is an attack on a part of their identity they have struggled to accept and value.

In 1998 and 1999 national attention was drawn to gay bashing by two horrendous incidents. They resulted in congressional hearings and community candlelight marches throughout the country. In October 1998, 21-year-old Wyoming college freshman Matthew Shepard was pistol-whipped so hard that he was disfigured, burned with cigarettes, and then bound to a fence in freezing weather by two men and left to die. In July 1999 the Servicemember's Legal Defense Network (SLDN) notified the media of the brutal murder of 21-year-old Private First Class Barry Winchell, who was bludgeoned to death with a baseball bat by fellow soldiers while asleep in his bed in the barracks at Fort Campbell, Kentucky. During the court-martial, fellow soldiers testified that Winchell was mercilessly taunted with antigay slurs in the months preceding his murder, beginning after an army sergeant violated the "Don't ask" policy and inquired about Winchell's sexual orientation. In response to his death, the Department of Defense issued an action plan for each of the military services to address such issues as eliminating mistreatment, harassment, and inappropriate comments or gestures; training; reporting of harassment; enforcement of policies prohibiting harassment; and measurement of antiharassment program effectiveness. The SLDN in March 1999 documented a 120 percent increase in reports of antigay harassment, including death threats, within the armed forces.

Perpetrators of hate crimes against Gays and Lesbians

According to a 1984 NGLTF survey, one-third of the respondents had been either verbally or physically abused by family members. Otherwise, almost all of the perpetrators of antigay and antilesbian violence were strangers. The strangers tended to be adolescent or young adult males, often attacking in groups. Unlike the offenders in other bias-motivated crimes or incidents, it is not uncommon for perpetrators to leave their own turf to hunt down gays or lesbians ("gay bashing").

One example involves four young members of a white supremacist group, barely out of their teens, who committed extreme antigay and antilesbian violence in Salem, Oregon, in 1992. The four were accused of the firebomb murders of two persons when they lobbed a Molotov cocktail into the apartment where a black lesbian and a white gay man lived. According to newspaper accounts, "The murder indictment said motive could be found in the defendants' perception of the race, color and sexual orientation of the victims" (Lambda, 1992, p. 6).

A persistent prejudice against gays exists among youth, regardless of their level of education. In surveys conducted in 2000, 40 percent of 16- to 18-year-old high school students whose scholastic achievement earned them a position in *Who's Who among American High School Students* stated that they were biased against homosexuals. The findings were basically unchanged from a 1998 survey. By contrast, only 15 percent said they were prejudiced against Hispanics and 13 percent said they were prejudiced against blacks.

Some allege that many of the perpetrators of bias against gays and lesbians have been police officers. "The police have been cited as perpetrators in hundreds of cases reported to the NGLTF and they are frequently mentioned in the anecdotal evidence presented by other agencies serving the gay and lesbian communities. The reports have included verbal abuse, physical assault, entrapment, unequal enforcement of the law and deliberate mishandling of cases" (National Gay and Lesbian Task Force, 1992). When police officers, who are sworn to uphold the laws of the land, are the perpetrators of discrimination and even assaults on gays and lesbians, the law enforcement community must take notice. For example, an off-duty Philadelphia police officer was accused of physically and verbally assaulting a man that he and his five companions thought to be gay. The officer was suspended and then fired by the police commissioner. The officer was later acquitted in a nonjury trial. The judge wrote in his ruling that "the [court] had enough evidence to establish a prima facie case. However, the [court] clearly did not have a strong case" ("Ex-cop Wins Expungement of Gay Bashing Record; Plans to Rejoin Force," *Au Courant*, July 17, 1989, p. 3).

Officers of the Los Angeles Police Department (LAPD) were accused of beating a gay man while yelling "get out of the park you fucking queers" ("Reports of Anti-Gay/Lesbian Violence," *Reactions*, November 1, 1988, p. 7). A 1984 NGLTF survey discovered that 23 percent of gay men and 13 percent of lesbians responding reported being abused in some way by the police. A similar study by NGLTF in 1988 indicated that of the 4,835 harassment or violent incidents reported by gay or lesbian victims, 3 percent (205) were acts of police abuse. It comes as no surprise, then, that many gay people are reluctant to report assaults that are motivated by hate or bias or to rely on the criminal justice system to protect them. Police professionals must treat gays, lesbians, and transgender individuals within the community and their own workforce with respect and dignity regardless of their own personal biases.

Some police departments have written orders that specifically state what constitutes unacceptable conduct for their employees. For example, the Alameda, California, Police Department has a general order (80-1 [A-1]: 21:02) that specifically addresses discrimination and racial remarks and requires courtesy and respectful treatment of all persons. It states: "Discrimination or racism in any form shall never be tolerated." Other general orders in that department deal with harassment in the workplace based on race, religion, color, national origin, ancestry, disability, marital status, gender, age, or sexual preference. Violation of these orders carries disciplinary ramifications up to and including termination of employment.

Application of such agency orders is an extremely relevant issue with regard to the gay and lesbian community. Even in departments that supposedly impose severe discipline for such misconduct, in cases involving gay or lesbian complaints, the discipline meted out is often nothing more than an official reprimand. Increasingly, the complainants in antigay discrimination cases are fellow law enforcement officers. For example, between 1993 and 1998, the Los Angeles Police Department settled six separate lawsuits filed by gay and lesbian officers against their coworkers. Although the city paid out over $3 million, none of the officers named in their suits were ever disciplined. In a seventh case, in which a heterosexual LAPD detective was harassed because he was perceived to be gay, one of the harassers was transferred and one received a reprimand ("Cop's Bias Suit Costs 1.2 M to Settle," *Daily Journal,* September 29, 1995; and "LAPD Officer Files Suit, Claims Colleagues Sexually Harassed Him," November 5, 1997; Grobeson, 2000).

Police Relations with the Gay and Lesbian Communities

Historically, in most cities and counties in the United States, relations between the police and the gay and lesbian communities have been strained. Many homosexual persons believe that the police regard them as deviants, criminals, and second-class citizens who are unworthy of protection or equal rights. Because of this perception, many gay and lesbian crime victims do not report crimes to the police or cooperate with investigations. Even though negative attitudes and stereotypes will probably continue, progressive police departments have found that communication and mutual respect between the department and the gay and lesbian communities are in the best interests of all concerned. However, according to Sgt. Grobeson, even departments that demonstrate strong public relations efforts, including uniformed staffing of booths and participation in annual gay pride events, have been documented as tolerating antigay behaviors by officers. He also states that, surprisingly, the complaints generated are not only by members of the gay and lesbian communities but also by fellow officers. A few cases that support his contention are located in Chapter 2 of this text, within the "Gays and Lesbians in Law Enforcement" section.

Examples of police departments wherein outreach and communications have resulted in cooperation between the agencies and the gay community include San Francisco, Boston, New York, and Baltimore. These departments have observed a noticeable difference in reporting by lesbian and gay crime victims, fewer complaints of police abuse, and a general improvement in relations between law enforcement and the gay and lesbian communities.

Researcher Kevin Berrill (1992) observed that there are numerous ways to improve relationships between the justice system and gay and lesbian groups. One of the keys to good relations, according to Berrill, is regular, institutionalized communication at the department, in committees and councils, and in public forums. In addition, he mentions the following:

- The creation of task forces and councils to establish ongoing dialogue and networking on important issues
- Public forums that allow police officials to meet the gay and lesbian community and help the officials to recognize that gays are a constituency with legitimate needs and concerns
- The appointment of a police official to be a liaison with the gay and lesbian community to respond to complaints and requests

- The involvement of prosecutors in the development of policies, procedures, communications, and awareness training to improve relations between the criminal justice system and gay and lesbian groups and individuals.

When laws are violated by a gay or lesbian individual, whether acting alone or as part of a group, the usual criminal justice procedures should be followed—investigation, arrest, prosecution, and incarceration. Almost every community has extremist and even militant segments, and the gay community is no exception. These activist groups, often advocating AIDS-related funding and research, may require additional attention and special interaction with area law enforcement. The goal of the agency liaison and management should be to avoid costly litigation and to communicate effectively with persons representing such groups. Departments should have an assigned liaison officer meet with these groups in an attempt to agree on acceptable behavior before any public demonstration occurs. Some groups obtain press coverage by orchestrating arrests by the police; in such cases, liaison and close monitoring by field supervisors, a press relations officer, a police video unit, and a department manager would be an absolute necessity. This methodology has been successful with agencies in the San Francisco Bay Area, resulting in no physical confrontation with groups, no negative press or photos and no legal action. However, even the best police outreach efforts may prove ineffective. For example, some activist groups have refused to communicate with police during their "actions." Nevertheless, police officers should not permit negative publicity from previous incidents with any group to stop them from attempting to make positive contact prior to scheduled public events. The willingness of the police to work with any community group, particularly gay activist groups, always results in positive publicity for police managers and their departments.

WAR-RELATED HATE CRIMES

War-related hate crimes are not new in America and date from the French-Indian War, the Plains Wars against Native Americans, and the Mexican-American and Cuban-American Wars to World War I, World War II, and the wars in Korea and Indochina; in all these wars, Americans associated with the "enemy" became victims of hate crimes. The Gulf War in Iraq in the early 1990s proved to follow the patterns of previous wars with respect to the perceived enemy (i.e., many Arab Americans were the targets of hate violence). Acts of hatred directed toward the peoples living in the United States from countries we have fought during these wars or police actions have been common. During the Vietnam War, however, war-related hate crimes were not common since there were not many Vietnamese living in the United States at that time. (Those prone to discriminate and hate "outsiders" expressed their sentiment after the Southeast Asians arrived in the United States.)

In 1992 "Japan bashing" in the United States was resurrected. The Japanese prime minister made comments about lazy American workers. These comments, combined with the 50th anniversary of the Pearl Harbor bombing and the World War II Japanese internment order, brought increased threats to Japanese Americans as well as a stepped-up "Buy American" campaign aimed at boycotting foreign, especially Japanese-made, products. The Japanese once again became targets of bias and, in some cases, hate violence, even though others had, for the most part, learned to live peacefully with Japanese Americans. The American Arab Anti-Discrimination

Committee indicates that an unfortunate trend usually follows any conflict in the Middle East, in that there is a corresponding backlash against Arab Americans in the form of hate crimes. The number of hate crimes reported against Arab Americans mushroomed during and immediately following the Gulf War.

LAW ENFORCEMENT RESPONSE STRATEGIES

Public confidence and trust in the criminal justice system and, in particular, law enforcement are essential for effective response to hate/bias crimes. Residents in communities where people of a different race, ethnic background, religion, or sexual orientation reside must be able to trust that they will be protected. They must believe that the police are not against them, that the prosecutors are vigorously prosecuting, that the judges are invoking proper penalties, and that parole, probation, and corrections are doing their share to combat crimes motivated by hate or bias. If people believe that they have to protect themselves, tensions build, communication breaks down, and people try to take the law into their own hands. For example, in Los Angeles in 1992 following the trial verdict of the four officers charged in the Rodney King incident, Koreans were defending their property by shooting it out with looters. Many of the looters were stealing for personal gain, but there are indications that many were using the opportunity to take out their frustration and hatred for members of a different race during the turmoil of the riots.

Recommendation to Communities to Fight Crimes Motivated by Hate

Following are recommendations to fight crimes motivated by hate:

- Train every patrol officer in the department to recognize hate crime. Patrol officers must understand and support a department's policies on hate crime and know how to respond when hate crime occurs. Topics should include recognizing bias-related incidents, utilizing standard criteria to determine bias and assess perpetrator intent, interviewing victims and witnesses, collecting and preserving evidence, referring victims to appropriate community agencies, and standardizing documentation of hate incidents and crimes.
- Train victim assistance providers, judges, and prosecutors.
- Establish a multiagency task force in areas where hate crime occurs and give it the full support of every elected official and law enforcement agency (as well as other community agencies and organizations) involved in the investigation and prosecution of hate crime. A team approach provides experienced personnel and dedicated resources to investigate incidents and leads more quickly.
- Seek out every source of state and federal law enforcement assistance in your community and make it available to the investigators and/or task force investigating or preventing hate crimes.
- Create the position of liaison officer, who is a contact person between spokespersons within the minority and gay community and the department.
- Adopt a written policy for each law enforcement agency, signed by the executive leader, to make responding to hate violence a priority.
- Comply with the Hate Crimes Statistics Act.
- Enact a penalty-enhancement hate crime statute at the state level.

In 1998 the International Association of Chiefs of Police (IACP) held a conference, the Hate Crime in America Summit. The organization produced 46 recommendations to prevent hate crime, respond to hate crime, and measure effectiveness of prevention and response efforts. The total report can be found on the IACP Web site. The summit participants' 20 major proactive initiatives to help communities prevent bias-motivated incidents and hate crime are as follows:

1. *Increase public awareness.* Citizen involvement and awareness are essential to the success of any program to reduce prejudice and prevent bias-related crimes.

2. *Create multidisciplinary planning processes to develop coordinated approaches to prevent and respond to hate crime.* Every community should maintain or develop a strategic crime prevention planning process that includes a focus on hate crime and view planning as an ongoing responsibility, not just a onetime project.

3. *Create local human rights commissions or other forums to promote community harmony and stability.* All citizens should be encouraged to talk about their differences and commonalties and to share their visions of safe and healthy communities.

4. *Focus public attention on issues of prejudice, intolerance, and the ways hate crime affects community vitality and safety.* Community and justice system leaders, particularly police chiefs, must continue to speak out forcefully against intolerance, bigotry, and hate crime, not only in the aftermath of high-profile incidents but at all times.

5. *Develop public information to promote values of tolerance and social equality.*

6. *Raise awareness of the goals and activities of organized hate groups.* Hate groups are less effective in sowing seeds of social unrest and conflict when their activities (including those publicized on Web sites) are brought to light.

7. *Develop national, regional, and/or state task forces to understand and counter the influence of organized hate groups.*

8. *Educate children and young adults.* Teaching our children to respect differences and celebrate diversity is essential to prevent development of prejudiced attitudes that can lead to hate crime.

9. *Involve parents in efforts to prevent and intervene against the bias-motivated behavior of their children.* Parents should be engaged in hate crime prevention and conflict resolution in their children's schools.

10. *Foster a "zero-tolerance" atmosphere in schools and colleges.* Written codes of conduct for students, teachers, and other employees should be developed, publicized, and enforced.

11. *Incorporate hate crime education into existing curricula.* Schools and colleges should encourage faculty to incorporate hate crime education into existing curricula in subject areas such as health, geography, social studies, history, and civics.

12. *Reinforce diversity training and multicultural education at early ages.* Multicultural education diminishes reliance on stereotyping and reduces the chances of miscommunication between members of different cultural groups.

13. *Provide conflict resolution training to all children.*

14. *Intervene with students who express discriminatory beliefs before their behavior escalates.*

15. *Educate community groups and leaders.* They should have the skills and knowledge to recognize and actively resist intolerance and hate-motivated actions in their neighborhoods and jurisdictions.

16. *Inform vulnerable groups and individuals about ways to protect themselves from bias-motivated incidents and crime.* They should be informed, also, of the importance of reporting bias-related incidents and the support available.

17. *Provide knowledge and impart skills to recognize and defuse high-risk situations.*

18. *Develop mechanisms for ongoing problem solving within local communities.*

19. *Encourage responsible and accurate media coverage.* Responsible coverage means treating victims with dignity and sensitivity.

20. *Improve accuracy and completeness of information about incidences of and responses to hate crimes.* Citizens need to know the facts about hate crimes and current responses to them so that they can more effectively prevent hate crime and deal with its impact on communities (International Association of Chiefs of Police, 1998, pp. 3–6).

Model Management Strategy Policies

Mike Oliver, chief of police of Belmont, California, developed a hate crime management strategy in law enforcement as part of his Command College Independent Study Project for the state of California. The policies he recommended follow (Commission on Peace Officer Standards and Training, 1992).

Policy one.   The establishment of an antiracist, antidiscrimination, pro-conflict-resolution posture on the part of law enforcement, including the following components:

1. *Police department mission statement.* The mission statement should articulate the department's antiracist, antidiscrimination, pro-conflict-resolution posture.
2. *Written hate crime policy.* A written policy should be developed that addresses the department's antiracist, antidiscrimination, pro-conflict-resolution posture; the departmental expectations regarding responses to hate crime incidents; and the departmental expectations regarding response to hate crime victims.
3. *Complaints.* Procedures should be instituted that ensure citizen complaints of bias and prejudice on the part of departmental employees are thoroughly and vigorously investigated.
4. *Formal resolution.* The police department management staff should encourage the mayor/council to issue a resolution that outlines the antiracist, antidiscrimination, pro-conflict-resolution posture of the city, and encourage the community to report all criminal and noncriminal hate-related incidents to the police department.

Policy two.   The establishment of a workforce education program to include:

1. *Hate crime.* To educate employees regarding the department's antiracist, antidiscrimination, pro-conflict-resolution posture, and the expected response to hate crime incidents and victims of hate crime.
2. *Cultural awareness.* To foster an understanding of and sensitivity toward the diverse cultures in the community.
3. *Conflict resolution.* To assist employees in managing the variety of disputes confronting them in performance of their duties.

Policy three.   The establishment of a cooperative hate crime prevention effort with other law enforcement agencies to include:

1. *Intelligence gathering.* The police department should gather and maintain information regarding organized hate groups and local hate crime activity.
2. *Networking.* The police department should develop a program of regular meetings with other law enforcement agencies to share hate-crime-related information.

Policy four.   The establishment of a cooperative hate crime prevention effort with the community using the following tactics:

1. *Community task force.* The police chief should appoint a task force of police department, community, religious, school, and victim advocate leaders that would meet regularly to share and discuss hate crime and related community concerns.

2. *Race relations officer (community relations officer).* A command officer should be appointed to be the liaison between the police department and minority and community groups. This officer should serve on the community task force and should investigate all noncriminal hate-related matters as well as all complaints of bias made against police department employees.

3. *Recruitment.* The police department should make every effort to recruit qualified minority candidates and to promote qualified minority officers.

4. *Community activities.* The police department should develop a program encouraging all employees to become involved in community activities.

Policy five. The establishment of a cooperative hate crime prevention effort with the schools. The purpose is to develop and implement programs that educate students about hate crime and build bridges between the student population and the police department. Suggested programs include:

1. *Police and Community Together (PACT).* A program that couples a police officer and a social studies teacher at the middle and high school levels to instruct hate crime and cultural awareness issues.

2. *Adopt-a-Cop.* A program that involves classes of sixth-grade students who "adopt" a police officer volunteer for the school year. The officer spends one or two hours per month in the classroom, addressing hate crime and cultural awareness issues as well as other issues of importance. Since hate crime is perpetrated primarily by teenagers and young adults, this policy targets the majority of that population.

Policy six. The police department should ensure that the citizens of the community are informed of the positive and innovative hate crime strategy that has been developed and implemented. An understanding of the cooperative partnership formed among the police department, other law enforcement agencies, the community, and the schools is imperative for the strategy to be successful. pp. 21–25

The Command College project of Robert Shusta, captain in the Concord, California, Police Department, entitled "The Development of a Model Plan for Cities Experiencing Multicultural Impact," contained many of these same recommendations. It included the following important elements as well:

1. *Chief executive.* Police executives must speak out publicly on these issues and make certain that people inside and outside of the department know that hate/bias crimes, discrimination, and racism reduction or elimination is a high priority. The chief executive should create a values statement for the organization that stresses the philosophy of the organization to protect and support the doctrine of individual rights.

2. *Human relations commissions.* Cities and counties should establish human relations commissions where they do not exist. Law enforcement agencies should report both criminal and noncriminal racial incidents to the local human relations commission, as they occur, and they should follow up with the final disposition of each incident.

3. *Dispositions.* Law enforcement should quickly and effectively communicate its investigative action and final disposition of racial crimes to victims of these crimes and to citizens who file complaints of police misconduct.

4. *Victim assistance.* Law enforcement and victim advocates need to provide immediate, practical assistance and support services to victims of hate violence.

5. *Interpreter programs.* Law enforcement must identify interpreters within the agency as well as community resources for language translations for emergency situations and planned interviews.

6. *Media utilization.* Marketing the reduction or elimination of discrimination and racism should involve use of the media. Law enforcement and the community

should work with local newspapers, radio, and television to develop public education programs on cultural events, information exchange, and racial and cultural issues. The media must be sensitized to the minority communities, their culture, and their heritage. Sensationalistic journalism regarding persons of color, ethnic background, religion, and sexual orientation must be discouraged.

7. *Legislation support.* Criminal justice executives should become actively involved in supporting local, state, and national legislation to improve race relations, reduce crimes motivated by hate or bias, and assist victims in their recovery.

8. *Law enforcement computers.* Law enforcement should expand its utilization of computers to track hate/bias crimes (including those who use the Internet to recruit members for supremacist groups and to espouse hate doctrines), gangs, and crimes involving minorities and immigrants as victims or perpetrators. pp. 32-34

Free or low-cost resources for teaching tolerance are also available from the Southern Poverty Law Center (www.splcenter.com/teachingtolerance/tt-mainbtm.html). The organization began the Teaching Tolerance project in 1991 in response to an alarming increase in hate crime among youth. A number of other guideline handbooks are available for teaching about hate crime. An excellent source of instructors' material, including videotapes, is available from the National Organization of Black Law Enforcement Executives (e.g., *Hate Crime: A Police Perspective Training Manual,* published in 1991). There are also specific courses available from most states' Peace Officer Standards and Training (POST) that cover such subjects as hate crimes guidelines for agency policy and training, hate crime investigation, sexual orientation guidelines, cultural diversity guidelines, and culture-specific courses (e.g., Muslim, Jewish, American Indian). The IACP is also a source of training material and roll-call videotapes about hate crime investigations and officer training. Its guidebook *Responding to Hate Crimes: A Police Officer's Guide to Investigation and Prevention* highlights the essential components of an effective response for police officers who are the first to arrive at the scene of a bias crime. The book outlines steps for authorities to take to preserve the evidence, approaches to assisting victims, and strategies for preventing hate violence. IACP also provides a pocket guide that is an easy reference for officers. Information is available via the Internet (www.theIACP.org). The Center for Democratic Renewal (CDR) in Atlanta, Georgia, a national organization assisting community-based groups to fight prejudice and hate crimes, developed a handbook, *When Hate Groups Come to Town,* in 1995. In addition, CDR has published other materials related to responding to hate groups and should be contacted for more information. The Justice Department has developed an excellent new hate crime training curriculum for law enforcement officials and continues to fund training opportunities across the country. (For further information, contact the U.S. Department of Justice Response Center at 800-421-6770.) The Anti-Defamation League (ADL) has developed a number of hate crime resources and prevention initiatives. The ADL has a wide range of information available via the Internet (www.adl.org).

In recent years, some progressive law enforcement agencies have developed strategies to address the problems of hate violence. Some of these strategies have become models for others in the criminal justice system, with the most successful approach involving the whole community. A few of the more notable contributions recognized as models by the U.S. Department of Justice have been the Boston Police Department and the Baltimore, Maryland, County Police Department.

SUMMARY

Racism and crimes motivated by hate are two of the most challenging issues confronting the United States today. Our nation is one whose ancestry includes people from around the world who are guaranteed the rights to be free of discrimination and violence. Yet we continue to witness incidents of hatred manifested in violence toward people perceived as "different." Racism and the resulting hate violence, bias treatment, and discrimination cause divisions between people and deny them their dignity. Racism is a disease that devastates society. Police officers should be at the forefront in the battle to combat such criminal behavior within society. Law enforcement must lead in the protection of human and civil rights of all citizens.

The presence of hate/bias crimes and incidents is often attributed to changing national and international conditions, immigration, and ethnic demographic change translated to a local environment. As immigrants, persons of color, or persons of different religious beliefs or sexual orientation move into previously unintegrated areas, increased threat of hate/bias crimes can be expected. The efforts of communities in the confrontation of these issues along with law enforcement agencies is critical. It is not just a problem for the criminal justice system, but rather must be addressed jointly by schools, business, labor, and social services. In taking the lead, law enforcement agencies can motivate other groups to join with them in their efforts to reduce hate violence.

Progress toward tolerance among peoples, mutual respect, and unity has been painfully slow in our country and marked with repeated setbacks. Criminal statutes and civil remedies to curb the problem in various jurisdictions across the nation have also been enacted slowly. Divisive racial attitudes, anti-immigrant sentiment, the increased number of hate/bias incidents, and the deepening despair of minorities and the poor make the need for solutions even more pressing.

DISCUSSION QUESTIONS AND ISSUES*

1. *Hate/Bias Crimes and Incident Reduction.* Make a list of how you would design a community-based program to reduce the number of hate/bias crimes and incidents in your area.

2. *Move-in Violence.* Discuss in a group setting what strategies might be used by a community to reduce the impact of move-in violence on a new immigrant.

3. *Victims of Hate/Bias Crimes or Incidents.* Have you been the victim of a hate/bias crime or incident? Share the experience with others in a group setting: the circumstances, the feelings you experienced, how you responded, and what action was taken by any community-based agency or organization.

*See Instructor's Manual accompanying this text for additional discussion issues and questions.

REFERENCES

Anti-Defamation League. (1991). *1990 Audit of Anti-Semitic Incidents.* New York: Anti-Defamation League of B'nai B'rith, Civil Rights Division.

Anti-Defamation League. (1999). *1999 Audit of Anti-Semitic Incidents.* New York: Anti-Defamation League of B'nai B'rith, Civil Rights Division.

BERRILL, KEVIN. (1986, October 9). Testimony before the House Judiciary Committee's Subcommittee on Criminal Justice: Second Session on Anti-Gay Violence, Serial no. 132.

BERRILL, KEVIN. (1992). *Dealing with the Criminal Justice System.* Washington, D.C.: National Gay and Lesbian Task Force.

BORGQUIST, DARYL. (2000, December 27). Media affairs officer, U.S. Community Relations Service, Washington, D.C., personal communication.

California Attorney General's Commission on Racial, Ethnic, Religious, and Minority Violence. (1986, April). *Final report.* Sacramento, CA.: Author.

California Office of Criminal Justice Planning. (1989). "Emerging Criminal Justice Issue. When Hate Comes to Town: Preventing and Intervening in Community Hate Crime." *1,*(4), 1.

DEES, MORRIS. (1987, December). "Gay-Bashing Prevalent among Hate Crimes." *Klanwatch Intelligence Report,* 5.

FINN, PETER, AND TAYLOR MCNEIL. (1988, May). *Bias Crime and the Criminal Justice Response: A Summary Report.* Washington, D.C.: National Institute of Justice.

FREY, WILLIAM H. (1998, June–July). "New Demographic Divide in the U.S.: Immigrant and Domestic Migrant Magnets', " *Public Perspective, 9,* pp. 14–15.

FRITSCHE, DAVID. (1992, May). *America on Fire: The Anatomy of Violence.* Reno, Nev.: Dynamics Group.

GAMBERT, RIVA. (1993, October). Associate director of the Jewish Community Relations Advisory Council of the Greater East Bay, personal communication.

GROBESON, MITCHELL. (2000). Retired sergeant, Los Angeles Police Department, personal communication.

International Association of Chiefs of Police. (1998). *Responding to Hate Crimes: A Police Officer's Guide to Investigation and Prevention.* Available at www.theiacp.org or from the National Criminal Justice Reference Service at 800-851-3420.

Lambda Update: Civil Rights News from Lambda. (1992). "Basement Apartment Firebombing in Salem, Oregon." Washington, D.C.: Lambda Legal Defense and Education Fund.

MCDEVITT, J. (1989, September). *The Study of the Character of Civil Rights Crimes in Massachusetts (1983–1987).* Report of the College of Criminal Justice. Boston, MA: Northeastern University Press.

MCDEVITT, JACK (1993). Hate Crimes: The Rising Tide of Bigotry and Bloodshed. New York: Plenum Press.

National Asian Pacific American Legal Consortium. June 2000 report.

National Gay and Lesbian Task Force. (1986). *Anti-Gay Violence: Causes, Consequences, Responses: A White Paper by the Violence Project of NGLTF.* Washington, D.C.: Author.

National Gay and Lesbian Task Force. (1991). *Anti-Gay Violence, Victimization, and Defamation in 1990.* Washington, D.C.: Author.

National Gay and Lesbian Task Force. (1992). *A Fact Sheet on Violence against Lesbians and Gay Men.* Washington, D.C.: Author.

National Institute against Prejudice Violence. (1992, March). 10 Percent of U.S. Population Victimized, *Forum, 6* (1), pp. 2–6.

National Organization of Black Law Enforcement Executives. (1991). *Hate Crime: A Police Perspective Training Manual.* Washington, D.C.: Author.

New York State Governor's Task Force on Bias-Related Crime. (1988, March). *Final Report.* Albany, N.Y.: New York State Printing Office.

QUINDLEN, ANNA. (1992, October 27). "Gay OK? Yes or no? Bigotry Put to a Vote." *Contra Costa Times,* A-2.

SCHLESINGER, ARTHUR, JR. (1991, July 8). "The Cult of Ethnicity, Good and Bad." *Time,* p. 17.

SHUSTA, ROBERT M. (1987). "The Development of a Model Plan for California Cities Experiencing Multicultural Impact," Class IV Post Command College, Sacramento, Calif.

Southern Poverty Law Center. (1987). *"Move-in" Violence: White Resistance to Neighborhood Integration in the 1980's.* Montgomery, Ala.: Southern Poverty Law Center, Klanwatch Project.

Time Magazine (2000, March 7). "Who's Who Among American High School Students." p. 30.

U.S. Attorney General's Commission on Racial, Ethnic, Religious, and Minority Violence. (1986, April). *Final Report.* Washington, D.C.: U.S. Government Printing Office.

U.S. Bureau of the Census. (1980, 1990, 1994). *Distribution of the Population by Type of Residence and Race.* Washington, D.C.: Author.

U.S. Commission on Civil Rights, Intimidation, and Violence. (1990, September). *Racial and Religious Bigotry in America* (Clearinghouse publication 96). Washington, D.C.: U.S. Government Printing Office.

WALLACE, STEVEN. (1987). "Elderly Nicaraguans and Immigrant Community Formation in San Francisco." Unpublished doctoral dissertation, University of California, San Francisco.

WALLACE, STEVEN. (1992, November 9). Doctorial Student, personal communication.

World Almanac and Book of Facts. (1988). Mahwah, N.J.: World Almanac.

WRIGHT, ROBIN. (1993, June 8). "Ethnic Strife Owes More to Present Than to History." *Los Angeles Times.* pp. A1, 13.

WYNN, DENNIS. (1987, October). Justice Department, Community Relations Unit, personal communication

12

HATE/BIAS CRIMES:

Reporting and Tracking

OVERVIEW

This chapter discusses a nationwide reporting system and clearinghouse for hate crimes data collected from state and local police. Criminal justice leaders in every sector of the United States must have standardized and comprehensive statistics as one tool to analyze hate crime/bias trends. Using these data, they must direct their resources more effectively against crimes of hate or bias and civil rights violations. In the first section of the chapter, we define the problem and establish why data collection is important. The second section continues with a discussion of the various organizations that monitor hate crimes and hate groups. In the third section, we discuss hate crime laws including the Hate Crimes Prevention Act and the purpose of special legislation. In the fourth section, we explore conditions in communities requiring monitoring and subsequent deployment of law enforcement and community resources (community-oriented policing) that will prevent or at least reduce hate/bias crimes and incidents. The final section examines the responsibility of law enforcement officers, supervisors, and managers in reporting and tracking these crimes and the usefulness of such data in forecasting and planning. We also present methods of forecasting.

COMMENTARY

The importance of reporting and tracking crimes motivated by hate and bias is evident in the following quotes:

> In a society convulsing with change, the central need of management is for far more
> sensitive information . . . especially anticipatory information . . . about the environment

in which the [organization] must function. . . . It is important for [organizations] to know about social stresses, potential crises, shifts of population, changes in family structure, political upheavals and to know about these early enough to make adaptive decisions. (Tofler, 1985, p. 4).

Local and national responses to bias crimes continue to be severely impeded by a lack of comprehensive and cooperative data concerning the number, location, and types of bias crimes. This data would assist in evaluating the effectiveness of bias crime legislation and the need for data collection remains as pressing as ever. (National Organization of Black Law Enforcement Executives, 1991, p. 16).

Evaluate Outcomes of Prevention and Response Efforts. Ensure that all hate incidents and crimes are documented thoroughly and consistently. To assess correlation among characteristics of victims, perpetrators, and the situations in which hate crimes occur, detailed information about these variables should be routinely collected by first responders and stored in central data repositories accessible to researchers. (International Association of Chiefs of Police, 1999, p. 22).

DEFINING THE PROBLEM

Changing demographics in almost every part of the United States require that all localities deal with issues of intergroup relations. The ideal of harmony in diversity is offset by increased stress in the social fabric of a community that often leads to bigoted or violent acts. Newspaper headlines across the country provide convincing examples of disharmony on a daily basis. Hate/bias crimes are not a new phenomenon; they have been present for generations. The need for law enforcement to maintain accurate and thorough documentation of such crimes is crucial.

Data must be collected at local levels, then sent in a standardized fashion to the state and national clearinghouse so that proper resources may be allocated to hate/bias crime investigations and victim assistance. Such a system provides the necessary information not only to the criminal justice system but also to public policy makers, civil rights activists, legislators, victim advocates, and the general public. The data provide a reliable statistical picture of the problem. Agencies collecting data have been able to strengthen their arguments and rationale for new hate crime penalty enhancements. The information is used in criminal justice training courses and to educate communities on the impact of the problem. Energy must be devoted to tracking and analyzing these crimes: "A single incident can be the tragedy of a lifetime to its victim and may be the spark that disrupts an entire community" (New York State Governor's Task Force on Bias-Related Crime, 1988, p. 32).

Increased public awareness of and response to such crime has largely been the result of efforts by community-based organizations and victim advocate groups. By documenting and drawing public attention to acts of bigotry and violence, these organizations laid the groundwork for the official action that followed. It is extremely important that hate groups across the United States be monitored by criminal justice agencies. Documenting a problem does not guarantee that it will be solved, but is a critical part of any strategy to create change. Documenting and publicizing hate/bias crimes and incidents raise consciousness about the problem within the community and the criminal justice system. It is a simple but effective first step toward mobilizing a response.

HATE CRIMES DATA COLLECTION

Purpose of Hate/Bias Crime Data Collection

Establishing a good reporting system within public organizations (e.g., human relations commissions) and the justice system is essential in every area of the country. Hate/bias crime data are collected for the following purposes:

- To help police identify current and potential problems
- To assist police in responding to the needs of diverse communities
- To help with diversity recruiting
- To provide information for training of criminal justice personnel on the degree of the problem and reason for priority response

When the police have more information about crime patterns, they are better able to direct resources to prevent and resolve problems. The data can provide the information needed to develop preventive and investigative strategies. Tracking hate/bias incidents and crimes allows criminal justice managers to deploy their resources accordingly when fluctuations occur. Hopefully, this will allow an agency to deploy its resources to prevent such crimes. Aggressive response, investigation, and prosecution of these crimes demonstrate that police are genuinely concerned and that they see such crimes as a priority. As departments visibly show their commitment to addressing hate/bias crime, the diverse communities they serve will be more likely to see policing as responsive to their concerns. (A secondary benefit for a responsive agency is that blacks, Asians, Hispanics, gays, and women would be more apt to consider law enforcement as a good career opportunity.) Agencies must also make it a priority to provide training to all department personnel on hate violence and civil rights violations, including such topics as victims' needs, effective responses, and investigation methods. This education would raise awareness and hopefully lead to more apprehensions, arrests, and discipline of the perpetrators.

Agencies that implemented policies to deal with hate/bias crimes in terms of reporting, investigating, treating victims, and collecting and analyzing data during the 1980s proved to be leaders in the field. The policies and procedures of the police departments of Boston, New York, San Francisco, Los Angeles, and the Maryland State Police have been used as models for dealing with hate/bias crimes or civil rights violations.

The Boston Police Department began recording and tracking civil rights violations in 1978 when it created its Civil Disorders Unit. Boston was probably the first law enforcement agency in the United States to record and track such crimes. The Maryland State Police was also a forerunner when it began to record incidents on a statewide, systematic basis as part of a pioneering governmentwide effort to monitor and combat hate violence in 1981.

Nevertheless, some law enforcement executives have expressed two primary concerns about implementing a hate/bias data collection system. Despite the known benefits, these concerns center on

- The time and expenses associated with establishing a reporting system
- The reputation that a city or county would gain due to the collection and publicity of hate crime data (especially with increases normally attributed to more reporting)

Departments in the United States that have implemented a reporting policy in fact found few problems and associated costs. In these cases the reporting was incorporated into an existing Uniform Crime Report (UCR) system to which they already submitted data. The training of police personnel to identify, report, investigate, and resolve such crimes was the only additional expense. Furthermore, the community's image was not damaged by the typically large numbers of hate/bias crimes being reported. First, agencies collecting data utilized local media to publicize the implementation of the reporting system. The media explained that as the department encouraged victims to document these crimes, there would be an associated increase in the numbers. The increase did not necessarily mean that more community members were being victimized; rather, their reporting of the crimes and incidents simply made them known. Departments should always stress to the public that they need the information to assist them in allocating resources to address the problem effectively.

Congressional Directive: Federal Hate Crime Legislation

In response to a growing concern about hate/bias crimes, the U.S. Congress enacted the Hate Crimes Statistics Act (HCSA) of 1990. The act required the attorney general to establish guidelines and collect data "about crimes that manifest evidence of prejudice based on race, religion, sexual orientation, or ethnicity, including, where appropriate, the crimes of murder, non-negligent manslaughter; forcible rape; aggravated assault, simple assault, intimidation; arson; and destruction, damage or vandalism of property" (U.S. Department of Justice, 1990). In 1994 the Violent Crime Control and Law Enforcement Act passed by Congress expanded coverage of the HCSA to require Federal Bureau of Investigation (FBI) reporting on crimes based on "disability." The U.S. attorney general delegated his agency's responsibilities under the act to the FBI. The Uniform Crimes Report (UCR) section of the FBI was assigned the task of developing the procedures for, and managing the implementation of, the collection of hate crime data.

The national clearinghouse for hate/bias crimes data enables the criminal justice system to monitor and respond to trends in those localities that voluntarily submit the information. States and/or localities enacting legislation involving hate crime reporting in the 1970s, 1980s, and early 1990s responded more effectively than those that did not enact legislation and reduced the numbers of incidents of hate/bias in their communities.

Uniform Crime Report System

The approach adopted by the U.S. Department of Justice incorporated a means of capturing hate crime data received from law enforcement jurisdictions into the already established nationwide UCR program. The FBI had begun the process of upgrading the UCR program to collect and publish much more comprehensive data on the victims, offenders, and the circumstances of crime. Modifying the program required the addition of only a single new data element to the National Incident-Based Reporting System (NIBRS), which had the capability to flag criminal incidents as motivated by bias or hate. The U.S. Department of Justice encouraged law enforcement agencies to follow the spirit of the federal legislation and voluntarily collect data. Only 2,771 law enforcement agencies of the approximately 16,000 in the United States that participate in the UCR program submitted hate crime data voluntarily in 1991. By 1997, 21 states and the District of Columbia had passed statutes requiring collection of data on hate crimes, though their definitions and reporting requirements vary. As of 1998, 10,730 law enforcement agencies submitted hate crime data. This was a marked improvement, yet not a total, voluntary compliance and two states did not report at all. Because the number of agencies reporting hate crimes voluntarily varies each year, it is not particularly useful to compare rates of hate crimes between years. Also, hate crimes are believed to be drastically underreported because many victims do not report their attacks to police for various reasons (discussed in Chapters 11 and 13 of this text).

Almost all states lack a central repository for police intelligence on hate crimes. That means an investigator working in one city of a state might not even know about a critical piece of information gathered in another location during a different incident. In 2000 California unveiled what it called the first high-tech database in the country aimed at combating hate crimes. The state implemented a database computer system allowing police departments statewide to call up names, mug shots, and even the types of tattoos that identify particular individuals or groups linked to hate crimes.

Objective Evidence: Bias Motivation

The following is intended to assist officers in making decisions about whether a crime is bias motivated. Motivation is subjective, and therefore it may be difficult to know with certainty whether a crime was the result of the perpetrator's bias. Because of this difficulty, bias, per the HCSA, is to be reported only if investigation reveals sufficient objective facts leading a reasonable and prudent person to conclude that the offender's actions were motivated, in whole or in part, by bias. The specific types of bias to be reported are as follows (U.S. Department of Justice, 1990, p. 15):

RACIAL BIAS

> Anti-white
> Anti-black
> Anti-American Indian or Alaskan Native
> Anti-Asian/Pacific Islander
> Anti-multiracial group

RELIGIOUS BIAS

> Anti-Jewish
> Anti-Catholic
> Anti-Protestant
> Anti-Islamic (Moslem)
> Anti-other religion (Buddhism, Hinduism, Shintoism, etc.)
> Anti-multireligious group
> Anti-atheist or antiagnostic

ETHNICITY/NATIONAL ORIGIN BIAS

> Anti-Arab
>
> Anti-Hispanic
>
> Anti-other ethnicity/national origin

SEXUAL ORIENTATION BIAS

> Anti-male homosexual (gay)
>
> Anti-female homosexual (lesbian)
>
> Anti-homosexual (gays and lesbian)
>
> Anti-heterosexual
>
> Anti-bisexual

To help investigators determine whether an incident has sufficient objective facts to classify it as a hate/bias crime, the UCR provides guidelines stressing that no single fact may be conclusive. The guidelines indicate that facts such as the following, particularly when combined, support a finding of bias (U.S. Department of Justice, 1990):

- The offender and the victim were of different racial, religious, ethnic/national origin, or sexual orientation groups. For example, the victim was black and the offenders were white.
- Bias-related oral comments, written statements, or gestures were made by the offender that indicate his or her bias. For example, the offender shouted a racial epithet at the victim.
- Bias-related drawings, markings, symbols, or graffiti were left at the crime scene. For example, a swastika was painted on the door of a synagogue.
- Certain objects, items, or things that indicate bias were used (e.g., the offenders wore white sheets with hoods covering their faces) or left behind by the offenders (e.g., a burning cross was left in front of the victim's residence).
- The victim is a member of a racial, religious, ethnic/national origin, or sexual orientation group that is overwhelmingly outnumbered by members of another group in the neighborhood where the victim lives and the incident took place. This factor loses significance with the passage of time (i.e., it is most significant when the victim first moved into the neighborhood and becomes less and less significant as time passes without incident).
- The victim was visiting a neighborhood where previous hate crimes had been committed against other members of his or her racial, religious, ethnic/national origin, or sexual orientation group and where tensions remain high against his or her group.
- Several incidents have occurred in the same locality, at or about the same time, and the victims are all of the same racial, religious, ethnic/national origin, or sexual orientation group.
- A substantial portion of the community where the crime occurred perceives that the incident was motivated by bias.
- The victim was engaged in activities promoting his or her racial, religious, ethnic/national origin, or sexual orientation group. For example, the victim is a member of the National Association for the Advancement of Colored People (NAACP), participated in gay rights demonstrations, or the like.
- The incident coincided with a holiday relating to, or a date of particular significance to, a racial, religious, or ethnic/national origin group (e.g., Martin Luther King Day, Rosh Hashanah).

- The offender was previously involved in a similar hate crime or is a member of a hate group.
- There were indications that a hate group was involved. For example, a hate group claimed responsibility for the crime or was active in the neighborhood.
- A historically established animosity exists between the victim's group and the offender's group.
- The victim, although not a member of the targeted racial, religious, ethnic/national origin, or sexual orientation group, is a member of an advocacy group supporting the precepts of the victim group.

Examples of Reporting Hate Crime Incidents

The U.S. Department of Justice's report entitled *Summary Reporting System: Hate Crime Data Collection Guidelines* (which was generated after passage of the 1990 act) contains a series of examples related to the reporting of hate crime incidents. These examples are intended to ensure uniformity in reporting data to the state and the FBI's UCR Section.

Example 1. While driving through a predominantly Mexican American neighborhood, an African American male stopped his car to repair a flat tire. A group of Mexican Americans leaving a bar across the street accosted the driver and then attacked him with bottles and clubs. During the attack, the offenders called the victim by a well-known and recognized epithet used against African Americans and told him that he was not welcome in the neighborhood. This incident would be reported as anti–African American because the victim and offenders are of different races, the offenders used a racial epithet, and the facts reveal no other reason for the attack than the stated one (i.e., to keep African Americans out of the neighborhood).

Example 2. Overnight, unknown persons broke into a synagogue and destroyed several religious objects. The perpetrators left a large swastika drawn on the door and wrote "Death to Jews" on a wall. Although valuable items were present, none was stolen. This incident would be reported as anti-Jewish because the offenders destroyed religious objects and left anti-Semitic words and graffiti behind, and theft did not appear to be the motive for the burglary.

Example 3. A 29-year-old Chinese American male was attacked by a 51-year-old white male wielding a tire iron. The victim suffered severe lacerations and a broken arm. The incident took place in a parking lot next to a bar. Investigation revealed that the offender and victim had previously exchanged racial insults in the bar, the offender having initiated the exchange by calling the victim by well-known Japanese epithets and complaining that the Japanese were taking away jobs from "real" Americans. An anti–Asian/Pacific Islander offense would be reported based on the differences in race of the victim and offender, the exchange of racial insults, and the absence of other reasons for the attack.

Example 4. An adult white male was approached by four white teenagers who requested money for the bus. When he refused, one of the youths said to the others, "Let's teach this (epithet for a homosexual) a lesson." The victim was punched in the face, knocked to the ground, kicked several times, and robbed of his wristwatch, ring, and wallet. When he reported the crime, the victim advised that he did not know the offenders and that he was not gay. The facts are ambiguous. Although an epithet for a homosexual was used by one of the offenders, the victim was not gay, such epithets are sometimes used as general insults regardless of the target person's sexual orientation, and in this case the offenders' motivation appeared to be limited to obtaining money. Therefore, the incident would not be designated as bias motivated.

Example 5. A small neighborhood bar frequented by gays burned down after being closed for the night. Investigation revealed that the fire was deliberately set, but there were no witnesses or suspects. Although the fire was deliberately set, the fact that the bar was frequented by gays may have been coincidental. Therefore, the incident is not reported as bias motivated. Two weeks later, three white adult males were arrested on a tip from an informant. They admitted burning down the bar, saying they did it to keep gays out of the neighborhood. As a result, this incident should now be reclassified as a bias crime.

Example 6. Six African American men assaulted and seriously injured a white man and his Asian male friend as they were walking through a residential neighborhood. Witnesses said that the victims were attacked because they were trespassing in an "African American" neighborhood. An anti–multiracial group bias incident should be reported because the victims and offenders were of different races and witnesses reported that the victims were attacked because they were not African American.

Additional Guidelines and Examples

Following are additional guidelines for assessing whether a hate/bias crime has occurred:

1. *Need for case-by-case assessment of the facts.* The aforementioned guidelines and examples are not all-inclusive of the types of objective facts that evidence biased motivation. Therefore, reporting agencies must examine each case for facts that clearly prove that the offender's bias motivated him or her to commit the crime.

2. *Misleading facts.* Agencies must be alert to misleading facts. For example, the offender used an epithet to refer to the victim's race, but the offender and victim were of the same race.

3. *Feigned facts.* Agencies must be alert to evidence left by the offenders that is meant to give the false impression that the incident was motivated by bias. For example, students of a religious school vandalize their own school, leaving antireligious statements and symbols on its walls, in the hope that they will be excused from attending class.

4. *Offender's mistaken perception.* Even if the offender was mistaken in his or her belief that the victim was a member of a racial, religious, ethnic/national origin, or sexual orientation group, the offense is still a hate crime as long as the offender was motivated by bias against the group. For example, a middle-aged man walking by a bar frequented by gays was attacked by six teenagers who mistakenly believed the victim had left the bar and was gay. Although the offenders were wrong on both counts, the offense is a hate crime because it was motivated by the offenders' anti-gay bias.

5. *Changes in findings of bias.* If, after an initial incident report was submitted, a contrary finding regarding bias occurs, the national file must be updated with the new

finding. For example, if an initial finding of no bias was later changed to racial bias or a finding of racial bias was later changed to religious bias, the change should be reported to the FBI's UCR Section.

These guidelines are from the U.S. Department of Justice's *Summary Reporting System: Hate Crime Data Collection Guidelines* (1990). The quarterly hate crime report format, instructions, and forms for reporting hate crimes to the FBI's UCR Section can be obtained from the U.S. Government Printing Office, Washington, D.C.

MONITORING HATE/BIAS CRIMES AND INCIDENTS

Importance of Monitoring Hate Groups

Monitoring extremist groups is an important obligation of law enforcement. Activities by all these groups are tracked through a nationwide criminal justice reporting system. There are also sources of hate/bias crime data other than those agencies that voluntarily collect it; however, the statistics are not comprehensive. The data these organizations do collect confirm that bias incidents and violence against a wide assortment of peoples are on the rise.

Klanwatch

Klanwatch, a project of the Southern Poverty Law Center (Montgomery, Alabama), considers its primary responsibility to monitor white supremacist groups on a national scale and to keep track of hate crimes. The group disseminates this information to law enforcement agencies through a bimonthly publication, the *Klanwatch Intelligence Report*. The center began as a small civil rights law firm in 1971. Now it is internationally known for its hate/bias publications, tolerance education programs, legal victories against white supremacist groups, and tracking of hate groups.

Anti-Defamation League

The Anti-Defamation League (ADL) was founded in 1913 "to stop the defamation of Jewish people and to secure justice and fair treatment to all citizens alike." The ADL has been a leader of national and state efforts and has assisted in the development of legislation, policies, and procedures to deter and counteract hate-motivated crimes. The organization is also respected for its research publications and articles dealing with hate-motivated crimes. The organization developed a recording system that has served as a model of data collection nationwide since its launch in 1979.

National Gay and Lesbian Task Force and NGLTF Policy Institute

The National Gay and Lesbian Task Force (NGLTF) works to eradicate discrimination and violence based on sexual orientation and human immunodeficiency virus (HIV) status. The NGLTF was founded in 1973 to serve its members in a manner that reflects the diversity of the lesbian and gay community. In 1991 the task force was restructured into two organizations—the NGLTF and the NGLTF Policy Institute—to improve its lobbying efforts and expand its organization and educational programs. Both groups are headquartered in Washington, D.C. The task force has consistently reported increases in homophobic attacks, which it tracks.

Center for Democratic Renewal

The Center for Democratic Renewal (CDR; formerly the National Anti-Klan Network), another organization tracking bias activity, reported that there were 50,000 active hate group members and 150,000 supporters nationwide in 1990 and their numbers are rising ("Hate Group Numbers Rising" *Fresno Bee*, November 12, 1990, p. A–1). Since 1982 CDR's strategy to end bigoted violence has concentrated its efforts not only in tracking bias activity but also in educating society through publications and assisting victims by way of various programs. The organization has been active in pushing law enforcement and government agencies to use existing laws to protect people from hate violence and in helping to build coalitions to educate the public of the need for new legislation that would punish perpetrators.

Simon Wiesenthal Center

The Simon Wiesenthal Center, based in Los Angeles, is a human rights group named for the famed Nazi hunter. It monitors the Internet worldwide for tactics, language, and symbols of the high-tech hate culture. The center shares its information with affected law enforcement agencies. The organization, in some states, also operates Holocaust exhibits that are used as shocking examples of atrocities committed toward Jewish people during World War II. Police academies and in-service advanced officer training often use the exhibits for training on hate violence.

HATE CRIMES LAWS

Federal laws provide criminal and civil causes of action for victims of hate crimes in the United States, regardless of whether they are citizens. (State and local laws are not discussed in this book.) The U.S. Congress has provided criminal and civil remedies to victims of racially motivated violence. Not all acts of hate violence are prohibited by federal law. Federal statutes forbid violence by private parties only when there is an intent to interfere with a federally protected right—that is, one specifically guaranteed by a federal statute or the U.S. Constitution. Nevertheless, these rights are broad when a perpetrator's motive is tainted by racial hatred. Similar protection is provided to victims of crime when motivated by sexual orientation.

A victim of a hate/bias crime that violates a federal law can initiate criminal prosecution of the perpetrator by reporting it to a local office of the FBI. That office then assigns an investigator to the case. A victim may also contact the local U.S. attorney's office or the criminal section of the Civil Rights Division at the U.S. Department of Justice in Washington, D.C. In addition to criminal prosecution, a victim can also pursue a civil suit if the facts support a civil action under the federal statutes. The victim can seek both damages and injunctive relief in civil action against the perpetrator of violence that is motivated by racial hatred.

In general, the federal criminal statutes are intended to supplement state and local criminal laws. Procedurally, the U.S. Justice Department will not become actively involved in prosecuting a particular action until local authorities have concluded their case. After a person is convicted or acquitted in state courts, the Justice Department evaluates the end result before determining whether to prosecute under federal statutes. There is no set time within which the Justice Department makes its decision.

According to the ADL, only 11 states did not have any hate crime law as of 1999. Many states had also enacted "penalty-enhancement" statutes, which were upheld unanimously by the United States Supreme Court in June 1993 in its decision of a Wisconsin case. The Court upheld the constitutionality of Wisconsin's state hate crimes law and enhanced sentences. In upholding the law, the Court made a clear distinction between freedom of thought versus conduct in the commission of a hate crime. The test case, *Wisconsin v. Mitchell,* involved a young black man who admitted that he assaulted a white teen solely because of his race. Mitchell was convicted of aggravated battery, which carries a maximum two-year prison sentence in Wisconsin. But prosecutors invoked the state hate crimes law, which permits a seven-year sentence and Mitchell was sentenced to four years. Mitchell appealed, and the Wisconsin Supreme Court rejected the extended sentence, maintaining that the hate crimes law was unconstitutional because it infringed on First Amendment rights of free thought. The court had further reasoned that an assault is the same whether the victim is "attacked because of his skin color or because he was wearing British Knights tennis shoes." In reversing the Wisconsin decision, U.S. Supreme Court Justice Rehnquist acknowledged that the only reason for the longer prison sentence was Mitchell's discriminatory motive in choosing the victim.

Penalty enhancements are legal when the defendant intentionally selects his or her victim based on the victim's race, religion, national origin, sexual orientation, or gender. Many states have also enhanced criminal penalties for vandalism aimed at houses of worship, cemeteries, schools, and community centers.

Hate Crimes Prevention Act

In 1999 the Hate Crimes Prevention Act (HCPA) was submitted to the 106th Congress. The intent of the legislation was to eliminate gaps in the federal authority to investigate and prosecute bias-motivated hate crimes. As of September 2000, the bill had still not become law. It had passed the Senate but not the House of Representatives, and state and local law enforcement officials were still playing the primary role in the prosecution of hate violence. The federal government had the authority to address only a limited number of cases, either because the crimes have a particular federal connection or because local officials are either unable or unwilling to handle the case effectively. Present law empowers federal authorities to intervene only when a crime is motivated by race, religion, or national origin and at the time the crime is committed the victim is engaged in a "federally protected activity." Such activity includes voting, serving on a jury, going to work, or enrolling in or attending public school. In addition to adding the new categories, the legislation would eliminate the protected activity requirement for federal intervention. The HCPA would expand and strengthen existing federal hate crimes laws in two ways. Under current law, 18 U.S.C. Sec. 245, the government must prove both that the crime occurred because of a person's membership in a designated group and because the victim was engaged in certain specified federally protected activities aforementioned. Second, the HCPA would authorize the Department of Justice to assist local prosecutions and, where appropriate, investigate and prosecute such cases. Some opponents of the bill said it would provide "special protection" for gays and lesbians. It became a political campaign issue during the elections in November 2000 (Federal Hate Crime Response Initiatives: 2000 ADL report).

Why Special Legislation?

Some law enforcement leaders argue that there is no need for special legislation dealing with hate/bias crimes because there are already statutes and laws covering the specific crime or crimes committed by the perpetrator. For example, an assault by one person on another is prosecutable in all jurisdictions. Therefore, the argument runs, why would such an assault be prosecuted differently even if it was motivated by a person's hate or bias toward victims because of their color, ethnic background, religion, or sexual orientation? Localities and states headed by leaders with this perspective have no system for identifying, reporting, investigating, and prosecuting hate/bias crimes. Thus there are deficiencies in the very way most law enforcement agencies and prosecutors process hate crimes.

First, incidents are not classified by racial, ethnic, sexual orientation, or religious motivation, making it virtually impossible to tabulate hate violence acts, spot trends, and perform analyses. Second, an inaccurate characterization of certain types of hate violence crimes occurs. For example, cross burnings are variously classified as malicious mischief, vandalism, or burning without a permit. Swastika paintings are often classified as graffiti incidents or malicious mischief.

Hate/bias crime laws and penalty enhancement send a clear message to the perpetrator and the public that these crimes will not be tolerated and will be treated as serious offenses. As discussed in Chapter 11, an attack of any kind on a person because of prejudice and bigotry is reprehensible and deserves special attention and enhanced penalties. There are some key differences that make hate/bias crimes more serious than standard offenses. Crimes of this sort deny the free exercise of civil rights, sometimes frightening the victim from exercising freedom of speech, association, and assembly. Furthermore, these crimes tend to be more violent than nonbias crimes. Often, the attacks are acts of terrorism intended to punish the victim for being visible (i.e., a person who looks or acts different is easy to single out by a bigoted person). Finally, these acts against individuals are also often meant to terrorize entire communities.

TREND MONITORING IN MULTICULTURAL COMMUNITIES

Monitoring conditions in a community provides useful information for forecasting potential negative events and preparing accordingly. Futurist William Tafoya (1990) has suggested that responsible forecasting should go beyond issue identification. He and other social forecasters contend that the framework for evaluating any predictions should include an analysis of economic circumstances, social and cultural conditions, and the political environment. Tafoya warns:

> It is a grave error for law enforcement executives to dismiss social maladies as being not within their purview. These conditions constitute the setting within which police officers must daily cope. They not only exacerbate, but are breeding ground for crime, drug use and violence. It is also a mistake to sweep aside such concerns as a function of bias and bigotry alone. Indeed, racism is a major component of the problem. But there are other ingredients in the witches' brew that transforms the essence of equity today. (Tafoya, 1990, p. 21).

For this reason, most law enforcement agencies in the United States are establishing true forms of what most call community-oriented policing (COP). Enlightened police executives recognized that they had not been operating as partners with the communities and neighborhoods that they serve and began doing so. COP is the current means of accomplishing that objective.

Identifying Communities at Risk

Community profiling. Law enforcement agencies experiencing demographic changes in their communities are well advised to perform an analysis of what is taking place: community profiling. Profiling involves a demographic analysis of the community with regard to ethnicity/national origin, race, religion, and sexual orientation groups. Such a profile must include a sense of time: What can the community and law enforcement personnel expect from profiled groups with regard to the observance of holidays and religious or cultural ceremonies? For example, because they are or feel threatened, more Japanese American students miss school during the U.S. observance of Pearl Harbor Day, than any other day of the year.

Progressive agencies send out listings to their patrol officers of religious and cultural holidays and world crisis events that could affect the area they serve. If officers wait to identify at-risk communities until hate crimes are committed in their patrol neighborhood, they are not fulfilling their professional responsibilities. Knowing how to identify at-risk communities and then committing resources to resolve problems is proactive police work and is crucial to preventing conflict. While this involves more departmental time and personnel initially, the ultimate savings in terms of preventing community disruption is well worth the time.

Neighborhood and police partnership. Neighborhoods (citizens and all those institutions encompassed) together with the police are the best means of identifying communities at risk. The term *at risk* refers to communities having a high level of criminal activity or disorder and usually a higher number of incidents of civil rights violations—hate/bias crimes, discrimination, and bigotry. How does a city determine if a neighborhood is at risk? Who is responsible for the assessment? What strategies can be utilized to reduce the at-risk status? The best approach is community policing, described in Chapters 1 and 15, whereby police assist the community to protect itself and enhance the quality of life. Officers and citizens meet to discuss the neighborhoods' most serious problems and work together to resolve them.

Community policing strategies can certainly be applied to efforts to reduce racial tension. Mike Scott, director of administration at the Ft. Pierce, Florida, Police Department, said: "Officers often recognize some kind of racial tension going on in a part of their city, but they can't seem to pinpoint it. They can feel it, they can see the incidents occurring on the streets, and people whispering about it, so there's a vague sense of tension. Unfortunately, that's where a lot of officers are left hanging" (Parker, 1991, p. 11).

Community policing encourages officers to delve into such observations and feelings to determine not only what is happening but also who is involved, what their motivation is, and where they are from. To be effective, officers who patrol highly diverse areas must have some grasp of cultural awareness and cross-cultural communication. Morris Casuto (1992), director of the San Diego Regional Office of the Anti-Defamation League and instructor at both the San Diego Police Academy and the San Diego County Sheriff's Training Academy, stresses: "If officers are scrambling to understand communities only after a crime is committed, it is a terrible indictment of their lack of professionalism."

Additionally, officers must know neighborhood leaders and ways to locate them quickly in the event that they are needed to provide general assistance or to control rumors or people. Neighborhood leaders can provide invaluable help when it comes to dealing with victims who distrust police. Officers should consider themselves as first-line intelligence assets for their community. For example, they should watch for graffiti and/or other materials posted on walls, fences, telephone poles and buildings. These markings could signal an operation in progress of racists or a locally active hate group.

Rana Sampson, a community policing training coordinator for the Police Executive Research Forum (PERF), stresses that a problem-focused approach provides officers with a solid understanding of social, economic, and environmental problems in the community. Sampson stated: "When officers start understanding the problems of the community, it means they're starting to work with the community. . . . When they start working with the community, they realize that 80 percent of the people are really good. A much smaller percentage of people are actually engaged in negative behavior" (Parker, 1991, p. 12).

There are limits as to what the police can do without community help, but with many groups, they have a traditional role identification to overcome. However, when officers patrol neighborhoods daily, they can interact with citizens to engender trust and can be the best resources to monitor, report, and determine occurrences while using problem-oriented policing strategies. Herman Goldstein, University of Wisconsin law professor and the architect of the problem-oriented policing (POP) concept, said:

> The police department, more than any other agency of government, must have a bird's eye view of the dynamics within its community, including the demographics, agendas of various groups, and an in-depth understanding of the hopes, aspirations

and frustration of various groups. . . . This will give the police a feel for the mood and tensions that exist within a community. That's the first step toward dealing with racial tension." (Parker, 1991, p. 13).

Role of community human relations commissions. Many cities and counties nationwide have established community human relations commissions (HRC). Created as independent agencies, they are responsible for fostering equal opportunity and eliminating all forms of discrimination. These objectives are accomplished by means of investigating, mediating, and holding public hearings on problems that arise from discrimination prohibited by federal, state, and local laws. Most HRCs will not investigate incidents of discrimination where such a function is preempted or prohibited by state or federal legislation. In cases where there is a violation of state or federal law, the HRC refers the complainant to the appropriate local, state, or federal agency. It then monitors the progress of the complaint. Each HRC has established procedures that govern how it receives, investigates, holds hearings, and mediates or resolves complaints. Confidentiality is a protected right of the complainant in discrimination cases reported to HRCs of civil rights violations. As established by state or federal law, the names of the parties may not be made public, with few exceptions, without the written consent of both. Human relations commissions should also be part of the community–police partnership in which they all take responsibility for educating their community about its ethnic makeup. This includes serious and sustained efforts to bring people together for dialogue.

Community Relations Service (CRS). The Community Relations Service, an arm of the U.S. Department of Justice, is a specialized federal conciliation service available to state and local officials to help resolve and prevent racial and ethnic conflict, violence, and civil disorder. When governors, mayors, police chiefs, and school superintendents need help to defuse racial or ethnic crises, they turn to CRS. They help local officials and residents tailor locally defined resolutions when conflict and violence threaten community stability and well-being. Created by the Civil Rights Act of 1964, CRS is the only federal agency dedicated to preventing and resolving racial and ethnic tensions, incidents, and civil disorders. CRS gathers data in seven areas: demographic balance, administration of justice (particularly police–community relations), employment, education, housing, health and welfare, and community relationships. The statistical data are then used to assess six critical factors:

1. The relationship of minorities to the administration of justice system
2. The impact of the economy
3. The level of minorities' inclusion and/or exclusion in the system and the number of minorities serving as elected officials, as part of the system
4. The quality of intergroup relationships
5. The level of violence currently in the city
6. The basic demographic influence

It is time-consuming to perform this type of analysis and develop a program based on the findings. Police departments have access to the same kind of data and a great deal of experience and expertise to complete the same type of analysis within neighborhoods if they choose to do so.

TRENDS TO MONITOR: STEEP TYPOLOGY

The acronym STEEP stands for "social, technological, environmental, economic, and political." There is often a connection between the economy, social conditions, and politics and the numbers of hate/bias crimes that occur. The relationship among a depressed economic situation, scapegoating, discrimination, bigotry, and violence against protected classes is explained in Chapter 11. It is important for agency personnel and officers involved in community-oriented policing to understand the basic economic, social, and political issues contributing to social unrest.

Economic Circumstances

Communities monitoring economic conditions in the late 1980s and early 1990s saw a recession that touched all parts of the world. Unemployment and poor economic times were at an all-time high. Several instances of crime, social unrest, riots, and disturbances in the United States have occurred during times of depressed economic situations. New, sudden, and massive immigrations (both legal and illegal) always affect the scramble for available jobs and services. Poverty, overcrowding, and wars have been pressuring more people to migrate than ever before, laying the conditions for what the United Nations reported as "the human crisis of our age" (United Nations, 1993). In Florida, for example, waves of refugees from Cuba and Haiti flooded the state. Many areas experienced real conflict as established residents who were already struggling now had masses of people competing with them for services and jobs. California continually experiences massive immigration (both legal and illegal) from Mexico, Central America and South America. The new immigrants (the weakest group) become the target for people's frustrations as their own sense of well-being decreases. The established ethnically and racially mixed groups in neighborhoods look at what they perceive as preferential treatment for the newcomers and react accordingly: "People who come from other countries are welcomed and treated better than people who have lived here for many years," says a black leader (Preston, 1989, p. A1).

Examples of immigrant/refugee settlement in economically depressed communities by the federal government are numerous. Placement of immigrants has frequently taken place without regard to the capacity of local resources to handle the influx. Polls reflect an increase in anti-immigrant attitude—a backlash against all newcomers, especially in such economically depressed areas. Eventually, police–community problems evolve with immigrants brought in under well-meaning national policy, but policy that has not been thoroughly worked through. Tracking influxes into communities plus awareness of political decisions should alert law enforcement executives and officers to relocation and acculturation problems of newcomers in local communities. Tracking also provides an opportunity to work with the community to develop transition management plans as well as preventive programs for keeping the peace. National immigration policies and politics have a tremendous impact on cities and counties, and therefore criminal justice agencies must monitor them and plan accordingly.

John Sullivan and Henry DeGeneste (1997) wrote for *Fresh Perspectives,* a Police Executive Research Forum publication:

> Urban tensions are fueled by a combination of . . . wealth disparity and the pressures of large scale migration, which are present not only in American cities, but in cities world-wide. . . . Wright [Robin Wright, a journalist for the *Los Angeles Times*] notes, "tensions in cities are often complicated by another dimension—racial or ethnic diversity." . . . [M]inorities are increasingly left stranded in urban outskirts—slums or squatter camps—excluded politically and financially. Their ensuing frustrations contribute to the volatility of urban life. Conflict (such as riots) resulting from urban decay, over-crowding, poor social services and ethnic tension has occurred in cities [also due to per-ceptions of police abuse] world-wide and can be expected to continue, particularly as swelling, migrant populations flock to cities. (p. 2)

This situation is not unique to the United States, but also can be found in Great Britain, France, and virtually all other developed countries.

Political Environment

The criminal justice system must monitor legislation, political events, and sensitive court trials. Executives of criminal justice agencies must scan what is going on not only in the United States and the jurisdictions they serve, but also in the world. (*USA Today, Newsweek,* and *Time,* to name a few publications, are sources of information; the *Economist* offers a more comprehensive worldwide perspective.) Often what goes on in the rest of the world affects populations in the United States. Law enforcement must be aware of foreign political struggles and their potential to fractionalize ethnic and racial groups in their community, leading to conflict. Police must have the abil-ity to recognize potential problems and strive to prevent or mitigate intergroup con-flict. Only by acknowledging their primary role in preventing and mediating conflict in the community can peace officers begin to remediate long-standing and emerging tensions. The criminal justice system cannot operate as though in a vacuum.

Social and Cultural Conditions

Typically, poverty and frustration with the system, the perception of racism, and un-equal treatment are conditions for social unrest. Diverse peoples living in close prox-imity can also contribute to potentially unstable social conditions. Furthermore, on the familial level, a decline in the cohesiveness of the nuclear family (including divorce) adds to stresses to microunits in the society. Unemployment, especially among youth, is another social condition with potentially dangerous consequences. "Some authori-ties believe that an alarming proportion of youth lack basic skills necessary to compete in an increasingly technologically-oriented job market. How will the frustration and joblessness of young people manifest itself tomorrow?" (Tafoya, 1990, p. 15).

And, finally, gangs and the heavy use of illegal drugs in general and their im-pact on neighborhoods make social and cultural conditions fertile grounds for ex-plosive events. None of these elements alone, however, account for community vio-lence. But all the factors, in combination with political and economic conditions, contribute to massive discontent. Officers frequently are frustrated that they cannot undo decades of societal precursors that set the stage for upheavals.

Overreaction

Overreaction (and underreaction) by a city or county law enforcement agency can be costly in terms of the resulting perception of the criminal justice system. In San Francisco, California, when a white truck driver was beaten and robbed in 1992, police flooded the neighborhood. The perpetrators were quickly arrested and no physical disturbance occurred in the aftermath. There was, however, an emotional reaction and cynicism by some members of the neighborhood (predominantly poor black) over the sudden police presence and anger over door-to-door police sweeps. "A black girl was killed here and only one police officer came, said a resident, referring to the 1990 slaying of a 23-year-old murder witness. But a white truck driver is beaten and everybody comes. They don't come when you need them, said the resident", ("White Truck Driver Beating Causes Neighborhood Outcry," *San Francisco Examiner,* October 11, 1992, p. B-1). Perceptions such as these must be changed. Community-oriented policing is one solution, combined with performing a neighborhood-at-risk analysis.

SUMMARY

The changing demographics of our communities, coupled with a bleak economic environment, constitute significant factors resulting in an increase in crimes motivated by hate or bias. Private organizations and law enforcement agencies monitoring these trends support this conclusion. It is clear that a national, standardized data collection process is essential so that the criminal justice system and respective communities served grasp the scope of the problem and allocate resources accordingly. Such a system would enhance the prospects for developing an effective response to crimes motivated by hate or bias. Similar monitoring approaches must also be utilized by schools and businesses to ensure that acts of bigotry are tracked and resolved quickly and effectively.

Criminal justice executives must monitor and respond proactively to the negative conditions in the social, political, and economic environment. Police officers and all other representatives of the institution of law enforcement operate daily in environments characterized by extremely negative conditions. The criminal justice system represents one part of the community, however, and it alone cannot provide the answers and responses that would combat hate/bias crimes in society.

DISCUSSION QUESTIONS AND ISSUES*

1. *Hate Crimes Monitoring Systems.* Does your law enforcement agency (where you work or in the community in which you reside) have a system in place for monitoring hate/bias crimes and incidents? If yes, obtain a copy of the statistics for at least the past five years (or as many years as are available) of the hate/bias crimes and determine the following:
   (a) What trends are noticeable in each category?
   (b) Do the categories measure essential information that will assist your law enforcement agency to recognize trends?

*See Instructor's Manual accompanying this text for additional activities, role-play activities, questionnaires, and projects related to the content of this chapter.

(c) What would improve the data collection method to make it more useful in measuring trends and making predictions?

(d) Has your law enforcement agency actually used the data to track the nature and extent of such crimes and incidents? Did it deploy resources accordingly? Provide the class with examples.

2. *Trend Monitoring.* Make a list of specific community social, economic, and political conditions and events occurring within the law enforcement jurisdiction in which you work or live. Which ones, if any, could potentially be connected to crimes motivated by hate? For each condition listed, make a comments column. Suggest what specific factors a peace officer or criminal justice practitioner should look for in the community that would assist the agency in forecasting trends and events.

REFERENCES

Anti-Defamation League. (1991). *An ADL Special Report. The KKK Today: A 1991 Status Report.* New York: Anti-Defamation League of B'nai B'rith.

Anti-Defamation League. (2000). *An ADL 2000 Report: Federal Hate Crimes Response Initiatives.* New York Anti-Defamation League of B'nai B'rith.

CASUTO, MORRIS. (1992, November 2). Director of the San Diego Regional Office of the Anti-Defamation League and instructor at the San Diego Police Academy and the San Diego County Sheriff's Training Academy, personal communication.

GWYNNE, S.C. (1992, September 28). "The Long Haul" *Time,* Volume 142, No. 41, 36.

HATAMIYA, LESLIE. (1991, August). *Walk with Pride: Taking Steps to Address Anti-Asian Violence.* San Francisco: Japanese American Citizens League.

International Association of Chiefs of Police. (1999, January). *Hate Crime: Recommendations from the 1998 IACP Summit.* Alexandria, Virginia, IACP Publishers.

KLUGMAN, JULIAN. (1986, December 1). U.S. Department of Justice, Community Relations Service presentation, Concord, Calif.

National Institute against Prejudice and Violence. (1986). *The Ethnoviolence Project Pilot Study, Institute Report 1.* Washington, D.C.: Author.

National Institute against Prejudice and Violence. (1991). *Striking Back at Bigotry.* Washington, D.C.: Author.

National Organization of Black Law Enforcement Executives. (1986). *Racial and Religious Violence: A Law Enforcement Handbook.* Washington D.C.: Author.

National Organization of Black Law Enforcement Executives. (1991). *Hate Crime: A Police Perspective.* Washington, D.C.: Author.

New York State Governor's Task Force on Bias-Related Crime. (1988). *Final Report.* Albany, N.Y.: New York State Printing Office.

PARKER, PATRICIA A. (1991, December). "Tackling Unfinished Business: POP Plays Valuable Position in Racial Issues." *Police,* 19.

PRESTON, JULIA. (1989, January 18). "Trouble Spreads in Troubled Black Areas." *Washington Post,* p. A-1.

SULLIVAN, JOHN, AND HENRY DeGENESTE. (1997, July). *Fresh Perspectives.* Policing a Multicultural Community.

TAFOYA, WILLIAM L. (1990, December–January). "Rioting in the Streets: Déja Vu?" C. J. the Americas, 2(6), 21.

TOFLER, ALVIN. (1985). *The Adaptive Corporation.* New York: McGraw-Hill.

United Nations, 1993 Annual Report. Department of Public Information. UN Printing Office, New York, New York.

U.S. Department of Justice. (1990). *Summary Reporting System: Hate Crime Data Collection Guidelines.* Washington, D.C.: U.S. Government Printing Office.

WILSON, WILLIAM J. (1987). "The Truly Disadvantaged: The Inner City." In *The Underclass and Public Policy.* Chicago: University of Chicago Press. pp. 17–23.

13

HATE/BIAS CRIMES:

Investigations, Control, and Victimology

OVERVIEW

In this chapter we discuss the importance of hate crime investigations and treatment of the victims. We illustrate the need for departmental establishment of clear policies specifying responsibilities and procedures. This chapter contains a list of factors an investigator should examine to determine if an incident is hate motivated and covers information on the need for properly trained law enforcement officials to carry out investigations and prosecutions. We also discuss organized hate groups, the increase in hate activity, and response alternatives. Finally, the chapter presents model policies for follow-up investigations and ends with community programs to reduce hate crimes and incidents.

COMMENTARY

The need for quick and effective investigation and prosecution of hate/bias crimes is exemplified in the following quotations

> Victims of racially and religiously targeted incidents incur damage to their homes and property, injury to their bodies and sometimes death. In addition to physical suffering, being victimized because of one's race, religion, or national origin brings negative attention to one's differences, injures one's dignity and self-esteem, and makes one feel unwanted in the community, yet because most crimes against racial and religious minorities are not extremely violent, victims are usually not given any special attention or assistance. (National Organization of Black Law Enforcement Executives, 1985, p. 24)

> Hate crimes are anathema to a free and democratic society. The destruction and fear that these acts cause, not just for the individual victim but for an entire group of citizens,

have ramifications well beyond the actual crime itself. This is why we must vigorously investigate, indict and punish those who unleash their bigotry through cowardly acts of abuse, vandalism and violence. Local law enforcement agencies play a large role in combating and deterring hate crimes. Police training in how to identify a hate crime and how to deal with a victim's trauma is essential for an effective law enforcement response. (Former U.S. Attorney General Richard Thornburgh, in Anti-Defamation League, 1990, p. 2)

INTRODUCTION

As mentioned in Chapters 11 and 12, criminal justice agencies must make hate/bias crimes and incidents a priority response, from the initial report through prosecution. To ensure that such crimes receive priority and are treated seriously by all personnel, each agency must have a written policy that establishes what the procedures and responsibilities are within that organization. Only when policies and procedures are in place, combined with feasible community programs, will society begin to control and reduce hate crimes. Those policies and procedures define how a law enforcement agency will investigate hate/bias crimes and incidents.

HATE/BIAS CRIME AND INCIDENT INVESTIGATIONS

The following provides a basic overview of general and specific procedures and protocol that law enforcement agencies and the district attorney's or prosecutor's office should use in response to crimes and incidents motivated by a person's race, religion, ethnic background, or sexual orientation (RRES).

General Procedures

Assigned officer/first responder. When the assigned officer arrives on the scene and determines that the crime or incident may have been motivated by hate due to RRES, the officer is to

1. Stabilize the victim
2. Apprehend the responsible
3. Protect the crime scene and evidence
4. Request a field supervisor (follow department policy)
5. Conduct a preliminary investigation, including neighborhood survey for witnesses when appropriate
6. Provide assistance to the victim and refer to the appropriate legal or service agency
7. Collect and process evidence
8. Complete an offense report form and code as an RRES
9. Complete report with supervisor approval prior to end of the shift; direct copies to required division commanders and follow-up unit

Patrol field supervisor. Upon arrival at the scene of an RRES crime or incident, the patrol field supervisor is to

1. Assist in the stabilization of the victim
2. Interview the officer receiving the complaint
3. Verify that the crime or incident is an RRES
4. Determine if additional personnel are necessary and ensure that evidence collection occurs
5. Take steps to see that the situation does not escalate or recur
6. Supervise the preliminary investigation
7. Assure the victim that a total investigation will be conducted
8. Ensure that all physical remains of the crime or incident are removed after processing of evidence is completed; if the remains cannot be removed (i.e., paint on walls), the supervisor will attempt to impress on building or property owners the need for complete restoration as soon as possible
9. Notify the watch commander or senior supervisor on duty
10. See that all reports are properly completed and submitted prior to the end of the shift
11. If appropriate, provide for increased patrol in the area for as long as necessary, but at least for several days following the crime or incident
12. Identify training needs relative to RRES crimes or incidents

Watch commander. After being notified of an RRES crime or incident, the watch commander should

1. Report to the scene immediately if the crime or incident is determined to be serious
2. Notify appropriate persons or units, such as the command duty officer, investigations, or specialized unit responsible for follow-up, depending on the nature and seriousness of the crime or incident
3. Ensure that the chief of police or deputy chief is notified of serious crimes or incidents
4. Determine whether press releases should be made or that the press information officer is notified
5. Review all reports completed by patrol officers and/or field supervisors prior to their submission

Assigned investigator or specialized unit. After being notified of an RRES crime or incident, the investigator(s) should

1. Check an extended neighborhood area to identify and interview witnesses when appropriate
2. Coordinate investigative work and evidence analysis with the crime scene investigations unit
3. Conduct surveillance and other techniques to identify and apprehend perpetrator or perpetrators
4. Coordinate victim assistance with appropriate legal or service agency
5. Maintain liaison with original reporting officer to keep him or her informed of the status of the case
6. Keep the victim informed through personal contact regarding case status
7. Prepare case for prosecution and refer to the district attorney's office

Crime prevention, community relations, or specialized unit. After being notified of an RRES crime or incident, the crime prevention, community relations, or specialized unit should

1. Perform appropriate administrative follow-up investigations to resolve noncriminal incidents that were motivated by RRES
2. Conduct public meetings; meet with neighborhood groups, residents in target areas, and other groups to allay fears; reduce the potential for counterviolence; and provide safety and protection information
3. Assist victims and their families
4. Establish liaison with formal minority organizations and leaders
5. Provide preventive programs, such as antihate seminars for schoolchildren

Training unit. After being notified of an RRES crime or incident, the training unit should

1. Include human and cultural relations training programs in both in-service and advanced officer training programs
2. Use minority and community leaders' input for development of cultural awareness, human relations, hate/bias crimes, and other types of training programs
3. Prepare bulletins pertinent to cultural and human relations subjects
4. Ensure that all officers attend assigned cultural and human relations in-service courses; those failing to attend shall be identified to division commanders and remedial training provided
5. Review and revise training programs to reflect changes in the community and in society
6. Assist field training officers in development of appropriate recruit training that deals with cultural awareness, human relations skills, and information

Specific Procedures for Patrol and Investigative Officers

The preceding information is a generic listing of responsibilities associated with first responders and units that deal, in some capacity, with hate/bias crimes or incidents. From this outline, and using guidelines available from federal and state organizations (or police and sheriffs' departments with model protocols), specific procedures should be developed and implemented at each agency.

Models for Investigating Hate/Bias Crimes

The following are suggested guidelines for law enforcement agencies without standardized protocol for follow-up of hate/bias crimes and incidents. The suggested formats are based on the size of the department.

Small department (agencies of 1 to 100 sworn). A small department may not have the staffing depth to have a specialized unit or investigator who can deal solely with hate crimes. Officers in small departments are usually generalists, meaning that they carry any type of case from the initial report through the investigation and submission to the district attorney. Therefore, all personnel should receive cultural and racial issues awareness training and learn the requirements of handling crimes and incidents motivated by hate. The officer who takes the crime or incident report must have it approved by his or her supervisor. Some small departments have allowed patrol officers to specialize in the investigation of certain crimes; they might be involved in either providing advice and direction or actually taking the case and handling it to its conclusion. These officers are usually the ones allowed to attend training and conferences that will teach and update them on the investigations of these crimes and incidents. Some departments have a patrol supervisor perform the follow-up investigation and submit the case to the prosecutor's office. It is important that the officer and his or her supervisor keep command officers informed of major cases. Small agencies with a detective follow-up investigations unit must be sure that they are trained in aspects of dealing with crimes motivated by hate.

Medium-sized department (agencies of 100 to 500 sworn). The following is a model suggested for a medium-sized department with a crimes-against-persons investigations unit and an administration unit responsible for community relations or affairs. The format follows this protocol: The responding patrol officer takes the initial report and decides if what occurred was indeed a crime or incident motivated by hate or bias and then completes a preliminary investigation. Then the officer documents the findings on the department offense report form and follows the policy and procedure as established by the agency. The report (which may or may not already be classified as a hate/bias or civil rights violation, depending on department policy) is approved by the officer's supervisor and watch commander. Then it is forwarded to the investigations unit that follows up on such cases (usually the crimes persons unit). The report is reviewed by the investigations unit supervisor, who again evaluates whether a crime or incident did or did not take place. If it is decided that it is an RRES crime, the report is assigned to a crimes persons investigator who specializes in this type of investigation.

A copy of the report is also forwarded (through the appropriate chain of command) to the administration or community relations unit for follow-up. The staff of the latter unit is also trained to handle hate/bias and civil rights violations investigations and to provide victim assistance. The administrative follow-up would include

- Investigations required
- Referrals and support for the victim
- Conducting of public meetings to resolve neighborhood problems
- Conflict resolution
- Liaison with the diverse organizations in the community and victim advocates

Some cases may require that the criminal investigator and administrative officer work jointly to resolve the crime or incident under investigation.

Large departments (agencies of 500 plus sworn). Most large departments have enough staff and the need for a specialized unit. There are many advantages to having a specialized unit that focuses on crimes motivated by hate/bias or civil rights violations. The investigators become familiar and experienced with the law and special procedures required and can handle more complex, sensitive cases. Investigators who are allowed to specialize can form networks with victim advocate organizations and other community-based agencies. They work closely with the district attorney's office (probably with a special bias unit within that agency), establishing the working relationships and rapport important to successful prosecutions. The investigators develop a sense of pride in their efforts and a commitment to provide a competent investigative and victim assistance response. Since the primary function of the unit is hate/bias crime investigations, officers can sometimes develop a knowledge of individuals and groups that commit such offenses and become more aware of where the incidents occur. Detectives in departments who handle a multitude of cases do not have the time to track and monitor these crimes and therefore may not spot trends. Specialized units can evaluate the field performance of the patrol officers who have handled such crimes and can provide suggestions for improvement or commendations when the response has been effective or innovative.

There are disadvantages to specialized units. Often, when there is a specialized unit, patrol officers believe that what is happening in the neighborhood in which they work is not their problem—it is the problem of the specialized unit. The officer takes reports and transfers responsibility for resolution of problems identified to the specialized unit. Patrol officers may be unaware of a problem or its magnitude or even what resources are being marshaled to resolve it unless there is good communication between them and the members of the specialized unit. The disadvantages are surmountable, however, especially if the department uses community-oriented policing strategies. Community-oriented policing usually involves a higher degree of communication among agency units and with the community.

One Model Hate Crime/Civil Rights Violations Investigative Unit

The Boston Police Department established its Community Disorders Unit (CDU) in 1978. Lieutenant Detective William Johnston (1992), commander of the unit, explained: "staff for the unit are selected for their investigative and people skills and not for their ethnicity, race, or sexual orientation. They are police officers first!"

CDU investigators receive 2.5 days of training on laws and procedures, then work within the unit reviewing policy, protocol, and cases, before receiving a caseload of their own. The unit has a central file clipboard that is mandatory reading for all members of CDU each workday, as it contains a summary of all civil rights violation cases received. The unit has two shifts that cover 17 hours per day five days per week and are on call after hours and on weekends for major cases.

According to department policy, the uniformed officer taking the preliminary report does not make a decision as to whether the incident is a civil rights violation (hate/bias crime). He or she establishes what took place, gathers evidence, takes statements, makes an arrest if possible, then simply checks a box on the report form routing the case to the Community Disorders Unit. The officer must also notify the patrol supervisor, who in turn alerts his or her superiors. In major cases, the CDU is also apprised of an event that might be a civil rights violation. The supervisor of the CDU decides whether the case involves this type of violation covered by the state statute. Above Lt. Johnston's desk, however, is the following sign:

> Neither the victim, the perpetrator, the local detectives, the CDU investigator, the Commander of the CDU, the Police Commissioner, the Mayor, nor any other mortal creature determines whether an incident is a civil rights violation.

Only the facts gathered during a competent, thorough investigation make that determination!

Johnston believes it is unfair to have the officer make a decision because he or she has too many other responsibilities at the crime scene during the preliminary investigation and not enough time or expertise. "Let the experts do it," explains Johnston.

The Community Disorders Unit's primary function is to investigate thoroughly all cases involving an alleged civil rights statute violation. They may then seek complaints in court and assist in the prosecution of such cases. In cases in which a responding patrol officer has made an arrest on another criminal charge unrelated to the civil rights violation, Community Disorders Unit personnel, after follow-up investigation, may seek additional complaints under the Massachusetts Civil Rights Law. CDU members are active in the community; they attend various meetings and are continually networking and aware of what is occurring in neighborhoods.

The department has been in the forefront of designing innovative, proactive strategies, many of which are described elsewhere in this part of the book, to deal with civil rights issues. CDU members have been involved in training and/or providing their protocol to other agencies.

HATE/BIAS CRIME PROSECUTION

District Attorney's Office

Many district attorneys' offices in the United States now have attorneys and/or units that specialize in hate crime prosecution. These agencies have established policies and procedures designed to effectively and efficiently prosecute such crimes. There are compelling reasons for district attorneys to devote special attention and resources to these crimes. The chief of community services of the Norfolk County, Massachusetts, district attorney's office wrote:

> A prosecutor has discretion to influence, if not determine, what might be called the public safety climate that citizens in the communities he serves will experience. . . . To establish a public safety climate that fosters the full enjoyment of civil and political rights by the minority members of our communities requires a focused political will directed to that end as well as resources and capacity. (Agnes, 1989, p. 3)

The most effective and successful approaches that build a climate of public safety have been those that

- Established specialized hate crimes or civil rights violations units
- Standardized procedures to prosecute hate crime cases (this standardization should include vertical prosecution of cases)
- Appointed attorneys to be liaisons with various ethnic, racial, religious, and sexual orientation groups in the community
- Provided all attorneys on staff with cultural awareness or sensitivity training

Prosecutors Offices That Target Hate/Bias Crime

District attorneys' offices with specialized hate/bias crime or civil rights units that can serve as models are the following:

San Francisco District Attorney's Office Hate Crimes Unit
Hall of Justice
850 Bryant Street
San Francisco, CA 94103
415-552-6400

Suffolk County District Attorney's Office Civil Rights Unit
New Courthouse
Pemberton Square
Boston, MA 02108
617-725-8600

Queens County, New York, District Attorney's Office
Anti-Bias Bureau
125-01 Queens Boulevard
Kew Gardens, NY 11415
718-286-6598

Special Problems in Prosecuting Hate/Bias Crimes

Attorneys who handle hate/bias crimes indicate that there are four potential obstacles to successful prosecutions:

1. Proving the crime was motivated by bias
2. Uncooperative complaining witnesses
3. Special defenses
4. Lenient sentences

It is often difficult to identify hate-motivated crimes or incidents accurately. Usually, no single factor is sufficient to make the determination, and sometimes the incident is disguised by the perpetrator such that it does not appear to be a hate/bias crime. Even cases that have been well investigated may lack sufficient evidence to prove that the crime was motivated, beyond a reasonable doubt, by hate or bias. Generally, prosecutors follow established guidelines for determining whether a crime was bias related. Criteria such as the following are assessed:

- Plain common sense
- The language used by the perpetrator
- The severity of the attack
- Lack of provocation
- History of similar incidents in the same area
- Absence of any apparent motive

The National Attorneys Association developed a comprehensive desk manual for prosecutors for identifying, responding to, and preventing hate violence. The desk manual contains information about case screening, investigations, trial preparation, and sentencing alternatives. The manual could be useful in the development of a training curriculum specifically designed for prosecutors.

Despite some difficulties in these prosecutions, the experience of the previously mentioned district attorneys' offices suggests that targeting these cases is the most productive approach to combating crimes motivated by hate or bias. District attorneys can play a major role in educating judges on the nature, prevalence, and severity of hate violence crime and in encouraging effective sentences for this offense. They can also be very effective in their working relationships with and encouragement of police officers investigating these crimes. The effort involves each member of the criminal justice system, but the prosecutor has one of the most important roles.

Special defense is sometimes argued. One such example is the "homosexual panic" or "gay advance" defense, in which the person charged with an attack claims self-defense or temporary insanity in response to a sexual advance. This sort of defense, on occasion, has resulted in lenient sentences or acquittals.

In an unprecedented move, a judge ruled in September 2000 that two white supremacists members of a criminal street gang suspected in a vicious Sacramento, California, hate crime are eligible for enhanced penalties under a new state law. California enacted the Terrorism Enforcement and Prevention Act, which adds time to the sentence of those convicted under its provisions. The two suspects, members of the World Church of the Creator, faced 15 years in prison instead of 7 for an unprovoked attack wherein they beat, almost to death, a 16-year-old minority high school student.

HATE/BIAS CRIME AND INCIDENT CONTROL

Hate/bias crimes and incidents can be controlled only through the combined efforts of the community (schools, private organizations, government agencies, churches, service organizations, and families), federal and state legislatures, and the criminal justice system. This holistic approach is examined in Chapters 11 and 12. It is also important to profile communities to determine if they are at risk of strife or conflict caused by social, economic, and environmental conditions that result in such crimes and incidents. According to national and regional statistics, juveniles commit approximately 50 percent of all hate crimes in which the perpetrators are known. This fact must be addressed within all communities. There must also be monitoring of the Internet because it has now become the communication medium of choice for the new generation of haters. In addition, it is essential to investigate (including the use of informants, surveillance, and infiltration), monitor, and control organized hate groups. The aggressive prosecution and litigation against these groups is also critical.

Organized Hate Groups

Understanding hate groups is essential when policing in a multicultural society. Loretta Ross, Program Research Director of the Center for Democratic Renewal based in Atlanta, Georgia, summarized well the urgent need to address and effectively deal with the presence of hate groups in America:

> America has moved into a new era of white supremacy. The new tactics used by white supremacists and far right organizations must be exposed so that we can work together to mitigate their effectiveness. . . . The ground-breaking progress gained by the civil rights movement of the 1960s in the United States has steadily eroded over the past decade, and the issues and incidents of racism as well as anti-Semitism, homophobia, and violence against women are ones that need to be addressed with increasing urgency. (Ross, 1995, p. 1)

Birch Bayh, in a *Newsweek* article entitled "Let's Tear Off Their Hoods: The Increasing Violence by the KKK and Other Right-Wing Hates Adds Up to a Record of Shame," wrote:

> To those who are startled to hear that the KKK is alive and well, one can only ask, Where Have You Been? Have no doubt about it, the Klan—which lynched helpless black Americans, murdered civil-rights workers, burned its crosses and spread its divisive venom of prejudice across the land—has not disappeared. It continues to hawk its poison to anyone who will listen. To make matters worse, the Klan today has been joined by other harbingers of hate such as the Skinheads, the Aryan Nations, Posse Comitatus, the Covenant and the Sword, the Arm of the Lord, White Aryan Resistance (WAR) and the strident right-wing political cult of Lyndon LaRouche. (Bayh, 1989, p. 8)

There are similarities among the mentioned groups, not the least of which is that each organization's bigotry and prejudice are based on religion, race, ethnicity, and sexual orientation. No two groups are the same, however. They range from the seemingly innocuous religious sects or tax protesters to openly militant, even violent, neo-Nazi skinheads and Ku Kluxers. In most cases, no single organization or person dominates a particular movement. Frequently individuals are members of several different groups at the same time. Many sources confirm that white supremacism is on the rise due to increases in certain hate group membership. The Intelligence Report by the Klanwatch indicated that record numbers of white supremacist groups were active from coast to coast in the 1990s.

Although the numbers of white supremacists in America are small in comparison with the total population, their influence should be recognized. According to Ross (1995)

> Because the percentage of whites who actually belong to white supremacist groups is small, there is a general tendency to underestimate their influence. What is really significant is not the number of people actually belonging to hate groups, but the number who endorse their messages. Once known primarily for their criminal activities racists have demonstrated a catalytic effect by tapping into the prejudices of the white majority. (p. 7)

Defining the White Supremacist Movement

The Center for Democratic Renewal (CDR, 1992) published *When Hate Groups Come to Town: A Handbook of Effective Community Responses,* wherein it defines the white supremacist movement:

> The white supremacist movement is composed of dozens of organizations and groups, each working to create a society totally dominated by white Christians, in

which the human rights of lesbians and gay men and other minorities are denied. Some groups seek to create an all "Aryan" territory; others seek to re-institutionalize Jim Crow segregation. (p. 41)

The Southern Poverty Law Center (SPLC), located in Alabama, tracks active hate groups in the United States. In 1999 the organization identified 457 active hate groups by gathering information from their publications, citizens' reports, law enforcement agencies, field sources, and news reports. The number of groups known to be active was determined by surveying marches, rallies, speeches, meetings, leafleting, published literature, and criminal acts. Some white supremacist groups consist of only a few members, while others have tens of thousands.

SPLC divided the hate groups identified into six categories or types: Ku Klux Klan, neo-Nazi (which includes Aryan Nations and World Church of the Creator), racist skinhead, Identity, black separatists, and other. The "other" classification consists of 82 other groups that have similar ideologies of hate but that do not fall under the aforementioned major categories. The largest of these are the Council of Conservative Citizens and the National Association for the Advancement of White People. Both of these organizations have chapters in many states across the nation.

Neo-Nazis and Klans

Concern about the activities of neo-Nazis and Klans should be obvious from the following:

[Midwest. 1994–95] Members of the white supremacist Aryan Republican Army go on a seven-state crime spree, leaving behind pipe bombs as they rob 22 banks from Nebraska to Ohio. (Kaplan et al., 1998, p. 17)

[Wise County, Texas. April 1997] Federal officials arrest four Ku Klux Klan members who plan to blow up a natural-gas refinery and use the disaster as cover for an armored-car robbery. (Kaplan et al., 1998, p. 6)

[San Diego. 2000] The FBI tape-recorded Robert Nichol Morehouse, 53, telling an unidentified FBI informant how he might kill Morris Casuto, San Diego's regional director of the Anti-Defamation League, set fire to a synagogue and shoot down an airplane. . . . [T]he FBI set out to investigate a Lemon Grove–based group of white supremacists for sweeping allegations of "domestic terrorism" and civil rights violations. ("Domestic Terrorism Alleged in Lemon Grove," *San Diego Union Tribune,* December 11, 2000)

According to SPLC, in 1999 there were about 138 different Ku Klux Klan and 130 neo-Nazi groups in the United States, some of which have chapters in multiple states. The largest neo-Nazi and Klan groups include the following:

Neo-Nazi-Type Groups	Klan-Type Groups
Aryan Nations	Alabama White Knights of the KKK
Knights of Freedom	America's Invisible Empire Knights of the KKK
National Alliance	American Knights of the KKK
Nationalist Socialist Movement	Imperial Klans of America
World Church of the Creator	Invincible Empire Knights of the KKK
	Knights of the White Kamellia
	New Order Knights of the KKK
	White Shield Knights of the KKK

The ideology of Klan members, neo-Nazis, and other white supremacists has been clear since the formation of these groups. They commonly advocate white supremacy, anti-Semitism, homophobia, and racism.

During the 1950s and 1960s, about a dozen Klan groups in America had membership totaling about 100,000, with units, or klaverns, in every state, in Canada, and in overseas military posts. Research by the Anti-Defamation League (1991) established that there had been "a ten year decline in the nationwide strength of the Ku Klux Klan" (p. 13). This decline of Klan membership continued through the 1990s; however, whereas its membership decreased, that of neo-Nazi and racist skinhead organizations increased. Some speculate that membership may be the result of violent civil unrest and/or riots, when some whites look for protection in numbers. The Klan also lost membership as a result of counteractions by law enforcement, civil rights groups actions (including successful lawsuits), and internal power struggles.

> Torches of the Ku Klux Klan, perhaps the most dreaded group to march on U.S. soil, no longer ignite terror across the nation. They have no organization. The back of the organized Klan is broken [due to successful lawsuit verdicts] and it will never come back. (Loh, 1994, p. A9)

While there is evidence that Klan groups are on the decline, there has been an increase in membership in neo-Nazi, Hitler-inspired groups including the National Alliance and the World Church of the Creator. The Klan is not currently well organized and has few members, most of whom are isolated. Yet some observers of hate groups think that the hard-core members are going underground and continuing their operations but avoiding the spotlight.

The most violent group is that of neo-Nazi skinheads, and their movement is growing in the United States (as of 1995, they had approximately 3,500 members) and in countries such as Germany and Austria. Young people from 13 to 25 are required to commit a hate crime as part of an induction into the organization. They openly idealize Hitler. In the 1990s they were responsible for nearly one-fourth of all bias-related murders in the United States. They have committed murders and hundreds of assaults and other violent crimes; most of their victims are African Americans, Latinos, Asian Americans, gays and lesbians, and the homeless.

World Church of the Creator (WCOTC). The World Church of the Creator, classified as a neo-Nazi-type group, was founded in 1973 by Ben Klassen. Its existence ended in mid-1990 by a combination of the suicide death of Klassen and the imprisonment of other leaders. In 1996, however, the WCOTC was reborn and has again become "America's most dangerous white supremacist group. . . . Based in Florida and North Carolina, the World Church of the Creator has been recruiting violent Skinheads from all across America. The group's rallying cry is 'Rahowa,' which stands for RAcial HOly WAr" (World Church of the Creator America's Most Dangerous Supremacist Group *Southern Poverty Law Center Newsletter,* September 21, 1992, pp. 42–44). They are also violently anti-Christian.

In 1993 members of this group plotted to start a race war in Los Angeles by machine-gunning parishioners of a major black church in southeast Los Angeles and planned an assassination of prominent civil rights leaders. Klassen, according to the *Southern Poverty Law Center Newsletter,* described Adolph Hitler as an " 'astute' political leader and 'the greatest man the White Race has ever produced. . . . The most important step we can take is to cleanse our racially polluted society,' and that a race war is 'the only and ultimate solution' to the Jews and 'mud races' that he believed were a threat to the white race." In July 1999 WCOTC member Benjamin Smith committed suicide after killing two and wounding eight Asians, blacks, and Jews over a three-day shooting spree. At the end of 1999, the WCOTC was said to have 31 chapters and claimed 9,000 members, although civil rights groups place membership at 200.

Aryan Nations and The Order.   The group Aryan Nations was formed in the early 1970s and operates out of Northern Idaho. It is considered primarily an identity group but also embraces neo-Nazi philosophy. The organization preaches that God's creation of Adam marked "the placing of the White Race upon this earth," that all non-whites are inferior, and that Jews are the "natural enemy of our Aryan (white) race" (Berkowitz, 1999). Aryan Nations was severely damaged by the $6.3 million verdict against the notorious hate group, its leader, Richard Butler, and three former members in September 2000. The verdict was for an assault on an innocent mother and son, mistakenly believed to be part of a Jewish conspiracy that had targeted Aryan Nations. This assault took place near the organization's 20-acre Idaho compound. Steps were being taken in late 2000 to seize the assets of the Aryan Nations as a result of the verdict.

During the early 1980s, an organization called the Silent Brotherhood, also known as The Order, was created and its members planned to overthrow the U.S. government. To raise money for its planned revolution, The Order engaged in a crime spree involving murder, counterfeiting, bank robberies, and armored-car holdups. The death of its founder in a shoot-out with federal officers in 1984 and incarceration of many members ended the group's revolutionary existence. However, the group is still very active on the Internet (Berkowitz, 1999).

The National Alliance.   A neo-Nazi group, the National Alliance, believes it is part of nature and subject to nature's laws only; therefore, members are able to determine their own destiny. They profess that those who believe in a divine control over mankind absolve themselves of responsibility for their fate. They also believe that they are members of the Aryan (or European) race and are superior to other races.

Racist Skinheads

Membership by young adults in racist skinhead groups in the United States has mushroomed since 1986, "growing . . . from just 300 nationwide to a peak of perhaps 3,500 in 1991" (Center for Democratic Renewal, 1992, p. 46). The SPLC identified 40 different racist skinhead groups active in the United States in 1999. Because skinheads are migratory and often not affiliated with groups, SPLC indicates their numbers are hard to assess.

The influence of adult white supremacist groups on racist skinheads and neo-Nazi skinheads has been substantial. The youth participate in adult hate group rallies and show a great deal of solidarity with them(World Church of the Creator

America's Most Dangerous Supremacist Group *Southern Poverty Law Center Newsletter,* September 21, 1992, p. 46). Skinhead groups have developed their own leadership and appeal, distinct from adult Klan and neo-Nazi groups (Ross, 1995). The adult hate groups seek to replenish their membership ranks from the racist skinhead groups.

According to the CDR, although most skinheads (easily recognized by their closely shaven heads) are explicitly racist, some have banded together to oppose bigotry—Skinheads against Racial Prejudice (SHARP). However, these skinheads do not represent the majority and have very little, if any, substantial influence on others.

T. J. Leyden, a former skinhead now working with the Simon Wiesenthal Center's Task Force against Hate, says that he did some of his most successful recruiting (for membership in white supremacists groups) on U.S. military bases. As a Marine, he would "target young, scared white kids who just wanted a group to fit in with." Lately, Leyden says, he has seen white power groups backing off from recruiting full-time active-duty military. Instead, the groups are pushing their young recruits to join the National Guard units. "It's just one weekend a month, and it's a lot easier to hide their racist sentiments that way" (Johnson, 2000, p. A14).

In November 2000, five skinheads who admitted an attempted firebombing (using a Molotov cocktail) of a synagogue were sentenced to up to 15 years in prison. All five self-proclaimed white supremacists, ages 19 to 26, agreed to plead guilty to federal hate crime and bombing-related charges that kept them from maximum sentences of up to 30 years. Photographic evidence of their Reno, Nevada, home (which served as the group's "clubhouse") showed walls covered with Nazi flags and hate material ("Reno Skinheads Sentenced," *San Diego Union Tribune,* November 7, 2000).

Identity

Identity describes a religion that is fundamentally racist, anti-Semitic, and antihomosexual. According to the Southern Poverty Law Center, as of 1999, there were 46 active Identity groups across the United States organized under different names but with similar ideologies. "Because many of its core beliefs are now held by members of different Klan and Neo-Nazi organizations, Identity binds the movement across the country" (Center for Democratic Renewal, 1992, p. 41). The goal of Identity groups is to broaden the influence of the white supremacist movement under the guise of Christianity. They form their views of diverse people based on a particular interpretation of the Bible. For example, they may say that "it teaches that people of color are pre-Adamic, that is not fully human and are without souls. Identity followers believe that Jews are children of Satan and that white people of northern Europe are the Lost Tribes of the House of Israel"(World Church of the Creator American's Most Dangerous Supremacist Group *Southern Poverty Law Center Newsletter,* September 21, 1992, pp. 42–44). The movement takes the position that white Anglo-Saxons—not Jews—are the real biblical "chosen people," and that blacks and other nonwhites are "mud people" on the same level as animals and therefore are without souls (Berkowitz, 1999). Identity followers believe that the Bible commands racial segregation. They interpret racial equality as a violation of God's law.

Christian Identity.   One Identity group is the Christian Identity. Followers of this belief, founded in California by Wesley Swift after World War II, use the Bible as the source of their ideology. It is a quasi-theological movement of small churches, tape and book distribution businesses, and radio ministries.

Posse Comitatus.   Another Identity group is Posse Comitatus, which means "power of the country" in Latin. The group is antitax and anti–federal government. The Posse believes that all government power is rested in the county, not at the federal level.

Christian Patriots.   The followers of this Identity group belong to many different organizations, all of which espouse white supremacy. The core beliefs are as follows:

- White people and people of color are fundamentally two different kinds of citizens, with different rights and responsibilities.
- The United States is not properly a democracy, but a republic in which only people with property should vote.
- Democracy is the same as "mobocracy," or mob rule.
- The United States is a Christian republic, with a special relationship between Christianity and the rule of law.
- Internationalists (usually identified as Jews) and aliens (sometimes identified as Jews, sometimes as immigrants and people of color) are attempting to subvert the U.S. Constitution and establish one-world socialism or, alternatively, the New World Order.
- The Federal Reserve banking system is unconstitutional and a tool of the "International Jewish Banking Conspiracy." (Center for Democratic Renewal, 1992)

Black Separatist

The SPLC in 1999 identified 21 black separatist groups active in the United States under two different names: the House of David and the Nation of Islam. Black separatist groups are organizations whose ideologies include tenets of racially based hatred. Black separatist followers share the same agenda as white supremacists of racial separatism and racial supremacy. The two movements also share a common goal of racial purity and a hatred of Jews. One example of a black separatist, militant organization espousing hatred of Jews is the Black African Holocaust Council (BAHC). BAHC, based in Brooklyn, New York, was established in 1991. Membership is restricted to African Americans and Native Americans. The organization publishes a monthly magazine, the *Holocaust Journal,* which is replete with anti-Semitic and antiwhite rhetoric. BAHC holds monthly meetings and conducts weekly lectures and study groups on antiwhite or anti-Semitic issues. On the first weekend of every November, the council holds what it calls the Black African Holocaust Conference in honor of ancestors who were victims of the slave trade. Although the Council denies it, observers of the organization have connected it with the Nation of Islam. Cornel West, a noted scholar and philosopher, wrote of the Nation of Islam and black supremacist doctrine:

> The basic aim of Black Muslim theology—with its distinct Black supremacist account of the origins of white people—was to counter white supremacy. Yet this preoccupation with white supremacy still allowed white people to serve as the principal point

of reference. That which fundamentally motivates one still dictates the terms of what one thinks and does—so the motivation of a Black supremacist doctrine reveals how obsessed one is with white supremacy." (West, 1993, p. 99)

In the past, there has been collaboration between black separatists and some white supremacist groups. Ironically, in the 1960s, Tom Metzger, leader of the White Aryan Resistance, attended meetings and rallies of black separatists and Nation of Islam to endorse their anti-Semitic propaganda. In 1985 Metzger attended a Farrahkan rally in Los Angeles:

> He later told *The Washington Post* that "People should not be surprised" by his support of [Nation of Islam]. "They're the black counterpart of us. According to Metzger, representatives of Farrakhan had invited him to the rally. . . . *The Washington Times* reported that Farrakhan and Metzger had formed an alliance to promote their racial-separatist, anti-Jewish ideologies." (Anti-Defamation League, 1994)

Despite the differences between black extremists and white supremacists groups and their mutual contempt, these groups are able to join rhetorical forces to demean and slander Jews.

White Supremacists and the Political Arena

C. T. Vivian, 1992 chairperson of the Center for Democratic Renewal, highlighted the increase in the numbers of white supremacists attempting to gain political power through electoral campaigns by sponsoring and supporting candidates who advocate their beliefs. The most notable example was former Klansman David Duke, who had won a seat in the Louisiana state legislature in 1989. He then made a bid for the Louisiana senate and governorship in 1990 and ran for president of the United States in 1992. He lost all three races but was able to convince 55 percent of Louisiana's white population to vote for him for governor. While still in the legislature, he continued to sell neo-Nazi literature and he founded the National Association for the Advancement of White People (described as a Klan without robes). Duke had promoted himself as a defender of white rights who must act on their perceived group interests as whites.

Vivian expounded: "Even if they [hate mongers] lose every election, their politics have gained a new currency that we long ago had hoped was forever devalued. It is important to remember that white supremacists' commitment to the niceties of electioneering is tactical, not long term. Their goal is still to replace the hope of democracy and pluralism with the fear of racism and bigotry" (Vivian, 1992). Research by the CDR illustrated that Duke and his organization, the National Association for the Advancement of White People, raised and spent about $5 million on campaigns between 1989 and 1991.

The early 1990s witnessed leaders of the two largest Klans instructing their followers to restrain from racist rhetoric and to avoid implication in violent crimes. They wanted to avoid criminal prosecution or civil lawsuits while selling their ideology and exploiting national issues such as affirmative action, immigration, drugs, and acquired immunodeficiency syndrome (AIDS) to their advantage (Boland, 1992). The more militant supremacist groups, however, did not agree with the peaceful and political approaches and continue to advocate armed revolution and violence. They remain a threat and concern for law enforcement and communities.

The ADL and other authorities tie the economy to white supremacist movements and popularity in the United States. "The economy is the key. If it's bad, then everyone is looking for scapegoats, and the white supremacists are happy to oblige. They point to immigration, to affirmative action, and tell white people that is where the jobs have gone" (Rosenfeld, 1992). These authorities agree that when the economy is bad, middle-class, mainstream people seem to look for scapegoats, and some listen to the white supremacist message and either sympathize or even, overtly or covertly, join the movement. This same phenomenon occurred before and during World War II in Germany, resulting in the extermination of 13 million "hate crime victims" (e.g., Jews, gypsies, gays, the mentally ill). White supremacists who appear respectable and reasonable, as we have seen in the past, can gain support politically when large numbers of people are dissatisfied with the economy and believe that minority groups are responsible.

Response Alternatives to Organized Hate Groups

Departments must actively work to fight and control organized hate groups, tracking their activities, establishing when they are responsible for crimes, and assisting in their prosecution. Intelligence gathering is crucial to efforts to reduce and prevent hate/bias crimes. Equally important is networking and sharing hate group activities information with other criminal justice agencies. Many have called this approach a cross-disciplinary coalition against racism. It involves state and regional commitments by criminal justice agencies with other public and private entities. All the institutions jointly develop and implement components of multitiered intervention strategies targeting enforcement, education, training, victim assistance, media relations, political activism and advocacy, and ongoing self-evaluation.

The fight begins with an understanding of the size and scope of the various supremacist groups, their movements, and their publications. The effort includes having a knowledge of their leaders so that organized, multitiered responses can be developed. In 1993 there were bombings at the offices of the National Association for the Advancement of Colored People (NAACP) in the states of Washington and California by members of a skinhead organization. At about the same time, the Federal Bureau of Investigation (FBI) broke up alleged plots among white supremacists, one to launch a race war in Los Angeles by placing a bomb in a prominent black church and the other to kill Rodney King. Such ongoing incidents demonstrate the need to continually monitor, investigate, and prosecute the persons and organizations responsible. When hate crimes of this magnitude are perpetrated against one group in the community, law enforcement must immediately alert any potential organizations that may also be targeted. The Jewish community was critical of law enforcement when a synagogue in Sacramento, California, was firebombed. Community leaders felt that warnings should have been disseminated after an NAACP headquarters in Tacoma was bombed and another in Sacramento gutted by arson. One synagogue president pointed out: "Had we learned [about the NAACP bombing] . . . we would have notified all other congregations, the NAACP and other minority organizations. . . . This was something that could have potentially been prevented if law enforcement had the sensitivity, the direction and the competence to advise us" (Jewish Community Critical of Law Enforcement Lack of Notification, *San Francisco Chronicle,* July 29, 1993, p. A-20).

One example of networking on the West Coast is the Bay Area Hate Crimes Investigators Association (BAHCIA), which provides training on hate crimes investigations and disseminates information on crimes, hate groups, and individuals active in their respective jurisdictions. Membership includes persons who specialize in hate crime cases from law enforcement, district attorneys, public agencies, and private organizations from the nine Bay Area counties. The association was formed "to address the dramatic increase in the incidence of hate violence, and the special needs of law enforcement officers and investigators who work on hate crime cases." The association bylaws mention that the mission of BAHCIA is to establish a cooperative effort among local, state, and federal agencies, with the purpose of eliminating hate crime in the greater Bay Area. Besides monthly meetings, it sponsors annual Hate Crimes Investigators' Conferences. (Contact the San Francisco Police Department Hate Crime Unit at 415-553-1133 for more information.)

Law enforcement leaders should be aware of and consider the implications of black, Hispanic, Asian, homosexual, or Jewish officers being requested to provide protection to an organized hate group whose history of bigotry and violence have included the officers' own groups. Supervisors must be sensitive to the difficult and frustrating position into which these officers are placed. The CDR publication *When Hate Groups Come to Town: A Handbook of Effective Community Responses* (1992) offers some excellent material for understanding the various movements, their leaders, response strategies, and resources.

The Future of Organized Hate Groups

Organizations and officials tracking hate groups have offered predictions on the evolution and future of hate groups. Groups that have traditionally shunned or actively opposed each other for ideological reasons will join forces against their "common enemies." For example, Tom Metzger of White Aryan Resistance, a "pure racist" who has always shunned religion, has been associating with Christian Identity groups such as Aryan Nations (Anti-Defamation League, 1999). As mentioned, black separatist groups have associated with white supremacist groups.

Another disturbing trend is the age and gender of new recruits to supremacists groups. New members are younger than in the past (including teenagers) and many are young women. Organized hate is no longer the exclusive domain of white men over 30 years of age. Loretta Ross wrote an article for the *Public Eye,* sponsored by Political Research Associates in Massachusetts, titled "White Supremacy in the 1990s." She wrote that

> Since the 1980s, women have joined the racist movement in record numbers. . . .
> This new and dangerous increase accounts for nearly one-third of the membership
> of some hate groups. The increase in the number of women, coupled with a strate-
> gic thrust to reform the public image of hate groups, has expanded women's lead-

ership. These new recruits do not fit the stereotypical image of wives or their husbands' arms. In fact, many of them are college-educated, very sophisticated, and display skills usually found among the rarest of intellectuals of the movement.

The Internet has become the medium of choice for recruiting young members for hate groups and for deciminating hate dogma:

> The Internet is giving old-fashioned bigotry a new lease on life, enabling people to spread hate instantaneously and anonymously around the world, says a Jewish organization that tracks anti-Semitism. It makes available, to a potential audience [of millions], their messages of hate and seeks to recruit today's affluent and educated youth to their cause ("Bigotry Online Now a Threat Group Says," *Contra Costa Times,* February 27, 1997, p. A3).

The Southern Poverty Law Center (2000) also emphasizes the danger of the Internet:

> There are now over 250 million people on the worldwide Web with 150,000 more signing up everyday. Increasingly what they find when they log on is hate. The gospel of hate is being projected worldwide, more cheaply and effectively than ever before, and it is attracting a new demographic of youthful followers to the Neo-Nazi movement. (p. 7)

As of September 2000, SPLC was tracking over 350 hate sites, including some specifically targeting women and children. SPLC has developed its own Web site (www.splcenter.org) with a special cyber campaign, "Hate Hurts," about the impact of hate. The Internet provides the hate group the ability to send unwanted mass e-mailings simultaneously into millions of homes. These Web sites entice viewers with on-line games, comic strips, and music or simply a friendly pitch from another kid. College and university sites are being bombarded with messages and lures from such groups. The Internet in some areas is also being used to provide tips on how to target groups' opponents with violence.

It is also predicted that white supremacists will continue to commit traditional crimes (e.g., cross burnings, vandalism) but will also venture into high-tech activities such as computer system infiltration and sabotage. Their political activism will include "white rights" rallies, protests, and demonstrations; election campaigns by racist candidates; and legislative lobbying. These activities are expected to incite countermovements and will create very labor-intensive situations for law enforcement to handle (Rosenfeld, 1992).

Observers of hate groups have also noted the shift of tactics by white supremacists in the United States. Discovering that supremacists no longer could effectively recruit members using the ideology of open racism with the focus on persons of color, Jews, immigrants, and the like, they are now targeting lesbians and gays. Loretta Ross wrote that hate groups since the mid-1990s have been refocusing their energies because

> They are worried that they can never convince the majority of white Americans to join them in their netherworld. While many whites may share their prejudices, very few are willing (any longer) to act on them by openly carrying a Klan calling card or an Uzi. This situation demands a new strategy that combines old hatreds with new rhetoric. White supremacists desperately need to reinvigorate their movement with new recruits by manipulating white fears into action. (Ross, 1995, p. 2)

This new approach does not imply that supremacists no longer hate people of color, Jews, and so on. Rather, it means that they are refocusing their energies; that they are exploiting white fear of change; and that they have adopted not only homophobia as a prominent part of their new agenda but also antiabortion, profamily, and pro-American values, in addition to their traditional racist and anti-Semitic beliefs. Ross says that the broadening of issues and the use of conservative buzzwords have attracted the attention of whites who may not consider themselves racist but do consider themselves patriotic Americans concerned about the moral decay of "their" country.

Jury verdicts against supremacists groups also lead to predictions about their future actions. For example, a $6.3 million jury verdict on September 7, 2000, against the Aryan Nations caused this violent racist group to go underground. SPLC, which led the prosecution of Aryan Nations, now predicts that the group will split into small terrorist units and utilize the Internet to continue recruiting, galvanizing, and inspiring their members to commit violent hate crimes independent of a larger organization. "The victory by SPLC founder Morris Dees against an organized hate group will drive more violent racists underground and turn them into what the movement has staked its future on: individual domestic terrorists bent on action" ("Hate Group Changes Tack After Court Loss," *Contra Costa Times,* September 17, 2000, p. A15). Federal and local law enforcement officials have long been aware of the ability of the Internet to galvanize and inspire hate group adherents to action.

Community Programs to Reduce and Control Hate/Bias Crimes

Some solutions to reduce hate/bias crimes involve going back to basics. Programs or solutions must involve grassroots institutions: families, schools, workplaces, and religious organizations. Partnerships between the criminal justice system and these institutions are often more successful in crime reduction programs than is the criminal justice system alone. However, some institutions that once built positive values or exercised some control over people are no longer working or have diminishing influence. The broken or dysfunctional family, for example, contributes significantly to society's problems, including the increase in criminal activity.

An effort must be made to reinstitute values that reinforce noncriminal behavior; law enforcement must be an integral part of that movement. The status quo policing approach (reactive) will not work anymore. "People have clearly begun to recognize that our strict law enforcement arrest approach isn't getting the job done,"(personal communications with Shusta, December 2000) says Darrel Stephens, former executive director of the Police Executive Research Forum. Progressive criminal justice executives and communities realize that crime has many complex causes and that police departments are not the first or only line of defense. They conclude that if crime is to be controlled, there must be a community alliance or partnership and that the causes must be attacked from multiple fronts.

Generic Community Resources and Programs

Following are examples of community resources and programs that can be established:

1. *Hot line:* Similar to those available for domestic violence and rape victims and suicide prevention. The staff is trained to provide victim assistance in terms of compassion, advice, referrals, and a prepared information package.

2. *Human relations commission:* Established in many cities and/or counties that have staff available to assist victims of hate crimes or incidents and hold hearings and provide recommendations for problem resolution.

3. *United States/State Department of Justice Community Relations Unit (**Community Relations Service [CRS]**):* With headquarters in Washington, D.C., the CRS has 14 regional and field offices and provides services to every state in the United States. The Justice Department has trained staff who, when notified of a problem, will participate and mediate in community meetings in an attempt to resolve conflicts. These units are not an investigative or enforcement body. Created by the 1964 Civil Rights Act, they are the only agency that Congress has assigned the task of providing direct help to communities to resolve disputes, disagreements, and difficulties relating to discriminatory practices based on race, color, or national origin. Their staff will respond when requested by state or local officials or citizens and organizations. They may also assist on their own initiatives when they perceive that a community requires help. They occasionally get referrals from state and federal courts. The triracial, bilingual CRS staff have knowledge of, and experience in, techniques of racial and ethnic dispute resolution. They assume the role of a neutral third party and apply conciliation and remediation techniques to settle the problem. CRS has also effectively worked with state and federal correctional institutions, helping them to develop and train prison conflict response teams to mediate individual and group conflict. Many states have similar justice agencies that perform these services.

4. *Conflict resolution panels:* Included are specially trained staff of city or county employees who can assist agencies and/or victims (including groups) in the resolution of conflict, such as that caused by hate or bias.

5. *The media:* Cooperation in building public awareness on the problem of hate/bias violence via articles on causes and effects, resources, and legal remedies is essential.

6. *Multilingual public information brochures:* Provided by government agencies on the rights of victims, services available, and criminal and civil laws related to hate and bias.

7. *Storefronts:* Police substations, established in the neighborhoods of communities with high concentrations of ethnic minorities, that are staffed by bilingual officers and/or civilians. The staff takes reports and provides assistance to the members of that community.

8. *Community resource list:* List of organizations that specialize in victim assistance. Examples are the Anti-Defamation League of B'nai B'rith, Black Families Associations, Japanese-American Citizens Leagues, the National Association for the Advancement of Colored People, and the Mexican-American Political Association, to name a few. National organizations that might be contacted as a resource are listed in Appendix C. The importance of having established networks with minority leaders and organizations cannot be overstressed. These leaders are extremely important for criminal justice agencies and should be identified and cultivated in advance to assist in a timely fashion with investigations, training, victim aid, and/or rumor control. If an agency experiencing serious hate/bias problems does not react quickly and effectively, victims and their community groups gain media attention because they publicly question an inadequate response or resolution. Only when a system involving trust and respect is already in place will such a network

prove its worth when violence occurs in the agency's community. A good relationship with representatives of diverse communities is essential because it can help broaden the department's (sworn and nonsworn personnel's) understanding of different cultures, ethnicities, and races. The same is true of members of gay and lesbian groups. When community members are utilized within departments, they can also help convince reluctant victims and/or witnesses to cooperate with investigators. Furthermore, they can encourage more victims to report incidents.

The key to a successful law enforcement response to hate crimes is building a partnership with victimized communities. There are many components and processes in building such a partnership. Other activities and events characterizing a joint effort would include educating the public at large, providing organizational networking opportunities, monitoring the media, and implementing federal, state, and county programs. The activities for each are described in the following sections.

Educating the public at large.   Prejudice and bias, which can ultimately lead to violence against someone of a different racial, ethnic/national origin, religious, or sexual orientation group is often the result of ignorance about the group targeted. In many cases there has been little or no firsthand exposure by persons with bias to the racial, cultural, religious, and/or sexual orientation group from which to base their understanding; thus the bias may be due to learned stereotypes and negative media images.

One key to combating ignorance is to educate the public at large as well as criminal justice system employees about the history, diversity, cultures, languages, and issues of concern of the various groups within the community. This can be accomplished through neighborhood forums, workshops, and speakers' bureaus. The speakers' bureaus would be composed of groups of people prepared and well versed on the issues who would be able to speak at community meetings, schools, and other forums. Criminal justice employees, of course, would be trained in the workplace and/or in training courses offered in service or at an academy. Most cities and counties have organizations that represent community-based groups that can assist in developing and implementing such education at local elementary and secondary schools, in churches, and on college and university campuses. The education presented (via speakers, videos, pamphlets, and so forth) should be factually correct and should not stereotype or caricature the community. (To check the accuracy of material presented, organizers of educational programs should have at least two or three minority community members provide input on the content of the program delivered. Preferably, they would represent the different subgroups within the community.) Neighborhoods and communities should be encouraged to observe their various heritages through the celebration of holidays and other special days via fairs and festivals. Calendars show that there are more holidays for different religions and cultures in the United States than anywhere else in the world: Chinese New Year, St. Patrick's Day, Cinco de Mayo, and Kwanzaa, to name a few.

Organizational networking.   National and local organizations must network to share information, resources, ideas, and support. A few of the organizations would include the NAACP, the ADL, the Committee against Anti-Asian Violence, the

National Gay and Lesbian Task Force, and the National Institute against Prejudice and Violence. Such advocacy organizations can furnish an invaluable bridge to victim populations and assist in urging citizens to come to the police with information about hate crimes. Many of these organizations have conducted research on hate violence laws, law enforcement models, and statistics on hate violence and can provide legal assistance and emotional support to victims of hate violence. Most of these organizations have also published books and reports covering such topics as how to respond to bigotry, trends in racism, and community organizing. Through networking, organizations or groups know who their allies are, increase their own resources and knowledge about other minority groups, and can form coalitions that make a greater impact on the community and the criminal justice system. They can also assist criminal justice agencies in dealing with community reactions to hate violence and help the victims of violence cope with the experience.

One example of organizational networking involves the Phoenix, Arizona, Police Department. In 1994 a hate crimes advisory board with representation from most of Phoenix's ethnic groups was created. The knowledge that members have and share about their communities' cultures and potential hot spots is highly beneficial. The board has since expanded into the Central Arizona Hate Crime Advisory Board to reflect its expansion throughout the state. The original board had 12 members but as of 1997 had grown to more than 80 participants. The board is the police department's conduit to the community. The importance of networking cannot be overemphasized. These partnerships with human rights groups, civic leaders, community leaders, and law enforcement can advance police–community relations by demonstrating a commitment to be both tough on hate crime responsibles and aware of the special needs of hate crime victims. In 1997 the Phoenix Police Department also instituted a Bias Crimes Investigations Detail.

Monitoring the media.   Minority organizations and the criminal justice system must monitor the media, which can be a foe or an ally. The media must be used strategically for education and publicity about hate/bias crimes and incidents, about multicultural and multiracial workshops, and about festivals and other cultural events. They must be monitored in terms of accuracy of reporting and must submit corrections when necessary. Negative editorials or letters to the editor pertaining to an affected group should be countered and rebutted by an op-ed piece from management within the involved criminal justice agency. Organization leaders or their designated spokespersons should become the primary sources of information for reporters to contact.

Federal, state, and county programs.   Police executives should seek out every source of federal, state, and county law enforcement assistance programs and make the information available to investigators and/or task forces investigating or preventing such crimes. Where the usual support organizations (e.g., ACLU, NAACP, ADL) do not exist, churches often are advocates for people facing discrimination and/or who are victims of a hate incident or crime. Many religious institutions are prepared to provide support and assistance. For example, the Concord (California) Hispanic Ministry acts frequently as an advocate for Latinos with tenant–landlord problems in addition to providing Spanish-language masses, family counseling, and religious classes. Jewish synagogues have always provided assistance of all sorts to their members.

The police executive must often take the lead within the community in the ambitious endeavor to implement special programs to reduce and control hate/bias crimes. Special programs must involve line officers and the average citizen in solving problems in the areas in which they live and work. The message to law enforcement and to communities not taking a proactive stance is that the status quo is not good enough anymore.

Communities with Special Programs

Some jurisdictions have used a community approach to decrease the numbers of crimes and incidents of all types, including those motivated by hate/bias. Some exemplary programs include the following:

1. *Block watch volunteers program.* The Northwest Victim Services (NVS) is a nonprofit organization created in 1981 in Philadelphia. NVS and the police of the highest-crime-rate districts in Philadelphia (the 14th and 35th) formed a partnership that utilizes the organized block watch program in that city. Carefully selected, screened, and trained block watch volunteers not only perform the usual functions of neighborhood watch (crime prevention) but also perform a vital victim assistance role. They provide emotional support for victims, who are often frightened or unfamiliar with the criminal justice process and accompany them to the various trial stages—arraignment, preliminary, and so on.

2. *Task force on police Asian relations.* In localities that have large Asian populations, task forces have been created that consist of criminal justice members, educators, victim/refugee advocates, and volunteer agencies, plus a representative of each Asian group living or working in the community. The purposes are several: to train criminal justice employees on communication techniques that improve relations and make them more effective and efficient in dealing with the Asian community; to prepare Asians on what might be expected from the various criminal justice components, especially the police; to open lines of communication between law enforcement and Asians; and to encourage Asians to report crimes and trust the police. Agencies in California that have created such task forces and that could be contacted for additional details are the San Francisco, Westminster, Garden Grove, Anaheim, Fresno, San Jose, and Huntington Beach Police Departments. These task forces could certainly be expanded to include other ethnic and racial groups as well. The city of Boston and other cities have effectively used the task force approach to resolve neighborhood problems. The results are similar to those discussed previously with regard to Asian task forces (i.e., they exchange information and curtail rumors; they identify problems and work on solutions; and, perhaps most important, they allow citizens to help with and approach problems on a joint basis).

3. *Rapid response strategy.* The Boston Police Department has a program to address any problem that shows a pattern. The strategy has been particularly effective in preventing and reducing civil rights violation crimes. The police department first identifies the problem from police reports, interviews with known victims, attendance at community meetings, and discussions with informants. If a pattern exists that includes a particular day and time for incidents, the department gathers a group of area residents together where the incident is occurring. They are asked to observe (sometimes anonymously) the vicinity in which the incidents are taking place. They are provided with a special hot line number to report activities rather than the usual police emergency line. The hot line is staffed by a police officer or civilian (with an interpreter available, if necessary), who is equipped with a walkie-

talkie. One or more unmarked police vehicles are strategically placed on the periphery of the target area, along with any other officers needed, depending on the seriousness of the crime or activity expected. Calls coming from the observer to the base station are logged, and officers are dispatched when necessary via the walkie-talkies. Response time is generally less than 2 minutes; thus many crimes are prevented and/or the perpetrator is caught in the act or shortly thereafter. The effectiveness of this approach is due to the minimum amount of police staffing required for maximum coverage and the fact that some of the burden is placed on community members, who share in their own protection.

4. *Citizens' patrol.* Following a series of attacks (including one fatal) on gays and lesbians in the Hillcrest community of East San Diego, California, the police responded by appointing a task force to investigate the crimes and provided more officers to patrol the area's streets. They also organized a citizens' patrol, whose volunteer members began driving Hillcrest's streets, watching for and reporting suspicious activity. Even when the task force was disbanded after the arrest of the suspect, the citizens' patrol remained. The patrol's membership even increased, and two-citizen teams with cellular telephones regularly drive problem-area streets. Both police and community leaders say there has been a noticeable decrease in violent street crimes and a feeling that Hillcrest is safer.

5. *Mobile crisis unit.* In 1984 San Joaquin County (the first of many in California) organized a mobile crisis unit modeled after a pioneering program in Arizona. The unit is available 24 hours a day to counsel victims at crime scenes, transport victims, console families, make referrals to social services agencies, and provide instant information on the criminal justice process. The staff monitor police and sheriff radio frequencies and respond when requested.

6. *Network of neighbors.* The human relations commission in Montgomery County, Maryland, has a "memorandum of understanding" with the police that when a hate crime occurs, the police department immediately notifies the commission. The commission in turn contacts the volunteer of the Network of Neighbors who lives closest to the victim. The network member visits the victim as soon as possible to assure the person of community support and to assist with other needs. The volunteers receive training on victim assistance and referrals. The New York City Police Department modeled a similar Good Neighbor Program after Montgomery County's Network of Neighbors.

7. *STOP program.* The Montgomery County, Maryland, office of the Human Relations Commission (OHRC) has a program that educates juvenile perpetrators of hate violence about the impact of their behavior on victims and the entire community. The program, which began in 1982, sends first offenders to the STOP program instead of through the court system. The OHRC staff requires that juvenile perpetrators and their parents attend five 2.5-hour sessions. Sessions include written and experiential exercises, discussions, films, and homework relating to their specific incident and the impact of hate and violence in general. Juveniles are also required to perform 40 hours of community service.

Such community models can play a vital role in reducing violence in neighborhoods. Successfully implemented programs can reduce individual violence, ranging from street crime to domestic abuse to drug-related crimes. Civil unrest, which can often include gang violence and open confrontations among various segments of society, can also be reduced.

> Building bonds of trust between the police and the community also allows community policing to contribute to the goal of promoting color-blind policing, where people and their police form new partnerships that offer the promise of reducing the potential for civil unrest. ("Police Build Bond With Community," *FBI Law Enforcement Bulletin,* May 1992, p. 11)

HATE/BIAS CRIME AND INCIDENT VICTIMOLOGY

For the most part, perpetrators of hate crimes commit them to intimidate the victim and members of the victim's community so that the victims feel isolated, vulnerable, and unprotected by the law. Many victims do not report their attacks to police out of fear and believe their best defense is to remain quiet.

The Criminal Justice System Response

Interest in victims of crime has increased markedly in recent years. Meaningful assistance to victims of major crimes became a priority only in the 1980s. The growth of a body of "victimology" literature and the emergence of numerous victim advocate and rights organizations began at about that time, reflecting a growing concern about crime, the victims of crime, and their treatment by the criminal justice system. The public mood or perception had become (and may still be) that the criminal justice system cares only about the defendant. The perception was that the defendant's rights were a priority of the system, while the victim was neglected in the process.

Possibly one of the forerunners of the movement to improve the system was the President's Task Force on Victims of Crime created by President Reagan in April 1982. The task force made 68 recommendations in its final report for addressing the problems of victims. The recommendations called for action by police, prosecutors, judges, and parole boards in making specified improvements in their respective operations. The preface included the following statement by the task force chairman, Lois Haight Herrington:

> Victims who do survive their attack, and are brave enough to come forward, turn to their government expecting it to do what a good government should—protect the innocent. The American criminal justice system is absolutely dependent on these victims to cooperate. Without the cooperation of victims and witnesses in reporting and testifying about crime, it is impossible in a free society to hold criminals accountable. When victims come forward to perform this vital service, however, they find little protection. They discover instead that they will be treated as appendages of a system appallingly out of balance. They learn that somewhere along the way the system has lost track of the simple truth that it is supposed to be fair and to protect those who obey the law while punishing those who break it. Somewhere along the way, the system began to serve lawyers and judges and defendants, treating the victim with institutionalized disinterest. (President's Task Force on Victims of Crime, 1982, Preface)

In 1982 the Omnibus Victim and Witness Protection Act, which, among other features, requires use of victim impact statements at sentencing in federal criminal cases, was signed into law. The legislation also provided, in federal cases, greater protection of victims and witnesses from intimidation by defendants or their associates, restitution by offenders to victims, and more stringent bail laws. In 1984 the Comprehensive Crime Control Act and the Victims of Crime Act authorized federal and state victim compensation and victim assistance programs. By 1987 more than 35 states had enacted comprehensive legislation protecting the interests of the victim, compared with 4 states before 1982.

As a result of the task force recommendations, state and federal legislation, and other research by public and private organizations (most notably the National Institute of Justice), improvements were made in victim services and treatment as well as in the criminal justice system.

Law Enforcement and the Victim

In the law enforcement field, courses in recruit academies and in-service, advanced officer programs typically include training about victimization. The training usually covers such topics as sociopsychological effects of victimization, officer sensitivity to the victim, victim assistance and advocacy programs, and victim compensation and restitution criteria and procedures for applying. Classes normally stress the importance of keeping victims informed of their case status and of the criminal justice process. How patrol officers and investigators of such crimes interact with victims affects the victims' immediate and long-term physical and emotional recovery. Proper treatment of victims also increases their willingness to cooperate in the total criminal justice process. Because of this training, the victims of hate crimes began receiving special attention and assistance in progressive cities and counties all over the country.

Victims of hate/bias violence generally express three needs: (1) to feel safe, (2) to feel that people care, and (3) to get assistance. To address needs one and two law enforcement agencies and all personnel involved in contacts with victims must place special emphasis on victim assistance to reduce trauma and fear. Such investigations sometimes involve working with people from diverse ethnic backgrounds, races, and/or sexual orientation. Many victims may be recent immigrants with limited English who are unfamiliar with the American legal system or have fears of the police rooted in negative experiences from their countries of origin.

> How immigrant and refugee communities generally perceive the criminal justice system is a principal factor in determining how best to serve those communities. These perceptions are often based upon the experiences of these groups with the criminal justice systems in their native lands. In many Asian countries, for example, there is a history of police corruption. The reporting of a crime may not only be futile but could invite unwanted and costly attention. The turmoil of war and the instability of political leadership have also dissuaded many from depending upon government institutions. (Ogawa, 1990, p. 14)

Therefore, the officer or investigator not only must be a skilled interviewer and listener but also must be sensitive to and knowledgeable of cultural and racial differences and ethnicity. He or she must have the ability to show compassion and sensitivity toward the plight of the victim while gathering the evidence required for prosecution. As with other crime victims, officers involved in the investigation must

- Approach victims in an empathic and supportive manner and demonstrate concern and sensitivity
- Attempt to calm the victim and reduce the victim's alienation
- Reassure the victim that every available investigative and enforcement tool will be utilized by the police to find and prosecute the persons responsible for the crime
- Consider the safety of the victims by recommending and providing extra patrol and/or providing prevention and precautionary advice

- Provide referral information such as counseling and other appropriate public support and assistance agencies
- Advise the victim of criminal and civil options (Concord, California, Police Department, 1988)

The stress experienced by victims of hate/bias crime or incidents may be heightened by a perceived level of threat or personal violation. Just like the victims of rape or abuse, many become traumatized when they have to recall the details of what occurred. Sometimes transference takes place whereby the victim, because of what happened to him or her, transfers his or her anger or hostility to the officer. The officer must be prepared for this reaction and must be able to defuse the situation professionally without resorting to anger himself or herself. It is imperative that investigators and officers make every effort to treat hate crime victims with dignity and respect so that they feel a sense of justice. Insensitive, brash, or unaware officers or investigators may not only alienate victims, witnesses, or potential witnesses but also create additional distrust or hostility and cause others in the community to distrust the entire police department.

Addressing the victim's need to get assistance requires that the community have established resources that can assist the victim and the victim group (e.g., gays, Hispanics). Few communities have the resources necessary to offer comprehensive victim services. Even where resources are available, victims are often unaware of the services due to poor public awareness programs or the failure of the criminal justice system to make appropriate referrals because of a lack of training or motivation. A key resource is available interpreters for non-English-speaking victims and witnesses. Ideally, jurisdictions with large populations of non-English-speaking minorities should recruit and train an appropriate number of bilingual employees. If the jurisdiction does not have an investigator capable of speaking the same language, an interpreter system should be in place for immediate callout. Victims must be informed that services for hate crime victims are available in areas where those resources are present. Victims of hate-motivated incidents are encouraged to report the circumstances to the National Hate Crimes Hotline (at 1-800-347-HATE).

Readers wishing additional information about victims can refer to *Victims of Crime,* by Robert A. Jerin and Loura J. Moriarty (1997). It is a well-developed textbook for the field of victimology that has many criminal justice applications. The first three chapters concern victims and the police, victims and the courts, and victims and corrections. The next three chapters address domestic violence, women as victims, children as victims, and the elderly as victims. Additional chapters look at nondomestic violence, sexual assault, and hate crimes.

SUMMARY

The degree to which the criminal justice system, especially law enforcement agencies, responds to acts of hate and bias intimidation, violence, or vandalism sends a message to victims, communities (especially the groups to which the victims belong), and perpetrators. If the criminal justice system reacts swiftly and effectively or is proactive, perpetrators will know that their actions will result in apprehension and prosecution and that such acts will not be tolerated. Those sympathetic to perpetrators may be deterred from similar hate/bias actions. The fears of the victims' groups will be calmed, and trust toward the criminal justice system will be established. Other members of the community who are sensitive to the impact of hate/bias crimes and incidents will also react favorably when state and federal laws are vigorously enforced. Where vigorous enforcement occurs, trust and goodwill are generated between the community and the criminal justice system, leading to long-term benefits for all.

DISCUSSION QUESTIONS AND ISSUES*

1. *Resources.*   Find out what resources exist in your community to assist victims of hate/bias crimes.
   (a) Which groups provide victim assistance?
   (b) Which coalition groups exist, and what types of community outreach programs are offered?
   (c) What types of pamphlets or other written materials are available?
   (d) Which groups have speakers' bureaus?
   (e) Which groups are working with local law enforcement agencies with regard to response programs or cultural awareness training?
   (f) Which groups are working with the district attorney's office?
   (g) What types of legislative lobbying efforts are taking place, and who is championing the work?

2. *Role of Human Relations Commissions.*   What is the role of the human relations commission (HRC) if one exists in your area?
   (a) Does it have a specific task force on hate crimes?
   (b) Does it have any type of tracking system for recording statistics on hate crime?
   (c) What is its relationship with local law enforcement agencies and district attorneys' offices regarding hate crime?
   (d) What is its relationship with community organizations concerned with hate crimes?
   (e) Has it produced any brochures, pamphlets, or other materials on hate crimes?
   (f) Does it provide multicultural workshops or sensitivity training regarding different ethnic, racial, or lifestyle groups?
   (g) Have there been occasions when the HRC has gone beyond the scope of its charter or stated goals that resulted in negative exposure or media attention? Describe the circumstances.

3. *Role of Your District Attorney's Office.*   Assess the role of your district attorney or prosecutor's office by determining the following:
   (a) Does it have a special hate crimes or civil rights unit?
   (b) Do hate crimes cases receive special attention?
   (c) Are misdemeanor and felony hate crimes processed differently?
   (d) How does the office determine if it will prosecute a hate crime case?
   (e) What types of training do assistant district attorneys receive regarding hate crimes?
   (f) What types of community outreach does the office provide regarding hate crimes?

---

*See Instructor's Manual accompanying this text for additional activities, role-playing activities, questionnaires, and projects related to the content of this chapter.

(g) Does the office take civil as well as criminal action regarding hate crimes? Does the office file for injunctions on behalf of victims?

(h) What is the office's relationship with other community groups and agencies, such as the local human relations commission?

4. ***Victim Assistance.*** Identify avenues of victim assistance in your area. Research and document the following:

(a) Does your state have a crime victims' assistance program? Does it offer victim compensation? What about a victims' bill of rights?

(b) What services does the local department of mental health offer?

(c) Do any community groups, rape crisis centers, or crime victim services agencies in the area offer counseling to hate crimes victims?

(d) Are any mental health care professionals willing to donate their services to victims of hate crimes?

A good resource for victim assistance networks in your area is the National Organization for Victim Assistance (NOVA), based in Washington, D.C. (202-393-6682).

REFERENCES

AGNES, PETER S. (1989). "Public Safety in the 80's: New Cultural Dimensions in Society. A Modern Prosecutor's Response to the Challenges Posed by Cultural Diversity," unpublished paper, Norfolk County, Massachusetts, District Attorney's Office.

Anti-Defamation League. (1990). *Hate Crime: A Training Video for Police Officers, Discussion Manual.* New York: Author.

Anti-Defamation League. (1991). *Law Enforcement Bulletin, 7, pp. 5–7.*

Anti-Defamation League. (1994). *Uncommon Ground: The Black African Holocaust Council and Other Links between Black and White Extremists.* New York: Author.

Anti-Defamation League. (1999). *1999 ADL Audit of Anti-Semitic Incidents.* New York:

BAYH, BIRCH. (1989, April 17). "Let's Tear Off Their Hoods: The Increasing Violence by the KKK and Other Right-Wing Hates Adds Up to a Record of Shame." *Newsweek*, 8.

BERKOWITZ, HOWARD. (1999, September 14). Hate on the Internet, Congressional testimony.

BOLAND, MIRA (1992, June). " 'Mainstream' Hatred." *Police Chief*, 30–32.

Center for Democratic Renewal. (1992). *When Hate Groups Come to Town: A Handbook of Effective Community Responses* (p. 41). Atlanta, Ga.: Author.

Concord, California, Police Department. (1988). "Response to Racial, Religious, Ethnic, or Sexual Orientation Complaints." *Department Training Bulletin*, 7(27). pp. 1–2.

International Association of Chiefs of Police (1999). *Responding to Hate Crimes: A Police Officer's Guide to Investigation and Prevention.* Alexandria, VA: Author.

JERIN, ROBERT A., AND LOURA J. MORIARTY. (1997). *Victims of Crime.* Chicago, Ill.: Nelson-Hall.

JOHNSON, DOUG. (2000, August 21).Former Skinhead Denounces Hate Groups, *Contra Costa Times*, p. A14.

JOHNSTON, WILLIAM. (1992, October 7). Commander of the Community Disorders Unit, Boston Police Department, personal communication.

KAPLAN, DAVID E., MIKE THARP, MARK MADDEN, AND GORDON WITKIN. (1998, January 5). "Terrorism Threats at Home." *U.S. News and World Report*, p.17.

LAH, JULES. (1994, December 18). *Contra Costa Times.* Flames of Fear Burn Out. P. A9.

National Organization of Black Law Enforcement Executives. (1985). *Racial and Religious Violence: A Law Enforcement Guidebook.* Landover, Md.: Author.

National Organization of Black Law Enforcement Executives. (1999, August). *Hate Crime: A Police Perspective Training Manual.* Washington, D.C.: Author.

OGAWA, BRIAN. (1990). *Color of Justice: Culturally Sensitive Treatment of Crime Victims* (pp. 215–216). Sacramento, Calif.: Office of the Governor, State of California.

President's Task Force on Victims of Crime. (1982, December). *Final Report.* Washington, D.C.: U.S. Government Printing Office.

ROSENFELD, HENRY O. (1992, June). "Establishing Non-Traditional Partnerships to Mitigate the Future Impact of White Supremacist Groups." Peace Officer Standards and Training, Sacramento, Calif.

ROSS, LORETTA. (1995). "White Supremacy in the 1990s." *Public Eye*, pp. 1–12.

Southern Poverty Law Center. (1987, February 5). *"Move-in" Violence: White Resistance to Neighborhood Integration in the 1980's*. Montgomery, Ala.: Author.

Southern Poverty Law Center. (1992, February). *Klanwatch Intelligence Report*. Issue 59, p. 4.

Southern Poverty Law Center. (2000, September). Klanwatch Intelligence Report Issue 99, Montgomery, Ala.

VIVIAN, C. T. (1992, May). "Bullets and Ballots in South Africa and USA." *Monitor, 25,* 2.

WEST, CORNEL (Editor). (1993). "Malcolm X and Black Rage." In *Race Matters*. New York, NY: Random House, Inc., pp. 9–13.

PART FIVE

Cultural Effectiveness for Peace Officers

14 PEACE OFFICER IMAGE AND CULTURAL SENSITIVITY
15 POLICE OFFICER PROFESSIONALISM AND PEACEKEEPING STRATEGIES IN A DIVERSE SOCIETY

Part Five concludes this volume by highlighting some of the themes from previous chapters, while discussing broad concepts on the emerging role of peace officers within a twenty-first-century multicultural society. The chapters analyze these changes primarily from the perspective of altering the reader's image of law enforcement and understanding the impact of this shift on one's behavior as a public servant. We examine why those who serve the public are expected to be more cosmopolitan—that is, more tolerant and less ethnocentric in their outlook and dealings with citizens—than in the past. Chapter 14 reinforces the meaning of cultural sensitivity and provides a model for understanding cultural differences.

Chapter 15 considers peace officer professionalism and peacekeeping in a diverse society by first defining and presenting the interwoven concepts of leadership, professionalism, and synergy. The analysis focuses on cooperation in statewide and regional law enforcement. One section links professionalism to ethics and interactions with diverse groups, emphasizing the special obligation that peace officers have in upholding respect for human dignity. In the following section, "Career Development and Professional Opportunities," we present ideas for advancing in one's career in law enforcement, underscoring the value of training and mentoring that contributes to improved professional behavior on the job. In this second edition, new input has been provided on how police executives can boost the morale of their officers. The last part of the book focuses on selected peacekeeping strategies for use in a multicultural society, especially through community-based policing, creative crime prevention among youth, the curbing of litigation against police officers, and planned law enforcement innovations. Finally, the summary reiterates the need for police officer professionalism, tolerance, and the understanding of diversity. It stresses the responsibility leaders in law enforcement have for demonstrating a leadership style that respects the pluralism in our society.

In addition to the Instructor's Manual for this text, further resource material is provided here in the form of four appendixes. These supplementary aids correspond to various chapters in the book. They include assessment instruments as well as a listing of consultants and services related to the content of this text.

14

PEACE OFFICER IMAGE AND CULTURAL SENSITIVITY

OVERVIEW

This chapter considers the changing role image of peace officers that will result in increased cultural awareness and effectiveness in law enforcement in the twenty-first century. Given the impact of greater diversity on both peacekeeping and enforcement, we explore how cultural understanding can be translated into more effective community policing. To increase cultural awareness, readers are provided with a simple model for quick analysis of differences in various cultures, ethnic groups, and generations. The content strengthens the case that improved police performance and professionalism are dependent on cross-cultural skills and sensitivity among peace officers.

COMMENTARY

Diverse images of law enforcement are evident in the following quotes:

> In the sense that image has a profound impact on the actual human interactions, sensitivity to how people perceive police is a very positive indicator. . . . The alternative available to police, which is to isolate themselves from public opinion, is to seek more favorable public opinion. . . . If the police and general community were to agree that keeping the peace was the law enforcement job, the problem would continue in that reality dictates that police arrest law violators and enforce laws in general, not merely keep the peace. (Coffee, 1990, p. 245)

> After a day of relative quiet, a Midtown Manhattan rally to protest the acquittal of four police in the shooting death of Amadou Diallo turned into a fast-moving march yesterday, with more than 2,000 protesters sweeping down Fifth Avenue and one large group marching about four miles to City Hall. (Rashbaum, 2000, p. 1)

These two commentaries underscore a common reality—the image of law enforcement projected to the public by police persons, their organizations, and the media (Hancock and Sharp, 2000). In the first quotation, a noted criminal justice author has emphasized the importance of the public image created by law enforcement agencies and their personnel. The second report concerns the shooting death of an innocent man by four officers that caused not just a major protest but a near riot in an urban area where there is a delicate balance in racial harmony among the population.

IMPACT OF IMAGES ON HUMAN BEHAVIOR

People create images, both accurate and inaccurate, of themselves and others, as well as images of their roles. Our behavior is then influenced by these mental images, and others respond to the image projected, which may not necessarily reflect reality. The most powerful of these images is the one we have of ourselves, and then those formed about our multiple roles. We also formulate images of our organizations and our nation. In fact, we can even form images of the criminal justice system and its activities, as the authors did in the book *Visions for Change: Crime and Justice in the 21st Century* (Muraskin and Roberts, 1999). We will consider this topic in a later section, but let us start by examining our images of law enforcement as an emerging profession that you, the reader, can mold and influence, now and in the future.

Peace officers today are both knowledge and service workers who must focus on effective performance, according to Norman Boehm, former director of the California Commission on Peace Officer Standards and Training. Thus, he believes police departments must become both learning organizations and enforcement agencies. Boehm maintains that the latter have the responsibility to provide officers with the new knowledge, skills, and behaviors to be effective on the job. "Smart cops," in every sense of that adjective, are becoming the norm (Barlow, 2000; Cromwell and Dunham, 1997).

Such an image of peacekeepers may explain why so many justice agencies are mandating a two- or four-year college degree for entering recruits and why the report of the Police Executive Research Forum, *The State of Police Education: Policy Direction for the 21st Century* (Carter, 1992), describes in detail the benefits of an educated officer. Brainpower, not brawn, is what will make for effectiveness in the vastly changing world of this new millennium.

Exhibit 14.1 differentiates between perceptions of the disappearing and emerging police work culture. Contrasting the two views helps to explain why, within the criminal justice field, a different image of law enforcement must be created of the peace officer and then projected to the public. This is but a synopsis of the transition under way in the world of work and law enforcement, which in turn alters our images of various justice roles. In the latter, the shift and trends seem to be away from the traditional approaches—from reactive to proactive; from just enforcement and crime fighting toward prevention and detection of criminal activity, toward preserving the public peace and service, and toward protecting life and property; and from just public-sector policing to synergistic security services by both public and private sectors working in cooperation (Hunter, Mayhall, and Barker, 2000).

Darrel Stephens, former director of the Police Executive Research Forum (PERF), put the situation quite simply: "Mechanically bean counting of arrests and putting squad cars on the street is no longer enough." These observations are from

Exhibit 14.1   Law enforcement role transitions.

TRADITIONAL WORK CULTURE	*EVOLVING WORK CULTURE*
Attitude Reactive; preserve status quo	Proactive; anticipate the future
Orientation Enforcement as dispensers of public safety	Enforcement and peacekeeping as helping professionals
Organization Paramilitary with top-down command system; intractable departments and divisions; centralization and specialization	Transitional toward more fluid, participative arrangements and open communication system; decentralization, task forces, and team management
Expectations Loyalty to your superior, organization and buddies, then duty and public service; conformity and dependency	Loyalty to public service and duty, and one's personal and professional development; demonstrate leadership competence and interpersonal skills
Requirements Political appointment, limited civil service; education—high school or less	Must meet civil service standards; education—college and beyond, lifelong learning
Personnel Largely white males, military background and sworn only; all alike, so structure workload for equal shares in static sharply defined slots	Multicultural without regard to sex or sexual preference; competence norm for sworn and unsworn personnel; all different, so capitalize on particular abilities, characteristic, potential
Performance Obey rules, follow orders, work as though everything depended on your own hard efforts toward gaining the pension and retirement	Work effectively, obey reasonable and responsible requests; interdependence means cooperate and collaborate with other; ensure financial/career future
Environment Relatively stable society where problems were somewhat routine and predictable, and authority was respected	Complex, fast-changing, multicultural society with unpredictable problems, often global in scope, and more disregard of authority, plus more guns/violence even among juveniles.

one who has served as head of the police department in St. Petersburg, Florida, and is now chief in Charlottesville-Mecklensburg, North Carolina (see foreword to this book). He has demonstrated his position on preventive, community-oriented policing. In a graduation address to police executives at California's P.O.S.T. Command College (January 15, 1993), Stephens stated his conviction that citizens are the first line of defense in preventing and fighting crime, not the crime fighter who reacts after the crime is committed. Therefore, he advocates a problem-solving type of law enforcement that collaborates with the varied community groups within departmental jurisdiction.

Image Projection

Within this larger context, comprehending the significance and power of image and its projection becomes critical for would-be peacekeepers. Image is not a matter of illusion or mere public manipulation of appearances. Behavioral scientists have long demonstrated the vital connection between image and identity, between the way we see ourselves and our behavior. Realists among us have always known that life's "losers," many of them convicted felons, lack an adequate sense of identity and suffer from feelings of poor self-worth. Some people raised in dysfunctional families go so far as to engage not only in self-depreciation and abuse but in self-mutilation as well. Aware of these factors, one state established a special commission to promote self-esteem among school youth, so as to curb crime and delinquency.

Behavioral communication may be understood in terms of senders and receivers of messages. Exhibit 14.2 suggests that we view the multiple images we form

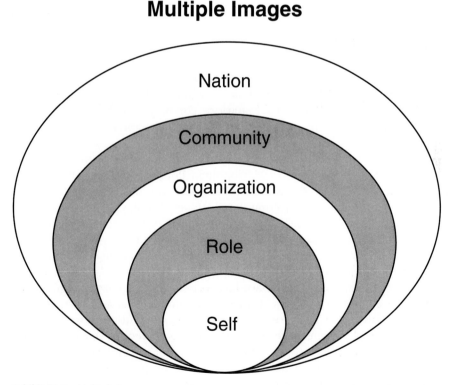

Multiple Images

Exhibit 14.2   Multiple images

in terms of concentric or spiraling circles, centered on the all-important self-image at the core (Harris, 1994). As we see ourselves, we project an image to which people respond. Normally, we set this receiver up, more often than not, for the reactions and treatment we receive—the exception being when the receiver is biased or prejudiced toward certain types or races of people. Our self-concept has been long in development, the outcome not just of life experience but of others' input to us. If a child continuously receives negative feedback from parents and teachers, he or she begins to believe in personal worthlessness. Usually, these young people fail to achieve unless an intervention calls into question their distorted concept of self. Such persons are likely to project weak images that often prompt others to take advantage of them. On the other hand, if they have self-confidence and project a positive image, both verbally and nonverbally, an acceptable response from others is probable. (Again, except for bigoted persons, who reflect an inner bias and refuse to accept people different from themselves, the problems and conflict are within the individuals, as is the case with frustrated youth known as skinheads.) The best antidote to underachievement or even racism is for a person to have a healthy self-image.

Furthermore, if a person is confused about self-identify, as is often the situation with adolescents, people tend to respond in an uncertain way toward that person. Therefore, in the selection of police candidates, law enforcement officials seek those with a strong self-image and appreciation of their own worth. Police academy training should reinforce, not undermine, this self-confidence. Police supervisors are well advised to provide regular *positive reinforcement* of their officers' sense of self.

We play many roles in the course of life—male or female, married or single, child or parent, student or mentor. However, our concern here is specifically on vocational roles within the criminal justice system and the changing images projected by its practitioners. In terms of behavioral communication theory, as police officers see themselves, they project an image to the public, and citizens usually respond to that image (see Longworthy and Travis, 1999).

Two illustrations—one old, one new—illustrate this point. In 1829 Sir Robert Peel established the London Metropolitan Police, projecting an image of a paid, professional force to which the British public positively responded, calling them "peelers" or "bobbies." Rejecting the old adage "employ a thief to catch a thief," he recruited these new police from the military (rather than from criminal backgrounds, as was then the custom) and compensated them with adequate salaries so they would be less inclined to accept bribes or indulge in other irregularities (Gilbert, 1990).

Since then the role of police has evolved as society has changed in its perceptions of values and priorities, justice and criminality, law and enforcement (Carter and Radalet, 1999; Champion and Rush, 1997). Currently, for example, the average citizen seems less concerned about police enforcement of vice and traffic laws and more concerned about their combating gang violence and domestic violence, especially physical abuse of children, spouses, and the aged. Understandably, the North American public today, particularly among minorities and the disenfranchised, has high expectations about being treated humanely and fairly when encountering police in an economically developed country. However, new arrivals in the United

States and Canada, whether through legal or illegal entry, bring "cultural baggage" from their homeland, including negative images of police there, which may be that of oppressors and bribe takers. For them, professional police in the new homeland have to act in such a way as to overcome or counteract these perceptions from the past in a different place.

Modern media have a powerful influence on how the public perceives police. It begins with fictional police as depicted in novels and mystery stories, expands to reports of police activities in newspapers and magazines, and extends to radio and television broadcasts about policing; today U.S. movies and television "cop shows" are viewed internationally. The range of media impact on images of law enforcement is extensive.

With the coming of the information age and its new communication technologies, local police actions may become international incidents. With the help of satellites, television, and computers, the inhabitants of our planet react as a global village. Thus, the ultimate diminishment of law enforcement's image occurred worldwide in 1991. This was the watershed case that took place with the beating of an African American, Rodney King, by a few members of the Los Angeles Police Department. This unfortunate event was captured on videotape and played repeatedly over the airways internationally. It underscores another new reality: criminal justice representatives are now subject to extra scrutiny and accountability when citizens use camcorders to capture their activities for possible review, even on the Internet. In 2000, just before the Republican Convention, Philadelphia's municipal administration was embarrassed in this, "the City of Brotherly Love," when police were again caught on video severely beating a minority criminal. The only mitigating factor in the undermining of that police force's image on the national media is that both white and black officers were involved in applying what they thought was "reasonable restraint." Furthermore, that department did admirable policing during the actual convention.

Perhaps the following two mini cases will clarify this important point about how unprofessional police officers can create negative images of law enforcement in general and their own departments in particular.

Case One: The Changing Images of the New York Police Department (NYPD)

Almost 8 million people live and work in metropolitan New York, a population larger than many countries represented there in the United Nations building. Toward the end of the decade of the 1990s, many of its citizens were pleased that the police crackdown on crime had increased arrests and made their streets safer. Then two incidents occurred to undermine their confidence in the NYPD force of more than 25,000 police. The first centered on the court case against five white policemen accused of arresting, beating, and torturing a Haitian immigrant, Abner Louima. On June 8, 1999, a jury consisting of eight whites, three Latinos, and one black convicted two officers—Justin Volpe and Charles Schwartz—of violating Louima's civil rights. The case and verdict triggered massive protests and broke the "blue wall of silence" that keeps police from testifying against one another. Four of the officers had supported Louima's testimony as to what happened but maintained their own innocence. Finally, Volpe pleaded guilty to brutalizing Louima in a squadroom bathroom after his arrest. The officer admitted ramming a broomstick up the victim's rectum as he lay handcuffed, causing the prisoner to suffer internal injuries that included a ruptured bladder and colon that kept Louima in the hospital for two months.

The second event occurred some seven months later, again involving an immigrant, but this time from Guinea, Amadou Diallo. When four white officers from the Street Crime Unit were cruising a Bronx street for possible criminals, they spotted what they thought to be a suspicious black man. As it turns out Diallo was simply an innocent person standing in front of a building that was his own home. When the four plainclothes officers approached him that night, waving their badges, the 22-year-old street vendor ducked into his small vestibule. When the officers demanded Diallo stop and raise his hands, he reached into his pocket, turning (according to them) in a manner that led the police to believe he may have been pulling a gun. When officer Sean Carroll mistook the black wallet in Diallo's hand for a weapon, he shouted "gun." In the confusion of the heated exchange, the policemen fired a total of 41 bullets at Amadou, striking him 19 times and killing him. In the court case that followed, the defense argued that the officers had broken no department guidelines about arrests and had to make a split-second decision to protect their own lives. The prosecutor argued that Mr. Diallo might have acted in an evasive manner because he feared four white strangers coming at him suddenly. A jury in Albany, New York, found the four officers not guilty of murder and several lesser charges. The Diallo family, dismayed by the verdict, is expected to file a multimillion-dollar lawsuit against the City of New York. The U.S. attorney for the southern district of New York will also review the shooting to see if it violated federal civil rights laws. The NYPD is reexamining its "stop-and-frisk tactics" to ascertain if they violate basic rights of citizens (in temporarily stopping, detaining, questioning, and searching suspects). Further, the city council discovered in its hearings on the case that the so-called elite squad from the Street Crime Unit involved in this questionable shooting had received virtually no specialized training (the unit's members were supposed to receive over 12.5 days of extra training) and that three of the officers in question had been in the unit only three months and received no team training together. In light of this information and the unit's limited number of African American members, the police commissioner has been redefining the Street Crime Unit.

In New York City, the aftermath of this verdict included daily angry outcries that justice had not been served and thousands marching in protest to city hall. A year after these events, *New York Times* reporters interviewed neighborhood locals from one end of the city to the other on their reactions to the whole situation. Following are some of the more salient replies, which show a subtle shift in New Yorkers' attitudes toward the police and deep anxiety over the fatal barrage and the acquittals:

1. To look at me you would not know if I sold drugs or owned a business. But if you are from this community, you would know who I am.

2. After something bad like this happens, the healing starts, but then there is another episode. So you have to ask yourself, "Are things really going to change?"

3. At the time, I worried that the police were using horrific force to fight crime. Now I have a more balanced view—sometimes the police do it well and sometimes they make mistakes.

4. I do not think police do things carelessly. I think they can become unnerved like most human beings.

5. I am a security guard, but aggressive police tactics take too large a toll on the African American communities. I don't think we have to put up with cops harassing us because of our color. They are supposed to stop criminals, not anybody who is black.

6. Though a music producer, three times I have been stopped and frisked by police in unmarked cars. I felt humiliated. I felt I had no right to walk the streets. . . . Yet crime has cleaned up. You can walk down the street and feel secure. You know they are on the beat and out there for your safety.

7. There are police who have become friends with our teenagers. I don't think all the kids think police are bad, but they do feel betrayed when things like this happen.

8. As a Bronx barber, I feel very reassured when I get regular courtesy visits from police. But I do not recognize the officers who stop me for questioning after I lock up at night. And what is worse, they do not know me.

9. There is really, really an unhealthy atmosphere in New York right now. It's not even a racial thing anymore, whites against blacks. But there is a divide between the police and all the rest of us.

10. I believe police have done well in lowering crime in New York, and the Diallo shooting was an honest mistake. In that neighborhood, if I was a white cop and I saw a black guy reach in his back pocket, I'd be on the edge. You hate to stereotype, but I can understand why they were afraid.

Learning Analysis

In the preceding two incidents that produced such repercussions among New Yorkers and Americans outside that city, a total of nine officers were involved from among the many thousands of NYPD members.

1. If you were among the five officers involved in the Louima occurrence that began at a nightclub melee, what would you have done differently to improve police image?

2. If you were commander of the Street Crime Unit involved in the Diallo killing, what could have been done with this group of officers beforehand to avoid the problems they later created?

3. As an outcome of these incidents, the New York Police Department instituted these changes:

   - Issued palm cards to officers that reminded them to be respectful to the public
   - Instituted the Board of Visitors

What other departmental changes would you recommend to improve their public image and services? With the influx of a wide variety of new immigrants into New York City, specifically how can police be better prepared for dealing with them?

Sources: "Cop Convicted in Attack on Haitian," *San Diego Union,* June 9, 1999, p. 2; "Marchers Protest Diallo verdict, Taunting Police along the Way," *New York Times,* March 5, 2000, p. 1; and "Diallo Case Views More Nuance View of Police," *New York Times,* March 5, 2000, pp. 1, 27, 31.

To put these matters into historical perspective, readers might read a new book on the NYPD written by two former police officers (Lardner and Reppetto, 2000). The authors remind us that fatal shootings of civilians by the NYPD are at a modern low. The 11 New Yorkers killed in such incidents last year were less than one-fifth the number killed in the early 1970s. In comments on this volume, the reviewer concludes:

> NYPD, a work in progress of popular history that takes place mainly in the distant past, teaches us several things about police in New York City. The first is that in the 155 years since the NYPD became a more-or-less professional crime-fighting force, nothing has changed—brutality is still an issue, as is incompetence, as is tension between white cops and black citizens, and only extreme vigilance keeps the lid on corruption.
>
> The book also teaches us, however, that everything has changed. The NYPD is today possibly one of the best police forces in the world, but this wasn't always so. It is famously good at crime control, its detectives are sophisticated; its science is good, its tactical capacity excellent. It is integrated by sex and race (not enough, but what agency is?), and its men and women, sometimes despite the department's leadership, generally perform their jobs professionally. It is also, despite the rash conclusions of some on the anti-cop left, a force in control of itself. (Goldberg, 2000, p. 6)

Case Two: The Deteriorating Image of the Los Angeles Police Department (LAPD)

Los Angeles is a sprawling, multicultural metropolis subject to both city and county supervision, with numerous law enforcement agencies. For many decades, the city's police department had a reputation for educated and well-trained personnel, as well as for an efficient and effective crime-fighting force. But in the decade of the 1990s, LAPD's repute was threatened by three major actions that caused citizens to question that image. First, there was the harsh police beatings of Rodney King, an African American, over a serious traffic violation, something that caught international attention by repeated showing of television clips of inappropriate arrest conduct. Second, there was the unprofessional police behavior during the Watts protest riots that followed in 1992. Both events led to major investigations of the department, along with significant changes in administration, communications, and training. Third, there were the scandals that erupted in September 1999 because of the department's CRASH Unit (an acronym for Community Resources against Street Hoodlums), which operates out of local precincts. Specifically, the problems centered on that unit within the Ramparts Division. Ramparts is the most populated district of Los Angeles, with 375,000 people of mixed races, many of them recent immigrants from Mexico and Central America. Within this packed area of eight square miles just west of downtown skyscrapers, there are family restaurants, repair shops, and small businesses.

The scourge of this "neighborhood" is 30 gangs, guilty of increasing violence— rape, robbery, murder. They also attract many of the youth from newcomer groups. As a countermeasure, CRASH was formed to monitor and police gang activities. It was to be an elite special unit, but like its New York counterpart (Street Crime Unit), both developed what was described as a *cowboy culture*. LA's secretive antigang unit within the Ramparts Division became an exclusive fraternity with its unique jackets and special patches; some members even got identical tattoos. Members had little interaction with their colleagues, becoming so standoffish that regular supervisors and officers avoided involvement with them, even when they called for backup support. Unfortunately, the Ramparts Division squad eventually became a lawless unit, guilty of widespread corruption and illegal activities in its zeal to curb the gangs.

Their guilty behavior was revealed by one of their own, Rafael Perez, when he was accused of stealing eight pounds of cocaine from the police evidence locker. Hoping to decrease his sentence, Office Perez described a series of further crimes committed by himself and other CRASH members, including the shooting by him and his partner of a gang thug and then planting a gun on him. As a result, over 800 convictions in which he was involved have been overturned by the courts. He has fingered 2,500 officers who participated in illegal actions and arrests, ranging from outright perjury and beatings to theft and drug dealings. Thus far, 32 judicial cases have been reversed. The investigative net is widening, along with public demands for a permanent nonpolice review board to oversee the LAPD. In light of all this, the core issue is how to improve police–community relations with a force that is supposed to be dedicated to *protect and serve.*

Learning Analysis

In both the New York and Los Angles cases described, the criminal justice professor Samuel Walker observed that there is a long history of problems with special police units. An author of a new book on civilian oversight of police departments, this University of Nebraska scholar noted that such special units loosen the bonds of supervision and are an invitation to trouble because they act on a political message: *Get tough, get results, and we are not going to ask questions about how you do it!* Readers should ask themselves three questions:

1. What can police administrations do to ensure that members of special units behave professionally and in a legal manner?
2. How can the honest majority of police officers in both New York and Los Angeles counteract the negative image created by *rogue cops* among them?
3. When the public confidence in the criminal justice system is undermined by scandals or inappropriate behavior by some personnel, what can police leaders, officers, and their unions do to restore community support for its police department?

At the start of the twenty-first century, the U. S. Justice Department began an investigation of allegations of civil rights abuses by the LAPD and excessive use of force by their personnel over the period 1996–1999. In the aftermath of the previously described cases, the public has demanded greater oversight of that department.

The principal lesson to be learned from these two departmental cases in the two largest cities of the United States is that the organizational image of a reasonably effective agency with a large workforce can be undermined by the unprofessional and illegal actions of a relatively small percentage of officers (see Palmiotto,

Sources: "Police Crime—LA More," *Economist,* February 2–5, 2000, p. 23; "Squads That Tripped Up Walking Bad," *New York Times,* March 5, 2000, p. WK6.

2001). The bottom line is that it is not enough for a peace officer to be a competent professional; he or she must also assist by preventing or reporting wrongdoing by colleagues.

TWENTY-FIRST CENTURY PEACE OFFICER IMAGES

Adopted in various American states, the term *peace officer*, which we utilize in this book, is a concept that might reverse negative publicity. Law enforcement personnel must take pride in the term and internalize its meaning. By projecting this image and its corresponding behavior, police are more likely to impress favorably the citizenry. Interestingly, it is terminology that was very popular in the old west and often used in the old cowboy movies. This term is also in use nationally within the U.S. Department of Justice, as well as within certain regions. For example, the California code (section 830) defines a peace officer as including sheriffs, police, marshals, constables, inspectors, investigators, district attorneys, state highway patrol and police division, state university and college police, and designated personnel in the departments of justice, corrections, fish and game, parks and recreation, and forestry. This broad designation applies to members of the national guard when on duty during states of emergency, as well as to U.S. federal marshals. It can encompass a wide range of related criminal justice occupations, such as arson investigators; park rangers; coroners; investigators of child support and fraud; security officers in municipal and public utilities; harbor, port, and transportation security officers; and public housing security. Similarly, in the state of Texas, the term *peace officer* is in widespread use; its Commission on Law Enforcement Standards and Training uses the term for constables, sheriffs, city police, specialized police, and the Texas Rangers. But do practitioners appreciate the implications of this nomenclature by which they are widely known?

Within this wide spectrum of peace officers, the image is strengthened by their being "sworn" to uphold the law, their adherence to standards and training, their badge and weapon, and sometimes their uniforms and insignia. But the true significance of these two words has yet to be fully realized by most who operate under the umbrella term of *peace officer*. Do most so engaged really perceive themselves as peacekeepers? Does their training regularly include developing skills in conflict resolution and facilitation, in human relations and the managing of cultural differences, in group dynamics and crowd control? Those who officially uphold the law are increasingly being asked to intervene and resolve domestic and neighborhood conflicts, to maintain order during protests and civil disobedience, to manage youth gangs and limit their criminal behavior, as well as to assist the elderly, runaway adolescents, the homeless, and those who would do harm to themselves. With adequate services not available for the mentally sick or disturbed, police are increasingly being asked to deal with these *walking wounded* on our streets.

In the United States, particularly marked by both real and artificial (media) violence, guns and other weapons are common and the supply seemingly plentiful. Police are being called into schools to deal with serious deviant behavior by alienated youth that may range from substance abuse and fighting to shootings and bombings (Crews and Montgomery, 2001). The spread of terrorism in many countries places new pressures on law enforcement agencies at all levels—not just to try preventing or punishing the zealous culprits but also to care for the victims traumatized by misguided or evil people, some of whom are anarchists or mentally ill. Consider, for instance, the major contributions performed by police in helping the bombing victims at the Olympics in Atlanta, Georgia; the World Trade Center in New York City, and Littleton High School in Colorado. So whether it is for crowd or riot control, assisting victims of natural or man-made disasters, or curbing crime and drugs, police in this century require more-than-adequate training, equipment, and compensation for the diverse public services they must render.

Thus, society asks those in law enforcement to fulfill a multiplicity of roles, from apprehension of criminal offenders and participation in court proceedings to preserving civil order, controlling traffic, and coping with accidents and emergencies of all sorts. Essentially, these varied functions come down to keeping the peace and civil order; the emphasis placed on either or both aspects is interpreted by the individual police department and officer under their mandate of "law enforcement."

Furthermore, police today are being asked to serve not just locally and nationally but globally. In pursuit of international drug traffickers, Internet criminals, and money launderers, local law enforcement may have to engage in cross-border activities. There is a continuing need for new applications of police experience and service to deal with new crimes and needs. A case in point: Under the auspices of the United Nations (UN), police officers were recruited to be part of an international peacekeeping force to serve in Kosovo. Their job was to assist North Atlantic Treaty Organization (NATO) troops in keeping peace between the warring Serbs and Albanians, while training a local civilian police entity. One qualified San Diego police veteran volunteered for this difficult humanitarian assignment. After months on the job, Todd Terrabonne confessed in a newspaper interview that he was ill prepared for what he faced in this former Yugoslavian province ("S.D. Cop Finds Crime and Life in Kosovo a Challenge," *San Diego Union Tribune*, 1999, p. B-4). He found there was no 911 system, no court system, no laws, no maps, no reliable electricity or running water, and no coroner's van. During his year abroad in that war-ravaged land, Terrabonne had to cope with explosions, ethnic hatreds, hoards of homeless, freezing weather without adequate heat, and a lifestyle most Americans could not fathom. The crime situation ranged from weapons violations and illegal house occupations to organized crime and prostitution. Apart from lack of language skills, he felt ill prepared to understand the local cultures and history, as well as the differing styles of law enforcement within the international police force. Recruited by the State Department, this peace officer particularly wished that he had been trained by that agency in conflict resolution (see Hart, 1999). The force of 1,800 volunteers had limited success in preparing the local, divided citizenry to take over and police themselves because the international law enforcers were themselves inadequately prepared. While engaged in this humanitarian service, the officer found the Balkans confusing and most welcomed the comforts of home.

All over the world there are societies in which citizens are engaged in civil conflict and war. With the intervention of institutions within the UN, NATO, European

Union (and so on), attempts are made to restore peace and order in these ravaged lands whose populations are in extreme need. One critical and constant call is for uncorrupted, well-trained, professional police to go to such places where there is dire need (e.g., Haiti and Africa). Throughout the next century there will be demands for either international peacekeepers or police trainers to serve in such hot spots, especially within developing countries. This is a whole new dimension and opportunity for professionals within the global criminal justice systems. Furthermore, domestic police are also challenged to deal justly with the disturbed and diverse refugees from these conflicts who immigrate to First World economies.

Influencing the Public Positively

Once again, psychologists remind us that the image we have of our role affects not only our behavior but also the behavior of those to whom we project this image. The U.S. Marine Corps, for example, is currently undergoing a change of image from warriors to peacekeepers and humanitarians. What if all those described previously under the definition of peace officer really saw themselves as such, authentically projecting that image to the public? What if they were actually to become peace practitioners rather than symbolic enforcers of authority? That implies functioning as preservers of equal justice under the law. What if such professionals, by their attitude and behavior, manifested that keeping the peace truly was the job of law enforcement? If they did, such a change in role image and actions among agents of the law might prompt the majority of the law-abiding community actually to perceive them more positively—as peace officers in fact as well as in name. Rather than fear police, citizens would turn to them as resourceful problem solvers. Neighborhood police who interact with the community are more likely to improve public perception of law enforcement, in contrast to police who rarely leave their squad cars or come into difficult areas as members of special units. There is much to be said for "cops" from the past who knew and patrolled their neighborhoods on foot.

COSMOPOLITAN PUBLIC SERVANTS

Cosmopolitan may be defined as common to or representative of all or many parts of the world; not national or local; not bound by local or national habits or prejudices. The use of the term *cosmopolitan* is carefully chosen with reference to public servants in general and peace officers in particular. Government sectors at all levels have long referred to their employees as public servants. Although the words *public servant* may not be highly regarded by some police officers, they are still commonly used in American society. The term is adapted on some city police cars by the motto emblazoned on their sides, "To protect and serve." At issue for police officers is what type of public servant is desirable in terms of attitudes, values, and actions. Among the publicly employed, someone who is "cosmopolitan" is more multicultural in perspective and open to people from throughout the world, in contrast to one who is full of local prejudices; thus both immigrants and the native-born receive the same impartial treatment and respect.

A cosmopolitan officer would have a more accepting, pluralistic view of people and their differences. He or she would be the opposite of someone who is provincial or ethnocentric—that is, locked into the cultural conditioning of one's own upbringing (often referred to as "rednecks"). Although ethnocentrism was discussed in Chapter 1, we review the definition again here: "Belief in the inherent superiority of one's own group and culture; it may be accompanied by feelings of contempt for others who do not belong; it tends to look down upon those considered as foreign; it views and measures alien cultures in terms of one's own culture." This attitude is found in the antisocial, white Aryan movements such as the Ku Klux Klan, the skinheads, and other fascist groups worldwide, most of whose members suffer from low self-esteem and lack self-confidence. These groups of hate-mongers somehow give the participants a feeling of belonging, of power.

The cosmopolitan officer does not show disdain for new émigrés, refugees, or groups that are "foreign" to his or her own background. Instead, he or she strives to understand the differences from a positive perspective. New immigrants and members of diverse ethnic and racial groups offer an opportunity for peace officers to expand their own view of life by altering personal perceptions, attitudes, and knowledge of human beings. The law enforcement person who is cosmopolitan demonstrates openness, tolerance, flexibility, and sensitivity with regard to cultural diversity among individuals and groups. Such a person is curious to learn about people's similarities and differences. Thus, when working in an ethnic neighborhood (i.e., when not responding to calls for service), these officers listen, observe, and ask questions about the citizens' cultural preferences, dislikes, and lifestyles (Alpert and Dunham, 1988). This approach contributes to establishing trust and rapport with citizens.

An officer might increase his or her cross-cultural understanding by employing the following methods:

- Sampling the ethnic food in local restaurants and showing interest in its preparation
- Seeking to comprehend the family structure and child-rearing practices in local ethnic groups
- Inquiring about the local customs, values, myths, taboos, and so on
- Learning and using some words from the foreign languages spoken in neighborhoods

Such activities can be incorporated as part of community-based policing strategies.

With increased heterogeneity within local populations, many states and agencies have inaugurated training programs so that criminal justice personnel will learn to become more sensitive to cultural differences among the people they seek to serve. For example, the *Ohio Police Chief Magazine* (June 1992) reported on that state's Human Diversity Initiative, which includes an advisory committee that assists law enforcement trainers who orient officers on such matters. The committee includes police chiefs and representatives of the Asian, African American, Hispanic, female, elderly, low-income, and homeless segments of the larger community. This type of approach is important for law enforcement today, when there is a trend toward community-based policing in increasingly diverse neighborhoods. This strategy is more akin to Japanese-type policing—intensive, friendly, and more forgiving of petty misbehavior but ruthless with presumed criminals ("Japanese Policing is Culturally Different," *Economist,* April 16, 1994, pp. 38–40). The police in Japan are widely dispersed in the neighborhoods for which they are responsible and expected to patrol while being helpful to citizens.

Finally, changing demographics alter the position of what has traditionally been termed as a "minority group" within a society. In some U.S. states (e.g., California), Caucasians are becoming the minority and Latinos the majority. How will the latter treat the former when they are the dominant group? And how will law enforcement change with larger numbers of officers from Hispanic origins? Obviously, the makeup of a police force should be somewhat representative of the community it serves.

COMMUNITY-BASED APPROACH TO POLICING

Cosmopolitan officers are comfortable with contemporary community-based policing,* described as a problem-solving approach (Oliver, 2001; Peak and Glensor, 1999). Community-based policing enables officers to work with civilians outside the conventional channels by officers meeting with community groups and learning of their concerns. It is more than a return to the old beat cop and traditional crime-fighting approach. The strategy involves unconventional and creative ways of dealing with crime and peacekeeping at the neighborhood level (e.g., developing an aggressive neighborhood watch program). However, as the two case studies cited earlier point out, problems can arise when special unit officers, often in civilian dress and unmarked cars, come into a community where they do not know the locals and vice versa.

As a result of the Christopher Commission recommendations in 1991 relative to the Rodney King incident, the Los Angeles Police Department is again moving toward a community-based approach, trying to determine community, not just departmental, priorities. Given the negative image policing received as a result of that event and the riots that followed, it should be encouraging to the law enforcement community to know that under new leadership, the LAPD is vigorously engaged in practices such as the following:

- A sergeant countered a string of bank robberies in the Wilshire district by cultivating relationships with local bank managers, having his picture taken with them, and placing the life-sized enlargement visibly in the banks, along with police hats on the managers' desks; the result was a dramatic decrease in robberies.
- An officer learned to read neighborhood graffiti and the messages behind them, so as to thwart gang plans and activities.
- In the south-central vicinity, 10 officers were engaged in "Operation Cul-de-Sac," which consists of barricading streets in a target area to cut down on drive-by shootings and drug peddling; they patrol the neighborhood on bicycles and develop rapport with the residents.

---

*Community-based policing is also discussed in Chapters 1 and 15.

- In the Harbor Division, six officers are free from regular assignments to work with community leaders on alleviating a host of local problems, ranging from gang warfare to graffiti and removal of abandoned cars, to refuse dumping on the streets and evicting tenants involved in drug pushing.
- Officers visit ghetto elementary schools to discourage students from joining gangs, to take them on ride-alongs, and to help them get away from the ghetto to summer camp.
- Officers work with local city council representatives and community associations to resolve community problems, such as rehabilitating a number of undesirable apartment houses; as a result, monthly complaint calls to police about drug and alcohol problems have dropped from 30 to 0.

But those engaged in nontraditional peacekeeping confess that not all officers and the police bureaucracy are supportive of this community approach; only a small percentage of the total force is involved directly in these innovative activities. Professor James Q. Wilson at the University of California, Los Angeles, a recognized authority on the subject, observed: "When you allow officers to set their own hours and to work with community people, first-line supervisors become very nervous. They have a feeling their officers are becoming social workers, or as they sometimes put it, are 'carrying rubber bullets.' A strong, devoted police chief can gain support for it, but even those most enthusiastic . . . are not completely selling it to their departments" ("Changes Desired in Police Practice," *Los Angeles Times,* June 3, 1991, p. A-22).

Critics of community-based policing claim that fiscal constraints limit the number of personnel that can be devoted to this type of peacekeeping if regular emergency response calls are to be effectively answered. Their solution is to get taxpayers and government to provide more funding for law enforcement to undertake these additional duties and to train special units of community service officers.

In these transitional times when urban areas are swamped with new immigrants, substance abusers, mentally ill people, escalating gang warfare, and gun violence, it is not easy to convince law enforcement officials to change their standard structures and practices, even in more multicultural communities. Yet in an increasingly diverse society, the traditional image of the police officer must change, especially through practice of greater cross-cultural sensitivity.

Twenty-first-century peacekeeping should learn from the law enforcement mistakes of the past and continually make improvements. For example, following the spring 1992 riots, a special commission under William H. Webster, former director of the Federal Bureau of Investigation (FBI), studied police response during community disorders in Los Angeles, concluding that the LAPD failed to apply standard tactics that would have held the disorder to a relatively confined area. Since then, 16 hours of riot training have been provided officers in maneuvers by police squads to intercept convoys of gang cars, tips on rescuing hostages, and other techniques in crowd control Thus, later that same year, the image of the LAPD as a professional police organization of 10,000 members was somewhat improved because of preventive actions related to a protest rally on behalf of four south-central gang members (arrested previously for the beating of a truck driver, Reginald O. Denny, during the prior riots). This time the headline in the *Los Angeles Times* (December 16, 1992) read: "LAPD Widely Saluted for Swiftly Quelling Incident." The public applause for the department resulted from the way officers handled a rock- and bottle-throwing situation at the same flashpoint of the riots earlier that year. In the fragile social environment within the inner city, police were quickly placed on tactical alert, mobilized rapidly, and responded with strong force. Law enforcement's image can be revitalized and public confidence restored by demonstrating the effective use of standard police practice, while innovating with new techniques and tactics.

This is precisely what happened in Reno, Nevada, in 1992. In preparation for a riot in Reno following the acquittal of the Los Angeles police officers who beat Rodney King, the Reno Police Department's community policing program was successful in preventing a social uprising by organizing its own protest march through the streets of Reno with the police chief leading the procession.

CULTURALLY SENSITIVE PEACEKEEPING

General Omar Bradley observed that the success of a leader is realized in the effectiveness of those who lead. Perhaps the bottom-line message of the preceding section can best be summed up in the philosophy of Robert K. Greenleaf, who believed that to change society, its leaders must first be seen as servants (Greenleaf, 1991). Public service does not mean subservience, but it does imply a willingness to help and show sensitivity to those in need, as well as to consider the perspective of the taxpayer. In today's diverse, multicultural society, cross-cultural communication is at the core of law enforcement (Levine and Adelman, 1993). Throughout this book, we have emphasized that cultural understanding and skills can be a powerful aid in more effective policing. Those in any branch of the criminal justice system are essentially in the "people business." The more its practitioners can learn about human behavior, its motivation, and its deviance, the better they can accomplish their jobs.

Understanding Culture

Cultural anthropology is one of the behavioral sciences that can contribute much insight. It reminds us, as we learned in earlier chapters, that culture is a distinctly human capacity for adapting to the circumstances in which we find ourselves and that the knowledge gained from this experience can be transmitted to subsequent generations. Our cultural heritage conditions our thinking and affects our behavior, often unknowingly—that is, we are aware of only some of these cultural influences, and much of it is in our unconscious mind. Within nationalities and ethnic groups in local communities, it is largely culture that sets the rules that govern behavior. Indeed, understanding human culture is a key to effective enforcement and peacekeeping, as well as management of criminal justice systems (Elashmawi and Harris, 1998).

Culture is our social environment, the way people cope or adapt to their physical or biological surroundings. Thus customs, practices, traditions, and taboos for survival and development are passed through generations among a particular people. Culture is the history of people in groups—what they believe and value, what they fear and exclude, how they learn and work, and how they create families and institutions to facilitate their lives. It preserves that group's cohesion and consensus, even its prejudices. Therefore, we tend to accept the common lore and myths of our unique community, practicing its "truths" about acceptable behavior and blocking out what is contrary to this wisdom from the past—unless we acquire knowledge from elsewhere, outside our own tradition. Experiencing culture shock when living in an alien environment often causes the expatriate to question some of his or her cultural inheritance. Culture helps us to make sense out of that part of the planet or space that we inhabit; it provides ready-made solutions to simple problems, establishing a pattern for living and forming relationships (Harris and Moran, 2000).

Hall and Hall (1987) offer the following insights, which may have special meaning for peace officers:

> Each cultural world operates according to its own internal dynamic, its own principles, its own laws—written and unwritten. . . . Any culture is primarily a system for creating, sending, storing, and processing information. Communication underlies everything. . . . Culture can be likened to an enormous, subtle, extraordinarily complex computer. It programs the actions and responses of every person, and these programs can be mastered by anyone wishing to make the system work.

Those in law enforcement who are culturally aware comprehend the characteristics of culture in general and are able to integrate these traits with specific cultures, whether of a foreign country, a minority group, or an organization. Those who are leaders in this regard acquire knowledge of cultural influences on individuals and their patterns of behavior. Such astute officers are able to distinguish between cultural universals and cultural specifics. They can appreciate cultural themes and diversity. Sensitive peacekeepers translate such understandings into effective relationships with people who are different, whether in their own agency or in the community.

Cultural Implications for Law Enforcement

Cultural insensitivity by agents of the criminal justice system can often have tragic consequences that may result in harassment, civil disturbances, and even death. In an early chapter we discussed the dangers related to cultural stereotyping (false or fixed notions and myths about a type of person). Television reports in 1992 highlighted this problem in terms of undercover cops who may be of African American, Latino, or Asian heritage. The two cases in point occurred in the Nashville Police Department and the New York City Transit Authority Police, where in both incidents white policemen may have fallen into the "stereotyping trap"—in one case beating and in the other shooting a fellow officer carrying out his undercover duty because he looked suspicious merely because he was a black man. The outcome for the latter organization was the introduction of cultural awareness training for transit police. The problem is worldwide within the law enforcement culture. CBS's program *60 Minutes* broadcast a feature (January 11, 1993) on inadequate policing by the British criminal investigative services. False arrests by London "bobbies," often on the basis of cultural misperceptions, has cost the government heavy payments to the victims of what appeared to be racial prejudice by police. Now retraining is under way to help the United Kingdom's police cope better with a multicultural society that is also becoming more violent.

Cultural misunderstandings by police often occur over racial issues. Yet anthropologists and biologists increasingly dismiss the word and concept of *race* as not having validity for human populations. Genetics is what is important to them; of the total genetic diversity of the human species, less than 8 percent can be attributed to racial differences (e.g., skin color and some physical characteristics). About 85 percent of genetic diversity can be found between different geographic groups within a race. Some social scientists maintain that race is a social construct and that we make it up to distinguish ourselves from others. Physical differences among people often relate to climatic adaptation. It helps to explain why those in some parts of the world (e.g., Eurasians) have been so innovative in creating civilizations and technologies.

In this century, we witness increasing social interactions and marriages between people of varied backgrounds. It creates a problem for census takers who like to put the population in neat racial categories. Professor Bernardo Ferdman of the California School of Professional Psychology (renamed Alliant University) observes about his graduate students:

> A new degree of fluidity of identity, a dissatisfaction with traditional categories of race or even ethnicity. ("Race—Murky Definitions Cloud Issue of Who, What We Are," *San Diego Union-Tribune,* April 9, 2000, p. A-10)

Thus, in this twenty-first century, better designations and classifications may emerge among the mixed and diverse generation of baby-boomers. Race fades in importance within a multiethnic society where interracial and interreligious dating and intermarriages are more common. But this trend is also very threatening to a small percentage of the population with weak self-esteem; such *racists* become so obsessed with matters of racial purity that they take a step backward to concoct countless ways of dividing and labeling people and form organizations and publications to protest the racial mixing. Their perceptions are distorted and their actions warped when it comes to racial matters. Their aim is to promote exclusion, not inclusion, which is the basis of democratic society. In the past century we have been exposed to the horrible results of *ethnic cleansing* in many European and African countries. Obviously, such a mind-set should not be present among civil servants supported by the general tax-paying citizen.

Applying the Concept of Culture

To be culturally sensitive, one learns about differences in *macrocultures*—mainstream or majority cultures, such as Japanese, Russian, Mexican, French, or Italian. Even more critical for law enforcement officers is the need to then gather information and insight about the *microcultures* encountered in such societies within the course of daily life. These ethnic cultures are found in abundance within local communities, such as American Indians, Irish Americans, African Americans, Asian Americans, and Mexican Americans. But the classification of subcultures may also be widely applied, as when we analyze the culture of youth or seniors, drug addicts or alcoholics, white-collar professionals, or even criminals.

Furthermore, like corporations or agencies, institutions have unique *organizational cultures.* Hence, there is a distinct *police microculture* throughout the world that is transformed into *agency or departmental culture.* This is an important consideration when seeking interagency cooperation on a case or project; although all may be in the field of law enforcement, each entity has a unique organizational culture that can encourage or discourage collaboration. It is also possible to analyze the cultural differences of specialization within the criminal justice field. Although the cultures of police, sheriffs, marshals, and correctional officers have much in common, there are also distinct differences caused by the nature of their law enforcement duties. Finally, the workplaces of some agencies are locked into a traditional industrial or military model, whereas others are attuned to a more innovative, team-oriented, postindustrial work culture (Harris, 1998; Senn and Children, 1999).

Vocational groupings worldwide have a commonality of culture, whether military, managerial, or police. During the 1960s, the National Commission on the Causes and Prevention of Violence commented on the U.S. police force as being for the most part white, upwardly mobile, lower middle class, conservative in ideology, and resistant to change. Therefore, the commissioners observed that young police officers of that decade, sharing the attitudes and biases of the majority culture, might experience (1) fear and distrust when dealing with minorities and (2) mild cultural shock when working in the urban ghettos of America, especially if faced with militant hostility.

Commenting on this disappearing law enforcement subculture, Coffee et al. (1990) confirm that it consisted largely of Caucasian men from working- or middle-class background, many with military service backgrounds. Being of the conventional culture with limited contact with diverse groups, recruits experience a process of occupational socialization whereby they become identified with police associates and with their procedures, problems, and values. In other words, they adopt the cultural outlook or mind-set of their colleagues in law enforcement, developing their own secure *miniworld* or cultural oasis. Immersed daily in this police microculture with its humor and pathos, its peak energy highs and boredom, its stresses and dangers, this culture shapes their perceptions and attitudes, their role views and sense of responsibility, and their commitment to safeguard one another. It often leads to a *we (police)/they (public)* attitude. Readers can decide for themselves whether this socialization process and outlook is still present among justice personnel in the twenty-first century in their locality. What is evident throughout North America is that police departments are recruiting more educated and diverse personnel.

Furthermore, police constantly interact with the criminal subculture, the hazardous "underworld" of the unsavory, the deviant, and the brutal. When engaged in undercover work, police temporarily assume the characteristics, dress, language, and behavior of criminals. Sometimes, they become so immersed in this illegal microculture that they lose their own sense of identity and perspective, adopting the role of the rogue cop. Further, some police retreat into a "we/they" isolation— "they" being not only the perpetrators of crime but also all nonsworn officers and civilians. Thus, many police are more comfortable with "their own kind," whether they come from another agency, another state, or another nation. However, with increasing professionalism and education, as well as the recruitment of more women and diverse groups, police culture everywhere is being altered rapidly. Peace officers are becoming more comfortable and skillful in interacting with a variety of peoples and cultures at all levels of society.

Changing Police Cultures

In the article "Taking Police Culture Seriously," law professor Andrew Goldsmith (1990) of Melbourne, Australia, makes these astute observations:

> Police culture tends to be seen negatively, as a contrary and perverse influence on "proper" exercise of police discretion. It is seen as often subversive of the ideals and demands of legality. Yet most modern societies are essentially dependent upon rule-based forms of police accountability. Police culture needs to be approached more positively, as a potential resource in the formulation of rules governing police powers and practices. This requires that police administrators and officers participate in negotiated rulemaking, a process similar to collective bargaining, in which police cultural perspectives are drawn upon.

Traditional police cultures are in transition away from the more rigid military and bureaucratic cultures of the past to the more flexible, corporate-like, proactive, and high-tech cultures of the future. Law enforcement leaders should become change agents in this twenty-first century process. To facilitate the changeover, police administrators and managers need to apply methods of cultural analysis to their own unique work environment.

Ways of Analyzing Cultures

There are many ways to study a culture, such as a systems approach that might analyze cultures in terms of kinship, education, economics, politics, religions, associations, health, and pastimes. However, Harris and Moran (2000) provide a simple model that will enable those in law enforcement to get a grasp of a culture, whether on a large or small scale, irrespective of the grouping. These 10 benchmarks can be used to better comprehend a foreign organizational or local culture, especially minority or ethnic groups. Exhibit 14.3 summarizes these characteristics for cultural analysis, first in terms of cultures in general and then specifically in the context of police culture.

A police officer in emergency situations is obviously not going to have the time to do an in-depth cultural analysis. However, especially in community-policing types of situations, the officer can undertake some preparation before beginning an assignment in a given area where citizens will largely be from unfamiliar ethnic groups. Most people have preconceived notions or only a stereotypical understanding of cultural groups with which they have not previously had contact. The categories listed in this exhibit are areas where one often finds predictable cultural variations. The more information an officer or agent can gather about the cultural patterns of a distinctive community group, the less likely he or she is to make false assumptions about people. Knowledge of these cultural patterns would help the officer understand the behavior and actions of groups and contribute to an overall ability to establish rapport and gain trust.

Exhibit 14.3 Characteristics for cultural analysis.

1. **Sense of self and space**. Examine how people in this cultural group perceive themselves and distance themselves from others. Culture not only helps to confirm one's identity but provides a sense of space, both physical and psychological. Such cultural conditioning of behavior may dictate a humble bearing in one culture or macho posturing in another. Some cultures support rugged individualism and independent action, while others teach that self-worth is attained in group conformity and cooperation. In some cultures, such as American, the sense of space dictates more physical distance between individuals, while in Latin/Asian cultures, less distance is desirable. Some cultures are very structured and formal, while others are more flexible and informal. Some cultures are very closed and determine one's place very precisely, while others are more open and dynamic. Each culture validates self in unique ways.

Police culture, for example, expects officers to project a sense of authority and assertiveness, to be respected and in control, to be curious and suspicious, to act with social appropriateness and a sense of duty, to uphold the law, and to serve the common good. Sense of space is experienced in terms of a precinct or district, a patrol area ("beat"), or a neighborhood in community-based policing.

2. **Communication and language**. Examine the communication system in the culture, both verbal and nonverbal. Apart from the national or regional language that might be spoken, study the dialects, accents, slang, jargon, graffiti, and other such variations. For example, there are differences in the way the English language is spoken in England and within the British Isles and Commonwealth nations; in North America, between the Canadians and the Americans (and within the latter between regions and groups, such as black English). Levine reminds us to go Beyond Language to comprehend the full communication by seeking the meanings given to body language, gestures, and signals.

The police culture has its own jargon and code system for communicating rapidly within the field of law enforcement; organizational communications dictate a formal system for reporting, for exchanges with superior ranks, for dealing with public officials and the media. A code of silence may exist about speaking to outsiders concerning police business and personnel.

3. **Dress and appearance**. Examine the cultural uniqueness relative to outward garments, adornments, and decorations or lack thereof; the dress or distinctive clothing demanded for different occasions (e.g., business, sports, weddings or funerals); the use of color and cosmetics; the hair and beard styles, or lack thereof; body markings.

In police culture, policy, regulations and even custom may determine a uniform with patches and insignia of rank, plus certain equipment to be worn and even the length of hair permissible. Exceptions may be permitted for those in administration, detective, or undercover work.

4. **Food and eating habits**. Examine the manner in which food is selected, prepared, presented, and eaten. According to the culture, meat, like beef or pork, may be prized or prescribed, or even forbidden all together—one person's pet may be another's delicacy. Sample national dishes, diverse diets, and condiments for tastes do vary by culture (realize that cultural groups can be conditioned to accepting some food or seasoning that your own body would not tolerate without reactions. Feeding habits may range from the use of hands or chopsticks to the use of utensils or cutlery (e.g., Americans and Europeans do not hold and use the fork in the same manner). Subcultures can be studied from this perspective (as in soldier's mess, executive dining rooms, vegetarian restaurants, prescriptions for females, etc.). Even drinking alcohol differs by culture—in Italy, it is more associated with eating a meal, while in Japan and Korea it is ritualized in the business culture as part of evening entertainment and strengthening business relations, sometimes done to excess.

In police culture, the emphasis has been on fast foods, hearty meals (preferably "complimentary," although official regulations require payment by officers for all such services); customs include that the patrol car sets the eating time for both partners, as well as off-duty relaxation and comradery in a "cop's drinking hole," sometimes marked by too much alcoholic consumption. The new generation of police is more concerned about healthy foods, keeping physically fit, and stress management—including diet, exercise, no smoking, and no substance abuse.

5. **Time and time consciousness**. Examine the time sense as to whether it is exact or relative, precise or casual. In some cultures, promptness is determined by age or status (e.g., at meetings—subordinates arrive first, the boss or elder last). Is the time system based on 12 or 24 hours? In tribal and rural cultures, tracking hours and minutes is unnecessary, for timing is based on sunrise and sunset, as well as the seasons, which also vary by culture (e.g., rainy or dry seasons vs. fall/winter/spring/summer). Schedules in the postindustrial work culture are not necessarily 8 hours; businesses may operate on a 24-hour basis because of telecommunications and electronic mail. Chronobiologists are concerned under such circumstances about the body's internal clock and performance, so analyze body temperature and composition relative to sleepiness, fatigue, and peak periods (e.g., as with jet fatigue when passing through time zones).

The police culture operates on a 24-hour schedule with sliding work shifts that do affect performance; some departments adopt the military time-keeping system of 24 hours. Normally, promptness is valued and rewarded; during police operations, timing is precise, with watch synchronization of all involved.

6. **Relationships**. Examine how the culture fixes human and organizational relationships by age, sex, status, and degree of kindred, as well as by wealth, power, and wisdom. In many cultures, marriage and the family unit are the most common means for establishing relations between the sexes and among parents, children, and other relatives. In the Far East, this is accomplished through an extended family that may involve aunts, uncles, and cousins living in the same household. Many cultures also operate with the male head of household as the authority figure, and extend this out from home to community to nation, explaining the tendency in some countries to have dictators. In traditional cultures, custom sets strict guidelines about boy—girl relations prior to marriage, about treatment of the elderly (in some cultures, they are honored, in others ignored), about female behavior (wearing veils and appearing differential to males in contrast to being considered an equal). "Underworld" or criminal cultures sometimes adopt a family pattern with the "godfather" as the head and various titles to distinguish roles.

In police culture, organizational relations are determined by rank and protocol, as well as by assignment to different departmental units. Although policy may dictate that all fellow officers and citizens be treated equally, unwritten practice may differ. The partnership system usually forgoes close relations and trust between individuals whose life and welfare is dependent upon the other. Postindustrial policing is moving more toward developing team relationships.

7. **Values and norms.** Examine how the culture determines need satisfaction and procedures, how it sets priorities, and values some behavior while decrying other practices. Thus cultures living on a survival level (e.g., homeless) function differently from those which are affluent. In some Pacific Island cultures, for instance, the more affluent one becomes, the more one is expected to share with the group. Cultural groupings with high security needs value material things (e.g., money and property), as well as law and order. In the context of the group's value system, the culture sets norms of behavior within that society or organization. Acting upon a unique set of premises, standards of membership are established affecting individual behavior—for example, the conventions may require total honesty with members of one's own group but accepts more relaxed behavior with those from other groups. Other standards may be expressed in gift-giving customs, rituals for birth/marriage/death, and guidelines for showing respect, privacy, and good manners. The culture determines what is legal or illegal behavior through a codified system or custom; what may be legal in one culture may be illegal in another.

In police culture, for instance, subordinates are expected to show respect for officers of superior rank, while the reverse may be tolerated for those who have broken the law. Publicly and by departmental regulations, a code of ethics is in place in which bribery and corruption are punishable offenses. A department of internal affairs ensures that alleged transgressors of such norms are investigated and tried or exonerated. This culture also espouses traditional American values of duty, loyalty, patriotism, and so on.

8. **Beliefs and attitudes**. Examine the major belief themes of a people and how this affects their behavior and relations among themselves, toward others, and what happens in "their world." A cultural "universal" seems to be a concern for the supernatural, evident in religious adherence and

practices, which are often dissimilar by group. "Primitive" or tribal cultures are described as "animists" because they experience the supernatural in nature (e.g., "Indians" or Native Americans)—a belief to which modern environmentalists resonate. The differences are apparent in the Western cultures with Judeo-Christian traditions, as well as Islamic, in contrast to Eastern cultures, dominated by Buddhism, Confucianism, Taoism, and Hinduism. Religion, or the lack of it, expresses the philosophy of a people about important realities of life's experiences. Some cultural groups are more fundamentalist and rigid in their religious beliefs, while others are more open and tolerant. The position of women in a society is one manifestation of such beliefs—in some, the female is enshrined, in others treated like an equal by the male; in others, she is subservient to the male and treated like chattel. A people's belief system is often dependent on their cultural stage of human development—hunting, farming, industrial, or postindustrial; advanced technological societies seems to substitute a belief in science or cosmic consciousness for more traditional beliefs.

In police culture, for example, there has been a strong belief in group loyalty, pragmatism, power, and public service. God and religion have been acknowledged in oaths, in religious societies of police officers, by appointment of department chaplains, and during burial ceremonies of officers who die in the line of duty. Until recently, the law enforcement culture tended to be "chauvinistic," but that is changing with the introduction of more female officers and education of the workforce on diversity issues.

9. **Mental processes and learning.** Examine how some cultures emphasize one aspect of brain, knowledge, and skill development over another, thus causing striking differences in the way their adherents think and learn. Anthropologist Edward Hall suggests that the mind is internalized culture and involves how a people organize and process information. Life in a particular group or locale defines the rewards and punishments for learning or not learning certain information or in a certain way. In some cultures, the emphasis is on analytical learning—abstract thinking and conceptualization, while in others it is upon rote learning or memorization; some cultures value logic, while others reject it; some cultures restrict formal education only to males or the wealthy, while others espouse equal education for all. While reasoning and learning are cultural universals, each culture has a distinctive approach. However, the emergence of the computer and telecommunications as learning tools are furthering the globalization of education.

In police culture, recruit academies and other forms of in-service training may differ by locality as to content, instructional emphasis, and method. Anti-intellectualism among some police is being undermined by professional development and standards established by the federal/state governments and their credentialing processes, as well as by criminal justice curricula in higher education. As a result, modern police are moving from a more reactive, pragmatic, action-oriented behavior based on feelings and experience toward a proactive, thoughtful, analytical, and informed response. Professional competence is judged now by high performance and level of learning, not just by years on the job and connections.

10. **Work habits and practices.** Another dimension for examining a group's culture is their attitude toward work, the types of work, the division of work, the dominant work habits and procedures, and the work rewards and recognitions that are provided. Some cultures adopt a work ethic that says it is desirable for all to be so engaged in worthwhile activities—even sports and the arts, while others preclude labor for income. Work worthiness is measured differently by cultures as to income produced, job status, or service to the community. In Japan, for example, cultural loyalty is transferred from the family to the organization, which is dependent upon the quality of individual performance. Classification of vocational activity is somewhat dependent on the culture's stage of development—a people can be characterized primarily as hunters, farmers, or factory or knowledge/service workers, with the trend away from physical labor toward use of mental energy aided by new technologies. The nature of work, as well as the policies, procedures, and customs related to it, are in transition. In the postindustrial culture, there is more emphasis on the use of advanced technologies, such as automation and robotics, as well as upon quality of working life—from compensation and benefits to stress management or enhancement of one's potential on the job. In conjunction with work, a culture differs in the manner and mode of proffering praise for good and brave deeds, outstanding performance,

length of service, or other types of accomplishment. Promotions, perks, and testimonials are all manifestations.

In police culture, a hierarchial structure has organized work into specializations, divisions, and other such operational units engaged primarily in law enforcement and crime fighting. Job performance varied from "workaholics" to those who just put in time. Today the trend is toward peacekeeping and crime prevention, toward teamwork and community-based policing, toward obtaining citizen cooperation. Rewards and recognitions in the past have been largely commendations, advancement in rank, and retirement dinners, but now are being expanded to include assignments for professional development, interagency exchanges, and even sabbatical leaves for educational advancement.

Source: Excerpted with permission from Philip R. Harris and Robert T. Moran. (2000). *Managing Cultural Differences* (5th ed.). Boston: Butterworth-Heinemann. This parent book with *Instructor's Guide* is part of the 12 titles in the MCD Series of volumes available from Butterworth-Heinemann (225 Wildwood Ave, Woburn, MA 01801; 781-904-2500; Web site: www.BH.com).

Admittedly Exhibit 14.3 offers only 10 general classifications for cultural analysis, whether a nation, an organization, a profession, a group, a generation (e.g., youth or seniors), or an ethnic or racial group. There are other dimensions of culture, but the categories provided here help peace officers more quickly and systematically comprehend cultures, such as those described in Part Three of this book. The same approach can also be applied to study the "underworld" or criminal culture and its various subcultures (e.g., bank robbers, car thieves, hijackers, drug pushers, or sexual perverts). Further, during international travel, whether on duty or for vacation, these same major characteristics can be observed to make the intercultural experience more meaningful. When law enforcement officers from other countries visit, these guidelines are useful for getting them to talk about their national or police cultures. All of the aspects of culture noted are interrelated; there is a danger in trying to compartmentalize this complex concept and miss the sense of the whole.

Using Culture to Create Positive Police Images

If the representatives of law enforcement are more culturally aware and sensitive, they are more likely to project to the public a positive image as peacekeepers. Following are examples of actual newspaper headlines affecting the image of the department involved. Although the media do not always accurately report what happened, we know that there are still instances of police insensitivity. Some negative headlines have included statements such as the following:

- Report on Police Cites Racism, Excessive Force
- Law Enforcement: Officials Deny That Deputies Are Using Excessive Force as Agency Faces More Turmoil
- Policewomen Call Sexual Harassment Endemic in Their Department
- On the Beat, Police March to a Changing Set of Rules
- Police Abuses Laid Bare, but Solutions Fall Short

On the plus side, there are numerous reports of law enforcement agencies engaged in constructive cross-cultural communication with the communities they seek to protect. One story concerned a special unit being established by the San Diego Sheriff's Department to patrol Native American reservations, which are being overrun from the outside by drugs and violence. Federal Public Law 280 transferred criminal jurisdiction and enforcement on reservations to some states. In this instance, the tribal chairmen requested the deputies for their rural, remote areas, which have become a kind of no-man's land. Four officers now make the East County reservations their sole focus, and the Native Americans appreciate the improved service. Word has spread among the inhabitants that the "law is back in town and he's not so bad." A *Los Angeles Times* article (June 17, 1991) describes Terry Lawson's experience on the Barona Indian Reservation:

> He's also taken a good look at how he carries himself, and has made a few changes. In his conversations with new Indian contacts, he noticed they rarely interrupted him. He now tries to return the favor. And he no longer relies on a handshake to make a good first impression—some Indians find that presumptuous, particularly from a stranger. "You've got to make sure they offer their hands first," Lawson said, sharing some hard-won knowledge. Also don't talk to one person about another person—many Indians are offended by that. . . . We're learning things the hard way, and I'm sure we're going to step on ourselves a lot more. When something bad happens, you're going to have a deputy who knows the tribal chairman by his first name, and who the Indians know by his first name. We're talking about personalized service.*

But do deputies have to learn about American Indian cultures the hard way? The issue is how much cross-cultural training was provided to officers for this unique assignment (refer back to Chapter 10). If police are culturally sensitized, it will facilitate their mission and interactions. For example, suppose that they had used the foregoing method of cultural analysis before and during their initial encounters with the local tribes.

Throughout this book the underlying message to law enforcement has been that patrolling or observing on the basis of one's own cultural background may result in distorted perceptions. Instead, peace officers should try to get into the unique world of the community being served. For example, gestures have different meanings in varied cultures. In India, men and women do not usually hold hands in public. Men may hold hands, and women in some rural areas may walk behind the men; when asking questions of some people, especially from southern India, the gesture of rolling the head from side to side (which is similar to the "no" head movement in the West) signifies "I'm listening" or "I'm in agreement." Now transpose this gesture into a North American urban area where a native of southern India is stopped by a police officer for running through a red light. The officer asks, "Did you see that red light?" If not yet acculturated to the ways of the United States or Canada, the response from the immigrant may be a head roll from side to side, a gesture that means "yes" in India. This response would probably confuse the officer, who may presume the Indian to be lying (i.e., the officer would interpret the Indian's head movement as "no"). Think back to the Diallo case and how the four white officers approached this black immigrant. The newcomer from Africa did not have the benefit of American black parents who warn their children about police exchanges: "shut your mouth, keep your hands in plain view, and make no sudden movements." The stop and frisk policy in certain neighborhoods looks suspiciously like unequal enforcement, especially when the New York State's attorney general report indicates that blacks are likely to be stopped twice as often as whites. Such actions give credence to civil rights claims that stopping black people at random is often based on race alone. Research by the psychologists Alpert and Dunham (1988) confirmed that ethnic prejudice frequently leads to mindless branding and stereotyping, as well as distorted perceptions.

Interpersonal interactions are complicated, especially when cultural, class, or economic differences are present. Real peacekeeping requires cultural sensitivity if officers are to fully comprehend what is taking place. Black male teenagers with braids and baggy pants may be normal youngsters and not necessarily gang members. To adults, adolescent dress and appearance may seem weird, as these youth try to distinguish themselves from others. Similarly, homeless persons, often dirty and bedraggled, can easily be misjudged because of their appearance and circumstances. The *San Diego Union-Tribune* (February 12, 2000, p. 3), for instance, reported a confrontation between police and a homeless person that was also caught on videotape. The mentally ill man had been hitting people with a tree branch; when officers ordered him to drop the "weapon", he charged them. Three officers shot and killed this unfortunate person. Twenty homeless people and activists then protested the unjustified and excessive force by law enforcement, crying "we refuse to be counted among the disappeared ones." The city administration ordered a public review of the case. Were the police culturally sensitive to the plight of poor street people? Could the three officers have used less lethal means to disarm this angry human being waving a tree branch? If so and they had succeeded, how would this approach have affected the image of police in their community? Finally, how could a knowledge of cultural differences help to improve both the images and services of those in law enforcement?

SUMMARY

For professionals in any facet of the criminal justice system, change begins with the practitioners' image of their role, which is then projected to the public. In the evolving new work culture Harris (1998) describes, adhering to the image of peace officer is appropriate and requires that those in public service become more cosmopolitan in their outlook and approach. Effectively dealing with cultural issues within the field of law enforcement then becomes a means for exercising leadership that demonstrates that sensitive peacekeepers capitalize on cultural uniqueness.

Since culture gives a people identity, the issue is how much of a person's cultural heritage is to be absorbed or retained in the process of acculturation after relocation (e.g., to the new homeland or new region of one's country). The late consultant Janice Hepworth maintained that one of the greatest strengths of the United States is "its elasticity" in that regard.

The challenges for law enforcement, in particular, are to recognize and appreciate diversity within both the community and the workforce, while using such insights advantageously. Human diversity must become a source of renewal rather than intolerable conflict within our agencies, communities, and society. To accomplish this goal within criminal justice systems, intercultural training must become an integral part of the human resource development of peacekeepers (Moran, Harris, and Stripp, 1993; Wederspahn, 2000). The type of peacekeeping advocated in this chapter also requires competent supervision and management with police administration (Holden, 1994; Whisenand and Rush, 1998).

DISCUSSION QUESTIONS AND ISSUES

1. *Cultural Impact.* Consider the long-term influence of the institution of slavery on the African American family in general and their male youth in particular. What is the implication of this negative heritage for today's black citizens as a whole and its influence within the subcultures of police officers and criminals? Identify hopeful trends that repair or redress the damage of slavery and discrimination on this valuable segment of the American population.

2. *Extended Families and the Law.* Many Asian, Near Eastern, and Middle Eastern cultures function with an extended rather than a nuclear family. When such immigrants come to North America, they attempt to carry on this larger family tradition (e.g., food preparation of large meals, working hard in a family-owned business, remodeling and enlarging houses or estates, acquiring several automobiles or a fleet, intermarriage with relatives). Consider how such customs may cause the new arrivals to violate local laws and regulations relative to killing animals, child labor, multiple-family dwellings and occupancy, multiple-car parking on public streets, and so forth. Have you observed anything in this regard about Indo-Chinese, Cuban, Haitian, Asian, Indian, Pakistan or other immigrants? What can a patrol officer do to help these newcomers from breaking laws of which they are unaware?

3. *Community-Based Policing.* Community-based policing requires a change in attitude, as well as in strategies and techniques. Consider how you would apply this approach if, for example, you were a peace officer in California's Fresno Valley. After the Vietnam War, over 60,000 H'mong refugees were resettled there in appreciation for their services to their American allies, as well as to protect them from Communist retaliations. An aboriginal people coming from a tribal culture in the agricultural stage of development, these Laotians found it hard to adjust to a modern, technological society, even when relocated to a rural setting. However, their kids are soaring—studying hard, picking up English quickly, doing well in math. Unfortunately, some of their youth are also forming gangs. Meanwhile, their adults suffer from culture shock, fearing their children are becoming too Americanized and losing too much of their own cultural heritage. What police challenges and problems would be found in a community with such a microculture? Can you identify other such refugee groups that have been suddenly relocated from a tribal or rural culture to modern North America?

4. *Culture and Crime.* With inadequate border management and increased illegal entry, a criminal element from abroad slips into the United States and preys on the vast majority of law-abiding immigrants from the "old country," particularly through extortion. Earlier in this century, such thugs and "crime families" were mainly from Europe; today they come in increasing numbers from the former Soviet Union, Latin America, Caribbean Islands, and Asia. Consider how law enforcement nationally can share information and tactics to

combat such threats (e.g., from Hong Kong triads, Salvadoran death squads, Russian black marketers, Jamaican Mafia, and Asian gangs). At the same time, how can peace officers gain the confidence of the law-abiding immigrants, many of whom have been culturally conditioned against police in their homelands? What insights can you share on these matters of concern to law enforcement?

5. **Case Studies.**   Discuss the additional learning to be gained by the two case studies provided in this chapter. What lessons go beyond the NYPD and LAPD and can be applied to other law enforcement agencies?

REFERENCES

ALPERT, G. P., AND R. G. DUNHAM. (1988). *Policing Multi-Ethnic Neighborhoods.* Westport, Conn.: Greenwood Press.

BARLOW, D. E., AND M. H. BARLOW. (2000). *Police in a Multicultural Society-An American Story.* Prospect Heights, Illinois: Waveland Press, Inc.

BARLOW, H. D. (2000). *Criminal Justice in America.* Upper Saddle River, N.J.: Prentice-Hall.

CARTER, D. L., AND L. A. RADALET. (1999). *The Police and the Community.* Upper Saddle River, N.J.: Prentice-Hall.

CARTER, D. L. ed. (1992). *The State of Police Education: Policy Direction for the 21st Century.* Washington, D.C.: Police Executive Research Forum.

CHAMPION, D. J. AND G. J. RUSH. (1997). *Policing in the Community.* Upper Saddle River, N.J.: Prentice-Hall.

COFFEE, A. (1990). *Law Enforcement: A Human Relations Approach.* Upper Saddle River, N.J.: Prentice-Hall.

CREWS, G. A., AND R. H. MONTGOMERY. (2001). *Chasing Shadows: Confronting Juvenile Violence in America.* Upper Saddle River, N.J.: Prentice-Hall.

CROMWELL, P. J., AND R. J. DUNHAM. (1997). *Crime and Justice in America: Realities and Future Prospects.* Upper Saddle River, N.J.: Prentice-Hall.

ELASHMAWI, F., AND P. R. HARRIS. (1998). *Multicultural Management 2000.* Boston: Gulf Publications Series/Butterworth-Heinemann.

ESSED, P. (1991). *Understanding Everyday Racism.* Newbury Park, CA: Sage.

GILBERT, E. L. (ed.). (1990). *The World of Mystery Fiction.* Bowling Green, Ohio: Bowling Green State University Popular Press.

GOLDBERG, JEFFREY. (2000, September 17). "New York's Finest." *New York Times Book Reviews,* p. 6.

GOLDSMITH, ANDREW. (1990). "Taking Police Culture Seriously." *Policing and Society,* 1, (2), 91–114.

GREENLEAF, R. K. (1991). *Servant Leadership: A Journey into the Nature of Legitimate Power and Greatness.* Mahwah, N.J.: Paulist Press.

HALL, E. T., AND M. R. HALL. (1987). *Hidden Differences.* Garden City, N.Y.: Anchor/Doubleday.

HANCOCK, E. W., AND P. M. SHARP. (2000). *Public Police: Crime and Criminal Justice.* Upper Saddle River, N.J.: Prentice-Hall.

HARRIS, P. R. (1994). *High Performance Leadership.* Amherst, Mass.: HRD Press.

HARRIS, P. R. (1998). *The New Work Culture.* Amherst, Mass.: HRD Press.

HARRIS, P. R., AND R. T. MORAN. (2000). *Managing Cultural Differences* (5th ed.). Boston: Butterworth-Heinemann.

HART, L. B. (1999). *Learning from Conflict.* Amherst, Mass.: HRD Press.

HENNESSY, S. (1990). *A Cultural Awareness Trainer's Manual For Law Enforcement Officers.* Scottsdale, AZ: Leadership, Inc.

HOLDEN, R. N. (1999). *Modern Police Management.* Upper Saddle River, N.J.: Prentice-Hall.

HUNTER, R. D., P. D. MAYHALL, AND T. BARKER. (2000). *Police Community Relations and the Administration of Justice.* Upper Saddle River, N.J.: Prentice-Hall.

KIRKPATRICK, D. (2000). *Managing Change Effectively.* Boston: Gulf Publications Series/Butterworth-Heinemann.

LANGSWORTHY, R. H., AND E. T. LAWRENCE. (1999). *Policing in America: A Balance of Forces.* Upper Saddle River, N.J.: Prentice-Hall.

LARDNER, J. AND T. REPPETIO. (2000). *NYPD,* New York: Henry Holt.

LEVINE, D., AND M. ADELMAN. (1993). *Beyond Language: Cross-Cultural Communication.* Upper Saddle River, N.J.: Prentice-Hall.

LONGWORTHY, R. H., AND L. F. TRAVIS, (1999). *Policing in America: A Balance of Forces.* Upper Saddle River, N.J.: Prentice-Hall.

MORAN, R. T., P. R. HARRIS. AND W. G. STRIPP. (1993). *Developing the Global Organization: Strategies for Human Resource Professionals.* Boston: Gulf Publications Series/Butterworth-Heinemann.

MURASKIN, R., AND A. R. ROBERTS. (1999). *Visions for Change: Crime and Justice in the 21st Century.* Upper Saddle River, N.J.: Prentice-Hall.

OLIVER, W. M. (2001). *Community-Oriented Policing.* Upper Saddle River, N.J.: Prentice-Hall.

PALMIOTTO, M. J. (2001). *Police Misconduct: A Reader for the 21st Century.* Upper Saddle River, N.J.: Prentice-Hall.

PEAK, K. J., AND R. W. GLENSOR. (1999). *Community Policing and Problem-Solving Strategies and Practices.* Upper Saddle River, N.J.: Prentice-Hall.

PONTELL, H. N. AND D. SHICHOR. (2001). *Contemporary Issues in Crime and Criminal Justice.* Upper Saddle River, N.J.: Prentice-Hall.

RASHBAUM, WILLIAM K. (2000, February 27). "Marchers Protest Diallo Verdict, Taunting Police along the Way." *New York Times,* p. 1.

SENN, L. E., AND J. R. CHILDREN. (1999). *The Secret of a Winning Culture.* Boston: Gulf Publications Series/Butterworth-Heinemann.

WATSON, E. M., A. STONE, AND S. DeLUCA. (1998). *Strategies for Community Policing.* Upper Saddle River, N.J.: Prentice-Hall.

WEAVER, G. AND M. R. HAMMER. (2000). "Cultural Considerations in Hostage Negotiations." Culture, Communications and Conflict. Boston, MA: Pearson Publishing. pp. 508–517.

WEDERSPAHN, G. H. (2000). *Intercultural Services: A Worldwide Buyers Guide and Sourcebook.* Boston: Gulf Publications Series/Butterworth-Heinemann.

WHISENAND, P. W. (1998). *Supervising Police: The Fifteen Responsibilities.* Upper Saddle River, N.J.: Prentice-Hall.

Resources

Readers may wish to request catalogs from specialized publishers. In the criminal justice field, Career and Technology, Prentice Hall, One Lake Street, Upper Saddle River, NJ 07458 (201-236-7000 or 800-526-0485; Web site *www.prenhall.com*)

In the cross-cultural field, Intercultural Press, PO Box 700, Yarmouth, MA 04096 (207-846-5168; fax: 207-846-5181) and Gulf Publications Series, Butterworth-Heinemann, 225 Wildwood Ave., Boston, MA 01801 (800-336-2665; Web site *www.bhusa.com*). Inquire about the *Managing Cultural Differences Series* and specifically the *Instructor's Guide and Intercultural Services: Worldwide Guide Buyer's Guide and Sourcebook.*

15

POLICE OFFICER PROFESSIONALISM AND PEACEKEEPING STRATEGIES IN A DIVERSE SOCIETY

OVERVIEW

This closing chapter considers issues of professionalism and leadership, as well as the future development of personnel within the criminal justice field. Given the trends toward greater multiculturalism with communities and the workforce, we examine specifically how this education and training can be directed toward the creation of greater cultural cooperation within neighborhoods and local law enforcement agencies. We then present strategies for peacekeeping in a diverse society: community-based policing, curtailing litigation against peace officers, crime prevention techniques, and planned law enforcement innovations—developments that should become integral parts of police policy in the twenty-first century. The chapter concludes with organizational trends in law enforcement contributing to effective peacekeeping in a diverse society (see Peak, 2000; Schmalleger, 2001).

COMMENTARY

The following quotes reflect the importance of professional development for law enforcement officers:

> In a paper presented to the Commission on "Recruitment, Selection, Promotion, and Civil Service," A. C. Germann outlined the criteria for a profession in general, and law enforcement in particular. These included being service-oriented; highly competent, being allowed autonomy and authority in the exercise of that competence; utilization of scientific knowledge and specialized techniques; strong career commitment based on that competence and accomplishment; valuing of free inquiry and loyalty to the

profession which relates more to the opinion of professional peers than to hierarchical supervisors; determination to influence change by actions to eliminate or ostracize all incompetent members of the organization. (President's Commission on Law Enforcement and the Administration of Justice, 1967)

The author of that national report in the late 1960s concluded that although there are many with professional competence and character in law enforcement careers, American police service "does not meet the standards of a profession to the degree that it should, even though it be a professional activity."

> Numerous current studies clearly demonstrate that the training of American police is deficient. Many police academies have a training curriculum consisting of approximately 400 hours. . . . Even when an academy is well structured . . . the curriculum concentrates on the law enforcement task, which occupies a relatively small portion of the police officer's time. Although most of the officer's time is devoted to service activities, training in the service function is, for the most part, de-emphasized or ignored at police academies. . . . Dedicated and responsible officers may be placed on the street unprepared for the experience they will face. They do not have a clear understanding of the true attitudes of the public they are policing. They may not have an appreciation of the historical factors that shaped the larger community and its neighborhoods. They may not understand the sources of the fears and prejudices of the people in the community, including themselves. They may not be trained in the techniques necessary to defuse dangerous situations with finesse or to seek alternatives to arrest. Unfortunately, they are too often taught to respond to threats or hostility with force. Lack of training in such subjects as introduction to social theory, basic psychology, human development and behavior, constitutional law, minority history, ethnic studies, interpersonal relations and communications skills allows communication blocks to remain intact. (Hunter et al., 2000, 194–195)

> In the field of criminal justice education, there are not only classroom-oriented quality textbooks and teaching materials, but a whole range of techno-products in new mediums. There are CD-Roms for computer learning on such crimes as murder and drugs, or available CJ multimedia. Police professional development can be advanced by distance learning—such as a www guide to criminal justice and criminology, as well as an introductory criminal justice course or a CJ central supersite on the Internet (http://www.prenhall.com/cjcentral). (Prentice-Hall, 2000) paraphrased

POLICE LEADERSHIP IN PROFESSIONALISM AND SYNERGY

Lack of professionalism and inadequate personnel development can be very costly to any organization. But when it occurs within the public sector, it can prove damaging to both individuals and their careers, as well as to agencies and society. The following subsections cover three key concepts, which will be defined because of their implications for law enforcement and peacekeeping within a multicultural society (see Barlow, 2000; Dantzker, 2000).

Leadership

Leadership is exercised when one takes initiative and shows the way, guides or influences others in a direction, and demonstrates how a process or procedure is performed. Leaders are said to possess a good mixture of conceptual, technical, and professional competence and to demonstrate judgment and people skills. Leaders are not only creative change agents but practical futurists, exercising foresight and the capacity for the "big picture" and the "long view" (see McGregor, 1991; Sullivan, 2000; Tamayo, 1999). Today as we transition into a new information age and work culture, leaders need to be both transformational and transcultural. That is, such high performers innovate in

- Transforming work environments from the status quo to the way it should be
- Renewing organizations, becoming role models in terms of transmitting intellectual excitement and vision about their work
- Helping personnel to manage change by restructuring their mind-sets and values

Leaders help to improve their organizations by preparing the next generation of supervisors and professionals. They do this primarily through the human resource development program that they initiate and/or supervise (Harris, 1998). At a more personal level, they become mentors and coaches to high-performing personnel with organizational potential (Lynn Learning Labs, 1998).

In terms of the intercultural, such leaders deal with persons equally, regardless of gender, race, color, religion, or cultural differences. They seek to empower a more diverse workforce in law enforcement. Further, culturally sensitive leaders cut across cultural barriers while combating prejudice, bigotry, or racism wherever found in the organization and community (Simons, Vazquez, and Harris, 1993). The description of the cosmopolitan provided in Chapter 14 applies to such leaders. Police supervisors, for example, exercise this leadership through anticipatory thinking, strategic planning, creative decision making, and effective communications (Moran et al., 1993; Whisenand and Ferguson, 1996). Similarly, chiefs of police provide leadership when they annually set forth their departmental goals orally and in writing for the benefit of the city council and their agency workforce, ensuring over the year that these goals are systematically achieved.

The Department of Justice in the state of California sponsors for law enforcement personnel the Center for Leadership Development, which conducts an annual Executive Leadership Conference. Other states in the United States have comparable offerings down to the level of supervisors.

Professionalism

Professionalism means approaching an activity, such as one's occupation or career, with a sense of dedication and expertise. In contrast to an amateur, a professional is a committed high performer. A professional possesses integrity and demonstrates competence—regardless of the role, career activity, or sport in which he or she is engaged. Some of the characteristics of professionalism, particularly with reference to law enforcement, were described in the opening commentary by A. C. Germann. When someone possesses this quality in criminal justice systems, that person is concerned about

- Doing an effective job or rendering an effective service
- Developing his or her career skill or competency level

- Ensuring ethical and sensitive behavior in himself or herself and other departmental members
- Capitalizing on diversity in people and organizations and seeking to develop human potential
- Keeping up on the latest developments in the criminal justice field

In law enforcement, professionals would make it a point to understand the law and legal system in which they work, as well as the key issues in the criminal justice field (Barlow, 2000; Calvi and Coleman, 2000; Schmalleger, 2001).

To increase their competence, these professionals are familiar with aspects of criminology and criminal and deviant behavior (Barkan, 2001; Bartol, 1999; Goode, 2001). Whether writing a report, conducting an investigation or an interview, or commanding a police action, professional peace officers do the work consistently well (Adams 1998; Gabor, 1994; Wallace et al., 2001). They are high performers who meet their own goals and targets, not just for self-advancement or to please command officers. Further, their performance observes the code of ethics expected of public employees (Goodman, 1998; Leighton and Reiman, 2001; Sonnenberg, 1995). With growing multiculturalism in both the community and workforce, law enforcement professionals support policies and programs that promote collaboration among people of diverse backgrounds (Harman, 1992). Furthermore, they curb among their colleagues or the community at the first signs of divisiveness, intolerance, discrimination, and even violence in the workplace (Peak and Glensor, 1999; Twilling, 1995).

Synergy

Synergy implies cooperation and the integration of separate parts to function as a greater whole and to achieve a common goal. Synergy occurs through working together in combined action, attaining a greater total effect than a sum of the parts. Cultural synergy builds on the differences in people to promote mutual growth and accomplishment. Through such collaboration, similarities, strengths, and diverse talents are shared to enhance human activities and systems. For team management and teamwork, synergistic relations are essential (Moran and Harris, 2000). In law enforcement, synergistic leaders

- Facilitate interagency and interprecinct cooperation
- Create consensus, which enables disparate people and groups to work together by sharing perceptions, insights, and knowledge
- Promote participation, empowerment, and negotiation within an organization or community, so that members work to mutual advantage and are committed to teamwork and the common good over personal ambition or need
- Demonstrate skills of facilitating, networking, conflict resolution, and coordination
- Are open-minded, effective cross-cultural communicators

Synergistic leaders give priority to the professional development of subordinates, especially through training and team building (Justice and Jamieson, 1999).

Thus leadership, professionalism, and synergy are three powerful, interrelated concepts. When combined within the criminal justice system in general, or law enforcement and peacekeeping in particular, they may alter one's role image and performance. The following descriptions demonstrate the application of these concepts to real situations. Leadership, professionalism, and synergy are illustrated next at both the organizational and individual levels in the context of the new work culture (Harris, 1994).

REGIONAL OR STATEWIDE COOPERATION IN LAW ENFORCEMENT

Society and communities today are so complex and interdependent that individual departments can best deal with certain enforcement challenges and crime problems through cooperation among criminal justice entities at all levels of government. Although cooperation is certainly more efficient and effective, for many traditional public safety agencies, it may require a paradigm shift in the thinking of its members. Effecting change means exercising a type of law enforcement leadership that actively promotes specific information interchanges, joint ventures, and task forces that operate on a statewide or regional basis. It would be contrary-thinking and unprofessional behavior not to work with another agency because of jurisdictional jealously and fear as to who will get the credit for success in the operation, or because of distorted desires to protect one's agency territory and budget. The overriding concern should be the public good by agencies working together to prevent and counter criminality in the community, while promoting the common good and civility.

Perhaps Hawthorne, a police executive, has summed up the need and problems best in his research, which is summarized in Exhibit 15.1.

Within the larger criminal justice system, there are already in place many commissions, councils, and other structures for promoting interagency collaboration. Law enforcement leaders with a sense of professionalism and synergy would ensure that all their command is committed to such collaborative action (see Langworthy and Travis, 1999). As a case in point, many matters of police

---

Exhibit 15.1   Regional law enforcement consolidation of services.

Reduced funding, increased demands for public services, technological advances in law enforcement, and the regional nature of crime in the '90s have all been identified as factors that could entice some communities to merge law enforcement agencies with those of neighboring communities. These mergers, however, could lead to a loss of community identity, reduced level of local control over the police, and the political perception that the city cannot take care of itself. This study examines the opportunities for the functional consolidation of certain law enforcement support services to achieve the benefits of consolidation, without the perceived negative impacts of full law enforcement mergers. It includes a guideline for conducting a feasibility study to determine possibilities for consolidation in any given area, as well as a transition management plan to aid in the implementation of such a project. Common pitfalls and success factors are also identified to assist in the successful implementation of a regional approach to any law enforcement support function. (Hawthorne, 1995)

training are best dealt with at a statewide or regional level, but with local agency input and participation (Pierce, 1997). For example, there are such joint, interagency programs for training with other public-sector personnel in human behavior, cultural diversity, or affirmative action. Again, in large metropolitan areas with several police jurisdictions, a consortium might be established to create an alliance for that locality to address specific law enforcement problems (e.g., ethnic gangs, juvenile delinquency, or emergency preparedness). Similarly, a regional, collaborative approach in peacekeeping might involve joint problem solving and activities on such concerns as hate crimes or recruitment of more women and minorities into criminal justice careers (Justice Research Association, 2000). Probably the greatest area for improvement of *synergistic* relations is between and among federal, state, and local law enforcement.

In the corporate world, people must often face the challenges of mergers and acquisitions. Today we see more consolidation of police services and more contracting out for either county or private policing than we have in the past. (Goggans, 1996; Simonsen, 1998). In the twenty-first century, especially in smaller townships and cities, it is conceivable that more police and fire departments may be combined into a single emergency services provider. These mergers require overcoming old organizational loyalties while learning to cooperate with new colleagues who have different perspectives, training, and skills.

Agency representatives come from differing organizational cultures. Therefore, any interagency collaboration or merger requires the practice of the kind of cross-cultural communication skills described in Chapter 5. Another illustration directly related to this book's theme would be in a border city with a twin urban area in another country (Johnson, 1994). For the United States, this synergy could be along the northern border with Canada or the southern border with Mexico, requiring international cooperation among public agencies that have similar missions but different cultural contexts, including legal systems. In such situations, local police departments of both nations should routinely share information and cooperate in combating crime or facilitating cross-border traffic. How much more could be accomplished if the many law jurisdictions along the American–Mexican border, for example, were to enter into informal or formal arrangements to cooperate and advance the professional development of each other? For instance, within the two sister cities of Juarez, the Mexican police could be most helpful to their northern colleagues in terms of language and cultural training, particularly with reference to those of Mexican origin living in Texas. In return, the Texas peace officers might assist in the technical and professional preparation of their Mexican counterparts. This cooperation might contribute to more humane treatment of American citizens who break the law when south of the border. In that Napoleonic law system, the supposed transgressor is considered guilty until proven innocent, just the opposite of the U.S. legal system, which is based on English Common Law.

For American, Canadian, and Mexican police, there are numerous other ways to be mutually supportive, ranging from information exchanges on criminology and specific criminals and groups to promotion of better bilateral relations and border law enforcement management. Once the North American Free Trade Agreement

(NAFTA) is fully implemented, we should expect increasing exchanges and transfers between the citizens of Canada, the United States, and Mexico (Moran and Abbott, 2000). When law enforcement in all three countries of North America cooperate, that process is facilitated. To overcome cross-cultural barriers, police jurisdictions and their personnel in adjoining countries have more to gain by thinking in terms of synergy across borders. One place to begin is to learn about the differences in each national culture's legal systems. Therefore, something is to be gained by joint training projects, such as among the customs service or border patrol agents of one or all three nations.

Police Professionalism, Ethics, and Diversity

Police professionalism, according to Hunter, Mayhill, and Barker (2000), requires self-awareness and a positive self-image, such as was discussed in Chapter 14. For professionalism to grow in law enforcement, the late Pamela D. Mayhill advocated not only greater technical skill training but also higher educational attainments, along with the setting of goals for career development. To reduce stress within the working environment of modern police, this criminal justice professor advocated an atmosphere of improved intra-agency communication, as well as supportive relations with the community (Anderson, Swenson, and Clay, 1995).

Police professionalism.   The principal purpose of criminal justice education, whether in universities, colleges, or academies, is improved performance and increased professionalism by those in law enforcement. What, then, seem to be the characteristics of a police professional? Some answers have been provided throughout this book, including earlier in this chapter when we discussed the concept of professionalism in general. A law enforcement professional is

- One who is properly educated and public service oriented
- One whose behavior and conduct on the job is appropriate and ethical, avoiding clear conflict of interests
- One who respects the dignity and humanity of everyone contacted in the course of his or her duties by treating all fairly and with equal justice
- One who is culturally sensitive to the differences and potential of others
- One who is aware of the impact of agency culture on the professional behavior of officers
- One who is a lifetime learner concerned about personal and career development for both one's self and others

The Florida Criminal Justice Executive Institute recently issued a monograph entitled *Against Brutality and Corruption*. It discusses how these twin evils can be countered within law enforcement by officers who demonstrate integrity, wisdom, and professionalism. Its author, Edwin J. Delattre (1991a), observes:

> We tend nowadays to neglect the immorality of professional incompetence! Many people who discuss ethics in different walks of life, whether in business or public service or the traditional professions, seem to believe that behaving honestly on the job and having the "right" attitudes about race, sexual orientation, and the environment are all that ethics requires. This view ignores our plain duty to be professionally competent and good at our jobs.

In the *Teacher's Guide* for another volume, Delattre (1991b) made the point to police academy instructors that all police training is directly relevant to ethics, which should include competent performance. We not only reinforce that observation, but add to it: All police professional development should contain adequate preparation in the understanding of culture and the attainment of cross-cultural skills. Our position is that ethical behavior by law officers also encompasses respect for human dignity, concern for human rights, and tolerance for diversity in the human family (Hurst, 1993; Miller, 1996; Ortega, 1993). Unethical behavior is present when officers are deliberately racist, acting with prejudice, bigotry, and intolerance toward a fellow officer, citizen, or foreign visitor. Such actions by public employees are simply unprofessional and unacceptable. The public will no longer overlook or tolerate such behavior by *peace* officers (Goodman, 1998; Leighton and Reiman, 2001).

Although the criminal justice system has made significant progress in recruiting and promoting women and members of diverse groups within the past decade, discrimination still holds sway within some law enforcement agencies and in the treatment of the public by their representatives. The case studies discussed in Chapter 14 provide ample evidence to confirm this reality. However, consider the observations of an insider within that system (see Exhibit 15.2).

Police ethics. At the core of professionalism should be one's sense of ethics (Muraskin and Muraskin, 2001). This may be manifested individually or through a group, such as society in general or a profession in particular, such as those sworn to uphold the law. Ethical practices are cultural expressions of a society or of an organization, or of a profession. The *Random House Dictionary* defines the term *ethics* as "a system of moral principles; the rules of conduct recognized in respect to a particular class of human actions within a particular culture as expressed by a group (e.g., medical ethics, police ethics, or Christian ethics), or by an individual (e.g., personal ethics)." The alternative definition is "a formal classification for study as a branch of philosophy dealing with values relating to human conduct, with respect to rightness and wrongness."

Certain ethical standards are cultural universals, generally accepted by humankind; other ethical practices are culturally specific, dependent on the attitudes and traditions of a particular group. Some ethical expectations are overt or open, while others are covert or hidden. For example, in parts of rural India one of the authors discovered that if an automobile driver were to hit someone, the expectation was that the driver did not stop but proceeded to the nearest town, where the incident was to be reported to the police. The practice did not condone hit-and-run driving, but faced a reality that in this developing country the justice system was inadequate, so people might be tempted to take its administration into their own hands with immediacy. Thus the driver, whether at fault or not, escapes to police in the next village to admit the accident. In contrast, in American culture the legal and ethical action for those involved in a car accident is to exchange information and/or to call the police and report the matter immediately from the site of the accident. The culture universal is that drivers must report accidents in which they are involved; the culture specific is that the procedure for doing this differs in national cultures. Police professionals should be aware of such differences.

Exhibit 15.2   Top civil rights official says discrimination persists.

Some believe we now live in a color-blind society, said Bill Lann Lee, the top official for civil rights at the United States Department of Justice. Despite *the advancement of minorities in education, population, and the workforce, there is still discrimination today,* said Mr. Lee in a lecture at the St. John's University Law School in Jamaica, N.Y.

> *The public's response to the shootings of [Amadou] Diallo and the brutal assault on [Abner] Louima are signs of a breakdown in trust in many of our nation's communities. Many people believe they are treated unfairly by law enforcement and that it is biased. For these reasons, many citizens don't trust police officers, and are unwilling to report a crime or to testify in criminal cases. For the most part, police officers do their job with honor and integrity.*

Mr. Lee commented that he could not discuss the Justice Department review underway on the shootings of Mr. Diallo by four police officers, stressing that federal jurisdiction is limited. We can only prosecute where there has been a willful deprivation of constitutional rights. He further observed that in national opinion polls, two out of three persons say they have confidence in police. When the question is posed to African-Americans, it's one out of four.

In his speech, Lee insisted that effective policing is law enforcement living up to a contract to the communities they serve by treating every citizen with respect and dignity. Every American must respect the law, and the law must respect every American. As acting assistant attorney general, Lee reported that since 1993, 200 law enforcement officers have been prosecuted for willful violation of constitutional rights. He reminded his audience that civil suits also have been brought for alleged patterns and practices of police misconduct, like the use of excessive force and failure by supervisors to discipline officers adequately.

Lee recalled that in 1994, Congress gave the U.S. Department of Justice the authority to punish wrongdoers. . . . [T]he Justice Department filed against the New Jersey State Police based on admitted evidence of racial profiling. As a result, the State of New Jersey agreed to prohibit its state troopers from making traffic stops because of race and national origin of drivers. [See also Chapter 1.]

In enforcing the Civil Rights Act of 1964, Lee noted that over the years, the civil rights division of the Justice Department has literally drawn hundreds of cases that changed the racial and gender makeup of the nation's law enforcement departments. Combating employment discrimination helps to reduce police misconduct. It opens up the talent pool so that the police forces reflect the diversity of the communities they serve. Also they are better able to form positive working relationships with community members. Further, they can more effectively deal with hate crimes which affect the lives of all, no matter what race, sex, or religion.

Lee quoted *Parade* magazine's report that up to 100,000 people in the U.S.A. and its territories are forced against their will to work in inhuman conditions. He added, One hundred and thirty-five years after the Emancipation Proclamation, we still see involuntary servitude and slavery in this democracy. He described Federal prosecutions against such illegal acts, as well as against discrimination in the purchase of a home. Another example is the enforcement of the Americans with Disabilities Act which protects some 54 million citizens. Lee declared that this bill was to integrate disabled people into the American mainstream by removing barriers in communications and architectural arrangements.

The assistant attorney general concluded: Civil rights are designed to cover everyone, not some people. Civil rights laws do not divide. They unite us as Americans! (Gonzalez, July 7, 2000, Vol. 1:3, pp. 1–4).

As a concept, ethics is closely associated with professionalism. Codes of ethics are vital to guide the behavior of practitioners of the learned professions (e.g., law or medicine) and to punish those who do not adhere to the agreed,

---

Exhibit 15.3   Professionalism.

This goal area is being included to emphasize our continuing obligation to deliver the highest quality police service in a manner that is seen as fair, impartial, and professional . . . Our objectives in this area for the coming year are:

1. Continued dedication to the principles of policing as articulated in our Mission, Vision, and Principles, and also in the Code of Ethics
2. To continue following the maxim of treating others as you would desire to be treated. . . . In each contact, whether internal or external, treating others in a respectful, professional manner is our first obligation and enduring concern
3. Continue to focus on building trust throughout the organization
4. Supervisors and managers should know the principles articulated in the City Leadership Statement, then act in a manner consistent with that directive Organizational leaders will be evaluated, in part, on their ability to carry out that directive (Memorandum to Members of the Police Department, January 25, 2000, from Chief of Police Bob Harrison, City of Vacaville)

---

enunciated conduct of behavior for those vocations. For peace officers, such codes promote self-regulation and discipline within a law enforcement agency (Boyd, 1993). Often these codes are written and sometimes are summarized within an agency mission statement. To be a professional implies not only competence and expertness, but adherence to higher standards of professional conduct (Bowman, 1991; Gellermann et al., 1990; Lewis, 1991).

In the best sense, professionalism implies having more than technical skills and refers to the moral contributions that professionals make in a complex, democratic society—the ethic of the calling. The ethical person is perceived as someone who has courage and integrity, is willing to resist corruption and unprincipled people by upholding humanity, justice, and civility. Such a peace officer tries to be loyal to his or her own conscience and avoids unprofessional behavior (e.g., use of excessive force, adherence to the *blue code of silence* during investigations, expressions of bias and bigotry, or acceptance of bribery).

To conclude this section, we provide in Exhibit 15.3 an excerpt from a departmental memorandum of the Chief of Police in Vacaville, California, which underscores our message here.

Police and diverse community groups.   Nowhere is law enforcement's sense of professionalism and ethics challenged more than the manner in which we treat diverse ethnic and racial group members, whether citizens or foreigners. Although North America consists of three nations marked by waves of immigration to Canada, the United States, and Mexico, the type of émigrés coming to their borders continuously changes. Apart from the indigenous Native Americans who were here first, immigrants from the fifteenth through the nineteenth centuries were mainly from Europe and Africa and were gradually assimilated into the mainstream population. But in the twentieth century, the newcomers were primarily from Asia, the Middle East, and the countries of the former Soviet Union; for them, the process of acculturation is ongoing over several generations.

What constitutes the term *minority group* is becoming increasingly debatable. For example, in some states (e.g., California) and cities (e.g., Miami, Florida), the Hispanic or Latino "minority" is becoming the majority, while Caucasians will become the minority group in such areas. One strategy for improving relations is obviously to bring more diverse members into law enforcement, a phenomenon that is taking place slowly in North America (see Muraskin, 2000).

Any new group integrating into the United States will present new law enforcement challenges that require changes in police tactics and behavior in the twenty-first century. Exhibit 15.4 describes one such emerging issue in the next decade.

Exhibit 15.4   New migrant communities.

While most immigrants to the United States concentrate on becoming Americans, there are new groups who have come as refugees, fleeing persecution, strife, and distant wars. Their minds and efforts are directed to their native countries and their suffering peoples. These include the Tamils of Sri Lanka, the Eritreans and Ethiopians of eastern Africa, the Congolese and Sierra Leoneans of western Africa, the Kurds of Iraq and Turkey, the Afghans from Afghanistan, the H'mong tribesmen of Laos, the Muslims from the Middle East, and even the followers of the Falun Gong sect from China, along with thousands of others, such as Serbs and Kosovoans from Yugoslavia. This diaspora usually arrives poor and live together in less desirable urban centers of the United States, striving to preserve their traditional cultures, especially their languages and music. Often such desperate peoples are at the agricultural or rural stage of human development, largely from peasant stock. Normally, they have little knowledge of English but are hard working and take jobs that more prosperous Americans no longer want. Their common concern is for relatives and friends in their homeland. Thus, they frequently send back a portion of their meager earnings here, take out bank loans, buy bonds, or engage in all kinds of voluntary relief work to assist the folks in their native countries. They seek information about those left behind through newsletters and newspapers in their native language, or even by using the Internet and maintaining Web sites.

Those left behind in the old country are very dependent on the generosity of these new immigrants; the economies of some of their Third World countries are entirely sustained on gifts from these exiles. For example, 35 groups support the destitute Sri Lankan Tamils who are totally dependent on their expatriates abroad. One Tamil bank takes in $350,000 billion a year in this way, about half as much as the Sri Lankan government's war budget.

The downside is that some of these American funds go to support divisions left behind from past misunderstandings, including civil wars. Of the 30 groups designated by the U.S. State Department as terrorists, most are doing their fund-raising in this country. In July 2000, 200 police officers in Charlotte, North Carolina, arrested a man suspected of raising money for the Hezbullah extremists in Lebanon and Palestine. Further, some of the old-country rivalries and feuds have been exported to the United States, often on the basis of clan loyalties—to further their narrow cause, conferences, petitions, and protests are organized, even on-line. All this contributes to furthering ethnic tensions, and sometimes illegal activities. For instance, the large Afghan community in Flushing, New York, is split between the supporters of the Taliban back home and their opponents. The 70,000 rural-mountain-type H'mongs in Minnesota fought with the Americans in the Vietnam War. They have thriving farmers' markets, but cooperation among themselves is undermined by clan divisions, along with arguments between moderates and radicals over military action in Laos against the still existing Communist government.

While most of these contemporary immigrants are law abiding, hard working, family oriented, and dedicated to education for their children, the realities described have great implications for law enforcement. Such upwardly mobile peoples are vulnerable to victimization by U.S. criminals, as well as by the lawbreakers among their own. The illegal activities of Russian–American Mafia in Bensonhurst, Brooklyn, confirm this unpleasant factor. (Adapted from "There Is Another Country," *Economist*, August 19th, 2000, pp. 26–27.)

CAREER DEVELOPMENT AND PROFESSIONAL OPPORTUNITIES

A professional peace officer masters the basics of his or her discipline or field, then moves on to higher, more innovative performance. Such a person not only possesses vision and a strong sense of mission but also has the capacity to bring out the best in others while coping with ever more complex situations (Block, 1991; Kirpatrick, 2000). Professional development in criminal justice systems should be considered within realistic limits, however. For example, there are limitations on the officials in charge as to what education, training, and support services are possible. Departmental constraints include declining budgets, expanding service demands—including increased 911 calls—and the quality of personnel now employed. Individual officers face constraints on their career development caused by job demands, family requirements, educational or financial limitations, and personal motivation.

For law enforcement organizations, human resource development (HRD) starts with recruitment and selection of qualified candidates. Apart from testing and basic qualifications, future peace officers must be chosen who have stable personalities, are educable and career growth oriented, and are representative of the multicultural communities in which they serve. In previous chapters, we have reviewed this challenge.

The ideal recruit should possess the potential to become the police professional described earlier in this chapter. Further, the academy curriculum must be relevant and constantly altered to prepare newcomers for the realities of their actual duties on the job in an ever-changing society. Just as a culture adapts, so do the laws that officers enforce and the duties they perform. For example, because of the diversity of the New York City population, its police academy, like others in the East and Midwest of the United States, devotes a third of the study time to learning from the social sciences; a large part of this segment deals with cross-cultural issues. Harris designed a similar program for the Philadelphia Police Department entitled "Police Development and Human Behavior," which provided academy students with the key concepts from the behavioral sciences of psychology, anthropology, and sociology. This program is encapsulated in his book *High Performance Leadership* (Harris, 1994).

Once sworn, the new officers must be given ample opportunities to advance in their careers, whether through in-service training or external study, so as to position themselves for promotions. Studies outside one's department, especially at colleges and universities, ideally should be subsidized by the agency. It is vital that those who rise into leadership positions within law enforcement be concerned about enhancing and capitalizing on the human assets. Within law enforcement, it begins by actions to promote one's own career development as well as that of one's coworkers (Brooks, 1987; Distelrath, 1989; Terborch, 1987). Then this concern expands to learning about current concepts and practices not only in policing and peacekeeping but also in human relations and cross-cultural communications. Those assigned to agency specialization need additional training in those fields of expertise, which may range from criminology and management information systems to training and personnel functions. For many, this continuing education may encompass new laws and technologies, as well as cultural diversity skills and knowledge of equal employment legislation. It is advantageous when police are included in a city- or countywide leadership or human resource program, so as to benefit from learning and interacting with other civil servants in their geographic area.

Many American states and Canadian provinces have provisions for such career development of their officers. Special institutes are often devoted to leadership development of supervisory personnel. However, it is at the higher levels of police and correctional administration that special attention should be given to career development in strategic management and planning.

Mentoring and Networking

Law enforcement agencies and their officers have always, to some extent, shared information and cooperated in crime fighting, as well as in career advancement, for mutual benefit. Perhaps the latter motive was the basis for the emergence of the Police Benevolent Associations and ethnic police organizations. Other examples are the traditional grapevine and informal supportive camaraderie within the global police, which traditionally has been called "brotherhood." What is proposed here is a cooperative strategy of mentoring and networking far beyond this previous collaboration. Such a formal strategy would advance both professionalism and career development, especially among women, minorities, and new recruits in the criminal justice system.

Mentors.   For some time, police have been paired together, often to share a patrol car. When on patrol, more experienced officers are often assigned as partners to less experienced employees, and in this way informal mentoring takes place. The strategy of mentors can be extended between sworn and civilian workers in the department or can even be expanded so that officers become mentors to troubled youth in the community (as in Big Brother/Big Sister programs). There is a need to adopt a formal system of mentors who are assigned initially to assist young recruits, especially women and minorities, to advance in their law enforcement careers (Murray and Owen, 1991). Chapter 3 offered initial insights on this subject.

Mentoring is simply a process whereby the more knowledgeable and experienced are connected to newer recruits, so they may share their insights and expertise (Cohen, 2000). The mentor may discover and encourage latent talents and abilities in the less experienced person. Mentoring can be of a limited duration or a lifetime relationship, as often happens between professors or teachers and their students. In law enforcement, it is a sign of a true professional when one is willing to devote time and effort as a mentor to help in a colleague's career development and empowerment. When a senior officer shares himself or herself with a junior officer in this manner, then both should benefit by the encounter and the emerging relationship. Essentially, the mentor develops the human potential of the mentee, particularly with regard to further education or training and leadership.

A related activity is the peer counseling team, where mature, well-balanced officers are trained to counsel and aid their peers in time of stress or personal emergencies. Counseling may be needed, for example, when an officer is engaged in a shooting and may be subject to trauma after the event, or when an officer experiences a new disability, suffers burnout, or becomes dysfunctional on the job (Janke, 1993). Similarly, the organization known as Alcoholics Anonymous utilizes a recovered alcoholic to help a new member. Peer counseling may be used with officers accused of misconduct (Jones and Carlson, 2001).

Boosting Officer Morale

In the twenty-first century, global society is both complex and diverse (Muraskin and Roberts, 1999). Policing urban areas can be very complex and stressful. It requires much training and skill for law enforcement to cope with the multiple demands made on it. Readers are only too well aware of increasing stressors that may lead peace officers to succumb to depression, burnout, nervous breakdowns, substance abuse, or other dysfunctional behavior.

Enlightened leadership, then, promotes wellness and fitness programs, staff development, and social gatherings. These and other such modern management practices facilitate improved performance, good mental health, comradeship, and job satisfaction among the workforce. Certainly, using human resource development as both a reward and an opportunity is one way to motivate officers. We asked a police executive who has benefited from such HRD strategies to comment on this matter, and his responses are included in Exhibit 15.5.

Exhibit 15.5 illustrates the value of leadership development in law enforcement and underscores the need for personnel offices to publicize the opportunities. A departmental newsletter, bulletin board, or Web site can inform officers of application procedures, scholarships, and grants. Should an officer qualify, then it is up to enlightened administrators to ensure the person's schedule is altered for part-time training or leaves are provided when appropriate.

PEACEKEEPING STRATEGIES IN MULTICULTURAL SOCIETIES

Within multiracial communities struggling with myriad problems of transition and integration, economic constraints, and rising crime, representatives of the justice system cannot afford to act capriciously and prejudicially. If social order is not to be replaced by chaos, law enforcement representatives of all types not only need to be culturally sensitive but also must actively avoid racist, sexist, and homophobic behavior that may trigger violent social protest. The police researcher Neil Lingle, in his futurist study on ethnic groups and culture, identified programs that can promote a cooperative and interactive relationship between peace officers and the community (e.g., coalitions and partnerships). His recommendations for law enforcement include the following (Lingle, 1992):

- More cultural awareness and sensitivity training of personnel
- More recruitment and promotion of minorities and ethnics with the help of police unions
- More information to officers on external factors affecting their performance (e.g., influence of wealth and economic power, as well as racial or ethnic and political power)

Exhibit 15.5   Motivating peace officers.

The nature of policing is such that improving morale is often an elusive goal. In a profession that requires its members to work odd and late hours, it is difficult to ask officers to sacrifice personal and family time in deference to community emergencies. To further ask these workers to assist in meeting your staffing commitments, to readily accept overtime or court time, is a challenge if they are not to fall prey to cynicism and complaining. Therefore, it is essential that executives are attuned to the inevitable stress of the job and take steps to mitigate the long-term damage it can cause, while creating a more supportive work environment.

Officer motivation can be improved when members understand the goals, objectives, and plans of an agency and how they play a part in these. The overall success of a department is ensured when officers can contribute to this process and know what we as executives are doing. In our case, a three-year strategic plan is developed by a cross section of our organization and finally refined by management. From this we promulgate annual goals and objectives that will positively influence the department's future. In other words, the members share in setting the plan that they ultimately will bring to fruition.

We also promote a work culture that emphasizes professionalism, respect for each other and the people we serve, and conducting business with a spirit of optimism and integrity. To this end, we encourage continuing professional development, especially by participation in advanced training opportunities. Our Youth Service Officers may attend the Delinquency Council Institute of the University of Southern California. Sergeants and lieutenants may apply for the FBI National Academy, while lieutenants are encouraged by their fifth anniversary of rank to complete the State of California's Law Enforcement Command College, which may also lead to a master's degree. The assistant chief is expected to take advantage of the Senior Management Institute for Police presented by the Police Executive Research Forum and the JFK School of Public Policy at Harvard University. A graduate of the latter two mentioned programs, I strongly support participation in such continuing education if the department is to cultivate twenty-first-century police mind-sets. For our workers to achieve their full potential, we are also assessing ways to implement mentoring programs for entry-level officers and staff members, as well as to assist midcareer supervisors.

As chief, I try to provide a role model in these matters. Having experienced the benefit of graduate-level leadership education myself, I not only require such education for promotion but also participate in curriculum revisions and alumni events sponsored by our state's Commission on Peace Officers Standards and Training. While a division commander and latter deputy chief in the City of Coronado, I was supported in taking advantage of the preceding programs, while also obtaining two master's degrees and beginning a doctorate in leadership. However, the most unique support rendered by the city manager and police chief enabled me to accept a Fulbright Fellowship to study policing abroad in the United Kingdom. Through a publication of the Police Executive Research Program, I learned of this opportunity sponsored by the Council for International Exchange of Scholars, in conjunction with the U.S. Information Agency. When my application was selected to receive this honor, I volunteered to use my available vacation and leave time for this purpose. My agency granted me a four-month paid leave of absence, so that I might go to England's Centre for Police and Criminal Justice at the University of Exeter. This cross-cultural experience permitted me not only to travel extensively in that country and form many professional relationships but also to visit a number of police training sites and learn of the British approach to law enforcement. As one of a handful of police officers to have been granted a Fulbright award, this proved to be one of the most invigorating personal and professional times of my life. Upon my return home, I verified that I had fulfilled the requirement for my doctoral internship, addressed a national conference on the British efforts to update their police code of ethics, and published four journal articles on my experience. I now have a better appreciation of a foreign culture and policing from a philosophical perspective. The value of professional development for police has been confirmed for me, as well as the need to allow for educational leaves for such purposes! (B. Harrison, October 5, 2000)

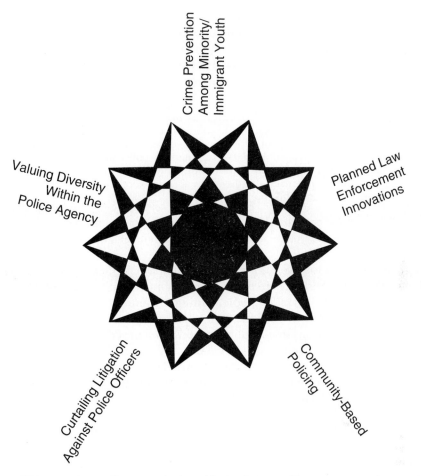

Exhibit 15.6   Peace officer strategies in multicultural communities.

- More study on how to confront institutional racism and the impact of minority employment and promotion on police policies and practices in the future

Those who would uphold law and order in twenty-first century should be more proactive and less reactive (Thibault, Lynch, and McBride, 2001). Furthermore, the new generation of peace officers must not only increase their knowledge in such matters but also promote positive law enforcement innovations (refer to Exhibit 15.6). In this next section, we focus on a few strategies for agencies to consider in their efforts to keep community peace in a multicultural society.

Community-Based Policing

The last two decades of the twentieth century brought problems to law enforcement that forced strategic changes within agencies. Because of greater population diversity in many communities, reduced budgets, increased illegal immigration, and social disorder, criminal justice entities were subject to increased scrutiny and public protest. Progressive law enforcement executives embraced a strategy of policing to meet many of these challenges, community-based policing (see Chapters 1 and 14) (Berg, 1993; Lopez, 1994; Slater, 1994). The transition to this strategy became evident in 1987 when the Philadelphia Police Commissioner's Council declared:

> A key concept . . . is that the police abandon the image of themselves as a "thin blue line," standing between the "good citizens" of the community on the one hand, and the "bad guys" on the other. Rather, they should favor an image of themselves as partners to the community in a joint effort to produce freedom from fear and victimization. . . . Finally, this concept acknowledges that unless the police work at establishing and maintaining a proper relationship with the community, they themselves can be seen as victimizers and troublemakers, rather than as peace-keepers. (Philadelphia Police Commissioner's Report, 1987, pp. 4–5).

For the most part, the Philadelphia Police Department has moved in this direction to change its image and tactics with the citizens of that "City of Brotherly Love."

Lee P. Brown followed this same approach when chief executive for police in Houston and New York City. In the latter municipality, with a force of 29,000 police, Brown earned high marks for implementing a community policing program that quadrupled the number of officers on foot patrol while sponsoring a crime-fighting partnership with citizens that resulted in a 6.7 percent reduction in reported crimes in early 1992. When Brown resigned to become a criminal justice professor at Texas Southern University, New York's then Mayor Dinkins praised him as among the world's best police administrators, who managed in 1991 to reduce crime in every category within the city "for the first time in some 36 years" ("Police Praised By Mayor," *Los Angeles Times,* August 4, 1992, p. A-2).

By 2000 community policing had contributed significantly to better public relations and even crime reduction in major American urban centers (Oliver, 2001; Stevens, 2001). The latest U.S. Department of Justice survey of violent crime confirms these improvements. In 1999 this report found a decline in every type of offense against citizens, except rape and sexual assault ("Compromise Reached on Racial Profiling Law," *San Diego Union-Tribune,* August 28, 2000, p. A-2). James Fox, criminal justice professor at Boston's Northeastern University, attributes the continuing crime decline to success in many areas, including better policing tactics, crime prevention programs, longer prison terms for convicted felons, drug market shift from crack cocaine, and the aging of the baby-boom population. Other criminologists also cite the strong American economy and stricter gun controls as contributing factors.

Law enforcement agencies adopting the community policing strategy have not only become partners within a community but advocates for public well-being. As a result, the role of the peace officer, especially at the line level, changes dramatically in those cities and counties using community-based policing. In addition, with increased contact between community members and police, there will be opportunities to educate the public as to the difficult practices and decisions that police have to make continually (see Exhibit 15.7).

Exhibit 15.7   The police department engages police critics.

Police swapped jobs with Sydney Ethridge yesterday. San Diego officers invited their most outspoken critic to step into their shoes during the department's first deadly-force training session for civilians. And then the officers evaluated whether Ethridge should have fired a paintball gun at a mentally ill, machete-swinging, suicidal woman played convincingly by Officer Cat Millett. The officers were impressed, and so was Ethridge. . . .

As President of the Coalition of African-American Organizations, she said, "what I actually learned was that there is a lot that is going through your mind in such situations, and that you have to make split-second decisions. It's not easy. She picked up the knife and started toward me. She left me with no choice."

For most of the officers, who spent Saturday without pay to pose as gun-toting robbers, bat-wielding assailants, and other unsavory characters, hearing those words made the cuts and bruises from the paintball rounds worthwhile.

About fifteen community members, invited by the National Latino Peace Officers Association's local chapter listened to lectures on deadly force and then broke into groups to experience simulations of actual police work. . . . In the debriefing to analyze what the participants learned, Ethridge added, "as we go through these scenarios, it gives me a greater understanding of how fast things happen, and your thought processes while making instantaneous decisions." (Thornton, 2000, pp. B1, B5)

To accomplish effective community policing, methods must be developed to enter into a problem identification and solving dialogue. Mastrofski and Greene (1991) emphasized that "if police are to increase a neighborhood's involvement in determining how it is policed, then three issues must be addressed: (1) to what extent should the community be organized, (2) who should be represented, and (3) what should the community do?" (p. 16)

In July 2000 Harris visited an old New York City neighborhood of Flushing, New York. While awaiting a plane change at nearby LaGuardia Field, he was surprised at how this once Caucasian area had completely changed into a largely Asian community, dominated by Chinese and Korean immigrants. When a nearby fast-food restaurant was invaded by outsiders who wounded seven customers, killing two, the new business leaders entered into a dialogue with their local precinct commanders. One outcome of improved community relations is that some larger enterprises in the vicinity, such as hotels, are utilizing off-duty police to strengthen their security forces.

Critical to the success of any community-based policing program is resolution of two issues: (1) How willing are citizens to accept some responsibility for community law enforcement? and (2) How willing are police officers to relinquish the social isolation of police cars in order to be involved with neighborhood citizens in police–community programs? These issues must be a part of a strategic, long-term plan by the chief executive desiring to implement community policing (CP) in his or her community. Chief Darrel W. Stephens, who wrote the foreword to this book, maintains that community- or problem-oriented policing is the future of law enforcement and is the next stage in the evolution of this profession.

How is the transition to this community orientation to be made? Typically, it takes an agency five to seven years to go from traditional policing to community policing. As a start, some departments have created citizen police academy programs that provide knowledge of CP, along with the requisite skills and resources to do problem solving. Other communities hold neighborhood forums to accomplish the same objective. As with change for most people, it takes time to transform the attitudes of typical officers toward such modern policing. Some have the mistaken notion there are community-oriented police officers—and then there are all those other real cops.

For long-term CP success, departments must recruit people who exhibit compassion, have good communications skills, and are problem solvers. Job descriptions and evaluations should be rewritten to emphasize and reward such abilities. Further, community policing also requires obtaining personnel, whether sworn or not, who have the local foreign-language skills to reach out to new ethnic communities.

This law enforcement approach is not incident or technology driven. Officers work in the neighborhoods on a decentralized basis, stressing regular contacts with citizens. They report back to their supervisor, who in turn transmits the information to the chief executive and his or her staff so that additional resources can be deployed as necessary. In addition to tactical plans, the agency should have a plan that calls for consulting with key community leaders before merely reacting in the event of a major crisis. Too often, police reaction has been the stimulus event for riots. Thus, Willie Williams, chief of the Los Angeles Police Department, wisely advised his force: "You just can't wait and look for the triggering mechanisms in the community. . . . Personnel must be trained to understand that they live and work in a diverse community, and to understand the different values and nuances of those people" ("Police Training For More Diverse Communities," *Los Angeles Times,* March 7, 1988, p. 24).

Obviously, community policing cannot function in a vacuum. It needs the support of not only the public but also other government agencies. Eldrin Bell, when the African-American chief of police for Atlanta, Georgia, declared at a conference hosted by the National Organization of Black Law Enforcement Executives and other organizations, "We cannot get to community-oriented policing until we have community-oriented government" (Bell, 1992). Chief Bell suggested that government be decompartmentalized, cleaned up, and made more community directed through use of community councils. He contended that by doing so community members and government employees work together to solve problems. The police are a driving force in the process.

Community-oriented policing is *proactive,* based on the neighborhood and the police identifying problems and directing resources to solve them. For example, as the police move more into the world of high technology, we see officers with laptop computers collecting information on and analyzing what is occurring in their neighborhood, including hate/bias crimes. Community-based policing involves additional expenses in cities or counties with already tight budgets. Public administrators and legislators must support CP efforts, lest they experience "Pay me now (providing budget for such strategies) or pay me later (the aftermath of riots, disturbances, distrust, and so forth)."

Exhibit 15.8 Equal justice?

How would you feel if the police regularly stopped you, for no apparent reason, demanding to know who you are and where you are going? Further, suppose they often search your car or belongings without sufficient cause because they consider your ethnic group more prone to criminality. How would you feel as the target of such frequent questioning and suspicion, especially if you can ill afford a lawyer to protect your rights? To make matters worse when charges are leveled against you, you may spend months languishing in jail, until an often incompetent, public attorney is assigned to you; then he or she usually advises you to plead guilty. Should you get a jury trial, it will not be composed of your peers or those from your ethnic group. In reality, if I am a young man from my ethnic group, the statistics prove that in the U.S., our rate of imprisonment is seven times that of the general population, for my kind are automatically thought by police as inclined to violence and crime.

People of color like me are arrested, convicted and killed more often than other citizens. In fact, among young persons within my group from the age of 20–29 years, one in three is in prison, on parole or probation. And who am I? —a black youth supposedly living in a democracy lauded as the home of the free and the brave. My ancestors were brought here as slaves. Like many of the poor in America, I am often denied the constitutional protections of which my countrymen are so proud. Whether on the streets, in a police station or courtroom, constitutional protections barely exist for the poor, particularly African-Americans. For example, in my economically deprived neighborhood, police regularly sweep through, stopping and arresting whomever they like. The courts have repeatedly refused to require the police to advise us that according to the Fourth Amendment of the Constitution, we have the right to refuse a search unless the police have a warrant or we are being arrested for a crime. Even when members of my group have an education and a job, we may be stopped by officers for "walking or driving while black." If white citizens were treated like we are by law enforcement, there would be a public outcry! For the vast majority of our people who have been stopped by police are subsequently proven innocent. There are no equal rights for my kind when it comes to search and seizure!(Adapted from Cole, 2000, p. 31)

Crime Prevention among Minority and Immigrant Youth

If it is to succeed, community-oriented policing must focus on positive relations, contact, and communications between young people and peace officers. This approach not only counters but actually prevents juvenile delinquency (Bartol and Bartol, 1999; Goode, 2001). A related challenge today is how to train officers to be successful role models for the benefit of young people, especially those from immigrant or "ghetto" groups. One aspect of this effort should make the case for equal justice in law and order, so as eventually to attract some of these youth into law enforcement careers (Shiner, 1996).

However, before such a goal can be realized, police officers have to change how they perceive deprived or disturbed youth and how they deal with them as human beings. Consider the message in Exhibit 15.8, based on a recent book that examines how the criminal justice system handles troubled youth from the underclass. Its author, David Cole, is a professor of law at Georgetown University.

Certainly Exhibit 15.8 provides some sobering thoughts for planned change in the way the criminal justice system treats youth from diverse racial and ethnic groups. But how about young people in general, what is the situation and what is working? Consider two cases.

Schools: Some law enforcement agencies contract with school districts to provide officers on a daily basis for security purposes, as well as to offer role models. Many officers get involved in educating youth on a voluntary basis in a variety of ways. Sworn officers are rightly proud of sponsoring projects such as the Police Athletic League (PAL), to involve neighborhood kids in constructive teamwork, or their Police Explorer Scout programs. Future studies by police executives propose a variety of youth strategies for this purpose, which range from a police high school curriculum to police cadet programs (Devore, 1989; Harding, 1990). In May 1992 the president of the United States publicly praised and advocated more efforts like the Los Angeles County Sheriff's Youth League, where off-duty police develop positive relations with the community's young people. So far police in schools and increased security in these facilities have not deterred violence in random actions by alienated students against classmates, as occurred at Columbine High School in Littleton, Colorado, in 1999. It would seem that more preventative programs to identify violence-prone youth have to be developed by both police and educators through cooperative efforts (see Meadows, 2001; Small, 1996).

Gangs: Perhaps the biggest challenges would appear to be in preventing or counteracting rising youth violence, especially among males between the ages of 12 and 24 (see Britz, Rush, and Barker, 2001). The problem is critical in the nation's inner cities, where unemployed, disadvantaged youths seek identity and support through destructive gang participation (Hebel, 1990; Hoffman, 1994; Huff, 1990; Jackson, 1991; Seaman, 1996; Thomas, 1990; Tognetti, 1991). As a case in point, the Los Angeles County district attorney, Ira Reiner, issued a May 1992 report on gang violence in that community, based on the mammoth county computer database called GREAT (Gang Reporting Evaluation and Tracking). He estimated 150,000 members in 1,000 gangs, made up largely of African Americans, Latinos, and some Asians. Although the figures may be less because of duplication in law enforcement agency data, misperception, or mislabeling of some young males, such groups are not the only cause of rising drug crimes and gun misuse. Yet gangs do account for a dramatic upswing in the murder rates (more than 800 homicides a year), often through senseless drive-by killings. As such gangs declare truces and work together, or link up with gangs in other cities for criminal activity, they can become a real threat to community stability if members' energies are not redirected. Often, the gang entities recruit by force or intimidation from among new immigrant groups, such as Asians (Wossener, 1995). Furthermore, gang activities have moved from urban to rural areas (Davidson, 1995).

To manage the deteriorating situation, the Los Angeles district attorney recommended the usual remedies: improved education, job training, and gang prevention programs. Although the statistics may be controversial, the 235-page report of the district attorney does have specific proposals that have significance for urban communities elsewhere:

1. Develop a countywide master plan for helping youth at risk of joining gangs, especially among minorities and immigrants
2. Overhaul the juvenile justice system, which often serves as a recruitment and training program for the gangs
3. Focus on the 10 to 15 percent of gang members who are hard-core criminals
4. Develop cooperative private-industry programs to provide training and jobs for inner-city youth

Nationally, other solutions may be forthcoming. Recent law enforcement studies, such as those cited earlier, point out a number of antigang and youth-oriented strategies. Some might receive financial support from foundations and corporations. Peace officers may assist nonprofit groups to write proposals for such private- or public-sector grants. Among the possibilities for criminal justice agencies to explore are the following:

- *Cooperation with the local clergy,* who maintain effective relations with gang members. For example, a coalition of Protestant and Catholic churches have formed the Southern California Organizing Committee, which promotes a "Hope in Youth" campaign. This is a five-year, public–private investment in a $20 million fund. With it, teams were formed in their church congregations to work with youth. One team member would be an outreach worker with a caseload of 25 youths at risk, leading them from gang involvement to alternative education or training and drug rehabilitation; a second team member would work with individual parents of gang members, while a third develops parent unions to empower them with regard to their children's education. Each church then would sponsor and mentor gang members in transition to a more mature way of life.
- *Assistance to local ethnic business organizations* that wish to work with gangs in community ventures and job development. One such association was formed between the Korean-American Grocers Association and two Los Angeles African American gangs, the Bloods and the Crips. Although gangs will increasingly occupy law enforcement time, agencies must be creative in devising nonarrest approaches to a community's disadvantaged youth, particularly in conjunction with other community organizations.
- *Creation of ethnic police benevolent associations* to provide role models and programs for disadvantaged youth of similar cultural heritage who are in gangs or are potential recruits. Hence, the black police groups get involved with young male African Americans, the Hispanic police officers' groups focus on young Latino males, and the police associations for Asian members attempt to serve the needs of young males from Chinese, Vietnamese, Korean, and Japanese backgrounds. The same strategy can be extended to ethnic police organizations for Italian Americans, Irish Americans, Polish Americans, and so on.

Forward-looking officers encourage and participate in a community task force that "gangs up" on the problem by brainstorming how to defuse the danger by providing positive places and group experiences for local youth through social activities, sports, voluntary service, and other constructive mechanisms. The goal should be to convert present-day gangs into team programs engaging in community rebuilding, while offering a gang alternative to youth who have not yet joined gangs but seek some group identity. Community conservation or ecology corps are one example of how young adults can be involved constructively. The plan for National Youth Service is another. Junior Achievement has already proved what businesspersons can do to involve youth constructively. Even bored middle-class or affluent youth would benefit by such outlets for their energies, in contrast to hanging around or "mall hopping." Such endeavors take a combination of public and private investment and personnel in which peace officers could provide needed leadership.

- *Counteracting hate groups* that reach out to a troubled generation of alienated white youth from urban, suburban, and even rural areas. White supremacists groups become surrogate families who use angry, disaffected young men and women. Some are from the underclass; some have parents in jail (1.5 million U.S. parents are in prison). Often their members are products of dysfunctional families and outside mainstream activities. Skinheads are enlisted to engage in hate crimes against racial, ethnic, religious, or gay groups that these dysfunctional youth have learned to despise. Many of these young people have themselves already been in prison, where they were recruited by such gangs as the Nazi Low Riders (NLR). Some, too, are frustrated middle-class kids who use the Internet Web hate sites to absorb neo-Nazi propaganda. Others are lower-middle-class youngsters discontent with society because of socioeconomic conditions; they wish to protest and may begin by getting together for something like graffiti tagging but end up engaging in hate crimes against their scapegoats. The problem is global in scope: Europe has its own violent young skinheads who attack immigrants. To undercut the white supremacists gangs, sometimes fueled by drugs and alcohol abuse, schools and colleges have begun programs to teach tolerance. What is needed is for both active and retired members of law enforcement to reach out with positive endeavors to help redirect the energies of these hate-filled youth into constructive enterprises.

- *Apprenticeships or internships for youth in law enforcement* have long involved interested young people on a part-time basis or during summer vacations (Taylor, 1999). Some have been at the high school level, organized through traditional police youth groups. However, with the increase of criminal justice studies in community colleges, colleges, and universities, innovative projects attempt to give these students some on-the-job, real-world experience in police, corrections, and justice activities. As a case in point, the criminal justice internships at New York's St. John's University are highly organized under a supervisor, Professor John McCabe, formerly chief of patrol in the New York Police Department. Those who have completed a majority of their criminal justice studies courses and meet the criteria can become interns thereby gaining entry into a facet of the justice system that may range from juvenile justice and district attorney office to the U.S. Marshals or drug enforcement agencies. The program to jump-start criminal justice careers provides three academic credits if successfully completed and has proved invaluable to the participants. St. John's University students in their junior or senior year who qualify are required to complete 120 hours, or eight hours a week, at the internship sponsor site. The program runs for 15 weeks, or one semester. The youth also must attend orientation sessions, as well as keep a daily log of their intern activities, verified and signed by their site supervisor. At the end of the process, participants prepare a term paper on their field experience and receive a letter grade. Some interns who work for a police department or federal agency are offered full-time positions on graduation. Obviously, these internships not only facilitate the transition to a criminal justice job but also help the person to determine whether this is his or her preferred career field. The benefits to the law enforcement entity that employs such interns also are numerous.

Curtailing Litigation against Police Agencies and Officers

Much innovation is necessary so that a police response will satisfy citizens, especially in multicultural communities, rather than provoke them to lawsuits against officers and their departments. Nonviolent peacekeeping is particularly critical in ethnic, immigrant, and racially diverse communities, where misperception and miscommunication may occur because of language barriers, along with differences in body language and nonverbal interactions. The principal problem in this regard relates to the use of force by law enforcement at the time of arrest, whether it is perceived as excessive or deadly. Agencies that analyze citizen complaints against officers usually find that this arena receives the most negative community feedback, especially from persons who feel disenfranchised.

America is a very litigious society. Throughout the United States, the last two decades of the twentieth century witnessed a dramatic increase in individual and class-action suits against law enforcement agencies for mistreatment and killing of citizens by police officers. Exhibit 15.9 examines such allegations for the past two decades and what it cost one agency—the Los Angeles Police Department. The

Types of Complaints Against the Los Angeles Police Department

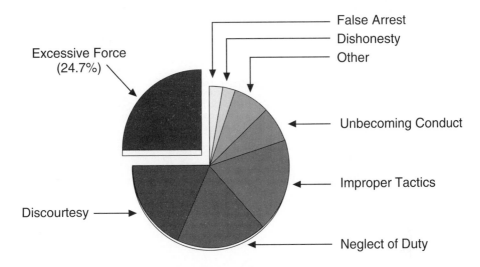

Frequency of Complaints Against the Los Angeles Police Department

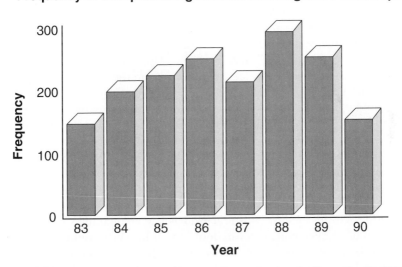

Exhibit 15.9   Excessive force and its costs. *Source: Los Angeles Times,* May 28, 1992.

scope of this national problem can be appreciated by citing statistics from one other city, Detroit. Between 1997 and 2000, that municipality had to pay $32 million because of lawsuits brought against the police. A city council analysis showed that 78 percent of the money so expended involved cases with only a small number of officers; 261 officers were named in more than one suit. The issue is what the city administration should do with such repeat offenders. Are these officers being unprofessional in their job behavior or simply victims of legal strategies by lawyers?

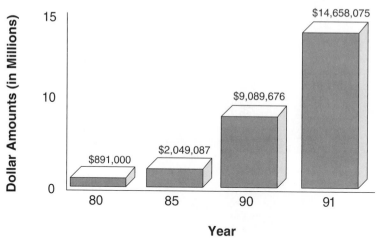

Judgments and Awards Paid by the City of Los Angeles

Exhibit 15.9 (continued)

The City of Los Angeles had to pay $14,658,075 in 1991, as a result of settlements, judgments, and awards related to excessive force litigation against its police. Then, in 1994, a jury awarded Rodney King $3.8 million to compensate for police actions. A federal judge ruled on August 28, 2000, that the Los Angeles Police Department can be sued as a racketeering enterprise in the so-called Rampart corruption scandal. This unprecedented decision, subject to judicial review by higher courts, could open this municipality to scores of lawsuits capable of bankrupting the city. U.S. District Judge William Rea ruled from the bench on a civil suit brought against the Los Angeles Police Department (LAPD) by a man who claims he was beaten and framed in 1997 for a crime by rogue police officers in the LAPD's Ramparts Division. Such illegal actions on their part caused 100 cases to be dismissed, resulting in five officers being charged with both conspiracy and even attempted murder. This latest ruling cleared the plaintiff to pursue the case under the federal racketeering statutes against conspiracies. His lawyers maintain the innocent man was a victim of a police conspiracy to deny him of his lawful rights as a citizen.

Many lawsuits against police agencies and their members are frivolous or unsubstantiated and are thus thrown out of court or are decided in favor of law enforcement. However, too many lawsuits result from inadequately screened or trained officers whose behavior on the job is not just unprofessional and unethical but outright biased and criminal. With greater public access to improved communications technology and increased information, citizens are fighting back when police trample their human or civil rights. When they win these legal suits, taxpayers ultimately have to pay for the insufficiencies or mistakes of their public servants in the criminal justice system.

Some analysts believe the problem is exacerbated because personnel in too many agencies operate more like soldiers than like peace officers (e.g., growth of

---

Exhibit 15.10   The militarization of police forces.

There is nothing inherently wrong with structuring police departments along military lines; agencies so designed exist in many democratic countries committed to the **rule of law**. However, a problem arises when an organization with a militaristic orientation entrusted with significant power comes to believe that it is literally engaged in combat. Over the past 30 years or more, almost every administration has waged its version of the "war on crime" and "war on drugs," a philosophy that has been embraced by many big-city police departments. . . .

The differences between city streets and a war zone is that in the former, police officers encounter fellow citizens with constitutional rights, while in the latter, soldiers seek out and destroy the enemy. According to testimony of convicted Los Angeles police officer, Rafael Perez, it is clear that some members of the Ramparts Division CRASH (Community Resources Against Street Hoodlums) thought of themselves and their jobs more in terms of soldiers than peace officers. . . . Although it is true that criminally active gang members are enemies of "law and order," they are not adversaries in the military sense. . . . After a lifetime of being taught that human life is sacred, [(police)] recruits are taught that they must kill their adversary on command.

One way of accomplishing this deadly goal is by dehumanizing the enemy; that is, by redefining him or her as less than human; an animal, for example. Once a designated group loses its status as human beings, members of that collective can be destroyed with few or any moral or ethical ramifications for the killers. . . . It is worth noting that this dehumanization process is made easier when the enemies are members of a different racial or ethnic group, a situation that is not uncommon concerning the composition of urban police forces and gangs. . . . Shooting parties not only exacerbate an already formidable "we/they" perspective regarding the police and gang members, but are likely to facilitate additional shootings. . . .

However, the unprecedented ruling by a federal judge that the LAPD could be sued under the Racketeer Influenced and Corrupt Organization Act (RICO) dramatically changes the way society responds to police corruption and brutality. . . . This should prompt local governments around the country to push for greater oversight of police behavior. It is not unusual for big-city departments to pay hundreds of thousands, if not millions of dollars, annually to settle police brutality charges. However, the estimated $300 million the City of Los Angeles might have to shell out in damage awards [(related to this case)] is an entirely different story. (Bryjak, 2000, p. G3)

Special Weapons and Tactics [SWAT] teams in departments). For 150 years, police departments have been organized on the military model. In the twenty-first century this may change because of increasing public dissatisfaction with law enforcement agencies, highlighted by legal settlements against officers. The extent of this questioning can be gauged somewhat by excerpts from a newspaper editorial written by a professor of sociology at the University of San Diego (see Exhibit 15.10; refer back to the LAPD mini case in Chapter 14 on the Ramparts Division to comprehend the implications of this criticism).

Consider if but a fraction of the enormous sums mentioned in Exhibit 15.10 were devoted to more creative training of officers in improved community relations, arrest tactics, and nonlethal, more peaceful apprehension; the taxpayers would certainly be more appreciative of police services (McErlain, 1991; Rivetti, 1988).

On the other hand, what of the officer's rights when accused of misconduct during a legal action? Brian Harris, a homicide detective of the Houston Police Department, astutely observed that in our judicial system the accused is presumed to be innocent until proven guilty. Therefore, he argues that under such circumstances, the public should afford sworn officers the same rights as the supposed victim. Until the evidence is presented and an inquiry commission or court has rendered a verdict, the public and media should not presume guilt. Further, there is the issue of intent. When an officer's life or well-being is threatened, he or she may not intend to hurt a perpetrator while defending himself or herself. Again, this is where training comes in, so that discipline and control are maintained in very difficult situations that police increasingly find themselves, while patrolling and seeking to ensure law and order in the community. Detective Harris concludes that training in basic police practice and its implementation by supervisors are the keys to effective performance on patrol: "When police create time and distance between themselves and the suspect, then they can conduct a safer encounter."

Planned Law Enforcement Innovations

Attempts are being made by the new generation of law enforcement leaders to develop innovative strategies, structures, and services that meet the changing needs of communities (Allevato, 1989; Galvin, 1987; Jordan, 1992; Lynch, 1998; Peavy, 1991; Riley, 1991; Schwab, 1992) as well as to improve interagency collaboration in serving those needs (Heller, 1992) or to evaluate the effectiveness of delivery of these services (Jensen, 1992). Many innovative peacekeeping strategies have already been described in this book. And each year, new opportunities unfold, such as using biometric technologies for identification of people by their eyes, smell, and other body characteristics ("New Ways of Identifying People," *Economist,* September 9, 2000, pp. 85–91), in addition to DNA profiles as evidence (Dwyer, Neufeld, and Scheck, 2000).

Some agencies have established an *innovation task force* made up of the most creative officers from all units of a department. In this approach, the chief asks the group to discover ways for police to encourage a "climate of understanding within the community, and combat a climate of fear" (words of President George Bush after the 1992 U.S. riots). To that end, the innovation team, along with community focus groups, described next, might study together new ideas of promise and develop action plans to implement them. Following are some examples of such innovations:

- Ongoing contact (in the form of both structured and unstructured meetings) with members of all minority and immigrant community organizations (including church leaders, business and civic leaders, school officials, and so forth); the ongoing nature of the program must be emphasized because, typically, law enforcement only meets with community leaders after a crisis.
- Bicycle or scooter bike patrols in problem and recreational areas; officers then interact with community members, especially where there are large concentrations of minority and immigrant youth.
- Crises management strategies not only for emergencies and disasters but also for social unrest—identifying and working with neighborhoods at risk (see Chapter 12).
- Neighborhood or shopping mall storefront police substations.
- Police concentration on repeat offenders and repeat locations for criminal activities.
- Law enforcement strategies with the homeless (Brummer, 1998; Knuthson, 1989; Plummer, 1991).

- Teams consisting of officers from diverse backgrounds regularly meeting with inner-city youth, engaging in such activities as sports, mentoring, and finding new ways to become role models.
- Preventative programs with schools to reduce school violence. For example, a Federal Bureau of Investigation (FBI) report issued in 2000 and titled *The School Shooter: A Threat Assessment Perspective* lists personal traits in teenagers that may lead to violence. Police and educators need to use this profile to help identify high-risk youth who manifest poor coping skills, access to weapons, drug and alcohol abuse, alienation and narcissism, inappropriate humor, and no parental or guardian monitoring of television or Internet use. In addition to these characteristics, be alert to dysfunctional family situations, as well as poor school and school interactions on the part of the troubled youngsters.
- Development of neighborhood child protection plans to reduce incidents of child abuse. Such plans should include constructive opportunities for youth to network with each other and with positive adult role models in their community. Such plans should also include business, civic, and religious organizations and the adoption of a particular high-risk neighborhood in which the police, community leaders, and family members make a commitment to protecting their youth.
- Program, in conjunction with other public service agencies, to protect the elderly from victimization by both economic and violent crimes (Bentz, 1996; Froom, 1996; Phelps, 1992).

With the increase in hate crimes and anti-Semitism described previously in this text, police should be seeking innovative strategies to counteract these crimes within their communities, such as the approaches reported in Exhibit 15.11.

Police supervisors in their departments should be actively encouraging the innovations described in Exhibit 15.11, as well as police innovators who contribute to cultural synergy and peacekeeping. For example, agencies might have an award for the Innovative Officer of the Month and display the person's picture in the squad room with a description of his or her innovative practice on or off duty.

ORGANIZATIONAL TRENDS IN LAW ENFORCEMENT

In concluding this textbook, it is useful to present two organizational trends that have become increasingly visible in certain private-sector organizations. We return to the law enforcement agency itself, because change must come from within the department before all personnel can demonstrate effectiveness and sensitivity in the community (Wagner, 1994).

Trend One: Transforming the Organizational Culture

The culture of law enforcement agencies must internalize changes and accept diversity within both the department and the community. In the past this culture typically was dominated by white males, principally of Irish or Italian backgrounds, who were often military veterans. With the influx of a multicultural workforce into the criminal justice fields, system change is necessary if the organizational culture is to reflect the needs and concerns of this new generation from a culturally diverse society (Simons et al., 1993).

Exhibit 15.11   Teaching tolerance.

- *In Police Academies.* Dr. Karin Ismaili, assistant professor of criminal justice at St. John's University, New York City, teaches twice a week at the New York Police Academy. He is part of a visiting professor exchange at that academy and teach recruits about policing in a diverse society. He provides a civilian perspective on the interactions with multicultural and minority groups. His multimedia presentation focuses patterns of stereotyping ethnic community members, including emphasis on street crimes in poorer communities and the downplaying of white-collar crimes. Ismaili reviews research studies on these subjects, such as the overuse of summons and arrests among minorities and its near exclusion in more affluent neighborhoods, or other manifestations of what may be perceived as police prejudices. These classes intend to reduce the anger-fear spiral among police when dealing with differences in people, and increase police understanding of unfamiliar communities. Dr. Ismaili's mission is to enable police to fulfill their duties within the law, without ethical and moral lapses. The other side of this teacher exchange occurs when the director of the Police Academy, Dr. John O'Keefe, comes to the university to teach criminal justice students about victimology and other social issues.

- *In Local Schools and Colleges.* Police have developed several programs conducted in schools and colleges about driver safety, child abuse, and drugs (e.g., the Officer Friendly project). Law enforcement could also cooperate with local educators to teach tolerance based on the learning materials developed by the Southern Poverty Law Center (400 Washington Ave., Montgomery, AL 36104; Web site: www.tolerance.org.). For example, SPLC distributes an attractive booklet titled *101 Tools for Tolerance: Simple Ideas for Promoting Equity and Celebrating Diversity*. The center has been an outstanding force in combating organized hate, especially through its complimentary newspaper, *SPLC Report*. The newspaper contains information on the Tolerance project, intelligence, and the center's litigation to counter the 8,000 hate crimes that the FBI says are committed every year.

One of the nation's leading diversity consultants, Elsie Cross, confirmed the reality of organizations' need to change. Throughout 20 years of working with many large corporate clients, this African American consultant recognized that most corporate cultures have actually been white male cultures, in which the majority controlled the power in the organization by dominating meetings, making all key decisions, establishing exclusive information loops, and choosing their own successors. To compensate for the past discrimination and to increase organizational effectiveness, Elsie Cross Associates recommends the following strategies for managing diversity and valuing differences (White, 1992):

- Introduce culture change to overhaul policies and procedures by means of focus groups and workshops that define basic assumptions, written codes, and rituals; incorporate this feedback into a revised mission statement that becomes a proclamation of the "new organizational culture vision and values."
- Identify the barriers that block individual or group diversity goals; identify the champions capable of building broad, internal coalitions around cultural awareness and group action against discrimination and for planned change.

- Require that the top command make at least a five-year commitment of resources to re-defining the agency culture toward more effective management of diversity.
- Hold managers accountable for implementing the diversity changes through regular evaluation of their efforts.
- Confront, not ignore, the pain of racism and sexism at the personal and group level in the organization.

This management model has proven successful, and Cross credits the National Training Laboratories for Applied Behavioral Sciences for helping her to develop it. The strategy is worthy of consideration by would-be law enforcement leaders in a multiracial and multicultural society.

Trend Two: Organizations Must Move beyond Awareness to Meet Today's Multicultural Challenges

Law enforcement leaders should ask themselves this question: Does our agency provide adequate training for officers in cultural awareness? If the answer is "no," then consider the implications of Exhibit 15.12.

When a law enforcement agency has provided the basic training in cultural awareness and inaugurated effective equal employment, affirmative action policies, it is time to adopt another strategic plan. George F. Simons, a consultant on diversity, believes we must move beyond mere avoidance of ethnic, racial, and gender discrimination or sexual harassment. Police supervisors and managers should not have to "walk on eggs" while at work trying not to offend women and minorities. For managing or training in a multicultural environment, this expert counsels that advanced diversity training that teaches people the skills to communicate and collaborate effectively with each other as colleagues, especially through mixed-gender, mixed-ethnic, and mixed-racial groups, should be conducted. Dr. Simons (1999) offers the following advice:

- Organizational policy that supports productive partnerships and creative sharing with diverse membership of representatives from majority and minority groups should be developed.
- Executives and other leaders should participate in special coaching programs that include assessment, mind management, and communications training that enables them to model behavior and values that inspire their associates to work ingeniously with differences.

To further promote police officer professionalism and peacekeeping strategies in a diverse society, officers must be able to look up to leaders who are not ethnocentric and biased in their manner of leading their agency and responding to the communities they serve. For a peace officer to reflect tolerance and understanding of all peoples, as well as to apply the principle of fair treatment to every police action and communication, he or she must have role models all the way up the chain of command, especially at the police chief level. The police chief should explicitly demonstrate pluralistic leadership. Early in this chapter, we discussed peace officers who are cosmopolitan or pluralistic in approach. Attaining this outlook cannot happen consistently without direction from the top. For this

Exhibit 15.12   Cultural sensitivity on the beat.

"Cultural Sensitivity on the Beat" was the title of a feature article by Miles Corwin on the first page of a national newspaper in January 2000. Its publication helped to facilitate a second edition of this book. The article's principal conclusion was that as police work in increasingly diverse communities, their academies are emphasizing recognition of ethnic customs. But in such training, the officers want practical advice, not "touchy-feely" lessons.

Following are other insights from this seminal review of current police practices:

- The State of California's Commission on Peace Officers Standards and Training now mandates that all law enforcement academies provide a minimum of 24 hours in cultural diversity and discrimination training. The LAPD Academy offers almost 100 hours of diversity training, in addition to requiring 82 hours in Spanish-language training.

- In Long Beach, California, all officers in the department take a three-day course in cultural sensitivity, while Monterey Park police, in addition to officer training in the subject, also sponsor an 11-week citizen academy for immigrants. This program includes information on what to do if you become a crime victim, how to file a report against a police officer, and how to use the 911 system.

- Police officers seek cultural training that is pragmatic, such as how to improve interviews with witnesses, suspects, and victims who come from different cultural backgrounds. For instance, it may help officers to understand that in communities where the culture promotes a sense of extended family, neighbors often have a concern and connection to the victim or the one arrested.

- Some foreign cultural practices are either unacceptable or illegal in the United States. Regardless of traditions in the home country, officers may have to stop or arrest persons so engaged (e.g., female circumcision [mutilation of the girl's genitals]; marriage by capture). In such instances, officers have to exercise discretion as to issuing a warning or making an arrest when the action is too egregious.

- The LAPD instituted the Asian Crime Investigative Section, which has led to the solution of a number of homicides because officers in the unit have intimate knowledge of Asian cultures. In Thai culture, for instance, the mere pointing of the sole of the foot at someone is such an insult that it might lead to murder. As a result, training in Vietnamese, Chinese, Korean, Thai, and Japanese cultures has been extended to other officers working in such communities.

- The University of Southern California sponsors the Delinquency Control Institute. One of its lecturers, Detective Rentein, says that officers who understand cultural traditions within their patrol area can be gatekeepers. She observes that once people have entered our legal system, it is hard to extricate them; once police understand local cultures, they can save immigrants from being caught up in the justice system. Peace officers' cultural insights can help them to do their job better, while minimizing tensions and conflicts within different ethnic communities. For example, in Gypsy culture, a body search of a woman is considered a defilement and may prevent marriage to another Gypsy. In fact, one Gypsy patriarch testified in a civil suit on this matter that such a search would be considered a defilement, resulting in the females so searched being ostracized from weddings and funerals. Thus, the City of Spokane, Washington, paid $1.43 million in a legal settlement when the judge ruled against police for conducting an illegal body search of 13 Gypsy women in their homes. (Adapted from the *Los Angeles Times*, January 10, 2000, pp. A1, A12)

Exhibit 15.13   Police pluralistic leaders.
Pluralistic leaders:

1. Look for ways to serve as catalysts for changing the work environment and community to welcome and value diverse people

2. Are committed to eliminating all the various "isms" (racism, sexism, etc.) that exist in their immediate work environment or neighborhood and speak to the greater concerns for equality, fairness, and other democratic ideals

3. Help diverse people to be seen fairly and to be valued in the work environment and broader community

4. Accept feedback about how to improve their relationships with those who are different by remaining open to change and growth

5. Acknowledge their own prejudices or stereotypes and see the limitations that these will bring to their work

6. Take time to assess their individual progress toward achieving the qualities and characteristics of a pluralistic leader

7. Mentor others who need to gain sensitivity toward diversity

8. Value differences among people and cultures as one of the great treasures of the human family and global community

Source: MGH Consulting, © 1993, reprinted with permission of MGH Consulting, 2454 Cameron Drive, Union City, CA 94587.

---

reason, we reprint in Exhibit 15.13, a list of characteristics and attributes of a pluralistic leader developed by MGH Consulting.

SUMMARY

In this final unit and chapter, as throughout *Multicultural Law Enforcement,* we have shared information and insights about improving public service in diverse communities. Our intention has been to help readers become more proactive with regard to the changing population, while anticipating future developments in both the law enforcement agency and society. Our basic premise is that the personal and professional development of modern peace officers requires cultural awareness training that reinforces creative agency policies and practices on this diversity or multicultural issue.

Part One of this book was devoted to the impact of increasing cultural diversity on the community, peacekeeping, and the law enforcement agency. Part Two centered on cross-cultural training and communication for peace officers. Part Three reviewed cultural specifics relevant to officers when they interact with people from Native American, African American, Asian/Pacific Islander, Hispanic/Latino, or Middle Eastern backgrounds. Part Four examined the matter of culturally and racially motivated hate crimes and response strategies.

Finally, in Part Five, we have offered an overview of how peace officers can improve their effectiveness in a multicultural workforce and community by practicing greater cultural sensitivity. Numerous concepts, methods, and anecdotes were provided to promote innovative, futuristic professional development of sworn officers and their associates. With the human family everywhere in profound transition during the twenty-first century, futurists expect further social disturbances. Thus, our analysis focused on planned changes in the image, operations, services, and skills of law enforcement practitioners within rapidly changing workforces and societies.

Readers are challenged to examine the concepts and techniques presented in these pages, as well as to implement those that are feasible within local agencies and communities. If the strategies proposed here are adopted, the law enforcement field will indeed provide more professional, diverse leadership within the public sector, while presenting positive models in that regard to the private sector. For the professionally minded who will go beyond the content of this book, several appendixes and the *Instructor's Manual* complement the main content of this text.

DISCUSSION QUESTIONS AND ISSUES*

1. *Police Culture.* Every group, whether ethnic, racial, vocational, or professional, has characteristics defining its culture. The police organizational culture is no exception. People who do not belong to a particular in-group often develop myths and stereotypes about another group in an attempt to categorize behavior they may not understand. Make a list of myths and stereotypes about police officers that exist among community members. After you have compiled and shared your list with others, discuss the following:

   (a) How did these myths or stereotypes arise?

   (b) Is there any truth to the myths or stereotypes?

   (c) Do they in any way affect communication with citizens or prevent you from doing your job well?

   (d) Do any of the stereotypes or myths create special difficulties or challenges with people from diverse backgrounds? If so, how?

   (e) What can a modern, professional police force do to counter or lessen the influence of such myths and stereotypes in the community?

2. *Protecting Human and Civil Rights.* Reread and discuss all the special exhibits in this chapter with a view to their implications for law enforcement. Particularly, review Exhibit 15.2, Top civil rights official says discrimination persists.

   (a) What is the role of the U.S. Department of Justice in protecting the civil rights of U.S. citizens?

   (b) What should law enforcement be doing to protect such rights within both agencies and the communities they serve?

   (c) What are some areas of civil rights that U.S. law protects and enforces?

   (d) What does it mean to say that police officers should do their duties with honor and integrity?

*See Instructor's Manual accompanying this text for additional activities, role-playing activities, questionnaires, and projects related to the contents of this chapter.

REFERENCES

ADAMS, T. E. (1998). *Police Field Operations*. Upper Saddle River, N.J.: Prentice-Hall.

ALLEVATO, S. (1989). "The Development of a Law Enforcement Plan for California Cities Committed to Quality Service through Community-Oriented Policing" (Order 8-0133). POST Commission, Sacramento, Calif.

ANDERSON, W., D. SWENSON, AND D. CLAY. (1995). *Stress Management for Law Enforcement Officers*. Upper Saddle River, N.J.: Prentice-Hall.

ARNOLD, J. (1995). "The Impact of Behavioral Profiling in the Identification of Police Misconduct in California by the Year 2005" (Order 20-0401). POST Commission, Sacramento, Calif.

BAPTISTA, C. (1998). "How Can the Internet Be Used to Benefit the Public and Its Service Agencies by Year 2005?" (Order 25-0505). POST Commission, Sacramento, Calif.

BARKAN, S. E. (2001). *Criminology: A Sociological Understanding*. Upper Saddle River, N.J.: Prentice-Hall.

BARLOW, H. D. (2000). *Criminal Justice in America*. Upper Saddle River, N.J.: Prentice-Hall.

BARTOL, C. R. (1999). *Criminal Behavior: A Psychosocial Approach*. Upper Saddle River, N.J.: Prentice-Hall.

BARTOL, C. R., AND A. M. BARTOL. (1998). *Delinquency and Justice: A Psychosocial Approach*. Upper Saddle River, N.J.: Prentice-Hall.

BARTOLLAS, C., AND S. MILLER. (2001). *Juvenile Justice in America*. Upper Saddle River, N.J.: Prentice-Hall.

BELL, ELDRIN. (1992, September 28). Keynote speech at conference sponsored by the National Organization of Black Law Enforcement Executives (NOBLE), the Police Executive Research Forum (PERF), and the Reno Police Department, Reno, Nev.

BENTZ, D. (1996). "How Will a Medium Sized Police Agency Provide for the Needs of the Elderly Populations by Year 2007?" (Order 21-0423). POST Commission, Sacramento, Calif.

BERG, G. (1993). "What Will Be the Status of Community-Based Policing in Large California Police Departments by the Year 2003?" (Order 16-0332). POST Commission, Sacramento, Calif.

BLOCK, P. (1991). *The Empowered Manager: Positive Political Skills at Work*. San Francisco: Jossey-Bass.

BOWMAN, J. S. (Ed.) (1991). *Ethical Frontiers in Public Managment*. San Francisco: Jossey-Bass.

BOYD, T. (1993). "A Model for Development of Police Officers' Understanding and Adherence to Ethical Standards" (Order 16-0313). POST Commission, Sacramento, Calif.

BRITZ, G. S., RUSH, J., AND THOMAS BARKER (2000). Gangs: An International Approach, Upper Saddle River, N.J.: Prentice-Hall.

BROOKS, R. E. (1987). "What Is the Future of Incentive Programs for Mid-Career Law Enforcement Officers?" (Order 4-0053). POST Center for Leadership Development, Sacramento, Calif.

BRUMMER, S. E. (1988). "How Will the Homeless Population Affect Services of a Medium Size Police Agency by the Year 2000?" (Order 6-0093). POST Commission, Sacramento, Calif.

BRYJAK, GEORGE J. (2000, September 3). "Opinion." *San Diego Union-Tribune*, p. G3.

CALVI, J. V., AND S. COLEMAN. (2000). *American Law and Legal Systems*. Upper Saddle River, N.J: Prentice-Hall.

CHAMELIN, N. (2000). *Criminal Law for Police Officers*. Upper Saddle River, N.J.: Prentice-Hall

CHAMPION, D.J. (2001a). *Corrections in the United States: A Contemporary Perspective*. Upper Saddle River, N.J.: Prentice-Hall.

CHAMPION, D.J. (2001b). *The Juvenile Justice System: Delinquency, Processing and the Law*. Upper Saddle River, N.J.: Prentice-Hall.

COHEN, N. E. (2000). *A Step-by-Step Guide to Starting an Effective Mentoring Program: The Mentee's Guide to Mentoring*. Amherst, Mass.: Human Resource Development Press.

COLE, DAVID. (2000). *No Equal Justice: Race and Class in the American Criminal Justice System*. New York: Free Press.

CREWS, G. A., AND R. H. MONTGOMERY. (2001). *Chasing Shadows: Confronting Juvenile Violence in America*. Upper Saddle River, N.J.: Prentice-Hall.

DANTZKER, M. L. (2000). *Understanding Today's Police* Upper Saddle River, N.J.: Prenctice-Hall.

DAVIDSON, S. (1995). "What Can Police Agencies in Rural Areas Do to Prevent Gang Violence in Schools by 2004?"(Order 19-0379). POST Commission, Sacramento, Calif.

DELATTRE, E. J. (1991a). *Against Brutality and Corruption: Integrity, Wisdom, and Professionalism*. Tallahassee, Fla.: Florida Department of Law Enforcement/Criminal Justice Executive Institute.

DELATTRE, E. J. (1991). *Character and Cops: Ethics in Policing*. Washington, D.C.: American Enterprise Institute for Public Policy Research.

DEVORE, L. R. (1989). "The Purpose and Function of the Police Cadet Programs in Medium Sized Police Agencies by the Year 2000"(Order 8-0138). POST Commission, Sacramento, Calif.

DISTELRATH, J. T. (1989). "What Will Be the Career Development Needs of Law Enforcement Managers by the 21st Century?"(Order 7-0115). POST Commission, Sacramento, Calif.

DWYER, J.,P. NEUFELD, AND B. SCHECK. (2000). *Actual Innocence*. New York: Doubleday.

EDEY, R. (1996). "The Impact of Organized Crime from the Former Soviet Republics by Year 2006" (Order 22-0447). POST Commission, Sacramento, Calif.

FROOM, R. (1996). "Preparing to Meet the Challenges of a Growing Elderly Population" (Order 21-0429). POST Commission, Sacramento, Calif.

GABOR, T. (1994). "Generalist or Specialist: What Will Be the Status of the Police Professional by the Year

2003?" (Order 17-0349). POST Commission, Sacramento, Calif.

GALVIN, G. T. (1987). "Community Based Policing" (Order 3-0037). POST Commission, Sacramento, Calif.

GELLERMANN, W.,ed (1990). *Values and Ethics in Organization and Human Systems Development.* San Francisco: Jossey-Bass.

Gonzalez, Julio C. (2000, July 7). "Top Civil Rights Official Says Discrimination Persists: *St. Johns Today.* Available Vol.1:3, pp.1-4.

GOODE, E. (2001). *Deviant Behavior.* Upper Saddle River, N.J.: Prentice-Hall.

GOODMAN, D. J. (1998). *Enforcing Ethics: A Scenario-Based Workbook for Police and Corrections Recruits and Officers.* Upper Saddle River, N.J.: Prentice-Hall.

GOGGANS, D. (1996). "In What Manner Can Leadership Aid in the Successful Integration of Organizational Values between Merging Law Enforcement Agencies?" (Order 23-0470). POST Commission, Sacramento, Calif.

GOSSELIN, D. K. (2000). *Heavy Hands: An Introduction to Domestic Violence.* Upper Saddle River, N.J.: Prentice-Hall.

GRENNAN, S., M. T. BRITZ, J. RUSH, AND T. BARKER. (2000). *Gangs: An International Approach.* Upper Saddle River, N.J.: Prentice-Hall.

HARDING, J. W. (1990). "Organized Youth Programs in Middle Sized California Law Enforcement Agencies"(Order 9-0165). POST Commission, Sacramento, Calif.

HARMAN, P. (1992). "Cultural Diversity Training for the Future: Is California Law Enforcement on Track?" (Order 14-0274). POST Commission, Sacramento, Calif.

HARRIS, P. R. (1994). *High Performance Leadership: HRD Strategies for the New Work Culture.* Amherst, Mass.: Human Resource Development Press.

HARRIS, P. R. (1998). *The New Work Culture: HRD Transformational Management Strategies.* Amherst, Mass.: Human Resource Development Press.

HARRIS, P. R., AND R. T. MORAN. (2000). *Managing Cultural Differences Instructor's Guide.* Boston: Gulf Publications Series/Butterworth-Heinemann.

HARRISON, BOB.(October 5, 2000). Chief of Police, Vacaville, Calif., personal communication.

HARRISON, E. R. (1993). "What Municipal Police Services and Financial Support Considerations Will Exist by the Year 2002?" (Order 15-0297). POST Commission, Sacramento, Calif.

HAWTHORNE, J.K.(1995). "Abstract of Regional Consolidation Of Law Enforcement Support Services (Order 23-0476)," In *Independent Study Project Catalog,* Sacramento, Calif: California Law Enforcement Command College, Commission of Peace Officers Standards and Training. (See Resources at the end of this chapter for information on how to obtain the full study.)

HEBEL, M. S. (1990). "The Impact of Disadvantaged Youth on Large, Urban Law Enforcement Agencies by the Year 2000"(Order 9-0166). POST Commission, Sacramento, Calif.

HELLER, S. (1992). "Addressing Community Problems through Interagency Cooperation"(Order 13-0259). POST Commission, Sacramento, Calif.

HERNANDEZ, J. (1999). "Can Distance Learning Improve the Quality of Training for the San Bernardino Sheriff's Department by Year 2003?" (Order 26-0530). POST Commission, Sacramento, Calif.

HOFFMAN, T. (1994)."What Will Be the Impact of Gang Related Homicides on Investigative Systems by Year 2004?" (Order 18-0373). POST Commission, Sacramento, Calif.

HUERRMAN, J. (1998). "Transforming Crime Prevention for the Twenty-First Century" (Order 25-0507). POST Commission, Sacramento, Calif.

HUFF, C. R. (Ed.), (1990). *Gangs in America.* Newbury Park, Calif.: Sage Publications.

HUNTER, R. D., P.D. MAYHALL, AND T. BARKER. (2000). *Police Community Relations and the Administration of Justice.* Upper Saddle River, N.J.: Prentice-Hall.

HURST, N. (1993). "Managing Cultural Diversity in Law Enforcement by Year 2003" (Order 16-0318). POST Commission, Sacramento, Calif.

JACKSON, K. D. (1991). "Impact of Gang Violence on a Police Department Serving an Emerging, Urbanized City" (Order 12-0234). POST Commission, Sacramento, Calif.

JANKE, G. (1993). "The Dysfunctional Police Officer: Management Strategies for the Future"(Order 15-0300). POST Commission, Sacramento, Calif.

JENSEN, P. (1992). "Evaluating Police Effectiveness by Year 2000" (Order 13-0264). POST Commission, Sacramento, Calif.

JOHNSON, J. (1994). "What Role Will Mid-Size Law Enforcement Agencies Play in Managing an Open Border between the United States and Mexico by the Year 2003?" (Order 17-0343).POST Commission, Sacramento, Calif.

JONES, J. R., AND D.P. CARLSON. (2001). *Reputable Conduct: Ethical Issues in Policing and Corrections.* Upper Saddle River, N.J.: Prentice-Hall.

JORDAN, R. (1992). "Police Strategies That Address Community Needs in the 21st Century." (Order 13-5207). POST Commission, Sacramento, Calif.

JUSTICE, T., AND D. JAMIESON (1999). *The Complete Guide to Facilitation: Enabling Groups to Succeed.* Amherst, Mass.: Human Resource Development Press.

Justice Research Association. (2000). *Your Criminal Justice Career: A Guidebook.* Upper Saddle River, N.J.: Prentice-Hall.

KIRKPATRICK, D. (2000). *Developing Supervisors and Team Leaders.* Boston: Gulf Publications Series/ Butterworth-Heinemann.

KNUTHSON, C. V. (1989). "Family and Youth Homelessness: How Will It Impact California Law Enforcement by the Year 2000?" (Order 8-0141). POST Commission, Sacramento, Calif.

KRAMER, L. C. (1987). "Will Changes in the Asian Population Impact Street Gang Related Crime in California?" (Order 3-0041). POST Commission, Sacramento, Calif.

LANGWORTHY, R. H., AND F.T. LAWRENCE, (1999). *Policing in America: A Balance of Forces*. Upper Saddle River, N.J.: Prentice-Hall.

LEIGHTON, P., AND J. REIMAN. (2001). *Criminal Justice Ethics*. Upper Saddle River, N.J.: Prentice-Hall.

LEWIS, C. W. (1991). *The Ethics Challenge in Public Service*. San Francisco: Jossey-Bass.

LINGLE, N. (1992). "People of Color and Culture: The Future of California Law Enforcement" (Order 13-0247). POST Commission, Sacramento, Calif.

LOPEZ, A. (1994). "What Impact Will Community-Based Policing Have on Individual Reward Systems of Major Law Enforcement Agencies by the Year 2002?" (Order 17-0346). POST Commission, Sacramento, Calif.

LYNCH, S. (1998). " Devoloping the Next Generations of Leaders in a Mid-Size Police Department." (Order 25-9516). POST Commission, Sacramento, Calif.

Lynn Learning Labs. (1998). *Mentoring: Passing the Torch*. Amherst, Mass: Human Resource Development Press.

MASTROFSKI, STEPHEN D., AND JACK R. GREENE. (1991). "Community Policing and the Rule of Law." In David Weisburd and Craig Uchida (Eds.), *The Changing Focus of Police Innovation: Problems of Law, Order, and Community. P. 120-128)* New York: Springer-Verlag.

MCERLAIN, E. J. (1991). "Deadly Force . . . An Age Old Problem . . . A Future Solution" (Order 12-0237). POST Commission, Sacramento, Calif.

MCGREGOR, E. B. (1991). *Strategic Management of Human Knowledge, Skills, and Abilities*. San Francisco: Jossey-Bass.

MEADOWS, R. J. (2001). *Understanding Violence and Victimization*. Upper Saddle River, N.J.: Prentice-Hall.

MILLER, S. (1996). "Communicating Effectively with Non-English-Speaking Customer Population in Mid-Size California Cities by Year 2005" (Order 22-0455). POST Commission, Sacramento, Calif.

MORAMOTO, B. (1989). "How Will Medium Size Law Enforcement Agencies Investigate High Technology Crime by Year 2003?" (Order 19-0391). POST Commission, Sacramento, Calif.

MORAN, R.T., AND J. ABBOTT (2000). *NAFTA: Best Practices*. Boston: Gulf Publications Series/Butterworth-Heinemann.

MORAN, R. T., P. R. HARRIS, AND W. G. STRIPP. (1993). *Developing Global Organizations: Strategies for Human Resource Professionals*. Boston: Gulf Publications Series/Butterworth-Heinemann.

MURASKIN, E., AND A. R. ROBERTS (1999). *Visions for Change: Crime and Justice in the 21st Century*. Upper Saddle River, N.J.: Prentice-Hall.

MURASKIN, R. (2000). *It's a Crime: Women and Justice*. Upper Saddle River, N.J.: Prentice-Hall.

MURASKIN, R., AND M. MURASKIN. (2001). *Morality and the Law*. Upper Saddle River, N.J.: Prentice-Hall.

MURRAY, M., AND M. A. OWEN. (1991). *Beyond the Myths and Magic of Mentoring*. San Francisco: Jossey-Bass.

OLIVER, W. M. (2001). *Community Oriented Policing: A Systemic Approach to Policing*. Upper Saddle River, N.J.: Prentice-Hall.

ORTEGA, D. (1993). *The Impact of an Ethnically Diverse Workforce on the Role of the Field Training Officer by Year 2002*. (Order 16-0322). POST Commission, Sacramento, Calif.

PALMIOTTO, M. J. (2001). *Police Misconduct: A Reader for the 21st Century*. Upper Saddle River, N.J.: Prentice-Hall.

PANICCIA, V. (1999). "What Will Be the Impact of Informational Technology on the Patrol Function of the Los Angeles Police Department by the Year 2004" (Order 26-0517). POST Commission, Sacramento, Calif.

PARKER, R. (1986). "The Impact of Emerging Technology on Law Enforcement Traffic Services" (Order 16-0329). POST Commission, Sacramento, Calif.

PEAK, K. J. (2000). *Policing America: Methods, Issues, Challenges*. Upper Saddle River, N.J.: Prentice-Hall.

PEAK, K. J., AND R.W. GLENSOR. (1999). *Community Policing and Problem Solving: Strategies and Practices*. Upper Saddle River, N.J.: Prentice-Hall.

PEAVY, J. D. (1991). "Don't Call Us, We'll Call You: Strategies to Increase Police Service Usage by Ethnic Minorities" (Order 12-0242). POST Commission, Sacramento, Calif.

PHELPS, P. B. (1992). "The Development of an Elderly Victimization Management Strategy for Law Enforcement" (Order 13-0256). POST Commission, Sacramento, Calif.

PIERCE, S. (1997). "What Will Be the Impact of Regionalized In-Service Training on the Davis Police Department by the Year 2002?" (Order 24-0500). POST Commission, Sacramento, Calif.

PLUMMER, L. C. (1991). "The Development of a Law Enforcement Plan to Generate Support for and Solutions to the Problem of Homelessness" (Order 12-0227). POST Commission, Sacramento, Calif.

Police Executive Research Forum. (1992). *Revisiting Community Policing: A New Typology*. Washington, D.C.: Author.

Prentice-Hall. (2000) *Criminal Justice Catalog*. Upper Saddle River, N.J.: Author.

President's Commission on Law Enforcement and the Administration of Justice(1967). Washington D.C.: U.S. Government Printing Press.

RILEY, R. W. (1991). "How Will Law Enforcement Reduce Community Fear of Crime in Major Urban Areas by the Year 2000?" (Order 11-0214). POST Commission, Sacramento, Calif.

RIVETTI, D. J. (1988). "What Is the Future of Less Than Lethal Weapons in Law Enforcement?" (Order 5-0086). POST Commission, Sacramento, Calif.

ROJAS, A., AND D. LOVE (2000). "Compromise Reached on Racial Profiling Law." *San Diego Union-Tribune*, pp. A2, A5.

SCHMALLEGER, F. (2001). *Criminal Justice Today: An Introductory Text for the 21st Century*. Upper Saddle River, N.J.: Prentice-Hall.

SCHWAB, S. (1992). "Restructuring Small Police Agencies: A Transition toward Customer Services" (Order 13-0260). POST Commission, Sacramento, Calif.

SEAMAN, S. (1996). "Impacting Youth Violence and Gangs: Community Creativity into Action" (Order 22-0457). POST Commission, Sacramento, Calif.

SEGURA, S. (1996). "Community Oriented Policing's Impact on Future Economic Development" (Order 22-0458). POST Commission, Sacramento, Calif.

SHINER, D. (1996). "How Can Small Law Enforcement Agencies Achieve Ethnic Diversity within Their Command by Year 2000?" (Order 22-0459). POST Commission, Sacramento, Calif.

SIMONS, G. F., AND B. ABRAMMS. (1999). *The Questions of Diversity: Reproducible Assessment Tools for Organizations and Individuals*. Amherst, Mass.: Human Resource Development Press.

SIMONS, G. F., C. VAZQUEZ, AND P. R. HARRIS. (1993). *Transcultural Leadership: Empowering The Diverse Workforce*. Boston: Gulf Publications Series/Butterworth-Heinemann.

SIMONSEN, C. E. (1998). *Private Security in America: An Introduction*. Upper Saddle River, N.J.: Prentice-Hall.

SLATER, G. (1994). "What Impact Will Cultural Diversity in Law Enforcement Have on Personnel Management By Year 2002?" (Order 17-0351). POST Commission, Sacramento, Calif.

SMALL, K. (1996). "Youth Violence Prevention: A Cost-Effective Strategy for Law Enforcement" (Order 22-0460). POST Commission, Sacramento, Calif.

SONNENBERG, R. (1995). "How Will Law Enforcement Respond to Ethnic Dilemmas within Changing Cultural Diversity?" (Order 19-0396). POST Commission, Sacramento, Calif.

STEVENS, D. J. (2001). *Case Studies in Community Policing*. Upper Saddle River, N.J.: Prentice-Hall.

STUCKEY, G. B., C. ROBERSON, AND H. WALLACE. (2001). *Procedures in the Justice System*. Upper Saddle River, N.J.: Prentice-Hall.

SULLIVAN, S. (2000). *Mastering Leadership* [audiovisual workshop]. Amherst Mass.: Human Resource Development Press.

TAMAYO, R. (1999). "What Will Be the Leadership Training Subject Delivery System for Middle Managers by the Year 2003?" (Order 26-0539). POST Commission, Sacramento, Calif.

TAYLOR, D. (1999). Jump Starting Your Carreer: An Internship Guide for Criminal Justice. Upper Saddle River, N.J.: Prentice-Hall.

TERBORCH, R. (1987). "Career Development: An Organizational Dilemma" (Order 4-0070). POST Commission, Sacramento, Calif.

THIBAULT, E. A., L.M. LYNCH, AND R. B. McBRIDE. (1998). *Proactive Police Management*. Upper Saddle River, N.J.: Prentice-Hall.

THOMAS, R. F. (1990). "A Response to Youth Gangs for a Mid-sized Police Department" (Order 0-0175). POST Commission, Sacramento, Calif.

THORNTON, KELLY. (2000, August 6). "Police Give Group Realistic Look at When Decisions Mean Life, Death." *San Diego Union-Tibune,* pp. B1, B5.

TOGNETTI, B. A. (1991). "Stategy for Addressing Illegal Youth Gang Activities by a Mid-Size Police Department" (Order 12-0230). POST Commission, Sacramento, Calif.

TRACY, M. (1993). "Impact of Emerging Communication Technology on Community Policing in a Medium Sized Police Force by Year 2000" (Order 19-0397). POST Commission, Sacramento, Calif.

TWILLING, G. (1995)."What Will Be the Role of Law Enforcement in Workplace Violence by the Year 2004?" (Order 19-0398). POST Commission, Sacramento, Calif.

WAGNER, L. (1994). "What Will Be the Status of Community-Oriented Policing and Problem Solving in a Mid-Size Agency by Year 2002?" (Order 18-0391). POST Commission, Sacramento, Calif.

WALLACE, H., C. ROBERSON, AND C. STECKLER. (2001). *Written and Interpersonal Communication Methods for Law Enforcement*. Upper Saddle River, N.J.: Prentice-Hall.

WHISENAND, P. M., AND F. FERGUSON. (1996). *The Managing of Police Organizations*. Upper Saddle River, N.J.: Prentice-Hall.

WHITE, J. P. (1992, August 9). "Elsie Cross vs. the Suits: One Black Woman Is Teaching White Corporate America to Do the Right Thing." *Los Angeles Times Magazine.* pp. 14–18, 38–42.

WOESSENER, L. (1995). "What Will Be the Impact of Asian Gang Mobility on Mid-Size Law Enforcement Agencies by the Year 2004?" (Order 20-0422). POST Commission, Sacramento, Calif.

Appendix A

MULTICULTURAL COMMUNITY AND WORKFORCE:

Attitude Assessment Survey*

The first set of questions ask for your opinions about how certain segments of the community view the police. Using the response sheets (Attitude Assessment Survey Response Sheet) on pages 425–428, put the number of the response that you think best describes each group's perception. Remember, give the response based on how you feel each group would answer the statements.

1. In your opinion, how would this group rate the job this police department does? (See response sheet.)
2. This group generally cooperates with the police.
3. Overall, this group thinks that police department acts to protect the rights of individuals.
4. This group feels that the current relationship between the police and the community is described by which of the following?
5. Overall, this group feels this department responds to citizen complaints about officers in an objective and fair manner.
6. This group thinks most contacts with police are negative.

The next questions ask for your opinions about procedures and practices within the police department.

7. Overall, police supervisors in this department respond to citizens' complaints about employees in an objective and fair manner.
8a. Most police officers in this department are sensitive to cultural and community differences.
8b. Most civilian employees in this department are sensitive to cultural and community differences.

Source: Adapted with permission from the Almeda, California, Police Department, March 1993.

9a. This department adequately prepares officers to work with members of the community who are of a different race or ethnicity than the majority of the population.

9b. This department adequately prepares civilian employees to work with members of the community who are of a different race or ethnicity than the majority of the population.

10. The police administration is more concerned about police–community relations than it should be.

11a. Special training should be given to officers who work with community members who are of a different race or ethnicity than the majority population.

11b. Special training should be given to civilian employees who work with community members who are of a different race or ethnicity than the majority population.

12. Special training should be given to assist officers in working with which of the following segments of the community?

13. How often are racial slurs and negative comments about persons of a different race or ethnicity expressed by personnel in this department?

14a. Persons of a different race or ethnicity in this city are subject to unfair treatment by some officers in this department.

14b. Persons of a different race or ethnicity in this city are subject to unfair treatment by some civilian employees in this department.

15a. Prejudicial remarks and discriminatory behavior by officers are not tolerated by line supervisors in this department.

15b. Prejudicial remarks and discriminatory behavior by civilian employees are not tolerated by line supervisors in this department.

16. Transfer policies in this department have a negative effect on police–community affairs.

17. Citizen complaint procedures in this department operate in favor of the citizen, not the employee.

18. Internal discipline procedures for employee misconduct are generally appropriate.

19. The procedure for a citizen to file a complaint against a department employee should be which of the following?

20. With regard to discipline for misconduct, all employees in this department are treated the same in similar situations, regardless of race or ethnicity.

21. What kind of discipline do you think is appropriate for the first incident of the following types of misconduct? (Assume intentional.)

This section examines your views about police–community relations training and community participation. Please circle the response that best describes your opinion.

22. Do you think training in police–community relations was adequate to prepare you to work with all segments of the community?

23. How often do you have opportunities to participate in positive contacts with community groups?

24. Do you think this department has an adequate community relations program?

25. What subject areas related to community relations would be helpful on an in-service training basis?

26. What do you think is the most important thing that citizens need to understand about the police?

27. How can the police department best educate the public about police policies and practices?

28. Listed are steps that police departments can take to improve police services as they relate to community relations.

Attitude Assessment Survey Response Sheet

Place the number that corresponds to your response in each column.

	Business community	Minority resident	Community leaders	Most residents	Juveniles
Question 1:					
(1) Very good					
(2) Good					
(3) Fair					
(4) Poor					
(5) Very Poor					
Question 2:					
(1) Most of the time					
(2) Sometimes					
(3) Rarely					
(4) Never					
Question 3:					
(1) Strongly agree					
(2) Agree					
(3) Disagree					
(4) Strongly disagree					
Question 4:					
(1) Very good					
(2) Good					
(3) Fair					
(4) Poor					
(5) Very poor					
Question 5:					
(1) Strongly agree					
(2) Agree					
(3) Disagree					
(4) Strongly disagree					
Question 6:					
(1) Strongly agree					
(2) Agree					
(3) Disagree					
(4) Strongly disagree					

Place check in column corresponding to your response for each question.

	Strongly agree	*Agree*	*Disagree*	*Strongly disagree*	*Don't know*
Question 7:					
Question 8a:					
Question 8b:					
Question 9a:					
Question 9b:					
Question 10:					
Question 11a:					
Question 11b:					

Check one response for each group.

Question 12:	Strongly agree	Agree	Disagree	Strongly disagree
African American/black (includes Caribbean, Haitian, and so forth)				
Asian				
Hispanic				
Homosexual				

Circle your response.

Question 13:	(1) Often	(2) Sometimes	(3) Rarely	(4) Never

Place check in column corresponding to your response for each question.

	Strongly agree	*Agree*	*Disagree*	*Strongly disagree*	*Don't know*
Question 14a:					
Question 14b:					
Question 15a:					
Question 15b:					
Question 16:					
Question 17:					
Question 18:					

Circle one response.

Question 19:

(1) Citizen sends complaint in writing to department.

(2) Citizen telephones complaint to department.

(3) Citizen comes to department.

(4) Any of the above are acceptable means.

(5) None of the above are acceptable means.

Please explain. _____

_____

_____

Question 20:   (1) Strongly agree   (2) Agree   (3) Disagree   (4) Strongly disagree

Check one response for each.

Question 21:

Type of misconduct	Verbal warning	Training/ counseling	Oral reprimand	Formal reprimand	Suspension	Termination
Excessive force						
False arrest						
Discrimination						
Use of racial slurs						
Criminal conduct						
Poor service						
Discourtesy to citizen						
Improper procedure						

Please circle the response that best describes your opinion.

Question 22:   (1) Yes   (2) No   (3) Did not receive training
If no, please describe why the training was not satisfactory.
Please explain. _____

_____

_____

Question 23:   (1) Frequently   (2) Sometimes   (3) Rarely   (4) Never

Question 24:   (1) Yes   (2) No   (3) Don't know
Please explain. _____

_____

_____

Question 25: _____

_____

_____

Question 26:   What do you think is the most important thing that citizens need to understand about the police?

_____

_____

_____

Question 27:

Circle one only.
(1) Through patrol officer contacts with citizens
(2) Through public meetings
(3) Through the media
(4) Selected combinations of the responses above
(5) Other (explain): _____

_____

_____

(6) Don't know

Please indicate how important you think each of the following should be to this administration by placing the number that best describes your response next to the appropriate question.

	1 *Somewhat*	*2*	*3* *Not at all*
Question 28:	*important*	*Important*	*important*
Hire more police			
Focus on more serious crime			
Improve response time			
Increase salaries			
Provide more training			
Raise qualifications for potential applicants			
Be more courteous to public			
Increase foot patrols			
Reduce discrimination			
Provide dedicated time for community involvement			

Appendix B

CULTURAL DIVERSITY SURVEY:

Needs Assessment*

There has been a great deal of discussion in recent years about whether the job of police officer has been changing. Some of the discussion revolves around issues related to contact with people from different cultural, racial, or ethnic groups. Please check or enter one answer for each question.

1. Comparing the job of officer today with that of officer a few years ago, I think that today the job is
   ( ) a lot more difficult
   ( ) somewhat more difficult
   ( ) about the same in difficulty
   ( ) somewhat easier
   ( ) a lot easier

2. When I stop a car with occupant(s) of a different racial or ethnic group than myself, I must admit that I am more concerned about my safety than I would be if I stopped a car with the same number of white occupant(s).
   ( ) strongly agree
   ( ) agree
   ( ) disagree
   ( ) strongly disagree

*Adapted with permission; police department wishes to remain anonymous.

3. If an officer notices a group of young people gathering in a public place and the young people aren't known to the officer, they should be watched very closely for possible trouble.
   ( ) strongly agree
   ( ) agree
   ( ) disagree
   ( ) strongly disagree

4. If an officer notices a group of young people from another racial or ethnic group gathered in a public place, the officer should plan on watching them very closely for possible trouble.
   ( ) strongly agree
   ( ) agree
   ( ) disagree
   ( ) strongly disagree

5. How often do you think it is justifiable to use derogatory labels such as "scumbag" and "dirtbag" when dealing with possible suspects?
   ( ) frequently
   ( ) some of the time
   ( ) once in a while
   ( ) never

6. When I interact on duty with civilians who are of a different race, ethnicity, or culture, my view is that
   ( ) they should be responded to a little more firmly to make sure that they understand the powers of the police
   ( ) they should be responded to somewhat differently, taking into account their different backgrounds
   ( ) they should be responded to the same as anyone else

7. When I encounter citizens of a different race, ethnicity, or culture who have committed a violation of the law, my view is that
   ( ) they should be responded to a little more firmly to make sure they understand the powers of the police
   ( ) they should be responded to somewhat differently, taking into account their different backgrounds
   ( ) they should be responded to the same as anyone else

8. When interacting on duty with civilians who have a complaint or a question and who are of a different race, ethnicity, or culture, I try to be very aware of the fact that my usual gestures may frighten or offend them.
   ( ) strongly agree
   ( ) agree
   ( ) disagree
   ( ) strongly disagree

9. When interacting on duty with offenders who are of a different race, ethnicity, or culture, I try to be very aware of the fact that my usual behavior may frighten or offend them.
    ( ) strongly agree
    ( ) agree
    ( ) disagree
    ( ) strongly disagree

10. How often have you run into a difficulty in understanding what a civilian was talking about because of language barriers or accents?
    ( ) frequently
    ( ) once in a while
    ( ) hardly ever
    ( ) never

11. How often have you run into a difficulty in understanding what an offender was talking about because of language barriers or accents?
    ( ) frequently
    ( ) once in a while
    ( ) hardly ever
    ( ) never

12. How often have you run into some difficulty in making yourself clear while talking to a civilian because of language barriers or accents?
    ( ) frequently
    ( ) once in a while
    ( ) hardly ever
    ( ) never

13. How often have you run into some difficulty in making yourself clear while talking to an offender because of language barriers or accents?
    ( ) frequently
    ( ) once in a while
    ( ) hardly ever
    ( ) never

14. How important is it that the police department provide training to make its members aware of the differences in culture, religion, race, or ethnicity?
    ( ) extremely important
    ( ) very important
    ( ) fairly important
    ( ) not too important
    ( ) not important at all

15. Personally, I believe that the training I have received on group differences is
    ( ) far too much
    ( ) somewhat too much
    ( ) about the right amount
    ( ) too little
    ( ) virtually nothing

16. The training in the area of group differences has been
    ( ) extremely helpful
    ( ) very helpful
    ( ) somewhat helpful
    ( ) not too helpful
    ( ) not helpful at all

17. My own view is that our department's quality of service could be improved by
    ( ) placing greater emphasis on hiring on the basis of the highest score obtained on the entrance exam, making no attempt to diversify by race, ethnicity, or gender
    ( ) placing greater emphasis on diversity by race, ethnicity, or gender and somewhat less emphasis on the numerical rank obtained on the entrance examination
    ( ) giving equal weight to both the score obtained on the entrance examination and diversification by race, ethnicity, or gender

18. What percentage of civilian or internal complaints against employees are adjudicated equitably?
    ( ) over 80 percent
    ( ) between 60 and 80 percent
    ( ) between 40 and 60 percent
    ( ) between 20 and 40 percent
    ( ) less than 20 percent

19. Some civilian or internal complaints are adjudicated more favorably toward people from diverse groups rather than toward the majority population.
    ( ) strongly agree
    ( ) agree
    ( ) disagree
    ( ) strongly disagree

20. I think that employees of a different race or ethnicity receive preferential treatment on the job.
    ( ) strongly agree
    ( ) agree
    ( ) disagree
    ( ) strongly disagree

21. The racial diversity of my coworkers has made it easier for me to see issues and incidents from another perspective.
    ( ) strongly agree
    ( ) agree
    ( ) disagree
    ( ) strongly disagree

22. To think that employees of a different race or ethnicity than myself receive preferential treatment on this job
    ( ) bothers me because I do not think it is justified
    ( ) does not bother me because I think it is justified
    ( ) is fair only because it makes up for past discrimination
    ( ) I do not believe minorities get preferential treatment

23. In certain situations, having a partner of a different race or ethnicity than myself is more advantageous than having a partner of my same race or ethnicity.
    ( ) strongly agree
    ( ) agree
    ( ) disagree
    ( ) strongly disagree

24. I have received negative feedback from members of the community regarding the conduct of other officers.
    ( ) strongly agree
    ( ) agree
    ( ) disagree
    ( ) strongly disagree

25. I have received negative feedback from members of the community regarding the conduct of officers who are of a different race or ethnicity in particular.
    ( ) strongly agree
    ( ) agree
    ( ) disagree
    ( ) strongly disagree

26. I have received more negative feedback from members of the community regarding the conduct of officers from different races and ethnic backgrounds than about the conduct of white officers.
    ( ) strongly agree
    ( ) agree
    ( ) disagree
    ( ) strongly disagree

27. In terms of being supervised
    ( ) I would much rather be supervised by a man
    ( ) I would somewhat rather be supervised by a man
    ( ) I would much rather be supervised by a woman
    ( ) I would somewhat rather be supervised by a woman
    ( ) It does not make a difference whether a man or a woman supervises me

28. In terms of being supervised by a man
    ( ) I would much rather be supervised by a nonminority
    ( ) I would somewhat rather be supervised by a nonminority
    ( ) I would much rather be supervised by a minority
    ( ) I would somewhat rather be supervised by a minority
    ( ) It does not make a difference to which group my supervisor belongs

29. In terms of being supervised by a woman
    ( ) I would much rather be supervised by a nonminority
    ( ) I would somewhat rather be supervised by a nonminority
    ( ) I would much rather be supervised by a minority
    ( ) I would somewhat rather be supervised by a minority
    ( ) It does not make a difference to which group my supervisor belongs

If this questionnaire is being used for a training class, please check the one answer in the following questions that best applies to you.

30. What is your sex?
    ( ) male
    ( ) female

31. What is your race?
    ( ) white
    ( ) African American or black
    ( ) Hispanic
    ( ) Native American
    ( ) Asian American
    ( ) other

32. How many years have you been employed by the police department?
    ( ) 0 to 5 years
    ( ) 6 to 10 years
    ( ) 11 to 20 years
    ( ) more than 20 years

33. What is your current rank?
    ( ) officer
    ( ) sergeant
    ( ) lieutenant
    ( ) captain or commander
    ( ) deputy chief
    ( ) chief

34. What is the highest academic degree you hold?
    ( ) high school
    ( ) associate's degree
    ( ) bachelor's degree
    ( ) master's degree

Appendix C

LISTING OF CONSULTANTS AND RESOURCES

The following is a partial list only of consultants who may be useful to law enforcement agencies (current as of January 2001). Please note that we are not personally familiar with each of the following and are, therefore, unable to endorse their services. The most complete listing of consultants and resources can be found in *Intercultural Services,* Boulder, CO, Butterworth-Heinemann (see next page).

CROSS-CULTURAL DIVERSITY CONSULTANTS

Consultant's Consortium. P.O. Box 490255, Miami, FL 33149. Design and implement training programs on human relations for law enforcement, intercultural diversity, and ethics for law enforcement.

Deena Levine & Associates. P.O. Box 582, Alamo, CA 94507. Telephone: 925-947-5627. Coauthor of *Multicultural Law Enforcement: Strategies for Peacekeeping in a Diverse Society.* Cross-cultural consultant for businesses and organizations.

Defense Equal Opportunity Management Institute (DEOMI), Patrick Air Force Base, Cocoa Beach, FL 32391, Telephone: 407-494-6976. DEOMI offers a variety of courses related to equal employment opportunity, civil rights, diversity, and human relations for the U.S. armed services. Training includes law enforcement, regulatory aspects, and legal compliance.

Elsie Y. Cross Associates, Inc. 7627 Germantown Avenue, Philadelphia, PA 19118. Telephone: 215-248-8100.

George Simons International. 740 Front Street, Santa Cruz, CA 95060. Telephone: 831-426-9608. Consulting practice of George Simons, leading diversity author and producer of videos and instruments on this subject. Website: gsimons@diversophy.com

The Gil Dean Group. 13751 Lake City Way, NE, Suite 210, Seattle, WA 98125. Telephone: 206-362-0336. Maintains a computer data bank and referral service for cross-cultural consultants. Also operates a book service and publishes a newsletter on diversity training.

Herbert Z. Wong & Associates. One Broadway, Suite 600, Cambridge, MA 02142. Telephone: 617-489-1930 or 781-749-2997. Coauthor of *Multicultural Law Enforcement: Strategies for Peacekeeping in a Diverse Society.* Management consultants engaged in organizational surveys, cultural audits, and workforce diversity training. Specialization in Asian cultures and the assessment of organizational culture for implementing the strategic advantages of diversity. Federal law enforcement and regulatory agency diversity assessment and training.

Intercultural Business Solutions. Gary Wederspahn, principal. 4838 W. Moorhead Circle, Boulder, CO 80305. Telephone: 303-494-5403. E-mail: Gary@intercultural-help.com; Web site: www.intercultural-help.com

Managing Cultural Differences (MCD) Authors' Network. 2702 Costebelle Drive, La Jolla, CA 92037. Telephone: 858-453-2271 or 800-231-6275. Ten authors and editors who produced the seven volumes of the MCD Series for Gulf Publishing. All experienced cross-cultural consultants.

ODT Inc. P.O. Box 134, Amhurst, MA 01004. Telephone: 800-736-1293. Principal distributor of diversity and upward management materials; consulting network.

Ondra Berry Deputy Chief. Law Enforcement Cultural Diversity Training. Reno, Nevada, Police Department. Telephone: 775-334-2197. Reno Police Department, P.O. Box 1900, Reno, NV 09505-1900.

Pelikan Associates. 6501 Bannockburn Drive, Bethesda, MD 20817. Telephone: 301-229-8550. Helen Pelikan's public and customized training programs on use of the Meyer-Briggs Type Indicator (MBTI). MBTI is a tool for working constructively with individual differences in a multicultural society.

PowerPhone, Inc. P.O. Box 1911, Madison, CT 06443-0900. Telephone: 800-53-POWER. Provides a two-day, interactive workshop for law enforcement on race relations and cultural awareness. Also has a similar program for police dispatchers.

Regional Training Center (RTC). 12760 High Bluff Drive, Suite 270, San Diego, CA 92130. Telephone: 858-792-6501. Susanne Foucault, Executive Director. A joint powers organization developing training and other resources. Provides the cultural awareness and leadership courses for law enforcement agencies in the Southern California area.

Simulations Training Systems. 210 Twelfth Street, Del Mar, CA 92014. Telephone: 619-755-0272. Produces simulation games and videos in cross-cultural and team management based on the research of Dr. Garry Shirts.

U.S. Commission on Civil Rights, 624 9th Street N.W., Washington, D.C. 20425. Telephone: 202-376-8312. The U.S. Commission on Civil Rights: (a) investigates complaints alleging that citizens have been deprived of their right to vote resulting from discrimination, (b) studies and collects information relating to discrimination on the basis of race, color, religion, sex, age, disability, or national origin; (c) reviews Federal laws, regulations, and policies with respect to discrimination and equal protection under the law; and (d) submits reports to the President and to the Congress on civil rights issues.

ANTIBIAS ORGANIZATIONS AND GOVERNMENT AGENCIES

American-Arab Anti-Discrimination Committee
4201 Connecticut Avenue N.W.
Suite 500
Washington, D.C. 20008
202-244-2990
Web site: www.adc.org

Anti-Defamation League (ADL)
442 Park Avenue South
New York, NY 10016
212-684-6950
Web site: www.adl.org

U.S. Department of Justice
Bureau of Justice Statistics
810 Seventh Street, N.W.
Washington, D.C. 20531
800-732-3277

Center for Democratic Renewal National Office
P.O. Box 50469
Atlanta, GA 30302-0469
404-221-0025
E-mail: cdr@igc.apc.org
A national clearinghouse that monitors hate groups; provides victim assistance, leadership training, and education.

Coalition against Anti-Asian Violence
c/o Asian American Legal Defense and Education Fund
99 Hudson Street, 12th Floor
New York, NY 10013
212-966-5932

Congress on Racial Equality (CORE)
30 Cooper Square
New York, NY 10003
212-598-4000
Web site: www.core-online.org

Equal Employment Opportunity Commission (EEOC)
1801 L Street, N.W.
Washington, D.C. 20507
202-663-4400
Web site: www.eeoc.gov

Gay & Lesbian Alliance Against Defamation (GLAAD)
150 West 26th Street, Suite 503
New York, NY 10001
212-807-1700
Web site: www.glaad.org

Human Rights Resource Center
30 N. San Pedro Road
Suite 140
San Rafael, CA 94903
415-499-7465

Provides unique historical and current information, technical assistance, and state-of-the-art training programs to law enforcement agencies, schools, and human rights organizations throughout the United States, Canada, England, and New Zealand seeking to prevent and solve various human rights problems within their respective communities.

Jewish Community Relations Advisory Council (JCRC)
National Office
823 United Nations Plaza
New York, NY 10017
212-490-2525

National Association for the Advancement of Colored People
Washington Bureau
1025 Vermont Avenue NW
Washington, D.C. 20009
202-638-2269
Web site: www.naacp.org

National Congress of American Indians (NCAI)
2010 Massachusetts Avenue N.W.
2nd Floor
Washington, D.C. 20036
202-466-7767
Web site: www.ncai.org

National Council of La Raza (NCLR)
1111 19th Street, N.W.
Suite 1000
Washington, D.C. 20036
202-785-1670
Web site: www.nclr.org

National Gay and Lesbian Task Force
1734 14th Street N.W.
Washington, D.C. 20009
202-332-6483
Web site: www.ngltf.org
Provides services for gay and lesbian crime victims.

National Hate Crime Reporting Hot-Line
800-347-HATE

National Institute against Prejudice and Violence
712 W. Lombard Street
Baltimore, MD 21201
410-706-5170

National Organization for Women (NOW)
1000 16th Street, N.W.
Suite 700
Washington, D.C. 20036
202-331-0066
Web site: www.now.org

The National Organization of Black Law Enforcement Executives (NOBLE)
908 Pennsylvania Avenue, S.E.
Washington, D.C. 20003

The Prejudice Institute
132 Stephens Hall Annex
Towson State University
Towson, MD 21204
410-830-2435
Conducts research on victimization and provides consultation and training to law enforcement personnel, victim assistance providers, and other agencies and community organizations.

Southeast Asia Resource Action Center (SEARAC)
1628 16th Street, N.W.
3rd Floor
Washington, D.C. 20009
202-667-4690
Web site: www.searac.org

Southern Poverty Law Center
400 Washington Avenue
Montgomery, AL 36104
205-264-0286
Provides legal services in discrimination, civil rights, and class action cases. Works to educate the public through films and publications. Monitors hate groups throughout the United States. Publishes *Klanwatch*.

U.S. Department of Justice Community Relations Service Headquarters
810 Seventh Street, N.W.
Washington, D.C. 20531
202-305-2935

Appendix D

SELF-ASSESSMENT OF COMMUNICATION SKILLS IN LAW ENFORCEMENT:

Communications Inventory

The following is adapted for law enforcement from Dr. Phil Harris's Communications Inventory in *High Performance Leadership* (1992). As you answer the questions, think about your cross-cultural communication with both citizens and coworkers in your department. (Many of these questions also apply to communication with people of the same background.) Find your areas of strength and your areas of weakness and make it a point to improve those areas. To check whether your perceptions of your communication are correct, have a coworker or partner fill out the questionnaire for you. Part of knowing where to improve involves self-awareness and an honest appraisal of your strengths and weaknesses.

Instructions: Circle the word that best describes your approach to the communication process.

1. In communicating, **I** project a positive image of myself (e.g., voice, approach, tone).
   Seldom   Occasionally   Often   Always

2. When appropriate, I try to show my "receiver" (the person with whom I am communicating—for example, victims, citizens making complaints, suspects, witnesses, and coworkers) that I understand what is being communicated from his or her point of view. I do this by restating this point of view and by showing empathy and concern.
   Seldom   Occasionally   Often   Always

3. I am sensitive to culturally different usages of eye contact and I establish eye contact where appropriate, but avoid intense eye contact with people for whom less eye contact is more comfortable.
   Seldom   Occasionally   Often   Always

*Harris, P. R. (1992). *High Performance Leadership: Strategies For Maximum Productivity,* Glenview, Illinois: Scott Foresman and Company.

4. I am aware of when my own emotions and state of mind affect my communication with others. (For example, I know my own needs, motives, biases, prejudices, and stereotypes.)

   Seldom   Occasionally   Often   Always

5. I refrain from using insensitive and unprofessional language while on the job (including language used in written and computer communications).

   Seldom   Occasionally   Often   Always

6. I try not to let the person with whom I am communicating push my "hot buttons," which would negatively affect my communication (e.g., cause me to go out of control verbally).

   Seldom   Occasionally   Often   Always

7. When speaking with individuals from groups that speak English differently from the way I do, I try not to imitate their manner of speech in order to be "one of them."

   Seldom   Occasionally   Often   Always

8. With nonnative speakers of English, I try not to speak in an excessively loud voice or use incorrect English (e.g., "You no understand me?") in an attempt to make myself clear.

   Seldom   Occasionally   Often   Always

9. I am aware that many immigrants and refugees do not understand police procedures and I make special efforts to explain these procedures (including their rights).

   Seldom   Occasionally   Often   Always

10. I check in a supportive manner to see if people have understood my message and directions and I encourage people to show me that they have understood me.

    Seldom   Occasionally   Often   Always

11. With nonnative speakers of English, I make a special point to simplify my vocabulary, eliminate the use of slang and idioms, and try to use phrases that are not confusing.

    Seldom   Occasionally   Often   Always

12. I make extra efforts to establish rapport (e.g., show increased patience, give more explanations, show professionalism and respect) with individuals from groups that have typically and historically considered the police their enemies.

    Seldom   Occasionally   Often   Always

13. I am sensitive to cultural or gender differences between me and the receiver.

    Seldom   Occasionally   Often   Always

14. I convey respect to all citizens while on duty regardless of their race, color, gender, or other difference from me.

    Seldom   Occasionally   Often   Always

15. When using agency communication channels or media, I communicate professionally, avoiding inappropriate or derogatory remarks.

    Seldom   Occasionally   Often   Always

Participant's initials _____

GLOSSARY*

Acculturation: The process of becoming familiar with and comfortable in another culture. The ability to function within that culture or environment, while retaining one's own cultural identity.

Affirmative action: Legally mandated programs whose aim is to increase the employment or educational opportunities of groups that have been disadvantaged in the past.

Alien: Any person who is not a citizen or national of the country in which he or she lives.

Anti-Semitism: Latent or overt hostility toward Jews, often expressed through social, economic, institutional, religious, cultural, or political discrimination and through acts of individual or group violence.

Assimilation: The process by which ethnic groups that have emigrated to another society begin to lose their separate identity and culture, becoming absorbed into the larger community.

Awareness: Bringing to one's conscious mind that which is only unconsciously perceived.

Bias: Preference or an inclination to make certain choices that may be positive (bias toward excellence) or negative (bias against people), often resulting in unfairness.

Bigot: A person who steadfastly holds to bias and prejudice, convinced of the truth of her or his own opinion and intolerant of the opinions of others.

Cosmopolitan: Literally, "a citizen of the world." A person capable of operating comfortably in a global or pluralistic environment.

Cross-cultural: Involving or mediating between two cultures.

Culture: A way of life developed and communicated by a group of people, consciously or unconsciously, to subsequent generations. It consists of ideas, habits, attitudes, customs, and traditions that help to create standards for a group of people to coexist, making a group of people unique. In its most basic sense, culture is a set of patterns for survival and success that a particular group of people has developed.

Discrimination: The denial of equal treatment to groups because of their racial, ethnic, gender, religious, or other form of cultural identity.

*Adapted in part with permission from George Simons, Carmen Vazquez, and Philip Harris. (1993). *Transcultural Leadership: Empowering the Diverse Workforce*. Houston, Texas: Gulf Publishing Company.

Diversity: The term used to describe a vast range of cultural differences that have become factors needing attention in living and working together. Often applied to the organizational and training interventions in an organization that seek to deal with the interface of people who are different from each other. Diversity has come to include race, ethnicity, gender, disability, and sexual orientation.

Dominant culture: Refers to the value system that characterizes a particular group of people that dominates the value systems of other groups or cultures. *See also* Macroculture/Majority or Dominant Group.

Emigre: An individual forced, usually by political circumstances, to move from his or her native country and who deliberately resides as a foreigner in the host country.

Ethnic group: Group of people who conceive of themselves, and who are regarded by others, as alike because of their common ancestry, language, and physical characteristics.

Ethnicity: Refers to the background of a group with unique language, ancestral, often religious, and physical characteristics. Broadly characterizes a religious, racial, national, or cultural group.

Ethnocentrism: Using the culture of one's own group as a standard for the judgment of others, or thinking of it as superior to other cultures that are merely different.

Glass ceiling: An invisible and often perceived barrier that prevents some ethnic or racial groups and women from becoming promoted or hired.

Heterogeneity: Dissimilar; composed of unrelated or unlike elements.

Immigrant: Any individual who moves from one country, place, or locality to another. An alien admitted to the United States as a lawful permanent resident.

Macroculture/majority or dominant group: The group within a society that is largest and/or most powerful. This power usually extends to setting cultural norms for the society as a whole. The term *majority* (also *minority*, see below) is falling into disuse because its connotations of group size may be inaccurate.

Microculture or minority: Any group or person who differs from the dominant culture. Any group or individual, including second- and third-generation foreigners, who is born in a country different from his or her origin and has adopted or embraced the values and culture of the dominant culture.

Multiculturalism: The existence within one society of diverse groups that maintain their unique cultural identity while accepting and participating in the larger society's legal and political system.

Paradigm shift: What occurs when an entire cultural group begins to experience a change that involves the acceptance of new conceptual models or ways of thinking and results in major societal transitions (e.g., the shift from agricultural to industrial society).

Parity: The state or condition of being the same in power, value, rank, and so forth; equality.

Pluralistic: The existence within a nation or society of groups distinctive in ethnic origin, cultural patterns, religion, or the like. A policy of favoring the preservation of such groups with a given nation or society.

Prejudice: The inclination to take a stand for one side (as in a conflict) or to cast a group of people in a favorable or unfavorable light, usually without just grounds or sufficient information.

Race: A group of persons of (or regarded as of) common ancestry. Physical characteristics are often used to identify people of different races. These characteristics should not be used to identify ethnic groups, which can cross racial lines.

Racism: Total rejection of others by reason of race, color, or, sometimes more broadly, culture.

Racist: One with a closed mind toward accepting one or more groups different from one's own origin in race or color.

Refugee: A person who flees for safety and seeks asylum in another country. In addition to those persecuted for political, religious, and racial reasons, "economic refugees" flee conditions of poverty for better opportunities elsewhere.

Scapegoating: The practice of blaming one's failures and shortcomings on innocent people or those only partly responsible.

Stereotype: To believe or feel that people and groups are considered to typify or conform to a pattern or manner, lacking any individuality. Thus a person may categorize behavior of a total group on the basis of limited experience with one or a few representatives of that group. Negative stereotyping classifies many people in a group by slurs, innuendoes, names, or slang expressions that depreciate the group as a whole and the individuals in it.

Subculture: A group with distinct, discernible, and consistent cultural traits existing within and participating in a larger cultural grouping.

Synergy: The benefit produced by the collaboration of two or more systems in excess of their individual contributions. Cultural synergy occurs when cultural differences are taken into account and used by a multicultural group.

Transgendered: The term "transgendered" covers a range of people, including heterosexual cross-dressers, homosexual drag queens and transsexuals who believe they were born in the wrong body. There are also those who consider themselves to be both male and female, or intersexed, and those who take hormones and believe that is enough to complete their gender identity without a sex change.

White supremacist group: Any ongoing organization, association, or group of three or more persons, whether formal or informal, having as one of its primary activities the promotion of white supremacy through the commission of criminal acts.

White supremacy:*   Helan Page, an African American anthropologist, defines white supremacy in the U.S. as an "ideological, structural and historic stratification process by which the population of European descent . . . has been able to intentionally sustain, to its own best advantage, the dynamic mechanics of upward or downward mobility or fluid class status over the non-European populations (on a global scale), using skin color, gender, class or ethnicity as the main criteria" for allocating resources and making decisions.

*Source: Ross, Loretta (1995). *White Supremacy in the 1990s*. The Public Eye. Sponsored by the Political Research Associates. (www.publiceye.org/eyes/whitsup.html). Somerville, MA, p. 6.

Index

A

Acculturation, of American Indians, 256–257
Action plan, 109–110
Administrative guidelines, for cultural awareness training, 109–111
Adolescents
  African American, 176–177
  Asian/Pacific Americans, 156
  crime prevention and, 405–408
  Latino/Hispanic Americans, 208
African Americans, 166–167
  cross-racial perceptions of, 174
  culture, 167
  demographics, 169–171
  family, 174–177
  group identification terms, 172
  historical information, 167–169
  identity issues, 171–172
  language and communication, 177–182
  law enforcement issues, 182–192
  myths and stereotypes, 172–174
African American Vernacular English (AAVN), 178–179
Age demographics, for Latino/Hispanic Americans, 200
Agencies. *See* Law enforcement agencies
Agency culture, 375
Agency-specific cultural awareness training, 102–103
Aggressive behavior, African Americans and, 181–182
Alameda Police Department, 48–49

Alaska Natives, 253
American Indians, 249–250
  differences and similarities, 254–257
  family-related issues, 260–262
  historical information and background, 250–252
  identity issues, 252–253
  language and communication, 257–260
  law enforcement issues, 262–270
  tribes, reservations, and mobility, 253–254
Americanization, of Arab American children, 235
Anti-Defamation League (ADL), 312
Anti-Semitism, 288–292
Apprenticeships, 408
Approach, 236
Arab Americans, 221–222
  cultural practices, 235–240
  defined, 222–224
  demographics, 226
  differences and similarities, 226–228
  family structure, 233–235
  historical information, 225–226
  Islamic religion and, 231–233
  law enforcement issues, 240–246
  stereotypes, 228–230
Aryan Nations, 335
Asian Americans. *See* Asian/Pacific Americans
Asian/Pacific Americans, 138–139
  communication styles, 157–159
  defined, 139–141

demographics, 145–146
family, 154–157
historical information, 142–145
key motivating perspectives, 147–150
labels and terms, 150–151
law enforcement issues, 159–163
myths and stereotypes, 151–154
typology of, 141–142
Assigned investigator, 325
Assigned officers, 324
Assignments, diversity and, 50–51
Authority, African Americans and, 186–187

B

Bias crimes. *See* Hate/bias crimes
Birthrate demographics, for
    Latino/Hispanic Americans, 200
Bisexuals. *See* Gay, lesbian, bisexual, and
    transgender individuals
Black English. *See* African American
    Vernacular English
Blacks, 172. *See also* African Americans
Black separatists, 337–338
Block watch volunteers program, 346
Blue code of silence, 395
Body position, 129
Brotherhood, 56–57
Brutality, 187–188
Business organizations, ethnic, 407

C

Career, family versus, 57
Career development, 397–399, 400
Center for Democratic Renewal
    (CDR), 313
Chicano, 197. *See also* Latino/Hispanic
    Americans
Chief executive, 67–70, 109–110
Children
    African American, 176–177
    American Indian, 262
    Arab American, 235
    Asian/Pacific Americans, 156
    crime prevention and, 405–408
    Latino/Hispanic Americans, 208

Christian Identity, 337
Christian Patriots, 337
Citizens' patrol, 347
Clergy, cooperation with, 407
Clustering, 280, 283–284
Commitment
    of chief executives, 67–68, 109
    of cultural awareness trainers, 110
    recruitment strategies and, 79–80
Common sense, 96
Communication
    African Americans, 177–182
    American Indians and, 257–260
    Arab Americans, 237–240
    Asian/Pacific Americans, 157–159
    cultural awareness training and, 96
    gender and, 131–133
    Latino/Hispanic Americans, 209–211
    nonverbal, 127–131
    See also Cross-cultural communication
Communities
    African American, 183–186,
        188–189, 190
    hate/bias crimes and, 297, 316–318,
        342–347
    Jewish, 291–292
    Latino/Hispanic Americans, 200
    recruitment strategies and, 84–85
Community-based policing, 33–35
    Asian/Pacific Americans and, 160–161
    Latino/Hispanic Americans and,
        215–216
    peace officers and, 370–372
    peacekeeping strategies, 401–404
Community–police partnerships. *See*
        Police–community partnerships
Community profiling, 316
Community Relations Service (CRS),
        318, 343
Community relations unit, 326
Community resource list, 343–344
Community revitalization perspective, 35
Community-specific cultural awareness
        training, 102–103
Conflict Prevention and Resolution (CPR)
        Team, 286–287

Conflict resolution panels, 343
Conflicts
    cultural awareness training and, 96
    racially and culturally rooted, 46–48
Consultants, external, 106–107
Conversational distance
    Arab Americans, 237–238
    cross-cultural communication and, 129
Cooperation, regional or statewide,
    390–396
Cosmopolitan public servants, 368–370
County hate crime programs, 345–346
County law enforcement agencies, 75
Crime
    Asian/Pacific Americans and,
        159–160, 161
    culture and, 20–22
    Latino/Hispanic Americans and, 211,
        213–214
    minority and immigrant youth, 405–408
    See also Hate/bias crimes
Crime prevention units, 326
Criminal justice system, hate/bias crimes
    and, 348–349
Cross-cultural communication, 114–115
    attempts, 116–121
    gender and, 131–133
    interviewing and data gathering skills,
        126–127
    language barriers and law enforcement,
        121–123
    law enforcement context, 115–116
    non-English speakers and limited
        English speakers, 123–126
    nonverbal communication and, 127–131
Cross-racial perceptions, 174
Cultural awareness training, 92–95,
    111–112
    administrative guidelines for, 109–111
    applications, 101–102
    assumptions and resistance, 95–96
    design and evaluation of, 102–106
    external consultants and trainers,
        106–107
    law enforcement agency models for,
        108–109
    reasons for, 96–101
Cultural competence, 99
Cultural diversity. *See* Diversity
Cultural diversity training. *See* Cultural
    awareness training
Cultural groups, police knowledge
    of, 22–23
Culturally sensitive peacekeeping, 372–382
Cultural pluralism. *See* Multiculturalism
Culture
    African American, 167
    crime and, 20–22
    definition of, 19–20
    hate/bias crimes and, 320
    Middle Easterners, 235–240
    organizational, 413–415
    peacekeeping and, 372–382
    police incidents and, 17–20
    race and ethnicity and, 8–9
    See also Multiculturalism
Culture shock, Asian/Pacific
    Americans, 155
Customer perspective, 35

D

Data collection
    cross-cultural communication, 126–127
    hate/bias crimes, 306–312
Demographics
    African American, 169–171
    Asian/Pacific Americans, 145–146
    Latino/Hispanic Americans, 199–201
    Middle Easterners, 226
    undocumented immigrants, 15
Departmental culture, 375
Deployment perspective, 35
Deportation, 15–17
Desecration, 267–268
Differential treatment
    African Americans, 1812–183
    Asian/Pacific Americans, 160
    Latino/Hispanic Americans, 212
Discrimination
    policies, 64–65
    against women, 54–55

District attorneys' offices, 329–330
Diversity
African American, 169–171
Asian/Pacific Americans, 145–146
assignments based on, 50–51
Latino/Hispanic Americans, 199–201
in law enforcement agencies, 43–44, 45
professionalism and, 395–396
reactions to, 7–8
recruitment and, 74–85
societal, 8–17
See also Multiculturalism
Diversity training. *See* Cultural awareness
training
Domestic violence
Asian/Pacific Americans, 156–157
immigrants and, 15–17
Double standards, 57
Driving under the influence, 20

E

Earth, American Indian philosophy
toward, 255–256
Ebonics. *See* African American Vernacular
English
Economy, hate violence and, 284–285,
319–320
Education, about hate/bias crimes, 344
Elders, respect for, 260–261
El mestizaje, 197. *See also* Latino/Hispanic
Americans
Emotional expressiveness
African Americans, 180–181
Arab Americans, 238–239
Employees, recruitment strategies and, 84
Environmental risk, 214–215
Ethics, 393–395
Ethnic business organizations, cooperation
with, 407
Ethnicity
law enforcement agencies and, 44–51
race and culture and, 8–9
Ethnicity bias, 309
Ethnocentrism, 20
Excessive force, 187–188

Expertise, of cultural awareness
trainers, 110
Extended family, of American Indians,
261–262. *See also* Family
External consultants and trainers,
106–107
Eye contact, 129, 258–259

F

Facial expressions, 129
Facial expressiveness, 129
Facilitation skills, of cultural awareness
trainers, 110
Facilitators, selection of, 110–111
Family
African American, 174–177
American Indians, 260–262
Asian/Pacific Americans, 154–157
careers versus, 57
Latino/Hispanic Americans, 206–209
Middle Easterners, 233–235
Family violence. *See* Domestic violence
Fathers. *See* Parents
Federal hate crime programs, 345–346
Federal laws
anti-Asian, 143–145
hate crimes, 307
First responders, 324
Fishing, 268–269
Fraternal organizations, 49–50
Future of Women in Policing, 53–54

G

Gangs, 406
Gay, lesbian, bisexual, and transgender
(GLBT) individuals
in law enforcement, 58–66
victimization of, 292–296
Gender
African Americans and, 175
Asian/Pacific Americans and, 155–156
communication and, 131–133
Latino/Hispanic Americans and,
206–209

law enforcement and, 54–57
See also Women
Gestures
Arab Americans, 238
cross-cultural communication and, 129
Glass ceiling, 85
Greetings, 236
Grocers, Arab American, 241–242
Group identification terms
African Americans, 172
American Indians, 259–260
Asian/Pacific Americans, 150–151
Latino/Hispanic Americans, 201

H

Harassment policies, 64–65
Harassment. *See* Sexual harassment
Hate/bias crimes, 274–275, 302, 304–305,
    323–324, 350–351
anti-Semitism, 288–292
Arab Americans and, 242–244
controlling, 331–347
data collection, 306–312
defining, 305
gay and lesbian victimization, 292–296
historical perspectives, 275–277
introduction to, 277–280
investigations, 324–329
law enforcement response strategies,
    297–301
laws, 313–315
monitoring, 312–313
national scope of, 280, 281–282
prosecution, 329–331
STEEP typology, 319–321
trend monitoring, 316–318
urban dynamics theory, 280, 283–287
victims of, 287–288, 348–350
war-related, 296–297
Hate Crimes Prevention Act (HCPA),
    314–315
Hate Crimes Statistics Act (HCSA), 307
Hate groups
black separatists, 337–338
counteracting, 407–408

future of, 340–342
Identity, 336–337
monitoring, 312–313
neo-Nazis and Klans, 333–335
organized, 331–332
politics and, 338–339
racist skinheads, 335–336
response alternatives to, 339–340
white supremacist movement and,
    332–333, 338–339
Head of household, 234–235
Hispanic Americans. *See* Latino/Hispanic
    Americans
Historical information
African American, 167–169
American Indians, 250–252
Asian/Pacific Americans, 142–145
hate/bias crimes, 275–277
Latino/Hispanic Americans, 197–199
Middle Easterners, 225–226
Homophobic crimes, 292–296
Homosexuals. *See* Gay, lesbian, bisexual,
    and transgender individuals
Hospitality, 236–237
Hot lines, 343
Household demographics,
    Latino/Hispanic Americans, 200
Human behavior, peace officer image and,
    357–366
Human relations
cultural awareness training and, 93
hate/bias crimes and, 318, 343
Human relations training. *See* Cultural
    awareness training

I

Identity
African American, 171–172
American Indians, 252–253
See also Group identification terms
Identity hate group, 336–337
Illegal aliens, 14–17, 203
Image. *See* Peace officer image
Image projection, 359–361, 368
Immigrants, 11–14

Asian/Pacific Americans, 141
  crime prevention among youth, 405–408
  undocumented, 14–17
Implementation plans, 68
Indians. *See* American Indians
Inner cities. *See* Communities; Urban
  communities
Innovation task force, 412–413
Innovative neighborhood-oriented policing
  (INOP). *See* Community-based
  policing
Insults, 239
Internships, 408
Interpersonal relations skills training,
  105–106
Interruptions, 258
Interviewing skills, 126–127
Investigations, for hate/bias crimes,
  324–329
Investigative officers, 326
Iranians, 223–224. *See also* Middle
  Easterners
Islamic religion, 231–233
Israelis, 224. *See also* Middle Easterners

J

Jews, anti-Semitism and, 288–292
Job hazards, Latino/Hispanic Americans
  and, 214–215
Jurisdiction, 262–264

K

Kinship. *See* Family
Klans, 333–335
Klanwatch, 312
Koran, 231
Ku Klux Klan, 333–335

L

Labels. *See* Group identification terms
Language
  African Americans and, 177–182
  American Indians and, 257–260

Arab Americans and, 239–240
  cross-cultural communication and, 117
  Latino/Hispanic Americans and, 200
  limited-English and non-English
    speakers, 123–126
  See also Communication; Cross-cultural
    communication
Language barriers, 121–123
Language style
  African Americans, 179–180
  cross-cultural communication and, 117
La Raza, 197. *See also* Latino/Hispanic
  Americans
Large departments, 327–328
Latino/Hispanic Americans, 195–196
  communication styles, 209–211
  defined, 196–197
  demographics, 199–201
  family, 206–209
  gender issues, 206–209
  historical information, 197–199
  labels and terms, 201
  law enforcement issues, 211–218
  myths and stereotypes, 202–205
  typology of, 202
  values and sentencing, 22
Law enforcement
  African Americans and, 169, 182–192
  American Indians and, 262–270
  Asian/Pacific Americans and, 143,
    159–163
  cross-cultural communication and,
    115–116
  cross-racial perceptions in, 174
  gays and lesbians in, 58–66
  hate/bias crimes and, 291–292, 297–301,
    349–350
  innovations, 412–413
  language barriers and, 121–123
  Latino/Hispanic Americans and,
    211–218
  Middle Easterners and, 240–246
  organizational trends in, 413–417
  prejudice in, 23–29
  regional or statewide cooperation in,
    390–396

women in, 51–58
See also Hate/bias crimes; Peace officer
image; Peace officers;
Professionalism; *specific minority
groups*
Law enforcement agencies, 40–42, 71
changes in, 42–44
chief executive, 67–70
ethnic and racial issues within, 44–51
gay and lesbian communities and,
295–296
hate/bias crimes and, 326–328
litigation against, 408–412
recruitment, 74–85
retention and promotion, 85–88
Law enforcement executive. *See* Chief
executive
Laws
anti-Asian, 143–145
hate/bias crimes, 307, 313–315
Leadership
models, 69–70
in professionalism and synergy, 387–390
Legislation. *See* Laws
Legitimacy perspective, 35
Lesbian. *See* Gay, lesbian, bisexual, and
transgender individuals
Limited English speakers, 123–126. *See also*
Communication; Cross-cultural
communication; Language
Liquor store owners, Arab American,
241–242
Litigation, against police agencies and
officers, 408–412
Local hate crime programs, 345–346
Local law enforcement agencies, 75
Local laws, anti-Asian, 143–145
Looting, 267–268
Los Angeles Police Department (LAPD),
364–366

M

Machismo, 22, 207
Macrocultures, 374, 375
Mainstreaming, 6

Management plans, 68
Marianismo, 207
Media, hate/bias crimes and, 343, 345
Medium-sized departments, 327
Melting pot myth, 5–6, 95–96
Men. *See* Gender
Mentor programs
career advancement and, 398–399
for women, 57–58
Microcultures, 374, 375
Middle Easterners, 221–222
cultural practices, 235–240
defined, 222–224
demographics, 226
differences and similarities, 226–228
family structure, 233–235
historical information, 225–226
Islamic religion and, 231–233
law enforcement issues, 240–246
stereotypes, 228–230
Minority group, 396. *See also specific groups*
Mobile crisis unit, 347
Mobility, of American Indians, 253–254
Modesty, 241
Morale, boosting, 399
Mosaic, 5–6
Mosques, taboos in, 232
Mothers. *See* Parents; Single mothers
Motivation, for hate/bias crimes, 308–310
Move-in violence, 285–286
Movies, Arab American stereotypes in, 229
Multiculturalism, 4, 5. *See also* Culture;
Diversity
Multicultural society. *See* Society
Myths
African Americans, 172–174
Asian/Pacific Americans, 151–154
Latino/Hispanic Americans, 202–205
melting pot, 5–6, 95–96

N

National Alliance, 335
National Gay and Lesbian Task Force
(NGLTF), 312–313
National origin bias, 309

Native Americans. *See* American Indians
Negro, 172
Neighborhood-oriented policing (NOP).
    See Community-based policing
Neighborhood–police partnerships. *See*
    Police–community partnerships
Neighbors, network of, 347
Neo-Nazis, 333–335
Networking
    career advancement and, 398–399
    neighbors, 347
    organizational, 344–345
New York Police Department (NYPD),
    361–364
NGLTF Policy Institute, 312–313
Non-English speakers, 123–126. *See also*
    Communication; Cross-cultural
    communication; Language
Nonverbal communication
    African American, 179–180
    American Indians, 258–259
    Arab Americans, 237–240
    Asian/Pacific Americans, 157–159
    cross-cultural communication and,
        127–131
    Latino/Hispanic Americans, 209–211

O

Obscenities, 239
Offensive terms. *See* Group identification
    terms
Openness, 257–258
Operation Abscam, 230
Order, The, 335
Organizational change, managing, 68
Organizational culture, 375, 413–415
Organizational networking, 344–345
Organizational trends, 413–417
Organized hate groups. *See* Hate groups
Orientals, 140, 151
Overreaction, 321

P

Pacific Islanders. *See* Asian/Pacific
    Americans

Parents
    African American, 176
    American Indian, 262
Participants, in cultural awareness training
    courses, 111
Patrol field supervisor, 325
Patrol officers, 326
Peacekeeping
    culturally sensitive, 372–382
    strategies in multicultural societies, 399,
        401–413
Peace officer image, 356–357
    culture and, 380–382
    human behavior and, 357–366
    twenty-first century, 366–368
Peace officers
    Asian/Pacific American, 161
    community-based policing and, 370–372
    cosmopolitan public servants, 368–370
    Latino/Hispanic American, 216
    litigation against, 408–412
    morale, 399
    See also Professionalism
Peer relationships, prejudice and, 26–29
Perceptions
    African Americans and, 174, 186–187
    American Indian, 262
    Arab Americans and, 240
Personalismo, 208
Peyote, 264–267
Philadelphia Police Department Conflict
    Prevention and Resolution (CPR)
    Team, 286–287
Philosophy, American Indian, 255–256
Physical distance. *See* Conversational
    distance
Planning, recruitment strategies and, 80
Police. *See* Law enforcement; Law
    enforcement agencies; Peace officers
Police benevolent associations, ethnic, 407
Police brutality, 187–188
Police–community partnerships
    cultural awareness training and, 105
    developing, 69
    hate/bias crimes and, 316–318
Police fraternal organizations, 49–50

Police incidents, culture and, 17–20
Police knowledge, of cultural groups, 22–23
Police microculture, 375
Police stops, 264
Politics
   hate/bias crimes and, 320
   white supremacists and, 338–339
Population characteristics, changes in, 9–11
Positive reinforcement, 360
Posse Comitatus, 337
Prejudice
   cultural awareness training and, 105
   in law enforcement, 23–29
Problem-oriented policing (POP). *See* Community-based policing
Problem-solving perspective, 35
Professionalism, 386–387
   career development and, 397–399, 400
   cultural awareness and, 104
   police leadership in, 387–390
   racial profiling and, 31–33
   regional or statewide cooperation, 390–396
Profiling. *See* Racial profiling
Promotion, 85–88
Prosecution, of hate/bias crimes, 329–331
Public information brochures, multilingual, 343
Public servants, cosmopolitan, 368–370
Purchasing power, Latino/Hispanic Americans, 200

Q

Questions, 258

R

Race
   culture and ethnicity and, 8–9
   law enforcement agencies and, 44–51
Racial bias, 308
Racial profiling, 29–33
   African Americans and, 182–186

   cross-cultural communication and, 119–121
   Latino/Hispanic Americans and, 212–213
Racism, in law enforcement agencies, 44–48
Racist skinheads, 335–336
Ramadan, 232
Rapid response strategy, 346–347
Recruiters, selection and training of, 80–84
Recruitment, 74–75
   crisis in, 76–77
   difficulties in, 77–79
   local, county, and state law enforcement agencies, 75
   strategies, 79–85
Refugees, 141
Regional cooperation, in law enforcement, 390–396
Religion. *See* Islam
Religious bias, 308
Reservations, 253–254
Resources
   for hate/bias crimes, 343–346
   recruitment strategies and, 80
Respect
   American Indians and, 260–261
   Latino/Hispanic Americans and, 206, 207, 208
Retention, 85–88
Role barriers, 55–56

S

Sacred lands, 267–268
Safety, Latino/Hispanic American attitudes toward, 213–214
Schools, crime prevention and, 406
Self-awareness, 110
Self-disclosure, 257–258
Sensitivity training, 93, 94. *See also* Cultural awareness training
Sentencing, values and, 22
Sexual harassment, 54–55
Sexual orientation. *See* Gay, lesbian, bisexual, and transgender individuals

Sexual orientation bias, 309
Silence, 258
Silent Brotherhood, 335
Simon Wiesenthal Center, 313
Single mothers, African American, 176
Skinheads, racist, 335–336
Small departments, 326–327
Society
  American Indians and, 256–257
  diversity of, 8–17
  hate/bias crimes and, 320
  peacekeeping strategies in, 399–413
Specialized units, 325–326
Stance, 179–180
State hate crime programs, 345–346
State law enforcement agencies, 75
State laws, anti-Asian, 143–145
Statewide cooperation, in law enforcement,
    390–396
STEEP typology, 319–321
Stereotypes
  African Americans, 172–174
  American Indians, 259–260
  Asian/Pacific Americans, 151–154
  Latino/Hispanic Americans, 202–205
  Middle Easterners, 228–230, 244–245
STOP program, 347
Storefronts, hate/bias crimes and, 343
Strategic plans, 68
Support groups, 63–64
Support programs, 57–58
Swearing, 239
Synergy, 397–390, 391

T

Talking, 258. *See also* Verbal
    communication
Tapestry, 6
Targets, of hate crimes, 287–288
Target zone theory, 280, 283–284
Task force on police–Asian relations, 346
Television, Arab American stereotypes
    on, 229
Terms. *See* Group identification terms
"Terrorist" stereotype, 244–245

Threats, African Americans and, 181–182
Touching
  American Indians, 258–259
  Arab Americans, 236
Traffic stops, racial profiling and, 31–33
Trainers
  external, 106–107
  selection of, 110–111
Training
  gay, lesbian, and transgender issues,
      65–66
  recruiters, 80–84
  See also Cultural awareness training
Training units, 326
Transgender. *See* Gay, lesbian, bisexual, and
    transgender individuals
Transition plans, 68
Trend monitoring, 316–318
Trespassing, 267
Tribes, 253–254
Turks, 223–224. *See also* Middle Easterners
Typology
  Asian/Pacific Americans, 141–142
  Latino/Hispanic Americans, 202
  STEEP, 319–321

U

Underreaction, 321
Undocumented immigrants, 14–17
Uniform Crimes Report (UCR), 307–308
Universe, American Indian philosophy
    toward, 255–256
Urban communities
  African American, 188–189, 190
  Latino/Hispanic Americans, 200
  See also Communities
Urban dynamics theory, 280, 283–287
Use desecration, 267–268

V

Values, sentencing and, 22
Verbal communication
  African Americans, 180–181
  American Indians, 258

Arab Americans, 237–240
Asian/Pacific Americans, 157–159
Latino/Hispanic Americans, 209–211
See also Communication; Cross-cultural
    communication
Verbal expressiveness, of African
    Americans, 180–181
Victimization
    Latino/Hispanic Americans, 211–212
    hate/bias crimes, 287–288, 348–350
Violence
    economy and, 284–285
    move-in, 285–286
    See also Crime; Domestic violence;
        Hate/bias crimes

W

War-related hate crimes, 296–297
Watch commander, 325
We-they distinctions, 119

White supremacist movement
    defining, 332–333
    politics and, 338–339
Women
    African American, 176, 189
    Arab American, 241
    glass ceiling and, 85
    immigrant, 15–17
    in law enforcement, 51–58
    See also Gender
Workforce. *See* Law enforcement agencies
World Church of the Creator (WCOTC),
    334–335

Y

Youths
    African American, 176–177
    Asian/Pacific Americans, 156
    crime prevention and, 405–408
    Latino/Hispanic Americans, 208